TO THE STUDENT: A Study Guide for this textbook is available through your college bookstore under the title STUDY GUIDE for BUSINESS COMMUNICATIONS, SEVENTH EDITION by William C. Himstreet and Wayne M. Baty. The Study Guide can help you with course material by acting as a tutorial, review, and study aid. If the Study Guide is not in stock, ask the bookstore manager to order a copy for you.

BUSINESS COMMUNICATIONS

BUSINESS COMMUNICATIONS
Principles and Methods Seventh Edition

William C. Himstreet
University of Southern California

Wayne Murlin Baty
Arizona State University

KENT PUBLISHING COMPANY   A Division of Wadsworth, Inc.   Boston, Massachusetts

Senior Editor: Richard C. Crews
Production Editor: Nancy J. Crow
Text Design: Armen Kojoyian, Glenna Collett
Cover Design: Nancy Lindgren
Cover Art: Phil Bailey
Text Illustrations: Michael Prendergast
Production Coordinator: Linda Siegrist

KENT PUBLISHING COMPANY
A Division of Wadsworth, Inc.

The Changing World of Communication photo essay
Design: Nancy J. Crow
Picture research: Pembroke Herbert and Laurel Anderson/Picture Research Consultants
Photo credits: p. xvii, courtesy of CPT Corporation; p. xviii (T) Culver Pictures, Inc.; p. xviii (B) ©
Co Rentmeester; p. xix (T) Chicago Historical Society; p. xix (B) Harold Sund, courtesy Ohio
Edison Co.; p. xx (T) © Joel Gordon 1982; p. xx (B) Brown Bros.; p. xxi (TR) Free Lance
Photographers Guild; p. xxi (M, B) courtesy NASA; p. xxii (TL) © Joel Gordon 1983; p. xxii (ML)
© Joel Gordon 1982; p. xxii (BL) Dan McCoy/Rainbow; p. xxii (R) courtesy IBM Corporation;
p. xxiii (T) courtesy CPT Corporation; p. xxiii (B) Charles (Chase) McNiss; p. xxiv courtesy IBM
Corporation.

Printed in the United States of America
6 7 8 9 — 87 86

Library of Congress Cataloging in Publication Data

Himstreet, William C.
   Business communications.

   Includes index.
   1. Commercial correspondence.   2. Business report writing.   3. Communication in
management.   4. English language — Business English.   I. Baty, Wayne Murlin.   II. Title.
HF5721.H5   1984   658.4′5   83-23854
ISBN 0-534-02837-3

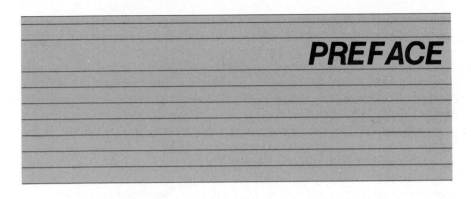

PREFACE

When we began work on the first edition of *Business Communications,* we did so because we thought we could write a better textbook than was then available. In the intervening 25 years, we've tried to make each edition better than the previous one. Whatever improvements have occurred from edition to edition have resulted from three ongoing experiences: (1) Our own learning from teaching and involvement in business communication, (2) the constant changes in business communication subject matter and course design—as revealed by the market research of publishers and by the academic research reported in professional journals, and (3) the thoughtful and helpful reviews of each edition by many instructors. Although the changes from edition to edition have seemed subtle to us, we realize that the cumulative effect has been dramatic when we compare this seventh edition with earlier ones.

Changes from Previous Editions

In some respects, this edition may contain more significant changes than did any of the previous ones. In addition to the usual updating of content and revising of end-of-chapter materials, we've incorporated material that, although perhaps not revolutionary, does reflect the impact of recent developments and research in business communication.

The business and government environment has been profoundly affected by the personal computer/word-processing explosion of recent years. A casual glance at the advertising in almost any metropolitan newspaper provides considerable evidence that technological developments are bringing the computer age within the monetary reach of all businesses and of most middle-income families. Although we cannot really anticipate the eventual impact of this development — frequently called *the communication revolution* — we have attempted to describe some of it and to look into the "crystal ball" just a little in Part I.

We do know that the computer and its microprocessor chip are not very intelligent things until humans tell them what to do and how to do it. And human input can be effective only to the extent that people understand communication principles and have the ability to write and speak successfully. Therefore, the focus of the book is on the development of those personal communication skills and knowledges needed by competent, upward-bound people.

Because of the widespread use of word processing in business, most management personnel will be faced with the task of dictating letters and memorandum via recording equipment for later transcription. In Chapter 6, we've added a detailed section on how to dictate, whether in a face-to-face situation with a secretary or in the word-processing mode. We believe this addition to the chapter coverage of message planning provides the foundation for a variety of approaches to the study of specific letter and memorandum problems.

Additionally, we have been influenced by an increasing interest expressed at professional meetings in the broad area of international communication. But there are constraints on how much classroom time can be devoted to this subject in the basic business communication course. At any rate, we've attempted to introduce in Part I some of the obvious problems of communicating with others whose cultures, value systems, and language are unlike our own.

This opening portion of the book combines our traditional chapter on communication theory and behavioral foundations with chapters on technology and international communication to provide a broad basis for the study of letters and reports in an increasingly complex environment.

Another development affecting the content of this edition is the role of the memorandum as the written message form most frequently prepared by most people in business. There is, as well, a growing emphasis on oral reporting. Rather than present these areas as minor parts of broader chapters on reports, we've devoted an entire chapter to memorandums, including case study problems that provide student opportunities to prepare memorandums while assuming a variety of roles in each case. Placement of this chapter presented a most difficult problem simply because memorandums are hybrids. They have characteristics of both letters and reports; but they are a primary means of communicating within organizations, and the memorandum format is often used for report preparation. We believe the placement of memorandums following the chapters on research methods and graphics permits considerable flexibility in the study of reports. The logic of problem solving and the use of graphics are valuable aids in memorandum preparation as well as in report preparation. With the memorandum chapter preceding chapters on short reports and formal reports, the study of report writing can be concluded at any of three points — memorandums, short reports, or formal reports.

To add more depth to the study and practice of speaking and oral reporting, Chapter 19 includes material on planning and making oral presentations, including the use of visual aids.

Features Retained from Previous Editions

Through successive editions of *Business Communications,* several "old standbys" have proven highly successful, so we've tried to improve on them as distinctive features of this edition:

1. The sentence-by-sentence analysis of letters provides the rationale for particular idea sequences and word choices.

2. The page-by-page critique of formal reports has been well accepted as an approach to giving the student an understanding of total report preparation and writing style.

3. The integration of listening practices, interviewing styles and methods, and interviewing for jobs as part of the employment application section (initiated in the sixth edition) has, from student comments, provided a valuable learning experience.

4. The coverage of letter writing is built on the three basic message plans rather than on separate chapters on specific letter types or subjects. This approach has been accepted as a valid way to develop genuine understanding of communicating through letters. We'd prefer our students to use some creativity within the limits of the basic plans rather than become users of lock-step check lists.

5. The final two chapters on organizational communication and management practices attempt to extend communication learnings into the organizational environment in which they will be put to practical use.

6. As in earlier editions, this seventh has been prepared with our conscious attention to the logical, simple-to-complex progression of content to assist the learning process. Additionally, we have attempted to practice what we preach by retaining a comfortable reading level.

A Total Teaching-Learning Package

A new package of teaching–learning materials complements the textbook and provides both teacher and student with a great variety of materials and activities.

1. The Instructor's manual and the Supplemental Teaching Aids of the sixth edition have been combined in a single Instructor's Manual to provide extensive teaching suggestions, testing materials, textbook problem solutions, and supplementary transparency masters for several textbook problems.

2. A package of fifty actual transparencies to use in lecture and discussion sessions and to reinforce textbook concepts is provided with all textbook adoptions.

3. A separate item, the *Study Guide,* takes students through a series of

exercises coordinated with the textbook. For each chapter, the *Study Guide* includes these sections:

    a. Check Your Knowledge, a set of short-answer items to assist in mastery of the textbook concepts.

    b. Communication Glossary, a matching problem designed to reinforce an understanding of terms used in communication theory and practice.

    c. Check Your Business English, a series of short exercises covering grammar and usage as an expansion of material in the textbook appendix.

    d. Check Your Spelling, a list of commonly used words in which the student corrects any misspellings.

    e. Case Problems, a series of short letter and memorandum writing problems.

The guide also includes a set of learning objectives for each chapter and an objective test for each of the six parts of the textbook. Answers to all but the case problems and the tests are provided in the study guide so the student may have immediate reinforcement of learning.

These additional materials were developed to simplify and to strengthen the study of business communication. We believe their use can provide more effective use of both in-class and out-of-class time. We hope their use will reduce the massive amount of paper reading and correcting that teachers face. The additional materials also provide more constructive and immediate feedback to students than assignments submitted to the teacher.

Course Design

A major objective of any course using this text should be to have students acquire the ability to write well enough to bring credit to themselves rather than to "just squeak by" in their careers. The text material is flexible so that emphasis can be placed on writing, and additional topics can be included to meet the goals of any basic course in business communication.

Several factors influence course design. How much prior applicable learning or experience do students bring with them? How much classroom time is available? What should be a desirable proportion of course time allocated to basic writing and usage skills, to oral skills, to letter writing, to memorandum preparation, to research methods, to written reports, to management principles, and to communication theory?

Ideally, at least a sixty-hour classroom meeting course provides time to cover most of the material. Certainly if everything in the book is to be covered in a 30- or 45-hour course, much of the coverage would be perfunctory. For a two-term course, Parts 1, 2, and 3 can be used for the letter-writing term and Parts 4, 5, and 6 for the report-writing term. We do think, however, that a heavier outside-of-class reading load and less in-class time can be used to cover Parts 1 and 6, with most in-class time being devoted to intensive coverage of the other parts. Further suggestions for course design are included in the instructor's manual.

To Students

To this point we've written primarily to instructors about the content and use of this book, and this probably hasn't been too exciting. But the book was really written for you—because we think this may be the most valuable subject you'll study. The primary causes for dismissal from jobs held by college graduates are weak communication skills and lack of ability in interpersonal relations. In other words, people are generally capable in their areas of technical expertise; but they frequently fail because of their inability to speak and write effectively and because of their failure to get along well with others.

From our own corporate experience, we know that good writing and speaking are often the only things that bring a young person's ability to the attention of superiors. Leonard Read, president of the Foundation for Economic Education, said:

> Thinking things through—finding answers to knotty problems—is perhaps best done in writing. Refinement demands that we visualize what is in the mind. Whatever cannot be made clear in writing probably is not clear in the mind. Clarity is a product of attentive practice and reflection.

And Daniel Webster philosophized:

> If all my possessions were taken away from me with one exception, I would choose to keep the power of speech, for with it I would soon regain all the rest.

These quotations typify what this book is about. We hope it will help you.

Our Thanks

First, we express our grateful appreciation to our wives—Maxine and Maxine—to whom we dedicated the first edition and who have somehow survived and helped us survive our 25 years with *Business Communications.* Second, we are indebted to our teaching colleagues and our students at Arizona State University and the University of Southern California for their insights, criticisms, and support. Finally, we offer sincere thanks to the following professionals who provided insightful comments, valuable suggestions, and helpful information for this edition:

R. Jon Ackley
Virginia Commonwealth University

Sherrill Amador
Southwestern College

Vanessa Dean Arnold
University of Mississippi

Vickie Lynn Boeder
Madison Area Technical College

George Boulware
Belmont College

M. E. Bowe
Community College of Denver

Carl H. Boyer
University of Toledo, Community and Technical College

William J. Burling
Pennsylvania State University

Eugene Calvasina
Troy State University

Joseph Cantrell
Foothill College

James L. Clark
Pasadena City College

J. R. Cole
University of Akron

Beth Crabtree
Guilford Technical College

Shela Criger
Mohave Community College

Frankie T. Davis
Palm Beach Junior College

Rodney Davis
Ball State University

Janette Day
Fullerton College

Wanda DeBoer
University of Northern Colorado

Marcia Dier
Clackamas Community College

Earl A. Dvorak
Indiana University

Margaret Ehrhart
Fairleigh Dickinson University

Gwendolyn M. Ellis
Grambling State University

Berta Gramling
Phillips County Community College

Carmen Griffin
Rio Salado Community College

Dave Hamilton
Sheridan College

Ellen G. Hankin
Rider College

Margaret Hebert
University of Houston

Rovena L. Hillsman
California State University

Larue Hubbard
Glendale Community College

Fred Jordan
Barry University

Debra K. Kellerman
St. Cloud State University

Elree Kellog
University of Utah

Erna Kemps
North Central Technical Institute

Morgan Kjer
North Hennepin Community College

Barbara Lea
West Valley College

Dorothy Leavitt
Sul Ross State University

Judy Leusink
Aims Community College

Jewel Linville
Northeastern Oklahoma State
University

Barbara Loush
Oakland Community College

Cynthia Lyle
Texas Tech University

C. R. McPherson
Louisiana State University-
Shreveport

Athyleen F. Nicholson
Fort Steilacoom Community College

Frederick E. McNally
California State University

James G. Patterson, III
Jackson Community College

Bernard J. Reilly
Oakland Community College

A. Ray Rustand
Pensacola Junior College

Larry Smeltzer
Louisiana State University

Carleen Spano
Miami-Dade Community College

Goldie Sparger
Surry Community College

Lois A. Sullivan
Bergen Community College

Alden S. Talbot
Weber State College

Billy E. Thompson
Austin Peay State University

Beulah Underwood
San Diego Mesa College

Robert Underwood
Ball State University

Anne C. Utschig
University of Wisconsin-Fox Valley

Douglas F. Warring
Inver Hills Community College

Max L. Waters
Brigham Young University

Jerry L. Wood
Northern Montana College

William C. Himstreet and Wayne Murlin Baty

CONTENTS

Part 1
COMMUNICATION ENVIRONMENT AND FOUNDATIONS   *3*

Chapter 1
Communication Foundations   5
Information Theory   7
Theory of Human
    Communication   10
Behavioral Concepts   12
Hierarchy of Communications
    Levels   19
Language and Culture   20
Summary   21
Exercises   22

Chapter 2
The Communication Technology
Revolution   24
The Rapid Acceleration of
    Progress   25
Word Processing and Personal
    Computers   26
Using the Executive Work
    Station   27
Using a Word-Processing
    Center   28
Electronic Mail   31

Teleconferencing   33
Summary   33
Glossary of Personal Computer and
    Word-Processing Terms   34
Exercises   36

Chapter 3
International Business
Communication   37
The Cultural Environment of
    International Business   38
Achieving Empathy   39
American Values and
    Stereotypes   39
Written Communication
    Problems   40
Semantic Problems and
    Translation   42
Nonverbal Communication
    Problems   43
Some Light at the End of the
    Tunnel   45
Summary   46
Exercises   47

Part 2
WRITING, PLANNING, AND DICTATING   49

Chapter 4
Using Words Effectively   51
    Messages Without Words   52
    Simple Words   54
    Categories of Words   56
    Frequently Misused Words   69
    Summary   71
    Exercises   72

Chapter 5
Using the Techniques of Style   76
    Phrases   77
    Sentences   85

    Paragraphs   98
    Compositions   103
    Summary   106
    Exercises   108

Chapter 6
Organizing and Dictating
Messages   113
    Organizing Letters   115
    Dictating Messages   121
    Summary   132
    Exercises   132

Part 3
COMMUNICATING THROUGH LETTERS   137

Chapter 7
Writing About the Routine and
the Pleasant   139
    Letters About Routine Claims   140
    Routine Letters About Credit   144
    Letters About Routine Orders   149
    Letters About Other Routine
        Requests   153
    Summary   156
    Exercises   157

Chapter 8
Writing About the
Unpleasant   164
    Saying "No" to an Adjustment
        Request   166
    Saying "No" to a Credit
        Request   171
    Saying "No" to Someone Who Has
        Ordered Merchandise   175
    Saying "No" to a Favor
        Request   179
    Summary   181
    Exercises   182

Chapter 9
Writing to Persuade   188
    Getting Ready   190
    Using an Attention Getter   192
    Introducing the Product   196
    Presenting Convincing
        Evidence   198
    Writing a Complete Sales
        Letter   206
    Writing a Persuasive Request for
        Action   211
    Writing Collection Letters   215
    Collection by Telephone and
        Telegram   225
    Summary   226
    Exercises   226

Chapter 10
Writing Special Letters   233
    Congratulatory Letters   234
    Letters of Recommendation   235
    Letters about Reservations   238
    Letters of Invitation   238
    Letters of Condolence or
        Sympathy   240

Thank-you Letters 241
Letters of Evaluation 242

Summary 246
Exercises 246

Part 4
COMMUNICATING ABOUT EMPLOYMENT   *251*

Chapter 11
Writing about Employment — The Application 253
   What Employers Want 254
   What Prospective Employees
     Need 255
   The Résumé 260
   The Application Letter 271
   The Letter of
     Recommendation 291
   Other Letters about
     Employment 294
   Summary 297
   Exercises 297

Chapter 12
Talking about Employment — Listening and the Interview 307
   Listening as an Interview Skill 308
   Types and Styles of Interviews 311
   The Job Interviewer's Role 313
   The Interviewee's Role in the Job
     Hunt 317
   Summary 324
   Exercises 325

Part 5
COMMUNICATING THROUGH MEMORANDUMS AND REPORTS   *327*

Chapter 13
The Report Process and Research Methods 329
   Characteristics of Reports 330
   Recognize and Define the
     Problem 334
   Select a Method of Solution 336
   Collect and Organize the Data 349
   Arrive at an Answer 351
   Summary 352
   Exercises 353

Chapter 14
Managing Data and Using Graphics 355
   Managing Quantitative Data 356
   Using Tables and Graphics 360
   Introducing Tables and Graphs in
     the Text 374
   Using Common Language to
     Describe Data 376

Summary 377
Exercises 377

Chapter 15
Preparing Memorandums 382
   Qualities of Memorandums 383
   Informational Memorandums 385
   Procedures and Instructions 390
   Persuasive Memorandums 395
   Helpful Guides for Memo
     Writers 395
   Summary 396
   Exercises 396

Chapter 16
Planning and Organizing Formal Reports 406
   What Are Formal Reports? 407
   The Growth of a Report 407

Complete Report Outline   419
Organizing Reports   420
A Sample Problem   427
Using Outline Symbols   431
Organizing Data   432
Summary   434
Exercises   434

Chapter 17
Preparing Short Reports   437
Characteristics of Short
    Reports   438
A Sample Short Report   439
Letter Reports   449

A Sample Letter Report   450
Proposals   450
Summary   455
Exercises   456

Chapter 18
Preparing Formal Reports   463
Composition   464
Special Parts   473
Physical Presentation   475
Report Critique   484
A Formal Report Checklist   508
Summary   511
Exercises   512

Part 6
ORAL COMMUNICATIONS AND COMMUNICATION MANAGEMENT 527

Chapter 19
Speeches, Oral Reports, and
Group Communication   529
Controlling Voice Qualities   530
Knowing the Audience   532
Making a Speech   533
Making an Oral Report   540
Communicating in Groups   547
Leading Conferences   551
Leading Committee Meetings   551
Running Banquets   555
Summary   556
Exercises   556

Chapter 20
Communication in
Organizations   558
Three Levels of
    Communication   559
Characteristics of Formal
    Organizations   559
Organizational Structure and
    Communication   562
External and Internal Systems   564

Communication Flow in
    Organizations   566
A Supportive Climate   568
Summary   571
Exercises   571

Chapter 21
Communication
Management   574
Communication Problems in the
    Organization   575
Tips for the Individual Manager   577
Suggestions for the
    Organization   578
Managing Written
    Communications   579
Summary   587
Exercises   588

Appendix   589
Pretest   590
I. Grammar   592
II. Mechanics   614
Posttest   649
Grading Symbols   672

THE CHANGING WORLD OF COMMUNICATION

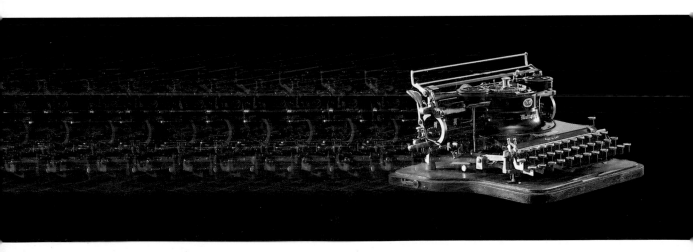

Thirty-six thousand years ago, Cro-Magnon man, thought to be the earliest language user, roamed parts of the earth. Consider those last 36,000 years compressed into one day. Each hour of that day would equal 1,500 years, and each minute would equal 25 years. Thus, if you are under the age of 25, you were born in the final minute of that day. But, some other important events have taken place in the final minutes of our compressed day.

About 11:54 P.M. on our imagined day, Samuel F. B. Morse introduced the telegraph. And between 11:54 and 11:57 P.M., which would be the remainder of the 19th century, the printing telegraph, the

trans-Atlantic cable, the telephone, the radio, and the motion picture camera were developed. The final three minutes of our day— only ¼ of one percent of recorded time—saw perhaps more significant technological advances than did the previous 23 hours and 57 minutes.

Dictation methods changed from clumsy recording on wax cylinders to the executive work station, recording on electronic tapes or discs in a computerized, word-processing environment. Typewriting has moved progressively from manual to electric to electronic machines. One-time stereotyped work roles have diminished and been replaced by task roles unrelated to sex. Now, most large offices are equipped with personal computers at individual work stations, easing the tasks of storing, retrieving, and processing information.

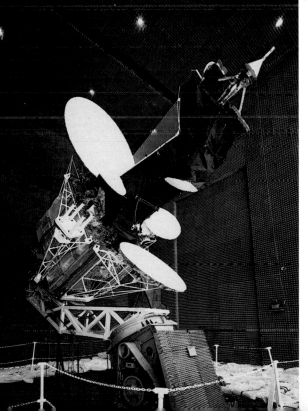

Radio relay stations and communication satellites have almost eliminated the need for the classic telephone company operator and the plug-in switchboard. The candlestick telephone proved a technological marvel of its day simply because it was not necessary to hang it on the wall. In its time it was the state of the art. Today, by telephone and computer, stockbrokers have up-to-the-second quotes on several thousand stock and bond prices and can send their buy and sell orders almost instantaneously. The telephone has become an integral part of our business lives. And, as a result of communications advances, many occupations will soon be located in the home rather than in the traditional business office.

Instantaneous, world-wide communication really began with the introduction of communication satellites. The space-age race was on with the launch of Sputnik in 1957; and the Telstar satellite put the United States in the experimental stages of space-age communication in 1962. Rapid, subsequent developments permitted the world to view humans walking on the surface of the moon. Now, of course, we have "live" television via satellite throughout the world.

The personal computer revolution, a contemporary of satellite communication, began with the development of the semi-conductor and the micro-electronic chip—greatly enlarged here, it is no larger than a small fingernail. Television computer games and home computers are the newest wonders coming from the micro-chip. The progressive shrinkage of space required for the computer's

"brain," along with the accompanying decrease in production costs, is making the personal computer a household tool rather than a luxury item.

With the addition of only a printer, the personal computer doubles as a word processor. Equipment designed exclusively for word processing can be adapted to perform mathematical computations, check spelling, produce graphics, and prepare documents in several different languages including Arabic and Japanese. When linked in a network, computers and word processors can communicate with one another as a form of paperless, electronic mail. Triple-duty is achieved when the personal computer is used as a teaching/learning tool.

Our excitement about the new communication technology may be tempered by thoughts about its impact on society. Billions of people can now witness the same events simultaneously; buildings are designed by computers; machinery and transportation can be controlled electronically; many formerly painful, manual labor tasks are being, and will increasingly be, performed by machine; and medical diagnoses and treatment are benefiting from new technologies.

Business is in the vanguard of the new communications. Cross-country or trans-Atlantic flights are no longer necessarily required. The conference call is familiar to most executives, as is the tele-conference.

What will be the effect of all this new communications technology on the quality of life, on life expectancies, on international relations, on the home as the focal point of the family, and on how we work and play? Are we reaching a time when we can truly control our environment and our destinies?

This progress occurred because of a critical need to communicate faster and more accurately. Communication, the cause, was also the cure. *The exchange of ideas* to effect progress takes place only through human language, still the greatest achievement of humankind. Skill in language use will always be the basic ingredient in progress. And, what marvels might someone be writing about at the conclusion of our next 360-century day?

COMMUNICATION ENVIRONMENT AND FOUNDATIONS

OBJECTIVES

1. To develop an understanding of the communication process.

2. To recognize how some concepts of human behavior affect communication.

3. To recognize how the rapid changes in technology are changing many communication methods.

4. To develop some insight into the problems of communication in an international business environment.

COMMUNICATION FOUNDATIONS

Information Theory
Theory of Human Communication
Behavioral Concepts
    Maslow's Need Hierarchy
    McGregor's Theories
    Transactional Analysis
    Communicating Interpersonally and
        the Johari Window
Hierarchy of Communication Levels
Language and Culture
Summary

> **com·mu·ni·ca·tion 1:** an act or instance of transmitting **2a:** information communicated **b:** a verbal or written message **3a:** a process by which information is exchanged between individuals through a common system of symbols, signs, or behavior **b:** personal rapport . . . **5a:** a technique for expressing ideas effectively **b:** the technology of the transmission of information.[1]

The dictionary definition of communication describes the aim of this book. The goal is to develop the reader's ability to communicate effectively in a business environment. Although the primary emphasis is on written communication through letters and reports, considerable attention is also given to various oral communications. Most principles underlying effective business communication are common to both written and oral communications.

Scholars, researchers, and scientists have long sought, in their own ways, to develop definitions of communication; and, no doubt, you have your own notion of what communication is and how it takes place. Your own definition of communication might incorporate one or all of Barnlund's three approaches to defining communication.[2] First, the *message-centered approach* consists of the transmission of an effective message. To communicate we must master the content, arrange it properly, and deliver it effectively. Public speaking, for example, is primarily concerned with message construction and delivery. Most of our letter-writing activities are message centered. Whenever our primary concern is the construction of a message for effect, the approach to communication is message centered.

If your definition emphasizes the transferring of a message from one person to another, you would be using what Barnlund calls the *transmission-centered approach.* This approach is concerned mainly with the flow of information, especially as it occurs in organizations such as business firms. In group conferences or meetings, where the exchange of information is essential and individual participation is encouraged, emphasis is on the transmission and reception of messages. Technical systems such as word processing and computer applications are transmission centered.

Barnlund's third approach is called *meaning centered;* it concerns the fact that we always seek meaning from what others say and do. People create meaning from whatever is going on around them, even though the messages they receive may have been sent unintentionally or may have been different from what was sent. For example, if someone unintentionally smiles at us, we tend to interpret the smile to make meaning of its occurrence and how it is related to any verbal message it may have accompanied. The meaning-centered approach emphasizes the idea that we are all unique persons with our own sets of unique lifetime experiences. To the extent that the sender and receiver of messages create similar meanings, communication is effective.

As you move through your study of business communication, you'll find that we use all three approaches in varying degrees. As a manager, you must be concerned with the transmission process and the flow of information. As a writer and speaker,

---

1. By permission. From *Webster's New Collegiate Dictionary.* 1980 by G. & C. Merriam Co., Publishers of the Merriam-Webster Dictionaries.

2. Dean C. Barnlund, "Toward a Meaning-Centered Philosophy of Communication," in *Basic Readings in Interpersonal Communication,* ed. K. Griffin and B. R. Patton (New York: Harper & Row, 1971), pp. 40–48.

your major concern is for the construction and delivery of an effective message. And as a sender and receiver of messages, you are obliged to be concerned with meaning. These three approaches to defining communication simply attempt to isolate aspects of the communication process for better understanding. Essentially, business people who want to be known as good communicators must combine *skill* in using language, *knowledge* of management and business operations, and *skill* in human relations.

As you review the contributions of the information theorists and scientists as well as those concerned with the aspects of interpersonal communication, you'll recognize the application of some of Barnlund's approaches to communication definitions.

INFORMATION THEORY

Electronic computers and satellites have posed almost as many problems as they have solved, but they have led to the development of communications systems involving vast amounts of data. The continuing research has contributed to the general knowledge of the communication process.

Samuel F. B. Morse, who in the nineteenth century developed the Morse code for use in telegraphy, may have been the first person to apply some form of mathematical analysis to communication. Morse assigned a short telegraphic dot to the most frequently used letter, *e*. For less frequently used letters, he assigned longer symbols, such as dash-dot-dash for *k*. His code used only two symbols, a dot and a dash. This code is the forerunner of the binary code now used on the disks, cards, and tapes that are the basic information elements of the computer. Through its decoding process, the computer produces printed matter from the symbols punched on cards or recorded as electronic impulses on tapes. What implication does such a mathematical system have for business communication?

What does *binary* mean?

When information to be communicated is composed of predictable symbols—dots, dashes, holes in certain places in cards, impulses on an electronic tape, or alphabetic characters—emphasis in communication need be given only to the unpredictable. Here, for example, are a pair of familiar sayings:

1. _ P_NN_ S_V_D _S _ P_NN_ __RNED.

2. _ ST_TCH _N T_M_   S_V_S N_N_.

Because we are familiar with the sayings "A penny saved is a penny earned" and "A stitch in time saves nine," we are able to recognize them even though vowels weren't used. Vowels omitted in context are highly predictable, so only consonants are actually necessary. Although we don't write without vowels, our chances of communicating adequately would be pretty good if we omitted them. Because of our backgrounds, we are able to predict certain elements in communications. Therefore, communication theory places stress on transmitting the unpredictable and letting the predictable take care of itself.

Do habits help us predict?

However, our ability to predict can often be a hazard. Note the following common sayings:

1. Sly as a a fox.	**2.** Eager as a a beaver.	**3.** Paris in the the spring.

Because we read in thought groups and are also familiar with the sayings, we may have failed to detect the repetition of a word in each saying. We tend to see and hear what we *want* to see and hear. And this habit is based on previous learning, prejudices, and conditioning circumstances. As we extend our understanding of the communication process, first from the perspective of the physical sciences and then from that of the humanistic sciences, we should recognize some of the problems in communicating.

At midcentury, Dr. Claude Shannon at the Bell Telephone Laboratories[3] developed a mathematical theory of the engineering aspects of communication. This theory applied basically to the technical problems involved in accurately transferring various types of signals from sender to receiver. Shannon saw the fundamental problem of communication as reproducing at one point, either exactly or approximately, a message selected at another point. Although he was concerned with mechanical or electronic communication, Shannon certainly selected the fundamental problem of all, communication. However, within the scope of his communication problem—getting the exact message from transmitter to receiver—he did not

Can a computer predict word meaning?

concern himself with the problem of semantics, since word meaning is not a problem in the process of sending coded matter from one piece of equipment to another. Shannon's schematic presentation of the communication process is similar to Figure 1-1.

At this point, some nontechnical definitions of terms used in communication theory are important.

Information is the property of a signal or message enabling it to convey something the recipient finds both unpredictable and meaningful. Loosely, information is the inside interpretation of an outside event. For example, when we touch a hot surface, our inside interpretation of the event may be "Ouch!" This interpretation is information and can be measured in bits of information. A computer may store millions of bits of information. On command, the computer is capable of recalling any

Is an information bit similar to a word in human vocabulary?

one or a combination of bits. In proper combination, these bits form meaningful messages. In human communication, bits of information are words or other communicative symbols that can be used to describe a person's interpretation of events. Simply, information is the stuff to describe a person's interpretation of events. More simply, information is the stuff of which messages are made.

---

3. Claude Shannon and Warren Weaver, *The Mathematical Theory of Communication* (Urbana: University of Illinois Press, 1949). For a concise description of the theory, see Francis Bello, "The Information Theory," *Fortune,* December 1953 [reprinted in *The Mighty Force of Research* (New York: McGraw-Hill, 1956), and in *Readings in Communications,* Francis W. Weeks, ed. (New York: Holt, 1961)].

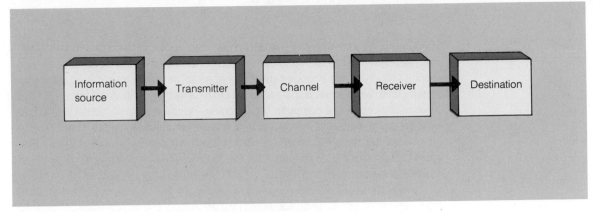

Figure 1-1   Simplified communication process.

A *message* is a transmissable combination of bits of information.

Encoding is the process of selecting and organizing bits of information into transmissable message language.

Decoding is the process of interpreting a message.

Feedback is a message or part of a message that the recipient returns to the sender so that the message may be modified or adjusted to make it clearer to the recipient. When one person responds to another's message, the response is called feedback.

Input is the sum of the experiences that build up the supply of bits of information in an information source such as a computer or a human mind. In other words, information fed into storage or memory for use in communication is input.

Output is the total information released from the information source for transmission.

If we look at Figure 1-2 and apply a simple situation, what goes on in communication becomes readily apparent. Suppose a satellite circling the earth passes through a change of temperature, and the change must be reported to earth. When the instruments detect the temperature change, the information source, which is a

What are the similarities between human communication and machine communication?

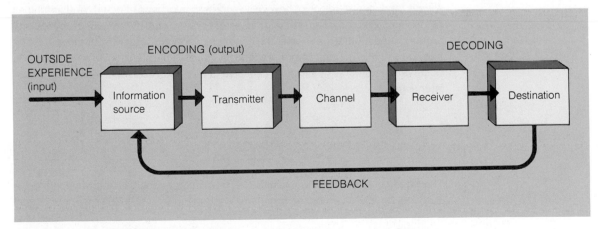

Figure 1-2   The communication process.

small computer in the satellite, selects those bits from its stored bits of information that best describe the change of temperature. After the bits have been placed in the proper sequence, the encoded message goes to the radio transmitter, where it is sent by radio waves over a channel to a radio receiver on earth. After being received, the message goes to a computer for decoding. Because both computers have been similarly programmed, if the message is not understandable to the decoding computer it will be rejected. Then the earth station will send a message back to the satellite asking for a modification of the original message. The message to the satellite is feedback.

In the communication process shown in Figure 1-2, disruptions in the message that require corrective feedback would probably occur in the transmission-reception process. Noise or static disrupts radio systems just as noise disrupts person-to-person discussions. Messages are also disrupted when too much information is transmitted. Transmission channels and receiving equipment, like human receivers and minds, can handle only limited quantities. Thus, one principle from information theorists that applies to all communication is *keep the message content within the quantity that can be handled by the communication system.* In other words, don't overload the channel.

Does decoding take place at the receiver or at the destination?

Communication is a process that remains incomplete until the message reaches its destination as undiluted or unchanged as possible. Proper encoding, clear transmitting and receiving, and accurate decoding are all involved. Thus, the main concern of information theorists is the most accurate method of selecting a message, transmitting it without noise, and reproducing it at the receiving/destination end. In addition, the proper selection of the channel and use of media are critical to the effectiveness of even the most carefully prepared message. Scientific research will continue to refine the various instruments now available, including the prototypes of equipment that can convert coded information into simulated human voices and the "talking" typewriters that can convert voice sounds into printed words.

Do specific words have the same meaning for all people?

However, whether spoken, written, graphic, or nonverbal, the message simply cannot be more effective than the quality of its preparation. A poor message will always be poor regardless of how well its transmission was effected. And as long as human beings are involved in the process of communication, semantics, behavioral patterns, and attitudes will enter the communication process. Furthermore, motivation enters into human communication; a bit of self-reflection may support the observation that "no individual can give an unequivocal definition of his own intentions."[4]

THEORY OF HUMAN COMMUNICATION

The theory of human communication has much in common with information theory. Both can be presented by the schematic chart in Figure 1-2. In the theory of human

4. Jurgen Ruesch, "Psychiatry and the Challenge of Communication," *Psychiatry* 17 (February 1954):5.

communication, the information source is the human mind. The transmitter is the voice, or whatever means humans have at their disposal to use in transmitting, and the channel becomes sight or sound waves. The receiver and the final destination, of course, are the sensory organs—ears, skin, nose, eyes—along with the mind of the recipient of the message. Thus physical scientists and behavioral scientists are talking about the same process. The physical scientists simply talk about machines and the behaviorists about people.

Dr. Jurgen Ruesch and his coworkers in the field of psychiatry have been instrumental in the development of theories of human communication.[5] Behavioral scientists working in the fields of sociology and psychology have strongly influenced business management by stressing interpersonal communication problems in the business environment. Basically, the various contributions to a theory of human communication have emphasized that difficulties in communication lie not so much with what we say or write but with what goes on in our own minds and in the minds of those with whom we are communicating. Bridging the gap between one mind and another primarily by the use of words is the communication task. It is not unlike the task of communicating from machine to machine.

Briefly, the theory of human communication advances the importance of such factors as social situation, role, status, rules, and instructions in understanding social action and personal intent.[6]

A *social situation* is established when people enter into the communication exchange and their behavior is organized around a common task. Within the communicative situation, people assume individual *roles* based on their parts in the activity; and these roles are mutually agreed to by the participants. On the college campus, a senior student assumes an authoritative role and the freshman a submissive role. *Status,* on the other hand, is closely related to role but is determined by officially prescribed duties and rights. A professor has more status than an assistant professor by virtue of the difference in titles. As their working relationship develops, however, the assistant professor might, through teaching ability and publications, play a more dominant role than that indicated by his or her status.

Within the business world, of course, such things as job titles, office furnishings, uniforms or other clothing, and a great variety of status symbols help us identify status. But more subtle clues are frequently identifiable to assist in the recognition of true roles. Frequently we find people whose own actions, time with the firm, close relationship with executives, and work habits result in their assumption of higher roles in the activities of the organization than their job titles and other status marks would indicate. Thus, good communicators must be conscious of role and status and must use this knowledge to identify the role and status of various individuals. In addition, they must develop skill in tailoring messages to the characteristics of the receiver.

Do you know of anyone whose role exceeds his or her status?

All games are played by *rules.* And the game of communications is no exception. Written and unwritten rules, such as company policies and practices, help

5. See Jurgen Ruesch, "Synopsis of the Theory of Human Communication," *Phychiatry* 16 (August 1953): 215–243.

6. Jurgen Ruesch and Gregory Bateson, *Communication, the Social Matrix of Psychiatry* (New York: Norton, 1951).

What unwritten rules govern classroom conduct?

Is the aroma of a cooking dinner a nonverbal clue?

determine who may talk to whom, how a message should be presented, the duration of a communication session, and what or what not to say. As people live and work in an environment, they gradually learn the rules of the game. In fact, they must learn them if they are to create a place for themselves within that environment.

Because not all messages are verbal (that is, conveyed through the use of words), the communication theorist must be aware of nonverbal communication. For example, facial expressions, gestures, other bodily actions — even the absence of any of them — are clues to whether a person is upset or pleased. And it is fairly easy, too, to recognize when a person's speech does not convey true intention. These nonverbal elements and their implications, along with roles and status, serve as secondary messages or *instructions* to assist the receiver in understanding the message. Both the sender and the receiver strengthen their communicative ability, then, as they develop greater understanding of human behavior to accompany their skill in using communication tools.

BEHAVIORAL CONCEPTS

Although many business activities have been taken over by highly sophisticated systems, those systems are still developed and operated by people. Within an organization — whether it be the home, the school, the industrial enterprise, or the governmental structure — coordination of human effort is the key to achieving goals. An understanding of human behavior is critical to effective communication whenever people interact with one another. Such an understanding provides the motivating force for task accomplishment.

Whether working with a single individual or with a group, a manager must keep in mind that each person is, and wants to be, his or her own person. Through past experience, we all have developed our own values, prejudices, likes, and dislikes. Although we all have some characteristics in common, the composite of our individual characteristics makes each of us different. We react in individual ways to messages.

Take the case where the boss storms into the office, rants, raves, and then stomps out. One employee's reaction is, "The boss was really angry. I've never seen her act that way before." Another might think, "That's no way for an executive to act." The first might appear frightened; the other might display disgust.

When a new piece of office equipment with time-saving possibilities and labor economies is introduced, a secure, competent employee might say, "Here comes the new machine!" From the tone of voice and facial expression, it is apparent that the employee is looking forward to the addition with pleasure. Another employee, far less secure and less competent, might use the same words, but indicate through tone and facial expression fears about being able to cope with the new equipment.

Because of the variety of possible reactions to a single message or event, business has turned to the behavioral sciences for information about possible management problems. This new attention to humans as dynamic beings with constantly changing needs and desires has led business to adopt policies and practices that are more people oriented than production oriented. The newer philosophy can be summed up as "The *right person* for the job is only a temporary solution because people change; the *right job* for the person is a more viable policy."

What does *viable* mean?

Maslow's Need Hierarchy

Abraham H. Maslow's concept of a hierarchy of needs has been widely cited as an excellent approach to understanding the changing nature of people's desires.[7] Maslow suggests a sequence of needs through which people successively move as they satisfy their wants and desires:

1. *Physiological needs:* to have food, shelter, and protection from the elements.

2. *Security and safety needs:* to be free from physical danger and to be secure in the feeling that physiological needs can be met.

3. *Social needs:* to be loved, to be accepted, and to belong.

4. *Ego needs:* to be heard, to be appreciated, to be wanted. These needs relate to status, and although economic status is often involved as a means of attaining social status, the satisfaction of ego needs ordinarily comes only with or after the satisfaction of economic needs.

5. *Self-actualizing needs:* to achieve one's fullest potential through professional, philanthropic, political, educational, and artistic channels.

As people satisfy needs at the first level, they are then motivated by those at the second level. As second-level needs are satisfied, those at the third level prevail, and so on. Keep in mind, though, that each of the need levels is always present. Lower-level needs simply diminish in importance as motivators as we satisfy them.

At what need level are most college students?

In the communicative process, we should be able to identify and appeal to need levels in various individuals. A simple review of advertising messages reveals how they are aimed. Ads for luxury cars appeal to ego needs, ads for breath fresheners appeal to social needs, and ads for fire alarms appeal to security needs.

If we accept Maslow's theory about need levels, then we should agree that a business environment that assists people to satisfy those needs is desirable. A satisfied worker is generally more productive than a dissatisfied one. The ability to apply behavioral knowledge to interpersonal relationships not only helps the individual, but it also strengthens the organization.

McGregor's Theories

In America, most people have fairly well satisfied the lower-level needs and are actively pursuing the satisfaction of social and ego needs. They want to be a part of

7. Abraham H. Maslow, *Motivation and Personality* (New York: Harper & Row, 1954).

things, they want to be recognized, they want to belong, and they want to be respected. This view of people has not always been held by those in management. Indeed, the view that people are probably motivated only to satisfy lower-level needs may still be held by management in some industries that employ mostly nonskilled labor. However, some striking changes have been made in labor contracts in industry in the past few years. The depressed automobile industry, for example, has developed contracts by which workers participate in a share-the-profits program. These workers are certain to develop some concern for the welfare of the industry.

Douglas McGregor attempted to distinguish between the older, traditional view of people and the emerging modern view — that management can be effective and production can be enhanced at the same time that management is assisting the individual to satisfy his or her higher need levels.[8] Basic to McGregor's theories of opposing management styles is the view that people cannot become mature if their experiences throughout life remain immature. Given the opportunity and the proper environment to be treated as mature individuals, people can develop maturity. At the risk of oversimplification, we give a succinct description of McGregor's two theories; he called the traditional style of management theory X and the new style theory Y.

1. *Theory X:* Strong control, concern for the job to the exclusion of concern for the individual; motivation derived primarily from external incentives.

2. *Theory Y:* A balance between control and individual freedom. As the individual matures, the need for external motivation decreases; concern of management is for the individual first and the job second.

In essence, as management moves from theory X styles to theory Y styles, external control gives way to self-control. Basic to theory Y, of course, are the assumptions that people are capable of change and that a gradual change to a permissive style in their leaders and in their environments will provide them with the impetus to change. In effect, theory Y advances the idea that if you treat adults as adults, permitting them to control their own destinies, they will act as adults and not as children. Although McGregor's concept is almost 25 years old, it has had a profound impact on recent education for management as well as on management practices, as has Maslow's 30-year-old development of the hierarchy of needs. As Americans are now well aware, the quality of working life is an important concern. Communication between worker and employer is now established as a two-way affair.

What style do you perceive in your classroom?

Transactional Analysis

In the past few years, *transactional analysis* (TA) has become popular as a means of analyzing behavior patterns in interpersonal relationships. Developed from psychia-

8. Douglas McGregor, *The Human Side of Enterprise* (New York: McGraw-Hill, 1960).

try, TA focuses on two-person exchanges of communication.[9] It is based on the premise that all persons have a set of ego states that are reflected in three broad categories:

1. *Parent:* The parent in each of us contains attitudes and behavior learned externally, usually from our parents. In effect, this is the "law and order" attitude. It is critical, prejudicial, but nurturing.

2. *Adult:* The adult in each of us contains the rational, objective intelligence that enables us to cope with the real world.

3. *Child:* The child in each of us contains the memories of our childhood experiences. It is impulsive, exciting, fun loving, and dependent.

When communication, which is a transaction, takes place between two people, one person provides a stimulus from one of the three ego states, and the other responds from one, as shown in Figure 1-3.

As long as the stimulus elicits the desired response and the stimulus–response lines do not cross, communication is satisfactory. As a simple example, a question from one person to another may begin a transaction: "Where did I leave my car keys?" Answer: "On the kitchen table." In this case, both the question and the answer come from the adult ego states of the two people, and the stimulus and response lines are parallel. Therefore, a complementary transaction has occurred. On the other hand, if the answer to the question is "Can't you keep track of anything!" the response is from the parent ego state to the child ego state of the one asking the question. An argument can ensue because stimulus and response lines have crossed. When lines cross, the transaction is not complementary, and arguments, problems, and misunderstanding will probably occur.

Transactional analysis in its therapeutic form is to be practiced only by experts. The important thing for us as business people is to become aware of the behavior exhibited by people when their messages are coming from a particular ego state. Certainly we can all recall some of the admonitions and rebukes of our parents when we were children: "Don't touch the stove!" "Go to your room!" "Brush your teeth and wash your hands!" "Don't cross the street!" "For heaven's sake!" These messages typify parent-type messages—bossy, dogmatic, and often unkind. At the same time, our parents had only our welfare in mind (or thought they did). The admonitions often led to good health practices, kept us from harm, and helped us in the growth process. As we matured, however, we tended to look on parental-type messages as invitations to fight back. Common sense should tell us, though, that fight-back behavior between adults won't resolve anything. In a work situation, messages from the parent ego state of a manager to a subordinate are characteris-

How do some baseball managers behave?

9. A thorough discussion of TA is beyond the scope of this book. The following books provide an interesting introduction to TA concepts, which are very helpful in understanding the human dynamics of communication. Eric Berne, *Games People Play* (New York: Ballantine, 1964); Muriel James and Dorothy Jongeward, *Born To Win* (Reading, Mass.; Addison-Wesley, 1971); and Thomas A. Harris, *I'm OK—You're OK* (New York: Harper & Row, 1969).

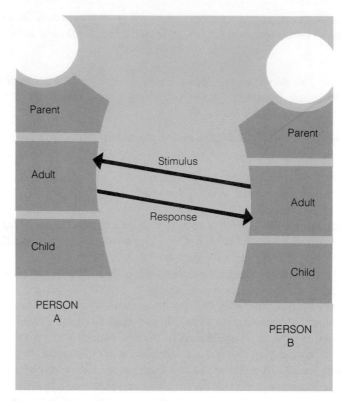

Figure 1-3   Transaction schematic showing three categories of ego.

tic of McGregor's theory X style of management. The sensitive subordinate will probably accept the admonition and wait for a time when the manager can be dealt with on an adult-to-adult basis. Probably the only other alternative would be for the subordinate to respond from the child ego state: cry or lash out in anger.

Becoming aware of situations in which the response and stimulus lines may cross can help us respond appropriately. Our communication behavior can be adapted.

Perhaps one of the most important concepts of TA is that of *stroking.* Research has indicated that when babies are left unattended or ignored for extended periods, they can develop actual physical problems as well as psychological ones. Babies require coddling, patting, and loving; and in TA terms, this is *stroking.* As adults, we also require stroking—but of a different sort. A simple "Good morning" is a stroke; and the reply, "Same to you," is another stroke. Although this exchange seems unimportant most of the time, imagine the reactions if the two were friends and no exchange took place. A pat on the back from the boss, a congratulatory phone call, and taking the time to listen to another's problems are examples of everyday stroking that occur in business. We all require stroking for our mental health, and attention to strokes can greatly improve communication and people's feelings about their work.

Have you received or given strokes today?

Figure 1-4 Before people meet, they know nothing about each other and something about themselves.

Communicating Interpersonally and the Johari Window

In addition to the contributions of Maslow and McGregor, the work of Joseph Luft and Harrington Ingram has expanded our knowledge of communication foundations. Their widely accepted Johari Window applies to two-way, interpersonal communication.

People engage in communication with others in the hope that the outcome may lead to trust in one another, mutual pleasure, and psychological wellbeing. The communication transaction is a means of sharing information about things, ideas, tasks, and selves. Before two strangers meet, what they know about each other might be depicted by the two circles shown in Figure 1-4.

After an introduction—"Hello, I'm John Green"; "Hello, I'm Jane Smith"— they know something about each other, if only each other's name and sex. They probably also gain an impression about each other through appearance and dress. At this point, the two circles begin to overlap, as shown in Figure 1-5 to indicate the surface things they know about each other.

As the transaction progresses, the overlap becomes greater and they learn

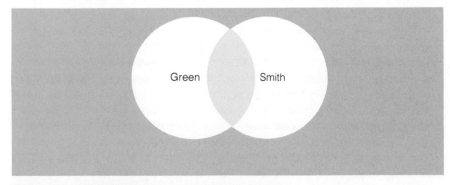

Figure 1-5 Knowledge about each other increases.

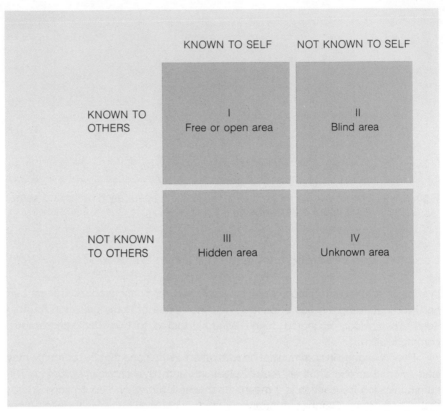

Figure 1-6   The Johari Window. Adapted from *Of Human Interaction* by Joseph Luft by permission of Mayfield Publishing Company. Copyright © 1969 by the National Press.

more and more about each other. Green may ask, "Care for a cup of coffee?" and Smith may answer, "Oh, I hate coffee, but I'd love tea." As a result of this exchange, Green learns a little more about Smith. Additionally, Smith may have gained some information about herself—that she was appealing enough to be invited to share coffee.

The nature of sharing is that people learn not only about others but also about themselves. Two simple circles do not provide for this concept, but the Johari Window, shown in Figure 1-6 (named for its creators, *Jo*seph and *Harri*ngton), does. The upper left-hand area, labeled "I," or "free area," represents what we know about ourselves, and what others know about us. Area II designates those things others know about us but that we don't know about ourselves: For example, you are the only person who can't see yourself as you really are. Mirror images are reversed. Things we know about ourselves but that others don't know about us is the hidden or secret area, III. Area IV includes things we don't know about ourselves and others don't know about us.

Each of these areas may vary in size to the degree that we can learn about ourselves from others and to the degree that we are willing to disclose things about

Can you really see yourself?

ourselves to others. Only through reciprocal sharing can people learn about themselves and about others. In communication practice, such sharing occurs only when people develop *trust* in one another. Of course, trust is something that must be earned. We are usually willing to tell people about our school records, our job tasks, and other items that aren't truly personal. But we share personal thoughts, dreams, and inner feelings only with selected others—with those whom we have learned to trust. Trust is a quality we develop from experience with others. Through performance, we earn the trust of others. The relationships existing between boss and employee, doctor and patient, and lawyer and client are those of trust, but of trust only in specific areas. In more intimate relationships—wife and husband, brother and brother, and parent and child—deeper, personal feelings are entrusted to each other. When a confidant demonstrates that he or she can be trusted, trust is reinforced and leads to an expansion of the open area of the Johari Window. In business, the boss–employee relationship is often strengthened to the point where nonwork elements can be discussed freely.

Who is your most trustworthy friend?

The idea that trust and openness leads to better communication between two people also applies to groups. People engaged in organizational development, O. D., are concerned with building large organizations by building effective small groups. They believe effectiveness in small groups evolves mostly from a high level of mutual trust among group members.[10] The aim of O. D. work is to open emotional as well as task-oriented communication. To accomplish this aim, groups often become involved in encounter sessions designed to enlarge the open areas of the Johari Window.

HIERARCHY OF COMMUNICATION LEVELS

Using the theories of communication and several of the behavioral concepts, we can establish a hierarchy for the effectiveness of communication situations:

1. Level one: The most effective communication occurs in a two-way, face-to-face situation where both verbal and nonverbal symbols and languages are apparent to both parties. Misunderstandings and inaccuracies can be resolved by observing the instructions accompanying messages and by providing appropriate feedback to assist in clarification. The most common examples of first-level communication are interviews, face-to-face discussion, small-group meetings, and conferences. The teaching–learning process is enhanced when conducted at this level simply because nonverbal elements and instant feedback are available.

2. Level two: The second most effective communication occurs in a two-way but not face-to-face situation. At this level, instant feedback is available but the nonverbal aids are not visible. Of course, the telephone call is the most common kind of communication at this level.

10. Harold J. Leavitt, *Managerial Psychology,* 4th ed. (Chicago: University of Chicago Press, 1978), p. 326.

Where does television fit?

3. Level three: The least effective communication occurs when it is necessary to rely only on written messages. Letters and written reports are read without the assistance of instant feedback and without the availability of many nonverbal aids.

Business certainly cannot be conducted solely at the first level. Constraints of time, distance, and money force us to resort to second- and third-level communication frequently. In addition, the complexity of the subject matter to be communicated may cause us to combine levels: for a very complex subject, we might well send a written document for study and follow up with a face-to-face discussion after the receiver has had an opportunity to study the document. In this way, feedback would be more meaningful. Of course, one-way communication may be necessary when legal matters are involved and written records must be retained. All too often, however, some people use written memorandums or letters for subjects that are routine—in frequently occurring situations in which a telephone call would be less expensive and speedier. In general, the cost of producing written messages is greater than the cost of telephone calls to handle the same subject when the labor costs of the writer and typist are considered.

Is your class schedule negotiable?

In any case, effective communicators will use the criteria of time, distance, money, and complexity of the subject when deciding which communication level to use for greatest effectiveness. Keep in mind that some messages do not call for immediate feedback. Policy matters determined by top management are generally put into practice only after considerable research and thought. They then constitute rules and guidelines for the conduct of the business and are best communicated at the one-way level. Agreements between labor and management, for example, end up as rules for a fixed time; further feedback is not necessary.

LANGUAGE AND CULTURE

No introduction to the study of communication would be complete without a brief discussion of the nature of *language.* As used in most contexts, language refers to a body of communicative symbols or signs, the significance of which is commonly known to a number of interpreters.

Human speech is no doubt the most highly developed of all languages. At the same time, we have a sizable sign language to accompany speech. For example, we all understand the thumbing-for-a-ride symbol. But we can never be sure of the intent of the hitchhiker, so he or she is frequently left standing. This insecurity about intent further complicates communication. In the meaning-centered approach to a definition of communication, as described at the beginning of this chapter, people were said always to attempt to attach meaning to things going on about them, observing symbols and interpreting them. "What did she mean by that?" is a thought that goes through most of our minds during our daily activities as a silent response to something we hear or see. Words, as well as gestures and facial expressions, are language symbols the sender of a message selects to express meaning. But meaning is developed by receivers of messages. Again, to the extent that both sender and receiver have the same experiences and, thus, attach similar meanings, communication is effective.

The study of word meaning in various contexts is *semantics,* a division of the broad science of language, which is *linguistics.* Other divisions of linguistics are *phonology,* the study of speech sounds; *morphology,* the study of the internal structure and forms of words; and *syntax,* the study of the arrangement of words in a sentence to show their relationship to one another. The study of business communication is concerned with all four divisions or branches. Semantic problems of meaning exist because of the varying life experiences of people. Cultural differences result from their geographic backgrounds, education, ages, occupations, and general life experiences. These create considerable variety in the interpretation of words. In our oral communication, we are concerned with proper speech sounds — phonology. Then morphology and syntax together constitute grammar and word usage, which are critical elements in both oral and written communication, particularly as we begin to rely on machine dictation as a part of word processing.

The study of language and communication can be exciting. Norbert Weiner summed up the fascination of language in this way: "The human interest in language seems to be an innate interest in coding and decoding and this seems to be as nearly specifically human as any interest can be. . . . Speech is the greatest interest and most distinctive achievement of [humanity]."[11]

SUMMARY

People engaged in the communication process are constantly and simultaneously involved in the two processes of encoding and decoding — they are acting as both sender and receiver at the same time. Even though you may sit quietly and motionless in the classroom, you send messages to your instructor through your facial appearance and your eyes. You are, thus, providing feedback to the instructor. The instructor, in turn, alters his or her behavior to adapt to your message; and this is the instructor's feedback to you. In a sense, then, communication is primarily dependent on feedback for effectiveness. In face-to-face communication, feedback is always present. In one-way, written communication, we have the problem of sending messages that we hope will be received and understood without the need for immediate feedback.

This absence of immediate feedback is the primary reason for studying written communication. Because it is at the least effective level, writing is the one communication skill that most people feel insecure about.

The behavioral sciences have contributed much to our understanding of the communication process, particularly to the idea that we must place primary consideration on the needs of the receiver when planning our messages. This considera-

---

11. Norbert Wiener, *The Human Use of Human Beings: Cybernetics and Society* (New York: Doubleday, 1954), p. 74.

tion of the receiver includes the wants, needs, and cultural backgrounds of people; it applies in communication ranging all the way from one-to-one discussion to international communication.

EXERCISES

Review Questions

1. Although computers and human minds play similar roles in information theory and in the theory of human communication, they have some differences. How do they differ?

2. Describe how McGregor's theory X management style and the parent ego state of TA are similar.

3. How is the adult ego state in TA similar to McGregor's theory Y manager?

4. What level of communication effectiveness would you use for the following situations?
  a. Notifying employees of a fire in the building.
  b. Notifying employees that the Friday after Thanksgiving is a paid holiday.
  c. Reprimanding an employee.
  d. Surveying the availability of restaurants and food prices for an annual department party.
  e. Getting agreement of management to a proposed annual department budget.

5. Describe some status symbols apparent on your campus.

6. How many semantic meanings can you think of for the word *fast?* For *fold?* Use a dictionary if you like.

7. How does "Some people are blind to their own faults" relate to the Johari Window? How do people learn about their own faults? From whom? If a person does learn about some previously unknown faults or attributes, how does this knowledge affect the size of some panes of the Johari Window?

Problems and Activities

1. At your instructor's direction, form pairs in the classroom. Your partner should be someone you don't know. Learn all you can about each other in four or five minutes. Evaluate your discussion in terms of trust, openness or self-disclosure, and the Johari Window.

2. In groups assigned by your instructor, discuss things that you consider barriers to your own ability to communicate in face-to-face situations, in writing, in speaking before groups. Make a list for a report to the class.

3. Clip a one-picture cartoon or photograph showing action from a newspaper or magazine. Remove the caption. Have three or four people privately provide a caption for the picture, telling them that anything goes. From what you know about the people, make an observational comment based on their replies. How similar were their observations?

4. Make a list of things you believe are included in most people's blind area of the Johari Window. Indicate those you think people would like to know about themselves and those you think people might not like to know about themselves.

5. Prepare a glossary of terms (terms and brief definitions) used in this chapter and new to you. They might come in handy at test time.

2

THE COMMUNICATION TECHNOLOGY REVOLUTION

The Rapid Acceleration of Progress
Word Processing and Personal
      Computers
Using the Executive Work Station
Using a Word-processing Center
Electronic Mail
Teleconferencing
Summary

By the time you read this sentence as a student of business communication, you may have had some exposure to a personal computer in high school or in your own home. But even so, you might not be aware of the kind of environment in which you will spend most of your working years. In fact, the lightening-like pace of developments in communication technology makes it almost impossible to foresee what things might be like in a few short years. The office of the future is already here . . . maybe.

THE RAPID ACCELERATION OF PROGRESS

About 36,000 years — 360 centuries — have passed since the Cro-Magnon, generally accredited to be the earliest language users, roamed parts of the earth. Yet, humans existed another 28,000 years before they could get past the limits of oral communication and hieroglyphic symbols. The oldest examples of writing date to just before 3000 BC in Sumerian inscriptions. Egyptian writing is known from about 100 years later and is the earliest example of the transfer of speech sounds (phonetics) to writing.

Greek writing evolved about 1000 BC, and its first two letters, alpha and beta, contributed to our word "alphabet." Twenty-five centuries passed before the printing press appeared in Europe to set the stage for mass communication through printed materials. Almost 99 percent of our authenticated history passed before the development of some form of mass communication; it was not until the 1800s that high-speed printing, a development of the Industrial Revolution, brought books and newspapers to the masses, thus contributing to the gradual eradication of illiteracy. The timing of communication developments and great social changes is not a coincidence. Printing accompanied the Renaissance, and high-speed printing and inexpensive newsprint came along with the Industrial Revolution.

What percentage of authenticated history preceded Columbus?

Each successive development has changed society. Early writing freed oral societies from the limitations of time and space. Their legacies could be transmitted in writing; and anthropologists and historians have not had to rely solely on hieroglyphs, pottery, utensils, and religious artifacts to study our more recent past. However, the world was essentially illiterate until the development of printing, which made literature available to other than the religious elite. As printing multiplied the dimensions of communication, people who weren't literate were encouraged to become so.[1]

Of course, high-speed printing and daily newspapers overcame all previous printing limitations and set the stage for even greater developments in communication. With the advent of the telegraph, telephone, radio, and later television, the world became an even smaller place; almost-instantaneous communication became commonplace. What a significant milestone we achieved when hundreds of millions were able to hear and see Neil Armstrong set foot on the moon!

Today we talk about personal computers, word processing, electronic mail, and

1. Frederick Williams, *The Communications Revolution* (Beverly Hills, CA: Sage Publications, 1982).

teleconferencing. Any chapter written on communication developments thirty years ago would have been relevant for a good fifteen years. But the communication explosion of the past fifteen years has eclipsed all previous developments in human history. The implications of these advances are imposing for modern society. We are no longer limited by such things as time, speed, and distance. Now the instantaneous transmission of both sight and sound has moved human communication from the speed of animals and people to the speed of light. Communication coupled with computer capability may change our society from one in which the individual travels to work, play, or study to one in which work, play, and study travel to the individual. As we review some aspects of the "new" communication systems or processes, keep in mind that the discussion is primarily a state-of-the-art summary. Change is so rapid that in a short time this discussion, too, may be looked on as "old stuff."

Does present technology qualify as revolutionary?

WORD PROCESSING AND PERSONAL COMPUTERS

A few years ago, "data processing" and "information processing" were terms used to designate the function of electronic computers. Those early computers were space-consuming devices that were highly sensitive to temperature changes. With the development of the microprocessor chip,* computers could be smaller without sacrificing capability. The computer was used to process data only, and the production of written material by automated devices was in its infancy. "Word processing" is a term describing a function that provides secretarial and stenographic service on a more efficient basis. The original concept involved automatic, error-free typewriting and increased productivity. Punched tapes and magnetic cards were used to record typed materials; and errors could be corrected directly on the tapes or cards so that error-free copy could be typed automatically, thus eliminating human mistakes. Early word processing of this type was used primarily for repetitive letter-writing situations. Recently, however, the smaller personal computer and the typewriter have been combined into our modern word-processing system. Modern word processing is an integration of sophisticated typing machines and computers, making possible the automation of most manual operations of the past. Word processing is rapidly becoming simply a part of a total, integrated, information-processing system.

Is a word processor a computer?

At the heart of the personal computer is the tiny microprocessor chip surrounded by several other miniature components and a keyboard for entering information. With the addition of a monitor (cathode ray terminal or personal television set), plus a way to load programs into the computer, and a printer, the package becomes a total word-processing information installation. The personal computer can also be linked to the mainframe of a large computer and, thus, have access to vast amounts of information.

In 1981, over one million personal computers were sold; and by 1985, accord-

---

* For definitions of a variety of word-processor and computer terms, see the Glossary at the end of this chapter.

ing to analysts of this new industry, personal computers—selling for well under $10,000 and designed to be used by one person—will be an $8 billion to $10 billion market.[2] Well-known firms (such as Apple, Commodore, Tandy, I.B.M., Digital, Xerox, Data General, Victor, Zenith, Wang, Nippon Electric, Texas Instruments, and CPT), along with some 150 others, have entered the market. Moreover, many of their products will be sold through major retail chains, making the computer as common as stoves, refrigerators, microwave ovens, and television in retailers' showrooms. A brief glance through your local newspaper will reveal ads for personal computers ranging in price from under $100 to several thousand dollars. Machines with both editing and printing capabilities do not cost much more than heavy-duty electric typewriters.

True or false: Smith-Corona no longer makes manual typewriters?

USING THE EXECUTIVE WORK STATION

The personal computer with word-processing capability has significant potential to save managerial time. Executives plan, motivate, control, make decisions, communicate, evaluate, delegate, and implement. They do not manufacture products, but they normally are the highest paid personnel in an organization. Their time is precious and expensive. Throughout the 1970s, computer terminals in executive and managerial offices were fairly common. As long as the terminal generated numerical data, the executive was "respectable." But for the executive to have a typewriter at her or his desk was not always respectable; perhaps, it was thought, he or she is "just a typist." Now the personal computer can serve several functions, and the executive can still be respectable.

Some executives, though, are hindered by technophobia—fear of change and of "smart machines." To use the information and word processor effectively, they must acquire some simple skills: in operating a keyboard (called keyboarding or typewriting), in composing and editing, and in dictating when necessary. These skills are necessary to use the "executive workstation," sometimes referred to as a management support station. It is an integral part of the new communication style.

The executive workstation allows the manager flexibility in arranging activities, scheduling conferences, using electronic mail, designing graphics, revising writing, and accessing large data bases.[3] In a well-equipped organization, computers can communicate with other computers. Each day an executive can query the computer about his or her schedule for that day or any future day. Plans can be made, and conferences can be scheduled with others in the organization simply by reviewing the schedules of others. Almost everyone in management knows through experience the difficulties of maintaining accurate daily schedules and of scheduling group meetings.

Can a computer lead to order out of chaos?

By typing any message on the keyboard, the executive can transmit that

2. Kathleen K. Wiegner, "Tomorrow Has Arrived," *Forbes*, February 15, 1982.
3. Betty R. Ricks, "The Neglected Managerial Communication Skills," *The ABCA Bulletin*, December 1981, p. 22.

message to any of the other personal computers in the organization's system. A light on the receiving station's equipment signals that a message is waiting. This internal communication system is only one minor application of "electronic mail," which is discussed later.

Mailing lists and telephone numbers of associates and customers may also be accessed through the computer. Such lists can be revised quickly whenever changes occur.

An exciting feature of many computers is the capacity to produce tables, graphs, and charts in a variety of formats to be printed for inclusion in written reports.

Students and business workers alike have the usual problem of composing at a typewriter or in longhand and then attempting to rearrange or edit the material. With the computer, the composition can be typed and displayed on the monitor, edited, and rearranged without retyping or rewriting the entire composition. The material can be stored for later recall and final typing of the entire manuscript. To support these writing activities, the executive workstation provides access to stored financial and other quantitative data. Thus, the personal computer is a data processor, a word processor, and a filing system.

Remember, however, that this entire concept of having a more efficient executive support system requires that the user (1) master some very basic skills, (2) disregard the implications of performing "menial" secretarial work, and (3) understand the time-saving, effective communication that can result.

Why do people resist change?

USING A WORD-PROCESSING CENTER

Word processing existed long before the personal computer revolution. Word processors were originally intended as replacements for typewriters and offered two distinct advantages. First, they provided faster typing with fewer errors; and second, they made revisions a simple task. Modern word processors continue to have these advantages; but they have expanded abilities, greater speed, and more flexibility than their predecessors.

The range of word-processing equipment is vast. The one-person, stand-alone version consists of a memory typewriter with a video display screen at one extreme. And at the other is the word-processing center — staffed by skilled transcriber – typists and supervisors or managers, and equipped with sophisticated typing equipment, cathode ray terminals, high-speed printers, copying and printing machines with graphic capability, and linkage to computers. In between these two extremes lies an abundance of variations. Thus, the decision of a business firm to adopt word processing need not be an "all-or-nothing" proposition. Office systems may be built a step at a time. Thus, a word-processing center may serve a single unit of an organization or the total organization. A schematic of a sophisticated word-processing network is shown in Figure 2-1.

The work of centers is high powered and the jobs often physically and emotionally demanding. Centers are usually made environmentally comfortable through the

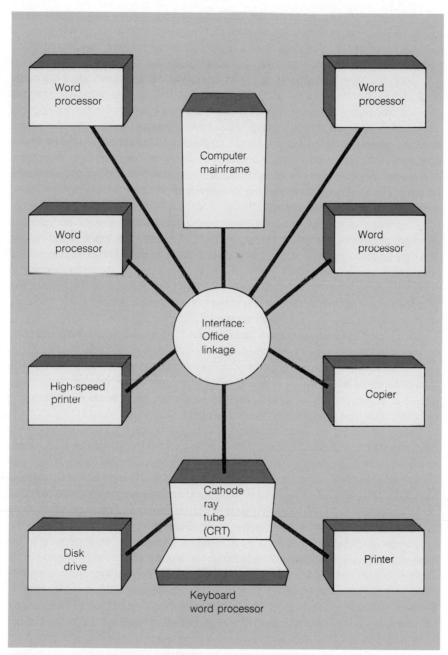

Figure 2-1   Word-processing communication network.

use of carpeted floors, air conditioning, good lighting, quality space design, and music. Skilled word-processing operators receive work either in rough-draft form or in the form of dictation by organizational personnel to recording equipment in the center. The operators then put the work in finished form.

Such formerly painstaking tasks as centering material, arranging columnar data, aligning decimals, and aligning right-hand margins are now automatic features of word-processing equipment. A display unit permits operators to prepare perfect copy before final automatic typing, thus making erasers and other correction materials obsolete. Additionally, optical scanners, storage units, and transmission devices tie the center into a total information system in the organization. The output of word processing may be returned to those requesting the work, or transmitted to an electronic storage or filing system, or relayed to an offset printer or high-speed printer for quantity reproduction.

The major difference between using your own word processor and using a word-processing center lies in the requirement of dictating as input to the center. The "garbage in, garbage out" cliché about computer input and output is true of word processing too when dictation is involved. The task of dictating by machine to a word processing center is far different from that of dictating to a responsive, live secretary who can ask questions and make corrections on the spot. In Chapter 6, we'll look at effective dictation techniques.

In addition to the obvious advantages of word processing, the word-processing centers provide economy of operation and more uniform production as well. Economy is achieved by reducing nonproductive secretarial time. Transcribers who formerly worked in individual or group offices can provide service for many more dictators. When centers are used, secretaries do not have to be present during dictation: thus, this time can be devoted to other office tasks.

What do you think "quality control" means?

More uniform production is achieved because tasks in word processing are often reduced to routines, quality control can be exercised uniformly by supervisors in word-processing centers, and work loads of word-processing operators can be equalized. In consideration of employee morale, uniform quality control and equal work loads through the use of word-processing centers are positive factors. Certainly, equal pay for equal work is a goal of both workers and management.

Can any of these problems be solved?

Among the problems of initiating word-processing centers are these: the reluctance of dictators to dictate to a machine rather than to a secretary; the necessity of convincing skilled secretaries or stenographers that moving to a word-processing center from an individual office is not demeaning; and the inability of the word-processing center to provide an immediate response to the dictator. In addition, technology has moved so rapidly that schools and other training institutions have lagged far behind in giving the kinds of training required and in the number of trained workers they can produce.

Although people problems appear to be foremost in the use of word processing, equipment selection and use is also of paramount importance. With the plethora of equipment available, anyone planning to acquire word-processing machines is likely to be bewildered by the range in capabilities and in cost. The language of computers applies to the language of word processing because the modern word processor and the personal computer are closely related—in fact, they usually are the same piece of equipment. For effective selection of equipment, one should look for machines with adequate display screens, advanced text-editing capabilities, easy-to-understand keyboards with simple words to describe what keys do, adequate software, and supporting service by the manufacturer following the purchase. Although it should not be difficult to narrow your choices down to a few using these criteria, you should consider the long-range use of the equipment. Must it be compatible with other electronic equipment in your office? Is the language of its programs transferable to other equipment? Is the storage adequate for your long-range plans? Does the printer produce quality work to represent you or your company?

Is a TV screen a display screen?

As with all computers, software programs also make word processors effective. With proper storage capacity, word processors perform mathematical calculations, check spelling of up to 100,000 words, and prepare documents in several different languages—including Katakana, the Japanese business language.

Will you really be using some form of word processing in your business career? A recent study of the written communication practices of managers found that about 2 out of 3 used a private secretary, almost half used a secretarial pool (sharing secretarial services with others), 1 out of 4 used a word processor or terminal, 1 out of 5 used stand-alone dictation units, and about 1 out of 7 used a central word-processing center. When asked what they thought they would be using in five years, 2 out of 3 anticipated using a word processor or terminal.[4] The use of a central word processor was expected by about 2 out of 5. Obviously (because of the overlap in the percentages), many managers use a combination of methods for the preparation of written material. Interestingly, the study revealed that lower-level managers used word processors or terminals more frequently than did middle- and upper-level managers. And by 1986, almost 70 percent of all managers polled expect to be using this medium. Yes, you'll be using word processing and dictating in your career—perhaps even in your first job.

ELECTRONIC MAIL

Some forms of mail transmitted electronically have been available for years—the telegram, the mailgram, the cablegram. Messages of these kinds travel faster than postal department messages, of course, and they provide written evidence about the communication. Currently, facsimile transmission (fax) represents a step forward in the use of electronic mail. Something like a copying machine, fax makes use of a scanning process to convert images into electronic impulses or signals that are transmitted over regular telephone lines to anyone having a like machine. Any kind of printed or typed document, including pictures or photographs, can be handled. The

What does fax mean?

4. Marie E. Flatley, "A Comparative Analysis of the Written Communication of Managers. . ." *The Journal of Business Communication* 19, no. 3 (Summer 1982).

primary users of fax are large businesses with offices scattered throughout the country. However, fax mail can be sent to stations that provide the service for those without fax equipment. Users simply pick up their electronic messages at this "mailing station," and they can also transmit messages through the station. Clearly, facsimile communication does compete with the service of the federal postal system. The competitive advantages of fax are the speed of transmission (only a few minutes for a page of information) and the reduced cost when volume is substantial and transmission occurs on a delayed basis during evening hours when telephone lines are at their lowest use and cost.

Now the computer enters the electronic mail picture. Lightweight computers the size of portable typewriters are used by some of our major news services and magazines to reduce the time to get stories from reporters in the field to editorial offices. All the reporter needs is an adapter or a three-way socket and a telephone to file stories. Once plugged into the wall socket, the computer is turned on and types "Ready." The reporter pushes a command button and types the story. When the typing is completed, the reporter dials a special telephone number of the receiving station, attaches the telephone handheld unit to the computer, and then commands the computer to transmit. Presto! The story arrives in printed form at the editorial office.

Perhaps the brightest prospect of electronic mail systems is their potential to reduce paper usage. Surprising to many, paper is expensive not simply in terms of its cost as a commodity but also in the immense cost of storing, filing, and retrieving written documents. To reduce paper use, electric typewriter impulses can go directly into an electronic system and be transmitted to a receiving station where the message is displayed on a television screen. When a computer is linked to the system, the message can be stored on either a hard or soft disk for later reference. To share information among several word processors, one manufacturer produces a hard-disk memory device that can store up to 22,000 pages of information. As many as eight word processors can retrieve information simultaneously, even if it is the identical piece of information.

List some advantages of electronic mail.

On the horizon, of course, is the prospect of our being able to do much of our day-to-day business electronically. Purchasing, paying bills, and banking are examples of activities amenable to electronic handling. Most utility bills are now prepared electronically and sent to customers through the postal service. The customer, in turn, writes a check and sends it back through the same postal service. Wouldn't it be nice to turn on your television set or home computer, dial your account number, have all your current obligations displayed, and then simply order payment by your bank through the system. No paper is involved, and your transactions are recorded and filed in a computer. When you want to reconcile your checkbook, you'll simply dial your account, observe it on your receiver screen, and reconcile it without the need to have your checks returned.

Can you suggest other home uses of computers?

Although most electronic mail now ends up on paper, as systems become available to a broader market and people lose their phobias about having to have a piece of paper in hand for peace of mind, much of the way we do business will change. We have talked about the "paperless" society for years. It is now imminent.

TELECONFERENCING

High costs of air travel, hotel rooms, food, and time lost while traveling have contributed to increased use of *teleconferencing* in business and government.[5] Except for the benefits that might accrue from face-to-face live meetings, electronically held conferences can be just as effective. Telephone companies have teleconferencing facilities available for business use. For a number of years, the telephone conference call, in which the phone company simply arranges for several people to be on the "line" at the same time, has been available. But current technology has gone far beyond that method.

Conferences can now be held using television cameras and receivers with feedback equipment, so participants can engage in a group discussion while observing one another. In this way, the facial expressions and gestures that add so much to communication are apparent. The major morning news programs on television make frequent use of two-way video equipment to show us both the interviewer and the interviewee; teleconferencing works the same way.

Educational programs on television bring the class to the student rather than the student to class. With closed-circuit television and feedback audio equipment, however, actual campus classes are sent to remote classrooms — often in a business organization's educational facility. Students in the remote classroom can "buzz" the actual classroom when they have questions to ask or answers to give to questions posed by the instructor. The same system, of course, can be used with ill or disabled students in elementary and secondary schools. Although the possibilities of teleconferencing in education are almost boundless, certainly the social and psychological personal growth that occurs when students attend school with other live students preclude any thought of universal use of electronic education.

Will television eliminate textbooks?

SUMMARY

Despite the technological developments that have led to an increasing capacity to communicate farther and faster, the ability of people to provide proper input to the communication process will always be the critical factor in communication effectiveness in the office and world of tomorrow. A personal computer can solve many problems; but it, too, is just "a dumb hunk of iron" without good software programs and proper input.[6]

The office of the future is essentially with us now, but the effects of this creature of technology on society may not be felt for some time. Historically, changes in communication technology have accompanied significant social changes — the

5. J. M. Nilles et al. *The Telecommunication – Transportation Tradeoff: Options for Tomorrow* (New York: Wiley Interscience, 1976).

6. J. A. Tannenbaum, "Small Businesses Learn that a Computer Without Software Is a "Dumb Hunk of Iron," *Wall Street Journal,* April 2, 1980.

printing press along with the Renaissance, high-speed printing along with the Industrial Revolution. The current revolution in communication technology — with its satellites, personal computer, electronic mail, word processing, and more sophisticated use of television — holds immense possibilities for the way we live, work, and play. More and more, the home may become the focal point for our activities. Video games, such as Pacman, were forerunners of home video educational packages. When people can interact with television on an intellectual basis, they tend to avoid the sedentary activity of merely watching. Children are perhaps learning as much about spelling and mathematics through electronics as they can in school.

In the future, many occupations involved with information processing (such as accounting, banking, financial analysis, statistics, and investing) may be conducted primarily from the home office. Sending the work to the worker rather than the worker to work, moving messages electronically rather than through the mail service, and using electronic records rather than paper records are all possible outcomes of the new communication revolution.

People present the major obstacle to the widespread adoption of innovations. Changes must occur in the way we feel about possible alterations in the traditional ways of doing things. Reluctance to change is a human trait we must cope with realistically. And when change is accepted, we still must acquire the skills and knowledges necessary to use the new technology. Because it is *people* who must provide the input to communication systems, they must be educated, or re-educated, to do it well. But when all is said and done, the capacity to write correctly and effectively, to organize ideas, to dictate efficiently, and to speak and listen well will remain the foundations for all human communication. Those are the things the remainder of this book is all about.

GLOSSARY OF PERSONAL COMPUTER AND WORD-PROCESSING TERMS

ASCII:	The American Standard Code for Information Interchange. It is the most common convention for representing data in the computer memory and is used to transmit data between computers.
BASIC:	A popular programming language for small computers.
BIDIRECTIONAL:	Describes printers that print both from left to right and from right to left.
BINARY:	The "base two" numbering system used by all computers to store and represent information.
BIT:	The basic unit of information in computer systems. All data are composed of combinations of bits.
BYTE:	Eight bits. A computer's words are composed of combinations of bytes. The storage capacity of computers

	is measured in bytes (for example, 64K = 64,000 bytes).
CHARACTER PRINTER:	A printer that prints one character at a time, the way a typewriter does.
CHIP:	Slang for "integrated circuit." A circuit is etched on a small piece of silicon (the "chip") and helps control the functions of a computer.
CIRCUIT BOARD:	A plastic board with electronic components on one side and a printed copper circuit on the other.
COBOL:	The Common Business Oriented Language, a high-level computer language.
CPU:	Central processing unit. It holds the silicon chips and is the brains of the computer.
CRT:	Cathode ray tube. The display screen of the computer and word processor. It is also known as a monitor, a screen, and a display unit.
CURSOR:	A mark on the display screen that shows where the next character will appear.
DISK OR DISC:	A magnetic storage device. Disks are either "floppy" or "hard." Hard disks have much greater storage capacity but are more expensive.
DISK DRIVE:	A device that operates the disks.
FILE:	A collection of records stored by the computer.
FORTRAN:	FORmula TRANslator, a computer language originally designed for mathematical and scientific use but now being used in business systems.
INSTRUCTION:	An action performed by the computer.
INTEGRATED CIRCUIT:	See *chip.*
INTERFACE:	A device that connects one part of the computer or word processor to another.
KEYBOARD:	The switch-actuated computer version of a typewriter.
KILOBYTE:	The standard unit of memory. One kilobyte equals 1,024 bytes.
LINE PRINTER:	A printer that prints an entire line at one time.
LINKAGE:	A device to connect word processors into a network.
MEMORY:	The place where a computer stores information and instructions.
MODEM:	A bundle of circuits enabling computers to talk to one another.
OFF-LINE:	Not connected directly to the computer system.
ON-LINE:	Connected to the computer system and available for access by other systems.
OUTPUT:	The information the computer produces on the CRT or on paper, or transmits.
PERIPHERALS:	Options or accessories that can be added to the basic

	computer, such as a printer or disk drive. Peripherals may cost more than the computer.
PROGRAM:	A series of instructions telling the computer what to do.
RAM:	Random Access Memory; the computer memory that can be called up from internal storage.
ROM:	Read Only Memory; the computer's permanent store of instructions which cannot be changed.
SOFTWARE:	Computer programs.
TERMINAL:	Device used for entering and retrieving computer information. Usually the terminal consists of a keyboard and display or printer.

EXERCISES

Review Questions

1. If the recorded history of man covers 36,000 years and this time were converted to one 24-hour day, you were probably born within the last minute of that day. Is this statement correct?

2. Some computers designed to play electronic games on home television sets are advertised at less than $100. What differences or improvements would you expect to have as you move upward to more expensive electronic items?

3. Are word processors and personal computers related?

4. What advantages accrue when word processing is made part of a totally integrated office information system?

5. What is meant by "technophobia," and what are its implications for increased use of computers and word processors?

6. What is "electronic mail"?

7. What is meant by the statement "Software makes the computer"?

8. If you were assigned the task of selecting word-processing equipment for an office, what would you do?

Activity

Visit a retail outlet for computers and word processors. Select two for evaluation. Prepare to discuss in class your reasons for preferring one over the other, assuming that you intend to use it for home or personal purposes.

INTERNATIONAL BUSINESS COMMUNICATION

**The Cultural Environment of
International Business**
Achieving Empathy
American Values and Stereotypes
Written Communication Problems
Semantic Problems and Translation
Nonverbal Communication Problems
The Language of Time
The Language of Space
Other Factors
Some Light at the End of the Tunnel
Summary

Chapter 2 described the technological developments that will continue to have an increasing impact on the way people will communicate; and fittingly the final chapter in Part One is concerned with another element of growing importance—communicating in an international business environment.

A few years ago, an American executive visited a new graduate school of business in Pakistan. As part of his tour, he was invited to the main office of the local electric utility company and observed sixty clerks preparing monthly customer bills by hand. Almost without a pause, he suggested that the installation of a computer system could reduce staff in the billing department by about 75 percent. His host replied, "When 95 percent of the people in my country are unemployed, why do you suggest that we do away with 45 jobs?"

Is automation always a step forward?

This story is not unusual: it typifies one of the problems of communicating with other cultures; and it demonstrates how a lack of preparation or knowledge can affect relationships. In our present era of sophisticated communication technology and increasing interdependence of nations, international communication will continue to involve more and more persons from business, government, and educational spheres. We must hope they will learn to conduct their work more effectively than did the visitor to Pakistan, because the success of our international programs will depend greatly on the personal communication effectiveness of those involved. Although this book is not the place for a course in cultural anthropology, a brief review of some factors affecting international communication is appropriate.

THE CULTURAL ENVIRONMENT OF INTERNATIONAL BUSINESS

The culture of a people is the sum total of their living experiences within their own society and is highly resistant to change. It could be described as "the way of life" of a people and includes a vast array of behaviors and beliefs. The following breakdown provides a broad (but not comprehensive) view of some critical factors that may differ greatly from culture to culture:

Language—spoken, written, nonverbal.

Values and attitudes toward materialism, time, work, change, dress, foods.

Religion—rituals, sacred objects, taboos, beliefs.

Law—civil, business.

Society—mobility, class.sytems, family, institutions, education.

Economic development—farming, large-scale agriculture, cottage industries, heavy industry, technology.

Culture enables us to acquire a language, which we use in common with others of the same culture; it provides us with standards for behavior and gives us the feeling of identifying with and belonging to a larger society.

Problems between cultures occur primarily because people assume that the elements of their own cultures are natural, appropriate, and acceptable to others. Obviously, however, this is not the case in practice; if it were, we would have little conflict or miscommunication.

Are capital-
ism and commu-
nism cultural influences?

ACHIEVING EMPATHY

A person who has empathy for another, in a total view, is "able to detect and identify the immediate affective state of another and also able to respond in an appropriate manner."[1] In other words, empathy is the ability to put yourself in another's "shoes" and to anticipate the other person's reaction to situations. Notice that this definition of empathy involves two skills: First, an empathic person can *identify* the feelings or emotional state of another; and second, the person can *respond* to this state effectively as a result of the accurate identification. In terms of international communication, we can extend the definition to include the recognition of some cultural factors that help or hinder communication. Perhaps total empathy is unachievable for we can never really *be* the other person nor can we possibly detect accurately all the factors that characterize a particular culture.

Because of the many things we have in common with close friends or relatives, we have opportunities to achieve maximum empathy. But when we attempt to communicate with strangers—even strangers from our own culture—the empathy "gap" widens considerably. As the stranger-type relationship evolves into friendship, participants in communication tend to develop greater trust in each other, and this trust leads to more self-disclosure and increased empathy. Obviously the same relationship can develop to a degree between people of different cultures, but the vast array of cultural differences will always be a limiting factor. To achieve intercultural empathy, a person would have to live in another culture—be immersed in it for a long time. The more reasonable alternative for Americans planning to work with those from other cultures is simply to study the other cultures thoroughly *prior to* engaging in the business relationship. In addition, Americans planning to work in the international arena should learn to understand themselves and their own cultural traits.

Is absolute
empathy achievable?

AMERICAN VALUES AND STEREOTYPES

Understanding ourselves is not always as easy as we might think. Many of our cultural traits are practiced so unconsciously that we may not be aware of them. We

1. Kathleen S. Verderber and Rudolph F. Verderber, *Inter-Act: Using Interpersonal Communication Skills* (Belmont, CA: Wadsworth, 1977), p. 39.

can, though, draw some broad generalizations about Americans—generalizations that others might also draw about Americans.

Since our beginning as a nation, we have grown and developed on account of the immigration of people from a great variety of cultures. Through the centuries most of us have blended into an American culture; but a tour through almost any major city will reveal pockets of people who, although immigrants, have banded together in their own enclaves and retained much of their native culture.

But apart from the cultural holdouts, the American stereotype does exist. The abundance of natural resources and our industrial might have made us appear affluent and wasteful in the eyes of foreigners. ''Visiting foreigners are often astonished to see cars less than ten years old heaped in junkyards. These cars would probably still be on the road in most countries because other cultures seem more inclined to foster an awareness of the need for conserving resources and preserving material goods.''[2] We attempt to control nature; many other cultures worship it as part of their religions. We also seem to seek status through the acquisition of high-priced things—certain automobiles, imported shoes, designer jeans—while many other cultures can get along with mass transportation, ordinary footwear, and a pair of pants.

Americans are also looked on as ''rugged individualists'' who are aggressive in their business affairs and seek to stand out ''above the crowd.'' Such individualism is not considered important in some other cultures—where the family, the group, and the organization take precedence over the individual. As we'll discuss later, Americans are considered straight-forward, get-to-the-point business people; and this is not necessarily a desirable attribute.

Do you have your own stereotype of a college professor?

Additional elements in the American stereotype are our attitudes toward formality, time, and change. We generally act informally, perhaps as part of our attempt to maintain our rugged-individualism reputation. Many foreign cultures place a high value on formality, rituals, and social rules. To Americans, ''time is money''; but in some other cultures, time is the cheapest of commodities and is an inexhaustible resource representing only the life span on earth as part of the longer period including the hereafter. Americans look on change as inevitable, but we attempt to initiate it and to control it. Many other cultures recognize change as inevitable but in no way attempt to initiate it.

Although all these characteristics are not undesirable—in fact, most of us would say they are desirable—they do constitute the picture of an American in the mind of many foreigners. We should keep in mind as well that we also have stereotypes for the foreigners with whom we'll be doing business.

WRITTEN COMMUNICATION PROBLEMS

The forthrightness of Americans is reflected in their writing style and would produce considerably different letters from the following one, which was prepared in an English company:

2. Arvind V. Phatak, *International Dimensions of Management* (Boston: Kent, 1983), p. 23.

Dear Sir,

With reference to our letter of August 20th, we attach hereto a statement showing a sterling balance due of £4.14.8 in respect of the film "Management by Objectives."

We trust you will find same in order and will favour us with your further remittance in early settlement.

Yours faithfully,

I. Wallace

I. Wallace
Accounts Dept.

This is an actual letter, and nothing has been changed. As critics of the letter, we would probably first say that it wasn't written in this century. Actually, it was written in 1977. Then we would go on to check all the redundant and trite phrasing, correct the spelling of "favor," and admonish the writer that "Yours faithfully" is appropriate only in a love letter. An American version would be something like the following example:

Dear Mr. Jones

Enclosed is our bill for $7.40 for your rental of the film "Management by Objectives."

We were pleased to serve you, and we hope you'll find the film helpful.

Sincerely

I. Wallace

I. Wallace
Accounting Department

Keep in mind that British colonies throughout the world adopted British practices, so you can expect to see a similar writing style from firms in many countries. If we look on writing style as an indication of the personality of the writer, we can be seriously misled. I. Wallace might be as natural and unstilted as the letter is stiff and stilted.

People in non-English-speaking countries have attempted to use English as the language of international commerce—a development for which we Americans should be profoundly grateful. Although the letters are neither English nor American in style, the writers' cultures are usually reflected in their writing. Japanese, for example, tend to write things in chronological order rather than in some of the sequences advocated in America. Their traditional letters also include opening and closing statements that reflect extreme degrees of humility and courtesy. Some openings carry greetings and ideas completely unrelated to the subject of the message. A typical opening sentence might be, "Winter cold is leaving and summer warm will soon come." A closing sentence might be "I pray that you have success." The "meat" of the letter falls between the opening and closing sentences. Even though these samples exhibit a high degree of courtesy, letters are not considered especially courteous in Japan — genuine courtesy is shown through personal visits or telephone calls. "The Japanese have always been — and particularly the younger generation are — 'allergic' to letter writing."[3]

SEMANTIC PROBLEMS AND TRANSLATION

In addition to the problems created by differences in writing style, the problem of semantics is one that is ever present. English words simply do not always have an equivalent meaning when translated into other languages, and the concepts which the words describe are often different as well. A study of the concept of profit held by Japanese and American business students concluded this way: "It is important for the American to understand that his definition of *profit* as solely corporate gain — involving as it will the maximization of short-term gains — conflicts with the Japanese definition, which necessarily involves a long-term view of things."[4] When the meaning of words is not agreed upon in advance, people may think they are talking about the same thing and only later discover that total misunderstanding has occurred.

In a humorous and helpful book about marketing overseas, David A. Ricks recites several examples of American advertising that resulted in double meanings when translated.[5] General Motors promoted its cars in Belgium with "Body by Fisher," a phrase familiar to Americans. But in Flemish, the translation was "Corpse by Fisher." "Come Alive with Pepsi" became "Come out of the grave. . ." in German, and "Bring your ancestors back from the dead" in parts of Asia. Even within English-speaking countries, words can vary greatly in meaning. For example, in your own experience, you probably relate the word "homely" to someone who is unattractive or even "ugly." Yet in England and in our own dictionaries, "homely" refers to someone who is plain, unpretentious with warm qualities.

How might "head shrinker" for psychiatrist be interpreted in another culture? "Living in the fast lane"?

Translation in international communication presents critical sending and receiving problems. Although the use of translators is helpful, we should be aware that translators are susceptible to the cultural problems that accompany translation.

Even Americans who are presumed fluent in another language must go through the process of mentally coding their ideas into the foreign language. Their word sequence and selection must be accurate because parts of speech may be used in different grammatical positions in other languages. As good practice, international communicators should keep words, sentences, and messages short and should

---

3. Saburo Haneda and Hirosuke Shima, "Japanese Communication Behavior as Reflected in Letter Writing," *The Journal of Business Communication* 19, no. 1 (Winter 1982): 23.

4. Jeremiah J. Sullivan and Naoki Kameda, "The Concept of Profit and Japanese-American Business Communication Problems." *The Journal of Business Communication* 19, no. 1 (Winter 1982): 38–39.

5. David A. Ricks, *Big Business Blunders* (Homewood, IL: Dow Jones–Irwin, 1983.

attempt to avoid slang, idioms, and humor. When speaking in English, the speaker should speak slowly, use correct pronunciation, and pause between sentences. Fortunately, most major trading nations have English as either a first or second language. We Americans do have the luxury of using our native tongue in most countries; but we must in keep in mind, of course, that we often have difficulty communicating accurately with people from other regions in our own country.

NONVERBAL COMMUNICATION PROBLEMS

The nonverbal languages of international communication are perhaps more important than the verbal languages, for it is in this area that cultural and social differences can provide significant barriers.

Is nonverbal both unspoken and unwritten communication?

The Language of Time

The value and meaning of time is not often understandable to Americans inexperienced in international affairs. The American stereotype of straightforwardness and get-to-the-point behavior leads us to make strict schedules, appointments, and arrangements. But this "programming" trait is not a world-wide custom; in fact, it is rare. Delays in meeting visitors, in responding to correspondence, and in taking action are often interpreted by Americans as signifying how unimportant they or their business are to the other person. Yet, the opposite might be true! In some cultures, the language of time says that important things take longer than do unimportant ones.

In parts of Central America, one should expect to be kept waiting for an appointment. Almost everyone who has visited Mexico and made arrangements for taxi service at a certain time is aware of the nonchalant attitude toward time. Seemingly, Mexicans operate in two time frames—the time on the clock and "Mexican time." "Mexican time" is "when I get there" to the taxi driver. Should this be your experience when you visit Mexico, don't get impatient about it—for two reasons: one, you are the outsider; and, two, the taxi driver will probably spend more than the agreed-upon time for your tour and not charge you more than the agreed-upon rate.

In the Middle East, Americans who insist on the meeting of deadlines will surely be left waiting. Interestingly enough, when the American finally is invited into the Middle Easterner's office, the interview will last as long as necessary to transact the business, even though the next visitor may be kept waiting for what might seem an interminable time. The nearest American parallel is a visit to the doctor's office.

The language of time is based on cultural factors often not understandable to others. Americans simply have difficulty believing that others are content to earn just enough to get by, to stay in one locality all their lives, and to find whatever recreation they have solely in the home or neighborhood. When these attitudes are present, time becomes a relatively unimportant consideration.

How important is "time" in your own day?

The Language of Space

Space operates as a language just as does time. In America, large offices are frequently reserved for executives as status symbols. In many parts of the world, large offices are for clerical workers and smaller ones for executives. Not much space is required for thinking and planning, so large areas are reserved as working spaces.

The distance between people functions in communication as "personal space" or "personal territory" in all cultures. In America, for example, for intimate conversations with close friends and relatives, we are willing to stay within about eighteen inches of others; for casual conversations, up to two or three feet; for job interviews and impersonal business, four to twelve feet; and for public distances, more than twelve feet.[6] The next time you are on an elevator in a public building notice how uncomfortable most people appear. They usually stare either at the floor or at the ceiling because their personal territory has been invaded and they must stand shoulder to shoulder with strangers.

But in many foreign cultures, men customarily kiss each other when they are introduced or when they meet. To the American "macho," this is normally an embarrassing situation; to the foreigner, it is no more personal than shaking hands. As a rule, we tend to move away when someone enters our personal territory. By observing the behavior of others, we can gain some idea of their concepts of personal territory, which can assist us in our own attempts to communicate.

Other Factors

Other nonverbal factors in international communication that spring from cultural backgrounds involve body movements and dress to a great extent. The familiar American symbol for "OK" or "everything is right" is made by forming a circle with the thumb and index finger. In other cultures it may mean zero, as in France, or money, as in Japan. The familiar "V" for victory symbol formed by raising the index and middle fingers may be an insulting sign in most of Europe. Hand motions are used much more in conversation by Europeans than by Americans. One of our stereotypes about Italians is that they can speak only if their hands are in motion.

We are familiar with our own habit of nodding our heads up and down to indicate "yes." In other parts of the world, this motion may mean simply that the person hears what is said. Unlike our movement of the head to say "no," other cultures' negative signs may be a simple backward jerk of the head, a waving finger in front of the speaker's face, or a finger waved back and forth in front of the listener, as we do when saying "no-no" to a small child.

In Saudi Arabia, Americans offend their hosts and contribute to communication breakdowns when they sit with their legs crossed in such a way that the sole of the shoe is visible. The solution of course is to sit with both feet flat on the floor.

The "business lunch" is an American tradition; and much business is trans-

Does the clothing style of any social or religious group affect your perception of them?

6. Edward T. Hall, *The Silent Language* (Garden City, NY: Doubleday), 1959, pp. 163–4.

acted on the golf course and tennis courts as well. However, in most parts of the world, dining and recreation are social functions and no place or time to conduct business.

These examples of nonverbal miscommunication are only a few of many that could be cited. As tourists, Americans can commit many blunders and have them overlooked. As representatives of businesses that are trying to make the proper impression, Americans can only hurt their causes by failing to become familiar with the major intercultural differences and some of the finer nuances.

SOME LIGHT AT THE END OF THE TUNNEL

A recent study was made of the use and problems of communication methods of firms with offices in both Hong Kong and California.[7] In descending order of frequency, the means of communication between the offices were telex, letter, telephone, visit, courier, computer, and telegram. The authors of the study indicated those involved in the study thought that cultural differences were not insurmountable in communication between offices but that time was needed to build mutual confidence and trust through exchange visits. Although training in the precise use of English was considered helpful, it wasn't foolproof: an American receiver still assumed that "scheme" used in a Hong Kong-initiated telex message meant "conspiracy" rather than "plan," as the writer had intended.

How does trust affect communication?

Business communication in English is now offered by colleges and universities in most of the major international trading countries.[8] Additionally, the Beijing Institute of Foreign Trade in the People's Republic of China provides English language courses in business correspondence and correspondence in foreign affairs.[9] Apparently, much of the world has accepted English as the language of international business.

Despite the difficulties of communicating effectively internationally, it is done. The study of business communication is growing throughout the world, particularly in English-speaking countries. American textbooks are widely used, and many have been translated for use in non–English-speaking countries. The writing style and format of business letters and other written messages may become universal, but significant gaps will remain in several areas.

Differences in legal aspects, export and import policies, political systems, religion, and business practices will continue to create problems. Semantic problems grow from these differences, leading some to suggest the usefulness of an international glossary or dictionary of business terminology. That sounds like a great idea, but what participants can agree on the meaning of the words used in the definitions?

---

7. John W. Gould et al., "Adequacy of Hong Kong–California Business Communication Methods." *The Journal of Business Communication* 20, no. 1 (Winter 1983): 33–40.

8. Herbert W. Hildebrandt, ed., *International Business Communication* (Ann Arbor: The University of Michigan), 1981.

9. Baolin Zong and H. W. Hildebrandt, "Business Communication in the People's Republic of China," *The Journal of Business Communication,* 20, no. 1 (Winter 1983): 25–32.

Why might an
American feel lonely at
3 P.M. in some countries?

The resolution of our problems in international business won't be that simple. Definitions grow from usage, and different people have long had different meanings for even simple words or terms. It takes time to work effectively in foreign countries, and some American firms have shown themselves to be very successful in their efforts to overcome the problems. Through educational and training programs, their representatives are prepared to undertake overseas assignments; and no new overseas employee is left on his or her own at the start of an assignment in another country. The crucial element is the capacity of the people engaged in international business to adapt to the culture of the strange country in which they find themselves.

SUMMARY

International business has been transacted for hundreds of years but never on the scale of the past twenty-five years. What was once "foreign trade"—the exchange of goods among countries—now is the commonly found business of the multinational firm. Billions of dollars have been invested by the major industrial countries in establishing plants in other countries. In most cases, these investments have been made by private firms—by the multinationals. The International Chamber of Commerce has estimated that just the American multinational firms alone account for about a third of the gross world production.

The business school graduate of today will almost certainly either work for a multinational or have to interact with one. For many people, the growing international business area will require them to work overseas as part of their career progress; and their success or failure will very much depend on skill in communicating in an intercultural environment.

Because other cultures differ markedly from our own in terms of language, religion, social structure, and values and attitudes, even the mastery of another language will not necessarily permit effective communication; but the person who has skill in using the language of the foreign country will become increasingly valuable to American firms.

Is some skill in a foreign language an asset?

Fortunately, English is fairly well established as the language of international business; and foreign countries have initiated educational programs to improve the English ability of their international business students and workers. Thus, the language barrier can be minimized, if not overcome. However, cultural problems will always exist. A growing awareness of the role of culture in communication and establishment of programs to educate and train participants in all forms of international affairs, including business, are both necessary:

> Since United States corporations face ever fiercer competition abroad, and their own power has diminished, the leaders of these enterprises have only one choice—to get smarter about the world.[10]

10. Louis Kraar, "The Multinationals Get Smarter about Political Risks," *Fortune,* 24 March 1980, p. 100.

EXERCISES

1.   How does a national "culture" benefit a people?

2.   How do cultural differences lead to communication problems?

3.   What is meant by "empathy"?

4.   What else might we add to the American stereotype as described in this chapter?

5.   Why might a translator be helpful in international communication? How might a translator be ineffective?

6.   Describe some aspects of the "language of time."

7.   Describe some aspects of the "language of space."

8.   Did cultural differences play a role in the problems the United States had in Viet Nam and in Iran? How?

9.   Select one of the following countries and develop what you think would be your stereotype of a business executive from that country: England, France, Saudi-Arabia, India, Japan, Israel, Brazil, Mexico.

10.   What are some cultural elements that might affect your communication with someone listed in exercise 9?

WRITING, PLANNING, AND DICTATING

OBJECTIVES

1. To strengthen writing skills.

2. To develop an understanding of how word selection and usage affects communication.

3. To provide a psychological background for planning interpersonal and group messages.

4. To develop an understanding of and skill in using dictation methods.

USING WORDS EFFECTIVELY

Messages Without Words
Simple Words
Categories of Words
Nouns
Pronouns
Verbs
Adjectives
Adverbs
Conjunctions
Prepositions
Frequently Misused Words
Summary

If we are to be successful in communication, we must recognize that a message can be transmitted both *with* and *without* words. Examples of unworded messages are metacommunications and kinesic communications.

MESSAGES WITHOUT WORDS

Is the spoken word the only means of conveying a message?

A *metacommunication* is a message that, although *not* expressed in words, accompanies a message that *is* expressed in words. For example, "Don't be late for work" gives that admonition (communication); yet the sentence may imply (but not express in words) such additional ideas as "You are frequently late, and I'm warning you," or "I doubt your dependability" (metacommunications). "Your solution is perfect" may also convey a metacommunication such as "You are efficient," or "I certainly like your work."

Whether we are speaking or writing, we can be confident that those who receive our messages will be sensitive to (1) the messages expressed in words and (2) the accompanying messages that are present but not expressed in words.

A *kinesic* communication is an idea expressed through nonverbal behavior. Messages can be conveyed through winks, smiles, frowns, sighs, attire, grooming, and all sorts of bodily movements. The science of kinesics seeks to gain knowledge about the impact of bodily movements on communication. Some examples of kinesic messages:

Action	Possible kinesic message
A wink follows a statement.	"Don't believe what I just said."
A professor is habitually late for class.	"I am busy." "I don't care much for students."
The boss starts to dial a number while a subordinate is talking.	"We're finished with our conversation; go away."
A group leader sits at a position other than at the head of the table.	"I want to demonstrate my equality with other members."
A receptionist offers a magazine to a client who must wait for a while.	"I want you to have something interesting to do while you wait."

What do kinesic messages have in common with metacommunications?

The list could go on and on. These unworded ideas (kinesic communications and metacommunications) have characteristics that all communicators should take into account:

1. *Unworded messages cannot be avoided.* Both written and spoken words convey ideas in addition to the ideas contained in the words used. All actions — and even the lack of action — have meaning to those who observe them.

2. *Unworded messages may have different meanings for different people.* If a committee member smiles after making a statement, one member may conclude that the speaker was trying to be funny; another may conclude that the speaker was pleased about having made such a great contribution; another may see the smile but have no reaction to it.

3. *Unworded messages may be intentional or unintentional.* "You are right about that" may be intended to mean "I agree with you," or "You are right on *this* issue, but you have been wrong on all others discussed." The sender may or may not intend to convey the latter and may or may not be aware of doing so.

4. *Unworded messages may get more attention than worded messages.* If an interviewee stamps out a cigarette on the floor while making a statement, the words may not register on the mind of the interviewer. Or, an error in basic grammar may get much more attention than does the idea that is being transmitted.

5. *Unworded messages provide clues about the sender's background and motives.* For example, excessive use of big words may suggest that a person reads widely or has an above-average education; it may also suggest a need for social recognition or insecurity about social background.

6. *Unworded messages are influenced by the circumstances surrounding the communication.* Assume that two men (Ward and Wood) are friends who work for the same firm. When they are together on the job, Ward sometimes puts his hand on Wood's shoulder. To Wood, the act may mean nothing more than "We are close friends." But Ward becomes a member of a committee that subsequently denies a promotion for Wood. Afterward, the same act could mean "We are still friends"; but it could also arouse resentment. Because of the circumstances, the same act could now mean something like, "Watch the hand that pats; it can also stab."

7. *Unworded messages can actually contradict the accompanying worded message.* "We appreciate your writing to us when you have a problem" may be taken to mean the opposite when nothing has been done to solve the problem or to explain the lack of action. When actions and words appear to be in conflict, receivers place more confidence in the message communicated by action. And keep in mind that when police discover that a suspect's words and actions are incongruent, suspicion about the suspect becomes stronger.

8. *Unworded messages may be beneficial or harmful.* Words or actions can be accompanied with unworded messages that help or hurt the writer's purpose. Metacommunications and kinesic communications can convey something like, "I am efficient in my business and considerate of others," or they can convey the opposite. They cannot be eliminated, but they can be made to work for communicators instead of against them.

No one can give a set of rules for interpreting unworded messages, but awareness of their presence and impact will improve chances of choosing the right word for the message we want to transmit.

When we select word symbols for the ideas we want to convey, we are *encoding*. Encoding is the task of the speaker or writer. When we decide what a message really means, we are *decoding*. Decoding is the task of the listener or reader. If communication is to be effective, both the decoder (receiver) and the encoder (sender) must play their parts well.

What are some consequences of selecting the wrong word?

The consequences of selecting the wrong word can be serious: (1) the message may be misunderstood completely, (2) the recipient may have to spend some time ascertaining the correct message, (3) the recipient could be so distracted by the error that the error gets more attention than the message itself, or (4) the recipient may lose some respect for the communicator. For example, the United States Senate was considering a man's qualifications to represent the United States at the arms limitation talks in Europe. Because the applicant's twenty-five-page memorandum (in which his views were set forth) contained numerous errors in word usage, spelling, etc., the senators questioned whether he *cared* enough to represent his country or whether he even *knew* enough to represent it.

One chapter can hardly discuss *all* problems of word choice, but it can explore some of the common problems: simple words, problems in various parts-of-speech categories, and frequently misused words.

SIMPLE WORDS

A good vocabulary is a great asset. High scores on predictive examinations can open academic and professional doors that would otherwise be closed. People with good vocabularies have definite advantages: they have an increased chance of being able to select the right word to use in a message for a certain person, and they have an increased chance of being able to understand spoken or written messages from others.

How is a good vocabulary useful?

If not properly used, however, a good vocabulary can be a liability. If the sender happens to select a word not in the receiver's vocabulary, the receiver (1) may not get the message at all, (2) may guess incorrectly and get the wrong meaning, (3) may lose time verifying the meaning, or (4) may wonder whether the sender selected the unusual word for the purpose of making an impression. Because of these risks, encoders should *rely primarily on plain, simple words.* For example, consider this statement:

> Usually about half of a college communication class will interpret ''mitigate,'' a word meaning to moderate or alleviate, as ''troublesome or aggravating.''[1]

Even though the words on the right in the following list may well be in the vocabulary of the recipient, the words on the left are still preferable:

---

1. Vanessa Dean Arnold, ''Join the Counterinsurgency against Word Excesses,'' *Business Education Forum,* February 1979, p. 24.

about	approximately
do	accomplish
improve	ameliorate
aware	cognizant
show	demonstrate
change	modify
publish	promulgate
ask	interrogate

The short, simple words convey ideas more efficiently (require less time and space), and they are less likely to draw attention to a writer or speaker's motive for using them. Those who deliberately use big words when little ones would do just as well are often thought of as social climbers. They are inclined to choose words from the column on the right in the hope their education and background will be recognized. According to E. Digby Baltzell, those in America's very highest social class are inclined to choose words like those on the left.[2] Already at the top, they don't need to impress others with a big vocabulary.

For college graduates just entering their first job, the temptation to reveal a good vocabulary is very real. Aware that without a college education they would not have the job they hold, they often seek to use words that will demonstrate their educational background: "To my recipient, I want my ideas to seem valid. Chances of achieving that objective are improved if I can reveal my educational background. Big words, which are not likely to be found in the vocabularies of the uneducated, should help to prove my point. To my superiors or colleagues, who will in all likelihood see a copy of what I have written, my big words will reveal my superior qualifications for the job I hold." Such thinking reduces the likelihood that messages will be expressed effectively. When recipients' thoughts turn from *what* is being said to the *way* it is said, the true meaning may be greatly distorted.

Imagine a sportscaster who frequently tosses in a very unusual word, occasionally takes time to define his words, and sometimes teases his cohort (who is a former player) for having a limited vocabulary. Not only do sports fans receive a description of what is happening in a game, they also receive such between-the-lines messages as "I'm more intelligent than most people." The accompanying resentment can actually interfere with a fan's enjoyment of the game.

Resentment is unlikely if an unusual word is understood and if it is apparently not used for the purpose of impressing. For example, two supervisors, Ruth and Wilma, are discussing methods of employee control. Ruth says, "Only two members of my team seem recalcitrant." She could have transmitted the same meaning by saying, "Only two members of my team seem to resent my efforts to control their work behavior." Knowing that Wilma knows the meaning of recalcitrant (perhaps sometimes uses it herself) and knowing that its use will not be taken as an attempt to impress, Ruth can safely use the word. The four-syllable word communicates as much as the fourteen syllables that would be used in place of it.

When the choice is between a simple, one-syllable word and a bigger word that

What are the advantages of using simple words?

What are the consequences of trying to use big words for the purpose of impressing people?

Under what conditions would use of a big, unusual word be appropriate?

2. E. Digby Baltzell, *Philadelphia Gentlemen* (Glencoe, Ill.: Free Press, 1958), pp. 50–55.

has the same meaning, the small word is normally more efficient. If Ruth says, "Let's turn out the lights," Wilma is likely to envision the act of turning out the lights; she is not likely to think, "Ruth could have said 'Let's terminate the illumination'; but she's afraid I would not understand." In other words, people are not likely to be offended when they receive messages that are stated in simple words. The use of simple words invites concentration on ideas; the use of complicated, unusual words risks calling attention to words.

CATEGORIES OF WORDS

In a book that discusses a wide variety of communication problems, a complete discussion of word usage is hardly possible. An English handbook, a dictionary, and a thesaurus should always be within easy reach. The following discussion touches on a high percentage of word-selection problems encountered in business communication.

Just as using a big, unusual word may result in receipt of the wrong message, misusing a small, common word may also result in receipt of the wrong message. And, just as using big words for the purpose of impressing can cause human relations problems, using small words in the wrong way grammatically can also cause human relations problems. Even when the correct message is received, a detected grammatical error can get more attention than the message itself. Such an error can cause the recipient to wonder about the sender's educational background or respect for others.

Word-selection problems exist in all parts-of-speech categories.

NOUNS

Pay special attention to the italicized words in each pair of sentences. Which do you prefer, the first sentence or the second?

> *Cancellation* of the requirement will occur in July.
> The *contract* will be canceled in July.

> That *decision* is to be made by the supervisor.
> The *supervisor* is to make that decision.

In both pairs, the first sentence employs an abstract noun as the subject; and the second employs a concrete noun as the subject. Just as the star in a film is the most important character, the subject in a sentence is the most important noun. The more vivid it is, the better. Since "cancellation" and "decision" are abstract nouns, they are hard to envision. Since "contract" and "supervisor" are readily envisioned, the meanings of the second sentences come through more clearly. Using an abstract noun as a sentence subject is certainly not an error; in fact, when an idea needs to be included but does not need emphasis, using an abstract noun as the subject may be

Compared with abstract nouns, why are concrete nouns normally better for use as sentence subjects?

desirable. Usually, however, writers and speakers will convey clearer messages if they *use concrete nouns as subjects.*

Note the italicized words in the following pairs of sentences:

> I shall appreciate your *help.*
> I shall appreciate your *helping me.*
>
> We were concerned about his *telephone conversation.*
> We were concerned about his *talking on the telephone.*

In the first sentence of the first pair, "help" is used as a noun (it tells what is being appreciated). Likewise, in the second sentence, "helping me" is also used as a noun (another way of expressing "help"). Now, notice the words that precede "help" and "helping me." Without a moment's hesitation, a receiver knows that the word preceding "help" should be in the possessive form ("your"). "I shall appreciate *you* help" would just not sound right. Since "helping me" serves the same purpose in the second sentence that "help" serves in the first, the word preceding "helping me" must be possessive also. In the second sentence of the second pair, note the use of the possessive form ("his") before "talking."

The expressions "helping me" and "talking on the telephone" are called *gerunds* (verbs used as nouns and characterized by an *-ing* ending). Each of the following sentences contains a gerund. Of the two words that precede the gerund, determine which one is correct:

> She was annoyed by (*me, my*) whispering.
> I shall appreciate (*Tom, Tom's*) submitting an application.
> We were not aware of (*them, their*) joining the group.

In each sentence, the second choice is correct. *Before a gerund use the possessive form.* To a recipient who is familiar with English, failure to use the possessive form before a gerund is distracting.

Which form of pronoun should be used to precede a gerund?

PRONOUNS   *Takes place of noun*

Note that each of the following sentences contains a masculine pronoun:

> When your auditor arrives, *he* is to go directly to the superintendent.
> A lawyer could probably solve the problem, but *he* would have to be a tax specialist.

The person who wrote these sentences was probably applying an age-old rule of English: when the gender of a noun ("auditor" in the first sentence and "lawyer" in the second) has not been revealed, use a masculine pronoun. When the English language began to emerge a few hundred years ago, women did not have the status they have today. In today's world, women can be auditors, lawyers, physicians, professors, and can practice other professions formerly restricted to men. Therefore, one who uses the masculine pronoun runs the risk of conveying a between-the-lines message that says "Women don't serve in professions" or "I don't think women *should* serve in the professions or have equal status with men."

A high percentage of women are accustomed to the old masculine pronoun rule. They use it themselves, fully aware that it is not really intended to offend. Surely, the statement, "One small step for man, one giant leap for mankind" was not intended to exclude one of the sexes. Neither does the statement, "Man does not live by bread alone" intend to imply "But women do live by bread alone." Some people are very sensitive to use of the masculine pronoun. To them, such usage can seriously interfere with correct reception of a message by inviting attention to a social issue instead of to the specific idea conveyed.

How can offensive pronouns be avoided?

Because clear receipt of the message is so important, a writer or speaker can scarcely afford the risk involved in using a masculine pronoun that could be taken as an offense. Offensive pronouns can be avoided in a variety of ways:

1. Avoid use of a pronoun completely.

   Original: When your auditor arrives, *he* is to go. . . .
   Revised: Upon arrival, your auditor is to go to the superintendent.

2. Repeat the noun.

   Original: . . . the courtesy of your guide. Ask *him* to. . . .
   Revised: . . . the courtesy of your guide. Ask *the guide* to. . . .

3. Use a plural noun.

   Original: If a supervisor needs assistance, *he* can. . . .
   Revised: If supervisors need assistance, *they* can. . . . (Since "they" can refer to men only, women only, or both, it avoids implying that supervisors can be men only.)

4. Use pronouns from both genders.

   Original: Just call the manager. *He* will in turn. . . .
   Revised: Just call the manager. *He* or *she* will in turn. . . . (Occasional use of "he or she" may not be particularly distracting, but repeated use can take attention away from the message.)

Although the English language has a common-gender pronoun (*they*) in the plural, it does not have such a pronoun in the singular (except for *it*, which is hardly appropriate for referring to people and *one,* use of which is seldom advisable.) Until such a pronoun emerges and is accepted, *avoid use of masculine pronouns that may be considered offensive.*

What is "second person"?

Another pronoun that frequently interferes with correct interpretation is *you. You,* always referring to the person or persons being addressed, is called a *second-person pronoun.* In the following sentence, what does *you* mean?

You never know what to expect.

"You" could be taken to mean (1) the speaker or writer, (2) the listener or reader, or (3) people in the group. Because three different meanings are possible, *avoid "you" when its antecedent is not absolutely clear.*

The following illustrations contain an error in pronoun usage:

> The recommendations arrived today; the judge checked *it* thoroughly.
> When the statement was first made, *they* were refuted.

Since "recommendations" is the noun to which the pronoun refers, the pronoun "it" should be changed to a plural form. Since "statement" is the noun to which the pronoun refers, "they" should be changed to the singular form, "it." Recognizing the lack of agreement, a reader or listener wonders whether more than one noun is involved or whether the wrong pronoun has been used. To avoid this confusion, *make sure pronouns agree in number with their antecedents.*

Sometimes, reaction to a message is strongly influenced by the choice of pronoun employed. If the first-person pronoun (*I*) is used frequently, the sender may impress others as being self-centered — always talking about self. When *I* is used, it appears as the subject; and the subject of a sentence gets emphasis. Knowing that overuse of *I* is discouraged, some people try to circumvent its use by inserting such words as *the undersigned, yours truly, this researcher,* or *this reporter.* Use of these expressions is just as bad as or worse than use of *I.* They may be taken as a devious way of inserting self into the message without use of the first-person pronoun. *Avoid overuse of "I" and other words that identify self.*

The following sentences employ the second-person pronoun. In which sentence is *you* less advisable?

> *You* typed a perfect copy.
> *You* made numerous mistakes on this page.

The first sentence contains a positive idea. The one to whom the sentence is addressed can hardly resent being associated with perfection. On the other hand, the second sentence contains a negative idea. Sensitivity about the mistakes is heightened when the one addressed is directly associated with the mistakes. If the speaker's desire is to be diplomatic (at least to be no more negative than necessary), the second sentence could be revised to avoid the use of second person: "This page contains numerous mistakes." For better human relations, *use second person for presenting pleasant ideas and avoid second person for presenting negative ideas.*

Like second and first person, third person has an influence on human relations. Note the difference:

> *You* will be severely challenged by tomorrow's test.
> Students who took the test last semester said *they* were severely challenged by it.

Whether the first sentence is preferred over the second depends on the speaker's purpose. If the intent is to heighten concern over the test, to emphasize its difficulty,

Why is agreement essential?

Should *this writer* be substituted for *I*?

For expressing negative ideas, should second person be avoided?

Does use of the third person assist in de-emphasizing a negative idea?

the second person is more effective. If the intent is to transmit the idea of difficulty with less emphasis, the third person is more effective. *Use second person for emphasis of an idea and third person for de-emphasis of an idea.*

Pronouns may appear in almost any position in a sentence. Selecting the right form to use is seldom a problem when the pronoun is at the beginning. Without stopping to think about it, English-speaking people will say *I went* instead of *me went, they went* instead of *them went.* Pronouns that serve as subjects of sentences are called *nominative-case* pronouns; pronouns that serve as objects are called *objective-case* pronouns. Errors in pronoun usage are more likely to occur when the pronoun is at the end of a sentence:

> The report was intended for Maria and *I*.
> Send copies to Phil and *I*.
> This quarrel is between Tony and *I*.
> The flowers are from Ed and *I*.

In the four sentences, "I" should be changed to "me." If a question should arise about whether to use the nominative-case pronoun, the answer becomes obvious when the sentence is read without the words that accompany the pronoun. Since no one would say "was intended for *I*," no one should say "was intended for Joan and *I*." Coming after the preposition "for," the pronoun should be in the objective case, "me." Since "send copies to *I*" would not sound right, "send copies to Phil and *I*" is not right.

Do objective-case pronoun normally appear as the *first* words in a sentence?

Because most errors in pronoun usage seem to occur in sentences involving two or more people, further illustrations are presented. In each pair of sentences, observe that objective-case pronouns follow the italicized prepositions.

> Wait *for* me.
> Wait *for* Neva and me.
>
> Send copies *to* us.
> Send copies *to* Dorothy and me.
>
> Give the difficult tasks *to* me.
> Divide the difficult tasks *between* Chester and me.
>
> Take a picture *of* me.
> Take a picture *of* my son and me.

In the preceding pairs of sentences, the first sentence has *one* object and employs an objective-case pronoun. The second sentence in each pair employs a *compound* object and also employs an objective-case pronoun.

Pronouns that serve as sentence subjects are *I, you, he she, we,* and *they.* Pronouns that serve as objects are *me, you, him, her, us,* and *them.* Usually, those in the second group will appear near the end of a sentence; those in the first, at or near the beginning. *Use objective-case pronouns to follow prepositions.*

In the following sentences, observe that pronouns follow verbs:

Mr. Shaw is taking *me* to the Harbor Club for lunch.
The systems analyst helped *me.*
The president encouraged *us.*
Georgia assisted *them.*
The officer stopped Tom and *me.*

Use of "Tom and *me*" does not mean that the objective pronoun is always used when two people are discussed. "Tom and *I* were stopped by the officer" uses a nominative pronoun because "Tom and I" serve as the subject of the sentence. *Use nominative-case pronouns as subjects of sentences, but use objective-case pronouns to follow verbs.*

VERBS

Every sentence contains two essential elements — the noun and the verb. Because verbs are used so frequently and because action is a critical part of a sentence, correct use of verbs is especially important. Observe the misuse of verbs in these sentences:

Only one of the officers *are* present.
The typists, not the secretary, *is* responsible.
Each of the following pages *have* been proofread.

For those whose native language is English, correct use of verbs is almost automatic: *They are, he is, she was, we were.* Whether to use *is* or *are* depends on whether the subject is singular or plural. Yet, because people are accustomed to using a plural form of the verb to accompany a plural noun or pronoun, they sometimes use the wrong verb when a noun appears between the subject and the verb. In the first sentence, notice that the subject is "one," a singular form. "Officers" is not the subject and therefore has no influence on the form of verb that is used: "Only *one . . . is* present." Likewise, "The *typists . . . are* responsible." *Each . . . has* been proofread."

Because subject-verb agreement is a basic principle of English, such errors are especially distracting. Even though recipients may be able to understand exactly what is meant, the message will not come through with the impact it deserves. Instead, the error may generate thoughts about whether the error resulted from haste, lack of respect, or lack of knowledge. To avoid such possibilities, senders must *use verbs that agree in number with the subjects of sentences.*

Agreement in person is also a necessity. The italicized verbs are used incorrectly:

He *don't* like to travel.
George *don't* make mistakes.
You *was* notified.

Why must verbs agree in number with their subjects?

Just as verbs must agree with subjects in number, they must also agree in person. "First person" describes a speaker or writer—*I* and *we.* "Second person" describes the one spoken or written to—*you.* "Third person" describes the one spoken or written about—*he, she, him, her, it, they, them.* In most usage, correctness is automatic: *I was* instead of *I were, she cooks* instead of *she cook,* and *they work* instead of *they works.* The most common errors are in the use of *don't* with third-person singular ("Alice don't live here any more") and *was* with second-person singular ("You was a kid once yourself"). "He *doesn't* like to travel," "you *were* notified," and George *doesn't* make mistakes." To avoid all the communication hazards that accompany a grammatical error, *use verbs that agree in person with their subjects.*

What is the difference between violation of *person* and violation of *number*?

In addition to revealing action, verbs reveal the *time* of action—past, present, or future. Observe the words that indicate time:

> We *received* your report last week, we *are studying* it, and we *will make* a decision tomorrow.

All three tenses are employed in this example. Using three tenses in the same sentence was *necessary* if events were to be properly placed in time. But sometimes, *unnecessary* changes in tense cause confusion and distraction.

> He *studies* (present) the proposal and *offered* (past) his reaction.
> John *offered* to pay but *fumbles* for his wallet.

Such sentences cause listeners or readers to wonder which is to be thought of—a present event or a past event. Each sentence should employ two present-tense verbs or two past-tense verbs, but not one of each. For consistency, *do not make unnecessary changes in tense.*

In English, two words are required for expressing verbs in infinitive form: *to be, to go, to write, to work, to study.* In other languages (French and German, for example), only one word is required for expressing infinitives: *aller* for "to go" in French, and *gehen* for "to go" in German. Even though the English infinitive is presented in two words, it is to be thought of as a unit. As a unit, it should not be split:

> **Incorrect:**   He was trying *to* rapidly *complete* his report.
> **Correct:**   He was trying *to complete* his report rapidly.

Why avoid split infinitives?

> **Incorrect:**   We want you *to* seriously *consider* the proposal.
> **Correct:**   We want you *to consider* the proposal seriously.

Although ideas in the incorrect sentences are not seriously distorted, a reader or listener could be distracted; the grammatical error may get more attention than the message itself. To avoid that possibility, *avoid splitting infinitives.*

Verbs are also categorized as either active or passive. In the following example, the first sentence employs an active verb; the second, a passive verb:

What is the
difference between
active and *passive*?

> Charlotte *edited* the script.
> The script *has been* edited.

Both sentences employ the verbs correctly. In sentences in which the subject is the *doer* of action, the verbs are called *active.* In sentences in which the subject is the *receiver* of action, the verbs are called *passive.* When sentences employ active verbs, receivers get a sharp picture. Recall that the two essential parts of a sentence are the subject and the verb. When the subject is the actor, clarity of ideas is heightened. When sentences employ passive verbs, receivers get a less distinct picture. In the second sentence, a reader becomes aware that something was done *to* the script, but who did it is not revealed, and the reader or listener gets a less complete picture.

Even when a passive sentence contains additional words to reveal the doer, the imagery is less distinct than it would be if the sentence were active:

> The script has been edited by Charlotte.

The word *script* gets the most attention because it is the subject. The sentence seems to let a reader know the *result* of action before revealing the doer; the sentence is less emphatic.

Because active verbs convey ideas more vividly, senders rely more heavily on active verbs than passive verbs. Passive verbs are useful, though, (1) in concealing the doer ("The script has been edited"), (2) in placing more emphasis on *what* was done and what it was *done to* than on who *did* the action ("The script has been edited by Charlotte"), and (3) in subordinating an unpleasant thought. Both of the following thoughts are negative:

Under what
conditions are
passive verbs advisable?

> You *failed* to fill in the form properly.
> You *have let* this machine become very dirty.

Both sentences are active. Because the subject "you" is the doer, the sentences are emphatic. But, normally, negative thoughts should be de-emphasized. To present an unpleasant thought emphatically (as active verbs do) is to make human relations difficult. When passive verbs are used, the sentences retain the essential ideas, but the ideas seem less irritating:

> The form *has not been* filled in properly.
> The machine *has been allowed* to become very dirty.

Just as emphasis on negatives hinders human relations, emphasis on positives promotes human relations:

Are active
verbs preferred for
conveying positive ideas?

> You *have filled* in the form perfectly.
> You certainly *keep* this machine clean.

Because the subjects ("you") are the doers, the sentences are emphatic; and pleasant thoughts deserve emphasis.

Sometimes, the expressions *past tense* and *passive verbs* are confused. *Past* and *passive* do have similar sounds, but they have different meanings. Passive verbs appear in sentences in which the subjects are acted upon; past-tense verbs appear in sentences in which events have taken place already:

> **Passive:** The work *has been done.*
> **Active:**   John *has done* the work.

Could a passive sentence be stated in future tense?

Note that such words as *have, had,* and *has* are frequently used when sentences are passive, but those words can be used also when the sentences are active—as in the second sentence. A passive sentence is not necessarily a sentence about a past event. In fact, a passive sentence can be in the future tense:

> The job *will be completed* before tomorrow afternoon.

Since the subject is not a doer, the sentence is passive—regardless of whether the tense is past, present, or future. Out of concern for clarity and human relations, *use active verbs to present important points or to present pleasant ideas; use passive verbs to present less significant points or to present unpleasant ideas.*

ADJECTIVES

Compared with nouns and verbs, adjectives play a less significant role in a sentence. Adjectives describe or give information about nouns. Compared with nouns and verbs, adjectives present fewer problems in usage. A common problem is use of adjectives that are too strong or too frequently used:

Why should business writers normally avoid overly strong adjectives?

> Sales have been *fantastic.*
> Mr. Jones presented a *ridiculous* plan.

Use of such adjectives can cause receivers to wonder about senders' objectivity. A person who wanted to report a highly satisfactory sales program would do well to avoid "fantastic" and, instead, give some details. Even though a plan may be worthy of ridicule, a person who comments on it would be better off to point out areas needing improvement. By labeling a plan "ridiculous," a speaker might risk being labeled biased or overly negative. Communication is normally more effective if writers and speakers *avoid use of adjectives that are used too frequently by others, are overly strong, or are overly negative.*

Sometimes, writers or speakers search in vain for the right adjective. Not finding one that presents the right shade of meaning, they can form an adjective by joining two or more words with a hyphen. At first, a writer may put down "We need *current* reports." Recognizing that "current" may be taken to mean "daily" or ''weekly,'' the writer can use a compound adjective:

> We need *up-to-the-hour* reports.

The compound adjective makes the description more precise. Notice that ''up-to-the-hour'' is used in the same way as ''current''—to describe the noun that immediately follows it. When two or more words are used to form a single-word describer of the noun that follows, a hyphen is used to join the words, and to present them as one. In spoken language, ''up-to-the-hour'' would probably be spoken a little faster than other words in the sentence. The speeding-up technique helps to demonstrate that they are used as one word. In written language, the hyphen serves the same purpose.

Why should compound adjectives be hyphenated?

Using or failing to use the hyphen in a compound adjective is more than just a matter of mechanical correctness or punctuation. Improper use of the hyphen can cause serious differences in meaning:

> *All night* seminars have been canceled.
> *All-night* seminars have been canceled.

In the first sentence, ''all'' is describing some things—''night seminars.'' The sentence means that every one of the seminars meeting at night has been canceled. In the second sentence, ''all-night'' is describing ''seminars.'' The sentence means that seminars lasting the entire night have been canceled. Further examples:

a *new car* salesman (The phrase means a new man who sells cars.)

A *new-car* salesman (The phrase means a man who sells new cars.)

His *two base hits* won the game. (The phrase means two hits, but they could have been singles, doubles, triples, or home runs.)

His *two-base hits* won the game. (The phrase means doubles, but the number of such hits is not revealed.)

Hyphens are used to join descriptive words that *precede* a noun and are used as one-word modifiers. Hyphens are not used when describers *follow* nouns:

Do nouns *follow* compound adjectives, or do they *precede* them?

> The boss made a *spur-of-the-moment* decision.
> His decision was made on the *spur of the moment.*

For accurate communication, writers must *use hyphens to join words that form a one-word modifier of a noun that follows.*

When nouns are described in more than one way, the hyphen is not employed. Observe the difference:

> Jane was asked to fill out a *long, complicated* questionnaire.

The questionnaire is long; it is also complicated. Either word could be omitted and the sentence would still make sense. Such adjectives are called *coordinate* adjectives. They are alike in that each describes the following noun. Since each describes separately, they are not joined with a hyphen; rather, they are separated with a comma. Careful writers and editors learn to *place a comma between coordinate adjectives.*

Messages are sometimes influenced negatively by another form of adjective — the superlative:

> This dryer is the *best* one on the market.
> The factory has the *worst* odor imaginable.

Superlatives are very useful words. Frequently, the extreme unit in a series needs to be identified — the *highest* or *lowest* score, the *latest* news, the *youngest* employee. But, when superlatives are totally unsupported — or even unsupportable — their use is questionable. Furnishing proof that no other dryer is up to the standards of this one would be extremely difficult. Proving that one odor is the worst imaginable is practically impossible. Knowing that such statements are exaggerations, the receiver may not believe them at all. In fact, one who has used a superlative to transmit an *unbelievable* idea may not be believed when she or he is able to offer support for a *believable* idea. For the sake of credibility, *use only supported or supportable superlatives.*

ADVERBS

Like adjectives, adverbs describe or modify. Adjectives describe or modify nouns; but adverbs describe or modify verbs, adjectives, or other adverbs. Examples:

> Tim writes *rapidly*. ("Rapidly" describes a verb.)
> Sue is an *extremely* efficient operator. ("Extremely" describes an adjective.)
> Juan works *very* rapidly. ("Very" describes an adverb.)

Superlatives can be either adjectives or adverbs. They are adverbs when they modify or describe verbs:

> Ernie types *fastest*.
> This item sells *best*.

Whether a superlative is an adjective or an adverb, the same principle applies: *use only supported or supportable superlatives.*

Like adjectives, adverbs can arouse skepticism or resentment if they are used without care:

> Our prices are *ridiculously* low.
> Our forecasts have been *fantastically* accurate.

For the sake of credibility, *avoid use of adverbs that are used too frequently by others, are overly strong, or are overly negative.*

The position in which an adverb is placed can make a genuine difference in the meaning of the sentence:

> *Only* John gets his vacation in summer. ("Only" modifies "John," meaning no other employee gets a summer vacation.)

> John gets his vacation in summer *only.* ("Only" modifies "summer," meaning John never gets a vacation at any other time.)

> John gets his *only* vacation in summer. ("Only" modifies "vacation," meaning John gets one vacation; it's in summer.)

> John gets *only* his vacation in summer. ("Only" modifies "gets," meaning John gets no other benefits.)

For the sake of clarity, *place an adverb close to the word it modifies.*

CONJUNCTIONS

Conjunctions assist in joining ideas. When the ideas are of about equal significance, *coordinate* conjunctions are employed:

> Maria did the typing and duplicating, *but* Gus did the collating.
> The reports are ready for editing, *and* the statements are ready for checking.

When the ideas are not of equal significance, *subordinate* conjunctions are employed:

> The clerk checked out *when* the job was finished.
> The reporter left *before* anyone could talk with her.

Note that the coordinate conjunctions "but" and "and" in the preceding sentences are preceded by a comma. The comma is sometimes appropriately omitted when the coordinating conjunction joins two ideas that are exceedingly short ("He left *but* I stayed.") Note that the subordinating conjunctions "when" and "before" are not preceded by a comma.

Punctuation of adverbial conjunctions is different from punctuation of coordinate conjunctions:

> The report arrived today, *but* it has not been evaluated. (Use a comma with conjunctions.)
> The report arrived today; *however,* it has not been evaluated. (Use a semicolon with adverbial conjunctions.)

What is the difference between coordinating and subordinating conjunctions?

How are adverbial conjunctions punctuated?

The words *however* and *therefore* appear frequently in business communication. Although they come between two related ideas, their relationship is a little closer to the second idea. The comma, which is a weak mark of punctuation, separates the adverbial conjunction from the second idea; the semicolon, a strong mark of punctuation, separates it even more definitively from the first. For accurate punctuation, then, *place a comma before coordinate conjunctions; place a semicolon before adverbial conjunctions and a comma after them.*

PREPOSITIONS

Prepositions are used to show a relationship between a noun or objective-case pronoun and some other word in the sentence. Examples:

The file is *in* the desk.	The file is *under* the desk.
The file is *on* the desk.	The file is *beside* the desk.
The file was taken *to* the desk.	The file was taken *from* the desk.

Prepositions do not appear at the beginnings or endings of simple sentences. Sometimes prepositions are unnecessarily attached to the ends of sentences.

May a preposition be used as the last word in a sentence?

Original: Where is the superintendent *at*?
Revised: Where is the superintendent?

Original: What did he do that *for*?
Revised: Why did he do that?

Yet, prepositions can be effectively placed at the ends of sentences.

Jan was less concerned about what she was living *on* than what she was living *for.*
Before you can take anything *out,* you must put something *in.*

For purposes of contrast, the key words "for" and "in" need emphasis. Last-word position affords that emphasis. *Place prepositions at the ends of sentences only when doing so serves a useful purpose.*

Prepositions are sometimes repeated for purposes of clarity. Do these sentences have the same meanings?

All majors must attain at least a C average *in* accounting, law, and finance.
All majors must attain at least a C average *in* accounting, *in* law, and *in* finance.

In the first sentence, one average is computed—an average of all grades made in the three disciplines combined. The single preposition implies a single average. In the second, three averages are computed — the average in accounting courses only must be at least a C; in law courses only, a C; and in finance courses only, a C. Three prepositions imply three separate averages. Under the terms of the second sentence, a student who had a D average in accounting, an A in law, and an A in finance would still not have satisfied requirements. *Repeat the preposition before each word in a series if doing so conveys the precise meaning intended.*

For a more thorough treatment of word-usage problems, consult an English reference book. The following words appear frequently in business communication. They present more of a problem for writers than for speakers.

FREQUENTLY MISUSED WORDS

1. *Affect, effect. Affect* is a verb meaning "influence"; *effect* is a noun meaning "result"; *effect* is also a verb meaning "to bring about."

> The change does not *affect* his pay.
> What *effect* will the change have?
> The manager wants to *effect* a change in the schedule.

2. *All right, alright. Alright* is considered substandard usage.

> The answers were *all right*.
> That's *all right* with me.

3. *Among, between.* Use *among* to discuss three or more, *between* to discuss two.

> Divide the earnings *among* the six workers.
> Divide the earnings *between* the two workers.

4. *Compare to, compare with.* Use *compare to* in pointing out similarities; use *compare with* in pointing out differences as well as similarities.

> He *compared* Kennedy *to* Lincoln. (He pointed out similarities.)
> He *compared* Kennedy *with* Lincoln. (He pointed out differences as well as similarities.)

5. *Consensus of opinion. Consensus* means "general opinion"; therefore, *of opinion* is redundant.

> The *consensus* was that we should withdraw.

6. *Credible, creditable. Credible* means "believable." *Creditable* means "praiseworthy" or "worthy of commercial credit."

The explanations were *credible.*
Mr. Jones did a *creditable* job for us.

7. *Different from, different than. Different from* is correct; *different than* is to be avoided.

That machine is *different from* mine.

8. *Disinterested, uninterested.* Use *disinterested* to convey neutrality or impartiality. Use *uninterested* to convey lack of interest or lack of concern.

Both employees agreed to accept the decision of a *disinterested* colleague. Because of severe financial pressures, the owner was *uninterested* in the discussion of social problems.

9. *Each other, one another.* Use *each other* when referring to two people; use *one another* when referring to more than two.

The two typists competed with *each other.*
The members of the group helped *one another.*

10. *Infer, imply. Infer* means "to draw a conclusion"; readers or listeners infer. *Imply* means "to hint" or "to set forth vaguely"; speakers and writers imply.

I *infer* from your letter that conditions have improved.
Do you mean to *imply* that conditions have improved?

11. *Irregardless.* Avoid this word. Use *regardless* instead.

12. *Its, it's. Its* is a possessive pronoun; *it's* is a contraction for "it is."

The phrase has lost *its* meaning.
It's time to quit.

13. *Less, fewer. Less* refers to things that cannot be counted; it also refers to money. *Fewer* refers to things that can be counted.

He concentrates more on accuracy, *less* on speed.
We can now do our work with *fewer* mistakes.

14. *Principal, principle. Principal* means "main" or "primary"; *principle* means "rule" or "law."

The *principal* runs the school.
The *principal* purpose is to gain speed.
The *principal* plus interest is due in thirty days.
The theory is based on sound *principles.*

15. *While. While,* meaning "at the same time that," should not be used as a synonym for such conjunctions as *but, though, although, and,* and *whereas.*

> You do the work sheet *while* I type a stencil. (Concurrent activities.)
> One man likes his work, *but* (not *while*) the other doesn't.
> *Although* (not *while*) we realize that your account is overdue, we think you should not pass up this opportunity.

Other frequently misused words are listed in the Appendix. See page 592.

SUMMARY

Worded messages are sometimes oveshadowed by unworded messages. An unworded message that accompanies a worded message is a metacommunication. An unworded message that is transmitted through action is called a kinesic communication. Writers and speakers should try especially hard to avoid transmitting messages that are incongruent with their words.

Errors in word usage cause lost meaning, lost time, distraction, and concern about the encoder's background. Some principles of effective word usage:

1. Rely primarily on plain, simple words.

2. Use concrete nouns as subjects.

3. Use the possessive form before a gerund.

4. Avoid the use of masculine pronouns that may be considered offensive.

5. Avoid *you* when its antecedent is not absolutely clear.

6. Make sure pronouns agree in number with their antecedents.

7. Avoid overuse of *I* and other words that identify self.

8. Use second person for presenting pleasant ideas and avoid second person for presenting negative ideas.

9. Use second person for emphasis and third person for de-emphasis of an idea.

10. Use objective-case pronouns to follow prepositions and verbs.

11. Use verbs that agree in number with the subjects of sentences.

12. Use verbs that agree in person with their subjects.

13. Do not make unnecessary changes in tense.

14. Avoid splitting infinitives.

15. Use active verbs to present important points or to present pleasant ideas;

use passive verbs to present less significant points or to present unpleasant ideas.

16.   Avoid use of adjectives that are used too frequently by others, are overly strong, or are overly negative.

17.   Use hyphens to join words that form a one-word modifier of a noun that follows; leave the words separate when they follow the noun they describe.

18.   Place a comma between coordinate adjectives.

19.   Use only supported or supportable superlatives.

20.   Avoid use of adverbs that are used too frequently by others, are overly strong, or are overly negative.

21.   Place an adverb close to the word it modifies.

22.   Place a comma before coordinate conjunctions; place a semicolon before adverbial conjunctions and a comma after them.

23.   Place prepositions at the ends of sentences only when doing so serves a useful purpose.

24.   Repeat the preposition before each word in a series if doing so conveys the precise meaning intended.

25.   Review the list of frequently misused words and avoid errors in their usage.

EXERCISES

Review Questions

1.   Should a writer strive to avoid metacommunications? Explain.

2.   List four consequences of selecting the wrong word in the process of conveying ideas.

3.   Even though simplicity in word choice is recommended, what are the advantages of building a large vocabulary?

4.   Should writers choose words that will impress others, or should they choose words that will clearly express ideas? Why?

5.   Under what circumstance would a communicator be justified in using a word that is not in the vocabulary of most people?

6.   List an advantage and a disadvantage of using the expression ''he or she'' as the subject of a sentence.

7.   For presenting unpleasant ideas, is second person normally recommended? Explain.

8. For presenting pleasant ideas, is third person normally recommended? Explain.

9. If an idea is to be de-emphasized, which will normally serve a writer's purpose better—second person or third person?

10. Which determines the form of verb to be used in a sentence—the noun that precedes the verb, or the subject of the sentence?

11. Which is more likely to result from use of a split infinitive—misinterpretation or distraction?

12. For presenting pleasant or important ideas, which type of verb is recommended—active or passive?

13. In business writing, are superlatives to be avoided? Explain.

14. How is the punctuation of an adverbial conjunction different from the punctuation of a coordinating conjunction?

15. What is the disadvantage of using descriptive words that are overly strong?

For each pair, what is the difference between (a) and (b)?

1. a. metacommunication
   b. kinesic communication

2. a. encoding
   b. decoding

3. a. noun
   b. gerund

4. a. abstract noun
   b. concrete noun

5. a. second person
   b. third person

6. a. nominative case
   b. objective case

7. a. past tense
   b. passive verb

8. a. active verb
   b. passive verb

9. a. adjective
   b. adverb

10. a. compound adjective
    b. coordinate adjective

11. **a.** coordinate conjunction
     b. subordinate conjunction

12. **a.** conjunction
     b. adverbial conjunction

13. **a.** "between the workers"
     b. "among the workers"

14. **a.** "Mr. Porter was compared to Mr. Berra."
     b. "Mr. Porter was compared with Mr. Berra."

15. **a.** "Tina inferred that raises were forthcoming."
     b. "Tina implied that raises were forthcoming."

For each sentence, state the type of weakness, and correct the weakness by revising the sentence.

1. Please terminate the illumination.

2. Reconsideration of the contract is expected at next week's board meeting.

3. I shall appreciate you sending the forms to me.

4. If a doctor is present, invite him to the exercise room.

5. Send the materials to Armen; it should reach him before September 19.

6. This researcher found no support for that hypothesis.

7. You added these columns incorrectly.

8. Every column has been added correctly.

9. That task was assigned to Martha and I.

10. Only one of the mistakes were attributed to carelessness.

11. George arrived late for the meeting and misses his opportunity to speak.

12. The Cardinals had another come from behind victory.

13. This stereo is the best on the market.

14. Bids are to be submitted before September 21; but, they are to be opened on October 1.

15. Where will the new plant be located at?

In each sentence, which of the parenthetical words is correct?

1. How much will that error (*affect, effect*) my grade?

2. First, check to see whether your absence is (*all right, alright*) with the supervisor.

3. Only three of our employees participated; they divided the proceeds equally (*between, among*) them.

4. After comparing Tom's results (*to, with*) Mary's, we will make our recommendation.

5. After all employees have used the device, a (*consensus, consensus of opinion*) will be taken.

6. Margarita's recommendations were different (*than, from*) Sue's.

7. Because Howard was (*uninterested, disinterested*) in the subject, he withdrew.

8. The four winners congratulated (*each other, one another*).

9. When the president spoke at last week's meeting, he (*implied, inferred*) that the contract was to be renegotiated.

10. (*Regardless, Irregardless*) of Mr. Wood's recommendation, Chester plans to apply for a one-year leave.

11. The technique has lost (*its, it's*) appeal.

12. Because quality-control standards have been relaxed, our unit has had (*less, fewer*) rejections this week.

13. The guiding (*principle, principal*) appeared to be "Defer taxes as long as possible."

14. Valarie was promoted to supervisor because she had done a (*credible, creditable*) job as cashier.

15. (*While, Although*) all questionnaires have been returned, they have not been tabulated.

USING THE TECHNIQUES OF STYLE

Phrases
  Certainties
  Demeaning Expressions
  Euphemisms
  Parallelisms
  Redundancies
  Clichés
  Expressions of Surprise, Doubt,
    and Judgment
Sentences
  Structure
  Expletives
  Tone
  Voice
  Emphasis

  Brevity
Punctuation
Paragraphs
  Coherence
  Readability
  Variety
  Type
  Emphasis
Compositions
  Unity
  Coherence
  Emphasis
  Grammar, Spelling, Punctuation,
    and Typing
Summary

The subject of the preceding chapter was words. The subject of this chapter is progressively larger units of thought: phrases, sentences, paragraphs, and compositions. Success in studying this chapter is at least partially dependent on a reader's willingness to think. When invited to answer a question, stop to present a mental answer. This prior intellectual involvement will increase the likelihood that the answer (which appears soon after the question) will be meaningful.

PHRASES

A phrase is a group of words that does not constitute a complete sentence. Texts in grammar have more complete discussions of phrases, but those selected for discussion here are those that present common problems in business writing.

Certainties

Read the following pairs of sentences, paying attention to the italicized phrases. Which—the first or the second—is better?

> I *am sure* you will agree that instructions are clear.
> Re-examine the instructions to see whether they are clear.

> *I know* you have read Chapter 10.
> Chapter 10 was assigned last week.

In each pair, the author of the first sentence seems to be making a declaration of certainty when certainty is hardly possible. If through prior discussion the speaker *can* be sure of agreement, the first sentence is unnecessary. If the speaker really *knows* the chapter has been read, the listener is probably already aware of the idea contained in the sentence. When the phrases "I know" and "I am sure" *cannot* be true, the speaker or writer who uses them risks transmitting a between-the-lines message that warns the reader by saying "Watch out—some of my other ideas may be stretched, too."

Why avoid expressions of certainty?

The expression "as you know" is to be avoided for the same reasons: the receivers either already know that they know and the words are unnecessary, or the words are simply inaccurate. *Avoid expressions of certainty when certainty is hardly possible.*

Demeaning Expressions

Read the following pairs of sentences. Which sentence seems more appropriate and why?

Marie is a *stew*.
Marie is a *flight attendant*.

That suggestion came from the *grease monkey*.
That suggestion came from the *lubrication person*.

Julio is a *hog head*.
Julio is a *locomotive engineer*.

What is a demeaning expression?

How do demeaning expressions interfere with effective communication?

In each of the preceding pairs, the first sentence can be taken as a put-down of an occupation. Like words that put down races or nationalities, words that put down occupations work against a writer's purpose. An expression that is designed to make an idea seem negative or disrespectful (sometimes called a *dysphemism*) is a demeaning expression. Because such expressions divert attention from the real message to emotional problems that have little to do with the message, avoid *demeaning expressions*.

Euphemisms

Although a demeaning expression makes an idea seem worse than it really is, a euphemism makes an idea seem better than it really is. For example, the idea of picking up neighborhood garbage does not sound especially inviting. One who does such work is often referred to as a *sanitation worker* or *sanitation engineer*. Contrasted with *garbage collector,* these words have pleasant connotations. As such, they are not objectionable. Other commonly used and accepted euphemisms are *passed away* for *died, allowed to resign* for *fired, senior citizen* for *aged, reprimanded* for *bawled out, cohabiting* for *shacking up,* and *customer service* for *complaint department*.

Are *all* euphemisms to be avoided?

Such expressions are generally recognized for what they are—distasteful ideas presented with a little sugar coating. Knowing that the sender was simply trying to be polite and positive, receivers are more likely to react favorably than unfavorably. Yet, euphemisms with *excess* sugar coating or those that appear to be deliberate sarcasm are to be avoided. For example, a secretary would probably rather be introduced as *secretary* than as an *amanuensis*. And the one to whom the secretary is introduced would probably prefer *secretary* also. To refer to a typist as *superintendent of the keyboard* is to risk conveying a negative metacommunication; such as, "We wish this typist held a more respectable position, but we do the best we can by making it sound good." To the receiver (and to the typist), just plain *typist* would sound better. *Use euphemisms when the purpose is to present unpleasant thoughts politely and positively; avoid them when they will be taken as excessive or sarcastic.*

Parallelisms

In the following pairs of sentences, the ideas are the same. Which is stated better and why?

We have three stated goals: to increase production, to expand our market, and recruiting skilled workers.

We have three stated goals: to increase production, to expand our market, and to recruit skilled workers.

Mark received a superior rating in hitting, fielding, and the technique of stealing bases.

Mark received a superior rating in hitting, fielding, and stealing bases.

In each pair, the second sentence is better. It presents similar ideas in a similar way grammatically—"to increase," "to expand," and "to recruit" in the first pair, and "hitting," "fielding," and "stealing" in the second pair. In both pairs, re-examine the first sentence. Because one of the three elements is presented in a form different from the others, that element looks as though it does not belong. In addition, the variation in construction suggests inconsistency on the part of the writer or speaker.

Why should the construction of related ideas be parallel?

When people get together for a certain purpose, they tend to have commonality in dress. A group attending a wedding would dress differently from a group attending a picnic. A person who is dressed for a wedding but attends a picnic appears to be out of place. When ideas appear together for a certain purpose, they should have commonality in grammar. If one of the ideas is presented in a different way grammatically, it also appears to be out of place. Commonality in grammatical presentation is called *parallel construction.* Just as geometry employs the word *parallel* to identify lines that run in the same direction, English employs the word *parallel* to identify ideas that are presented in the same way grammatically.

The principle of parallel construction applies not only to elements of a series that appear in a sentence, but also to major units in an outline, to subunits that appear under a major unit, and to headings that appear on typewritten pages. If one major heading appears in complete-sentence form, so should the others; if one subheading appears in question form, so should other subheadings under that division, etc. *Present multiple units in the same way grammatically.*

Redundancies

A redundancy is a phrase in which one word unnecessarily repeats an idea contained in an accompanying word. In each sentence, which phrase constitutes a redundancy?

In a paragraph, does use of a certain word for the third time constitute redundancy?

We need to review the basic fundamentals of law.
Consensus of opinion is that a promotion is warranted.
We have a free gift for you.

Since "fundamentals" are "basic," both words are not needed. Since "consensus" means "survey of opinion," both are not needed. Since a gift by definition is without charge to the receiver, "free" is not needed; "gift" is sufficient.

The following redundancies are common:

but nevertheless (but *or* nevertheless)
exact same (same)
exactly identical (identical)
full and complete (full *or* complete)
other alternative (alternative)
past history (history)
personal opinion (opinion)
true facts (facts *or* truth)
whether or not (whether)

What is the difference between redundancy and repetition?

Redundancy is not to be confused with repetition. In a sentence or paragraph, a certain word may need to be used again. Repetition serves a purpose and *is not* an error. Redundancy serves no purpose and *is* an error. Because such an error wastes words and risks distracting from the idea presented, *avoid redundancies.*

Clichés

Phrases that have become overused are called *clichés.* In each sentence, which phrase is well worn?

Please send a reply at your earliest convenience.
A booklet is being sent under separate cover.
Enclosed please find a copy of my transcript.

"At your earliest convenience," "under separate cover," and "Enclosed please find" have been used so much that they no longer appear original. Now, look at the same sentences without the clichés:

Please send a reply just *as soon as you can.*
The booklet is being sent *in a larger envelope.*
The enclosed transcript should answer most of your questions.

Why avoid clichés in speaking or writing?

Clichés can make reading monotonous, and they can make a writer seem like a copier. But they present a still more serious problem. Suppose Trisha is sitting in the waiting room of an office. A man enters and says to the receptionist, "I'm George; don't you look gorgeous today." After filling out forms, he takes a seat by Trisha and uses the same line. Because Trisha knows the line has been used before, she may not take it as any sort of a compliment. George has an expression he can use without thinking and possibly without meaning. Between the lines, a worn expression can convey such messages as these: "You are nothing special." "For you, I won't bother to think; the phrases I use in talking with others are surely good enough for you." Some more clichés are discussed on the following pages.

according to our records, our records indicate

Since everyone knows business firms keep records, the phrase "Our records indicate your last payment was due on January 5" is not necessary unless the person should contrast *his* or *her* records with others that are being discussed. If not, then the same idea is communicated more simply and directly by saying, "Your last payment was due on January 5." However, if the purpose is to contrast records, the phrases may be useful. ("According to the client's records, the account is paid; according to our records, it isn't.")

at an early date

The expression is vague. Be specific. *Soon* is an improvement. Giving the exact date is more helpful.

at this time

The expression means *now,* so why not say *now?* It is shorter and less overused. Also, the words may imply (without the writer's intent) that *another* time is being considered.

at this writing, at this point in time

When else could it be? Say now *if an expression is necessary.*

attached please find, please find enclosed, enclosed you will find

These expressions seem to imply that something has been hidden or that locating it may be difficult. In addition, they usually tell what is known already—that the letter is accompanied with other material. References to enclosures can be made in *sentences* that also say something else; such as "Refer to page 7 of the enclosed folder to see the basic steps of operation."

claim, complaint

In letters to customers, these words suggest negative thoughts. No one wants to learn that a letter asking for a legitimate adjustment has been branded as a *complaint.* And no one would be pleased to read a sentence that says, "You *claim* the cog was stripped when the drill was installed." To some people, the words *complaint* and *claim* suggest a request for something to which they are not entitled. "We appreciate your letter of March 18" is better than "We appreciate your complaint of March 18."

Why not refer to a complaint as a *complaint?*

have a nice day

Imagine yourself as seventh in line at a grocery-store checkout counter. By the time you are ready to leave, the clerk has said "Have a nice day" to the six who preceded you. Now, it's your turn. Do the words have much meaning? Because the same

What could be wrong with such a positive expression as "Have a nice day"?

expression is used for everyone, it may have little meaning for anyone. If the words are *not* really meant, the phoniness will probably be detected.

> *hereto, herewith, hereby, said, above, same, thereof, wherein, hereinafter*

All these words are overused law terms. They seem to convey an unneeded tone of legality and formality.

> *I have your letter, your letter has been given to me for reply*

These ideas will be understood without taking time to express them.

> *I remain*

Who would think of saying, "I remain," or "I shall remain," if the expression had not been learned from others? In business letters, the expression is useless and should be omitted.

> *no problem*

Although the words *deny* the existence of a problem, they are used in discussing something that *is* a problem. "If you don't have the cash, no problem; we accept credit-card purchases." Since a shortage of money is a problem, *no problem* is best omitted.

> *permit me to say*

Asking permission to make a statement is not necessary. Besides, asking permission and then immediately proceeding without it may imply that we are rude or are saying something that should not be said.

> *please contact me if you have any further questions.*

Why should we avoid ending a letter with "If you have any further questions . . ."?

If this sentence says exactly what is meant, and if the receiver has not encountered it frequently before, its use is not especially objectionable. However, it does have these disadvantages: (1) it implies doubt about whether other questions have been answered adequately, (2) it is especially out of place if the preceding discussion has not been about *questions,* and (3) it may actually encourage needless correspondence.

> *pursuant to your request, referring to your request, in reference to your letter*

These expressions often appear at the beginning of letters. Readers recognize them as coming from a person who would rather copy than think — someone who says the same thing at the beginning of all letters. Such beginnings can have meaning when they identify the reply with a specific piece of correspondence. But referring to previous correspondence is more smoothly done in an indirect manner. Instead of saying, "Pursuant to your January 21 request for a catalog, we are sending it to you today," say "The catalog you requested on January 21 was mailed today."

recent date

Be specific. State the exact date.

take this opportunity

Save time by getting right into the subject.

the writer, the undersigned

Such expressions suggest that we are trying to give the impression of modesty. Using *I* too frequently is monotonous; it also places greater emphasis on the writer than on the reader. But obvious attempts to circumvent *I* are just as bad. Instead of "I found that sales and collection departments actually have common goals," or "The writer found that sales and collection departments actually have common goals," rephrase to "The survey showed that sales and collection departments actually have common goals," or "Sales and collection departments, according to the survey, actually have common goals."

> Why shouldn't someone refer to himself or herself as *the writer?*

thanking you in advance

The expression seems to say, "I know you will do as I have asked you to do. After you do it, I will be grateful. Instead of sending a note of gratitude later, I'll just save time (and a stamp) by expressing my thanks now." To express gratitude for expected or requested action, "I shall appreciate your (action)" or "If you will (action), I shall be grateful" are less worn than "Thank you in advance."

this letter is for the purpose of, this will acknowledge receipt of

These words are usually just space fillers that warm up to the real message. Omit them and get right to the point.

trusting you will, trusting this is, we hope, we trust, I hope, I trust

Not only are these expressions overused, they introduce the unpleasant idea of doubt. If we say, "We trust this is the informatiion you wanted," we are suggesting our own doubts, and the reader may also begin to doubt. The expression should be omitted in most cases.

under separate cover

Instead of using this nebulous expression, we can be specific by saying that a package is being sent by express or parcel post.

wish to, would like to

These words may convey *no* meaning, or they may convey the *wrong* meaning. "We wish to say that we have considered the idea" probably means "We have considered the idea." "We would like to recommend Mr. Clark" may be taken to mean either, "We recommend Mr. Clark" or "Recommending Mr. Clark would be a pleasure, *if we could.*"

you know

This expression is more common in spoken than in written expression. "The technique is, you know, complicated. It took us, you know, many weeks to develop." The "you know" is distracting, meaningless, or inaccurate—all of which make it objectionable.

Can you add to this list?   The following list contains many other expressions that have become clichés:

above (as in "if the above is")   in regard to
acknowledge receipt of   in terms of
along this line   in the event that
are in receipt of   in the near future
as a matter of fact   inasmuch as
as the case may be   kindly (as in "kindly fill out")
as to   meet with your approval
as yet we have not heard from you   party (as in "another party wants")
at all times   please be advised that
at an early date   previous to
avail yourself to the opportunity   prior to
contact (as in "please contact us")   relative to
due to the fact that   same (as in "have cashed same")
for your information   take the liberty
in accordance with   we feel
in due course   we regret to inform
        would say

From a writer's or speaker's point of view, some of the preceding phrases are convenient; they can be used easily and quickly. But to avoid monotony, to keep from seeming to have no originality, and to avoid possible human relations problems, *avoid clichés.*

Expressions of Surprise, Doubt, and Judgment

Phrases that reveal a writer's surprise about reader's behavior can cause problems in human relations. Why are the following sentences risky?

I am surprised that you did not accept.
I just cannot understand your attitude.

"I am surprised" risks conveying something like "I am accustomed to normal behavior. Yours is abnormal and therefore bad or totally unjustified." "I cannot understand" takes the same risks. Such expressions are particularly offensive to receivers because they seem to place them in a position of recognized inferiority.

Similarly, expressions that reveal judgment of recipients' emotional balance are very risky. "I am so sorry you are upset" may be intended as a heart-felt apology, but the "I am sorry" can be completely overshadowed by "you are upset." It could mean "Your conduct is such that I recognize your lack of self-control. Because of your condition, you could not be thinking rationally." *Avoid expressions of surprise, doubt, and judgment.*

How could the clause "I'm surprised" cause a human relations problem?

SENTENCES

For a complete review of sentences, consult an English handbook. The following discussion identifies problems and techniques most likely to be encountered by business writers.

Structure

All sentences have at least two parts: *subject* and *verb*.

Sally	retired.
(*subject*)	(*verb*)

The rains	came.
(*subject*)	(*verb*)

In addition to subject and verb, a sentence may have additional words for completion of their meaning. These words are called *complements*:

Sally	retired	in her twenty-fifth year.
(*subject*)	(*verb*)	(*complement*)

The grade	was changed	to a B.
(*subject*)	(*verb*)	(*complement*)

The children	played	baseball.
(*subject*)	(*verb*)	(*complement*)

Observe from the preceding examples that a complement may be expressed in one word (the third sentence) or more than one word (the first and second).

A group of words that does not express a complete thought (that is not a sentence) is called a *phrase* or a *clause*. A phrase does not include a subject and a verb; a clause does. In the following examples, the phrases and clauses are italicized:

Phrases: One *of the workers* was absent.
The people *in that room* have voted.
The electrician fell *while replacing the socket.*

Clauses: *As the president   reported this morning . . .*
(subject)   (verb)
If construction   is begun in January . . .
(subject)   (verb)
. . . if I   can pay the rent.
(subject)   (verb)

Could a dependent
clause serve as
a complete sentence?

Clauses are divided into two categories: dependent and independent. A dependent clause does not convey a complete thought. The preceding illustrations are dependent. An independent clause does convey a complete thought; it could be a complete sentence if presented alone:

As the president reported this morning,   sales increased in May.
(dependent clause)   (independent clause)

If work is begun in March,   the job can be completed in July.
(dependent clause)   (independent clause)

I can keep my apartment   if I can pay the rent.
(independent clause)   (dependent clause)

Although an independent clause can be stated as a separate sentence, a dependent clause cannot. Without the remainder of the sentence, "As the president reported this morning" does not convey a complete thought and should not be presented as a separate sentence. When a *sentence fragment* (a portion of a sentence) is presented as a separate sentence, readers become confused and distracted.

Sentences fall into four categories: *simple, compound, complex,* and *compound-complex:*

Simple: The parents went to work.

Compound: The parents went to work, and the children went to school. (two independent clauses)

Complex: As I expected, the parents went to work. (a dependent and an independent clause)

Compound-complex: As I expected, the parents went to work; but they plan to return before five o'clock. (a dependent clause and two independent clauses)

In the preceding examples, notice the use of punctuation to separate one clause from another. When punctuation is omitted or used incorrectly, the result is usually a *run-on* sentence. Run-on sentences also result from use of too many clauses in one sentence.

Original: New forms have been ordered they should be delivered next Friday.

Revisions: New forms have been ordered. They should be delivered next Friday.

New forms have been ordered, and they should be delivered next Friday.

New forms have been ordered; they should be delivered next Friday.

The new forms, which were ordered last week, should be delivered next Friday.

Original: New forms were delivered today, the number of questions has been reduced from fifteen to five, this simplification will reduce office work by 25 percent.

Revision: New forms were delivered today. Because the number of questions has been reduced from fifteen to five, office work will be reduced by 25 percent.

A common problem in sentence structure is the placement of words, clauses, or phrases in the wrong position:

Original: We have taken the check to the bank, which was unsigned.

The sentence is confusing (or amusing) because it seems to imply that the bank was unsigned. That impression is given because the "which" clause is placed closer to "bank" than to "check."

Revised: We have taken the check, which was unsigned, to the bank.

Similarly, the following sentences have very different meanings:

The questionnaire, which has some serious defects, is being returned to the committee. (This sentence means the questionnaire is defective.)
The questionnaire is being returned to the committee, which has some serious defects. (This sentence means the committee is defective.)

The following sentences illustrate a very common (and sometimes very serious) type of error. What causes the confusion?

Being new to our city, I extend a welcome to you.
While taking an exam, the teacher noticed Sam was turning pale.
Typing at seventy-five words per minute, a few errors were made.

Re-examine all three sentences. Each is complex. Each begins with a dependent phrase. The dependent phrase speaks of action without revealing who the doer is. "Being new to our city" does not reveal *who* is new. "While taking an exam" does not reveal *who* is taking an exam. "Typing at seventy-five words per minute" does not reveal *who* is typing. Because the word *I* comes immediately after the idea of being *new,* the newness is attributed to the speaker. But, surely, the person being spoken to is the newcomer. The second sentence implies that "the teacher" was taking an exam. The third sentence implies that "a few errors" were doing the typing.

When a sentence begins by identifying action without revealing who the doer is, the subject of the independent clause gets credit for that action regardless of whether that credit is justified. Such sentences can be corrected in three different ways:

1.   Change the dependent phrase to a dependent clause:

> *Since you are new to our city,* I extend a welcome to you.
> *While Sam was taking an exam,* the teacher noticed he (Sam) was turning pale.
> *While Jane was typing at seventy-five words per minute,* she made a few errors.

In these revisions, confusion is removed because action and actor in the dependent clause are close together.

2.   Change the *subject* of the independent clause:

> Being new to our city, *you* are extended a warm welcome.
> While taking an exam, *Sam* turned pale and the teacher noticed his condition.
> Typing at seventy-five words per minute, Jane made a few errors.

Confusion is removed because the doer of the action mentioned in the dependent phrase is introduced immediately after the phrase.

3.   Begin the sentence with the independent clause.

> *I extend a welcome to you,* being new to our city.
> *The teacher noticed Sam was turning pale while taking an exam.*
> *A few errors were made* because the paper was typed at seventy-five words per minute.

Why is a dangling participial phrase a more serious error than a redundancy?

In these revisions, confusion is removed because the subject of the independent clause is not placed close enough to action of the dependent phrase to merit association with it.

The problem illustrated in the preceding sentences is the *dangling participial phrase.* "Being new to our city, I extend a welcome to you" is misleading because the dependent phrase dangles—is not properly attached to its doer. *When the dependent phrase identifies action without revealing the doer, present the doer immediately after the phrase.* In other words, the subject of an independent clause is presumed to be the doer of any action mentioned in a dependent phrase that precedes it.

Expletives

By definition, an *expletive* is a meaningless word. Find the meaningless word in the following sentence:

> There is to be an addendum made to the policy.

Try to grasp the true meaning of "there." Since it is not being used in the sense of contrast with *here,* it does not mean "location." Observe that the same idea can be presented in fewer words:

> An addendum is to be made to the policy.

In addition to being shorter, the revised sentence has another advantage: it presents words in the normal sequence of the English sentence—subject, verb, complement. In the original sentence, a reader is exposed to the verb ("is") before knowing what the sentence is about. Being unusual, such sentences make reading a little more difficult.

What are the disadvantages of employing expletives?

Expletive beginnings are not considered grammatical errors but are seldom advisable. Any sentence that begins with *There is, there are,* etc., can usually be improved upon. Also, sentences that begin with *It is* can usually be improved upon:

Are expletives considered grammatical errors?

> **Original:** *It is* probable that our rules should be changed.
> **Revised:** Our rules probably should be changed.

> **Original:** *It is* encouraging to note that sales have increased this month.
> **Revised:** Sales have increased this month; the figures are encouraging.

Although each of the preceding original sentences does have a subject ("It") that precedes the verb ("is"), the subject is vague; only after having read the entire sentence does a reader become aware of what "It" means. The revisions employ fewer words, and they employ the more conventional subject-verb-complement pattern. Of course the word *it* can serve as a first word when the antecedent is in a preceding sentence:

> . . . of this document. *It is* being revised. . . .

Seeing "It" before the verb "is," a reader knows that "it" stands for "document."

Such a pronoun can serve well as a coherence technique, and its use is not to be discouraged at all. *Avoid expletive beginnings.*

Tone

Tone is the way a statement sounds. Negative words are associated with unpleasant tone; positive words are associated with pleasant tone. In each pair of sentences, which sounds better?

> We cannot pay until September 1.
> We can pay on September 1.

> Construction will not begin before January 1.
> Construction will begin soon after January 1.

> You made a failing score.
> Your score was 63; passing scores were 70 and above.

The first sentence in each pair contains a negative word—"cannot," "will not," and "failing." In each pair, both sentences are sufficiently clear; but the positive words in the second sentence make the message more diplomatic. It sounds more pleasing and does a better job of promoting human relations. For good human relations, *use positive sentences—sentences that speak of what can be done instead of what* cannot *be done, of the* pleasant *instead of the* unpleasant.

Sometimes, the tone of a message can be improved by switching to the subjunctive mood. Subjunctive sentences employ such conditional words as *if, could, would, might,* and *wish.* Subjunctive sentences speak of conditions contrary to fact, of doubt, or of possibility. In each pair, the second sentence is subjunctive. Which seems more diplomatic?

> I cannot attend the convention with you.
> I *wish* I *could* attend the convention with you.

> I am unable to accept your invitation.
> *If* I accepted your invitation, I *would* have to miss my parents' anniversary party.

> I cannot pay until next month.
> I *wish* I *could* pay this month, but I must pay my taxes instead.

How can the subjunctive mood be employed to achieve good human relations?

Are human relationships more important than clarity?

In all three pairs, a negative idea is involved; but the second sentence transmits the negative idea in positive language. Positive language is more diplomatic. In the second and third pair, the revised sentence includes a reason. Because a reason is included, the negative idea seems less objectionable and tone is thus improved.

Tone is important, but clarity is even more important. The revised sentence in the preceding pairs sufficiently *implies* the unpleasant idea without stating it directly. If for any reason a writer suspects the implication is not sufficiently strong, a direct statement in negative terms is preferable. *For tactful presentation of an unpleasant thought, consider stating it in the subjunctive mood.*

Sometimes, the sting of an unpleasant thought can be reduced by placing that thought in the same sentence with a pleasant thought:

Original: Another seven points and your overall score would have been considered passing.

Revised: Another seven points and your overall score would have been considered passing, *but your score in chemistry was in the ninety-sixth percentile.*

Original: Because of increased taxes and insurance, you are obligated to increase your monthly payments by $50.

Revised: Because of increased taxes and insurance, you are obligated to increase your monthly payments by $50; *but, from last year's figures, your home is increasing in value at the monthly rate of $150.*

For improved tone, place a positive idea in the same sentence with a negative idea.

Can a negative thought be de-emphasized?

Voice

If a sentence is in the *active voice,* the subject is a doer of action. If a sentence is in the *passive voice,* the subject is not a doer; rather, the subject is acted upon. (See the discussion of active and passive verbs in Chapter 4.)

Active voice: Angela wrote the report.
Passive voice: The report was written by Angela.

The active sentence draws attention to Angela. The passive sentence draws attention to the report. Readers normally get more vivid imagery when sentences are active. The first sentence invites the reader to see a woman using a pen or a word processor. The second directs attention to a completed report. The choice of either active or passive voice is determined by the writer's purpose.

Why is the active voice normally preferred?

From the discussion of tone, recall that positive ideas should be emphasized and negative ideas should be de-emphasized. Which sentence places more accent on the *positive* idea?

Jerry completed the job ahead of schedule.
The job was completed ahead of schedule.

Why use the active voice for pleasant ideas and the passive voice for unpleasant ideas?

Since a person ("Jerry") is the subject of the first sentence, and since people are easily envisioned in action, the first sentence is more vivid. *For presenting positive ideas, use the active voice.*

Which of the following sentences places greater emphasis on the *negative* idea?

> Jerry completed the job two months behind schedule.
> The job was completed two months behind schedule.

Again, the first sentence, which is active, is more vivid. But normally negative ideas should be toned down. Because the idea is negative, Jerry would probably appreciate being taken out of the picture. Because the second sentence is in the passive voice, it places more emphasis on the job than on who failed to complete it. *For presenting negative ideas, use the passive voice.*

Emphasis

A landscape artist wants some points in a picture to stand out boldly and others to get little attention. A musician sounds some notes loudly and others softly. Likewise, a writer or speaker wants some ideas to be *emphasized* and others to be *de-emphasized.* Normally, as we have seen, pleasant and important ideas should be emphasized; unpleasant and insignificant ideas should be de-emphasized.

We have seen how clarity can be influenced by sentence structure. Emphasis is also influenced by sentence structure. Which sentence places more emphasis on the idea of John's taking a job?

> John took a job in insurance.
> John took a job in insurance, but he really preferred a job in accounting.

For stating a very important idea, is a simple sentence better than a compound sentence?

The first sentence has one independent clause. Because no other idea competes with it for attention, its idea is emphasized. *For emphasis, place an idea in a simple sentence; for de-emphasis, place an idea in a compound sentence.*

Which sentence places more emphasis on the idea of John's taking a job?

> John took a job in insurance, but he really preferred a job in accounting.
> Although he took a job in insurance, John really preferred a job in accounting.

Observe that the first sentence is compound; the second, complex. In the first sentence, the idea of taking a job is in an independent clause. Because an independent clause would make sense if the rest of the sentence were omitted, an independent clause is more emphatic than a dependent clause. In the second sentence, the idea of taking a job is in a dependent clause. By itself, the clause would not make complete sense. Compared with the independent clause that follows ("John really preferred. . . ."), the idea in the dependent clause is de-emphasized. *For emphasis, place an idea in an independent clause; for de-emphasis, place an idea in a dependent clause.*

Should very significant ideas be placed in dependent clauses?

Which sentence places more emphasis on the idea of *success?*

> The mission was successful because of. . . .
> The mission was successful; this success is attributed to. . . .

In the second sentence a form of "success" is repeated. *For emphasis of a word, let it appear more than once in a sentence.*

In each pair, which sentence places more emphasis on *success* and which on *failure?*

> The project was a success; without your efforts, it would have been a failure.
> Your efforts contributed to the success of the project; otherwise, failure would have been the result.

> Success resulted from your efforts; failure would have resulted without them.
> The project was successful because of your efforts; without them, failure would have been the result.

In the first sentence, "success" and "failure" appear as the *last* words in their clauses. In the third sentence, "success" and "failure" appear as the *first* words in their clauses. For attention, words that appear first compete only with words that follow; words that appear last compete only with words that precede. *For emphasis of a word, let it appear first or last in a sentence.*

In the following examples, the first sentence contains a general word and the second sentence contains specific words. Which gives the more emphatic picture?

> Wilford comes to work in a *truck.*
> Wilford comes to work in a *1984 Ford pickup.*

Because the second sentence gives a more detailed picture, it is more emphatic.

Another way to de-emphasize a negative point is to express it in general terms. Which sentence is more appropriate?

> **Specific:** Thank you for letting us know that *your credit card has been revoked and that your car has been repossessed.*
> **General:** Thank you for letting us know about *your financial situation.*

Because the general sentence is less vivid, it is less emphatic. Because the subject matter is unpleasant, general language is more appropriate. On the other hand, specific language is more appropriate if the subject matter is pleasant:

> **General:** Congratulations on *your recent honor.*
> **Specific:** Congratulations on *your selection as real estate woman of the year.*

Specific language has the effect of giving the honor the emphasis it deserves. *For emphasis of a positive idea, use specific language; for de-emphasis of a negative idea, use general language.*

In the following sentences, the ideas are the same; but the emphasis is different:

> The problems have been narrowed into three categories: absenteeism, tardiness, and alcoholism.
> The problems have been narrowed into three categories: (1) absenteeism, (2) tardiness, and (3) alcoholism.

In the second sentence, the words preceded by numbers get special attention. They are easier to locate when a page is reviewed. If the preceding and following sentences on the page contain no numbers, the words with numbers take on special significance. The significance can be magnified even further:

> The problems have been narrowed into three categories: absenteeism, tardiness, and alcoholism.

> The problems have been narrowed into three categories:
> **a.** absenteeism
> **b.** tardiness
> **c.** alcoholism

The second of the preceding examples employs a technique referred to as "tabulation." Units of a series are placed in a column and indented (instead of being placed side by side). Because each unit in the series is on a line by itself (where it does not have to compete for attention), and because the arrangement consumes more space on the page, a tabulated series is attention getting. On typewriter keyboards, a special "tab" key facilitates making the indention needed for typing columnar (tabulated) items.

A letter assigned to a unit has the same effect as a number. In the second sentence, each of the three elements is emphasized because it appears on a line by itself, where it is not competing with other words for attention. *For emphasis of units in a series, precede each element by a number or letter; for still further emphasis, tabulate the series.*

Careful writers employ punctuation marks for emphasis and de-emphasis, particularly when sentences contain appositives. An *appositive* is a word that purposefully repeats or explains a preceding word. Upon reading each of the following sentences, try to decide whether the appositive ("Cal Thomas") is emphasized or de-emphasized.

> The job was completed in two days by one man (Cal Thomas).
> The job was completed in two days by one man, Cal Thomas.
> The job was completed in two days by one man—Cal Thomas.
> The job was completed in two days by one man: Cal Thomas.

For a very significant idea, is specific language better than general language?

What is the effect of placing a number before each unit in a series?

Parentheses label an idea as parenthetical: it could be left out. An idea that could be omitted is not thought of as particularly important. Use of parentheses is like saying "The name is not especially important; but just in case it is of interest, here it is." The comma in the second sentence implies neither emphasis nor de-emphasis. "One man" and who that man is are of about equal importance. The dash in the third sentence is considered a strong mark of punctuation. Requiring two strokes of the typewriter key, the dash looks longer and stronger than a comma. In oral presentation, a word preceded by a long pause gets special emphasis. Likewise, a dash attaches special emphasis to an appositive. The colon in the last sentence serves the same purpose as the dash. Requiring two dots and two typewriter spaces after it, a colon is a strong mark of punctuation; it serves to magnify the appositive. *For appositives, use parentheses for de-emphasis, a comma for neutral emphasis, and a dash or colon for emphasis.*

For an appositive that is to be stressed, what punctuation marks could be used?

Another way to emphasize or de-emphasize an idea is to include words that label it:

> But most important of all. . . .
> A less significant aspect was. . . .

For emphasis or de-emphasis, attach words that label ideas as significant or insignificant.

Brevity

Ideas that are sufficiently implied need not be stated. For example,

What ideas can be left to implication?

> She took the test and passed it.

If she passed the test, she obviously took it. The sentence can be shortened:

> She passed the test.

Observe how the following sentences on the right have been improved by eliminating the words that can be implied:

The *auditor reviewed the figures and concluded* that they were accurate.	The *auditor concluded* that the figures were accurate.
The *secretary checked her transcript and found* three spelling errors.	The *secretary found* three spelling errors in her transcript.

Sometimes we can shorten sentences by using the following suffixes and making any necessary changes in word form: *-ful, -ly, -ing, -iest, -ed, -less, -able, -ible, -ic, -ical, -ous,* or *-ious*. For example:

She was a typist *who took great care.*	She was a *careful* typist.
He waited *in an impatient* manner.	He waited impatiently.
Stenographers lose time *when they have to use* the dictionary.	Stenographers lose time *by using* the dictionary.
the work *that he had not finished*	his *unfinished* work
the machine *that made the most noise*	the nois*iest* machine
the workers *who have the most skill*	the *most skilled* workers
Omit the expressions *for which you have no use.*	Omit *useless* expressions.
Only half of the material *could be used.*	Only half the material *was usable.*
a person *with a lot of energy*	an *energetic* person
arranged according to the alphabet	*in alphabetical order*
a speech *that was full of pomp*	a *pompous* speech
a person *of great industry*	an *industrious* person

The expressions on the right represent useful techniques for achieving economy. However, the ones on the left cannot be categorically condemned. We may sometimes use them to achieve the right *emphasis*.

Using a *compound adjective* often helps to reduce the number of words required to express an idea. A compound adjective is two or more words joined with a hyphen or hyphens and used as a single modifier of the noun it precedes.

He wrote a report *that was up to the minute.*	He wrote an *up-to-the-minute* report.
They were engaged in an enterprise *that was first class.*	They were engaged in a *first-class* enterprise.
His policy *of going slowly* was well received.	His *go-slow* policy was well received.

By using the compound adjectives, we reduce the number of words required to express our idea and thus save the reader a little time.

Punctuation

Speakers use pauses and voice inflection to assist listeners in extracting meaning from sentences. Similarly, writers use punctuation marks. For both writers and readers, knowledge of punctuation is essential.

In the preceding pages, sentences used to illustrate *other* principles also illustrate principles of punctuation:

Place a comma before the conjunction in a compound sentence.

> I wanted to pay this month, but I must pay my taxes instead.
> The reports are ready for editing, and the statements are ready for checking.

Place a comma after a dependent clause that precedes an independent clause.

> As I expected, the parents went to work.
> If work is begun in March, the job can be completed in July.

Place a comma before and after a parenthetical phrase.

> The typist, not the secretary, is responsible.
> Management does, as I learned today, plan to revise pay scales in January.

Place a comma between coordinate adjectives.

> Jane was asked to fill out a long, complicated questionnaire.
> The system provides cold, dry air.

For appositives, determine the punctuation by the amount of emphasis desired.

> We had one problem, weather.   (Neutral emphasis)
> We had one problem (weather).   (De-emphasis)
> We had one problem: weather.   (Emphasis)
> We had one problem — weather.   (Emphasis)

Place a comma after the units in a series (except the final unit, which is followed by a period).

> All majors must attain a C average in accounting, law, and finance.
> Our primary problems are in absenteeism, tardiness, and alcoholism.

Place a colon before a series if the series is preceded by a complete thought.

> The problems have been narrowed into three categories: absenteeism, tardiness, and alcoholism.
> Three items are essential: pencil, paper, and eraser.

Place a semicolon before an adverbial conjunction and a comma after it.

> The report arrived today; however, it has not been evaluated.
> Your efforts contributed to the success of the project; otherwise, failure would have been the result.

Place a semicolon between independent clauses when the conjunction is omitted.

> Your score was 63; passing scores were 70 or more.
> The recommendations arrived today; the judge checked them thoroughly.

Place a semicolon before the conjunction in a compound–complex sentence.

> As I expected, the parents went to work; but they plan to return before five o'clock.
> The parents went to work; but, as I expected, they returned before five o'clock.

Use hyphens to join words that form a compound adjective.

> He wrote an up-to-the-minute report.
> Diana applied for a two-week vacation.

For a more thorough review of punctuation, see the Appendix.

PARAGRAPHS

Just as a wall is made by attaching stones, a paragraph is made by attaching sentences. Without adhesive devices, the sentences would not convey messages effectively.

Coherence

What are some of the techniques for achieving coherence?

Although the word *coherence* is used sometimes to mean "clarity" or "understandability," it is used throughout this text to mean "cohesion." If writing or speaking is coherent, the sentences stick together and each sentence is in some way linked to the preceding sentences. The following techniques for linking sentences are common:

1. Repeat a word that was used in the preceding sentence.

> . . . to take *responsibility* for the decision. This *responsibility* can be shared. . . .

The second sentence is an obvious continuation of the idea presented in the preceding sentence.

2. Use a pronoun that represents a noun used in the preceding sentence.

> . . . to take this *responsibility*. *It* can be shared. . . .

Because "it" means "responsibility," the second sentence is linked directly with the first.

3. Use such connecting words as *however, therefore, yet, nevertheless, consequently, also, in addition,* etc.

> . . . .to take this responsibility. *However,* few are willing to. . . .

"However" implies "We're continuing with the same topic, just moving into a different phase." Remember, though, that good techniques can be *overused.* Unnecessary connectors are space consuming and distracting. Usually they can be spotted (and crossed out) in proofreading.

4. Use words that are frequently found together.

> The *girls* rejected the idea. The *boys* accepted, but with some reluctance.

The words "girls" and "boys" are commonly found together. If *student* appears in one sentence, *teacher* can be used as a linking word in the following sentence by continuing with a discussion of people in academics. The same would be true of such word pairs as *employer* and *employee, summer* and *winter, state* and *federal*—any words that are thought of in pairs.

Careful writers use coherence techniques to keep readers from experiencing abrupt changes in thought. *Avoid abrupt changes in thought, and link each sentence to a preceding sentence.* When the writing is coherent, reading is simplified.

Readability

Even though sentences are arranged in a sensible sequence and coherence techniques have been employed effectively, reading can still be difficult or fruitless. Two factors that contribute to readability are (1) length of sentences and (2) size of words. In an effort to determine the school grade level at which a passage is written, Robert Gunning[1] developed a readability formula:

What qualities cause a message to be difficult to read?

1. Select a passage of 100 words or more.

2. Find the *average sentence length* by dividing the number of words in the passage by the number of sentences. Count compound sentences as two sentences.

3. Find the number of *difficult* words per hundred. A *difficult* word is defined as a word with three syllables or more. Words are *not* to be counted as difficult if they (1) are compounded words made from smaller words, such as *however* or

---

1. Adapted from *The Technique of Clear Writing* (New York: McGraw-Hill, 1968), pp. 38–39, copyrighted by Robert Gunning and used with permission.

understand; (2) are proper nouns; or (3) are verbs that became three syllables by addition of *ed* or *es,* such as *imposes* or *defended.* Determine difficult words per hundred by dividing the number of words in the passage into the number of difficult words and multiplying the resulting figure by 100.

4.   Add the average sentence length and the number of difficult words per hundred.

5.   Multiply the resulting figure by 0.4, to arrive at the reading grade level at which the passage was written.

The following passage illustrates application of the formula: ("Difficult" words are underscored.)

> Each successive development has changed society. Early writing freed oral societies from limitations of time and space. Their legacies were transmitted* in writing; therefore, anthropologists and historians have not had to rely on hieroglyphs, pottery, utensils, and religious artifacts to study our recent past.** However,*** the world was essentially illiterate until the development of printing. Printing made literature available to other than the religious elite. Printing multiplied the dimensions of communication; those who weren't literate were encouraged to become so.**
>
> High-speed printing and inexpensive newspress paper overcame*** all previous limitations and led to mass communication. With the advent of the telegraph, telephone, radio, and television, the world became a smaller place and instant communication commonplace.*** What a milestone we achieved when millions of Americans**** (plus millions throughout the world) saw and heard Neil Armstrong begin his walk on the moon.

The passage contains 141 words in 11 sentences. The number of "difficult" words is 33.

Average sentence length (141/11)	12.8
No. of "difficult" words per 100	
(33/141 × 100)	23.4
Add 12.8 and 23.4	36.2
Multiply 36.2 by .4	14.48

The reading grade level is between 14 and 15. The resulting grade level is referred to by Gunning as the *Fog Index.* For most business writing, the desirable Fog Index is in the eight-to-eleven grade range. A writer need not be overly concerned if the index turns out to be a little over eleven or under eight. Trying to write at the grade level of the actual recipient is inadvisable. The level may not be known, and even those who have earned advanced degrees appreciate writing that can be read and understood

---

* Not a "difficult" word (because it is a verb that became three syllables by addition of " *ed.* ").

** Counted as two sentences (because it is a compound sentence).

*** Not a "difficult" word (because it is made from two separate words compounded into one).

**** Not a "difficult" word (because it is a familiar proper noun).

quickly and easily. *For quick, easy reading (and listening), use small words and short sentences.*

Variety

Although a short *average* sentence length is desirable, keeping *all* sentences short would be undesirable. The passage may sound monotonous, unrealistic, or elementary. A two-word sentence is acceptable; so is a sixty-word sentence, if it is clear. Just as sentences should vary in length, they should also vary in structure. Some complex or compound sentences should be included with the simple sentences.

Variety is just as desirable in paragraph length as it is in sentence length. A paragraph can be from one line in length to a dozen lines or more. But, just as average sentence length should be kept fairly short, average paragraph length should be kept short.

Paragraphs in business letters are typically shorter than paragraphs in business reports. First and last paragraphs are normally short (one to four lines), and other paragraphs should normally be no longer than six lines. A short first paragraph makes a letter look more inviting to read than a long first paragraph. A short last paragraph enables a writer to emphasize the parting words.

In business reports, the space between paragraphs comes as a welcome resting spot. Long paragraphs make a page look as if reading would be laborious. Paragraphs approach the danger point when they exceed eight to ten lines, depending on the subject matter.

Although variety is a desirable quality, it should not be achieved at the expense of consistency. Using *I* in one part of a letter and then without explanation switching to *we* is inadvisable. Using the past tense in one sentence and the present tense in another sentence is unwelcome variety at the expense of consistency. Unnecessary changes from active to passive voice (or vice versa) and from third to second person (or vice versa) are also discouraged. Generally, *strive for short paragraphs, but vary their lengths.*

Why is variety in sentence length and structure essential?

In letters, what is the advantage of employing short first paragraphs?

Should consistency be sacrificed to achieve variety?

Type

The principle of consistency also applies to the type of paragraphs employed. Paragraphs are of two basic types—deductive and inductive. *Deductive paragraphs* present the main idea in the first sentence and follow with details. *Inductive paragraphs* present the details and follow with the main idea. Readers appreciate consistency. Once they catch on to the pattern employed, they know where to look for main ideas.

When the subject matter is complicated and the details are numerous, paragraphs sometimes begin with a main idea, follow with details, and end with a summarizing sentence. But the main idea may not be in the first sentence; the idea may need a preliminary statement. For a writer, composition is simplified if a basic

Why should a writer strive for paragraphs that are consistently inductive or consistently deductive?

pattern (inductive or deductive) is selected and employed. That consistency simplifies the reader's task as well.

Consideration of the reader determines whether to use the inductive or deductive paragraph. Chapters 6–9 discuss planning before writing good-news and bad-news letters, using deductive for good news and inductive for bad news. The same principles hold for paragraphs. If a reader might be antagonized by the topic sentence in a deductive paragraph, antagonism can be avoided by leading up to the topic sentence (making the paragraph inductive). If a writer wants to encourage reader involvement (to generate a little concern about where the details are leading), inductive paragraphs are recommended. Inductive paragraphs can be especially effective if the topic sentence strikes the reader as confirmation of a conclusion the reader has drawn from the preceding details.

If a paragraph is inductive, might a reader know the content of the topic sentence before reading it?

These suggestions hardly apply to the first and last sentences of letters. Such sentences frequently appear as single-sentence paragraphs. But for reports and long paragraphs of letters, *strive for paragraphs that are consistently deductive or consistently inductive.* Regardless of which is selected, first and last ideas are in emphatic positions.

Emphasis

In sentences and paragraphs, where are the emphatic positions?

In sentences, the first and last words are in emphatic positions. In paragraphs, the first and last sentences are also in emphatic positions. An idea that deserves emphasis can be placed in either position, but an idea that does not deserve emphasis can be placed in the middle of a long paragraph.

In sentences that contain a series, each element in the series can be emphasized by placing a number before it. In paragraphs, sentences can be numbered and tabulated with the same effect. For example, a long report could close with a concluding paragraph that restates four supporting reasons for a conclusion. Emphasis on the reasons can be achieved by preceding each reason with a number, by presenting each reason on a separate typewritten line that is about an inch shorter than other lines, and by leaving extra space between the numbered reasons. Notice that the revised concluding paragraph attaches increased emphasis to the reasons:

Original: For our needs, then, the most appropriate in-service training method is programmed instruction. It is least expensive, allows employees to remain at their own work stations while improving their skills, affords constant awareness of progress, and lets employees progress at their own rates.

Revision: For the following reasons, programmed instruction is the most appropriate in-service training method:

1. Programmed instruction is least expensive.

2. Programmed instruction allows employees to remain at their work stations while improving their skills.

3. Programmed instruction affords constant awareness of progress.

4. Programmed instruction lets employees progress at their own rates.

In paragraphs, the first and last words are also in particularly emphatic positions. The word *I*, which is frequently overused in letters, is especially noticeable if it appears as the first word. It is still more noticeable if it appears as the first word in *each* paragraph. *However* and *but* are to be avoided as first words if the preceding paragraph is neutral or positive. These words imply that the next idea will be negative. Unless the purpose is to place emphasis on negatives, such words as *denied, rejected,* and *disappointed* should not appear as the last words in a paragraph. *Within paragraphs, emphasize a sentence by placing it first or last or by assigning it a number in a tabulated series.*

Why should *I* be used sparingly?

COMPOSITIONS

Just as sentences are formed from smaller units (words), and paragraphs are formed from smaller units (sentences), compositions are formed from smaller units (paragraphs). Regardless of whether a composition is a letter, a report, or a speech, problems encountered in sentence and paragraph construction are also encountered at the composition level.

Unity

If a letter has unity, it will cover its topic adequately but will not include extraneous material. It will have a beginning sentence appropriate for the expected reader reaction, paragraphs that present the bulk of the message, and an ending sentence that is an appropriate closing for the message presented.

What *is* unity?

If a report has unity, its introduction will identify the topic, reveal the thesis, and give a preview of upcoming points. The introduction may also include some background, sources of information, and the method of treating data. A unified report will also have a summary or conclusion that brings all major points together. Between the beginning and the ending, a unified report will have paragraphs arranged in a systematic sequence.

The sequence of paragraphs should be determined before the paragraphs are written—at the outline stage. Sequence is strongly influenced by the nature of the subject and by anticipated reader reaction. The following bases for sequence of paragraphs are commonly used:

What are some common bases for sequence of paragraphs?

1. *Time.* In reporting on a series of events or a process, paragraphs proceed from the first step through the last step.

2. *Space.* If a report is about geographic areas, paragraphs can proceed from one area to the next until all areas have been discussed.

3. *Familiarity.* If a topic is complicated, the report can begin with a point that is known or easy to understand and proceed to progressively more difficult points.

4. *Importance.* In analytical reports where major decision-making factors are

presented, the factors can be presented in order of most important to least important, or vice versa.

5. *Value.* If a report involves major factors with monetary values, paragraphs can proceed from those with greatest values to those with least values, or vice versa.

6. *Deduction-induction.* Good-news letters and routine messages are arranged deductively; bad-news letters and persuasive letters are arranged inductively. In reports, the major conclusion can be presented first and supporting paragraphs can follow (deductive); or the conclusion can be omitted from the introduction, and details can lead up to the conclusion.

Letters and reports have a beginning, a middle, and an end; readers must be able to sense the presence of these three parts. If the ending can't be easily linked to some word or idea presented in the beginning, unity has not been achieved. The effect is like that of an incompleted circle, or a picture with one element obviously missing. *Make sure that compositions form a unit with an obvious beginning, middle, and ending and that in-between paragraphs are arranged in a systematic sequence.* If the sequence is logical, coherence is easy to achieve.

Coherence

Just as sentences within a paragraph must adhere, paragraphs within a composition must also adhere. Connecting words, pronouns, repeated words, and orderly sequence are helpful. Especially helpful at the composition level is the *transition sentence.*

Why should you use transition sentences?

Unless a writer (or speaker) is careful, the move from one major topic to the next will seem abrupt. A good transition sentence can bridge the gap between the two topics by summing up the preceding topic and leading a reader to expect the next topic.

> Cost factors, then, seemed prohibitive until efficiency factors were investigated.

This sentence could serve as a transition between the *cost* division heading and the *efficiency* division heading. Since a transition sentence comes at the end of one segment and before the next, it emphasizes the central idea of the preceding segment and confirms the relationship of the two segments. Since the two can be easily presented in one sentence, the next heading is the most logical one to discuss next.

Should transition sentences be employed between *subtopics*?

Transition sentences are very helpful if properly used, but they can be overused. For most reports, transition sentences before major headings are sufficient. Normally, transition sentences before subheadings are unnecessary. Having encountered the previous subheading only a few lines back, a reader may readily see its relationship to the upcoming subheading. Also, transition sentences typically summarize; and the discussion under a subheading of a report is seldom long enough to merit summarization. *Place transition sentences before major headings.*

Emphasis

Just as emphasis is a critical factor in composing sentences and paragraphs, it is also critical at the composition level. The following techniques are commonly employed:

By what techniques can parts of an entire composition be emphasized?

1. *Position.* Beginning and ending positions are emphatic. The central idea of a talk or report appears in the introduction and the conclusion. Good transition sentences synthesize ideas at the end of each major division.

2. *Repetition.* A central idea is emphasized by transition sentences that repeat the essence of a discussion.

3. *Space.* The various divisions of a report or talk are not expected to be of equal length, but an extraordinary amount of space devoted to a topic attaches special significance to that topic. Similarly, a topic that gets an exceedingly small amount of space is de-emphasized.

4. *Headings.* Ideas that appear in headings get more attention than ideas that don't. Ideas that appear in subheadings are less emphatic than ideas that appear in major headings—a factor that should be taken into account at the outline stage. *Talking headings* (headings that reveal the conclusions reached in the following discussion) are more emphatic than general topic headings. For example, "Costs Are Prohibitive" is more emphatic than "Cost Factors."

5. *Nonverbal devices.* Ideas presented in graphs, charts, tables, or pictures are emphatic. Some ideas are more clearly presented in such devices. Also, the contrast in appearance is appealing.

Within a composition, achieve emphasis through position, repetition, space, headings, and nonverbal devices.

Grammar, Spelling, Punctuation, and Typing

Errors in grammar, spelling, punctuation, and typing can be harmful in many ways:

In what ways are grammatical and mechanical errors harmful?

1. They can cause a message to be completely misunderstood.

2. They can cause a reader to waste time.

3. They can cause distraction from the message.

4. They can cause a receiver to lose confidence in the sender—to wonder if the error resulted from haste, ignorance, or lack of respect.

Strive for perfection in grammar, spelling, punctuation, and typing.

SUMMARY

Larger units of messages have been defined as phrases, sentences, paragraphs, and compositions.

Phrases

1. Avoid expressions of certainty when certainty is hardly possible.

2. Avoid demeaning expressions.

3. Use euphemisms when the purpose is to present unpleasant thoughts politely and positively; avoid them when they will be taken as excessive or sarcastic.

4. Present multiple units in the same way grammatically.

5. Avoid redundancies.

6. Avoid clichés.

7. Avoid expressions of surprise, doubt, and judgment.

Sentences

1. When the dependent phrase identifies action without revealing the doer, present the doer immediately after the phrase.

2. Avoid expletive beginnings.

3. Use positive sentences—sentences that speak of what *can* be done instead of what *cannot* be done, of the *pleasant* instead of the *unpleasant* to emphasize the positive.

4. For tactful presentation of an unpleasant thought, consider stating it in the subjunctive mood.

5. For improved tone, place a positive idea in the same sentence that contains a negative idea.

6. For presenting positive ideas, use the active voice.

7. For presenting negative ideas, use the passive voice.

8. For emphasis, place an idea in a simple sentence; for de-emphasis, place an idea in a compound sentence.

9. For emphasis, place an idea in an independent clause; for de-emphasis, place an idea in a dependent clause.

10. For emphasis of a word, let it appear more than once in a sentence.

11. For emphasis of a word, let it appear either first or last in a sentence.

12. For emphasis of a positive idea, use specific language; for de-emphasis of a negative idea, use general language.

13. For emphasis of units in a series, precede each element by a number or a letter; for still further emphasis, tabulate the series.

14. For appositives, use parentheses for de-emphasis, a comma for neutral emphasis, and a dash or colon for emphasis.

15. For emphasis or de-emphasis, attach words that label ideas as significant or insignificant.

Paragraphs

1. Avoid abrupt changes in thought, and link each sentence to a preceding sentence.

2. For quick, easy reading (and listening), use small words and short sentences.

3. Strive for fairly short paragraphs, but vary their lengths.

4. Strive for paragraphs that are consistently deductive or consistently inductive.

5. Within paragraphs, emphasize a sentence by placing it first or last or by assigning it a number and tabulating.

Compositions

1. Make sure that compositions form a unit with an obvious beginning, middle, and ending and that in-between paragraphs are arranged in a systematic sequence.

2. Place transition sentences before major headings.

3. Within a composition, achieve emphasis through position, repetition, space, headings, and nonverbal devices.

4. Strive for perfection in grammar, spelling, punctuation, and typing.

These suggestions can assist encoders in presenting clear, tactful messages. Messages that employ these suggestions should be easily understood and positively received by decoders.

EXERCISES

Review Questions

1.   Why are such phrases as "I am sure" and "I know you will" to be avoided?

2.   Under what conditions are euphemisms to be avoided?

3.   Why should elements in a series be presented in parallel form?

4.   Which is more serious as an error—redundancy or a dangling participial phrase? Why?

5.   In addition to monotony, for what other reason should clichés be avoided.

6.   "I can understand why you are upset." Why should the sentence be avoided or modified?

7.   List the disadvantages of using expletive beginnings.

8.   State the formula for computing readability (Fog Index). To write at a lower readability level than you presently write, what modifications in style would you have to make?

9.   Is variety more important than consistency? Explain.

10.   What is the difference between inductive and deductive paragraphs?

11.   How can unity be achieved?

12.   What is the relationship between transitions and coherence?

13.   In addition to leading a reader to expect the next heading, what else should a transition sentence do?

14.   What is the difference between repetition and redundancy?

15.   List the reasons for trying to achieve perfection in grammar, spelling, punctuation, and typing.

Questions on the Principles of Emphasis

1.   Which position places more emphasis on a word?
   a.   the last word in the sentence
   b.   the middle word in a sentence

2.   If an idea is to be emphasized, which technique is preferred?
   a.   place it in a simple sentence
   b.   place it in a complex sentence

3. If an idea is to be emphasized, which technique is preferred?
   a. place it in a dependent clause
   b. place it in an independent clause

4. If an idea is to be subordinated, which technique is preferred?
   a. place it in a complex sentence
   b. place it in a compound sentence

5. If an idea is to be emphasized, which technique is preferred?
   a. place it in a simple sentence
   b. place it in a compound sentence

6. Which is more emphatic?
   a. active voice
   b. passive voice

7. Ordinarily, which ideas deserve more emphasis?
   a. positive ideas
   b. negative ideas

8. Which is more emphatic?
   a. specific words
   b. general words

9. Which is more emphatic?
   a. second person
   b. third person

10. Ordinarily, which technique is better for presenting a negative idea?
    a. second person
    b. third person

11. Which places less emphasis on a negative idea?
    a. the indicative mood
    b. the subjunctive mood

12. Which punctuation mark affords less emphasis on an appositive?
    a. colon
    b. parentheses

13. Which technique affords more emphasis?
    a. use a person as the subject of the sentence
    b. use a thing as the subject of the sentence

14. Which technique affords more emphasis?
    a. use a concrete noun as the subject of the sentence
    b. use an abstract noun as the subject of the sentence

15. Which is more emphatic?
    a. an idea that appears in a heading
    b. an idea that appears in a paragraph

Application of Emphasis Techniques

1. In which sentence does "credit" receive more emphasis?
   a. On June 7, we applied for credit.
   b. We applied for credit on June 7.

2. In which sentence does the date receive more emphasis?
   a. We applied for credit on June 7.
   b. Although we applied for credit on June 7, we have not had a response to our application.

3. In which sentence does the idea of denial receive more emphasis?
   a. Although our application for credit was denied, we were encouraged to make cash purchases.
   b. Our application for credit was denied, but we were encouraged to make cash purchases.

4. Which sentence is more emphatic?
   a. Tom hit a home run in the ninth inning.
   b. A home run was hit in the ninth inning.

5. Which sentence is more emphatic?
   a. Congratulations on your recent honor.
   b. Congratulations on your receipt of the "outstanding student" award.

6. Which sentence is less emphatic?
   a. We appreciate your letting us know about your condition.
   b. We appreciate your letting us know about your migraine headaches, your shingles, and your broken thumb.

7. Which sentence is less emphatic?
   a. If you found one of our hotel's blankets when unpacking your luggage, please return it to us.
   b. When people find one of our hotel's blankets when unpacking their luggage, they return it to us.

8. Which sentence places more emphasis on the positive?
   a. You will probably react very favorably to our first examination.
   b. Last semester, the students reacted very favorably to their first examination.

9. Which sentence places less emphasis on the negative?
   a. I will not help you with your assignment.
   b. I wish I could help you with your assignment.

10. Which sentence places more emphasis on "money"?
   a. We have a primary need: money
   b. We have a primary need (money).

11. Which sentence places more emphasis on "excuses"?
   a. We are not allowed to make one thing, excuses.
   b. We are not allowed to make one thing—excuses.

12. Which is more emphatic?
    a. George is expected to complete the plaster work tomorrow.
    b. The plaster work is expected to be completed tomorrow.

13. Which sentence is more emphatic?
    a. The building will be completed on or before June 8.
    b. Completion of the building is to be on or before June 8.

14. Which sentence places more emphasis on the units in the series?
    a. The firm needs money, materials, and management.
    b. The firm needs (1) money, (2) materials, and (3) management.

15. Which sentence places more emphasis on the units in the series?
    a. The firm has three needs: (1) money, (2) materials, and (3) management.
    b. The firm has three needs:
        (1) money
        (2) materials
        (3) management

Sentence-Writing Problems

For each sentence, define its weakness and rewrite it in such a way that the weakness is eliminated.

1. I am sure you will agree with my suggestion.

2. Check to see whether any finks have appeared at the entrance.

3. We will provide sanitary engineers for the dishwashing chores.

4. Follow these simple steps: move Lever 2 to the neutral position, turn off the switch, and the machine is to be unplugged.

5. The firm has a free gift for you.

6. Please return the questionnaire at your earliest convenience.

7. Your point of view came as a surprise to us, but we will consider your request.

8. After evaluating your work record, you are being promoted.

9. There are three customers in the waiting room.

10. You failed to fill in the form properly.

11. Charles did not know where the instructions were at.

12. Please try to quietly spread the word.

13. This calculator is the best you can buy for the money.

14. Flora asked for a three week vacation.

15. Only one of the answers are correct.

Editing the Punctuation

If a sentence is not punctuated correctly, make the needed changes.

1.   When you get time please check these figures.

2.   I plan to apply for a leave; but I have a few doubts about whether my request will be granted.

3.   The superintendent, not the foreman, signed the request.

4.   The committee is developing a clear, comprehensive statement.

5.   The following flavors are available: grape, lemon, orange, and cherry.

6.   The available flavors are: grape, lemon, orange, and cherry.

7.   The board considered the proposal this morning, however, the decision was negative.

8.   Your bid was received too late for consideration, it was not opened.

9.   If I can finish projects now under way, I will attend the convention, but I cannot answer definitely until Friday.

10.   The supervisor has adopted a wait-and-see attitude.

ORGANIZING AND DICTATING MESSAGES

Organizing Letters
When the Reader Will Be Pleased
When the Reader Will Be Displeased
When the Reader Will Be Interested
When the Reader Will Not Be
Interested
Dictating Messages
Methods of Dictation
Requisites for Good Dictation
The Dictation Process
Summary

Wilford had been working in the national headquarters of a meat-packing company for eighteen months. He had learned rapidly, had been promoted twice, and was considered capable of eventual movement into a high-level management position. Shortly after the sudden death of the superintendent at a small branch plant a few hundred miles away, Wilford received the assignment as superintendent. Immediately after arrival at the plant, he called a meeting of the six foremen. His opening sentence to the foremen was "We are going to increase output by 10 percent." He followed with details of his plans for achieving that goal. By four o'clock that afternoon, four foremen had resigned.

What is organization?

Wilford had one major idea and a few solid supporting details, but he made a serious mistake; his thoughts were poorly organized. Organization is the act of systematically categorizing ideas and arranging them in an appropriate sequence for later presentation.

What act should precede the act of *expressing*?

Writing a speech, a letter, or a report is a complicated endeavor. Chances of success are greatly increased if the task can be divided into small units. Because each unit can then be concentrated on fully, each unit can be more effective. Very broadly, composition can be divided into two tasks: (1) identifying the ideas that are to be included and arranging them in appropriate order, and (2) expressing the ideas. The first task is determining *what* to say and in what *order* it should be said. The second task is encoding. The first task is the subject of Chapter 6. Encoding was the subject of Chapters 4 and 5.

People who hate to write, who see themselves as poor writers, and who are seen as poor writers frequently turn out to be people who plunge into the task of writing without having first organized their material. A writer should postpone construction of sentences until an outline has been carefully constructed.

Why outline before composing?

If an outline has been made carefully, the reader will easily see the specific ideas that have been included and their relationship to one another, and the writer's task of composition will be much easier.

Writers cannot make outlines without turning over in their minds the ideas that will appear. Preliminary thinking about each idea makes expression of that idea much easier when the next step (composition) is undertaken. Naturally, if only one step is taken at a time, each step receives the writer's total attention. But trying to make simultaneous decisions about *what* to say and *how* to say it reduces the writer's chances of doing either task well.

Making the outline first builds the writer's confidence. When writers are confident that the right ideas have been designated for inclusion and that they are arranged in the right sequence, they begin to get the feeling that the second step (composition) can be undertaken with equal success.

Having made an outline, a writer can present ideas with the proper emphasis. One of the most common and beneficial techniques of emphasis is use of position in the discourse. If a writer decides to place a point first or last, that point is guaranteed emphasis without the writer's needing to worry about emphasis while writing.

What is one way a point can be emphasized?

With an outline prepared in advance, a writer will not stray from the subject. If an outline is *not* made before the actual writing is begun, the writer may either ramble (which makes messages difficult to comprehend and gives the reader a bad impression of the writer) or worry about the possibility of doing so. Both are serious handicaps.

An outline can also assist in promoting human relations. Wilford's lead-off statement caused the foremen to react negatively. After the first statement, they were deaf to supporting details. Instead of trying to understand the young superintendent's plans, they tried to refute them. If Wilford's presentation had been organized differently, the foremen could have joined in a discussion of details about their goals and techniques. As a result, the idea of increasing production by 10 percent could have come from them. Or, if Wilford had, at the appropriate time, asked whether they thought production could have been increased by as much as 10 percent, they might all have agreed. The problem stemmed from poor organization.

How can an outline assist in promoting human relations?

The organization of ideas is as essential as organization of things. Shopping at a supermarket would be a horrifying experience if storekeepers did not arrange thousands of items in such a way as to make them easy to find. By placing related items in groups, businesses make shopping possible. Likewise, by dividing ideas into groups and arranging the groups in a systematic order, writers make reading easier.

Regardless of whether a message is to be spoken or written, the same organizing principles can be applied.

ORGANIZING LETTERS

"Do you think before you write?" Most people would say "Yes." "Do you make an outline before you write a letter?" Most people would respond "Yes, I make one, but I don't bother to write it down. I just keep it in my head." Some succeed, but even those who do succeed would be better off if they took time to *put the outline on paper*.

Why put an outline on *paper* instead of just keeping it in the mind?

Before beginning to write any letter, a writer can profitably ask two questions: (1) What is the main idea to be included? and (2) What is the reader's reaction likely to be? The answer to the second question can be deduced from the answer to the first. For example, the main idea of a letter is to reveal that a request is being granted. Knowing the satisfaction that comes when their own requests are granted, writers can safely assume that the recipients will be pleased with the basic content of the letter. On the whole, writers can draw upon their own experiences to predict the reactions of others. The messages that would please them would please others; the messages that would displease them would displease others.

What two questions must be answered before letter writing is begun?

How is one person able to predict another's reaction?

To any message contained in a business letter, a reader is likely to react in one of the following ways: (1) by being pleased, (2) by being displeased, (3) by being interested but not emotionally involved, (4) by not being initially interested. Once a letter has been classified into one of these categories, it can be organized into a message that will be clear and at the same time facilitate human relations.

What are four possible reader reactions to a letter?

When the Reader Will Be Pleased

Writing good news is easy. For letters that will please, the following outline is recommended:

If a reader will be pleased, should the outline be deductive?

1. Present the big, pleasant idea in the first sentence.

2. Follow with essential details.

3. Close with a reminder of the main idea or a look to the future.

This outline has been applied in the following letter:

(1) Yes, <u>The Masks We Wear</u> is available for showing on August 18 as you requested.	(1) Presents pleasant idea.
(2) It is being mailed in time to reach your office on or before August 17. Please note the "instructions" card that is included with the film. Viewer comments are appreciated.	(2) Follows with needed details.
(3) See the enclosed folder for a list of related films.	(3) Ends with a reminder that a pleasant event could be repeated.

The preceding outline is *deductive;* it puts the main idea first. For letters that will likely evoke a pleased response, this outline has these advantages:

For conveying good news, what are the advantages of a deductive outline?

1. It gives emphasis to the positive idea. The positive idea has to compete for recognition only with the following sentences. If the positive idea is placed in the middle of a letter, the idea has to compete with the ideas that appear before *and* after, resulting in decreased emphasis.

2. It conditions the reader favorably for details that follow. Having had good news, the reader is in a pleasant frame of mind while being exposed to details and thus absorbs them more readily.

3. It gives the writer a dependable starting place. Knowing that beginning with good news is advisable, a writer can prepare an outline without much hesitation.

Confident that the deductive outline is good, a writer can now concentrate on expressing the ideas vividly.

When the Reader Will Be Displeased

Writing bad news is more difficult than writing good news. The difficulty is not in clarity; it is in human relations. Just as good news is accompanied with details, bad news is accompanied with supporting detail (reasons, explanations). If the bad news is presented in the first sentence, the reaction is likely to be negative: "They never gave me a fair chance," "That's unfair," "This just can't be." Having made a value judgment on reading the first sentence, readers are naturally a bit reluctant to change their minds before the last sentence—even though the intervening sentences present a valid basis for doing so. Having been disappointed by the idea contained in the first sentence, readers are tempted to concentrate on *refuting* (instead of *understanding*) supporting details.

Why avoid putting bad news in the first sentence?

From the writer's point of view, details that support a refusal are very important. If the supporting details are understood and believed, the message may be readily accepted and good business relationships preserved. Because the reasons behind the bad news are so important, the writer needs to organize the message in such a way as to emphasize the reasons. The chances of getting the reader to understand the reasons are much better *before* the bad news is presented than *after* the bad news is presented. If presented afterward, reasons may not even be read.

People who are refused want to know why. To them (and to the person doing the refusing) the reasons are vital; they must be transmitted and received. The process is simplified if the writer employs the following outline:

In refusal letters, do reasons deserve emphasis?

1. Begin with a pleasant or neutral statement that leads to supporting reasons. (The first sentence neither presents bad news nor leads a reader to expect good news.)

2. Present and analyze the facts. Give supporting reasons.

3. State the bad news.

Why avoid putting bad news in the last sentence?

4. Convey a pleasant or neutral idea in the closing sentence.

The following letter applies this outline:

(1) You are to be commended for your efforts to identify principles that apply to the insurance field.

(1) Introduces the subject without revealing whether the answer will be "yes" or "no."

(2) One of our primary concerns has been preservation of confidentiality. Each policyholder is assured that information provided will be seen by insurance officials only.

(2) Gives reasons.

(3) Therefore, permission to inspect 100 selected policies cannot be given.

(3) States refusal.

(4) If in your research you could use some of our blank policyholder forms, we can supply them for you.

(4) Closes on a more positive note by offering an alternative.

For conveying bad news, what are the advantages of an inductive outline?

The preceding outline is *inductive;* it places the main idea near the end of the letter. This sequence of ideas has the following advantages:

1. It sufficiently identifies the subject of the letter without first turning the reader off.

2. It presents the reasons *before* the refusal, where they are more likely to be understood.

3. It emphasizes the reasons by letting them precede the refusal.

4. It avoids a negative reaction. By the time the reasons are read, they seem sensible, and the refusal is foreseen. Since it is expected, the statement of refusal does not come as a shock.

5. It de-emphasizes the refusal by closing on a neutral or pleasant note. By showing a willingness to cooperate in some other way, the writer conveys a desire to be helpful.

Writers have two goals. One is clarity. What is the other?

When the inductive outline is employed, readers can get impatient with explanations that are too long and detailed. But when the deductive outline is employed to present negative information, readers can become angry. Through concise presentation of explanations, impatience may be reduced or avoided. Of the two emotional states (anger or impatience), the latter is less damaging to clarity and human relations.

When the Reader Will Be Interested

If a letter is to convey routine information, should the outline be deductive?

The suggested outline for presenting routine information is very similar to the outline for presenting good news:

1. Present the main idea in the first sentence.

2. Follow with essential details.

3. Close with a reference to the main idea or a look to the future.

The following letter illustrates this outline:

(1) Please send one copy each of the following free publications:	(1) Begins with the main idea.
(2) Small Marketers Aid No. 148, "Insurance Checklist for Small Business" Small Marketers Aid No. 71, "Checklist for Going Into Business"	(2) Gives specifics.

| (3) Thank you. Our counselors have found these booklets very helpful. | (3) Closes with a reference to the main idea. |

The preceding outline has the following advantages:

For routine letters, what are the advantages of the deductive approach?

   1.   It places emphasis on the main idea.

   2.   It saves the recipient time. The person who opens the letter can quickly identify the person to whom the letter should be sent for action or response. The first sentence tells that person the central idea of the letter.

   3.   It simplifies composition. Once the main idea is stated, remaining details can be expressed quickly and easily.

Deductive organization works well when the recipient is not expected to be involved emotionally. But such organization would hardly work if the purpose of the letter were to persuade.

When the Reader Will Not Be Interested

Typically, an unexpected sales letter is not received with great initial enthusiasm. Vitally interested in other letters that may have been received at the same time, a reader may have no interest at all in a sales letter and may even wish it had not been received. Under such circumstances, a deductive arrangement would hardly work at all.

Imagine the response to a letter that begins with "Send $300 and we will ship. . . ." Having been told first what to do, and having been given no reason for doing it, a reader is inclined to stop reading at that point. As shown in the following outline, the reasons for acting must precede the request for action:

In sales letters, should the main idea be presented first?

   1.   Begin with an attention-getting sentence, designed to make a reader put aside other thoughts and read further.

   2.   Introduce the product or idea, and try to arouse interest.

   3.   Present evidence of the proposal's validity.

   4.   Close by encouraging action.

The following letter illustrates application of this outline:

| (1) How to increase the range of the Hughes 500D without decreasing safety — for three years Jefferson Aviation worked on this problem. | (1) Seeks to gain attention by identifying a problem in which the recipient will almost surely be interested. |

(2) The effort paid off in January, 1978, when our range-extension fuel tank was awarded the official STC by the FAA.	(2) Introduces the product.
(3) With the crash-resistant tank installed under the rear seat, the Hughes 500D can still be licensed in the "normal" category.	(3) Begins presentation of evidence.
(4) By the time the tank had met these high standards, it had gone through experiment after experiment. . . . Demand is heavy. Orders are being taken on a first-come, first-serve basis.	(4) Discusses evidence in three paragraphs of detail not included here.
(5) For information about available delivery dates (or for answers to other questions), please call me or George Woods.	(5) Encourages the desired action.

Why must a proposal's advantages be presented before its acceptance is urged?

People cannot be expected to buy a product or accept an idea until after its advantages have been presented. The preceding outline employs the sequence-of-idea pattern long employed by successful sales people. It has the following justifications:

1.   The letter must begin by presenting an idea that will make the recipient put aside other ideas and continue to read.

2.   The letter must quickly introduce a product or idea that can be seen as a possible solution to a recipient's problems, or that will somehow bring satisfaction.

3.   The letter must present supporting evidence that the product or idea will bring satisfaction.

4.   The letter must reveal the specific action a recipient must take to get satisfaction.

For the most effective letter writing, do the thinking first. Identify the major idea to be conveyed, anticipate reader reaction, and make an outline on paper. If the letter is to convey good news or routine information, use a deductive outline. If the letter is to convey bad news or to persuade, use an inductive outline.

Having put an outline on paper, a writer is satisfied with (1) what the ideas are and (2) the order in which they will be presented. This satisfaction builds confidence and allows the mind to concentrate totally on the next problem—how to express the ideas. As students, most writers have had abundant experience with pen, pencil, typewriter, or even word processor; but many can benefit from the following consideration of dictation techniques.

DICTATING MESSAGES

Skill in dictating effectively in a word-processing environment is becoming increasingly critical. Word processing requires broad use of machine dictation to replace what is fast becoming the out-dated practice of dictating to a personal secretary. Many large companies have converted to word-processing systems for all levels of management except at the very top. And even at the top levels, the secretaries themselves frequently use word-processing equipment to prepare letters and reports.

Although the principles of dictating are similar for dictation either to a secretary or to a machine, some striking differences do exist. The comfort of having another person take shorthand dictation in a face-to-face situation is not present in machine dictation. Thus, many executives have found the transition from secretary to a machine extremely difficult. In addition to missing the feedback once provided by a secretary, the new machine dictator has problems associated with giving good instructions, making corrections, and speaking clearly.

Methods of Dictation

Your method of dictating depends to some extent on the manner in which your dictation will be transcribed.

1. Dictation to your own secretary—"live" dictation, taken by a person who becomes familiar with your dictating characteristics.

2. Dictation to a machine, with your secretary transcribing. Inexpensive cassette recorders provide great flexibility in dictation. You can dictate in the office, at home, in an automobile, in an airplane, and in any out-of-the-office situation. Your dictation tapes can be transcribed by being played back on modern transcribing equipment.

3. Dictation to a machine, with a word-processing center providing the transcription. In this case, the transcriber will probably not be familiar with your dictation manners and peculiarities.

4. Other dictation methods, such as by telephone calls or by direct secretarial transcription at the typewriter. These methods are not routine but are used typically in "rush" situations. They require a slow voice speed and clear articulation and pronunciation.

Requisites for Good Dictation

No matter which method of dictation you are involved in, certain requisites apply:

1. You must be skilled in the use of language and able to apply it in the dictation situation.

2.   You must be proficient in planning and organizing ideas for communication through letters and reports.

3.   You should have an understanding of good word usage, punctuation rules, and composition skills.

4.   You must have skill in giving appropriate instructions to the transcriber.

5.   Lastly, you must have confidence in your ability to apply requisites 1–4 to your dictation.

The Dictation Process

Dictation, as a process, can be divided into three stages: pre-dictation practices, dictation practices, and post-dictation practices. Some things you do before you begin to dictate will simplify and speed up your dictation. During the dictation, you will be much more effective and be able to simplify the transcriber's job if you adopt some of the techniques used by good dictators. When transcription is completed, you still have the job of reviewing the finished work before signing or otherwise releasing it.

Pre-dictation Practices

In learning to dictate, keep in mind that you will not always be replying to a message from someone else. In many cases, you'll have to initiate messages. Therefore, although the following discussion will contain frequent references to replies to messages, you should mentally attempt to relate practices to situations in which you will not be replying but will be originating the process. Some suggestions about steps to take before dictating:

1.   Read your incoming mail; then, underline or mark the highlights of each message. Particularly, note the items you will have to consider in preparing your reply. Make marginal notations.

2.   Sort the mail in priority order based on the importance of speedy replies. If your volume is significant, sort by *rush, important,* and *routine* categories.

3.   Gather the information necessary to prepare your reply. You may have to obtain previous correspondence from the files, verify facts or figures, or consult with other employees. If you are replying to a message, clip the supporting materials to the message. If you are initiating the communication process, you should simply clip your supporting information together.

For long messages, what are the advantages of a *written* outline?

4.   Prepare an outline for your message. The planning process described in this chapter should be of help to you. Your plan may be written or it may be simply mental. As you become proficient in letter planning and writing, you'll find that a mental outline is often adequate. Even experts, however, will suggest that a written outline should always be prepared for a long message. For longer, technical reports, a detailed outline is essential.

5. Either before or during dictation, number each item to be discussed. Whether the dictation is to a secretary or to a machine, the numbering system will usually prove to be a time saver when material must be referred to for clarification. Figure 6-1 shows a letter marked and ready for reply. Obviously some research had to be done to prepare for dictation, but notice how the outline has clearly defined how the reply will appear, as is shown in Figure 6-2.

How does the numbering of points assist writers and readers?

Dictation Practices

Although the following dictation practices are primarily designed for machine dictation, they can be adapted for dictation to a secretary. In dictating to a machine, you can speak more rapidly than you can in giving dictation to a secretary. A machine transcriber (secretary), as in word processing, can listen to short sections, stop the machine, and then type the short sections. On some transcribing equipment, the voice speed can be reduced.

1. Always begin dictating by indicating who you are, the type of message, and special instructions — such as the type of letter format and number of copies. Example: "Secretary, this is L. L. Moore, Credit Department. Please use the block form with open punctuation for this letter. One copy and the original are needed."

Why should special instructions to the typist *precede* (instead of follow) the dictation?

Incidentally, the block form with open punctuation used in Figures 6-1 and 6-2 is frequently preferred by word processors. This form places all items on the left margin (hence, blocked) and requires no punctuation at the ends of the inside address, salutation, and complimentary close. Variations of letter formats are shown in the Appendix.

2. If the person who will transcribe your dictation will have the letters to which you are replying, you need not dictate the inside address. Otherwise, you will have to dictate the address. Although some authorities say the zip code need be only on the envelope because it is an aid to the postal service, it should be included as part of the inside address for easy reference on your file copy.

3. Speak clearly and let your words flow as naturally as possible. Keep in mind, however, that dictation is not done in conversational style. When dictating, you are actually composing something that will have to be transcribed so that it can be understood. In conversation, your gestures, facial expressions, and voice inflections increase the likelihood of understanding; but they are apparent to the listener only in live dictation — and never to the final reader. Thus, your choice of words must be unambiguous because there will be no visual aid to comprehension, and your dictation voice speed will have to be much slower than your normal speaking speed — for the transcriber's sake and to be sure the message that ends up on paper is the message you had meant to send.

Should conversational tone be used in dictating?

CENTRAL LUMBER COMPANY
PO Box 42135
Portland, Oregon 98412

April 10, 19—

ABC Company
1118 Seventh Street
Los Angeles, CA 90007
Request for Credit Information

Mr. William Brown has applied for open-account credit with us
and has given your organization as a reference. Will you please
give us the information requested? Your reply will, of course,
be held in strictest confidence.

       Length of time sold on credit
       Highest credit extended
       Balance due or past due
       Normal paying habits

Thank you for your help. Please call on us when we can be of
further assistance.

H C Carlstead
H. C. Carlstead
Credit Manager

HCC/wpc

Handwritten annotations:
① *good risk*
② *10 years*
   $16,000
   Excellent
③ *enjoyed serving him*

Figure 6-1 Letter marked for reply.

ABC COMPANY
1118 Seventh Street
Los Angeles, California 90007

April 12, 19_

Mr. H. C. Carlstead
Credit Manager
Central Lumber Company
PO Box 42135
Portland, OR 98412

Dear Mr. Carlstead

We considered Mr. William F. Brown, about whom you requested confidential credit information, as a very good credit risk.

During the ten years in which we sold building materials to him on credit, his highest balance was $16,000. His payments were always prompt, and he reduced his balance to zero before moving to Oregon.

He was a pleasant customer, and we enjoyed serving him.

Sincerely

L L Moore

L. L. Moore

LLM/wp

Figure 6-2 Reply based on plan noted in Figure 6-1.

4. Dictate in thought groups as an aid to the transcriber. For example, in dictating "I am pleased to accept your invitation to speak on May 6," say "I am pleased to accept your invitation (PAUSE) to speak on May *six.*" Note that dates are expressed by cardinal numbers (i.e., 6, and not ordinal numbers, 6th) when the date follows the month. When you dictate "May six," the transcriber will type it as "May 6."

5. In dictating initials, speak slowly and overemphasize the pronunciation of the following letters: B, F, H, M, N, P, S, T, V, S, Z. In dictating ordinal numbers, overemphasize the pronunciation of second, fifth, sixth, seventh, fifteenth, seventeenth. When unusual words or names are used, spell them. For example, Aaron and Erin are pronounced similarly. To use Erin, you should say "Erin, that's capital E - r - i - n."

6. Use the phonetic alphabet used by telephone operators to clarify the letters used in difficult-to-understand names or words:

A	Alice	N	Nellie
B	Bertha	O	Oliver
C	Charles	P	Peter
D	David	Q	Quaker
E	Edward	R	Robert
F	Frank	S	Samuel
G	George	T	Thomas
H	Henry	U	Utah
I	Ida	V	Victor
J	James	W	William
K	Kate	X	X-ray
L	Lewis	Y	Young
M	Mary	Z	Zebra

For example, *Orvil* is spelled "O as in Oliver, R as in Robert, V as in Victor, I as in Ida, and L as in Lewis."

7. To indicate that a word such as *East* begins with a capital, say "Capital, East." To indicate that a word is entirely in capitals, say "Secretary, all capitals. . . ."

8. To indicate quoted matter, say "Quote" to indicate beginning quotation marks and "Unquote" to indicate closing quotation marks.

9. Always dictate the correct form of possessives when using a machine. For example, to indicate *Frank's,* say "Frank, apostrophe s."

10. Many transcribers need instruction in making special punctuation marks. For example, to make a dash (—) say "Secretary, make the dash by typing two hyphens without a space before or after." When hyphenated words are used, be sure to dictate the hyphens. To make an ellipsis (. . .) say "Secretary, make the ellipsis by typing three periods with space between." Incidentally, the ellipsis, used to show omission of words, always consists of only three periods when used at the beginning or in the interior of a sentence. When the ellipsis is at the end of a sentence, it should be followed by a period as in this case. . . .

Is punctuation the responsibility of the typist?

11. Become familiar with the equipment to make corrections in your dictation. When using cassette recorders, you can rewind to the point of correction and simply begin dictating again. The incorrect material will be erased and replaced by the new dictation. In many cases when dictating to word processors, you can simply say "Secretary, correction please. Change that sentence to . . . ." Keep in mind that you can often play back your dictation before it is typed.

12. When tabulations of numeric data are to be incorporated in the message, the material should be prepared in rough draft form and given to the secretary.

13. Dictate the closing instructions. If you use a title, dictate the title you prefer to have typed in parentheses before your name such as Dr., Mrs., Ms., Miss. If a business title is to be used, dictate it if it is not on the letterhead. Indicate the enclosures to be included, the names of people who will receive carbon copies, and any special ending instructions for the secretary.

14. If you are dictating to a word-processing center, end your dictation by saying, "Thank you, secretary." If the material is to be transcribed by your personal secretary, use the secretary's name.

Throughout your dictation, you should practice good dictation habits. To avoid the necessity of retyping, always give special instructions *before* the item is to be typed. For example, if a quote is to be indented, indicate that before the quote begins. For something to be centered, simply give the appropriate instructions: "Secretary, center the following title in all capitals."

The successful dictator knows that another person is always involved in that success—the secretary or transcriber. Throughout the discussion, the term *secretary* appears, but the dictation terminology varies from office to office. Some may use *operator* or *typist*. In any case, the courtesy and respect you show to the person doing your transcribing may have much to do with the quality of production you receive in return. As indicated previously, word-processing centers are rather high-pressure offices. Little by little the pay for working in them is increasing, and the quality of worker is increasing accordingly. To do your own part in this change, you should become an expert in using whatever equipment is available to you as a dictator. You should study the operations manual that accompanies your equipment. Additionally, visit your word-processing center to become familiar with what goes on at that end of the process.

Why should dictators study operations manual for word-processing machines?

Post-dictation Practices

Should dictators take time to proofread materials typed for them?

When your transcribed material is returned to you, you must never take for granted that it is perfect! No self-respecting person signs a letter without first reading it. People who sign letters are responsible for the contents and the quality. So, learn to proofread for both content and grammatical usage. If something is incorrect, you have no choice but to have it corrected. In this case, your skill in human relations and your personal sense of humility come into play. If a comma or an apostrophe is missing, you can often insert it with a pen. Most readers don't mind. On the other hand, extensive corrections in longhand will reflect negatively on you and your organization.

Some dictators, for example, insert a comma each time they take a breath. Others follow the unreliable rule of "If in doubt, leave it out." The misplaced or missing comma is a major cause of lack of clarity in writing. Although sometimes using the comma may be a matter of choice, a rule usually exists for using or not using it. You should learn those rules.

Secretaries can do some surprising things to your dictation if you are not careful. An address such as "70 Fifth Avenue" may be transcribed as "75th Avenue." Instead of saying "seventy," you as the dictator can avoid the problem by saying "7-Oh." When a sentence ends with the word "period," you can be helpful by dictating "Secretary, end the sentence by typing the word 'period' and type a period after it."

Proofreading is definitely your best insurance against embarrassing or confusing errors. When a rough draft is long or complicated, two persons should read the manuscript simultaneously, with one reading aloud while the other checks the manuscript. This technique is called *copyheld* proofreading. In a publisher's office, for example, the copyheld method is sometimes used after the manuscript is produced in galley form—the first printed copy. The work of oral reading and proofreading is accelerated by use of these shortened expressions to identify symbols other than words:

Instead of	Say
apostrophe	apos
capital	cap
comma	com
decimal point	point
dollars	doll
exclamation point	exclam
italics	ital
paragraph	para
period	point
question mark	query

quotation marks	quotes
semicolon	semi
underscore	score
zero	oh

As a rule, you should read down columns of tabular items rather than across rows. You should also try to indicate things orally in proper order: for example, in reading *West,* say "cap, West;" and if a word is to be in italics, say "ital" then the word.

More often than not, however, your proofreading will be an individual job. You will find this procedure helpful in proofreading your own materials: (1) Read the copy for sense at a comfortable rate of speed. (2) Read the copy again very slowly, and preferably aloud, to check on spelling, grammar, and mechanics. The following errors are often overlooked by proofreaders:

Should a proofreader try to check for content and grammar at the same time?

1. Misspelling of proper names.

2. Misspelling of words because of omitted, added, or transposed letters.

3. Incorrect addresses.

4. Incorrect abbreviations.

5. Mechanical errors, particularly those involving commas and semicolons.

6. Incorrect or omitted apostrophes (particularly, *it's* for the possessive *its*).

7. Errors in capitalization.

8. Hyphenation errors both in word division at the end of lines and in compound adjectives and nouns.

9. Omitted "enclosure(s)" references at the end of letters.

10. Omitted quotation marks at the end of a quote.

11. Incomplete sentences.

12. Failure to identify the form of a homonym, as in their–there, sail–sale, wear–ware, etc.

To type final copy from a rough draft, you should understand the meanings of several proofreaders' marks. As good practice, you might try using proofreaders' marks when you check your drafts. They permit you or another person to prepare final copy easily and without the normal scribbling that most of us use because we aren't familiar with professional methods. When using word-processing centers, your use of proofreaders' marks can be especially effective. First, learn the symbols for "insert" and "delete." Additional proofreader's marks are shown in Figure 6-3.

∧   the *caret* means to insert something that is indicated in the margin, and

℘   the *delete* means to take out.

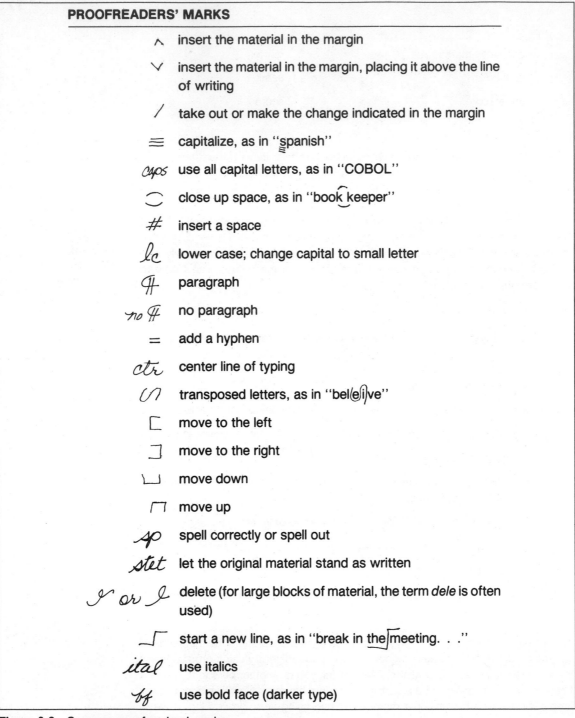

PROOFREADERS' MARKS

∧	insert the material in the margin
∨	insert the material in the margin, placing it above the line of writing
/	take out or make the change indicated in the margin
≡	capitalize, as in "spanish"
caps	use all capital letters, as in "COBOL"
⌒	close up space, as in "book keeper"
#	insert a space
lc	lower case; change capital to small letter
¶	paragraph
no ¶	no paragraph
=	add a hyphen
ctr	center line of typing
∽	transposed letters, as in "bel(ei)ve"
⌐	move to the left
¬	move to the right
⊔	move down
⊓	move up
sp	spell correctly or spell out
stet	let the original material stand as written
✐ or ℓ	delete (for large blocks of material, the term *dele* is often used)
⌐	start a new line, as in "break in the⌐meeting. . ."
ital	use italics
bf	use bold face (darker type)

Figure 6-3 Common proofreaders' marks.

The caret may also be inverted ∨ and placed above the line to indicate that an item is to be placed above the line of writing—a footnote reference, an apostrophe, or a quotation mark. When the delete sign appears this way ℐ, it means to take out the crossed-out item and close up the space it occupied. Remember that only the caret or delete is placed in the text where the change is to be made, and the proper material is noted in the margin of the paper. For example,

> As good practice∧ you might try

means to add a comma following the word "practice." Some commonly used proofreaders' marks included in Figure 6-3 are employed in Figure 6-4.

When you review your completed letters or other materials, check to make certain that you have all the enclosures included before the mail is sealed. Also make sure you sign the letters. If you are not available to sign the letters before mailing, instruct the secretary to sign them with your name followed by the secretary's initials. It's a terrible practice to have a notation such as "Dictated but not read" at the bottom of the letter. It seems to invite return of the letter with a new notation: "Received but not read."

Original copy:

¶ Today,∧due to societal change, (there is) a wide variety of magazines (that) concentrates (its) circulation appeal on women in the 18-34 age group. These magazines talk specifically to women who work,∧women with children,∧women vitally interested in good health. Three womens magazines that fall into this (catagory) are ⊙ Glamour, Mademoiselle and Cosmopolitan. (It) (is) these three printed media selections (that) will be evaluated by this study. All evaluations are based on the assumption that the Star Cosmetic Company will continue to advertise using one∧ page∧four∧color ads.

Retyping with the changes results in this copy:

Today, due to societal change, a wide variety of magazines concentrates circulation appeal on women in the 18-34 age group. These magazines talk specifically to women who work, women with children, and women vitally interested in good health. Three women's magazines that fall into this category are Glamour, Mademoiselle and Cosmopolitan. These three printed media selections will be evaluated by this study. All evaluations are based on the assumption that the Star Cosmetic Company will continue to advertise using one-page, four-color ads.

Figure 6-4 Proofread and marked copy with revised copy.

SUMMARY

Regardless of whether composition is done through use of pen, typewriter, or dictation, the thinking should be concluded before the expressing is begun. Such thinking is required for outlining and forces a writer to identify the ideas he or she wants to include and to arrange them in the most suitable order. The basis for determining the sequence of ideas is anticipated reader response. If a letter is to present routine information, or if it is to present good news, use a deductive sequence. If a letter is designed to persuade, or if it is to present bad news, use an inductive sequence.

When words are to be conveyed in writing, they may be spoken to another person who either types them directly on a typewriter or writes them on paper and later types them. Or, they may be spoken into a machine and later typed on a conventional typewriter or word processor. Success in dictating requires knowledge of the language, skill in organizing thoughts, a good command of punctuation and stylistic techniques, clarity in giving instructions, and confidence in one's dictation skill.

If the letter to be dictated is a response to a letter you have received, penciled notes on the received letter simplify the dictation of your response. Assigning a number to each item to be discussed is also helpful. Before dictating, think about the specific instructions a typist will need to type the page exactly as you want it. After your dictated messages have been typed, read them before signing and make sure the needed corrections are made.

EXERCISES

Review Questions

1. In what ways do writers benefit from making outlines before beginning to compose?

2. Which is normally better? (a) Put the outline on paper, or (b) Just keep the outline in mind. Explain.

3. Before preparing an outline, a writer needs to ask two questions. One is "What is the principal idea to be conveyed?" What is the other?

4. What is the difference between a deductive outline and an inductive outline?

5. Readers may react in one of four different ways to a message. List the four possible reader reactions.

6. (a) List the three-point outline recommended for letters that convey good news. (b) Name its advantages.

7. (a) List the four-point outline recommended for letters that convey bad news. (b) Name its advantages.

8. (a) List the three-point outline recommended for letters that convey routine information. (b) Name its advantages.

9. (a) List the four-point outline recommended for letters designed to persuade. (b) Name its advantages.

10. What are the advantages of dictating to a secretary instead of to a machine?

11. What are the advantages of using cassette recorders for dictation?

12. Who is responsible for the punctuation of dictated letters — the dictator or the typist?

Dictation Exercise

Assume you are a professor of business economics at your school and have received the following letter:

Dear Professor _____

You can be extremely helpful to the members of Delta Sigma Kappa, professional business fraternity. On October 17 at 6 p.m., we are holding our annual father-member dinner in the Windsor Room of the Bradbury Hotel.

We are excited at the prospect of having you speak on a current topic of your choice as you did two years ago. We can offer you good fellowship, a great audience, an excellent dinner, and a $100 honorarium.

Please let me know that you will accept our invitation. I'd also like to have a title for your talk to use in our program and in our invitation to our fathers. May I have your response soon.

Sincerely

Mavis Johnson

Mavis Johnson
President

You will accept the invitation. You want to know what time the dinner will begin if a cocktail party will begin at 6 p.m. as it did two years ago. The earliest you can arrive is 6:30 p.m. Your title will be "The National Debt — Who Owes It." (1) Mark the letter for dictation. (2) Prepare an outline. (3) Write a reply as though you had dictated it. (4) Be prepared to dictate your reply in class. You'll dictate without using your finished letter as a guide.

Proofreading Exercise

Assume you are using the copyheld proofreading method for a manuscript. Read the list of errors often overlooked by proofreaders to another member of your class; while you do, attempt to use some of the shortened expressions previously listed. Be sure to spell the unusual words and the homonyms.

Proofreading-marks Exercise

Use appropriate proofreaders' marks to prepare the following paragraph for final typing.

Compared with the task of conveying good news the task of conveying bad news is more challanging. If the message itself is justified and presented with tack the cordialy reader writer relationship may be preserved. If the mes sage is justified the writer will have solid reasons to support the decision. Ifthe reasons are read and under stood the decision may be accepted without resent ment.

COMMUNICATING THROUGH LETTERS

OBJECTIVES **1.** To develop skill in applying planning and writing techniques to the solution of business problems.

2. To develop an understanding of the communication tasks involved in a variety of business areas — ordering, handling claims, working with credit and collections, and selling by mail.

3. To acquire sensitivity to reader needs and desires.

4. To develop skill in using proper tone in messages while achieving goals.

WRITING ABOUT THE ROUTINE AND THE PLEASANT

Letters about Routine Claims
The Claim Letter
Favorable Response to Claim Letter
Routine Letters about Credit
Request for Information
Response to Request for Information
Request for Credit
Favorable Response to Request for
Credit
Letters about Routine Orders
The Order Letter
Favorable Response to Order Letter
**Letters about other Routine
Requests**
The Routine Request
Favorable Response to Routine
Request
Summary

Before we can begin writing letters, we must know what the messge is and feel confident that we can predict the receiver's reaction.

We must also remember that the receiver's reaction will almost surely fall into one of the following categories: (1) pleased, (2) displeased, (3) neither pleased nor displeased but interested, or (4) not initially interested. This chapter is devoted to a discussion of letters in the first and third categories. Letters in the first group are referred to as *good-news* letters, letters in the third as *routine* letters. These letters are discussed in the same chapter because they present ideas in the same sequence. As shown on the next page, both outlines follow a deductive arrangement —the major idea is presented first, followed by supporting details. In both, the third point (closing thought) may be omitted without seriously impairing effectiveness; but including it unifies a letter and avoids abruptness.

How are good-news and routine letters similar?

Good-news letter	Deductive pattern	Routine letter
Pleasant idea	_____	Big, important idea
Details or explanations	_____ _____ _____	Details or explanations
Closing thought	_____	Closing thought

By following this plan, we gain several advantages:

1.   We can write the first sentence with very little hesitation; and once past the first sentence, we can follow easily with the details.

2.   We have a beginning that is inclined to attract attention.

What are the advantages of the deductive arrangement for good-news and routine letters?

3.   In good-news letters, we put readers in a pleasant frame of mind right at the start; in this state, they are receptive to details of the correspondence.

4.   We may save time for readers; once they get the important idea, they can move rapidly through the supporting details.

This basic plan is applicable in several business-writing problems: (1) routine claim letters and "yes" replies, (2) routine requests and "yes" replies, (3) routine requests related to credit matters and "yes" replies, and (4) routine order letters and "yes" replies.

LETTERS ABOUT ROUTINE CLAIMS

Both routine claim letters and "yes" replies to routine claims employ the deductive approach.

The Claim Letter

A *claim* letter is a request for an adjustment. When writers ask for something to which they think they are entitled (a refund, replacement, exchange, payment for damages, and so on) the letter is called a *claim* letter.

These requests can be divided into two groups: *routine claims* and *persuasive claims*. Persuasive claims, which will be discussed in a later chapter, assume that the request will be granted only after explanations and persuasive arguments have been presented. Routine claims (possibly because of guarantees, warranties, or other contractual conditions) assume that the request will be granted quickly and willingly, without persuasion. When the claim is routine (not likely to meet resistance), the following outline is recommended:

1. Request action in the first sentence.

2. Explain the details supporting the request for action.

3. Close with an expression of appreciation for taking the action requested.

The following letters illustrate first an inductive and then a deductive treatment of a routine claim letter.

I recently ordered a 10-volume set of books (see attached copy of the order). They were delivered this morning.

Since they are to be presented as a gift, I want them to be perfect in every way. I have noted one problem, however: In Volume II, pages 17 through 32 are missing.

The volume is being returned in the package to which this letter is attached. I shall appreciate your sending a complete volume in exchange.

Now, compare the preceding letter with one that employs a direct approach:

(1) Please send a replacement copy of the book that is attached.	(1) Reveals the claim.
(2) When it was delivered in response to my order (see copy attached), pages 17 through 32 were missing.	(2) Presents reason.
(3) I shall appreciate your sending a complete volume in exchange.	(3) Closes with a confident reference to the action desired.

Favorable Response to Claim Letter

Businesses *want* their customers to write when merchandise ᵒor service is not satisfactory. They want to learn of ways in which goods and services can be improved, and they want to see that their customers get value received for the

What is the outline for a favorable reply to a routine claim letter?

money they spend. When saying "yes" to a claim letter, present ideas in the following sequence:

1. Reveal in the first sentence that the claim is being granted.

2. Explain the circumstances.

3. Close on a pleasant, forward-looking note.

We can reasonably assume that the writer of the claim letter thought the claim was a valid one. A response that says, in effect, "We're granting your request but we want you to know we don't have to," would be worse than refusing the request.

After having said "yes" in the very first sentence, we can't stop there. The request was made because something went wrong. If no explanation is given, the client may assume that we have no valid explanation, or that mistakes are commonplace in our business. If the claim clearly resulted from our own mistake, we should admit it frankly. Most people like to do business with others who have the courage to admit mistakes frankly. If we grant a claim in spite of the fact that the customer is somewhat at fault, we must explain it; otherwise, the same problem may present itself again.

How can adjustment letters increase business?

We can actually build business with adjustment letters. By making things right and explaining why they went wrong, we can gain a reputation as a business that stands behind its goods or services. A loyal customer may become even more loyal after a business has demonstrated its integrity. Adjustment letters can also work as low-pressure sales letters. Since we are sure to be writing about our product or service, we have the opportunity to speak of it in a favorable light—to reassure clients that they actually made a good choice. Such reassurance is known as using *resale*. In addition, we might be able to generate interest in some related item. Introducing a related item or service is known as using *sales-promotional material*. We can be reasonably sure that such resale and sales-promotional material will be read. We don't have that assurance when we send sales circulars.

What is the distinction between resale and sales-promotional material?

When might a claim be granted even though the customer is at fault?

Sometimes the adjustment department decides to grant some claims even though it has sufficient evidence to warrant refusal. For example, a woman who has ordered hundreds of dollars' worth of merchandise from a mail-order house during the past few years discovers that the two wash-and-wear white cotton dress shirts she got two months ago are turning a dirty gray, but her husband's other white cotton shirts are still snow white. She returns them for new ones. The customer-service department reviews her past purchasing record, discovers that this is her first complaint, and decides to send her two new white shirts even though she has evidently failed to follow the laundry instructions on the label. Thinking that her goodwill will be retained so long as she gets what she asked for, the adjustment department might send the following perfunctory letter:

(1) We have the two wash-and-wear shirts that you returned to us with the request that we exchange them for new ones.

(1) This obvious statement could have been omitted; however, it does serve as an introduction to the letter.

(2) We can imagine how disappointed you must have been with them, but we can explain the difficulty. (3) You have been sending your shirts to a laundry which evidently washes them by machine (we noticed the laundry marks in the collar).

(2) No need for such a vivid reminder of the disappointment.

(3) For this delicate point, the reader should not have been employed as the subject of the sentence.

(4) The washing instructions plainly visible on the label say "HAND WASH." (5) Did you call this to your laundry's attention? Some laundries do hand washes only if specifically instructed to do so.

(4) Forceful language; sounds too accusing.
(5) Ideas could have been introduced in more pleasant terms.

(6) Strong bleaches used in some washing machines will keep other cotton fabrics white, but they sometimes turn wash-and-wear cottons a "dirty gray."

(6) This explanation is necessary, but It should not precede the good news that the dirty gray shirts are being replaced.

(7) In view of your past record with us, however, we are sending you two new wash-and-wear shirts free. (8) Just follow the instructions on the label, and the shirts will give excellent service.

(7) Suggests that we should not grant your request but we are making an exception.
(8) A final reminder that she did not follow instructions on the label.

"Circumstances warrant refusal, but we are granting your request." What is the likely customer reaction?

The preceding example says "yes" grudgingly and then only after the other details have been presented. The following revision corrects these weaknesses.

(1) Two long-lasting, snow-white Dresso shirts are on their way to you. Your account will not be charged.

(1) Grants request; puts customer in a good frame of mind for understanding the remainder of the letter. Includes resale on the shirts.

(2) Compared with conventional shirts, Dresso wash-and-wears stay whiter, last longer, and remain more wrinkle free.

(2) Reassures the woman that she made a wise choice when she chose wash-and-wears, and leads into an explanation of how to get maximum results.

(3) But for maximum service, they must be washed by hand without strong bleaches.

(3) Uses the shirts (instead of the addressee) as subject of this sentence because it treats a negative idea. She will probably recall that she has not

been washing them or having them washed by hand. Through positive language, she is made to see her mistake.

(4) When you take them to your laundry, just ask them to follow the washing instructions that we have placed on the collar label.

(4) Presents a plan that will prevent future trouble. Refers unaccusingly to the laundry label, which has evidently been disregarded.

Why does the letter present resale and sales-promotional material?

(5) You should receive your annual catalog within a few days.

(5) Reminds her that we still expect her to order merchandise from us.

Notice that the preceding letter grants the request but does not employ the word *grant.* And it does not refer to the letter being answered as a *claim.* Although these words are convenient in talking *about* such letters, they are not good words to use *in* such letters. "We are *granting* your request" can also convey "We see ourselves as being in a position of power" or "We are acceding to your unjustified request." "We are adjusting your *claim*" can also convey "We are responding to your overly strong statement of dissatisfaction."

Confident that a routine request for an adjustment will be granted, a writer simply asks for it (in the first sentence and without seeming to complain).[1] Knowing that the recipient will be glad to learn that a request has been granted, a writer simply states it (in the first sentence and without apparent reluctance). The details and closing sentence follow naturally and easily.

ROUTINE LETTERS ABOUT CREDIT

Normally, credit information is requested and transmitted by form letters or simple office forms. When the response to a credit request is very likely to be favorable, the request should be stated at the beginning.

Request for Information

What is the outline for a credit-information request?

The network of credit associations across the country has made knowledge about individual consumers easy to obtain. As a result, exchanges of credit information are common in business. Study the following outline for an effective letter request for credit information about an individual:

1. Identify the request and name the applicant early — preferably in the opening sentence or in a subject line.

2. Assure the reader that the reply will be held confidential.

---

1. This principle was recommended by some of the pioneers in business-letter writing. See, for example, Edward Hall Gardner, *Effective Business Letters* (New York: Ronald, 1915), p. 106.

3. Detail the information requested. Use a tabulated-form layout to make the reply easy.

4. End courteously. Offer the same assistance to the reader.

The following request letter applies the outline:

May we have credit information about Mr. William F. Brown? He has applied for credit with us and has given your business as a reference.

After filling in the blanks on this page, use the back side for additional remarks if necessary. Your reply will be held in strict confidence.

Length of time sold on credit _____
Highest credit extended _____
Credit limit _____
Balance now due _____ Past due _____
Normal paying habits _____
Remarks _____

Thank you for your help. Please call on us when we can be of similar assistance.

The preceding letter showed another desirable arrangement for a credit request, which is to place the complete letter at the top of the page and to arrange the fill-in items at the bottom of the page.

Just as a theme or report is given a title, a letter can be given a title also. In a letter, the title is referred to as the "subject line" (point 1 in the preceding outline). The following subject lines are typical:

SUBJECT: REQUEST FOR CREDIT INFORMATION ABOUT
        MR. WILLIAM C. WARD

SUBJECT: CREDIT INFORMATION, JONES-ANDERSON CO.

Requests for credit information are acceptable either with or without a subject line. The subject line does provide quick, emphatic identification of what the letter is about.

If a subject line is used, the letter can be even shorter than the example we have seen. Printed forms on which the names of the reference and applicant can be filled in are certainly desirable when the volume of credit requests is great.

Why should we use an outline form to get credit information?

Response to Request for Information

Replies to requests for credit information are usually very simple — just fill in the blank and return it. If the request does not include a form, follow a deductive plan in writing the reply — the major idea followed by supporting details.

(1) We considered Mr. William F. Brown, about whom you requested confidential credit information on May 26, as a very good credit risk.	(1) Presents the major idea. Reminds reader of the confidential nature of the letter.
(2) During the ten years in which we sold building materials to him on credit, his highest balance was $70,000. His payments were always prompt. He reduced his balance to zero before moving away from Springerville.	(2) Gives the information requested.
(3) We found Mr. Brown a pleasant customer and enjoyed doing business with him.	(3) Ends courteously.

To whom is the person who gives credit information obligated?

In credit letters, writers have an obligation to themselves, as well as to the addressee and the credit applicant. Good advice is to stick with facts, as this letter did. Why say "I'm sure he will pay promptly," when "His payments were always prompt" is a strong recommendation? Is there any need to say he *is* a good credit risk when all we know is that he *was* so considered when he bought from us?

Request for Credit

When people want to begin buying on credit and assume credit will be willingly granted, they can place their request in the first sentence and follow with details:

(1) Will you please fill the enclosed order on a credit basis?	(1) Presents the major idea.
(2) If you need information other than that given on the enclosed financial statements, please write to me.	(2) Gives details.
(3) Current plans are to place a similar order every two weeks.	(3) Closes with a look to the future.

What ideas are included in a letter that grants credit?

This approach is recommended only when the writer's supporting financial statements are assumed sufficient to merit a "yes" response.

Favorable Response to Request For Credit

Effective "yes" replies to requests for credit should use the following outline:

1. Begin by saying credit terms have been arranged; or, if an order has been placed, begin by telling of the shipment of goods, thereby implying the credit grant.

2. Give some idea of the foundation upon which the credit grant is based.

3. Present and explain the credit terms.

4. Include some resale or sales-promotional material.

5. End with a confident look toward future business.

Before credit managers say "yes" to a request for credit, they must answer two basic questions: (1) Will this potential customer have the money to pay when the bills become due? (2) Will the customer be willing to part with the money at that time? To answer the first question, they consider the would-be customer's financial status and earning power. To answer the second question, they consider character. Ordinarily, they get information from the following sources: (1) the potential credit customer; (2) credit-rating associations; (3) those who are presently selling, or have previously sold, to the potential customer; and (4) others who may have some knowledge of the potential credit customer's ability to pay.

Most letters that say "yes, you may purchase on credit" are *form letters*. If a firm uses word-processing equipment, a typist gives the machine instructions identifying the specific form to be typed. Stored in the memory of the machine, the message will be typed automatically. Firms receive so many requests for credit that the costs of individualized letters would be prohibitive. Typically, the form messages read something like this:

Why should we use form letters when replying to credit requests?

We are pleased to extend credit privileges to you. Temporarily, you may purchase up to $200 worth of merchandise on time. Our credit terms are 2/10, n/30. We welcome you as a credit customer of our expanding organization.

Although such form messages are effective for informing the customer that credit is being extended, they do little to promote sales and goodwill. Whether to say "yes" by form letter or by individualized letter is a problem that each credit manager has to settle individually. If the list of credit customers is relatively short and few names are being added, individualized letters may be practical. A credit manager may also choose to use individualized letters if the workload in the department is such that letters can be sent without overworking present personnel or adding new workers. But even when credit grants are tailor made to fit the individual, they often fall short of their capacity to promote profitable business. Although the following letter is probably more effective than a form letter, it can still be improved:

(1) Thank you for your order for six Unicook microwave ovens.
(2) They are being shipped today.

(1) Delays the answer to the reader's question, "May I pay for them later?"
(2) Implies the answer to the question of credit extension—if they are being shipped, credit must have been granted.

(3) We are pleased to report that your credit rating was investigated and found to be satisfactory.

(3) "Pleased" and "investigated" could have been taken for granted. The applicant may feel under suspicion.

(4) Our credit terms are the usual 2/10, n/30.

(4) Since this letter is to a dealer, the explanation of terms is probably sufficient. In letters to consumers, more detailed explanation and interpretation are helpful.

What impression does a cliché make?

(5) Welcome to our growing list of satisfied customers.

(5) Uses a cliché. Since the dealer has read this many times before, it may be meaningless. By sending an individualized letter that explains what the dealer wants to know, the writer could *imply* the welcome.

(6) We trust that this will be the beginning of a long and profitable business relationship.

(6) A good credit manager would not have ended his letter with a standard remark that was worn out long ago.

In spite of its drawbacks, the preceding letter sounds about as good as the average credit letter that passes through the mail. It was not intended as a horrible example; it does, however, leave room for improvement.

From our discussion, we know why we should tell of the shipment and credit grant in the first sentence, we can see the wisdom of using resale and sales-promotional material, and we know the advantage of writing as if we expect future orders. But why should we discuss the foundation upon which we based our decision to grant credit? To prevent collection problems that may arise later. Just as lawyers work to prevent courtroom litigation and doctors work to prevent sickness, credit managers should work to prevent collection problems. Indicating that we are granting credit on the basis of an applicant's prompt-pay habits with present creditors encourages continuation of those habits with us. It recognizes a reputation to live up to. When financial situations become difficult, the purchaser will probably remember the compliment and try to pay us first.

Why discuss the basis for granting credit?

Why should credit terms be discussed?

Why would we discuss the credit terms? To stress their importance and prevent collection problems that may arise later. Unless customers know exactly when payments are expected, they may not make them on time. Unless they know exactly what the discount terms are, they may take unauthorized discounts. Furthermore, the mere fact that we take time to discuss terms in detail suggests that terms are important; it suggests that we expect them to be followed. The following revision applies these principles:

(1) Six Unicook ovens (known for uniform cooking without a rotisserie) should reach your store in time for your weekend shoppers.

(1) Presents good news. Reminds the dealer of an important advantage in stocking this particular oven. Indicates that the writer has some consideration for the problems of a dealer. Implies the credit grant.

(2) Pay us later.

(2) States specifically that credit has been granted. Leads to an explanation of the basis and terms of the credit arrangement.

(3) Because of your very favorable current rating and your prompt-pay habits with your other creditors, we are sending the shipment subject to the usual credit terms--2/10, n/30. (4) By paying this invoice within ten days, you save almost $150.

(3) Gives the dealer recognition for having earned the credit privilege. Gives a reason for the credit grant; it was not granted haphazardly. Introduces the credit terms.
(4) Encourages taking advantage of the discount. Talks about the discount arrangement in terms of profits for the dealer.

(5) The turn knobs used in previous models have been replaced by pushbuttons--a feature that homemakers really seem to appreciate. (6) For other kitchen items on open account, use the enclosed order form.

(5) Presents additional resale.

(6) Looks confidently forward to future orders.

Although the foregoing example was written to a dealer, the same principles apply when writing to a consumer. Of course, we have to talk to each in terms of individual interests. Dealers are concerned about markup, marketability, and display; consumers are concerned about price, appearance, and durability. Also, consumers may require more detailed explanation of credit terms. But be careful. Don't present an elementary lecture. For example, don't use such an expression as "EOM" and then follow it with, "This means 'End of the Month.'"

The preceding example performed a dual function; it said "yes" to an application for credit and it also said, "Yes, we are filling your order." But because of its importance, the credit aspect was emphasized more than the acknowledgment. In other cases (in which the order is for cash or the credit terms are already clearly understood), the primary purpose of writing may be to acknowledge an order.

What is the principal difference between a credit letter to a dealer and a credit letter to a consumer?

LETTERS ABOUT ROUTINE ORDERS

Like routine letters about credit, routine letters about orders put the main idea in the first sentence.

The Order Letter

Order letters create one half of a contract. They constitute the offer portion of a contract that is fulfilled when the shipper sends the goods, thereby creating the

What outline should be
used for an order letter?

acceptance part of the contract. Therefore, if we seriously want to receive shipment, we should make our order letter a definite offer. The outline for order letters is deductive:

1. Use order language in the first sentence. Say, "Please ship," "Please send," "I order," or use some other suitable language that assures the seller of the desire to buy. Avoid phrases like "I'm interested," "I'd like to . . . ," or similar indefinite statements.

List two possible
interpretations of "I
would like to order. . . ."

2. Carefully detail the items ordered. Be specific by mentioning catalog numbers, prices, colors, sizes, and all the other information that will enable the seller to fill the order promptly and without the need for further correspondence.

3. Include a payment plan and shipping instructions. Remember that the shipper is free to ship by the normal method in the absence of specific instructions from the buyer. Tell when, where, and how the order is to be shipped.

4. Close the letter with a confident expectation of delivery.

In addition to the application of the outline principles, notice the physical layout in the following order letter:

Please ship me the following items listed in your current winter catalog:

24 #2314 Black record Tower typewriter ribbons @ 2.50	$60.00
100 #2332 8 1/2 x 13 Bristol file dividers @ .29	29.00
2 #2408 White-out correction compound @ 2.04	4.08
	$93.08

The enclosed check for $100.54 covers the $6 parcel post charge and local sales tax of $1.46. I shall appreciate receiving the materials by April 8.

A retailer sending the first order to a wholesale house has a little more detail to include, particularly if a credit account is being opened at the same time.

Please send the following Mercury Brand Tools:

24 #16 Claw Hammers @ 3.40	$ 81.60
12 #8 Cross-cut Saws @ 7.50	90.00
12 #14 24" Squares @ 5.30	63.60
	$235.20

Deliver by highway express to Jameson Hardware Company, 1134 La Brea Avenue, Los Angeles, California. The enclosed credit application completely filled out with the assistance of your salesman, Jack L. Carter, should provide you with sufficient information to extend us open credit.

We are pleased with the quality of Mercury supplies. This order, which we hope to receive by December 1, should be only the first of many.

In large companies, the normal procedure is to use purchase-order forms for ordering. And most consumers buying from mail-order houses use the order forms enclosed with catalogs.

The most important thing we can do as customers is to make sure our order letter or form is complete in every detail and that we'll receive what we want. If we sell by mail, we'll want to use every work-simplification technique within our means to make the order system foolproof.

Favorable Response to Order Letter

When customers place an order for merchandise, they expect to get exactly what they ordered as quickly as possible. For most orders, we can acknowledge by shipping. No letter is necessary. But for initial orders or for orders we cannot fill quickly and precisely, we need to send *letters of acknowledgment*. Senders of initial orders like to know that they are going to receive what they ordered, they like to know their business is appreciated, and they need some information about the firm with which they are beginning a business relationship. If a regular customer's order is not being filled immediately, some form of explanation is expected. The explanation usually takes the form of a duplicated or printed sheet, similar to this:

Why should we send letters of acknowledgment?

Dear Customer:

We appreciate your order for _____.

You should receive it within _____ days.

Sincerely yours,

Forms like this are often sent as a matter of routine when orders can be filled immediately but will require considerable time in transit. Although the form is impersonal, it is appreciated because it acknowledges the order and lets the customer have some idea of its disposition.

Nonroutine acknowledgments, on the other hand, require an individualized letter. And although initial orders can be acknowledged through form letters, the letters are more effective if individually written. Most people who write letters have no difficulty in saying "yes"; but, because saying "yes" is easy, they can fall into the habit of making their letters sound too cold and mechanical:

(1) Thank you for your order, which we are very glad to have.	(1) Begins with a cliché.
(2) We extend to you a sincere welcome to our ever-growing list of satisfied customers.	(2) Says to this customer the same thing that has been said already to thousands of customers.
(3) We were delighted to send you a dozen Sure-Alarm clock radios.	(3) Sounds exaggerated and, thus, insincere.
(4) They were shipped by express today.	(4) Presents information that should have been presented earlier.
(5) We are sure you will find our firm a good one with which to deal and that our electronic units are unmatched in quality.	(5) Includes an unsupportable statement of certainty.
(6) Our latest price list is enclosed.	(6) States the obvious.
(7) Thank you for your patronage.	(7) Ends with a cliché.

Is this letter good enough to increase business? Let's see how the same letter sounds when it confirms shipment of goods in the first sentence, includes concrete resale on the product and business establishment, and eliminates business jargon.

(1) A dozen Sure-Alarm clock radios were shipped by Fastway air-express today.	(1) Sufficiently implies that the order has been received and filled. Refers to specific merchandise shipped and reveals method of shipment.
(2) The red ticket attached to each unit explains how the wake-up alarm works perfectly--even if the electric power fails.	(2) Points out a specific quality of the merchandise (uses resale).
(3) See the enclosed folder for price lists and forms for ordering additional radios or other high-quality electric units.	(3) Implies expectation of additional orders. Refers to enclosures without using an entire sentence to reveal their presence. Mentions related merchandise (uses sales-promotional material).

What three statements should be part of an acknowledgment letter?

The major purpose of the acknowledgment letter is to encourage future orders. An effective technique to achieve this goal is to state that the merchandise was sent, that it is good merchandise, and that future orders will be handled in the same manner. Don't expect to encourage future business by just filling the page with words like *welcome* and *gratitude*. They are overused words, and many people whose merchandise and service are poor overwork them. Appropriate action implies both gratitude and welcome. We can emphasize our appreciation by both action *and* words, but we should be careful. We should strive to make the words sound sincere and original.

LETTERS ABOUT OTHER ROUTINE REQUESTS

Notice how routine requests and favorable responses to them employ the same sequence-of-idea patterns.

The Routine Request

Most business people write letters requesting information about people, prices, products, and services. Because the request is a door opener for further business, readers accept it optimistically; but, at the same time, they draw an opinion about the writer based on the quality of the letter. The following outline can serve as a guide in the preparation of effective requests that are expected to be fulfilled:

1. Make the major request in the first sentence.

2. Follow the major request with the details that will make the request clear. If possible, use tabulations.

3. Close with a forward look to the reader's next step.

What outline should be used for a routine request?

Let's take a look at a vague request letter:

(1) Last night's <u>Daily News</u> included an article about your speech to a local investor's club. The reporter presented some of your thoughts on state and municipal bonds, but I would appreciate more details than were printed in the paper.	(1) Delays the real purpose of the letter.
(2) Do you have a copy of your speech? I'm sure some of the handouts you may have provided would be interesting.	(2) Presents the request rather vaguely.

Now let's see how the request could be handled more efficiently:

(1) May I have a copy of your speech to the Investor's Club on March 1?	(1) States request.
(2) Last night's <u>Daily News</u> included excerpts, just enough to whet the appetite for your complete discussion of state and municipal bonds.	(2) Presents details.

| (3) As a potential investor, I would certainly appreciate a copy of your speech and any printed materials you may have distributed. | (3) Expresses appreciation and alludes to action. |

Notice that the letter starts with a direct request for specific information. Then it follows with as much detail as necessary to enable the reader to answer specifically. It ends confidently with appreciation for the action requested. The letter is short; but, if it conveys enough information and has a tone of politeness, it is long enough.

The following request has an additional commendable technique — the subject line:

SUBJECT: REQUEST FOR INFORMATION ABOUT FLUSH-MOUNTED
               LIGHTING FIXTURES

How expensive is installation of the flush-mounted square lighting fixtures advertised on page 23 of the home section in the Times, April 17?

I am interested in replacing twelve old-fashioned bulb fixtures throughout my house. The ceilings are made of lath and plaster. Can the fixtures be installed without replastering?

Would new wiring be required for those fixtures holding two bulbs? My home is only six years old, and the present wiring is in good condition.

I shall appreciate your suggestions.

How is a subject line helpful?   The purpose of the subject line is to let the reader know what the letter is about — to establish the topic early. But we should not rely on the subject line for the remainder of the letter. We should avoid such hazy references as *the aforementioned subject* and *the above-mentioned subject.* Even worse, of course, is to refer to the subject line as *that* or *this.* Keep in mind that a pronoun needs a word antecedent that is easily located. Also, we should use enough words to establish clearly what the letter is about. Everything we can do to make answering our inquiry an easy task is to our own advantage.

Favorable Response to Routine

"Yes" is so easy to say that many people say it thoughtlessly. The following letter accedes to a request, but it reports the decision without much enthusiasm:

| (1) We have your letter in which you request an interview for the purpose of writing a master's thesis. | (1) States the obvious. |
| (2) As I interpret it, the person you need to talk with is Mr. Rudolph Smith, who is in charge of our suggestions program. | (2) Suggests "We had a good deal of difficulty in deciphering your message." |

(3) Right now, he has a busy schedule indeed; but he has so arranged his work as to leave a half-hour open for you--1:30 to 2:00, November 20.

(4) May we take this opportunity to assure you of our interest, and we wish you great success in your endeavors.

(3) Hints that the favor was difficult to grant and, therefore, granted reluctantly.

(4) Uses too many words, Is too general and perfunctory.

What is the most likely reaction to a statement that suggests sacrifice on the part of the writer?

With a little planning and consideration for the candidate's problems, the following letter could have been written just as quickly:

(1) Yes, our Suggestions Supervisor, Mr. Rudolph Smith, can talk with you from 1:30 to 2:00 on November 20.

(2) After he leaves for his two o'clock meeting, you may enjoy looking through our files of accepted and rejected suggestions. (3) Mr. Smith thinks they will be of special interest to you since you are doing a thesis on suggestion plans.

(4) After you have finished compiling the results of your study, we would like to see them.

(1) Answers the question in the first sentence.

(2) Reminds the reader that one half-hour is all that can be spared. The offer to show the files is a polite gesture.

(3) Reminds the candidate that Mr. Smith does have some interest in the project.

(4) Anticipates conclusion of the study (a pleasant thought!) and hints that the conclusions will be worth reading.

Why grant a request in the very first sentence?

Occasionally, successful business or professional people are asked special favors. They may receive invitations to speak to various social or school groups. If they say "yes," they might as well say it enthusiastically. Sending an unplanned, stereotyped acceptance suggests that the talk will be in the same style:

(1) I was pleased to have your letter of November 14 in which you invited me to talk to your students on Career Day.

(2) In reply, I wish to state that I have been in the insurance business for almost 25 years, having spent a good deal of time on the road as a life-insurance salesman and some time in the home office as an actuarian.

(1) Assumes that the expression of pleasure is of more interest than his indication of acceptance.

(2) Talks about self in language that was trite long ago.

Why should you avoid beginning most sentences with *I*?

(3) I have a talk that I could give on "Insuring your Career by Insuring your Friends," and I could supplement it with an eight-minute film on insurance careers.

(3) More talk about self.

Was this letter written inductively?

(4) I therefore consider it an honor and a pleasure to accept your invitation. I shall look forward to seeing you promptly at nine o'clock on Tuesday next.

(4) Finally accepts after having indirectly indicated acceptance. The eighth *I* in the letter. The sentence indicates that he may be a stuffy speaker.

The following revision accepts the invitation graciously, presents an idea of the contribution to be made, and ends with a reference to the event at which the speech is to be given:

(1) Yes, I accept your invitation to talk with your students on Career Day about a career in insurance.

(1) Accepts immediately. Reader is relieved. Now some other person won't have to be asked.

(2) Your students are probably interested primarily in the selling aspects, but the talk can include actuarial careers, too, if any should indicate interest.

(2) Employs a you-attitude.

(3) As a supplement to the discussion, they can see an eight-minute film. I'll bring the projector; perhaps you could arrange to have a screen in the room.

(3) Presents necessary details.

(4) I plan to see you in Owens Hall at nine o'clock next Tuesday morning.

(4) Ends by referring to the next step in the chain of events—a linkage of present and future states the expectation pleasantly.

Why were "yes" and routine letters discussed in the same chapter?

Whether we are writing an adjustment grant, a credit grant, an acknowledgment of an order that can be filled, or a favor grant, the key word that we will use is *yes.* For emphasis on the big, pleasant idea, plan to say "yes" at the beginning of the letter, follow with the necessary details, and close pleasantly.

SUMMARY

A deductive outline is recommended for letters that convey routine information or good news. A routine letter presents the main idea first. A good-news letter presents the good news first. Details and a closing sentence follow.

Typical routine letters are claims that are very likely to be granted, requests for credit information, requests for the credit privilege when supporting data are very convincing, order letters, and other requests that will almost certainly be granted. For these letters and favorable responses to them, the deductive outline has the following advantages: emphasizes the main or pleasant idea, simplifies composition, provides a beginning that attracts attention, puts readers in a good frame of mind when the first sentence is read, and saves time for the reader.

EXERCISES

Review Questions

1. Why are routine letters and "yes" responses to them discussed in the same chapter?

2. List the outlines that are recommended for routine letters and "yes" responses.

3. What is the disadvantage of beginning a reply with "Your letter requesting information has been given to me for reply"?

4. If a request is to be granted, is it better to reveal that the grant was made with reluctance, or to reveal that the grant was made with enthusiasm?

5. Should a subject line be used as the antecedent of a pronoun that appears in the first sentence of a letter?

6. In letters that request credit information, what is the advantage of employing a subject line?

7. For each pair, what is the difference between the paired elements?
   a. deductive and inductive?
   b. routine claim and persuasive claim?
   c. claim letter and adjustment letter?
   d. resale and sales-promotional material?

8. In a response to a letter that requests credit, why is use of the word "granted" inadvisable?

9. Which has the greater chance of being read—a sales message that appears in an adjustment letter, or a sales message that is sent separately? Explain.

10. If the decision is to grant a customer's questionable request, which tone is more appropriate for the adjustment letter—enthusiasm or reluctance?

11. Which is more common for soliciting credit information—form letters or personalized letters? Explain.

12. In a request for credit information, what are the advantages of tabulated-form layout as shown on page 145.

13.   In letters that request credit information and in letters that convey credit information, why is "confidential" a good word to use?

14.   In a credit-granting letter to a consumer, which is better? Devote one sentence to the credit terms, or devote a paragraph to the credit terms. Explain.

15.   In the first sentence of an order letter, why is use of "I would like to order" inadvisable?

Letter-Writing Problems

In composing solutions to the problems in this and remaining letter-writing chapters, proceed in the following manner:

1.   Before composing a letter, study the preceding chapter. Look primarily for principles that can be applied (not for expressions or sentences that might possibly be paraphrased or used word for word in the letter to be composed).

2.   Study the writing problem until you understand the facts.

3.   Assume you are the person who has the problem described.

4.   Anticipate reader reaction, and jot down on scratch paper the outline you will employ.

5.   Compose rapidly without looking at the definition of the problem and without looking at sample letters from the preceding chapter. (A sentence written to *define* a letter-writing problem may not be appropriate in a letter designed *to solve* the problem. Practice in adapting and paraphrasing is not needed; rather, the purpose of the assignment is to give practice in planning and expressing in such a way as to achieve clarity and to promote good human relations.)

6.   Before typing the letter, refer to the definition of the problem for such specifics as names, addresses, and amounts.

7.   Unless otherwise instructed, type the letter in one of the letter-format arrangements illustrated in the Appendix (Figures A-1, A-2, A-3, or A-4).

8.   If the nature of a problem is such that a letter is written by a consumer who would probably not have letterhead paper, use the format illustrated in Figure A-4, which includes a typed return address. If the letter is from someone in a business organization: (1) leave 2 inches of blank space at the top of the page (the space that would be taken up by the firm's letterhead); (2) select the arrangement illustrated in Figure A-1, A-2, and A-3; and (3) begin by typing the date in its appropriate position.

9.   After typing, proofread and make (as neatly as possible) any needed corrections in typing, grammar, spelling, and punctuation.

10.   Remember that the assignment was designed to give students experience in applying *principles* that can be applied in offices, but the mechanical *processes* of preparing a school assignment and producing an actual business letter are different. In a business office, the letter that you have written would probably have been dictated into a machine, transcribed in the word-processing center, edited and corrected on the screen, retyped by the machine in letter-perfect form at speeds up to 600 words per minute, and stored in the machine (if desired) for subsequent use as a form letter.

In the letter-writing problems, names and addresses are strictly fictitious. Unless otherwise instructed, type in your own name as sender.

1.   Assume you are in your fourth year as an undergraduate student. After graduation, you are considering pursuit of a master's degree. Write a letter requesting a catalog and other materials the university may have prepared for mailing to prospective students. Address: Registrar, Interstate University, 400 Popular Street, Floraville, CA 90114.

2.   As registrar of a university, acknowledge a student's request for a graduate catalog and other materials prepared for distribution to prospective students. For the up-coming year, tuition fees and housing costs are the same as stated in the catalog. If the student has any questions not answered in the catalog, they will be gladly answered by mail. Miss Jennifer Wells, 306 West Belton, Apt. 4, Ashby, NM 76431.

3.   As one who plans to attend a lithographers' convention about six weeks from now, write to the hotel in which it will be held. Give the date and approximate time of your arrival and planned departure. Accompanied by your spouse, you will need a room for two with a double bed. Since your spouse will want to do considerable sightseeing while you attend meetings, you would appreciate the hotel's sending a copy of the tour guide it provides. Since your envelope contains a $100 check to guarantee a room on the first night, call the reader's attention to the check. Portside Hotel, 1000 Waterbeach Road, New Orleans, LA 63114.

4.   Assume you are a member of a real estate brokers' group that has had monthly breakfast meetings for years. Usually, the speakers talk for about 15 minutes on some topic of current interest to brokers (inflation, economic forecasts, "wraparound" mortgages, etc.). The date for the December meeting is the 7th. As program chairman, you want this meeting to be different. One of the members is a well-known and well-decorated pilot who was at Pearl Harbor on December 7, 1941. Write a letter inviting him to speak. Mr. Joseph Wright, 347 West Walnut Street, Springfield, MO 65331.

5.   Your paint and wallpaper store has not previously ordered merchandise from Ambassador Wholesale. An order form is not available. The following items (for which a check is enclosed) are wanted: 6 double-roll bolts, $17.98 each, stock number W30X4817; 10 double-roll bolts, $23.98 each, stock number T31X3816; and 4 double-roll bolts, $18.49 each, Vinyl, V27X2917. The enclosed check ($544.36) includes $4.22 for taxes and $18.50 for transportation (by Cross-Nation Freight Lines). Ambassador Wholesale, 4421 West Elford, Chicago, IL 54331.

6. At Ambassador Wholesale, you have received an initial order for wallpaper and a check for $544.36. Except for four bolts of Vinyl-coated paper (which will be shipped from the Memphis warehouse), the entire order is being shipped today from the main warehouse in Chicago. Since the order is your first from this retail firm, a letter of acknowledgment would be appropriate. The likelihood that both parts of the order would be delivered at the same time is very small. If the merchant is not expecting two-part delivery, some unnecessary communication might result. Your letter also needs to make reference to an enclosed brochure that illustrates swatches of the most recent designs. Smith's Wallpaper & Paint, 144 South Bell Street, Eastford, MI 43117.

7. In response to an ad in a financial journal, George Wilson called a toll-free number and asked that a prospectus be sent to him. As one of the vice presidents in charge of the Yield-Right Fund, you have decided to include a personalized letter in the envelope with the prospectus. (The letter is stored in the word processor and used in response to all requests for this prospectus.) Although the prospectus contains complete details of the proposed investment, one point is selected for inclusion in the letter (a point that deserves great emphasis): The *Delphi Money Fund Report* has rated Yield-Right as the top performer of all money-market funds (with similar investment criteria) for the 12-month period ending October 31 of the current year. George Wilson, 454 N. 37th Avenue, Weston, PA 13342.

8. Before Edith went away to school, her parents called the Charge-Bank Credit Card Company and asked that she be issued a credit card with the parents' number on it. With this card, she could make purchases that would be paid for by the parents when they paid their monthly Charge-Bank bill. On the phone, Charge-Bank assured the parents that such arrangements could be made; but the request must be in writing. Write a letter authorizing Charge-Bank to issue a card to Edith. Charge-Bank Credit Card Company, P.O. 1227, Phoenix, AZ 85334.

9. When Joyce Adams left for college in another state, she drove a car to which her mother held title. When her mother received papers designed for renewal of license plates, the following instructions were included: "Drive your car to one of the Emission Control locations listed at the bottom of this page. If the car meets emission standards, a 'pass' certificate will be issued. Return the certificate with your payment and the accompanying papers." Requiring Joyce to drive home (about 1,000 miles) for the inspection would be unrealistic. A call to the state's Motor Vehicle Department told her mother how to proceed: "Write a letter to the Department, giving the name and address of person driving the car, reason for being out of state, date on which the car was driven from the state, and date of expected return to the state. Include a check for $1. In response to the letter, an exemption certificate will be mailed to you [the mother]. It is to accompany the check for the license fee and accompanying papers when you renew the license." After Joyce's mother complies with these instructions, the renewal sticker will be mailed to her, and she can then mail it to Joyce. Write the letter requesting exemption. From your imagination, supply the information requested: Motor Vehicle Department, State of CA, P.O. Box 980, Sacramento, CA 90114.

10. You are the director of personnel. You have received a well-written application letter and résumé from a college senior who will soon be graduated. She hopes to get a job as an administrative assistant in the word-processing department. Before an interview can be arranged, she must fill out the firm's standard application form. Because such correspondence is frequent, a short form letter has been prepared and stored for immediate recall by the automatic typewriter. All you have to do is provide the name and address and identify the form that is to be used. Directions: Reconstruct the letter that would emerge from the automatic typewriter. Use the following inside address: Ms. Carla Bright, 321 West 14th Street, Apartment 3, Mountain Pass, VA 18934.

11. You are an administrative assistant to Mr. Charles Wood, Vice President, Research and Development. While he is away for a two-week vacation, you are to open and read all his mail. You have authority to take care of some of his routine correspondence for him. However, you are to hold unusual and important letters until he returns. You do want to acknowledge their receipt. Prepare a form acknowledgment letter, which can be placed in the word-processing equipment, ready for immediate response. You will sign the letter.

12. You are responsible for credits and collections at a building-materials firm. So customers will understand credit items and procedures, you have printed a "credit terms" sheet. It is included with letters to new customers. A young man (new to the area and a recent recipient of a degree in construction engineering) is trying to get started in the business of building homes. He has submitted all the paper work essential in an application for the credit privilege. His financial condition is such that his application would have been rejected ordinarily, but his character references are very strong. For the time being, his credit limit is $90,000. Write a "yes" letter. In it, refer the reader to the "credit terms" sheet. Do not compose the sheet; just assume it has been composed already and is being enclosed. Calvin Bab, New-Home Construction Company, 2607 East First Street, Wilheim, CO 73504.

13. You do most of the correspondence for a small firm that sells do-it-yourself solar water heaters. Newspaper and word-of-mouth advertising are bringing in orders daily. The next two weeks present a problem. The specially designed coupling unit that attaches the solar unit to the existing hot-water tank is not available; it won't be available for two weeks. The plan is to go ahead and fill all orders and send a letter of explanation. The unit will be sent as soon as you receive your shipment. Since attaching the unit is the last step in a long series of instructions, it will probably arrive before a do-it-yourself homeowner would reach that step. Write a form letter that could be stored in the automatic typewriter's memory, ready for immediate use.

14. You are a woman expecting your first child in six months. Your physician has told you about a magazine to which you want to subscribe. *Young Ones* is published twelve times yearly. Its articles are of great interest to expectant women and to mothers of young children. Its advertising is limited to carefully selected merchandise related to health and child raising. For the first six issues, subscription is free. All you have to do is write and ask to be placed on the mailing list. *Young Ones, Inc., Westhaven, PA 23471.*

15.   You are responsible for planning a convention of pheasant farmers, to be held in a distant city. The city was selected because a famous pheasant farm is nearby. Participants will attend some lectures and banquets in the city and tour the Restless Feathers farm. Your present problem is selecting a hotel for the convention. Two hundred farmers, about half of whom will bring their spouses, will attend. You will need a banquet hall big enough to accommodate 300, three lecture rooms big enough to accommodate 75 people each, and hotel rooms for all attendees. The convention is to be on January 21, 22, and 23. You need some figures: costs to attendees for hotel rooms, and costs to the organization for all other expenses. Other information, such as distance from the airport and types of transportation available, would be helpful. Write a letter that can be sent to four different hotels. One of them: The Comrade Arms Hotel, 1427 N. Broadway, Remway, TX 45712.

16.   You ordered a combination radio and cassette player as a present for a graduating student. It arrived two days before the graduation party, but it would not work. You selected another gift and are returning the unit for a full refund. Gifts Unlimited, 753 S. Fifth Street, Westland, TN 38941.

17.   In a recent publication, you saw merchandise in which you have a special interest. If you had more information, you might purchase the goods. Write a letter to the distributor. Ask at least three questions. Assign a number to each question, leave blank space before and after each question, and type the questions on lines that are shorter than the typewritten lines of the first and last paragraphs. Such an arrangement on the typewritten page will give emphasis to the questions. Don't forget to arrange the questions in a logical order. Be sure to use parallel construction.

18.   While traveling on a summer vacation, you stopped at a fast-food restaurant. Favorably impressed with the food and the manner of operating the business, you talked with the manager about the possibility of getting a franchise and opening a similar restaurant in your hometown. According to the manager, "The first step is to write to the home office asking for the investment prospectus. It will answer almost all your initial questions." He provides the address to which you will write: Mr. Edward Wells, Manager, Franchising Department, Quick-Eat, Inc., 7843 West Portland Street, Hillsburgh, MD 12541.

19.   As manager of the franchising department for a national chain of fast-food restaurants, you have received a request for a prospectus. Along with the prospectus (which will answer most of the questions a prospective investor might have), send a letter. Encourage careful study of it, call attention to pages containing information worthy of special attention, and offer to answer questions. Mr. Neil Worthy, 718 N. Forge Street, Bunkerton, MO 64122.

20.   As manager of the credit department in a large wholesale firm, you have received a letter requesting permission to make credit purchases. Along with the letter came the small firm's financial statements and a list of credit references. Before permission can be granted, however, you need further information. The applicant must fill in the wholesale firm's credit-application form and return it. Write a letter of acknowledgment; request the recipient to fill out and return the form. Ms. Mary Atherton, P.O. Box 714, Allister, SC 13541.

WRITING ABOUT THE UNPLEASANT

Saying "No" to an Adjustment Request

Saying "No" to a Credit Request

Saying "No" to Someone Who Has Ordered Merchandise

Saying "No" to a Favor Request

Summary

Before we can begin writing any letter, we must determine what the message is and what the receiver's reaction will be. When the message is unpleasant (a "no" answer to a request, for example), we can expect the reaction to be one of disappointment. Our goal is to convey the message and to minimize the disappointment.

What are the objectives of a "no" letter?

If the sentence that contains the disappointing idea is placed at the beginning of the letter, the unpleasant idea receives emphasis. Promoting business harmony is difficult when emphasis is placed on negatives. Thus, the following outline is recommended:

What outline should we use for a "no" letter?

1. Begin with a neutral statement that leads to the reasons for refusing the request.

2. Present the facts, an analysis, and the reasons for refusal.

3. State the refusal.

4. Close with a related idea that shifts emphasis away from the refusal.

Notice that the reasons *precede* the refusal statement.

When we say "no," we should have a reason. We assume readers are reasonable. If we can make them understand our reasons, they may agree with us that their request should have been refused. When they agree with us, we have their goodwill—and future business.

No one can give us a foolproof formula for persuading our reader to agree with the "no." But we do have a dependable guiding principle. *The person we are writing to deserves an explanation.* Preferably, the explanation should precede the refusal. Presenting the refusal before the explanation has two disadvantages: (1) The reader may stop reading before the explanation. (2) After being disappointed, the reader may not be receptive to the explanation.

Why should explanations precede a statement of refusal?

Presenting explanations first is an effective technique for emphasizing reasons. The more clearly a reader understands our reasons, the less disappointed he or she will be when the refusal is stated. Naturally, even good letter planning and writing can hardly be expected to make readers just as happy with a refusal as they would have been with an acceptance. Rather, the goal is to get readers to understand the reasons for the refusal. The more clearly they understand them, the less likely they will be to think that the decision is illogical, unfair, or arbitrary.

Presenting reasons first does have a possible disadvantage, however. If the reasons are presented in a long, involved, roundabout way, readers may become impatient before the unpleasant idea is stated. Thus reasons should be stated vividly and concisely.

How can we
prevent a reader's
impatience when
reasons are given first?

Under what
condition might
we prefer to say "no"
in the very first sentence?

Concise, well-written explanations are unlikely to make readers impatient. Even if readers should get impatient, consider these alternatives: (1) While reading the preliminary explanations, readers become a little impatient. (2) After reading the refusal (which is presented first), readers feel that trying to understand the reasons is pointless or that they should concentrate on rebutting the explanations as they read. The second alternative certainly seems more damaging.

The outline suggested in this chapter is not intended to be the pattern for *every* refusal letter. Sometimes we may actually *want* to jolt a reader with an emphasized refusal followed by a subordinated explanation. For example, someone who has repeated a request after receiving a thorough explanation and a denial may (in our second letter of denial) need a forceful statement of refusal in the first sentence. Someone who has not responded favorably to repeated instructions may (in a memorandum) profit from a statement of bad news in the first sentence ("Change or lose your job.") If prior experiences have indicated that a certain person responds better after having been shaken, emphasize the seriousness of the problem. If the message is conveyed adequately and promotes the kind of reader-writer relationship desired, the process is acceptable. But, before taking this approach, we should give serious thought to the reaction it will produce.

Let's now analyze some business letters in which reader reaction is not considered. Then let's look at the same letters after they have been rewritten in the light of anticipated reader reaction. After these analyses of adjustment, credit, order, and favor refusals, we shall arrive at a list of specific *do*'s and *don't*'s for refusal letters.

SAYING "NO" TO AN ADJUSTMENT REQUEST

When business prudence dictates that we should say "no," our major writing problems are saying "no" as inoffensively as possible and presenting supporting reasons as convincingly as possible. We know our reader may be disappointed with a "no" answer; thus, we have to make sure our method of communicating "no" either mitigates or eliminates the disappointment. We do not want to report an adverse decision in an adverse manner; to do so is to make a customer for our competitors.

How would you say "no" to the following request?

Will you please correct the balance of my account.

Knowing that billing time was near, I stopped in your credit office on October 19, asked a clerk what my balance was, and paid in full with a personal check. A few days later, the store sent the enclosed statement showing a $27 balance.

Because no further purchases had been made, another customer's purchase apparently has been charged to my account. I shall appreciate your changing my account balance to the correct figure--zero.

The following letter explains (but not very well) why the request cannot be granted:

(1) Thank you for your letter of October 29.

(1) Employs a well-worn beginning, but does introduce the subject of discussion.

(2) However, I must inform you that you cannot be excused from paying the $27 balance of your account.

(2) Presents the refusal before explanation. Coming immediately after the polite "thank you," "however" signifies an abrupt change to a negative point.

Which should receive greater emphasis—the "no" answer or the reasons for the "no" answer?

(3) According to the credit contract, you agreed to pay for purchases you made. As indicated on your statement, you made a $20 purchase on September 21, a $44.17 purchase on October 1, and a $10.56 purchase on October 8. Apparently, the clerk read the total ($74.73) as $47.73 when asked about your balance.

(3) Presents explanations.

(4) By inadvertently transposing the first two digits, the clerk made an unfortunate error. But that error does not alter the fact that you did make the purchases for which you are being charged.

(4) Employs negative language.

(5) You are legally obligated to pay.

(5) Emphasizes (through active voice, short sentence, and second person) a truth; but such a forceful statement may be unnecessary. Business harmony is more likely to be achieved if cooperation can be obtained without introducing legality. A forceful statement of legality could be very appropriate in a subsequent letter—if this letter did not succeed.

(6) Payment received before November 15 will not be subject to an interest charge.

(6) Accents the negative.

(7) Thank you for writing and we hope you continue to avail yourself of our good merchandise and low prices.

(7) Employs a doubtful expression that could be taken to mean "I recognize that this incident may spell the end of the business relationship."

The following revision represents an improvement—both in sequence of ideas and in manner of expressing them:

(1) Thank you for making your latest payment before receiving a statement.	(1) Begins by emphasizing a positive point. Identifies the letter as being related to the account.
(2) A look at your purchase record revealed the answer to the question raised in your letter of October 27:	(2) Introduces explanations.

	Purchases	Payments	Balance
Sept. 21	$20.00		
Oct. 1	44.17		
Oct. 8	10.56		$74.73
Oct. 19		$47.73	27.00

(3) The clerk who reported your balance on October 19 apparently read the dollar digits in reverse order (47 instead of 74). If she had overstated your balance and you had paid the amount quoted, you would have had a credit toward future purchases. Since the amount was understated, your account shows the $27 balance.	(3) Continues with explanation. And reminds indirectly that the customer is expected to pay for purchases made —no more, no less.
(4) That balance can be paid now or simply added to your statement for November purchases.	(4) Employs positive language. Confidently implies a future business relationship.
(5) Our Fall Presale (for charge customers only) begins on November 3. (6) Most items will be reduced by 20 percent. When you charge purchases, remember to pick up Green Stamps from the office on the third floor.	(5) Closes with sales-promotional material that may be appreciated. (6) Emphasis is on the positive aspect of future transactions instead of the negative point that request was denied.

In adjustment refusals, why should we begin on a neutral point?

From the preceding letters, we can now draw some conclusions about what should and should not be done in adjustment refusals:

1.   Begin either with a thought upon which both reader and writer can agree, or with a neutral point upon which there will not be disagreement. The likelihood of strong disagreement about the important issue is decreased if both reader and writer have begun by agreeing on a less important issue.

2. Devote a major portion of the letter to an explanation. To be convincing, use sufficient detail—facts and figures are helpful.

3. Give the explanation before the refusal. By giving a logical explanation first, we make it possible for readers to see our logic. We may be able to prevent a negative reaction completely. *Preventing* a negative reaction is always easier than *curing* it.

4. Let readers know how they actually gain from the refusal. If we stop to think the problem through, we can usually see ways in which readers profit from our ''no'' answer. Perhaps by refusing such requests, we can either sell at lower prices, make quicker deliveries, or deliver better merchandise. Disappointment will be minimized if we can show that in the long run the recipient is the winner, not the loser, as a result of our ''no'' answer.

5. De-emphasize the ''no.'' Use the de-emphasis techniques discussed on pages 92–95, 102–103, and 105. Impersonal language, minimum space, embedded position, positive language, complex sentence structure, and the subjunctive mood are particularly helpful. De-emphasize the ''no,'' but make sure it is there and will be understood.

> How can the refusal be de-emphasized?

6. Use resale.[1] Remember, our goal is to say ''no'' and still retain the customers' business. One effective way to retain their business is to keep them sold on our merchandise and our services. A touch of resale may be appropriate in any part of the letter, but it is most effective after the explanation has been given.

7. Offer a counterproposal if the problem calls for it. Doing so suggests that we are considerate and not angry with the customer for having made a request we cannot grant.

> Why should we offer an alternative solution to the problem?

8. Close by either suggesting acceptance of the counterproposal or by using resale and sales-promotional material. This technique permits us to end on a more pleasant note; it suggests that we still confidently expect to retain the customer's business, and it may lead to another sale.

Perhaps we can now reinforce our knowledge of what to do by reviewing what *not* to do:

> What are the most common mistakes made in refusal letters?

1. Don't say ''no'' in the first sentence. Doing so invites a negative reaction. Agreement will be very difficult to reach if we present our most disagreeable thought first.

2. Don't say something that suggests that a ''yes'' answer will follow. Doing so makes the disappointing news sound all the more shocking when it is presented later.

3. Don't begin by talking about something only remotely related to the subject of the letter. For example, if the letter to the person who asked that the $27

---

1. See Edward Hall Gardner, *Effective Business Letters* (New York: Ronald, 1915), p. 121.

balance be canceled had begun with "The enclosed brochure describes our latest styles in car coats," the recipient would have expected a sales message to follow. Such a sentence would not have indicated a response to the request for exchange or refund.

4.   Don't give an elementary lecture. The following sentence neither conveys bad news nor leads the reader to expect good news, but it does arouse a negative reaction: "If businesses are to continue, they must satisfy customers."

5.   Don't begin by recalling the original disappointment too vividly. "We know how you must have felt when your balance showed a $27 debt" not only introduces an unpleasant thought but may lead the reader to expect a refund.

6.   Don't make the resale too strong in the beginning. The person who asked that the $27 balance be canceled would not agree with this beginning sentence: "Our computerized credit system is superior to old hand-added methods." Such a strong resale beginning invites disagreement from the start.

7.   Don't talk too long before getting to the point. By the time the receiver has read a half-dozen lines and still can't tell what it's all about, the reaction may be negative. The neutral or agreement beginning should lead naturally and quickly into an explanation.

8.   Don't let the explanation be so short or general as to be unconvincing. When we refuse, we have a reason. Give enough detail to make the reason clear.

9.   Don't hide behind company policy or the terms of the guarantee. For example, saying, "I'm sorry, but *company* policy forbids our canceling your $27 balance" would probably infuriate the customer. Giving reasons behind a policy takes up more space and time than simply stating a policy, but the effort is more convincing.

10.   Don't blame some other person when you are at fault. If you are caught passing the buck, you will lose goodwill.

11.   Don't sound accusing. When we want to remind people of their mistakes, we can usually employ third-person, impersonal language that gets the point across in an inoffensive way.

12.   Don't employ negative language unnecessarily. Be especially careful to avoid the following words and expressions:

cannot understand	error	shocked
damage	fault	surprised
defective	go wrong	unable
delay	inconvenience	unfortunately
dissatisfied	regret	wrong

13.   Don't use a tone that hints of bending over backward or giving blood when offering a counterproposal. Offer it willingly or not at all.

14.   Don't close by referring to the most unpleasant part of the whole letter—the "no" answer. Preferably, use resale, sales promotion, or some other off-the-subject ending.

15.   Don't close by revealing doubts about whether the explanation will be accepted. "We trust this is satisfactory" suggests "We ourselves doubt whether we have made the right business decision or presented it in the right way."

16.   Don't apologize for the action taken. We should take a course of action only when we have a good reason for doing so. We should be glad to stand behind our reasons.

Why should we avoid apologizing for the action taken?

17.   Don't close with a reminder of future trouble. "When this happens again, just . . . ." ends a letter with an unpleasant, negative thought.

18.   Don't use a worn expression as a closing statement. For example, "Thank you for your interest" and "We appreciate your consideration" have been used so much that a reader may wonder whether a writer really means them or is merely using them for the sake of politeness.

19.   Don't invite a prolonged correspondence. "If you have any further questions, please don't hesitate to write us" indicates that the case is still open, that pertinent information may not have been considered, and that through further correspondence the decision may be reversed. If we have good reasons behind our decision and have explained them well, the case can be considered closed. Further correspondence on a closed issue is a waste of time.

20.   Don't use an ironic ending. "When we can be of any *further* help, please call on us" is intended to indicate a helpful attitude, but such an ending is bitter when the extent of our helpfulness has been to say "no." The sentence could easily be taken to mean, "When you want us to refuse another request, just write us; we will be pleased to do so."

As we have seen, adjustment letters that say "no" follow a general sequence of ideas: (1) Begin with a neutral or factual sentence that leads to the reasons behind the "no" answer. (2) Present the reasons and explanations. (3) Present the refusal in an unemphatic manner. (4) Close with an off-the-subject thought. Naturally, the ending should be related to the letter or to the business relationship; but it should not be specific about the refusal. Although the same pattern is followed in credit, order, and favor refusals, those letters are sufficiently different to make a discussion of each profitable.

SAYING "NO" TO A CREDIT REQUEST

Once we have evaluated a request for credit and have decided "no" is the better answer, our primary writing problem is to say "no" so tactfully that we keep the business relationship on a cash basis. Since requests for credit are often accompa-

In a letter that
refuses credit, what is
a good counterproposal?

nied with an order, our credit refusals may serve as acknowledgment letters. And, of course, every business letter is directly or indirectly a sales letter. The prospective customers may be disappointed when they cannot buy on a credit basis; but if we keep them sold on our goods and services, they may prefer to buy from us on a cash basis instead of seeking credit privileges elsewhere.

When the credit investigation shows that applicants are poor credit risks, too many credit writers no longer regard them as possible customers. They write to them in a cold, matter-of-fact manner. They don't consider that such applicants may still be interested in doing business on a cash basis and may qualify for credit later.

Why discuss rea-
sons for a credit refusal?

In credit refusals, as in other types of refusals, the major portion of the message should be explanation. We cannot expect our reader to agree that our "no" answer is the right answer unless we give the reasons behind it. Naturally, those who send us credit information will expect us to keep it confidential. But if we give the reasons without using the names of those from whom we obtained our information, we are not violating confidence. We are passing along the truth as a justification for our business decisions. Both writers and readers benefit from the explanation of the reasons behind the refusal. For writers, the explanation helps to establish fair-mindedness; it shows that the decision was not arbitrary. For readers, the explanation not only presents the truth to which they are entitled; it has guidance value. From it they learn to adjust habits and as a result qualify for credit purchases later.

Why use resale
in a credit refusal?

Resale is helpful for four reasons: (1) It might cause credit applicants to prefer our brand. Thus they might be willing to buy it even on a cash basis. (2) It suggests that the writer is trying to be helpful. (3) It makes the writing easier—negative thoughts are easier to de-emphasize when cushioned with resale material, and by using resale material we sound confident of future cash purchases. (4) It can confirm the credit applicant's judgment—suggesting the applicant made a good choice of merchandise is giving an indirect compliment.

Assume a retailer of electronic devices has placed an initial order and requested credit privileges. After examining financial statements that were enclosed, the wholesaler decides the request should be denied. The following letter would be substandard:

(1) Your order of July 6 has been received, and your request for credit privileges has been given to me for evaluation.	(1) States ideas that could have been left to implication.
(2) At this time, we do not believe it is our best interest to sell to you on a credit basis.	(2) Reveals the negative decision before revealing the basis for it.
(3) As you may be aware, many leaders in the field of finance recommend that businesses maintain a 2-to-1 ratio of current assets to current liabilities.	(3) Presents an explanation, but unnecessarily raises doubts about the applicant's knowledge of financial matters.

(4) Since your current ratio is approximately 1 1/4 to 1, your orders will need to have payment attached. (5) We trust you will understand.

(4) Continues with figures that should have preceded the statement of refusal.

(5) Reveals that the writer has doubts about the strength of the explanation.

(6) An envelop is enclosed for your convenience in sending your check for $1,487.53, after which your order will be shipped.

(6) Employs worn expressions in referring to the enclosure.

(7) For a look at the latest in video games, see the enclosed folder.

(7) Does make a commendable effort to encourage additional orders.

Contrast the tone of the preceding letter with the tone of the one that follows:

(1) The items listed in your order of July 6 have been selling very rapidly in recent weeks.

(1) Implies receipt of the order. Leads to an explanation.

(2) Supplying customers' demands for the latest in electronic technology is consistent with sound business practices.

(2) Introduces explanation. Implies approval of *one* of the applicant's practices (supplying most recently developed items).

(3) One sound practice is careful control of indebtedness, according to specialists in accounting and finance.

(3) Leads to discussion of *another* practice that is the basis for subsequent refusal.

(4) Their formula for control is to maintain at least a 2-to-1 ratio of current assets to current liabilities. (5) Experience has taught us that, for the benefit of all concerned, credit should be available only to purchasers who meet that ratio.

(4) Provides further detail.

(5) Continues with the explanation.

(6) Since your ratio is approximately 1 1/4 to 1, you are encouraged to make cash purchases.

(6) Employs positive language in expressing the refusal.

(7) By continuing to supply your customers with timely merchandise, you should be able to improve the ratio.

(7) Looks confidently to the future and reminds the applicant of the commendable practice discussed in the second sentence.

(8) Then, we would welcome an opportunity to review your credit application.	(8) Encourages subsequent application and thus implies expectation of continued business relationship.
(9) To send your check ($1,487.53) for your current order, just use the enclosed envelope; your order will be shipped promptly.	(9) Reminds the merchant of the desired action.
(10) Other timely items (such as the most recent in video games) are shown in the enclosed folder.	(10) Employs sales-promotional material as a closing sentence. Uses ''timely'' as a reminder of the applicant's commendable business practice and as a technique for developing unity.

Whether a credit refusal is being sent to a dealer or a consumer, a retailer or a wholesaler, a prospective customer or an old customer who has lost credit privileges, the principles of writing are the same. Let's review them.

What are some techniques for writing credit refusals?

1. Begin with a thought upon which both reader and writer can agree, or begin by introducing a neutral idea upon which there will be no disagreement. Resale on the merchandise ordered (if an order is involved) is a dependable choice.

2. Lead naturally into a discussion of the reasons behind the credit refusal.

3. Give the reasons for the refusal. But employ a polite, tactful tone and impersonal language.

4. State the refusal without attaching emphasis to it. Let it come as a logical result of the reasons presented. Since some adverse information must be mentioned, temper the reaction by also indicating some favorable aspects of the credit report.

5. Invite readers to present their side of the story. Doing so will suggest that the case is not completely closed and that the writer is a fair-minded person who has some knowledge of human nature.

6. Sound confident of a future credit grant when the obstacle has been removed. Doing so will remind the addressee that credit privileges are earned. Once the addressee has earned it and become a credit customer, she or he will probably not cause problems for the collection department.

7. Offer to sell for cash as an alternative.

8. End by suggesting the action desired; use some resale on the goods or services if an order is involved.

What are some common errors in writing credit refusals?

Now that we have completed a review of what to do in credit letters that say ''no,'' we have a good idea of what *not* to do. But for the sake of emphasis, let's review the *don't*'s for credit refusals.

1. Don't say "no" in the first sentence.

2. Don't hint that the answer may turn out to be "yes."

3. Don't begin by talking about something unrelated to the subject.

4. Don't try to give an elementary credit lecture.

5. Don't begin with a routine "We're glad to have your order" or "Thank you for your order."

6. Don't talk too long before getting around to an explanation of the refusal.

7. Don't use accusing, negative, or personal language.

8. Don't sound like a sleuth by talking about the investigation.

9. Don't identify referents.

10. Don't talk about company policy.

11. Don't close with an apology; remember, we have good reasons for our decisions, and an apology may serve as a last-minute reminder of the refusal.

12. Don't close with a meaningless or outworn expression.

These lists of do's and don't's are long, but they should be easy to remember. Why? Because they are based on human nature. We can recall the list of things to do by asking what kind of credit refusal would make the best impression on us, and we can recall the list of things not to do by asking what aspects of a refusal would arouse the most resentment in us. We can follow the same procedure when we have to refuse an order.

SAYING "NO" TO SOMEONE WHO HAS ORDERED MERCHANDISE

For various reasons, we may not be able to send the merchandise that people have ordered from us.

Why might you refuse to fill an order?

1. We may be able to send it, but there will be a waiting period. (At such times we would acknowledge the order and write a letter saying "Yes, you will receive the . . . by. . . .")

2. We may not sell directly to consumers. (We would tell the customer where to buy the merchandise.)

3. We may not have what the customer ordered, but we have something that will serve his or her needs better. (We would hold the order until we have made the customer understand that we have something better.)

If the customer's shipment will be delayed, a good plan is to follow the deductive approach described in the previous chapter. But for orders that cannot be filled, the inductive approach recommended for all "no" letters is preferred. The following request has to be refused because the manufacturer to whom it is addressed does not sell directly to consumers:

Please send a valve for my Sunex solar heater. According to the Manufacturer's Installation Guide, the part number is S-54. Since I don't have a price list, just send it COD.

If a manufacturer received many similar requests, they would very likely be answered by form letter. But even form letters do not have to be so cold and indifferent as the following letter:

(1) We have your recent request that we ship you a ____.

(1) The receipt of the order could have been implied.

(2) Unfortunately, we do not sell direct to consumers. (3) Your nearest dealer is ____ whose address is ____ (4) May we suggest that you place your order there.

(2) Distribution through dealers has advantages; it's not necessarily "unfortunate." (3) Giving the exact name and address of a local dealer is commendable. (4) This suggestion misses a chance for resale.

(5) Thank you for your interest in our merchandise.

(5) The ending seems perfunctory.

People understand the practicality of form letters. They don't object to them because they are *forms;* but they do object to indifferent, matter-of-fact language. When stored in the memory of word-processing equipment, form letters can be individually typed. They look like letters written specifically for a certain person. The general plan of the following revised letter is to make customers' desire for the merchandise so strong that they will be willing to wait for it and to purchase it through conventional merchandising outlets:

(1) When we began the manufacture of solar heaters, the valves (like the one you ordered) were made of plastic.

(1) Introduces the subject and leads to an explanation.

(2) They are now made of a copper alloy, which gives much longer and more dependable service. (3) As manufacturers, we devote all our efforts to experimenting, making, and improving the Sunex. (4) Because we concentrate solely on these efforts (and leave selling and

(2) Provides resale on the item ordered.

(3) Begins the explanation.

(4) Reveals — in positive language — that sales are not made directly to consumers. Lets the reader see an ad-

servicing to retailers), we have been able to develop one of the most efficient solar units available anywhere.	vantage in the manufacturer's not selling to consumers directly.
(5) Your nearest retailer of Sunex parts is Western Supply Company, 217 N. 24th Street, Albuquerque, NM 75341.	(5) Closes by providing needed information.

If the merchandise involved in the preceding letter had been expensive, or if orders sent directly to the manufacturer were rare, it would have been better not to use a form letter. Both form letters and individual letters can benefit from applying the following suggestions:

1. Imply receipt of the order and confirm the customer's good choice of merchandise.

2. Wherever appropriate in the letter, use resale to make the customer willing to reorder through the proper channel.

3. Give reasons why sales are through dealers. Suggest or spell out how advantageously customers can buy through a dealer.

4. Use positive language to explain that the order is not being filled.

Sometimes, customers *order* one item when they can more profitably *use* another, as in the following order letter:

Will you reload the casings in the box to which this letter is attached.

In each casing, put 1 1/4 ounces of No. 8 shot with 32 grains of SR7625 powder.

Continuing our arrangement of last year, charge the total bill to my Mastercard No. 5302 1826 0520 X120.

The individual has ordered reloads that are inappropriate for the casings returned. Filling the order as submitted would be a mistake. Injury, or at least dissatisfaction, could result. Th following letter seeks to convince the recipient that the type of refill ordered is not the type of refill needed.

(1) The casings you sent to us have been received.	(1) Begins with an idea that could have been left to implication.
(2) However, we do not think it advisable to fill them as requested.	(2) Reveals the refusal before presenting the explanation. After a neutral statement, "However" immediately lets the reader know that negatives follow.

(3) The load requested is too heavy for the shells.

(3) Explains in general terms.

(4) In view of the condition of the shells, do we have permission to load them with 26 grains of powder and 1 ounce of shot?

(4) Needs more specific explanation. Commendably, seeks approval to send that which is usable.

(5) Your order will be held until we hear from you.

(5) Presents needed information, but the idea of "holding" the order seems a little negative. "Hear from you" is worn and literally implies oral communication.

Although such letters as the preceding letter may get the desired results, the following letter applies writing principles more effectively:

(1) The casings you sent to us can be filled with a variety of reload combinations.

(1) Implies receipt of the casings and the request that they be reloaded. Use of "variety" serves as an easy transition into a discussion of *two* of those combinations: the one requested and the one recommended.

(2) The copper portion of each casing is only 5/8 of an inch, and the plastic portion shows signs of wear. (3) They appear to have been reloaded once or twice previously. (4) If the requested load (32 grains of powder behind 1 1/2 ounces of No. 8 shot) is used, portions of the plastic casing can become lodged in the barrel. (5) The result could be at least a nuisance and at most a serious accident.

(2) Begins the explanation. Presents some specifics.

(3) Continues with explanatory details.

(4) Continues with explanation. Uses specific numbers to tailor-make the letter to this receiver; they serve to confirm the specific request. The receiver may not remember (and have no record of) what was ordered.
(5) Gives further evidence that the item ordered was not the item needed.

(6) Although we are not filling your order as requested, we would like your permission to reload with 28 grains of powder behind 1 and 1/8 ounces of No. 8 shot.

(6) Places the refusal in a subordinate clause for de-emphasis. Offers details of an alternative.

(7) The extra safety would more than compensate for the slight decrease in range. (8) Your choice of the SR7625 powder is ideal; we recommend it because it burns so cleanly.

(7) Reveals a disadvantage of the alternative, but de-emphasizes it by putting it in the sentence that states the primary advantage.
(8) Includes resale by confirming the sportsman's choice of powder.

(9) To authorize reloading according to our suggestions, just check
the appropriate square on the
enclosed card and return the card
in the enclosed envelope.

(9) Seeks confirmation of permission to
send what is needed instead of what
was ordered. Makes response easy.
On the card, one of the squares (the
options) could be to return the empty
shells. Mentioning that option in the
letter would give it undesired emphasis;
no reference is made to it.

The preceding letter involved no difference in price between the ordered item and
the needed item. If the needed item should cost more, its advantages should be
pointed out and then the extra cost stated.

Taking the time required for writing such a long letter to a customer may at first
seem questionable. The preceding letter (as is so often true) is about a circumstance
that recurs frequently. With one good draft in the file or in the word processor, the
next letter can be adapted and reproduced quickly and with very little effort.

Foreign Models Incorporated handles carburetors and other parts
for European cars only.

If you will place your order (which we are returning) with Pacific
Motors at 1301 South Jackson Street in San Pedro, you should have
your carburetor in a short time.

When you need to trade cars, come in and see our selections. We
have 14 different makes--from low-priced economy cars to the most
expensive European sports cars.

Remember, the sales-promotional material didn't cost anything so far as paper
and postage are concerned—we had to write anyway. And it's almost sure to be
read—something we can't say of all sales messages.

What is an advantage of including sales-promotional material in an order refusal?

When people say "no" in a letter, they usually do so because they think "no" is
the better answer for all concerned. They can see how recipients will ultimately
benefit from the refusal. If the letter is based on a sound decision, and if it has been
well written, receivers will probably recognize that the senders did them a favor by
saying "no."

SAYING "NO" TO A FAVOR REQUEST

Every business will at some time or other be asked for a favor. How would you
answer the following letter if you were a turnpike official who cannot grant the
request?

You can be a real help to the Better-A Fraternity here at State
University. And we don't think it will take any more effort than signing
and returning the enclosed card.

In the three years in which I have been driving to and from college on weekends, I have noticed a large pile of rocks on the right-of-way of the Turnpike just west of Kaywood. Since they are not being used and in no way make the right-of-way more attractive, we of the Better-A thought you might like to let us use them for constructing a wall around our house. We could rent a local truck and arrange to pick them up during hours when turnpike traffic is light.

May we have your authorization on the enclosed card? You will be helping us and we will be helping future members.

After having read thus far in this chapter, you would probably *not* answer in the following manner:

(1) Your request that we give your fraternity the rocks on the Turnpike right-of-way just west of Kaywood has been referred to me for reply.	(1) Begins with the obvious, but does lead to a discussion of the problem at hand.
(2) Unfortunately, we are unable to grant your request. (3) To give Turnpike property to any group whatever is a violation of the Turnpike Commission's policy. (4) Furthermore, although the rocks have been there for some time, we do have a plan for them. (5) When the Turnpike was constructed, the engineers advised the Commission to leave all usable stone on the right-of-way for later use in repairing drains that might be damaged by severe rainstorms.	(2) Begins with a word that telegraphs the refusal before any reasons are given. Employs the negative "unable" and the condescending "grant." (3) Hides behind policy. (4) Follows an unpleasant thought with "furthermore" which suggests that another unpleasant thought is to follow. Leads into the reason, which should have been given earlier. (5) Presents the reason, which by now may be unimportant to the reader because the refusal has been made already.
(6) We do hope you will understand our position and that you can find some rock that will be suitable for your wall.	(6) Seems polite, but also serves as a parting reminder of the disappointment.

What is wrong with giving company policy as a reason for refusing?

Why should we avoid using the sentence "We hope you will understand our position"?

Those who write letters like this probably think they are being considerate and tactful. After all, they have said that the refusal was "unfortunate," they have expressed hope that their position would be understood, and they have wished the receiver good luck in finding a solution to the problem. Some people may find the letter adequate; it does communicate. Is the following version, which incorporates some of the principles of good refusal letters, an improvement?

(1) The rocks on the Turnpike right-of-way were left there at the	(1) Employs a neutral beginning, which identifies the subject of the letter and

suggestion of Commission engineers. (2) When the Turnpike was completed, the Commission had plans for future drainage improvement and repair. (3) They foresaw that some rocks on the right-of-way would be useful when flash floods hit the drainage ditches in the Kaywood area.

leads into a discussion of the reasons behind the refusal. (2) Suggests the purpose for which the rocks are to be used.
(3) Presents the specific reason for the rocks and leads the receiver to expect the refusal that follows.

(4) Since the last three years have been very dry, little repair work has been necessary; but we think we should keep the rocks as insurance against heavy spring rains, which occasionally come to this area.

(4) Leads from the reasons into a statement of the refusal. Employs a long, complex sentence to de-emphasize the negative.

(5) Wishing I could contribute to your construction plans, I called Mr. Bill Watson at Watson Supply (347 West Walnut). (6) He sees some possibilities and would be glad to talk with you about them.

(5) and (6) Offer an alternative that could lead to a solution of the problem.

Why should we avoid alluding to the refusal in the last paragraph?

This inductive outline has the following advantages: it de-emphasizes unpleasant ideas, it emphasizes reasons for a decision, it reduces the possibility that reasons will be skipped in reading, and it decreases the possibility of negative reaction.

SUMMARY

From the original letters and their rewritten versions, we can see that all "no" letters have several characteristics in common. Adjustment refusals, credit refusals, order refusals, favor refusals all follow the same basic plan:

1. They begin with an agreement or a neutral statement.

2. They present the reasons behind a refusal before presenting the refusal.

3. They present the refusal without emphasizing it.

4. They include an alternative if appropriate.

5. They end on a pleasant or neutral note.

EXERCISES

Review Questions

1. List the objectives of a refusal letter.

2. List the four-point outline that is recommended for letters that present negative information.

3. What would be the disadvantage of saving the last sentence for conveying a statement of refusal?

4. As a first sentence, "Your letter of June 12 has been received" is neutral. It neither states bad news nor leads a reader to expect good news, but why should such a sentence not be used?

5. What would be the disadvantage of stating a refusal in the first sentence?

6. Under what conditions do you think refusing in the first sentence would be justified?

7. Which is more likely to be harmful to human relations—(a) presenting bad news in the first sentence, or (b) presenting explanations first and risking a reader's impatience? Explain.

8. In an inductive letter, how can a writer decrease the likelihood that a reader will experience impatience?

9. Should negative language be used for conveying negative ideas? Explain.

10. In a letter that conveys negative information, why is "However" a poor word to use as the beginning of the second sentence?

11. Which would be better for conveying a refusal—active voice or passive voice?

12. Which type of sentence is better for stating a refusal—simple sentence or complex sentence?

13. If a refusal is stated in a complex sentence, which is better? (a) State it in the dependent clause, or (b) State it in the independent clause.

14. In the explanations portion of a refusal, which is preferred—second person or third person?

15. State an advantage and a disadvantage of presenting a refusal in the subjunctive mood.

16. In adjustment letters, how do resale and sales-promotional material assist in promoting human relations?

17. Is "company policy" a good word to use in an explanation? Explain.

18. In a letter that refuses a request for an adjustment, should a writer apologize for the action taken? Explain.

19. Why should writers avoid ending with "If you have any further questions, please do not hesitate to write"?

20. In a letter that refuses credit, should the receiver be given an explanation? Why?

21. In a letter that refuses a request for a favor, what is wrong with "I am sure you can understand my position."

Letter-Writing Problems

1. Assume you were president of your senior class in high school. For the five-year reunion of the class, you have been invited to serve as master of ceremonies for a banquet. You cannot accept; the banquet is being held during the two-week period in which you will be in Europe on a business trip. Ruth Massey, 1111 Hawthorn Street, Houston, MO 65483.

2. As the one in charge of next fall's homecoming festivities, you have received a request from Charley Loud. After his graduation two years ago, he formed a music group and has had some success and publicity throughout the area. He offers to provide the music for the dance. You are not altogether wild about his music. Besides, his request was late for consideration; just last week, arrangements were completed with another group. Respond to his letter. Mr. Charley Loud, 478 Kings Street, Westbrook, ND 89114.

3. When George Smith quit his job as a reporter on your newspaper last year, you encouraged him to stay. To get a job in another state, he asked that you write a letter of recommendation for him. You wrote a strong one. Now, you have a letter from him asking for his job back. This year, you cannot afford to add another reporter, and the woman who replaced him is outstanding. You must write and reveal the bad news. Mr. George Smith, 9014 S. Pine Street, Southwood, IL 58112.

4. When the Southtown Drug store bought Halloween candy, it overestimated the amount that could be sold. The manager asked the wholesaler's representative about taking back the unsold portion. Not being satisfied with the representative's "no" answer, she wrote to the wholesale firm. Candy wrapped or packaged for special events is delivered to the store with special-colored forms. The forms (as well as catalogs of the wholesaler's merchandise) have vividly stated notices to the effect that the merchandise cannot be returned. As the wholesaler, write a refusal letter. Mr. John Baxter, Manager, Southtown Drug Store, 874 South First Street, Wells, IN 32117.

5. Mr. and Mrs. Edward Jones bought a couch that had been marked down from $400 to $120. Rather than pay delivery charges, they asked their son to haul it home for them in his truck. Upon delivery, two problems became apparent: a large stain on the back side and a spring on the bottom was not anchored. They called the store about the problem and learned the couch could not be returned. Neither would the store fix it free. Thinking a letter to the manager might get results, they wrote. The purpose of the sale had been to move out damaged merchandise or items from broken sets. Boldly displayed in the store were signs stating that the items were being sold on an "as is" basis and could not be returned. Tags attached to each item bore the same information. In refusing the request, you, as the manager, send the name and phone number of a small, independent operator who does good repair work. Mr. and Mrs. Edward Jones, 1133 E. Fourth Street, Alton, TN 45116.

6. You work for a firm that sells steel storage buildings, which buyers can assemble for themselves. As a manufacturer, you charge retail outlets approximately $125 per unit. Retailers get $200 or more for each unit. Hoping to save some money, someone has written a letter describing the unit wanted. A check for $140 was included (enough to pay for the unit, taxes, and shipping charges). As manufacturer, you are not in the retail business and don't want to be. Involvement in direct sales to consumers would take too much time and attention away from your primary concern — manufacturing. As specialists in their work, retailers can give consumers the attention and special assistance they deserve. The gambrel-style roof and channel-steel support beams are outstanding features of the unit ordered. Compared with buildings made by competing firms, the unit has more overhead storage space. (The letter you are about to write can be saved and adapted for use as a form letter, which can be recalled from the word-processing equipment when such a letter is needed again.) Included with the letter is a list of names and addresses of retailers who sell the buildings you manufacture. Mr. Melford Smith, 781 S. Oak Street, Woodland, CA 89412.

7. You work at the home office of a publishing company. Today, you received a letter from a student who is using an atlas purchased as a required book for a geography class. As a reference book, it has relatively infrequent use; but after the first month of the semester, the binding is coming loose. The student requests a new book or a check for the purchase price, $21.95. Instead of writing to the publisher, the student should have taken the atlas to the bookstore from which he purchased it. If the book was purchased new from the university's bookstore and was in the first semester of use, the bookstore would be authorized to replace it or give the customer a refund; the bookstore would be reimbursed by the publisher. Mr. Tom Collins, Dorm A, Room 221, City University, Junction City, GA 23145.

8. You are the dean of a business college. Today, you received a long questionnaire designed by a graduate student. Its stated purpose is to get confidential information that would assist in contrasting curricular requirements of AACSB schools with curricular requirements of non-AACSB schools. The American Association of Collegiate Schools of Business (an accrediting body that holds its members to very high standards) long ago adopted some strict rules about the type of research that could be done among its members. Earlier, members had been bombarded with so much research (of varying degrees of respectability) that administrators were spending too much time in filling out questionnaires. And some erroneous conclusions found their way into print. Apparently, the student did not know about the AACSB restriction. Write a letter of explanation for refusing to cooperate. Mr. Dan Edwards, 489 East First Street, Hall Town, MO 37149.

9.   As a college professor, you are the advisor for twenty students. Today, a letter came from an advisee's parent. It requested that you sign a "good student" form—a form that would, if properly signed and returned to the insurance company, reduce an insurance premium by $70. To qualify for the reduction, a student must have earned a B average or higher on the grade report from the preceding semester. Because the student's average for the preceding semester was a C—, you cannot sign. The parent's letter had pointed out that insurance firms "don't check out the facts anyway" and that a signature would be very much appreciated. Because of obligations to yourself, your advisee, the school, and the insurance company, you must return the form unsigned. Mr. Sam Smith, 789 West Elm Street, Common City, SD 56491.

10.   You are the personnel director for a large firm. For certain types of training, you encourage employees to enroll in night classes at a local university. For students who earn an A, the firm pays 100 percent of the tuition; for a B, 75 percent; for a C, 50 percent. For lower grades, no reimbursement is allowed. One employee has completed a course and written a memorandum requesting full reimbursement. His grade was a C. Write a memorandum that explains and refuses. Bill White, Purchasing Department.

11.   You own some professional buildings across the street from a church. Most of the tenants are lawyers and dentists; their offices are normally closed on Sunday. Some church members have been parking in the lot you have provided for tenants and their clients. The pastor has requested written permission for use of the parking lot on Sundays. He prefers that permission be granted as a favor to the church, but he would be willing to rent the lot on Sundays for a reasonable fee. Checking into the possibility of allowing church-member parking, you discover that doing so would result in an insurance premium that would far exceed the cost of a reasonable rent fee. The request must be refused. Reverend Vernon White, West Avenue Community Church, 684 West Avenue, Pinewood, SC 13479.

12.   You have been commissioned by a manufacturer of large earth-moving equipment to do some research. Specific objective: develop a laser-beam instrument that can be attached to grading machines used to level ground for irrigation purposes. Such an instrument could greatly simplify the process of leveling ground and thus increase efficiency and reduce costs. Having heard of your research project, a student has written to ask what you have learned thus far. You have made progress, but your results are to be reported only to the firm that is financing the research. The request must be refused. Mr. Ward Jones, 314 Wing A, Thomas Hall, City University, Chalmer, AZ 85343.

13.   You have been asked to serve as next year's president of a civic club. It meets twenty-five times per year. Last year, other obligations kept you from attending seven of those meetings; prospects don't look any better this year. You would be very willing to take the responsibility, but you know the job is important enough to receive more attention than you could give. Decline. Marve Mitchell, 619 Downey Street, Cedar Top, IN 23189.

14.   You own and operate a small retail store that sells Oriental furniture. In addition to selling items directly from the store, you take orders for merchandise that customers have selected from a catalog. Customers who order from the catalog are attracted by the lower price, but they realize the product delivered may not be exactly as envisioned. The waiting period for delivery can be many months. At the time an order is placed, you point out that customers are responsible for paying import duties upon delivery. Before sending the order, you collect in full for the items ordered and for the transportation charges. Your receipt bears a statement that import duties are to be paid by the customer at the time of delivery. In today's mail is a letter to which is attached a statement for $36.19 — the duty paid when an item was delivered. According to the letter, payment had been made in full and the charge (if valid at all) is not the purchaser's responsibility. A refund is requested. Write a denial. Mr. Edward Brown, 784 W. Jackson Street, Pocatello ID 84435.

15.   You own and manage a swimming-pool-supply store. You provide service, as well as supplies and repair parts. After testing a sample of the water brought in by a customer, you recommended that the pool be drained — the only way to rid the pool of excess stabilizer. Since draining would be a twenty-four-hour process, you were afraid the top portion of the pool sides would crack from exposure to dry air. As a precautionary measure, you recommended that the pool owner spray the exposed pool sides with a hose every half hour while the pool was draining. After the pool was refilled, the pool light shorted. Your charge for the new light and the service call was $96. Your service man told the customer what had happened. Turning the light on for nighttime spraying of the walls (when water had subsided below the light) had caused the bulb to overheat. The owner paid the service man in full, but later you receive a letter requesting a refund. The reason: you recommended that the walls be sprayed and spraying caused the light to burn out. Write a refusal. Mr. Bill Smith, 316 E. Fairmont, Rock Ledge, NM 73681.

16.   You are the credit manager for a major oil company. A student who is under the legal age has applied for a gasoline credit card. The application must be rejected. The student can either (1) reapply after reaching the legal age or (2) ask an adult to sign a form guaranteeing that charges against the account will be paid. The form will be included with your letter. A copy of the letter is to be stored in the memory of the automatic typewriter, where it can be recalled quickly and addressed to other youngsters who have a similar problem. A touch of resale on your products or service would be appropriate for inclusion in the letter. Mr. Gary Williams, 163 N. 21st Street, Cotton Grove, LA 34775.

17.   You are the credit manager for a manufacturer-distributor of sports equipment. The proprietor of a small retail store seeks permission to make credit purchases. Although her financial statements appear to justify credit purchases, other reports list her as negligent about meeting payment deadlines. Perhaps a little resale and sales-promotional material would assist in getting her business on a cash basis, but her credit-purchase request is to be declined. Ms. Lida Rinehart, 684 East Broadway, Elmwood, NV 91342.

18. You are a real estate agent. When Mr. I. B. Cheap decided to sell one house and buy another, you (1) sold his house for $10,000 more than he had at first planned to ask, and (2) arranged to get the house he wanted for $5,000 less than its seller originally asked. Since he had to give possession of his old house three weeks before he got possession of his new house, you let him move into one of your vacant houses for three weeks without charge. A problem arose, however, when movers were moving the original owner's possessions from the house Mr. Cheap bought. With the temperature 112 degrees and the entry door standing open to accommodate movers, the refrigeration unit ran constantly. By the time Cheap moved in, the unit was burned out and he was burned up. After he called, you sent a service man to replace the electric motor. Later, when the statement of charges ($200) arrived, Cheap mailed it to you with a note that it was your responsibility. Though he may have some legal grounds to expect payment, you think he should be willing to pay the bill. Write a denial. Mr. I. B. Cheap, 317 North Ash, Gila Corner, AZ 85304.

19. You own and operate a retail store that sells small electric motors. Mr. Ben Wood bought a 2.5-horsepower motor for use on the filtering system of his swimming pool. Before the purchase, you reviewed his figures on pipe size and distance from the pool. You told him candidly that the 2.5 horsepower size was too small for his needs, that his motor needed to be at least 3.5 horsepower, and that if he chose the 2.5 size the normal guarantee would not apply. On the sales ticket, you wrote "3.5 size recommended." When the motor burned out ten weeks later, he called to discuss exchange under terms of the guarantee. Not satisfied with the phone conversation, he wrote a letter requesting permission to bring the motor in for exchange. Permission is to be denied. Mr. Ben Wood, 4513 East Colton Street, West View, NM 79316.

20. You are the chairperson of a school standards committee. Cal West is a former student who has just been denied permission to re-enroll. In his last semester, he devoted twenty-five hours per week to a part-time job, took four three-hour courses, and earned a semester's grade index of 1.5 (on a scale in which 1 is a D and 4 is an A). After being out of school for one semester, he applied again for admission. Upon readmission, he had hoped to continue working twenty-five hours per week and attend four three-hour courses. On the application form, he stated he was confident of success this time because he had had a change of attitude. The committee thought his chances for success upon readmission were very slim. Aptitude test scores were no better than average; but, if he were ever to be eligible for graduation, he would have to make better-than-average grades. In major universities, the rule of thumb is that for every hour spent in class two hours should be spent in preparation. Adding twelve hours of class time, twenty-four hours of study time, and twenty-five hours on the job, you see that Cal is headed for at least a sixty-one-hour week. Because another attempt would probably mean another failure, readmission is denied. If he could either enroll for fewer courses or work fewer hours, his application would be reconsidered. Mr. Cal West, 671 N. 3rd Avenue, Glenwood, OK 38742.

WRITING TO PERSUADE

Getting Ready
Knowing the Product
Knowing the Reader
Knowing the Desired Action
Some Principles
Using an Attention Getter
Starting with the Product
Focusing on a Central Selling
  Feature
Addressing the Reader's Needs
Getting the Reader's Interest
Using an Original Approach
Keeping It Short
Introducing the Product
Being Natural
Being Action Oriented
Stressing the Central Selling Point
Presenting Convincing Evidence
Emphasizing the Central Selling
  Point
Using Concrete Language
Being Objective

Interpreting Statements
Talking About Price
Giving Evidence
Using Enclosures
Using Testimonials
Offering a Guarantee
Motivating Action
Writing a Complete Sales Letter
**Writing a Persuasive Request for
  Action**
Writing a Persuasive Claim
Asking a Favor
Writing Collection Letters
The Collection Series
Form Letters
Collection-Related Letters
The Language of Collection
  Letters
**Collection by Telephone and
  Telegram**
Summary

The letters previously discussed were designed to convey information or to get action. Some were designed to do both. Letters in this chapter are designed to get action, but they differ from previously discussed action-getting letters. The difference results from the circumstances surrounding the action desired.

In letters that contain orders, requests for information, or requests for adjustments, the assumption is that the reader will be willing to take the desired action once it is identified. For example, a supplier who has shipped the wrong merchandise will almost certainly want to correct the error. Explaining *why* the correction should be made is hardly necessary.

Sometimes, however, we must ask for action when the proposal will probably be rejected unless we show *why* it should be accepted. For example, we can hardly expect people to accept our proposal that they buy a product if our letter does not reveal *why* doing so would be beneficial. We can hardly expect business executives to provide classified information about their businesses without some preliminary explanation and assurance. Letters that involve these conditions are called *persuasive* letters. They are designed to provide readers with sufficient information to make them want to take the desired action.

When is persuasion necessary?

Persuasive letters, then, are sales letters: they *sell* a product or an idea. But, for various reasons, readers can be expected to resist taking the desired action:

Why might proposals be resisted?

1. Readers may (when our letter arrives) be thinking about something else. They may not want to consider another proposal. Also, they may have been expecting another message and thus find our letter disappointing. Therefore, our very first sentence will have to succeed in *getting attention*—in generating willingness to read.

2. Readers may sense no need for (or interest in) the proposal. They may be perfectly satisfied with circumstances as they are. A new idea may require changes in routine, a new product may not seem needed when an old one is apparently satisfactory—these thoughts may be distasteful. Therefore, the first sentences must have an interesting way of *introducing the proposal.*

3. Readers may resist (or choose to ignore) supporting evidence. They may not care about the proposal. They may have considered the proposal (or a similar one) before and have already made up their minds. They may not appreciate any additional information. They would only be interested in the proposal if they could identify *specific* reasons why acceptance would be beneficial to them. Unsupported generalizations and high-pressure talk will almost surely fail to persuade someone to do what is asked. Therefore, the sales letter must concentrate on *providing sufficient evidence* to convince readers of the proposal's merits.

4. Readers may agree that the proposal is good but then ignore it. They may be habitual procrastinators, or they may not bother to take action unless they are told exactly what to do. Therefore, the sales message closes by *encouraging action* on the part of the reader.

The preceding barriers to persuasive communication apply regardless of whether the letter attempts to sell a product or an idea and thus evoke action favorable to the writer. When the purpose is to get cooperation from others, preliminary planning is especially important.

GETTING READY

Before composing a sales letter, you need to know (1) the product and how it differs from competing products, (2) something about the people to whom the letters are to be directed, (3) the specific action wanted, and (4) the principles of sales-letter composition.

Knowing the Product

You cannot be satisfied with knowing the product in a general way; you need details. Get your information by (1) reading all available literature, (2) using the product and comparing it with others, (3) conducting tests and experiments, (4) watching others use the product, (5) observing the manufacturing process, and (6) soliciting reports from users. Before you write, you need concrete answers to such questions as these:

What questions must be answered before writing a sales letter?

1. What will the product do for people?

2. From what materials is it made?

3. By what process is it manufactured?

4. What are its superior features in design and workmanship?

5. What is its price?

6. What kind of servicing, if any, will it require?

Answers to these questions about the product are not enough; similar questions must be answered about competing products. Of particular importance is the question, "What is the major difference?" People are inclined to choose an item that has some advantage not available in a similar item at the same price. For example, some people may choose a brand of bread because it is made from a formula developed by fourteenth-century monks; others may choose bread because it contains no preservatives; and still others may choose bread because it is wrapped in two-layer paper.

Why is the major difference so important?

Knowing the Reader

Envision yourself as the person receiving the letter.

Is a sales letter to be written and addressed to an individual?[1] Or is it directed to a group? If it is addressed to a group, what characteristics do the members have in

1. See Albert J. Sullivan, "How to Write Your Next Sales Letter," *Printers' Ink*, 235 (June 22, 1951): 37–38.

common? What are their common goals, their occupational levels, their educational status? Formulating answers to these questions helps prepare you for effective composition.

Knowing the Desired Action

What do you want your reader to do? Fill out an order form and enclose a personal check? Return a card requesting a representative to call? Write for more information? Whatever the desired action, you need to have a clear definition of it before beginning to compose the letter.

Some Principles

The principles of unity, coherence, and emphasis are just as important in sales letters as in other letters. In addition, some other principles seem to be especially helpful in sales letters:

Return to Chapter 5 for a quick review of coherence and emphasis.

1. *Use concrete nouns and active verbs.* Concrete nouns and active verbs help readers see the product and its benefits more vividly than do abstract nouns and passive verbs.

2. *Use specific language.* General words seem to imply subjectivity unless they are well supported with specifics. Specific language is space consuming (saying that something is "great" is less space consuming than telling what makes it so); therefore, sales letters are usually longer than other letters. Still, sales letters need to be concise—they should say what needs to be said without wasting words.

Why are sales letters usually longer than other letters?

3. *Let readers have the spotlight.* If readers are made the subject of some of the sentences, if they can visualize themselves with the product in their hands, if they can get the feel of using it for enjoyment or to solve problems, the chances of creating a desire are increased.

4. *Stress a central selling point.* Few products have everything. A thorough product analysis will ordinarily reveal some feature that is different from the features of competing products. This point of difference can be developed into a theme that permeates the entire letter. Or, instead of using a point of difference as a central selling point, a writer may choose to stress one of the major satisfactions derived from using the item. A central selling point (*theme*) should be introduced early in the letter and should be reinforced throughout the remainder.

What is a central selling point?

5. *Use an inductive outline.* Over 75 years ago, Sherwin Cody summarized the basic steps in the selling process.[2] The steps have been varied somewhat and have had different labels, but the fundamentals remain relatively unchanged. The selling procedure includes four steps:

2. Sherwin Cody, *Success in Letter Writing, Business and Social* (Chicago: A. C. McClurg, 1906), pp. 122–126.

What are the four steps in the selling procedure?

a. getting the prospect's attention
b. introducing the product and arousing interest in it
c. presenting convincing evidence
d. encouraging action

All these steps are necessary in unsolicited sales letters.

Why are unsolicited sales letters more difficult to write than solicited sales letters?

Unsolicited sales letters differ from solicited sales letters in that the latter have been invited by the prospect; the former have not. For example, a letter written to answer a prospect's questions is a *solicited* letter; a letter written to someone who has not invited it is *unsolicited.*

Someone who has invited a sales message has given some attention to the product already; an attention-getting sentence is hardly essential. Such a sentence is essential, however, when the recipient is not known to have previously expressed an interest. The very first sentence, then, is deliberately designed to make a recipient put aside other thoughts and concentrate on the rest of the message.

USING AN ATTENTION GETTER

Why is the first sentence exceedingly important?

Various techniques have been successful for getting recipients to put aside whatever they are doing or thinking about and consider an unsolicited letter. Some commonly used methods·

(1) A ball-point that writes every time!	(1) A solution to a problem.
(2) Top-quality cigars at $14.89 a hundred!	(2) A bargain.
(3) A penny saved is a penny earned.	(3) A proverb.
(4) INCOME TAXES WILL GO UP 10 PERCENT, the papers are saying. You know what that means for those in our business.	(4) A news announcement.
(5) Our city spends more for alcohol than for education!	(5) An astonishing fact.
(6) It's "sale-ring" day at the local stockyards. Come along. Let's see what goes on.	(6) A story.
(7) "We have met the enemy and they are ours," cabled Commodore Perry. We get the same report from those who use our termite killer.	(7) A quote from a famous person.
(8) Whetstone--the Cadillac of sterling silverware!	(8) An analogy.

(9) What if the boss came to your desk and said, "We're going to increase production by 13 percent this week"?	(9) A what-if opening.
(10) Gasoline that will not knock! We have it.	(10) An outstanding feature of the product.
(11) A young sophomore approached his professor's desk at the end of the first class period of the semester and said, "Sir, I had this class last semester, but I flunked because the teacher was so brilliant. I think I can make an 'A' under you."	(11) An interesting anecdote.
(12) Why does Oriental wool make the best carpets?	(12) A question.
(13) Feel the piece of gingham attached to this letter. Notice. . . .	(13) A comment on an attached gadget.
(14) Here's a silver-plated spoon for your new baby. Accept it with our sincere compliments.	(14) A gift.
(15) The Latest Summer Styles Have Just Arrived Today, Mr. Smith:	(15) A fake inside address. (These lines would be arranged in the inside-address position, getting attention by location.)
(16) You should see. . . .	(16) A split sentence.

how easy it is to operate a tractor with power steering.

Regardless of the attention-getting technique we choose for any letter, we should ask ourselves some pertinent questions: (1) Is the attention getter related to the product and its virtues? (2) Does the first sentence introduce a central selling feature? (3) Is the attention getter addressed to the reader's needs? (4) Does the attention getter sound interesting? (5) Is the attention getter original? (6) Is the first paragraph short?

What are some characteristics of a good attention getter?

Starting with the Product

The beginning sentence must suggest a relationship between recipient and product. It must pave the way for the remainder of the sales letter. The sentences that follow the first sentence should grow naturally from it. (See the discussion of coherence in

What might be the reader's reaction if the attention getter has no relationship to the product or its virtues?

Chapter 5.) If readers do not see the relationship between the first sentences and the sales appeal, they may react negatively to the whole message — they may think they have been tricked into reading.

Ordinarily, we have no difficulty in thinking of some way to get attention. But the main problem is getting attention in an appropriate manner. Is the following attention getter related to the product and its virtues?

> Would you like to make a million?
> We wish we knew how, but we do know how to make you <u>feel</u> like a million. Have you tried our latest mentholated shaving cream?

The beginning sentence is short and, being a question, it's emphatic. But it suggests that the remainder of the letter will be about how to make a million, which it is not. All three sentences combined suggest that the writer is using high-pressure techniques. Since the mentholated cream does have virtues and these virtues are important, one of them could have been emphasized by placing it in the first sentence.

Focusing on a Central Selling Feature

Almost every product will in some respects be superior to the products of competitors. If it has no superior qualities intrinsically, we'll have to supply them extrinsically — favorable price, fast delivery, superior service. But we must emphasize a major selling point. As we've already learned, one of the most effective ways to emphasize a point is by position. An outstanding feature mentioned in the middle of a letter may go unnoticed, but put it in the first sentence and it will stand out. Notice how the following sentence introduces the central selling feature and leads naturally into the sentences that follow:

> Your <u>Gazette</u> delivery boy brings your paper at almost exactly the same time every day. You can almost set your watch by him.
> And the news stories are just as timely as he is punctual. For example. . . .

What is an advantage of introducing the central selling point in the first sentence?

Addressing the Reader's Needs

Few people will buy just because doing so will solve a problem for someone else. How would an office manager react to the following sales opening?

> We have just introduced a mechanical device that is selling faster than any of our other copy holders.

Why should you be more frequently used than I or me?

Would the manager really care about what *we* have just done? Numerous sales may be of interest to the writer, but readers are more interested in what's helpful to them.

Getting the Reader's Interest

Not only must the first sentence capture attention, it should generate a genuine interest. It must whet the appetite for more. The beginning that emphasizes the writer's needs is perhaps the only beginning more boring than the lecture:

> Experience has shown that a good duplicating machine should give easy-to-read copies, be easy to operate, and last for ten years or more. Let's examine the factual history of the Diplifax.

A statement of fact may not be particularly interesting if it is not an astonishing fact. And, if a statement is too elementary, it will offend. To express a simple thought that anyone would know is to say between the lines, "I don't think you are very intelligent."

Why should you avoid direct statements of commonly known facts?

Using an Original Approach

All the preceding attention-getting devices (and others, too) are useful. We can use any one of them without being copyists. For example, beginning a sales letter with an anecdote is all right, but we should not use one with which many people are already familiar. Good sales writing often shows in the very first sentence how a product can solve a reader's problem. However, when mentioning the feature, don't use the same peculiar combination of words other people are known to use. That's bad sales technique; it's also poor composition. People like to read something new and fresh; it gets their attention and interest. And writers should enjoy creating something new.

Keeping It Short

The spaces between paragraphs serve three purposes: (1) They show the dividing place between ideas. (2) They improve appearance. (3) They provide convenient resting places for the eyes. What is your psychological reaction to a fifteen-line paragraph? Doesn't the reading of it appear to be an arduous physical and mental chore?

A reader is encouraged to take that first step if it's a short one. If possible, hold the first paragraph to three or fewer lines. A one-line paragraph (even if a very short line) is perfectly acceptable. You can even use paragraphs less than one sentence long! Put four or five words on the first line and complete the sentence in a new paragraph. Of course, be careful to include key attention-getting words that either introduce the product or lead to its introduction.

Why should the first paragraph be short?

INTRODUCING THE PRODUCT

What are some
suggestions for
introducing the product?

Of all the possible ways to begin a sales letter, perhaps the most dependable is one that makes the reader think, "Here's a solution to one of my problems," or, "Here's something I can use." We may lead the addressee to this thought by introducing the product in the very first sentence. If we do, we've succeeded in both getting attention and arousing interest in one sentence. Good sales writing does not require that we have separate sentences and paragraphs for each phase of the letter — getting attention, introducing the product, giving evidence, and stimulating action. To follow such a plan would be to place our writing style in a straitjacket. But, if our introduction of the product is effective, we need affirmative answers to the following questions: (1) Is the introduction natural? (2) Is the introduction action centered? (3) Does the introduction stress a central selling point?

Being Natural

If the attention getter does not introduce the product, it should lead naturally to that introduction. One sentence should grow naturally from another. Notice the abrupt change in thought in the following example:

> Strained eyes affect human relationships.
> The Westview Association of Office Managers has been conducting a survey for the last six months. Their primary aim is to improve lighting conditions.

"Strained eyes" as first words of the first sentence are related to "lighting conditions"—the last words of the third sentence. But the thoughts are too far apart. No word or phrase in the first sentence is readily identified with the words of the second sentence. The abrupt change in thought is confusing. The writer may have sought diligently for an attention getter; this one is not particularly related to the sales message that follows. Has the relationship between the two sentences been improved in the second example?

> Strained eyes affect human relationships.
> That's one thing the Westview Association of Office Managers learned from their six-month survey of office lighting conditions. For light that is easy on the eyes, they're switching to BA's Kold Kathode. When you flip on your Kold Kathode lights, you get. . . .

The second sentence is tied to the first by the word "that's." The "light" of the third sentence refers to the "lighting" of the second. And the Kold Kathode is introduced as a solution to the problem of strained eyes.

Being Action Oriented

If we want to introduce our product in an interesting way, we won't simply bring it into the view of the reader and begin describing it. Remember, active voice is more emphatic than passive voice. Action is eye catching—it holds attention and interest more readily than does description. Remember, too, we normally expect *people* to act and *things* to be acted upon.

Why should you concentrate on action instead of description?

Place the product in your readers' hands and talk about their using it. They will get a clearer picture when they read about something happening than when they read a product description. And the picture is all the more vivid when the recipient is the hero of the story—the person taking the action. If we put readers to work using our product to solve problems, they will be the subject of most of our sentences.

A small amount of product description is necessary and natural; but too many sales writers overdo it, as in the following excerpt:

This 8mm projector is housed in a die-cast aluminum case. It has a 750-watt bulb, tilt-control knob, and easy-to-use, swing-out film gate.

See how each sentence has a *thing* as the subject. We're looking at a still picture. Now let's turn on the action. Let's let a *person* be the subject and watch that person *do* something with our projector.

Lift this projector. See how easy it is? That's because of the lightweight aluminum case. Now, swing the film gate open and insert the film. All you have to do is keep the film in front of the groove embossed on the frame. See how easily you can turn the tilt-control knob for raising or lowering your pictures on the screen. And notice the clear, sharp pictures you get because of the powerful 750-watt projection bulb.

In a sense, we don't sell products—we sell what they will do. We sell the pleasure people derive from the use of a product. Logically, then, we have to write more about that use than we do about the product.

Stressing the Central Selling Point

If the attention getter doesn't introduce a distinctive feature, it should lead to it. We can stress important points by position and by space. As soon as readers visualize our product, they need to have attention called to its outstanding features; the features are therefore emphasized because they are mentioned first. And if we are to devote much space to the outstanding features, we have to introduce them early. Notice how the attention getter introduces the distinctive selling feature (ease of operation) and how the following sentences keep the reader's eyes focused on that feature:

Your child can show vivid motion pictures of this year's birthday party — and from a projector so <u>easy to operate</u> that your child can do it easily.

Watch your child lift the Vido projector. See how <u>easy</u>? We kept the weight down to eight pounds by using an all-aluminum case. Let the youngster set it on a coffee table, chair, or kitchen table — <u>effortlessly</u>.

Now, swing the film gate open and insert the film. <u>All you have to do</u> is keep the film in front of the groove embossed on the frame. See how <u>easily you can turn</u> the tilt-control knob for raising or lowering your pictures on the screen. And notice the clear, sharp pictures you get because of the powerful 750-watt projection bulb.

Does stressing
one point mean
excluding other points?

By stressing one point, you do not limit the message to that point. For example, while *ease of operation* was being stressed, other features — tilt-control knob, swing-out film gate, 750-watt bulb — were mentioned. Just as a good film presents a star who is seen throughout most of the film, just as a good term paper presents a central idea that is supported throughout, just as a school yearbook employs a theme throughout, so should a sales letter stress a central selling point.

PRESENTING CONVINCING EVIDENCE

After we have made an interesting introduction to our product, we have to present enough supporting evidence to satisfy our reader's need. In presenting evidence, keep the following points in mind:

1. Continue to emphasize the central selling point.
2. Use specific, concrete language.
3. Be objective.
4. Interpret statements.
5. Talk convincingly about price.
6. Give experimental evidence.
7. Use enclosures to help convince.
8. Use testimonials and references.
9. Offer a guarantee or a free trial.

Emphasizing the Central Selling Point

We should keep one or two main features uppermost in the recipient's mind. When we present evidence, we should choose evidence that supports this feature or features. For example, it would be inconsistent to use appearance as an outstanding selling feature of compact cars while presenting abundant evidence to show economy of operation.

Using Concrete Language

Few people will believe us if we make general statements without supporting them with factual evidence. Saying a certain machine is efficient is not enough. We have to say *how we know* it's efficient and present some data to illustrate *how* efficient. Saying a piece of furniture is durable is not enough. Durability exists in varying degrees. We must present information that shows what makes it durable; we must also define *how* durable.

Why should we avoid unsupported generalities?

Especially in the convincing-evidence portion of the sales letter, we need all the information we have gathered about our product. We can establish durability, for example, by presenting information about the manufacturing process, the quality of the raw materials, the skill of the craftsworkers. For example,

Why are facts and figures important in the evidence section?

How can we guarantee your NCC carpet to last for 10 years? Because we use Oriental wool exclusively--every fiber of wool is at least 12 inches long. And the longer the raw wool, the greater the strength of the yarn. Count the number of knots per square inch. Our carpets have 400 knots in every square inch. Conventional carpets, which have an average life of about 5 years, have fewer than 100.

Evidence presented must not only *be* authentic; it must *sound* authentic, too. Facts and figures help. Talking about wool fibers of twelve inches and carpets with 400 knots to the square inch suggests the writer is well informed. These figures increase reader confidence. Figures are even more impressive if the reader can get some kind of internal verification of their accuracy. For example, the following paragraph not only presents figures, it gives their derivation:

We insulated 30 houses in Mesa last year. Before the insulation, we asked each homeowner to tell us the total fuel bill for the four coldest months--November, December, January, and February. The average cost was $408, or $102 a month. After insulation, we discovered the fuel bill for the same four-month period was $296, or $74 a month--a saving of $28 a month, or 25 percent.

Being Objective

We must use language that people will believe. Specific, concrete language makes letters sound authentic. Superlatives, exaggerations, flowery statements, unsupported claims, incomplete comparisons, and remarks suggesting certainty all make letters sound like high-pressure sales talk. And just one such sentence can destroy

What are some signs of subjectivity?

confidence in the whole letter. Examine the following statements to see whether they give convincing evidence. Would they make a reader want to buy? Or do they merely remind the reader of someone's desire to sell?

These are the best plastic pipes on the market today. They represent the very latest in chemical research.

The way to tell which pipes are best is to gather information about all pipes marketed and then choose the one with superior characteristics. We know that the writer here is likely to have a bias in favor of the product being sold. We don't know if the writer actually spent time researching other plastic pipes, and we also don't know if the writer would know how to evaluate this information. And, lastly, we certainly don't know if the writer knows enough about chemistry and chemical research to say truthfully what the very latest is.

Gardeners are turning handsprings in their excitement over our new weed killer!

Why should we avoid unsupported superlatives?

Really? Doesn't that statement seem preposterous? And, if we don't believe in the handsprings, can we believe in the weed killer?

Stretch those tired limbs out on one of our luscious water beds. It's like floating on a gentle dreamcloud on a warm, sunny afternoon. Ah, what soothing relaxation!

The adjectives in every sentence suggest subjectivity. Even though some people may be persuaded by such writing, many will see it as an attempt to inveigle them. Notice the incomplete comparison in the following example:

New Smoko cigarettes filter the smoke better.

Why are incomplete comparisons bad?

Better than what? Better than "old" Smoko cigarettes? Better than any other cigarette? Better than they would without a filter? We can't tell. And the writer of the sentence probably hoped we would conclude for ourselves that they filter better than any other cigarette. Instead of giving us a clear picture of what was meant, the writer has presented some generalities and hoped our imagination would supply a more colorful picture than the information justifies.

We are sure you will want to keep the whole box of cigars; but if after smoking five or six you decide to return the remainder, do so at our expense.

Can saying, "We are sure" actually arouse doubts?

Can the writer be sure? The mere provision for returning the cigars shows that the writer is *not* sure the recipient will want to keep the whole box.

Interpreting Statements

Naturally, your readers will be less familiar with the product and its uses than you will be. Not only do you have an obligation to give information, you should interpret it if interpretation is necessary. Point out how the information will benefit the reader. For example,

> And the new Karns refrigerator is frostproof as well as economical to operate.

Some prospects may not fully comprehend what "frostproof" means for them. If we make the most of this feature, we have to say *what* makes it frostproof and suggest *how* a frostproof refrigerator is superior to one that is not. The economy-of-operation feature need not have been introduced until the frostproof feature was fully exploited. The following revision interprets this feature:

Why should we bother to interpret statements?

> Open the door to the frozen-food compartment of your Karns. No frost anywhere--even if the door has been opened several times during the day. The moment you open the door, a small fan concealed in the back wall begins to circulate the air. The air isn't still long enough to deposit frozen particles of moisture. Take frozen strawberries or juice from the new Karns and open the cans without first having to remove frost.

The following excerpt from a sales letter uses a pocket calculator as the subject of the sentence. Notice, too, how it states dimensions in cold figures without interpretation:

> This calculator weighs 1 ounce. Its dimensions are 3 1/4 by 2 1/4 by 1/4 inches; and it comes in black, ivory, or turquoise.

In what respects is a 1-ounce unit superior to a 9-ounce one? Or is a 9-ounce unit actually better? If there is any advantage in having a calculator of these dimensions, what is it? What would be the disadvantage if it were twice as big?

Now see how interpretation makes the letter more convincing:

> Compare the weight of this calculator with the weight of a flashlight. The flashlight is probably heavier; the calculator weighs only 1 ounce! See how easily it fits inside a purse or jacket pocket. That's because its dimensions are 3 1/4 by 2 1/4 by 1/4 inches--only slightly bigger than a playing card.

The revision shows what the figures mean in terms of reader benefits. It also makes use of a valuable interpretative technique — the comparison. We can often make a point more convincing by comparing something unfamiliar with something familiar.

Since most people are familiar with the size of a playing card, they can now visualize the size of the calculator. The playing card comparison can also be used to interpret prices. For example, an insurance representative might write

The annual premium for this 20-year limited-payment policy is $219.00, or 60 cents a day--not much more than a cup of coffee.

Talking About Price

Most sales letters should mention price. They should either tell what the price is or say something to assure the reader that the price is not unreasonable. Logically, price should be introduced late in the letter—after most of the advantages have been discussed. Few people want to part with their money until they have been shown how they can benefit by doing so.

Why should we introduce price late in the letter?

People are inclined to react negatively to price. They may think it's too high, even when it is actually low. So we have to find ways to overcome price resistance. Here are some suggestions:

1. Introduce price only after having presented the product and its virtues.

2. Keep price talk out of the first and last paragraphs—unless, of course, price is the distinctive feature.

3. Mention price in a sentence that relates or summarizes the virtues of the product. In the sentence where price is mentioned, remind readers of what they get in return. The positive aspects (satisfaction from using the product) should be put beside the negative aspects (giving up money). If we have given convincing evidence, the positive features should remain uppermost in a recipient's mind; therefore, the emphasis is taken off the negative features.

Why should a complex sentence be used for stating price?

4. Mention price in a long, complex, or compound sentence.

5. Use figures to illustrate how enough money can be saved to pay for the expenditure. (For example, say that a $70 turbo-vent that saved $7 per month on summer electric bills would save approximately $70 in two 5-month summers, and that the vent would last for many summers.)

6. State price in terms of small units. (Twelve dollars a month sounds less than $144 a year.)

7. If practical, invite comparison of like products with similar features.

8. If facts and figures are available, use them to illustrate that the price is reasonable.

One letter, of course, probably wouldn't utilize all of these techniques for de-emphasizing price. The following excerpt shows how some of the techniques discussed can be applied.

After a few minutes' instruction, your office workers, too, can begin making perfect copies in six seconds or less; and, if you need 10 such copies a day, the $500 you spend for the machine can be saved in three months. Here are the figures. . . .

Giving Evidence

If we can present research evidence to support our statements, we have a good chance of convincing. For example,

Why should we introduce results of research?

We asked 100 farm laborers to wear our Worth white dress shirts for 60 days. We asked 100 other farm laborers to wear white dress shirts manufactured by Goodwear. Each night both groups of shirts were run through automatic washers and dryers, ironed, and supplied to the workers the next morning. After 60 days, only three Worth shirts had frayed cuffs and collars; 51 Goodwear shirts had frayed cuffs and collars. See the difference in the pictures on the enclosed folder.

Relating the experiment takes more space and time, but it is well worth the effort. Experimental facts are much more convincing than general remarks about the superior durability and appearance.

Using Enclosures

Ordinarily, the enclosure is less significant than the letter itself. The letter should make the recipient want to read the enclosure. Thus, the preferred technique is to refer to the enclosure late in the letter — only after the major portion of the evidence has been given. Since readers have already seen the enclosure, we should not call attention to it by saying "Enclosed you will find" or "We've enclosed a brochure." An enclosure is easily referred to in a sentence that also says something else:

Why should we avoid introducing the enclosure in the first paragraph?

Please compare the pictures on the enclosed folder.

Using Testimonials

If our product is really beneficial, some people are likely to report their satisfaction. If they don't write voluntarily, we can invite their comments through questionnaires or by attaching cards to the merchandise — cards the users are urged to fill out after they have used the merchandise for a certain time. One way to convince prospective customers that they will like our product is to give them concrete evidence that other people like it. Tell what others have said (with permission, of course) about your product's usefulness.

Offering a Guarantee

Guarantees and free trials convey both negative and positive connotations. By revealing willingness to refund money or exchange an unsatisfactory unit if necessary, a writer confesses a negative: purchase could be regretted or refused. However, the positive connotations are stronger than the negatives: The seller has a definite plan for ensuring that buyers get value for money spent. In addition, the seller exhibits willingness for the buyer to check a product personally and to compare it with others. The seller also implies confidence that a free trial will result in purchase and that a product will meet standards set in the guarantee. If terms of a guarantee are long or complex, they can be relegated to an enclosure.

Regardless of the kind of evidence we give, we give it for the purpose of motivating action.

Motivating Action

What are some characteristics of the action ending?

Our chances of getting action are increased if we (1) state the specific action wanted, (2) allude to the reward for taking action in the same sentence in which action is encouraged, (3) present the action as being easy to take, (4) provide some stimulus to quick action, and (5) ask confidently.

Mention the Specific Action Wanted

Whether the reader is to fill out an order blank and return it with a check, place a telephone call, or return an enclosed card, define the desired action in specific terms.

Allude to the Reward for Taking Action

Why should we allude to the reward for taking action?

For both psychological and logical reasons, readers are encouraged to act if they are reminded of the reward for acting. If our letter has been well written, we will have chosen a distinctive selling feature (the reward for using our product). We will have introduced it early—perhaps in the very first sentence; and we will have stressed it in the following paragraphs. The distinctive selling feature is the big idea we've tried to put across. We want it to stick in a recipient's mind. Thus we should also work it into our parting words—where it will be emphasized.

A distinctive selling feature is to a sales letter what a theme is to a speech. It's a thread of continuity running through every paragraph. A public speaker, for example, introduces a theme, follows it with analysis and interpretation, and ends with a final reference to the theme. A sales letter follows the same pattern. To end without a final reference to the selling feature (theme) would be like ending a speech without summarizing remarks. The picture must be complete. Something in the ending should remind the reader of the beginning and the middle.

Present Action as Being Easy to Take

People naturally hesitate to attempt something that is difficult or time consuming. Instead of asking readers to fill in their names and addresses on order forms or return cards and envelopes, do that work for them. If action is easy or consumes little time, they may act immediately; otherwise, they may procrastinate.

What is one way to reduce the likelihood of procrastination?

Provide a Stimulus to Quick Action

We want action, fast or slow; but we prefer fast action because it's more certain. The longer our reader waits to take action on our proposal, the dimmer our persuasive evidence will become. Reference to the central selling point (assuming it has been well received) helps to stimulate action. Here are some commonly used appeals for getting quick action:

1. Buy while present prices are still in effect.

2. Buy while the present supply lasts.

3. Buy before a certain date approaches — Christmas, Father's Day, the end of the season.

4. Buy now while a rebate is being offered.

5. Buy quickly to get product benefits quickly.

Prospects will not necessarily act because we tell them to act. The following expressions seem to shout *too* loudly for action:

Act today.

Do it now.

Don't delay.

Hurry, hurry, hurry.

Why wait?

Don't wait another minute.

Ask Confidently for Action

Sales writers who have a good product and have presented evidence well have a right to feel confident. Instead of "*If* you want to save time in cleaning, fill in and return . . . ," writers can demonstrate confidence in favorable action by stating "To save time in cleaning, fill in and return. . . ." Of course, writers will make a mistake if they sound overconfident. And conversely, statements suggesting lack of

Why should we avoid *hope* and *if* statements in the action ending?

confidence, such as "If you agree . . ." and "I *hope* you will . . . ," should be avoided. Between the lines, such thoughts convey, "I have some doubts about my product or my selling ability." If such doubts exist in the mind of the writer, they are generated in the mind of the reader.

For good appearance and proper emphasis, the last paragraph should be kept relatively short. Yet the last paragraph has a lot to do—it must suggest the specific action wanted, refer to the distinctive selling feature, present action as being easy to take, encourage quick action, and ask confidently. Observe how the following closing paragraph accomplishes these tasks:

(1) For perfect legal-document copies in six seconds or less,	(1) Final reference to the central selling feature.
(2) initial the enclosed order blank and mail it by January 1.	(2) Action made easy. Definite action defined.
(3) Those who order by January 1 will receive 1,000 free sheets of the specially treated copy paper.	(3) Stimulus to quick action.

The following version is an improvement because it places the central selling feature in the very last line:

Initial the enclosed order blank and mail it by January 1, and we'll ship you 1,000 free sheets of the specially treated copy paper along with the machine. And from now on, you'll get perfect copies of legal documents in six seconds or less.

Now that we have examined the major problems encountered in writing the various parts of sales letters, let's read and analyze some complete letters.

WRITING A COMPLETE SALES LETTER

The following letters illustrate the principles discussed in preceding pages. Although the improved examples may seem long, each can be typed on a single page of letterhead paper. Typically, sales letters are longer than letters that present routine information or convey good news. Specific details (essential in getting action) are space consuming.

The following sales letter is unsolicited:

(1) Will you take a few seconds to read this letter? (2) It describes a wonderful proposition I'm sure you will not want to miss.	(1) Begins by asking a small favor. Contains nothing to identify the subject of the letter. (2) Uses a *thing* as the subject of the sentence. Invites some skepticism by using *wonderful* and *I'm sure*.

(3) We want you to start taking the Gazette. (4) The Gazette is worth your money any way you look at it.

(3) Presents writer-centered introduction to the proposal. (4) Introduces the idea of parting with money before having given satisfactory reasons for doing so.

(5) The first page contains the very latest in news from home and abroad. (6) The editorial page contains interesting commentaries on local and international affairs. (7) You are sure to enjoy the sports page and the comic strip, which are featured daily.

(5) Describes the product instead of the satisfaction gained from using it. (6) Employs (once more) a sentence in which a *thing* is the subject. (7) Uses reader as subject of the sentence, but in this sentence doing so is risky. Recipient may not care for sports and comics.

(8) Each day the Gazette carries valuable coupons that can be applied on purchases at some of the local food stores. (9) In addition to saving you money in this way, the Gazette saves you time and effort through its Classified Ad section.

(8) Continues with the product as subject of the sentence. Gives no support for the general word "valuable." (9) Continues with product-centered sentence. Bringing "you" into the picture is commendable, however.

(10) Still another advantage of the Gazette is its prompt delivery. (11) Your paper will be delivered regularly at about 6:15 each evening.

(10) Uses an abstraction as subject of sentence—a technique that makes writing less vivid. (11) Employs another *thing* as subject of sentence. Doesn't say *why* prompt delivery is advantageous.

(12) The subscription price is only $7.

(12) Tends to emphasize price by placing it (a) in the last paragraph; (b) in a short, simple sentence; and (c) at the end of a sentence.

(13) Please return the enclosed card now so we can start delivering your paper this week. (14) Don't delay.

(13) Refers to action wanted, but the reference to action comes after the statement of price, not after a reminder of the good points of the paper. (14) Seeks quick action (in a negative way), but suggests pressure.

The following letter corrects some of the weaknesses in the preceding one. Observe how *punctual delivery*—the one feature in which the *Gazette* is different from other papers—has been developed as a central selling point.

(1) The person who delivers your Gazette will bring it at almost exactly the same time every day.

(1) Uses the central selling point as a device for getting attention and identifying the subject of the letter.

Identify the central selling point and notice how much stress is given to it.

(2) And the news stories are just as timely as he or she is punctual. (3) For example, you can read up-to-the-minute accounts of important local and national events less than two hours after they have occurred. (4) That's because we keep our news wires open right up to the four o'clock press time.

(5) When important news breaks just before press time, our skilled reporters and printers can arrange to include it in today's Gazette; you can read it this evening shortly after six o'clock. (6) Tomorrow at the same hour, you can begin reading about tomorrow's news.

(7) When you can depend on receiving your paper at the same time each day, reading it naturally becomes a habit—a habit that's easy to fit right into your regular routine of family living. (8) Whether you want a first-hand report of Washington affairs, a baseball or football score, or a local wedding, you can turn to the Gazette regularly.

(9) You can turn to the up-to-date Classified Ad section for anything you want to buy, rent, or locate. (10) In spite of the inviting front-page stories and the sports, society, and editorial pages, many people have told us they look first at the advertising--especially at the grocery sale ads featured daily. (11) They say the ads enable them to save many times the $7 monthly subscription rate. (12) For example, this week's Thursday paper will carry a coupon that lets you buy nationally advertised

What techniques are employed to keep price from seeming objectionable?

(2) Employs a sentence closely related to the first.
(3) Proceeds to give detail to support the idea of timeliness. Uses the reader as the subject of the sentence.
(4) Continues with additional detail to support the time theme.

(5) Gives more support for timeliness. Ties timeliness in with punctual delivery. Employs concrete nouns and action verbs.
(6) Further emphasizes the central selling point.

(7) Suggests an advantage of punctual delivery.
(8) Refers to features of the paper in a sentence in which the reader is the subject. "Regularly" serves as a reminder of the central selling point.

(9) Lets the reader take the paper in hand and use it to solve problems.
(10) Tells of additional features that make the *Gazette* a good paper to receive daily. "Daily" is a good word choice because it is related to the central selling point.
(11) Employs the pronoun "they" as a coherence device. After having presented most of the sales points, introduces price in a sentence that suggests a reward for paying the price. Subordinates price by presenting it in a long paragraph. (12) and (13) Give figures to support the idea of saving money.

instant coffee for $5.29 (regularly $5.59) and $1.59 frozen TV dinners for $1.39. (13) Similar coupons are featured daily.

(14) You can keep up with the local and national news as a matter of habit. (15) You can take advantage of local advertising as a matter of economy. (16) By subscribing in plenty of time to get Thursday's paper, you can save 60 cents on this week's grocery bill.

(14) Uses "habit" as a reminder of the central selling point.
(15) Seeks to summarize (as does 14) the advantages of subscribing.
(16) Follows the summary of advantages immediately with a mention of the action necessary to get them. Shows the reward for quick action.

(17) Please sign and return the enclosed card. (18) Your delivery girl or boy will then leave the Gazette on your steps around 6:15 each weekday evening. (19) Look at your clock when Thursday's paper comes; from now on you can expect to receive the Gazette at almost exactly the same time.

(17) Indicates the specific action desired. (18) and (19) Present a final reminder of the central selling point.

What are some characteristics of the action ending?

The following letter employs similar techniques of style and organization:

(1) When the doctor gives you instructions, how often have you thought, "I wish you had time to explain" or "On medical matters, I wish I were better informed"?

(1) Seeks to gain attention by introducing an experience the recipient has probably had. Presents "informed" as the central selling point.

(2) To inform people on such topics as home care of patients, first aid, or detection of illness, Medical Publishers is introducing the Handbook of Health.

(2) Introduces the product as a solution to a problem. Employs "inform" to achieve transition from the preceding sentence and to reinforce the central selling point.

(3) In it, you can read about symptoms before calling at the doctor's office. (4) Having done some reading first, you are informed--you have improved your chances for effective communication with your doctor.

(3) Begins presentation of evidence. Employs a pronoun for coherence with the preceding sentence. Uses reader as subject in an active-voice sentence. (4) through (11) Continue with presentation of evidence. Note especially that the reader is the subject of the sentences, the sentences are active, and "informed" receives considerable stress.

(5) From the Handbook of Health, you can become even better informed after calling at the doctor's office. (6) If the doctor used words unfamiliar to you, you can turn to the 3,000-word encyclopedia of medical terms that appears in the back of the book. (7) If you really don't understand why a certain treatment was recommended, just look it up. (8) Whether you want to be better informed on such topics as infectious diseases, skin disorders, pregnancy, laboratory tests, or operations, you can turn immediately to one of the handbook's 30 chapters. (9) You can read and understand quickly because each chapter author (a medical specialist in the subject discussed) took great care to write in language that intelligent, concerned patients can understand. (10) And for concrete illustrations of points discussed, you can see vivid diagrams and three-color pictures (more than 1,000 such illustrations appear in the 1,212-page Handbook). (11) See excerpts of sample pages on the enclosed sheets.

(12) Handbook of Health (which will keep you informed and able to converse easily with your physician) sells for $18--about 1 1/2 cents per page.

(12) Presents price in a sentence that reinforces the primary reward for paying that price.

(13) To get the informative Handbook of Health, you have but to initial the enclosed card (see instructions printed on it). (14) By mailing the card before March 1, you will also receive a complimentary copy of our 74-page booklet "Physical Fitness and You."

(13) and (14) Associate action with reward for taking action, identify specific action desired, make action easy, and reward quick action.

The preceding letters were designed for readers who were not expecting them. They needed an attention getter. But when sales letters are sent to recipients who have expressed an interest or made an inquiry, writers already have attention; they can begin quickly to give information. Aside from the attention getter, solicited and unsolicited sales letters employ the same pattern.

What is the difference between solicited and unsolicited sales letters?

In answering a series of questions about merchandise or services, a writer has a choice of answering questions in the order in which they were asked or in some other order. If the first and last questions are being answered affirmatively, the questions can best be answered in the order in which they were asked. However, if the first answer is negative, beginning with an immediate answer to it might risk placing too much emphasis on the negative. For maximum impact, answers should be arranged to begin and end with positive answers.

WRITING A PERSUASIVE REQUEST FOR ACTION

The purpose of the preceding letters was to sell products. Similar writing techniques are used when the purpose is to persuade someone to take action favorable to the writer. Typical among persuasive requests are claim letters and letters that request special favors.

Writing a Persuasive Claim

Claim letters are often routine since the basis for the claim is a guarantee or some other assurance that an adjustment will be made without need of persuasion. However, when an immediate remedy is doubtful, persuasion is necessary. In a typical large business, the claim letter is passed on to the claims adjuster for response.

In modern businesses, any reasonable claim will probably be adjusted to the customer's satisfaction. Therefore, venting strong displeasure in the claims letter is of little value. It can alienate the claims adjuster—the one person from whom cooperation is sought. Remember, adjusters are human beings, too. And very likely, they have had little or nothing to do with the manufacture and sale of the product. They did not create the need for the claim letter.

From the point of view of the claims adjuster, claims should be welcomed. Only a small percentage of claims are from cranks; the great bulk are from people who believe they have a legitimate complaint. The way in which the adjuster handles the claim determines, to a large extent, the goodwill of the company. For the adjuster, granting a claim is much easier than refusing it. Because saying "no" is one of the most difficult writing tasks, the writer of a persuasive claim letter has an advantage over the adjuster.

Why do businesses appreciate claim letters?

Notice how the following claim letter presents a sincere statement of the situation and appeals to the business character of the firm. The letter begins with a point on which the reader and writer can agree, presents an adequate description of the reason for the claim, reviews steps needed to remedy the cause, and relies on the letter's basic theme for the closing appeal:

> Your "customer satisfaction after the sale" advertising was one of the main reasons for my stopping in your showroom recently.
>
> On February 1, just one month ago, I purchased a new "factory-fresh" Cardinal from you, and it functioned well for two weeks. I followed the new-car breaking-in instructions to the letter and had little difficulty. But two weeks ago the front wheels developed a frightening vibration that forced me to bring the car to your shop for inspection.
>
> The service manager inspected the wheels, said the bushings had been damaged, and immediately had the old bushings replaced. Later that day, we tested the car together, and it worked satisfactorily. The service manager then asked me to sign the service slip indicating my willingness to pay the repair and parts charges of $115.75. In the discussion that followed, he stated that the bushings could not have been damaged by normal operation but only by careless driving over rough terrain. I refused to pay. He refused to make the bill "no charge." There the matter stood until today, when I received a bill from you for $115.75.
>
> Because I had not driven the car over rough terrain and had taken care of it during the breaking-in period, I can only conclude that the bushings were damaged in the 60 miles the car was driven before I purchased it. Perhaps the damage to the bushings occurred during demonstration trips by salespeople.
>
> Please write "no charge" on the attached bill, proving that your advertising is backed by the integrity you claim.

Knowledge of effective claim writing should never be used as a means of taking advantage of someone. Hiding an unjustifiable claim under a cloak of untrue statements is very difficult and strictly unethical. Adjusters are fair-minded people who will give the benefit of the doubt, but they are not give-away specialists who will satisfy a grumpy customer simply to avoid a problem. An ethical business follows the Golden Rule.

Asking a Favor

Occasionally, everyone has to ask someone else for a special favor — action for which there is not much reward, not much time, or not much inclination. Consider an invitation extended to a prominent person to be the speaker at a professional meeting. Assume that we have no money to offer. Will a deductive letter be successful? The following letter illustrates a direct request in what is really a persuasive-request situation:

(1) The Society of Real-Estate Appraisers will hold its annual seminar and dinner at the Tilton Hotel on May 23.

(1) Begins with an announcement that may be of little interest to the recipient.

What are some common errors in writing invitations?

(2) We would like very much to have you join us and be the principal speaker at the dinner meeting, which will begin at 7 p.m.

(2) Extends the invitation before letting the person see any reason for accepting.

(3) Spouses of the members will be guests at the dinner meeting; and we, of course, invite your spouse to attend. I'm sure your background and writing in the field of real estate will enable you to select a subject of interest to us.

(3) Fails to suggest a topic, but instead implies that the chosen topic might not be of interest to the group.

(4) Will you let me know promptly that your busy schedule will still enable you to accept our invitation?

(4) Risks refusal because "busy schedule" provides an excuse.

Now note the contrast between that letter and the one that follows:

(1) Your recent article "Are Appraisers Talking to Themselves?" in the Appraisal Journal has drawn many favorable comments from local real-estate appraisers.

(1) Begins on a point that is related and of interest to the receiver.

(2) The South-East Chapter of the Society of Real-Estate Appraisers, in particular, has felt a strong need for more information about appraisal report writing from the point of view of a specialist in real-estate education. About 200 members will be attending our annual seminar dinner meeting. They would be very glad to meet you, and they would be especially interested in hearing you discuss "Appraisal Report Writing."

(2) Presents details before making the request. Revealing membership enthusiasm for the topic before making the request helps to increase the reader's enthusiasm for the proposal.

What is the advantage of presenting some details before making the request?

(3) By accepting this invitation to be the featured speaker, you'll be able to assist the appraisal profes-

(3) Presents the invitation and attaches it to the advantages of acceptance.

sion. You'll also have the opportunity to meet several new members
of our group.

(4) Your spouse is also invited to be our guest at the meeting. It will be held at the Tilton Hotel on Thursday, May 23, at seven o'clock. We can promise you a pleasant evening and an attentive audience.	(4) Provides details that will be useful if he accepts.
(5) We would appreciate having, with your acceptance, one of your photographs for display purposes.	(5) Seeks specific action.

Note that the preceding letter employs an inductive approach. When a deductive approach is employed in a persuasive situation, chances of getting cooperation are minimal. For example, what might be a probable reaction to the following beginning sentence?

Will you please ship, without charge, one Quick-Master teaching machine and one program on office safety?

If the first sentence gets a negative reaction, a decision to refuse may be made instantly. Having said "no," the reader may not read the rest of the letter or may hold stubbornly to that decision in spite of a well-written persuasive argument that follows the opening sentence.

What outline should be used for a persuasive letter?

The following letter employs an inductive approach. (Note the extent to which it applies principles encountered earlier.)

Almost 70 people in our management-trainee program need to become familiar with your teaching machines and programed instruction.

Each year, a group of about 70 new employees enters the program. Eventually, they will assume positions of responsibility at the home offices or at branch offices throughout the country. Many will at some time be responsible for in-service training within their departments.

Their present training provides some instruction in safety, but not to the extent to which it would be treated in a teaching-machine unit. Many in the program have yet to see and use a teaching machine such as your Quick-Master, which was shown in the May 17 issue of Sunday Supplement. They need to learn from direct experience about its potential.

If they could actually use your Quick-Master, if they could come to appreciate the advantages of planned reinforcement and the feeling of accomplishment that accompanies a correct response, they could become real boosters of programed learning.

In return for the opportunity to acquaint this select group with Quick-Master, would you send a complimentary Quick-Master and the safety program? Every trainee would have opportunity to see it, use it, and become sold on its advantages for in-service training.

Your sending the machine and program will enable us to enrich our training and will get Quick-Master some well-deserved promotion.

Letters in this chapter have been directed toward getting a reader to take some type of action—to buy a product or to accept an idea and act accordingly. The recommended sequence-of-idea pattern has been (1) get attention, (2) introduce the idea or product, (3) present evidence, and (4) encourage action.

WRITING COLLECTION LETTERS

As in other persuasive letters, the primary purpose of a collection letter is to get action (payment). A secondary goal is to hold a customer's goodwill.

What are the two goals of a collection letter?

Like other persuasive letters, collection letters are written inductively. However, collection letters are shorter. Normally, customers know that they owe (no need to devote space to informing them). They expect to be asked for payment (no need for an attention getter and no need for an apology). If a letter is short, its main point (pay is expected) stands out vividly. Compared with a long letter, a short letter has a greater chance of being read in its entirety. In a long letter, the main point could appear in the skipped-over portion or compete for attention with minor points.

Why are collection letters shorter than other persuasive letters?

Knowing that slow-pay customers may not respond to the first attempts at collection, businesses that use collection letters normally use a series (if the first letter does not bring a response, a second letter is sent; then, a third, etc.).

The Collection Series

An effective series of collection letters incorporates the following characteristics: timeliness, regularity, understanding, and increasing stringency.

What are the four characteristics of an effective collection series?

1. *Timeliness.* Procrastination is a bad habit for anyone. For the collection writer, putting off until tomorrow is an especially bad practice. The longer debtors are given to pay, the longer they will usually take. Most people react favorably to deadlines. Deadlines stick in our minds, put our world out of balance, and provide the motivation to act. Thus effective collection efforts should be made promptly, and they should encourage payment by certain dates.

2. *Regularity.* We should never let the obligation out of the debtor's mind. Although we can't send a collection letter every day, we can base the time lapse between letters on our previous experience with debtors and on a knowledge of the overall effectiveness of our collection practices. A regular system for mailings impresses on debtors the efficiency of collection practices.

3. *Understanding.* Understanding involves adaptability and skill in human relations. The collection series must be adaptable to the nature of the debtor. Good-pay risks should probably be given more time to pay than debtors with poor-pay reputations. We should recognize that many debtors have very good reasons for not having paid on time. They should be given every opportunity to meet their obligations or to explain why they are unable to do so.

Understanding also influences the regularity of the collection series. Letters should not be sent so close together that the debtor won't have a chance to pay before the next letter arrives. No one likes to receive a collection letter after the bill has been paid. Some collection letters paradoxically accuse the debtor of trying to avoid payment and then end with a sentence that says, ''If you have already paid, please ignore this letter.'' This notation is appropriate on friendly, printed reminders only.

4. *Increasing stringency.* The fourth characteristic of the collection series is increasing stringency in letter tone as the seriousness of the delinquency increases.

Most collection authorities classify the letters in the series according to names descriptive of the seriousness of the problem. We can call these classes the *collection series.*

How many letters are in a collection series? The number of letters varies with the collection philosophy of the company and the nature of the debtor. We will have to write as many letters as necessary to collect the money or until collection is hopeless and must be attempted through legal action. For our study purposes, the following stages are used: (1) reminder, (2) inquiry, (3) appeal, (4) strong appeal or urgency, and (5) ultimatum.

1. Reminder

Many people will pay promptly when they receive a bill. Shortly after the due date, a simple reminder will usually bring in most of the remaining accounts. The reminder is typically a duplicate of the original statement with a rubber-stamp notation or printed statement saying ''second notice,'' ''past due,'' or ''please remit.'' To send a collection letter at this stage would be risky, indeed, for goodwill. The assumption is that the obligation has been overlooked and will be paid when the reminder is received. Very often, companies will use two or three reminders before moving to the letter-writing stage. Remember, letters cost money. They should be used only when we are reasonably sure collection is going to be difficult.

Colored gummed stickers may be attached to the statement for their attention-getting qualities. Or the duplicate copies of statements may be prepared on colored paper. The aim at the reminder stage is to make sure the reader recognizes the reminder element. But this step should be accomplished as though the reminder were a routine procedure (which it is). Under no conditions should the debtor think he or she is being singled out for special attention. For that reason, initialed handwritten reminders should be avoided at this stage.

Why should a reminder letter look routine?

2. *Inquiry*

After sending the normal number of reminders without success, we must resort to letters. In some cases these are form letters; in other cases they may be form letters individually typed to emphasize the personal touch. In all letters at the inquiry stage, though, the assumption must be that something has prevented the debtor from paying. The aim is to get some action from the customer, either in the form of a check or an explanation. These are the guideposts to follow in writing effective inquiry letters:

What is the desired action of an inquiry letter?

1. Because reminders have failed to bring payment, something is wrong.

2. Action on the part of the debtor is necessary. Either a payment or an explanation is expected.

3. Offer to help in any way possible — short of forgetting the indebtedness, of course.

4. Make it easy for the debtor to reply, but do not provide excuses for nonpayment.

The following letter effectively demonstrates the inquiry technique:

(1) The January payment on your refrigerator is now past due, and the February payment will soon be delinquent.	(1) Reviews the problem briefly to break the ice.
(2) We believe something special has prevented you from continuing your prompt paying habits. (3) Perhaps we can help you with your problem.	(2) Mentions a possible problem to set the stage for the inquiry. (3) Reveals attitude of helpfulness.
(4) Will you please either send a check for $87.46 to cover the January and February payments, Mr. Scott, or give me an explanation of your difficulty and your plans for meeting your obligation.	(4) Gives the reader a choice of actions, both of which are favorable to the writer, and uses the reader's name to ensure a friendly tone.

That letter did not provide an excuse for nonpayment. Nor did it mention that the customer had merely overlooked paying. These are two very important principles the inexperienced collector often violates. Frequently, too, inquiry letters mistakenly ask whether something is wrong with the goods purchased or service provided. If people are attempting to avoid payment as long as possible, they will be glad to tell us something was wrong with our product or service.

Why should we avoid mentioning possible excuses for nonpayment?

One letter of helpful inquiry is sufficient because any additional ones will only give the debtor the idea we will continue to wait. The increasing-stringency characteristic is best incorporated by reducing the proportion of helpful talk as we proceed from one stage to the next. Helpful talk can be used in the appeal and ultimatum stages, but it should not predominate as it does in the inquiry stage.

3. Appeal

Should a collection letter list *three* reasons why the debtor should pay?

By writing a short letter that is restricted to one appeal, a collection writer (1) increases the chances that the entire letter will be read, (2) places emphasis on the appeal employed, and (3) reserves something new to say if an additional letter is needed.

Typically, collection letters employ appeals selected from the following list:

1. *Fair play.* Cooperation, loyalty, honesty.

2. *Closure.* According to the closure principle in Gestalt psychology, people gain satisfaction from concluding that which they have begun, from taking the final step—paying—in a business transaction.

3. *Pride.* Reputation, prestige, accomplishment, ownership.

4. *Fear.* Loss of credit privilege, loss of possessions, and the possibility of litigation.

Does ". . . or your account's condition will be reported to a credit-rating agency" constitute a threat?

Each of the preceding appeals can be used to help a customer see the advantage of paying, but certain appeals should not be used. A threat of physical violence is outside the scope of rational behavior and is illegal. A statement of intent to destroy a credit reputation (by telling friends, relatives, employers, etc.) is also inadvisable and illegal. However, creditors are normally within legal limits when they provide facts about an account to firms or individuals entitled to receive such information. Appeals to fear, being negative, should be employed only after more positive appeals have been given a chance to solve the collection problem.

Several avenues are open when the indebtedness reaches the rather crucial appeal stage. For those debtors who have ignored the notices, reminders, and inquiries, the collection writer must (1) select the appeal most suitable for the individual case and (2) determine the best method of developing that appeal. The delinquent customer whose account has reached this stage must be persuaded to pay.

Going back to the basic appeals, we know a person can be persuaded to act when a challenge has been made to ambition, security, or reputation. Character, of course, is the most cherished part of reputation. People want to be known for their honesty, loyalty, and cooperativeness. Ambitions are usually achieved through the attainment of some position or the ownership of some valued possession. Security, as an appeal, must be approached indirectly. In the typical family, the head of the household provides the family with the necessities and luxuries of life. The threatened loss of any of these items is a challenge.

Retailers who are in debt are probably most concerned about staying in business, making a profit, achieving ambitions, and building good reputations. Retail consumers, on the other hand, are not so concerned about the profit motive as about squaring their accounts and maintaining personal security. Knowing these traits, the collection writer can vary appeals, increase their sensitivity, and get at the heart of the problem. The appeal letter involves the area of human emotions. It must appeal, collect, preserve goodwill, and leave the door open for further business.

We can establish these two guides, then, for the appeal letter or letters:

1.   Keep in mind the personal nature of the appeal. It is written for one person or for one company. We should personalize the letter by calling the reader by name if the use of the name falls naturally into place as we compose.

2.   Write the letter from the reader's point of view. We shouldn't plead our own poverty as a reason why payment should be made. Instead, we should select an appropriate appeal and drive it home. We should concentrate on one appeal. Multiple-appeal letters don't provide time or space to develop any single appeal properly.

Should the writer's need for money be used as an appeal?

Appeals to Fair Play   In the following example of a fair-play appeal, notice how the debtor is encouraged to pay primarily because it is the right thing to do.

(1) Two months ago we shipped 24 dozen Amazon Golf Balls to you as the first purchase charged to your new account.

(1) Reviews the situation as an agreeable way to begin.

(2) The mutual contract we entered into was based on two things. The first was our ability to make delivery as agreed. The second was your ability to pay as agreed—an ability, incidentally, that was apparent in comments we received about you from your credit references.

(2) Informally reviews the nature of a contract to establish the basis for the fair-play appeal; also establishes ability to pay.

(3) You'll have to agree that we kept our part of the bargain. You'll have to agree, too, that the only way to complete the agreement is for you to send a check for $156 today.

(3) Develops the fair-play appeal by describing the necessary action.

(4) Slip the check in the enclosed envelope now--while this letter is before you.

(4) Requests action.

**How are pride and
fair-play appeals similar?**

Appeals to Pride   Words such as *mutual, fair, cooperative, agreed,* and *bargain* point to the two-sided nature of the credit transaction. These words are useful in appeals to pride as well as to fair play. Appeals to pride can, of course, incorporate appeals to fair play; but our emphasis in the pride appeal should deal primarily with reputation, prestige, accomplishment, or ownership. In the following examples of appeals to pride, notice how talk about a product can be related to the pride variations. The first letter is a typical form appeal to pride:

(1) "Excellent" and "good" were the reports we received when we ran our routine check on your credit rating. As a result, we were pleased to open a credit account for you.	(1) Reviews the circumstances as a wedge for developing the appeal.
(2) You must be proud of such a rating. Let us help you retain that pride by keeping your account in our "preferred" file, Miss Wright.	(2) Introduces the pride element. And develops the appeal.
(3) All you have to do is pay your 30-day past-due balance of $17.86 promptly.	(3) Requests action.

The following letter is a personalized appeal to the customer's sense of pride.

(1) As a prominent lumber dealer in Ashton, you know the advantages of a good credit reputation. It can help bring business success, positions in local government, and prominence in community affairs.	(1) Establishes basis for the appeal and adapts the letter to the debtor.
(2) I think you'll agree, Mr. Johansen, that your credit reputation helped you achieve these things-- achievements of which you should be rightfully proud.	(2) Begins the appeal talk.
(3) We are proud of the part we may have played through the years by extending you credit.	(3) Builds additional appeal by talking about what he owes us.
(4) So that neither your pride nor ours will be shaken, won't you sit down right now and make out a check for $300 to balance your account.	(4) Requests action while emphasizing the appeal.

So far, our appeals to fair play and pride have intimated only lightly, if at all, that the debtor might lose some tangible possession or be forced to become involved in a distasteful credit or legal entanglement. Typically, these are fear appeals reserved for the strong appeal or ultimatum letters.

4. Strong Appeal or Urgency

The strong-appeal letter emphasizes urgency. It says, in effect, "We must have the payment by return mail." By developing the basic appeals and insisting on payment for the debtor's own good, the writer adds stringency. Partial payments may be satisfactory, offers to accept time notes may be made, or full payment may be demanded. Comments about the cost of a lawsuit are common in urgency letters.

What is the advantage of having a vice-president's signature on an urgency letter?

To emphasize the crucial status of the delinquency, the strong-appeal or urgency letter may be signed by a top executive rather than by a member of the collection staff.

Although implications about the loss of credit or possessions may be used, the best psychology is to let the reader know we are still willing to square things without undue embarrassment, as the following letter does:

Just in terms of interest earned, the $1267.50 you have owed us for the past 60 days could have earned $24.00. We are concerned about the interest, but we are more concerned about retaining your goodwill and collecting the money rightfully due us.

Neither of us looks forward to expensive litigation, nor does either of us relish the implications of submitting your account as "nonpay" to the Wholesale Furniture Dealers Association. Yet both things can happen.

We certainly want your check within the next five days; but as a courtesy to you, we will accept your 60-day note at 9 percent so that you can retain your credit.

You must do one of these things, Mrs. Jenkins. The action you take now is extremely important to you and your business.

The appeal stages—both mild and strong—must of necessity be involved with human sensitivity, perhaps more than any other letter-communications problem. The deftness with which the writer handles the collection problem determines which customers are retained for the firm. At the same time, the account has reached a rather critical stage at which our assumption is that the customer will definitely pay only after a persuasive challenge to a sensitive point.

To develop the strong appeal from the mild appeal, keep these suggestions in mind:

1. Change the appeal from one of challenging the debtor's *retention* of a favorable credit rating, a good reputation, or a prized possession to definitely implying that the debtor is about to *lose* something of value or *face a distasteful dilemma.*

2.   Decrease the persuasive tone. Become more demanding.

3.   Instead of talking about why the debtor *doesn't* pay, talk about why he or she *must* pay.

4.   Offer the debtor a choice between two or more things, none of which enables him or her to get off the hook.

5.   Let the debtor know clearly that the weight of evidence and the legal aspects definitely favor us and not the debtor.

5. *Ultimatum*

What is the basic message contained in an ultimatum?

When strong appeals fail to do their work, the collection writer must take the only remaining course of action: a letter that says, "You must pay now of your own volition or we will use every possible legal means to enforce collection." The debtor has only one choice. He or she must pay or face the consequences. Whatever recourse we have to final collection must be mentioned in the letter. We must make the most of the fact that we use the courts, a collection agency, or an attorney to enforce collection. Unfortunately, accounts getting to this stage may be as costly to the lender as they are to the borrower. Furthermore, if payment is not made, we're sure to lose the customer; if payment is made, we'd probably be hesitant about engaging in further credit transactions with the same customer.

Why should we avoid giving a lecture on credit?

Despite this dilemma, our letter should not use language that will make us susceptible to legal recourse by the customer. We must keep our self-control, show some impatience, and stay above the name-calling level. Any effort we can make to retain goodwill is worthwhile. Above all, we should avoid preaching because debtors who get to this stage do not react favorably to advice about how they should have acted. In the following ultimatum letter, the tone has changed from "must pay" to "now or else."

When we agreed some three months ago to ship automotive supplies, you agreed that you would pay the $1,265 within 30 days. Yet the 30 days went by, then 60. Now more than 90 days have elapsed.

During this time, we have sent you several overdue notices and letters--all without a single word of reply from you. Our patience is exhausted, but our interest in you and your welfare is not.

As members of the National Retail Credit Association, we are compelled to submit your name as "nonpay" unless we receive your check for $1,265 by June 6. The effect of a bad report could very well restrict your ability to purchase supplies on credit. In addition, our legal department would be forced to bring suit for collection.

As you yourself know, we have every right to enforce legal collection. You have until June 6 to retain your good record and to avoid legal embarrassment.

Notice how the ultimatum letter reviews the sequence of events, past and future, to indicate the seriousness of the matter. If the ultimatum letter does not collect, the only recourse left is to tell the debtor the account is being prepared for collection and that we are taking whatever steps promised. The account is no longer in our hands.

What do you think about following the first ultimatum with a second?

Form Letters

Many organizations use form letters to handle nearly all collection problems. The following principles establish the framework for companies planning to use form-letter series:

Under what conditions are form letters appropriate?

1. The collection problem must be frequent. Personal finance companies, department stores, banks, and savings and loan associations are examples of organizations that can make good use of form letters.

2. Secured loans made by financial institutions such as banks, savings and loan associations, and finance companies give the lender the advantage of repossession or foreclosure if payment is not made.

3. The collection problems must be uniform. All letters must apply to the same types of problems.

Frequently the letters in the series are coded to indicate the collection stage at which they are to be used. In a finance company, for example, there is likely to be a complete series for debtors who have failed to make the first payment, another for those who have made the first payment but missed a later one, and still another series for those who have made all payments but the final one. One major oil company has a book of over 200 form collection letters, each covering a uniform collection problem.

Except for the most routine early stages in the collection process, even form letters should be individually typed so they can be personalized with names, amounts, and dates. One rule holds true: If the letter is an obvious form, don't try to camouflage it. The debtor will recognize a mimeographed or auto-typed letter as a form—particularly when the fillers are typed with a different typewriter.

Present-day word-processing equipment greatly simplifies use of form letters in collecting overdue debts. Having typed an inside address, a typist has but to give the automatic typewriter instructions on which form to type. It will type the remainder of the letter at speeds up to 600 words per minute.

How does word-processing equipment simplify collection work?

Collection-Related Letters

The purpose of previously discussed letters was to get the debtor to *pay;* some letters, however, are designed to get the debtor to *conform.* For example, the following letter is an inquiry in which the debtor is asked whether another due date for payment would be desirable:

> Thank you for your March 1 payment, which was received yesterday, March 15.
>
> We are certainly satisfied with the regularity of your payments, but we do wonder if a different due date is advisable. Your payments are usually made around the 15th of each month.
>
> If a change to the 15th would enable you to meet your payments on time, make a notation to that effect at the bottom of this letter and return it to me promptly. Otherwise, please make your payments on the first as scheduled.

In the following case, the debtor pays exactly one month late, and as a result will eventually cost the lender a month's interest income. Therefore, the writer attempts to extend the time limit by one month, and also attempts to extract the additional interest.

> Your June 1 payment was received today, July 1. Although we thank you for this payment, we are concerned about the July payment which is now due.
>
> To avoid collection problems, please make this payment promptly. If payment is difficult at this time, we suggest that you request a one-month extension on the payment period of your loan. This would put your payments back on schedule and enable us to put your account back in the good-pay file. To do this, you should attach the late charge of $5, covering the interest payment for one month, to this letter and return it to me promptly.

The problem of collecting unearned discounts is one that plagues many businesses. As a vivid example, one furniture dealer pays his accounts some thirty to fifty days after they are due. And when he pays, he deducts whatever discount terms were given for prompt payment. On a $500 bill due on June 1, with terms of 3/10, n/30, he might pay on July 15 with a check for $485—the bill less the prompt-pay discount of 3 percent. Obviously, a business with several debtors employing the same tactics could lose a considerable sum unless it did something about it. Fair play, of course, is the primary appeal in such letters. "Do unto others" is an effective approach. Some of the furniture dealer's creditors sent printed notices (such as the one that follows) along with the next billing:

> The additional amount on your bill represents the discount that you may have inadvertently deducted when you paid your last bill after the discount period.

Persistent deduction of the discount then brings a letter something like this:

The business you have brought our way is certainly appreciated. In fact, we are pleased to list you among our most prominent retail outlets.

We are not so pleased, however, about your handling of your discount privilege. The 2 percent is given for prompt payment within 10 days of the first of the month. The money we receive early by offering the discount enables us to take similar discounts on our own obligations. Were it not for these savings, the cost of our product would have to be increased by 2 percent. Thus the increase would have to be passed on to you and our other customers.

Because our business is based on either receiving full payment in a month or a discounted payment within 10 days, we ask that you help yourself and us by fairly observing the discount terms. In a mutually cooperative spirit, will you please send your check for $37.86 to balance your account.

The Language of Collection Letters

Throughout the discussion of collection problems, we have seen that certain words are particularly effective. The mutuality of business problems and the resultant appeal to fair play have made *mutual, fair, cooperative, agreed,* and *bargain* good words to use in collection letters. The adverb adds stringency to collection language. Instead of being *important,* a problem has become *very important* or *extremely important.* Words and phrases such as *must, compelled,* and *no other alternative* are important in the strong-appeal and ultimatum letters.

As is true with other persuasive letters, a collection letter is successful if it gets results without adversely affecting goodwill.

COLLECTION BY TELEPHONE AND TELEGRAM

At any stage in the collection process, telephone messages are effective if they are made on a local basis. Long-distance calls, of course, denote seriousness and urgency. Not only are telephone calls effective as reminders and inquiries, they are inexpensive compared with the cost of letter preparation. In addition, the telephone approach to collections gets two jobs done at the same time. Not only can we complete the reminder or inquiry stage, but chances are we will also get a firm answer, with the strong possibility that future letters will be unnecessary.

What advantages do telephone conversations have over letters as collection devices?

Those who use the telephone for collecting should become familiar with applicable state laws. Some states have restrictions on the *number* of calls about a debt and the *times* at which such calls can be made. And, of course, conventions of courtesy apply. Legal or illegal, a call at 3 A.M. is not advisable.

Telegrams should be used only in the last stage of collections. They are more expensive than either local telephone calls or letters, and our appeals are necessarily limited because of the high rates for additional wording.

Registered mail has much the same urgency effect as telegrams. When any of these rapid means of communication is used, the debtor is sure to feel the urgency of the matter, and our chances of collection are increased.

SUMMARY

The purpose of a persuasive message is to get action. People are not inclined to act because they are *told* to do something, but they will do something if they *want* to. The technique of persuasion, then, is to arouse desire.

When a writer's purpose is to sell a product or to request a special favor, ideas should appear in the following sequence: get the reader's attention, introduce the product or request, present evidence that the reader gains by buying or complying, and ask for action. The typical persuasive message is longer than the typical routine message; evidence of reader benefit is necessary and space consuming.

Compared with other persuasive letters, collection letters are shorter. Debtors already know that they owe money. A short letter that presents one good reason for paying has a better chance of success than a long letter that presents many reasons. In the collection series, each letter presents one appeal. If no response results, the next letter presents a different appeal. Collection by mail is often done by form letter. If a business has word-processing equipment, the letters are typed by computer. Collection by telephone or telegraph is sometimes more effective than collection by letter.

EXERCISES

Review Questions (Sales letters)

1. Compared with routine letters, the typical sales letter is longer. Why?

2. Name the four parts of a sales-letter outline.

3. Should a sales letter have four paragraphs? Explain.

4. If a product has four commendable features, should the sales letter devote separate paragraphs to each feature with about equal emphasis on each? Explain.

5. (a) Why is use of general (instead of specific) language discouraged? (b) Under what condition could general language be used?

6. Which makes more use of an attention getter—a solicited sales letter or an unsolicited sales letter? Explain.

7. If a question is to be used as an attention getter, which is better—a question that can be answered with one word, or a question that would require a sentence or more in response? Why?

8. Which sentences are normally more interesting—sentences that use a person as the subject, or sentences that use a product as the subject? Why?

9. (a) What are the disadvantages of using paragraphs as long as 10 or 12 lines? (b) How is the white space between paragraphs helpful?

10. Should the first paragraph be one of the longest? Explain.

11. Of the four points in the outline for a sales letter, to which is most space devoted? Explain.

12. Should superlatives be used in sales letters? Explain.

13. Why are incomplete comparisons to be avoided?

14. Which is normally better—introduce price after discussing the virtues of a product, or introduce price before discussing the virtues of a product? Why?

15. Which is normally better for introducing the price of a product? A simple sentence or a complex sentence? Explain.

16. List some techniques for overcoming price resistance.

17. Should the central selling point be alluded to in the final paragraph of a sales letter? Explain.

18. The "action ending" should strive for *quick* action. Why?

19. Are such expressions as "Do it now" and "Don't delay" advisable in the final paragraph? Explain.

20. In a solicited sales letter, should questions be answered in the same order in which they were asked? Explain.

Review Questions (Other persuasive messages)

1. What is the difference between a persuasive claim and a routine claim?

2. Which is longer a routine claim or a persuasive claim? Why?

3. In a persuasive claim letter, should a writer vent strong displeasure? Explain.

4. How does the writer of a persuasive claim have an advantage over an adjuster?

5. In a persuasive claim letter, which is better procedure? (a) Begin with a point on which agreement is likely and proceed to discuss a point on which agreement is less likely. *or* (b) Begin with a point on which agreement is unlikely and proceed to discuss a point on which agreement is more likely. Explain.

6. In a letter that requests a favor, which is better? (a) State the specific request in a simple sentence. *or* (b) State the request in a complex sentence that also alludes to a reader benefit for cooperating? Explain.

7. List the two primary goals of a collection letter.

8. Compared with other persuasive letters, are collection letters longer or shorter? Why?

9. In a collection series, why should the inquiry precede the first letter of appeal?

10. In a collection series, how many appeals should be included in each letter? Explain.

11. List some qualities that an effective collection series should possess.

12. In an inquiry letter, should possible reasons for nonpayment be mentioned? Explain.

13. In every collection letter, should the specific amount owed be stated? Why?

14. If a debtor has not responded to an ultimatum that payment be made by a certain date, is a second ultimatum (setting a new deadline) advisable? Why?

15. How is word-processing equipment useful in producing collection letters?

16. Compared with collecting by letter, what are the advantages of collecting by telephone?

17. What kinds of legal restrictions do some states place on collection by telephone?

18. At which stage are telegrams more effective — early in the collection series, or late in the collection series?

19. Which stage in the collection series could more profitably include sales-promotional material — the early stages, or the late stages?

20. In the early stage of a collection series, would resale be appropriate? Explain.

Letter-Writing Problems

1. From a newspaper or magazine, clip a picture of an advertised product. Using principles presented in the preceding chapter, write an uninvited sales letter. Attach the picture to the letter.

2. Select a sales letter that you (or a friend) have received. Make a list of principles it applies and violates. Rewrite the letter.

3. Assume you are the proprietor of a new business that sells mopeds. You hope to sell mopeds to students who have been driving their cars to a large university in your city. The gas-saving advantage is apparent. So is the parking advantage. So is the initial investment (compared with automobiles). Some facts about the engine: 48.8 cc, 2-cycle, gas tank holds 0.9 gallons. Transmission is single speed, automatic. Clutch is centrifugal. Muffler is chrome plated. Brakes are of the drum type and are moisture resistant, hand controlled. Throttle is mounted on the handlebar. The moped has lights for the front and rear. Has functional pedals. Has a chain guard. Other features are described on an enclosed folder. Price: $549. In writing a letter, choose a central selling point that will appeal to college students.

4. Assume one of your above-ground swimming pools was pictured in a magazine, and a prospective customer has written for information about it. Yes, you can make immediate delivery on the vinyl-tank pool. The vinyl is well supported with lightweight aluminum walls that won't rust. Pools make excellent places for children to cool off on hot days. The drain is made to fit a garden hose. Yes, you have a pool to fit the customer's yard; you think a pool ten feet in diameter will allow plenty of room around the sides. The pool sells for $149 plus shipping charges. An illustrative booklet and an order blank are enclosed. Mr. Charles Wells, 318 S. 14th Street, Westfall, CA 90112.

5. Mr. Robert Wright is the manager of a local retail store, one of a nationwide chain. He is civic minded and has an exceptionally good background in marketing. For him, Saturday is an extremely busy day. Five weeks from this coming Saturday, your Marketing Club meets for a banquet (at which new members will be initiated), and you want him to be the speaker. You want to hear his views on how well today's applicants are suited for entry-level jobs. Mr. Robert Wright, Manager, Melvin's, 317 E. Main Street, Wellsford, OK 65349.

6. Assume you are a graduate student planning to write a thesis on women holders of the Ph.D. degree. You have developed a questionnaire for them, and you have developed a questionnaire to be filled out by an equal number of men who hold the same degree. That questionnaire is eleven pages in length, and you fear that it will be tossed aside because of its size; recipients may not want to take the time required for filling it out. Prepare a persuasive letter that is designed to make recipients *want* to fill out and return the questionnaire.

7. When your college of business administration was constructed several years ago, major businesses were invited to pay for furnishing rooms. They paid for carpeting, tables and chairs, and wall decorations. Having selected the room for which it was responsible, a business could choose the carpet and decorate the walls with small artifacts or pictures related to that firm's history, product, or service. In each room is a small plaque identifying the sponsoring firm. Now, a new wing is being added; local firms are again being invited to furnish one of the rooms. Write a form letter that could be placed in a word processor and (with appropriate modifications) sent to a number of local businesses. Assume an enclosure has been prepared already. It shows an architect's drawing of the new wing, room sizes, and estimations of costs for furnishing carpeting, tables, and chairs for rooms of various sizes. Firms are not expected to respond by sending a check; they are to call or write to the dean and express an interest in participating.

8. Typically, college graduates who apply for admission to professional schools are required to fill out admission forms that ask (among many short-answer questions) an open-ended question: (a) "Why do you want to be a (lawyer, physician, dentist, therapist, nurse, engineer, etc.)?" *Or*, (b) "Why have you selected *this* school instead of others?" Usually, a space limitation is given — such as, one page or 200 or 500 words. The answer gives students an opportunity to present pertinent information, to demonstrate skills in organizing and writing, and to persuade. Using the principles of persuasion, write your answer to question (a) or to question (b). Assuming you are in your last semester as an undergraduate student, tailor your answer to your specific plans.

9. Students on your sprawling campus have a problem: bicycles and skate boards. The interval between classes is 10 minutes. For some students, the entire 10 minutes is spent in hurrying to the next class. Those who try to save time by using skate boards or bicycles are becoming a nuisance and a safety hazard. You think you have figured out a solution to the problem. Write a persuasive letter to the school newspaper's editor.

10. Two years ago, Marla Novakov became Miss America after attending your college for one year. Although she received the most publicity during her year as reigning queen, she is still thought of as a celebrity. She has just been awarded a degree from another well-known school. Marla's parents still live in your city; she visits them occasionally. Marla frequently receives invitations to speak (for pay). Recently, she was an announcer for a parade that preceded a nationally televised football game. As the one in charge of programs for your business club, write a letter inviting Marla Novakov to speak on "Coping with Stress and Time Pressure." Within limits, you could adjust your meeting date. Perhaps it could be set for a time when she visits her parents. Your club does not pay its speakers. For completeness, supply an inside address to your letter.

11. Because so many students ride bicycles to school, your city council has designated a portion of College Avenue as a "bike path." Motorists do not invade the bike path, and bike riders leave the rest of the street to motorists. Just a few blocks from school, a railroad track crosses College Avenue. The portion that crosses the bike path is exceedingly rough. It is dangerous, especially for students who have night classes. According to the city, the responsibility for repair is with the railroad. Calls have not brought results. Surely, the railroad can fix the crossing so bikes can pass over it easily (so it will be just like the crossing one mile farther down the track; at that intersection, the crossing is very smooth; but the street has no bike path). Supplying an inside address, write a persuasive letter to the railroad company.

12. Assume a national association of credit-collection managers wants to make college students familiar with their monthly publication—*Collection Power.* Each month, it contains articles written by professionals in the collection field; it frequently contains samples of collection series that have proved effective. If majors in business could see and read the publication, they might become interested in collections and credit as a career. The association has decided to give students in selected colleges and universities a one-year subscription. As secretary of the association, write a letter to business professors. Ask for names and addresses of their students. Each student will be placed on the mailing list for one year. A copy of the most recent edition is to accompany the letter. (Assure the teachers that the list of names will be used for no other purpose.)

13. For this year, you are president of Beta Gamma Sigma, the honorary fraternity in your college of business administration. Preceding presidents have succeeded in persuading *local* business personalities to speak at the initiation banquet. Persuading a *national,* even *international,* authority to speak would be a great accomplishment. You have discovered that Dr. Peter Drucker (eminent author and lecturer in management) is scheduled to address a large convention of business people in your city just two days before your initiation banquet. Surely, he would enjoy a couple of extra days in the beautiful weather and would like to talk to students in the top 10 percent of their class — students who attend the largest school of business in the country. (Before writing, perhaps a peek at some of his books would be of some assistance.)

14. You know that Barbara Leander is a very busy woman. She has the interests of your university at heart; otherwise, she would not have donated a quarter of a million dollars to construction of the school's baseball stadium. Ms. Leander was a business major. As dean of the business college, invite her to serve on your advisory council. It meets twelve times per year. Ms. Barbara Leander, 143 Harrison Street, Tempe, AZ 85281.

15. You have an idea that could help many people, particularly those who suffer from muscular dystrophy. You could conduct a well-publicized relay — from Phoenix to Las Vegas. After one runner has run for a mile, he could be picked up and another runner would take his place on the road to Las Vegas. With ten well-conditioned runners taking turns, the event should not be too strenuous. It could be timed so that the group would reach Las Vegas at the right time to appear on the Jerry Lewis telethon. You can work out details of finding volunteer participants, serving as the one in charge of the group, etc.; but you need a sponsor. Because the event would make news, a sponsor would get some advertising value from having provided such needs as running shoes, T-shirts with a "run for those who can't" slogan, and a van to haul food and water, as well as runners. Prepare a letter designed to persuade a local automobile dealership to serve as the sponsor. Mr. George De Marino, President, Valley Chevrolet, 471 West Lancaster Road, Phoenix, AZ 84132.

16. You are the credit manager for a store that sells building materials. A local carpenter was in the home-building business in a limited way. For three years, he had made charge purchases and always paid at the end of each month. A recent increase in interest rates made selling his homes very difficult. He closed out his operation and left town — owing $1100.

    a. Write an inquiry letter.
    b. Since it brings no response, write two separate appeals letters.
    c. Since the appeals letters bring no response, write an urgent appeals letter.
    d. Other letters having failed, write an ultimatum letter.

Mr. Hanson Edwards, 113 N. 14th Street, Phelps, MO 65341.

17. You are the manager of an automobile supply company. When the Mansfield Service Station sent its most recent order, you checked the account before filling the order. The past-due balance is $950, and the credit limit placed on the account is $1000. The owner of the station has placed the new order for $600 in tires and batteries. Write to the owner seeking some action on his part. You want to keep the account open by collecting for the present order before shipping the merchandise. Mr. Roy Swartz, Mansfield Service Station, 314 N. Broadway, Central City, MI 34112.

18.   Prepare a letter to send to Mr. Thomas Kaas. You, as the credit manager of a finance company, notice that he pays every month; but his payments are exactly a month late. Each month, you figure you lose a month's interest on his $200 account. Mr. Thomas Kaas, 784 N. Elm Street, Independence, MO 73159.

19.   You manage the Tune-of-the-Month Club. You sell stereo records to club members who contract for four records a year at eight dollars a record. A bill accompanies each record mailed. Because of the small amount involved in each sale, collection costs can be excessive. You decided that just one collection letter will be mailed to delinquent accounts. If payment is not received, the account will be sold to a collection firm for 20 percent of its value. Prepare the letter. As a form, it will be stored in your word-processing equipment for repeated use.

20.   You are the manager of an appliance store. Prepare a letter that can be used as a form letter. It will be sent to customers who have made their payments regularly and have now made the final payment on their accounts.

WRITING SPECIAL LETTERS

Congratulatory Letters
Writing Congratulations
Replying to Congratulations
Letters of Recommendation
Requesting Recommendations
Writing Recommendations
Letters about Reservations
Letters of Invitation
Writing Invitations
Replying to Invitations
Letters of Condolence or Sympathy
Thank-You Letters
Letters of Evaluation
Positive Qualities
Negative Qualities
Summary

Every business person occasionally faces circumstances that vary from the usual day-to-day operations. Many of these situations require letters that provide an opportunity to create goodwill for both the business and the individual. This chapter discusses these situations and provides examples of these letters and messages. The purposes of the chapter are to provide (1) a modified handbook for unusual-circumstance letters and (2) an opportunity to develop a sensitivity about communication opportunities often overlooked by business people. In many cases, of course, the problem is not overlooked but simply avoided because of the business person's insecurity about social etiquette or procedures.

CONGRATULATORY LETTERS

Writing Congratulations

How many times a year do you overlook an opportunity to congratulate someone?

All too often we read about the election, promotion, or other significant achievement of a colleague or acquaintance and think that a note or telephone call of congratulations would be in order—only to procrastinate until it is too late. On the other hand, a successful executive takes advantage of the situation to build goodwill for the company and for herself or himself. Some executives accomplish this goodwill gesture by using one of a supply of note cards, which is always available. However, although handwritten messages are acceptable, typed ones permit more to be said. The thoughtfulness of sending letters of congratulations is genuinely appreciated. And when the letter is the only one the person receives, it really stands out.

What is your preference—handwritten or typewritten notes?

In addition to promotions and elections, such events as births, weddings, and engagements call for acknowledgment. We should always acknowledge the events when those involved are employees in our firm.

Here is an example of a short letter of congratulations on the occasion of a promotion:

> I just learned of your promotion to the post of Vice-President of Security, Inc. Please accept my warmest congratulations and best wishes for every success.

For an engagement, the letter may take a more warm and enthusiastic tone, as in the following example:

> Your good news just arrived, and I wish you and Stephen every possible happiness. He has always seemed to me like a wonderful person, and now I know he's also a lucky one. Please congratulate him for me.

Replying to Congratulations

In almost all cases, letters of congratulations should be answered. A typed acknowledgment might take the following form:

Many thanks for your nice words about my promotion and for the good wishes. I look forward to continuing to work with you at the Chamber of Commerce. I always enjoy it.

Some replies take a tongue-in-cheek tone, particularly when the promotion is to a rather high-pressure position:

Thank you for your good thoughts about my promotion. I'm not certain whether congratulations or condolences would have been appropriate.

The job is going to be demanding, especially as I make the transition. I'm going to give it my all, however; and your thoughtfulness is going to help ease the burden. Again, I truly appreciate your support.

Notice the friendliness displayed in letters of congratulations. Because they are usually sent to friends and acquaintances, congratulations messages and acknowledgments are casual, warm, and sometimes witty. We should not delay our message until it is too late to take advantage of the immediacy of the accomplishment.

LETTERS OF RECOMMENDATION

Requesting Recommendations

Requests for recommendations and recommendation letters themselves are closely related to congratulatory messages because they also tend to say something nice about someone. In general, requests for information about a person arise because the person has given someone as a reference. Often the person who lists someone as a reference has asked permission to do so. (If not, then he or she has left the door open for a negative recommendation.) Sometimes, job seekers can greatly assist their references by alerting them to imminent requests for information. For example, months (or even years) may have elapsed since an employer or professor agreed to future service as a reference. The following letter alerts the recipient to possible receipt of a letter requesting a recommendation:

Would you consent to giving a letter of recommendation if you could not give a favorable one?

Although nine months have passed since I received permission to use your name as a reference, you may be receiving a request soon.

Interstate Cable Corporation is considering my application for a job as sales representative. In case some of the information may be helpful in preparing to write a letter of recommendation, I am attaching a copy of my résumé.

You knew me as Susan Garcia (my wedding to Arnold Jackson was four weeks ago).

My interest in a sales career is stronger than ever. I shall certainly appreciate the time you spend in responding to a request for information about me.

To the recipient, such a letter is a courtesy. It may assist the writer in producing a recommendation letter that is more up to date, more detailed, and more convincing. The employer's request for a letter of recommendation should be as specific as possible about what is wanted. For example, here's a letter requesting a faculty member to submit a recommendation for admission of a student to an honor society:

Sally Ann Jones is being considered for election to the Order of the Laurel, the all-university recognition society for outstanding women students. Because she has given your name as a reference, will you please give us your candid opinion of her in terms of the following items:

1.   Her ability and willingness to go beyond the normal course requirements.

2.   Her classroom participation, leadership indications, and respect for other students.

3.   Her potential for future success.

Because final selection will take place on May 1, may we have your response by April 25. Thank you very much for your help.

In the preceding letter, notice the effect of assigning numbers to attributes and typing them on shortened lines with space before and after. The arrangement emphasizes positive qualities and simplifies review of them.

Writing Recommendations

The most common recommendation is one for employment, which is discussed in Chapter 11. Less common are letters of recommendation or reference for employees leaving employment, nominations for awards, and membership in clubs or societies.

Letters of recommendation about employees or friends take two forms. One is the solicited recommendation requested by an organization, and the other is the unsolicited letter requested by the individual to incorporate in an employment dossier or in a personal reference file. The first will be addressed to a specific person or organization; the second may be headed by "To Prospective Employers." Generally, the solicited letter will reply to specific concerns as outlined in the request letter. The unsolicited letter will be broader in nature and contain statements about work performance, attitude, and potential.

If the person being written about can be endorsed with enthusiasm, we should use a deductive approach. If the endorsement cannot be strong, an inductive plan permits the use of negatives and leaves open the possibility of subordinating them.

Remember, we can de-emphasize ideas by placing them in the dependent part of the sentence and emphasize them by placing them in the independent part. We can increase impact by also using the name of the person talked about in the independent part. Note the difference caused simply by changing the location of the name in the following pair of sentences:

> Although *John's* golf is only fair, *his* amiability and integrity should make him a good club member.

> Although *his* golf is only fair, *John's* amiability and integrity should make him a good club member.

What is the meaning of *amiability*? Do you think it's a good word to use here?

Because readers pay more attention to the independent part of a sentence, John's strengths have been placed in the independent clause in each sentence. However, people also pay more attention to proper nouns than to pronouns. Therefore the second sentence improves John's chances by placing his name in the independent clause.

In the following letter (also recommending a person for club membership) notice how the writer has endorsed the candidate enthusiastically while subordinating his golfing ability.

> As a member of Riverside Country Club for over twenty years, I heartily endorse the nomination of Charles Swanson for membership.
>
> Charles is well known in civic affairs, owns property near the Club, and is a respected attorney. Although his golf is only fair, Charles's amiability and integrity should make him a good club member.
>
> I would be pleased to represent him at the membership interview if desired.

Normally, an employee who is leaving a job should ask the employer for a letter of recommendation. Our particular strengths may be forgotten if we wait several months (or longer) to ask for a recommendation. And there is a chance our employer may go out of business, or our supervisor may also have left the company and be difficult to locate.

Study the following outline for a letter of recommendation, then read the letter employing that outline:

1. Establish the subject.

2. Give details about the person's qualities.

3. End with a summarizing statement or a forward-looking thought.

To Prospective Employers:

> Leland Johnson served as an Internal Auditor on my staff from 1977 to 1981. He left ABC Company on January 20, 1981, to find employment in the Miami area and to care for two elderly parents.

Mr. Johnson is a true professional in his field and effected many economies in our office and production facilities. He identifies problems clearly, tackles them with skill, and backs his recommendations with concrete evidence.

His loyalty and integrity, in my opinion, are beyond question. Despite the sometimes sensitive nature of the internal audit task, Mr. Johnson has been able to develop strong acceptance from employees on whose problems he has worked.

I can recommend him without reservation and would be delighted to re-employ him should he return to our area.

This same message could serve as a *letter of introduction* simply by addressing it to an individual and by preceding the opening sentence with "I'm pleased to introduce Mr. Johnson."

LETTERS ABOUT RESERVATIONS

The simple letter of reservation for hotel accommodations should be specific in terms of (1) the request for the type of room; (2) dates, arrival time, and departure time; and (3) request for confirmation. For example,

Please reserve a single room for me for the nights of June 15, 16, and 17. I shall arrive about 6 p.m. on June 15 and depart at noon on June 18.

Will you please send a prompt confirmation.

If the writer will be attending a convention at the hotel in which a reservation is requested, the letter should include the name of the group that is convening. In setting room priorities, management may give preference to convention attendees and provide special rates for them.

LETTERS OF INVITATION

Like most other special letters, invitations and responses to them are deductive and relatively short.

Writing Invitations

An informal invitation resembles a business letter. When sent from a business office, the letter is sometimes typed on executive stationery, which is smaller than the regular business letterhead. Wording should be conversational, as though the writer were extending the invitation orally. As a matter of style, the inside address may be placed at the end of the letter. For example,

> We are pleased to invite you to be our guests at the Installation Ball of the Chamber at the Beachrider Hotel on January 5.
> As was recently announced, Robert Dodson, our Executive Vice-President, will be installed then as president of the Chamber of Commerce for the coming year. A cocktail reception at seven o'clock will be followed by dinner and dancing.
> Will you please let me know by December 29 whether you will attend. I will be glad to see you there.
>
> Cordially

Mr. and Mrs. Theodore Smith
444 Commonwealth Drive
Beverly Hills, CA 90037

Replying to Invitations

All invitations should be acknowledged promptly. When a telephone R.S.V.P. is not mentioned, either a typed or handwritten reply is satisfactory and should use the same conversational style as used in the invitation.

> **What is the meaning of R.S.V.P.?**

Although many formal invitations are handwritten, especially for smaller groups, formal invitations are generally printed and follow formats provided by the printer (Figure 10-1). When the affair includes formal wear, the invitation should include the notation "black tie."

The replies to such invitations should follow a similar pattern with wording such as the following example:

> Mr. and Mrs. Charles Longworth accept with pleasure the invitation of the Board of Directors of the Massachusetts Investment Company for dinner on Saturday, the twelfth of June, at seven-thirty o'clock.

A simple, one-paragraph letter is satisfactory, particularly when the invitation is from a business concern and contains a fill-in line for the names of those invited. At the most formal level, however, the reply should be prepared in longhand and arranged in the same format as the invitation.

The refusal of an invitation is like the acceptance:

> Mr. and Mrs. Charles Longworth regret they are unable to accept the kind invitation of the Board . . .

Although formal etiquette calls for handwritten replies to invitations, business protocol does permit use of typewritten messages.

The Board of Directors

Massachusetts Investment Company

request the company of

_____

at dinner

on Saturday, the twelfth of June

at seven-thirty o'clock

744 North New York Avenue

Chicago, Illinois

Black Tie   R.S.V.P.

Figure 10-1   Formal invitation format.

LETTERS OF CONDOLENCE OR SYMPATHY

A letter of sympathy to the family of a friend or business associate who has died should be written promptly. Yet, the sympathy message presents a difficult writing problem, with the result that these messages are often put off until too late or are not sent at all. One way to solve the problem, although a little impersonal, is to send a card (called an *informal*), which may be purchased at any stationery store, and prepare a short handwritten message: "Deepest Sympathy." Telegrams may also be used with messages such as "Deeply saddened by your loss. Sympathy to you and your family." Although etiquette now allows typed messages to be sent when the deceased is a business associate, a handwritten message provides a much more personal tone than does any other kind.

The simplest plan for such messages is (1) start with a statement of sympathy, (2) follow with sentences about mutual experiences or relationships, and (3) close with some words of comfort and affection. The following letter is to the widow of a deceased acquaintance:

I was deeply sorry to hear of your sad news. Jim was a fine man with whom I spent many enjoyable and constructive times. He will be greatly missed by all of us who knew him and who worked with him in building a better community. Please accept my warmest sympathy and best wishes.

When a close relative (such as spouse, son, daughter, mother, or father) of a close friend dies, we should write the friend a letter of sympathy. Printed sympathy cards may also be used; but, in general, the closer the relationship, the greater the need for personal written messages of condolence or sympathy.

THANK-YOU LETTERS

Following the receipt of a gift, attendance as a guest, an interview, or any of the great variety of circumstances in which a follow-up letter of thanks might be desirable, a thoughtful person will take the time to send a written message. As with all other special letter situations, our message should reflect our sincere feelings of gratitude. When couples have been guests, one person usually sends the thank-you message for both. The message should be informal; a simple handwritten message is sufficient. When written in a business office to respond to a business situation, the message may be typed on office stationery. Here's a message of thanks for a weekend visit. Rather than the routine, thank-you-for-a-lovely-weekend thought, the letter includes something specific that the writer enjoyed.

We had a wonderful time this weekend, and Jack and I still have our rosy glows from the swimming and sunshine. The Barkers were just as charming as you said they'd be. You were kind to invite us. Thanks again for everything.

A thank-you note covering a business situation might have the following tone:

This note is simply to thank you for your letter of introduction, which enabled me to see Mr. Albert Jenkins in San Diego. He said many nice things about you, by the way.

Although nothing really definitive came from our meeting, I think we did lay the groundwork for future relationships. I very much appreciate your taking the time to help me and look forward to an opportunity to return the favor.

In cases such as those covered by these two letters, thanks could be conveyed as well by telephone calls; but the notes seem much more thoughtful.

All gifts received should also be acknowledged by a thank-you note. In longhand, we should identify the gift, tell why we like it, and describe how we'll use it. Here's an example:

Bill and I are delighted with the beautiful silver candy dish you sent us. We plan to use it on our coffee table where everyone will see it first thing. Thanks so very much for your kindness.

LETTERS OF EVALUATION

Even though evaluation is not our purpose, we can hardly escape noticing when the attitudes and performances of others are especially good or especially bad. For those who deserve high marks, letters can encourage; for those who deserve low marks, letters can alert.

Positive Qualities

How can a compliment be worth more than money?

When someone has performed exceptionally well or exhibited a commendable attitude, a tangible reward may not be possible or even advisable. From the bestower's point of view, an intangible reward (such as a letter) is easy and inexpensive. From the recipient's point of view, the value of an intangible reward can be much greater than any reasonable tangible reward. (Recall Maslow's hierarchy of needs.)

Why are *written* compliments so effective?

Especially effective are letters that recognize positive qualities or performances. People are not usually reluctant to *say* "Thank you," "A great performance," "You have certainly helped me," etc. Yet, because people seldom bother to *write* such messages, such messages are especially meaningful — even treasured. Compared with those who merely *say* nice things, people who take time to *write* them are more likely to be perceived as sincere.

In an intangible way, how do letters of commendation benefit their writers?

Although a letter of commendation is intended to recognize, reward, and encourage the receiver, it also benefits the sender. Contributing to another's happiness, paying tribute to one who deserves it, encouraging that which is commendable — such feelings can contribute to the sender's own sense of wellbeing and worth. Such positive thinking can have a salutary influence on the sender's own attitude and performance.

Yet some of the potential value (to sender and receiver) is lost if a letter is perfunctory, such as the following example:

> Your speech to our Business Breakfast Club was very much appreciated.
> You are an excellent speaker, and you have good ideas. Thank you.

Should a letter that commends be couched in general terms?

To a speaker who has worked hard preparing and who has not been paid, such a letter may have *some* value. After all, the author cared enough to write. Yet, such a letter could have been sent to any speaker, even if its author had slept through the entire speech. A note closed with *sincerely* does not necessarily make the ideas seem sincere. Because the following revision is more specific, it is more meaningful:

> Before noon today, I found myself applying some of the principles you discussed at this morning's Business Breakfast Club.
> I jotted down each of your three suggestions on the Money Market;

and, thanks to all the supporting figures you presented, I am convinced of their validity.

Thank you for an interesting, thought-provoking talk.

The revision does not sound so much like a form letter. At least its author was aware of the three points made and that each was supported. The letter conveys gratitude, an intangible reward; but a different approach could result in a tangible reward as well. A letter of commendation could have been addressed to the speaker's employer:

Mr. Will Jones (financial analyst at your Lockwood office) gave a very interesting, informative speech at this morning's Business Breakfast Club.

In a well-organized and witty presentation, he offered three suggestions on the Money Market (along with supporting facts and figures). From members' reaction during the question-and-answer period that followed, I sensed that his ideas were clearly understood and appreciated.

Possibly Mr. Jones has let you know that he was to give a talk this morning, but I just want you to know that he gave an outstanding talk — totally consistent with the image your bank projects.

With such letters in his file, Mr. Jones's chances for promotion or other tangible rewards are increased; but the intangible reward alone makes the effort worthwhile.

Such letters should be written for the purpose of commending deserving people; they should not be written for the purpose of possible self-gain. However, sometimes those who take time to write such letters receive some unexpected benefits too.

As an undergraduate student, Henry Kissinger wrote a letter of appreciation to a Prussian general who had spoken at his university. Touched by such thoughtfulness, the general invited Mr. Kissinger to dinner. Concluding that the young man had unusually keen insights into international affairs, the general was instrumental in getting Kissinger admitted to graduate study.

Although generous praise is seldom objectionable, a letter or memo of commendation may not fully achieve its purpose if it reaches the point of exaggeration or uses language that is hardly believable:

Mr. Combs, who conducted the ten-week seminar that was concluded this week, is by far the best and most informed discussion leader we have had.

He was fantastic. I learned more from him than from all the others combined. Thanks for selecting him.

(As a within-the-firm communication, the message would be typed as a memorandum.) In the writer's mind, the statements may be true; but, in the reader's mind,

Why write to an *employer* *about an employee who has gone beyond the call of duty?*

Is self-gain a legitimate motive for writing a letter that commends?

Are exaggerations advisable?

they may seem unbelievable. Because the language is strong and the statements are not supported, the memo could arouse thoughts about how bad other leaders were; or it could arouse questions about the writer's motives. The training director would probably be more impressed with the following memo:

> I commend Mr. Frank Combs for his effectiveness in the ten-week seminar that concluded this week.
>
> In the first session, he began by defining a problem and pointing out relevant factors. Then he formed small groups for specific discussion. After collecting a "solution" from each group, he synthesized the groups' thoughts and helped us derive a sensible solution. In sessions two through ten, he always began by re-emphasizing principles from the preceding session.
>
> Because he gave us credit for being able to think, and because he was willing to listen, we were willing to listen. From his wealth of knowledge and experience, we learned much that we can apply on our jobs.

Does strong language strengthen a compliment?

Although the preceding message does not employ strong language, it conveys a stronger compliment. Without the words "best" and "fantastic," it reveals *why* the participant's reaction was favorable.

Who benefits from a commendation letter sent to the subject's employer?

The net effects of the preceding memorandum are positive: (1) the writer feels good for having passed on a deserved compliment, (2) management gains some assurance that a training program is effective, (3) the person about whom the letter was written is encouraged to continue an effective technique, and (4) subsequent trainees may have an increased likelihood of exposure to a similar program. Even when communications point out negatives, the intent should be to get results that are positive.

Negative Qualities

Why are people hesitant about writing letters that point out negatives?

A person who has had a bad experience as a result of another's conduct may be reluctant to write about that experience. Assume, for example, that the discussion leader in the preceding illustration had been ineffective. Before writing about the problem, a trainee would recognize the rollowing *risks:* (1) being stereotyped as a complainer, (2) being associated with negative thoughts and thus thought of in negative terms, or (3) appearing to challenge one of management's prior decisions (choice of the leader). Yet such risks may be worth taking because of the benefits:

When another person has made or is making mistakes, what can be gained by writing a letter?

(1) the writer gets a feeling of having exercised a responsibility, (2) management learns of changes that need to be made, (3) the person about whom the letter is written modifies techniques and is thus happier and more successful, and (4) present and future trainees may be exposed to programs that are more beneficial.

Are letters that seek revenge advisable?

In the decision to write about negatives, the primary consideration is *intent*. If the intent is to hurt or to get even, the message should not be written. Of course, false information would be unethical and illegal.

A memo or letter that reports negatives results from evaluation, but evaluative words are discouraged. Instead of presenting facts, the following message judges:

> Mr. Frank Combs, discussion leader in our seminar, is positively the worst of all our leaders.
>
> Because of his lack of promptness, his ineffectiveness in presenting concepts, and his negative attitude, I consider the seminar a complete waste of time.

In the mind of the trainee, the first sentence may be fair and accurate; but in the mind of the reader, "worst" may seem overly harsh. It may convey the tone of a habitual fault-finder. Without details, the charges made in the second sentence lack force. If *complete waste of time* strikes the receiver as an exaggeration, the whole message loses impact. Overall, the memo is short, general, and negative. By comparison, the following revision is long, specific, and positive:

(1) Looking back over the last ten weeks of seminars, I realize I have had exposure to the excellent leaders you spoke about in our orientation.

(1) Introduces a discussion of seminar leadership.

(2) Of the four leaders, three are just as good as or better than you said they would be. However, some aspects of Mr. Combs's performance need to be called to your attention:

(2) Tries to convey fair-mindedness and establish credibility by acknowledging good points in a memo that discusses bad points.

What is the effect of including a positive in a letter that points out and stresses negatives?

1. (3) On three occasions (May 1, May 8, and May 22) he arrived twenty minutes late without apology or explanation.

(3) Presents a statement of fact without labeling it in negative terms. Judgment is left to the reader.

What is the effect of assigning a number to each point?

2. (4) His discussion leadership consists of rapid-fire lecture. In all sessions combined, about fifteen minutes were devoted to discussion of ways in which principles can be <u>applied</u> in the work we will be doing.

(4) Includes another verifiable fact. A training director who had promised give-and-take discussions does not need to be told how bad the lecture technique is.

3. (5) Written case analyses submitted on May 22 were scheduled for return and discussion the following week. Now, six weeks later, the papers have yet to be returned.

(5) Continues with a verifiable statement. If such conduct is deplorable, outrageous, or insulting, the reader will be aware of it without the writer's use of such terms.

(6) I see Mr. Combs as a well-informed person who could become an excellent discussion leader.

(6) Confesses a positive and thus seeks to add credibility to the preceding negatives.

(7) Overall, the seminars have been very helpful to me. In the spirit of helpfulness, I am passing this confidential information to you.

(7) Ends on a pleasant note. Employs "confidential" as a safeguard; the information is intended for professional use only, not designed to hurt and not to be thought of as gossip.

Because one person took the time to write a memo, many could benefit. Although not always easy or pleasant, writing about negatives can be thought of as a civic responsibility. For example, a person who returns from a long stay at a major hotel might, upon returning home, write a letter to the management commending certain employees. If the stay had not been pleasant and weaknesses in hotel operation had been detected, a tactful letter pointing out the negatives would probably be appreciated. Future guests could benefit from the effort of that one person.

Whether negative evaluations are presented in writing or in conversation, the same principles apply: have a positive intent, be factual, use positive language, and leave judgment to the recipient.

Why should you avoid use of judgmental terms?

SUMMARY

Would a letter to a hotel or business where you had been treated well be a goodwill gesture? Would it be necessary?

Although routine business affairs dominate most of our time, special situations provide opportunities for us to put our best foot forward. The way in which we display our sensitivity to human relationships marks the kind of people we are. Special letters provide one way to demonstrate that sensitivity.

EXERCISES

Review Questions

1. What are the advantages of keeping congratulatory messages relatively short?

2. Compared with oral communication, what are the advantages of using written communication to convey congratulatory messages?

3. Compared with congratulatory messages that are handwritten, what are the advantages of congratulatory messages that are typewritten?

4. Should letters of congratulation be answered? Explain.

5. If a letter contains a congratulatory message, what nonverbal message is conveyed by sending the letter a few weeks after the congratulatory event?

6. What does a job seeker gain by alerting a reference about the possibility of a request for a recommendation letter?

7. What does a job seeker gain by providing a résumé for the person who may be asked to write a recommendation letter?

8. In a recommendation letter, what is the advantage of using a typing format that employs enumeration and tabulation of each quality discussed?

9. If you, as personnel director, received an unsolicited recommendation letter, which salutation would you prefer and why? (a) To Whom It May Concern, or (b) To Prospective Employers.

10. Recommendation letters may be written either inductively or deductively. Explain.

11. In a recommendation letter, which portion of a sentence would provide less emphasis for a negative quality — the dependent clause or the independent clause?

12. Upon leaving a job, what does an employee gain by asking the employer for a recommendation letter?

13. In a letter that reserves a room for purposes of attending a convention at a hotel, what information should be included?

14. When R.S.V.P. appears on an invitation, what determines whether the response is to be in writing or by telephone?

15. Although "thank you" letters are short, why should they include something specific?

16. A supervisor receives a letter that commends one of her subordinates. To the subordinate, what are the intangible benefits? And what are the tangible benefits that could accrue?

17. A sales representative genuinely appreciates the extra efforts an employee has expended on his behalf. How does the representative benefit from writing a commendation letter to the employer?

18. "I want something from Mr. Jones. After he sees this commendation letter from me, my chances of success will be improved." Is the motive commendable? Explain.

19. In a letter that calls attention to another person's failures, which would be better: (a) present facts and leave evaluation of them to the reader, or (b) present the facts and reveal the negative results from your own evaluation?

20. In a letter that calls attention to another person's failures, what should be the writer's intent?

Letter-Writing Problems

In the following letter-writing problems, supply the names, addresses, and specific facts of each problem. Although you have freedom to use your imagination, be especially careful to apply principles discussed in the preceding chapter.

1.   In this morning's paper, a picture of an acquaintance caught your eye. A systems analyst for three years, she was promoted to chair her department. Write a congratulatory letter.

2.   After selling your coin collection to a buyer from another state, you learned that the buyer's check "bounced." An assistant vice president at your bank showed extraordinary human understanding. Not only was she successful in keeping your anxiety level from soaring, she eventually was successful in getting your money for you ($10,000). Write a letter of commendation to her boss.

3.   As president of a bank, respond to the letter described in the preceding problem. Let the bank customer know that the letter was genuinely appreciated.

4.   To the most recent guest lecturer in your class, write a "thank-you" letter.

5.   From this morning's student newspaper, you have learned that a classmate in one of your courses last semester was killed in an accident. Write a condolence letter to the classmate's parents.

6.   After a severe wind-and-thunder storm in which your house was damaged, an insurance claims adjuster reached a satisfactory settlement with you. But your personal reaction to the adjuster was very negative, and you wrote to his boss. Pretending you are the boss who received that letter, write the letter you think the boss should send to you as a response.

7.   Your stylist has done your hair for the last time. He (or she) is retiring at the end of the week. Write a letter that will make him or her feel good.

8.   An insurance adjuster was tactful, efficient, and fair in settling your accident claim. Write a letter of appreciation to the adjuster's supervisor.

9.   Assume an elderly, eminent ophthalmologist removed a tissue growth from your eyeball. The operation was very delicate; results were perfect. Your last trip to the physician's office was routine. Upon paying your account before leaving, you were told that Dr. Sooter-Smith was retiring. You were the last patient in a career that spanned more than fifty years. Write a letter that she will treasure.

10.   According to the papers, your congressman in Washington voted for a bill that you very much wanted to see passed. The bill is strictly in line with your political philosophy. Write a letter of appreciation and encouragement.

11.   A competitor's warehouse burned. You have about 4,000 square feet of space that is available to him for five weeks—if he wants to use it. No charge.

12. An acquaintance has just been released from the hospital. Her convalescence time is expected to be about six weeks. Send a letter that will help to keep up her morale.

13. You were among those being considered for promotion. You were not promoted, but a friend in another department was. Write the friend a congratulatory letter.

14. One of the employees whom you supervise is quitting and moving to another state. For her husband's health, a dry climate was recommended. By all standards, the employee's record is exceptionally good. Write a recommendation letter that she can show to prospective employers.

15. A certain employee has, over the last year, been a frequent contributor to the suggestion box. Five suggestions have been incorporated into operating procedures. With each suggestion has gone a monetary reward. But, after the most recent suggestion, you want also to reward her with an expression of appreciation and encouragement. Send her a memorandum. (Assume you are the top official in the firm.)

16. You have been promoted to a position of much greater responsibility. Write a response to one of those "congratulations, you deserved it" notes you have been receiving.

17. A friend has applied for admission to Mortar Board, an honorary society with exceedingly high standards. A good grade index helps; but *service* is weighted heavily, too. Assuming you are writing about a very deserving candidate, write a letter supporting the application.

18. Assume a student committee is trying to select a teacher of the year. Students have been invited to write nominating letters. Pick a teacher from a preceding semester, and write a letter of support.

19. Compared with other teachers you have had, one of last semester's teachers was far below standard. Maybe he doesn't know; maybe he thinks he's doing an outstanding job. Maybe his administrators don't know. In an effort to help him, to help the school, and to help students who take his classes later, write a letter. Address it to his dean or departmental chairperson.

20. You and your spouse spent the weekend with friends in another city. Upon returning home, write a thank-you letter.

COMMUNICATING ABOUT EMPLOYMENT

OBJECTIVES   **1.** To develop an understanding of the job-search process.

2. To compile an effective personal résumé.

3. To develop skill in preparing application letters that reflect creativity, indicate personal strengths, and encourage favorable action.

WRITING ABOUT EMPLOYMENT—THE APPLICATION

What Employers Want
What Prospective Employees Need
Locating a Job Opportunity
Matching Job Requirements
   with Qualifications
Working and Worrying
The Résumé
Starting with the Résumé
Perfecting the Résumé
Including Detail
Emphasizing Important Points
Selecting a Kind of Résumé

The Application Letter
The Unsolicited Letter
The Solicited Letter
Special Problems
The Letter of Recommendation
Other Letters About Employment
Job-Inquiry Letters
Application Follow-ups
Job-Acceptance Letters
Job-Refusal Letters
Thank-You Letters
Summary

Asked "How can one become a millionaire?" an American financier replied, "It's easy. Just find the right person to do your work and stay out of the way."

To an employer, is finding the right employee a major problem?

For an employee, few decisions are more important than choosing the right job. For an employer, few decisions are more important than choosing the right employees. Because finding the right person is so important, businesses are willing to spend huge amounts for recruitment. They pay transportation costs for interviewees, they pay the expenses of high-salaried recruiters who travel to distant cities, they maintain interviewing offices, and they solicit the help of public and private employment offices. All these efforts are designed to match employers' needs with employees' qualities.

WHAT EMPLOYERS WANT

What qualities do employers look for in employees?

To continue earning a profit by providing high-quality goods or services, employers look for high-quality employees. They may not see each of them in every person hired, but they are looking for the following qualities:

1. *Employees who can do what must be done.* Education, training, and experience at other jobs assist in predicting whether an applicant can actually do the job.

2. *Employees who can get along with others on the present work force.* This quality can be assessed by statements (even between-the-lines statements) in application letters, in personal interviews, and in references. As a cause for dismissal, failure to do a job well is less frequent than failure to get along with others.

3. *Employees who are planning to remain on the job for a reasonable time.* Through career-objective statements on résumés and through interviews, prospective employees' goals can be assessed. Because training employees is expensive and because tolerating a new employee's relatively low production is also expensive, employers prefer to select workers who will stay on the job long after the initial training period is over.

4. *Employees who are loyal to the employer.* To assess this quality, interviewers invite discussion about previous jobs and employers. Application forms, application letters, and résumés frequently provide clues about attitudes toward employers. Employers appreciate employees who assist in projecting a positive corporate image.

5. *Employees who are industrious.* Through interviews, application letters, résumés, and application forms, employers hope to find evidence that a prospective employee is willing to spend the energy required to do a job well. Subjective as they may be, the following conditions can suggest laziness: poorly organized

correspondence, sloppy erasures, strikeovers in typing, misspellings, and slouching in a chair during an interview.

6.   *Employees who can communicate.* A necessity on any job, this quality can be easily judged by scrutinizing the application letter, the résumé, and the verbal skills exhibited in interviews. Lack of skill in using the language may be associated with lack of job skill or knowledge.

7.   *Employees who have integrity.* Although integrity is a very desirable quality, it is difficult to judge in applicants. Even people who profess to have integrity are often regarded with suspicion. From correspondence or interviews, an employer needs assurance that the prospective employee would measure up to high standards of ethics.

8.   *Employees who plan carefully.* An applicant who arranges a résumé carefully, supplies information promptly, arrives promptly for an interview, and presents a realistic statement of career objectives is giving some indication of willingness to look ahead. Applicants who plan their personal lives carefully are likely to be looked upon as workers who would plan their workday carefully.

How can carelessness in typing and spelling defeat an applicant's purpose?

9.   *Employees who are free of serious personal problems.* Serious personal problems can reduce job effectiveness. Although interviewers are prohibited by law from delving unnecessarily into applicants' personal lives, interviewees can beneficially volunteer information that depicts them as being able to give a job the attention it deserves; such as a happy home life, freedom from alcoholic addiction, freedom from problems of indebtedness, etc.

10.   *Employees who are in good health.* Because health problems often result in absence or substandard production, employers like to have assurance that applicants are in good physical and mental condition. (A physically handicapped person is different from an unhealthy person. When properly matched with a job, the physically handicapped can be ideal employees who are seldom or never absent and whose production meets high standards.)

Although the preceding list is not arranged to show any consensus about order of importance, it is true that employers understandably devote most of their attention to the first two qualities—*doing the job* and *getting along with people.*

Aware of the qualities that employers want employees to have, job applicants should have little difficulty in deciding what to talk about in their job-hunting efforts.

WHAT PROSPECTIVE EMPLOYEES NEED

From a job seeker's point of view, the following questions need to be answered: Where are the jobs? How well do my qualifications match the jobs to be applied for? What is the best way to prepare a résumé? How do I write an effective application letter? How do I conduct myself in an employment interview?

Locating a Job Opportunity

**What are some good
sources of job information?**

In answer to the question "Who needs the knowledges and skills I have to offer?"
you can find out about possible jobs from the following sources:

Libraries

The following library sources are helpful:

1. Annual reports from major firms
2. *Black Enterprise* (each year's June issue)
3. *Career,* the *Annual Guide to Business Opportunities*
4. *College Placement Annual*
5. Company house organs (newsletters)
6. *Dictionary of Occupational Titles*
7. Dun and Bradstreet's *Million Dollar Directory*
8. Dun and Bradstreet's *Middle Market Directory*
9. *Engineering Index*
10. *Forbes* ("Annual Directory Issue," published May 15 each year)
11. *Fortune*
12. Moody's *Manuals*
13. *Occupational Outlook Handbook*
14. Science Research Associates' occupational information pamphlets
15. Standard and Poor's *Register of Corporations, Directors, and Executives*
16. *Thomas' Register of American Manufacturers*
17. Trade or professional journals
18. United States Civil Service Commission
19. *Wall Street Journal*

Newspapers and Magazines

The most obvious source is an advertisement for a position in the classified section
of the newspaper. When responding to a newspaper ad, do so as promptly as
possible. Early responses may receive heavier consideration. Using your previously
prepared résumé and letter of application as a guide, you can make any needed
revisions and mail a response soon after reading the ad.

Another source of job information in newspapers, and in magazines too, is in articles. If any business or industry is reported to be expanding or moving into your area, you can assume that they need additional employees. Your present employer's in-house publication for its own employees may have information about advancement opportunities for you (without changing employer).

Professional Organizations

Much job information is exchanged at meetings of professional associations. Some journals of professional organizations have help-wanted and position-wanted columns. Officers of professional organizations, through their contacts with members, are sometimes very good sources of information about job opportunities.

Employment Agencies

Because bringing employers and job seekers together is their business, employment agents can be especially helpful. Private agencies charge a fee, customarily based on the first month's salary; but the payment may be spread over several months. Naturally, the agency makes more profit if it finds you a high-paying job. A note of caution: Find out who pays the placement fee, the employer or employee, before you sign anything. Also, check the percentage of the fee—unscrupulous agents sometimes take advantage of first-time users.

School Placement Bureaus

More useful than employment agencies, perhaps, are school placement bureaus, sometimes referred to as the office of career services. These bureaus are in an ideal position to assist both applicants and employers, being able to supply students with information about job opportunities and employers with information about job applicants. Information about openings comes from company recruiters who visit campuses for interviews and usually leave informative handouts that students can read. Information about students is supplied by the students to the bureau, leaving it with a set of credentials ready for quick release to prospective employers.

What are the advantages of registering with your school's placement bureau?

Normally, students are invited to have recommendation letters from teachers submitted to the bureau for inclusion in the set of credentials. As the law now stands, students have a right to see the letters written about them unless they have signed a statement waiving that right. Each student should use his or her judgment about signing such a form, but signing the waiver can increase employer confidence in the recommendation. When the form has been signed, the writer of the recommendation letter can proceed with confidence that the letter cannot be shown to the applicant. Hence, the writer may exercise the freedom to include pertinent negatives. Seeing the signed waiver, the employer will expect the letter to be more frank and thus more useful.

Should applicants waive the right to see letters written about them?

Acquaintances

What is the
meaning of *nepotism*?

Friends who are already employed in a firm can usually give you some information about its employment needs. Some firms encourage their employees to recommend prospective workers. If information about employment comes from a friend or relative, you should try to ascertain whether the firm has policies against hiring friends or relatives.

You can also get information about possible jobs from your professors. Through consulting work and other contacts with business, professors have frequent opportunities to become aware of unfilled positions.

Direct Inquiry

Perhaps the most useful way of finding out about job openings is to make direct inquiry to a firm, either by writing, phoning, or walking in. If a firm is in need of employees, letters of inquiry about jobs are welcomed. A short, simple letter asking whether employees are needed in a certain field may bring you an application form and an invitation to apply. Such letters can be addressed to the personnel director by name, if possible. (If the name cannot be found in the library, you can find it by using the telephone.)

Sometimes other job information can be obtained quickly by using the telephone. By talking with the personnel director or other responsible officials, you may be able to discover open positions and request application forms.

A very simple way to learn about job opportunities is to go directly to the firm and ask. Even though no appointment has been made, someone at the firm may be able to give out job information or even conduct a short interview. Going to the employer's office has advantages over either writing or calling. You are there and someone must talk to you, if only to say "no." A letter can be thrown out and a phone hung up, but a person must be talked with. Also, you have a chance to make a strong favorable impression.

An Advertisement of Yourself

Just as employers who need workers can advertise their needs, so can job-seekers advertise their needs. As specifically as possible, the ad should indicate the type of job wanted; and it should highlight outstanding qualifications. Whether the ad invites response to a box number or to a phone number, it could bring numerous leads.

Matching Job Requirements with Qualifications

Before you try to convince an employer that you can do a job well, you must first convince yourself. You need a clear definition of what the job entails and your specific preparation for it.

Information about what a job entails can be found in a variety of ways:

1. *Occupational courses in school.* Students who have taken courses in such disciplines as accounting, finance, advertising, salesmanship, management, word processing, etc., will surely have some idea about the work done at entry-level positions. Yet, you should seek additional information.

2. *The Dictionary of Occupational Titles.* The *Dictionary* lists thousands of jobs along with a description of the work done. Naturally, a job title at one firm may involve duties slightly different from those performed under the same title at another firm.

3. *A visit to a company plant or office.*

4. *Conversation with former employees.*

5. *Conversation with employees who perform a similar job at another firm.*

6. *Information supplied by the firm's employment office.*

In addition to learning as much as possible about the duties required on a job at a certain company, you should also learn about the company itself. Thoroughly read the annual report and study pamphlets distributed by the firm's employment office.

In job hunting, as in solving other problems, putting ideas on paper is a useful technique. For a vivid picture of the ways in which *what the job requires* matches *what you can offer,* you can easily develop a worksheet. If job requirements are listed in one column and your qualifications are listed in another, their compatibility (or lack of it) can be seen readily. If the two columns don't match very well, you may appropriately decide to seek another type of work. If they do match well, pointing out that commonality of relationship should be easy at later stages in the job-getting procedure.

Why should we list job requirements and what the applicant can offer on the same sheet of paper?

Working and Worrying

Searching for a job (while trying to survive without one) can be extremely challenging, time consuming, and frustrating. It requires careful planning and record keeping. If done well, it requires at least as much daily energy as would a full-time job. Sending a letter or two and then just doing nothing until a reply comes back is not the way to proceed. Instead, the job hunter should keep moving—always working toward the goal of finding the right job. No one should wait aimlessly at home for a few days after an interview (just hoping for positive results). Instead, efforts to get other interviews should be in progress. Several interviews in one day should be welcomed if they can be arranged.

Such efforts may require as much emotional energy as physical energy. But the job seeker should not tolerate the additional handicap of worry. The reason for any rejection may be a circumstance over which the applicant has no control whatever. Many are the happy employees who were rejected one day only to get a much better job the next. And keep in mind that bitterness over failure to get one job could be reflected in the interview for the next. From the very beginning of the job search, think positively; it will be reflected in your writing as well as in interviews.

THE RÉSUMÉ

The typical job application normally consists of two parts: a letter of application and a résumé or data sheet. The two are attached, with the letter on top.

Starting with the Résumé

Why should we prepare the résumé before writing the application letter?

Although the letter is seen first, it should be written *after* the résumé has been prepared. Just as making an outline forces beneficial thinking about a report that is to be written, making a résumé forces beneficial thinking about an application letter that is to be written. Having prepared the résumé, you can easily identify the ideas to include in the letter and the sequence in which to present them.

Perfecting the Résumé

Why should we strive for perfection in grammar, punctuation, typing, and spelling?

You can hardly expect to be hired solely on the strengths of the letter and résumé (an interview will almost certainly precede hiring). In the selection process, the interview is vital; but if infirmities are detected in the preceding papers, an interview may never take place. Therefore, paperwork is also vital. Knowing how much a job may mean to an applicant, the person who sees the paperwork is likely to look on it as the best the applicant can do. Errors in content, style, organization, and mechanics risk being looked upon as inexcusable.

Including Detail

What makes employers willing to read an application letter that is long?

Applicants who have little confidence in their writing or who are fearful of making errors are inclined to argue for brevity in letters and in résumés. The prospective employer, however, has a serious decision to make and (after making the decision) will need to justify it. Because justification is difficult when information is scant, the employer (or the employer's agent) appreciates specifics.

No one can say just how long letters and résumés should be, but applicants are more likely to err on the side of making them too short than too long. Suppose, for example, an employer is half way through reading a page. So far, the applicant is satisfactorily presenting information that shows a positive relationship between qualifications and job requirements. Will the page be put aside just because it is long? Not likely. In fact, the reaction is more likely to be "Give me more; this is the kind of information I need." Yet, a brief résumé would be better than a long résumé that contains irrelevant or insignificant information. Unimportant information is time and space consuming; in addition, it competes for attention with important information.

If all your pertinent data can be arranged on one page, one page is long enough. If an additional page is needed, include it. If two pages are required, they should be planned. Two pages with generous margins would demonstrate better planning than would two pages with narrow margins and only four lines on the second page.

Should application letters be restricted to one page?

Emphasizing Important Points

In the process of analyzing job requirements and qualifications, you should be able to determine which is more impressive, your education or your experience. If you are just emerging from school and have had little part-time experience, education will be your main qualification. If you have considerable related experience, that will probably be your main qualification.

Under what condition would an applicant list *education* before *experience*?

Because the first position in a series is emphatic, the most outstanding qualification should be presented first. With an appropriate title distinctly set apart from surrounding data, it will get primary attention. Items that appear under the *experience* or *education* headings are likewise preferably presented in order-of-importance sequence. Application forms prepared by employers usually invite applicants to list previous jobs in reverse chronological order. From the employer's point of view, the arrangement simplifies identification of job hoppers; it also enables the employer to account for all an applicant's time over a certain period. From the applicant's point of view, however, emphasizing a certain experience and demonstrating how closely related it is to the job sought is more important than stressing *when* the experience was accumulated.

Should a résumé list all the jobs held, and should they be listed in chronological order?

Selecting a Kind of Résumé

By the time an employer has finished reading an application letter and data sheet, answers to two questions should be apparent: (1) What educational and work experiences has the applicant had? (2) How are those experiences related to the job sought? Answers to these questions can be presented by the applicant in either of two ways:

1. A résumé that *lists* and *explains,* plus an introductory application letter that is relatively short.

2. A résumé that *lists,* plus an application letter that explains and is relatively long.

From reading about academic and work-oriented experiences, employers want a clear picture of what was done, what was learned, and how those experiences are related to the job sought. *Where* this information is presented (résumé or application letter) is much less important than *whether* it is presented.

In the résumé in Figure 11-1 (pages 263–264), the applicant has decided to include explanatory material (his accompanying letter would be introductory and short). In studying the résumé, note the features contained in the following list:

1.　The title reveals (a) the name of the applicant, (b) the job sought, and (c) the name of the firm from which the job is sought.

2.　Address and phone number are placed in an easily located spot.

3.　Objectives are consistent with the accompanying application and present the applicant as one who (by doing a job well) plans to be moved upward.

4.　Because recent experience is more closely related to the job than education, experience is presented first—for emphasis. The title ties experiences to the title of the job sought.

Why should we include information about what was learned while on a job?

5.　In addition to presenting duties and responsibilities, the experience section concludes by summarizing *what the experiences have taught.* In presenting this information, an applicant should try especially hard to list points in which the employer will be interested.

6.　The education section lists only related courses. Grade average is explained. (An applicant with only an average grade index would possibly choose to omit it.)

7.　Like the experience section, the education section attempts to explain how the academic experience has been job related. Also like the experience section, the education section identifies some important principles that were *learned.* The principles have been selected carefully—principles in which the employer is most likely to be interested. Inclusion of such statements helps the employer to see that the applicant knows what to expect on the job. In addition, it enables the applicant to use some of the vocabulary used on the job. And, it helps to contrast the applicant who has *learned* from courses with other applicants who merely report that they have *taken* courses.

Why should we identify principles learned in school?

8.　Because personal information is less important than education and experience, it is placed in a less emphatic position. Although personal information is very difficult for employers to *require,* applicants can beneficially reveal information that depicts them as having no personal problems that would interfere with their work.

9.　References are not included, but their availability is noted. Other methods are to omit the reference section completely or to present a list of people who could write credibly about an applicant. Omitting references completely could imply that the applicant does not know much about the job-seeking process, or that the applicant is afraid references would be negative. Presenting references could be beneficial; the applicant is apparently confident that positive support is available, and (if the employer desires) references *could* be solicited before the interview. However, such solicitations could become an embarrassment on the present job.

JAMES B. WOOD
Applicant for Office Manager with
JONES-WILFORD CORPORATION

Address: 721 East 21st Street, Fremont Hills, CA 94321

Telephone: (214) 555-2140

Professional Objectives: (Current) To become an
office manager.
(Long-range) To serve in higher
levels of management.

Experiences Related to Office Management

Assistant Office Manager, Camwood Investment Corporation
(1981 to present). Share (but to a lesser degree than the office
manager) responsibility for the entire office operation. Have
primary responsibility for appraising employee performance.
Was successful in initiating a change from evaluation by
checklist to results-oriented appraisal. The new system is
consistent with top management's practice of MBO and has been
enthusiastically accepted by employees. Have responsibility for
filing OSHA reports and for spotting and correcting any
condition that might violate OSHA standards.

Supervisor, Word-Processing Center, Camwood Investment
Corporation (1979-1980). Gathered information and wrote a
report that resulted in installation of our word-processing
center. Assisted in the transition from old hot-type equipment
to computers. Conservatively, the new system saves Jones-
Wilford at least $25,000 yearly. Assisted in training employees
to operate the new equipment. Was direct supervisor of 14
employees.

Bookkeeper and Cashier (part-time), Royal Dipper (a
restaurant) (1977-1978). Kept financial and personnel records.
Made payments to suppliers and employees, made bank deposits.

Secretary, Society of Advanced Management (1983-1984).
Have responsibility for doing correspondence and keeping
records and an opportunity to become acquainted with top office
managers in the area.

These experiences have demonstrated (1) the need for
keeping abreast of current techniques and the latest
technological developments; (2) an even greater need for
carefully selecting, training, and rewarding employees; and (3)
the necessity of keeping up with daily work while still allowing
time daily for planning ahead.

Figure 11-1   Résumé containing explanatory material. Accompanying letter is short.

Education for Office Management

Currently taking night courses toward an M.B.A. at State University (expected graduation, Spring 1986).

Courses in administrative services:
  Principles of Office Management
  Records Management
  Theory of Administrative Communication
  Business Report Writing
  Electronic Data Processing

Other related business courses:
  Principles of Management
  Business Policy
  Business Communication
  Human Relations in Business
  Business Programming
  Personnel Management

Honors:
  Dean's List, three semesters
  Beta Gamma Sigma (honorary fraternity for business majors)
  Pi Omega Pi (honorary fraternity for majors in administrative services)
  Grade average: 3.52 (on 4-point scale)

During the undergraduate years, attendance at local SAM meetings helped to reveal the relationship of theory and practice. Writing a school report on "Human Relations in the Office" turned out to be a valuable experience; it was excellent preparation for the tasks of appraising employee performance. Because of the computer-oriented courses, communication with computer personnel is greatly simplified. In various courses and in various ways, the academic exposure stressed the need for (1) always being ready for change, (2) always trying to bring about change, (3) always striving for self-improvement, (4) always being sensitive to human needs, and (5) always exhibiting high levels of integrity.

Personal Information

Have been married for four years. One son, two years old. Have been a homeowner for two years. Excellent health. Swim and play tennis.

References

References will be supplied on request.

Figure 11-1 continued.

JAMES B. WOOD
Applicant for Office Manager
with
JONES-WILFORD CORP.
January 15, 1984

Address: 721 East 21st Street   Telephone: (214) 555-2140
           Fremont Hills, CA 94321

Job Objectives: Office management (immediate)
                  Middle or higher management (eventual)

Experiences Related to Office Management

Assistant Office Manager
Camwood Investment
Corporation
(1981 to present)
Bookkeeper and Cashier
(part-time)
Royal Dipper (a restaurant)
(1977-1978)

Supervisor, Word-Processing
Center
Camwood Investment
Corporation
(1979-1980)
Secretary, SAM (local chapter)
(1983-1984)

Education for Office Management

B.S., State University (1978)

Courses in administrative
services:
   Principles of Office
      Management
   Records Management
   Theory of Administrative
      Communication
   Business Report Writing
   Electronic Data Processing

M.B.A., State University (night
classes: expected graduation,
Spring 1986)

Other related business courses:
   Principles of Management
   Business Policy
   Business Communication
   Human Relations in
      Business
   Business Programming
   Personnel Management

Figure 11-2   Résumé to accompany a long, explanatory letter.

Honors:
    Dean's List, three semesters
    Beta Gamma Sigma (honorary fraternity for business majors)
    Pi Omega Pi (honorary fraternity for majors in administrative
       services)
    Grade average: 3.52 (on a scale in which 4 is an A and 3 is a B)

Financing:
    Except for 1st and 2nd years, education was totally self-
       financed.

Personal Information

Married, one child (2 years old)   Excellent health
Have owned a home for 2 years   Recreation: swimming, tennis

References

References will be supplied on request.

Figure 11-2   continued.

RÉSUMÉ   E D W A R D A. R O S S   April 14, 1984

University address   Permanent address

21 Founders Hall   347 E. Fifth Street
Central State University   Green Stick Village
Plattsburg, NM 63114   Mountain Home, NM 63215

Phone (517) 321-4471   Phone (517) 274-3122

Department in which job is sought: Forecasting

Can offer an employer the following attributes:

CAN LEARN QUICKLY	With one semester to go as a major in Economics, the grade-point average is 3.67 (on a 4-point scale). GRE score, 670 quantitative and 643 verbal (for many schools, 500 is acceptable for admission to graduate study). As a new, part-time clerk in a clothing store, was commended by the supervisor for learning the system faster than any clerks previously employed.
KNOW MATHEMATICS AND COMPUTER	Quantitative courses taken include linear algebra, calculus, business statistics, and econometrics. Computer courses provided experience with four different languages. Skill in typing (60 wpm) is an advantage in using machines efficiently. Almost always successful in "balancing" (on the first try) with the cash register at the end of a day in the store.
CAN COMMUNICATE	Think before beginning to communicate, listen carefully, have human empathy for others: such principles were stressed in oral communication courses, and the clothing-store job provided abundant opportunities to practice them. Courses in written communication and report writing (with generous feedback) provided ideal experience in gathering data, organizing ideas, and

Figure 11-3   Résumé stressing attributes, to accompany a short letter.

	meeting high standards of style and mechanics. Fluency in Spanish was exceedingly useful on the job.
AM DEPENDABLE	Have missed only three class sessions in seven semesters. Have occasional responsibility for locking the store at closing time, sometimes take cash to the bank. Have never been late to work or absent. Was highly commended for a school report, "Ethics in Business."
HAVE STABLE PERSONAL LIFE	Come from a happy, success-oriented family. Have exceptionally good health. Willing to work in (or be transferred to) other sections of the country. Am fascinated by latest advances in electronic technology.
WILL PROVIDE REFERENCES	On request, references can be obtained from present employer, former professors, and a local banker.

Figure 11-3 continued.

RÉSUMÉ

MARY ALICE JACKSON

Objective
To work in a word-processing unit (immediate). To assume increased responsibility in office administration (eventual).

Education
A.A. degree, Tri-City College, Weston, OK Major, Office Administration. Courses most related: word-processing, office procedures, typewriting, note-hand, office management, elements of business enterprise, computer programming, and written business communication.
Grade average, 3.40 (on a 4-point scale).

Extracurricular work: secretary, student council (one year); solicitor, help-the-needy program during Christmas holidays.

Honors: dean's list, three semesters.

Experience

1983-present
Receptionist-typist in Student Aid office at Tri-City. Greet those who come to the office, give instructions on filling out forms, check and route forms, type letters and reports, and transcribe from machines or handwritten notes.

1981-1983
Clerk at a grocery store. Operated cash register, sometimes did light record keeping, sometimes assisted new clerks. Overall, an ideal experience in practicing accuracy and meeting people.

Figure 11-4 Résumé stressing dates.

1978-1981   Candy Striper at Good Samaritan Hospital. Ran errands, read for patients, listened to patients who needed an audience. Was (in the third year) president of the candy stripers and supervised a Christmas party for 16 patients.

Special Skills   Read and write Spanish
Take notehand at 90 words per minute
Type 70 words per minute (with accuracy)

References   Can supply references from former professors and employers.

Address   982 West 27th Street, Weston, OK 73182

Telephone   (917) 341-7432

Figure 11-4   continued.

Of course, the present employer will eventually learn of an employee's efforts to seek another job; but that information need not be revealed until (as a result of an interview) the applicant is being seriously considered. Also, if an employer customarily checks with references only after interviews, specific references are not needed before the interview — they compete for attention with more important information.

Are there any *disadvantages* to including references?

In the résumé in Figure 11-2, the applicant has omitted explanatory material (his accompanying letter would be explanatory and long). In studying this résumé, observe that it employs the same type of heading and that ideas are presented in the same sequence as those presented in Figure 11-1 — and for the same reasons. Depending on personal taste, headings in Figure 11-2 could be placed at the left margin and headings in Figure 11-1 could be centered.

Should the application letter repeat information contained on the résumé?

No one format is considered correct; if space appears to have been used wisely and if information is easy to find, the format is acceptable.

Pay special attention to Figure 11-3. This résumé would accompany a short application letter. Intended for submission to the forecasting department of a telephone company, it has some especially good features. Instead of using "Experience" and "Education" as main headings, it employs attributes. Just emerging from four years of college and with only a limited amount of part-time experience, the applicant chooses to emphasize the *attributes* that would be most appealing to the employer. As left-side headings, the attributes stand out vividly. The lines to the right of each heading give details that suggest a close relationship to the job sought. The arrangement provides an emphatic answer to the employer's most pertinent question: Does this applicant have what it takes to do the job well? Each of the five listed qualities (attributes) can be seen and reviewed easily; it has abundant space above, on the left, and below.

Note that the applicant in Figure 11-3 does not include dates. Although the résumé does not use "Experience" and "Education" headings, it draws heavily on education and experience for subject matter. To the employer, whether the applicant *has the qualities* essential for success on the job is much more important than whether they were developed in school or at work. *When* an attribute was developed is not a critical matter. With attributes as a basis for division, this résumé allows an applicant to emphasize the *match-up* of qualifications with job requirements.

Figure 11-4 illustrates a format that is common. Because it is not directed to any specific employer, it can be mailed to many. For those who want to stress chronology, it emphasizes dates.

The résumés in Figures 11-2, 11-3, and 11-4 can be arranged neatly on *one* page (even though two pages are employed for presentation in the text). The type of résumé employed determines the type of application letter.

THE APPLICATION LETTER

The following letter would accompany a résumé that both lists and explains (such as Figure 11-1).

Under what conditions should the application letter be short?

(1) Subject: Application for office
              manager's job

(1) Reveals immediately the purpose of the letter.

(2) In deciding whether to apply for your office manager's job, I made two lists: (3) What the office manager would have to do and what I have been doing.

(2) Leads to an introduction of the résumé.

(3) Implies that some careful thought went into the decision to apply. Could identify the writer as one who solves problems systematically.

(4) Because the lists matched so well, I am sending my résumé. (5) After you have studied it, please call or write to me and suggest a time when we can discuss the job (and my work and education experiences) in more detail.

(4) Introduces the résumé as possible solution to the employer's recruiting problem.

(5) Invites scrutiny and a response. Seeks an interview without the worn expression "May I have an interview at your convenience."

(6) At my present job, Tuesday is a day of long-standing obligations; but any other day would be fine.

(6) Employs this sentence only because it is essential. If the employer is really interested, a day other than Tuesday can be arranged. By including the sentence, the applicant may be conveying loyalty to the present employer and determination to meet obligations —favorable qualities in any applicant.

Under what conditions should the application letter be short?

In contrast, the following letter would accompany a résumé that lists but does not explain—like the one in Figure 11-2:

(1) Subject: Application for office manager's post.

(1) Reveals the specific purpose of the letter. Use of the subject line can assist in achieving a first sentence that is not excessive in length.

(2) In comparing your needs with my university and work experience, I saw a great amount of compatibility.

(2) Begins immediately to discuss points of interest to an employer— what the applicant has to offer.

(3) As a member of the Administrative Management Society, I enjoyed a tour of your facilities last year. Mr. Forest had already told me about your latest automated systems for data storage and retrieval and about your plans for a word-processing center.

(3) Introduces the discussion by revealing some knowledge of the firm and the job sought.

(4) Although your equipment and systems are more sophisticated than those with which I am now working, most of the day-to-day problems Mr. Forest encounters at Jones-Wilford are also encountered on my present job.

(4) Seeks to reveal a relationship between the job held and the job sought.

(5) One of my primary responsibilities is appraising employee performance. For the first few months, evaluation was by checklist. (6) After doing some research and writing a proposal, I succeeded in getting that changed to a "results-oriented" appraisal.

(5) Begins presentation of details about a present-job responsibility that is almost sure to be new-job responsibility (if hired).
(6) Reveals an accomplishment.

Why include details?

(7) The new system is consistent with top management's practice of MBO and has been enthusiastically accepted by employees.

(7) Presents some evidence of having kept up with current thinking ("results-oriented appraisal" is a fairly new concept) and of being team oriented.

(8) Early in my employment with Camwood Investment Corporation, I gathered information and wrote a report that resulted in the installation of our word-processing center. Conservatively, the new system saves at least $25,000 yearly. As supervisor of fourteen employees, I assisted in training employees to operate the new equipment.

(8) Continues with an account of experience that demonstrates good preparation for the job sought. Tells (in addition to what was *done*) the *desirable consequences* of his efforts.

(9) Experiences at Camwood Investment and other jobs have taught me the necessity of (a) keeping abreast of current technological developments; (b) carefully selecting, training, and rewarding employees; and (c) keeping up with daily work while still allowing some time daily for planning ahead.

(9) Presents experience as a *learning* experience. Selects points that will be an obvious advantage to the one selected for the job. Tacitly reveals knowledge of important determinants of success on the job sought.

(10) While I was a student, attendance at local AMS meetings helped me to see the relationship

(10) Points out the practical nature of academic experiences.

of theory and practice. (11) Writing a school report on "Human Relations in the Office" turned out to be valuable preparation for the tasks of appraising employee performance.

(11) Presents a specific academic experience as being related to the office manager's job.

Why enumerate some points that were stressed in school?

(12) Because of computer-oriented courses, communication with computer personnel is greatly simplified. (13) In various courses and in various ways, the academic exposure stressed the need for (a) being ready for change, (b) trying to bring about change, (c) striving for self-improvement, (d) being sensitive to human needs, and (e) exhibiting high levels of integrity.

(12) Identifies the usefulness of certain courses.

(13) Seeks to identify principles (picked up in the academic experience) that are associated with success in the management field.

(14) After you have examined the attached résumé, please call or write to me and suggest a time when we can discuss the office management job (and my background) in more detail.

(14) Seeks an interview.

(15) On my present job, Tuesday is a day of long-standing obligations; but any other day would be fine.

(15) Reveals that choice of the interview time is primarily up to the reader.

What is the basic outline for an application letter?

Assuming a listing-type résumé is to accompany it, the preceding application letter follows the basic sales-letter plan: get attention and interest, identify specific preparation to do a job, give sufficient evidence to be convincing, and ask for action. The primary difference is in the product we have to sell. Instead of selling a *thing,* we are now selling our *own merits.* But, in either case, we're selling an idea — we have what the recipient needs.

As indicated earlier, the writing task is simplified if we have preceded it with a thorough job- and self-analysis. And for most of us, the writing is almost sure to be more effective if we first review some of the important aspects of composition: coherence, concreteness, convention, emphasis, originality, simplicity, sincerity, and empathy. For example, the following letter violates many principles of good application-letter writing:

Why should we avoid a beginning sentence that discusses the graduation date?

(1) On June 15 of this year, I will receive my B.S. degree in business administration from Western Sea University. (2) I understand that

(1) Uses a writer-centered opening. The emphatic announcement of graduation may suggest that the applicant considers a degree, *as such,* to be

you have an opening in your management-trainee program.

(3) Please consider me an applicant for the position.

(4) I entered Western Sea as a freshman four years ago. (5) Since that time I have had all the business courses listed on the attached résumé. (6) I think the course I took in Office Management was especially helpful in training me for the position you have to offer. (7) While in school, I was active in the school organizations and clubs listed on the attached résumé. (8) I am sure you will agree that these activities provide good background for management. (9) Getting along with people, you know, is so important in our fast-moving world.

(10) While in school, I worked part time as an expediter for Flywood Aircraft. (11) This job not only provided me with funds, it gave me that business perspective that is so valuable to a management trainee.

(12) You will find me able and willing to learn. (13) Please write to the references on the enclosed résumé; they have expressed a willingness to supply information about me.

---

sufficient qualification. Although a degree is important, businesses are interested in what the applicant is prepared to do.
(2) Indicates the specific job for which the applicant is applying; could also have told the source of information.

(3) Uses a standard statement. Use of such worn expressions can cause readers to conclude that the candidate has nothing outstanding to offer.

(4) Uses "*I*" for the third time. "*I*" is especially conspicuous as the first word of a paragraph. By writing about what was done four years ago, the applicant suggests he or she may intend to present qualifications with an emphasis on autobiography. (5) Calls attention to the enclosure too early in the letter. (6) Needs to tell specifically *how* the course helped. (7) Continues with the emphasis on "*I*."
(8) Needs to show how these activities contributed to effective job preparation. Doing so would have indicated that the applicant knew what the job would require. "I am sure you will agree" is questionable. The reader may not agree. (9) Attempts to point out the advantages of a varied extracurricular life, but seems to lecture.

(10) Presents factual information listed on the résumé.
(11) Makes a commendable attempt to interpret the part-time experience as helpful, but the funds idea is irrelevant. "That business perspective" is too vague and general to be really helpful.

(12) Sounds a little too presumptuous.
(13) Employs an overused expression ". . . willingness to supply."

Why hold the use of *I* to a minimum?

Why should we avoid repeating the facts stated on accompanying résumé?

Why should we avoid stereotyped expressions?

(14) May I have an interview at your convenience? (15) You may reach me by telephoning 555-8334.

(14) Presents a good idea in the appropriate paragraph for it, but uses another stereotyped expression. (15) Employs "*may* reach," which suggests "I *permit* you to. . . ." Repeats the telephone number unnecessarily, since it is given on the résumé.

What are some common errors in writing application letters?

All applicants can benefit from giving their own letters a thorough sentence-by-sentence analysis. Here is a summary of don'ts for those who write application letters:

1.   Don't copy a letter written by some other person.

2.   Don't write an autobiography.

3.   Don't overwork *I, me,* and *my.*

4.   Don't be unduly humble.

5.   Don't beg or ask for sympathy.

6.   Don't sound too casual.

7.   Don't lecture.

8.   Don't brag.

9.   Don't use a present employer's stationery.

10.   Don't express dissatisfaction with a present employer.

11.   Don't emphasize graduation unnecessarily.

12.   Don't use worn expressions.

13.   Don't write in vague, general terms.

14.   Don't simply repeat résumé information.

15.   Don't say you are qualified; instead, give evidence.

Let's examine some parts of application letters written for different job-getting occasions — unsolicited application letters, solicited application letters, and sundry employment letters.

The Unsolicited Letter

Why do firms like to receive applications for jobs that have not been advertised?

For several reasons, firms like to receive applications for jobs they have not advertised. (The practice of sending unsolicited applications is very common. IBM, for example, is said to receive between 2,500 and 3,000 such letters daily.) With a file of unsolicited applications, a firm can achieve several objectives:

1. Save advertising costs.

2. Fill jobs more quickly because the personnel department can look in the file and be in touch with an applicant in a short time.

3. Save personnel-department time because the personnel department may find a suitable worker from a small file of unsolicited letters (an advertisement may bring fifty or a hundred invited applications, all of which require some attention).

4. Avoid possible goodwill-losing situations because some who have applied may be embittered when they are not employed.

5. Get applicants who possess the qualities of initiative and foresight.

6. Be fairly certain that any present employee who may not be measuring up to performance standards can be replaced.

From applicants' points of view, the unsolicited application letter also has advantages:

What are the advantages to the applicant who writes an unsolicited letter of application?

1. It increases the number of jobs for which the writer can apply.

2. It meets with less competition than it would have if it were sent in response to an advertisement.

3. It could *create* a job if it persuaded the employer to believe that a new person was needed to do something not now being done.

4. It may assist in getting a better job because highly preferred jobs are often filled before any applications are invited.

5. It may suggest initiative on the part of the writer.

Basically, the unsolicited letter of application is a sales letter. When such a letter accompanies a listing-type résumé, it follows the fundamental steps of selling—getting attention, arousing interest, presenting convincing evidence, and asking for action.

Getting Attention and Interest

In application letters, the choice of attention getters is more limited than in other forms of sales letters. Here are some commonly used attention getters:

What are some possibilities for a beginning sentence?

1. Present outstanding qualifications.

2. Describe job requirements.

3. Use the name of someone in the organization.

4. State the source of job information.

5. Use some catch phrase that leads to the presentation of qualifications.

One of the most dependable attention getters introduces the qualities most necessary for performance of the job sought. Such a device does its job if it makes the recipient think "Here's a person who can do what we want done." A secretary began an application by saying

When you need a secretary who can type 70 words per minute, take shorthand at 125, and transcribe notes at 50, call me.

An applicant for a part-time job with an accounting firm began the letter this way:

Three college courses in tax accounting and one season's experience in filling out individual income-tax returns--with this preparation, I could help you with this year's tax-return overload.

Another closely related technique quickly reviews the requisites for a job and proceeds to show the applicant's possession of those requisites. For example,

"Trainees must have college degree with major in finance and economics, and excellent references." Please check to see how well my background fits these trainee specifications, as listed in your "Information Booklet No. 44."

Why should we refer to the source of information about a vacancy?

Sometimes we can gain attention by referring to the source of job information. By using this technique, we create the same effect that strangers experience when they discover they are both friends of the same person. The disadvantage, of course, is that the letter gets off to a slower start — the writer's preparation for doing the job is somewhat delayed. But the technique may be well worth the price; the source mentioned may have considerable status with the employer. The name of a present employee, or the name of some person whom the employer regards highly, may be very effective in getting attention:

When Mr. Adam Smith of your department spoke to our fraternity last March, he said you often added young marketing majors to your summer sales force.

Or

Dr. Anna Porter, head of our Business Administration Department and an active member of your chapter of PIRA, told me today that you usually hire two or three accounting graduates every year.

References to magazine articles, newspaper articles, annual reports, or house organs are often used as attention-getting devices:

When you make the change to electronic data processing, about which you wrote in this week's Fortune, will you need to employ an experienced programer?

Or

From the Gazette's July 13 story about your plans to market pork on the West Coast, I concluded that you may want to hire a well-trained, experienced sales representative.

The catch-phrase opening is sometimes effective. Not only will a good one get attention, it will get attention in an appropriate manner. But it has to be in good taste, and it has to be closely enough related to the job to lead naturally into a review of qualifications. A catch-phrase opening would be especially appropriate if we are applying for a job requiring imagination — as a commercial artist, an architect, a home-furnishings sales representative, an insurance agent, or a claims adjuster. Some illustrations:

What are some advantages and disadvantages of opening with a catchy phrase or sentence?

What do you see in the sketch at the right? Is it a girl placing a pound of your Meato Wieners in a baby carriage? Is it a grandma placing a pound of your Meato Wieners in a grocery cart? Now look again. The picture changes from one to the other right before your eyes, but Meato Wieners are prominent in both. That's just one of the types of art work I could do for you as an artist in Meato's advertising department.

Or

Zollfrei, exempte d'impots, insenta de direitos al fandegarios-- whether you say it in German, French, or Portuguese, it still means "tax free." As an expediter in your foreign shipping department, I could handle correspondence in all of these languages; I speak and write them fluently.

Regardless of the manner in which we seek to attract attention, our attention-getting paragraph should lead the employer to expect an application for a specific job or a specific type of work. The first paragraph should lead naturally into a discussion of the applicant's preparation for a job.

Why should the first paragraph reveal the type of work applied for?

Presenting Qualifications

If we can get attention by summarizing our outstanding qualification in the first sentence, fine. Then we can proceed to give the supporting details. But if we use some other attention getter, we will need to introduce our qualifications as quickly afterward as possible. The natural tendency is to plunge into a historical account of past experiences, as the following second paragraph does:

> While I was a student at Wilcoy High School, I majored in business subjects--bookkeeping, salesmanship, and business law. Then, after studying business for two years at the Hays Business College, I took a job as collection agent with Porter and Sons, where I am still employed.

Why should we avoid placing the emphasis on autobiography?

Many applicants use this approach because it employs the narrative style of writing. Sequence of ideas is not a problem because the applicant writes about experiences in chronological order. But its disadvantages probably outweigh its advantages. Remember, the reader wants to know whether we can do the job for which we are applying. Our autobiography may sound very much like hundreds of others. Then, too, the narrative approach is conducive to using too many *I*'s. Remember the admonition to write to others in terms of their own interests. Readers are primarily interested in the phase of our experience most related to the job. And they expect us to point out the relationship. Does the preceding example tell anything not included on a résumé? The letter should not *repeat* the facts given on the résumé—it should *interpret* them. For example,

What is the relationship of the application letter to the accompanying résumé?

> In business courses at school and in two years' experience as a collection agent, I have wrestled with a variety of human-relations problems--legal, psychological, and sales promotional. The relationship to claims adjusters' problems was apparent to me--acting always within the limits of law and ethics, saying the words most likely to influence a particular client, and constantly promoting the sales of the company product.

How can an applicant reveal knowledge of job requirements without seeming to lecture?

Notice that the revision employs *I* only once; it does not mention the factual details about where the applicant went to school, courses taken, or the name of the firm. These facts can be included on the résumé. Notice, too, that the emphasis is not on chronology. Rather, it is on the relationship of the applicant's experience to the requirements of the job. Furthermore, we get the impression that this applicant knows what would be expected of a claims adjuster. The last sentence is long, but it is not too complicated for easy reading. For example, consider the less effective sentences that follow:

> A claims adjuster must always act within the limits of law and ethics, must choose words most likely to influence a particular client, and must be constantly promoting the company's product.

Or

> I learned from experience that a claims adjuster must . . .

Or

> It is my understanding that a claims adjuster must . . .

The person reading the application letter does want some assurance that the applicant understands what the job entails. Don't begin with, "It is my understanding that. . . ." Imply the understanding by showing experiences and training closely related to the job. Then back up the statements with convincing evidence.

Giving Convincing Evidence

A Phoenix firm was sorely disappointed in each of sixty responses to its ad for a new employee. Not one of the applicants was invited for an interview. By far the most frequent criticism of the letters received was insufficient information.

Few people will believe we are prepared for a job just because we state that we feel qualified or we are sure we have the necessary qualifications. They need evidence — concrete evidence. But we shouldn't go into detail about every little point in our favor. Doing so makes the letter too long; it runs the risk of writing too much. Rather, we should choose one or two major points (such as education or a major phase of our experience) and give enough details about it to be convincing. The preferred technique for selling a product by letter is to select one or two prominent features and stress them. The same principle applies in application letters. Young graduates with little experience may give educational background the primary emphasis. They might say in a general way that they ". . . had two courses in industrial management and one course in office management." However, how much better it would be to convince the reader that something had been *learned* from the course! The following sentences do not guarantee that the candidate learned from the courses, but they do suggest that he or she knows what it's all about and has some idea of what would be expected on the job:

> In the office and industrial management courses, we worked with realistic problems in time-and-motion study, wage incentive plans, suggestion systems, and forms control. I did a research paper on induction-training programs, such as you have for your beginning office workers.

Naturally, the candidate chose to emphasize those aspects of education most nearly corresponding to the requirements of the job.

In an application for a collection job with a larger firm, an applicant could write

> After having successfully completed two years as collection manager for Maxwell and Edwards, I feel that I am now ready for a similar position in a larger firm.

Chances would be improved by giving the facts behind that word *successful*. For example,

> When I received the responsibility for collections two years ago, our loss from bad debts was almost 2 1/2 percent. This year, the loss from

Why should we avoid statements such as "I feel ready" and "I know I would be successful"?

Why can't the evidence section be limited to general statements?

bad debts was exactly 1 percent. Yet there had been no change in our sales or credit policy.

My collection letters were based on the assumption that clients knew they owed us and expected us to ask for the money. Time-worn collection expressions were avoided completely. As much as possible in the early stages, the letters stressed a resale appeal.

The details seem convincing. Without boasting of success, the applicant gives evidence of it. Furthermore, the candidate uses the language of the job.

How can we reveal familiarity with the firm's goals and procedures and still avoid statements of the obvious?

To give further evidence of preparation for a job, we should weave something into our writing to show we are familiar with the firm and its future plans or present problems. Of course, we shouldn't put ourselves in the position of telling something already well known:

In addition to opening three new branches this year, your bank is installing drive-in windows in all its branches and switching to electronic calculating machines.

The sentence does little more than reveal a knowledge of company affairs. Use an indirect method of revealing this knowledge; let this information reveal itself in a sentence saying something more important. For example,

In addition to taking finance courses and working part-time as a teller at the ABC Bank, I'm now completing an eight-week course in the programing of the XXX computer--the same model State Bank is now making preparations to install.

A following paragraph could profitably allude to specific knowledge or experiences gained from the course.

Asking for Action

As with sales letters, someone writing application letters should define the desired action before beginning to write. Whether we want the employer to invite us to an interview, give some indication of interest, or file the application for future openings, that desired action should be kept in mind. The final paragraph is the natural place to define action. *Call* and *write* are more vivid words to use than *contact.*

What should the last paragraph include?

The following points should be kept in mind when you are writing the closing paragraph:

1. Mention the specific action wanted—just ask for it, don't demand it.

2. Try to sound natural and original—too many application letters end with a trite expression such as "May I have an interview at your convenience."

3. Express gratitude because a favor is being asked for — but use first person and future tense instead of the present tense ("Thank you for calling. . . .") or the presumptuous "Thank you in advance."

4. Try to work in a final reference to the most outstanding feature of preparation for the job — this final reference adds *emphasis* because of its last-paragraph position; it shows *coherence* because of its relationship to the preceding discussion; it indicates *unity* because of its tie-in with the first sentence. It makes the whole letter now seem complete, as the following closing paragraph does:

Please examine the attached résumé and write to the references if you wish. Then, I shall appreciate your calling me to suggest a time when we could discuss the possibility of putting my collection experience to work for you.

Now that we have examined the major parts of an uninvited letter of application, let's examine a complete letter. The following letter is not a model; it is an example of how the principles we have been considering can be put into action. The accompanying résumé would *list* information; it would not interpret.

(1) Having studied accounting for four years and practiced tact for twenty-four, I could be the "tactful auditor" for which you advertised in the Journal of Accountancy (April issue).

(1) Identifies the specific job wanted, introduces a qualification for it, and reveals the source of information.

What are three major things we want the first sentence to do?

(2) As an accounting major, I especially liked Auditing Theory and Practice. In it, I could see specific application of principles encountered in my human relations and psychology classes. Social scientists' research findings were thoroughly evident in our auditing discussions of autocratic, custodial, collegial, and supportive leadership styles.

(2) Begins by discussing educational background. Since experience is limited, stress on education is a compensating factor. Seeks to show how courses are related to job requirements.

(3) Questions about leadership and motivation seemed to recur throughout the course: What really motivates executives? Why are auditors actually feared at so many levels? How can those fears be overcome? How can an ego be salvaged? The professor's most

(3) Continues to point out ways in which education has been good training for a job that requires tact.

frequent admonition was "Consider the human element." That element was the focus of my term report in auditing, "Auditors Consider Egos"; in psychology, "The Auditor as a Psychologist."

(4) These reports gave me an opportunity to apply principles of organization, human relations, and clarity as learned in Business Report Writing. It taught me how such techniques as passive voice, third person, positive language, and the subjunctive mood could be used to get ideas across to executives without offense.

(4) Interprets résumé information. (Business Report Writing is listed on the résumé). Seeks to point out the value of that class.

(5) Working with executives has been part of my responsibilities as a part-time assistant at Globe-Howell, Inc., for the past four months. Working with auditors, cost accountants, and tax accountants, I came to appreciate seasonal necessities for working long and irregular hours, keeping information confidential, trying to be right the first time, listening carefully, and getting along with others.

(5) Introduces experiences as being related to education and to the job sought. If the experience had been longer or richer, it could have been introduced before education. Also seeks, without lecturing, to reveal a knowledge of what accountants are expected to know and do.

(6) References on the enclosed sheet have said they would be glad to comment on my knowledge of accounting and my relationships with others. Whether you want to call or write, I welcome a chance to discuss the "tactful auditor" job with you.

(6) Uses an action ending that once more emphasizes the quality in which the employer is interested.

If references were not listed on the résumé, the first sentence in the last paragraph could be deleted. After the last sentence the writer could add, "At that time, I could supply a list of people who would be glad to comment on my knowledge of accounting and my relationships with others."

When placed on standard-sized stationery, the preceding letter fills one page. If it seems lengthy, remember that its purpose is to show how the applicant's background is suitable for the job. To be persuasive, a message has to be presented in detail, enough detail to let the employer picture the applicant as one who has qualities not possessed by competing applicants. Remember that, for employers, finding the right person to do their work is important. As long as a letter presents evidence of suitability for a job, the employer will read eagerly.

The letter does not mention salary. That problem can be discussed later. To discuss salary in the initial application letter is to risk magnifying its importance.

Why should we avoid discussing salary in the initial letter?

The letter also doesn't reveal why the applicant wants to change jobs or why a job is being sought from this specific firm instead of some other. To include too many minor points is to risk taking emphasis away from primary qualifications. Also, the possibility of appearing to complain about a present employer arises when we attempt to explain why we would rather work for another.

All questions cannot be answered in a letter of application; some are most appropriately discussed in an interview. In some job-getting situations, the letter of application is actually preceded by an interview during which a letter is invited.

The Solicited Letter

Whether our application letter is solicited or unsolicited, the principles of presenting qualifications are the same. The primary difference is in the beginning paragraph. In the solicited application letter, no attention-getting device is necessary. The firm is already devoting some attention to filling its vacancies. We already have a contact. Start with the contact (the source of the invitation) and proceed from there. A good beginning for an invited application will ordinarily (1) refer to the source of the invitation, (2) indicate the specific job for which the candidate applies, (3) suggest the candidate's major qualifications. For example,

Why is a solicited application easier to write than an unsolicited application?

As you requested in our discussion yesterday, I have prepared the attached résumé of my educational and experience background for cost-accounting work.

Figures 11-5 and 11-6 illustrate a solicited application letter and résumé.

In responses to blind ads, we should follow the principles that apply to other solicited application letters. But we should also keep in mind that the advertiser has placed us in a rather awkward position by not telling the name and location of the business. Without these details, we may have difficulty matching our preparation with the job. The best policy may be a reserved response. For example, we may not want to give references, just indicate a willingness to supply them on request. We wouldn't want our references to receive requests from firms with whom we would not care to work.

What are the special problems of answering a blind ad?

If the blind ad asks us to state the salary expected, we will have to mention salary in some way. Of course, we run the risk of starting to work for less money than we deserve if we suggest a low salary. On the other hand, we run the risk of placing ourselves completely out of consideration if we suggest a high salary. Perhaps the best way out is to say we are willing to accept the standard or

1639 Oakhaven Drive
Temple, CA 91006
January 3, 1983

Mr. John Larson
Sales Manager
Robert Mondavi Winery
7801 St. Helena Highway
Oakville, CA 94562

Dear Mr. Larson:

Thank you for contacting me regarding the position of
Marketing Assistant that you have available at this time. I
believe I could do a good job for the Robert Mondavi Winery
because of both my related work experience with Bronco Wine
Company and my marketing courses at the University of
Southern California.

The courses in marketing management and retailing listed on
the enclosed personal sketch have given me a sound background
in Marketing. This specialized training, along with the
knowledge obtained in working for a Bachelor of Business
Administration degree, should enable me to implement your
marketing procedures.

Working as an assistant to the Sales Manager of Bronco Wine
Company, one of the two distributors for Robert Mondavi wine
in Southern California, gave me experience in dealing with
people and increased my understanding of the business. Mr.
Edgar, the Sales Manager of Bronco Wine Company, gave me
varied assignments with commensurate responsibilities.

For example, I organized Wine Seminars for many of the larger
California wineries. My responsibilities included finding
accommodations for the Seminars, working closely with specific
wineries, contacting the prospective audience, preparing charts
and speeches and giving presentations. For this kind of work, I
have found my teaching background to be a valuable asset. I
also arranged wine tastings for charitable and other
organizations which gave me additional experience in dealing
with people and a chance to use some of the knowledge acquired
in class and on the job.

Figure 11-5 Solicited application letter.

During my teenage years my stepfather worked as a Sales Manager for a Wine Import Company, so I have been exposed to the business end of wine from a young age. Sometimes I feel that I have wine, not blood, running through my veins. I would really like to be a part of your company since it has the reputation of producing superior wines and for having a progressive attitude toward business methods.

Please telephone me at 213-555-6897 to arrange a mutually convenient time when I can further discuss with you my qualifications for your position of Marketing Assistant.

Sincerely yours,

Christine Barry

Christine Barry

Enclosure

Figure 11-5 continued.

ADDRESS: 1639 Oakhaven Drive, Temple, California 91006
TELEPHONE: 213-555-6897

CAREER OBJECTIVE

To be a Marketing Manager in a company involved in the wine
business.

RELATED WORK EXPERIENCE

July 1980 to present: Part-time assistant to the Sales Manager
of Bronco Wine Company. Duties have been concentrated
in the areas of presenting Wine Seminars to retailers and
restauranteurs and planning and participating in Wine Tastings
for several of the larger California wineries including Robert
Mondavi, Gallo, Sebastiani, Beringer, Beaulieu, Krug, Christian
Brothers, and Sterling.

OTHER WORK EXPERIENCE

College Assistant: November 1980 to January 1982. Auditor
                      for EOP Program and Student Assistant for
                      two professors at Pasadena City College.

Volunteer Work: 1964 to present. Various activities including
                      church, hospital, social services and school-
                      related jobs.

Teaching: June 1967 to November 1972. Six years of
                      teaching First Graders in London and
                      Pittsburgh.

PROFESSIONAL EDUCATION

Bachelor of Business Administration, University of Southern
California, June 1983, with a major in Marketing, and emphasis
on retailing and marketing management. A average in both
major and minor courses including the following classes related
to Marketing:

Marketing Management	Marketing Analysis and Strategy
Promotion Management I	Retail Management
Promotion Management II	Consumer Behavior
Sales Force Management	Marketing Research

Figure 11-6   Solicited résumé.

Associate of Arts, Pasadena City College, June 1981, with a 4.0 grade-point average.

Diploma of Education, Goldsmiths' College, London University, June 1966, with a 4.0 grade-point average.

HONORS AND AWARDS

University of Southern California:
    University scholarships 1981 to 1983

Pasadena City College:
    Awards: Academic Excellence
                             Outstanding Student Assistant
    Honors: Business Mathematics
                             Business Law
                             Accounting
    Dean's Honors List: Fall 1980
                             Spring 1981

PERSONAL DATA

Birth date and place: Born December 29, 1952
                         Ebbw-Vale, South Wales
Physical condition: Excellent health
Family status: Married since 1972
                         2 boys: John   aged 9 years
                                  Justin aged 5 years
Hobbies: Reading, listening to music, gourmet
                         cooking, antiquing, ballet, racquetball,
                         tennis, and travel

REFERENCES

References will be furnished upon request.

Figure 11-6 continued.

customary salary paid for the job, or that we would like to discuss the salary with them. Advertisers place us in an awkward position when they ask us to state a salary when we don't yet know the full duties or circumstances of the job.

Special Problems

Although every job-hunting contingency is not included in the following list, it does include many of the frequently encountered circumstances that make writing difficult:

1. No experience in the job sought. Use an "attributes" résumé (such as Figure 11-3). Stress the aspects of academic or work experiences that are related to the job sought. For example, a waitress applying for a management job has had experience in getting along with people, solving some unusual crisis-type problems, making change, appearing for work at appointed hours, making plans for the day, etc. Such experiences may have helped in developing the same qualities essential for success in the management job.

Sometimes, unpaid volunteer work provides experience that can be referred to in applying for a paying job.

Reporting special interests or participation in unusual events may partially compensate for shortage of experience. A young man applying for his first accounting job included (in his personal-details section of the résumé) a statement about his participation in a well-publicized fund-raising effort. He had been a member of a team that ran 300 miles to gain publicity for the Muscular Dystrophy campaign. In all his interviews, the event was a highlight of the conversation. His physical endurance, tenacity, concern for others, and willingness to do something he was not forced to do — all these attributes were seen as useful in accounting. He selected from several job offers.

2. Experience is in *other* types of work. Use an "attributes" résumé. It will force emphasis on the commonality of the work done and the work sought. As each attribute is discussed, an applicant may need to draw heavily from educational experiences as well as job experiences that have developed attributes needed for success on the job sought.

3. Experience in too many jobs. Again, the "attributes" résumé can be employed to take emphasis away from the *number* of previously held jobs. Or, if a conventional résumé is used, the experience section could be restricted to the most related jobs only (with a notation that some other jobs had been held). A list of other jobs could (if asked for) be provided at the interview.

4. Time unaccounted for. Although employers' application forms are often designed to reveal unaccounted-for time, an applicant (in preparing the résumé) is under no obligation to account for all time spent. For example, a person who has been institutionalized for reasons of health or behavior may have completely conquered personal problems. Reporting them in the earliest written materials could reduce chances for an interview (during which questions the interviewer asks could be answered at once).

5. Scanty formal education. On the résumé, avoid use of "education" as a heading (see Figure 11-3). Stress courses that have been taken. Stress points that have been gained from experience or from education you *have* had. Indicate any plans for night courses or seminars. Report training programs if any were provided on previous jobs.

6. Education that is too general. Stress pertinent aspects of the courses most closely related to the job sought (See Figure 11-3). Make the most of part-time or full-time work experiences. Consider taking specifically related courses, or reveal plans to take them.

7. Physically handicapped or too old. Although many employers try hard to accommodate those who have a disadvantage, such matters are best saved for the interview. If written materials discuss a "handicap," an interview may not take place. Having attained an interview, the applicant may be able to make a very favorable impression.

8. Fired from previous job. In the application letter and résumé, make no statements about having been fired. Be prepared, though, to discuss previous jobs in the interview if asked about them.

9. Self-terminated from previous job because of low pay or poor treatment. Omit from application letter and interview. These points are hard to discuss without "knocking" a previous employer.

10. The line between fact and fiction. Falsifying information is deplorable for moral reasons; it is also deplorable for pragmatic reasons. Pretending to have held jobs that were not held or to have attended schools that were not attended could be detected and thus block a job offer that would have been made otherwise. Or, false information could help an applicant get hired for a job he or she cannot do well. Some newly hired employees have been extremely embarrassed (and terminated) upon discovery of falsified information in the pre-employment papers.

Especially when applications are for high-level positions, some firms now submit application documents to verification agencies (who make it their business to check the accuracy of statements). One such agency reported that, of forty applicants who listed Stanford University as their alma mater, eight had never attended Stanford at all!

THE LETTER OF RECOMMENDATION

Recommendation letters may be written inductively or deductively. If the applicant can be endorsed with enthusiasm, the deductive approach is preferred—it gets to the point quickly and adds emphasis by placing the endorsement first in the letter. If

When might a letter of recommendation be written inductively?

for some reason the applicant cannot be recommended, the inductive plan would serve well—it allows for inclusion of negatives, but avoids giving them more emphasis than they may deserve.

Why use the deductive approach for requesting information about people?

Normally, a person who gives us as a reference is a person whom we can give a good recommendation. Since personnel managers are well aware of this probability, they are inclined to think of references as having a bias in favor of the applicant. However, they have a right to expect sincere evaluations. Before writing a letter of recommendation, consider the following points: (1) the letter must be fair, (2) it must include pertinent information, and (3) it must have legal safeguards.

1.   The letter must be fair to applicants and to prospective employers. Helping applicants to get jobs for which they are ill qualified may be a serious injustice to them and to employers. Similarly, failure to help applicants who are well qualified is an injustice.

2.   The letter must include information pertinent to the job applied for: length of present employment, nature of present job, performance on present job, personal qualities related to the job, and other information that might help in evaluating the applicant.

3.   The letter must have legal safeguards. Some commonly used safeguards: labeling information as confidential, stating that information is given for professional purposes only, stating that information is given only because it was requested. Such statements reduce the likelihood that their authors will be convicted of libel. Lawsuits can arise from statements made in recommendations. As a result of recent legislative enactments and court decisions, some employees can legally request to see contents of their personnel folders. Lawsuits could result if writers were not cautious.

These enactments have weakened the influence of recommendation letters. Knowing that a letter *could* later be seen by its subject, writers have become less inclined to mention negative information even though doing so could be ultimately beneficial to applicant and employer. Knowing that a writer is aware that a letter could be seen by the applicant, personnel managers expect a strong bias in favor of the applicant. Some college and university placement bureaus place a very noticeable stamp on their recommendation forms: "Statements may be read eventually by the student about whom they are made." Others give students an option of signing away their rights to see whatever is written on the recommendation form. Many students have signed such forms in the hope of increasing confidence in statements made about them.

What are the advantages of using form letters to request information about prospective employees?

Typically, businesses use forms for getting information about applicants. Use of forms helps a business to get the specific information needed. In addition, filling out a form is usually an easier task than writing a letter; thus, a form may be returned sooner than a letter would be.

The following letter requests information, but does not employ a form:

(1) Please send confidential information about Mr. Charles Ross, who is applying for a job as teller in the Saguaro Bank.

(1) Gets to the point quickly. Assumes that the reference will be glad to cooperate. Indicates the answer will be kept confidential.

(2) Of special interest to us are his dependability and his interest in banking as a career.

(2) Reveals type of information desired.

(3) We shall appreciate your evaluation of his performance at United.

(3) Expresses appreciation.

The preceding letter would probably get information about the specific points raised. The response follows a deductive approach:

(1) Mr. Charles Ross, about whom you requested confidential information, is a good teller.

(1) Identifies the purpose of the letter. Reminds the reader that the information is considered confidential and that it was requested. Lets reader know that the letter is about an acceptable applicant.

(2) He has worked as a part-time teller here at United for the past two years while he was in his third and fourth years at Western College. (3) Finance was his major; and, as he has implied many times, he thinks of banking as his lifetime work.

(2) Reveals length of time worked and nature of the work.

(3) Answers a question raised in the request for information.

(4) Because he is accurate in handling money and keeping records, and because he is punctual in reporting for work, I rate him as a most dependable young man. (5) In two years, he was always on the job at the appointed time. On the two occasions when he could not report for work, he informed me well in advance.

(4) Gives information that was requested.

(5) Gives some supporting data for the preceding statement about dependability.

(6) His working relationship with other employees has always been cordial. His courtesy to customers will almost certainly be an asset when he gets into loan work, as he eventually plans.

(6) Gives added information.

(7) Mr. Ross's considerate attitude, his dependability, and his academic training in finance combine to make him one of the best tellers we have ever employed.

(7) Summarizes major attributes and thus implies strong support of the application.

How do we proceed when we are asked for information about an applicant who is not qualified?

The preceding letter describes a deserving applicant. An applicant who is not deserving or who would not be satisfactory should not be recommended. If he or she has weaknesses or characteristics that would preclude satisfactory performance, a factual letter that discusses both strengths and weaknesses would be appropriate; but remember to include legal safeguards and bear in mind that statements *could* later be seen by the applicant. Abusive, condemning language would be inappropriate.

If weaknesses are very serious, we can write a short letter in which we acknowledge the request and invite the recipient to call us if the applicant is in contention for the job.

OTHER LETTERS ABOUT EMPLOYMENT

Other job-connected letters include job-inquiry letters, application follow-ups, job acceptances, job refusals, and thank-you letters.

Job-Inquiry Letters

Why choose the deductive approach for writing a job-inquiry letter?

Inquiry letters are sometimes mailed when applicants know the firm will not regard them as applicants until they fill out an application form. In that case, they may write to request a form. Although the request for the form is a fairly routine letter, candidates increase chances of getting the form if they at least give enough information about themselves to assure the personnel department that they have some of the requisites for the job mentioned. For example,

May I please have an application form for work in your actuarial department. I am finishing my college work, which included several courses in mathematics, statistics, and insurance. I plan to make my home in your city after school is out in June.

Such a letter is, of course, not so effective as a complete letter of application. But, because of its directness and shortness, it does enable candidates to make job contacts they would probably otherwise not make. If an applicant wanted a position for which applicants were relatively scarce, some sort of response would be almost certain.

Application Follow-ups

Follow-ups can be well worth the time required to write them. If applicants do not receive a response to an application within a short time, they can reinforce it with a second letter. Doing so (1) keeps the file active, (2) provides a convenient way of reporting additional experiences related to the job, and (3) creates an impression of diligence—of knowing what is wanted and going after it methodically. For example,

> Since I wrote to you about a junior-accounting position in January, I've completed three additional courses in accounting and have been doing some part-time, individual income-tax work for Mr. Hugo Smith of this city.
>
> Please keep my application in the active file and let me know when you need to add another junior accountant.

Job-Acceptance Letters

Acceptance letters are easy to write. As in other letters that convey good news, they begin by accepting the job in the very first sentence, follow with any necessary details, and end naturally with a pleasant look toward the time when the employee is to report for work:

Why accept in deductive fashion?

> Yes! I accept your offer of a job in the Accounts Payable Department.
>
> Here are the security-clearance forms and health record. I'll bring a photostatic copy of my birth certificate when I report for work on Monday morning, July 1.
>
> Thank you for introducing me to some of the accountants when I talked with you last week. I shall enjoy working with them.

Job-Refusal Letters

Refusals logically follow the inductive approach—reasons first, then the refusal, and a pleasant ending. When the job we wanted goes to some other candidate, we want to know about it and we want some justification. Employers feel the same way. They like to know as quickly as possible whether a job offer has been accepted; and, if possible, they would like to know *why* a job offer has been declined. As a courtesy, we should tell them. We should be tactful, as in the following example, because we may want a job with this firm later.

Why refuse in inductive fashion?

> Yours was one of the most interesting job interviews I had in my search for tax-accounting work. I especially remember your ideas on the percentage-depletion problem.
>
> As you pointed out, opportunities in Petrolio are exceedingly good for those who are primarily interested in costs. But since my major

interest is in tax accounting, I have taken a job with Mills Mining Company where my responsibilities will be restricted to tax accounting exclusively.

I appreciate the time you spent with me.

The first sentence lets the personnel manager know the candidate had other interviews—a good way to lead up to the statement about accepting a job with another company. In the second sentence, the applicant reminds the reader of knowledge gained in the interview—a compliment to the interviewer. After these remarks, reasons easily follow; and the refusal is given in polite, positive language. The letter closes with an expression of gratitude.

Thank-You Letters

Why write a letter of appreciation for an interview even though you have been rejected?

Thank-you letters are appropriate after an interview, even when applicants think they have no chance for the job. Even after an interviewer has indicated there is no chance for a job, the candidate still owes a small debt of gratitude. Courtesy requires a note of appreciation:

I certainly appreciated your taking time to talk with me last week about the job in your data-processing department.

As you suggested, I am enrolling in a computer course this summer. Later, after my knowledge and skill have improved, I would be glad to talk with you again.

An employer who receives such a letter would react something like this: "This applicant recognizes weaknesses and is doing something about them; I will keep this person in mind."

Many competitors for a job will neglect this small courtesy of sending a thank-you note. The simple expression of gratitude could decide the case in the applicant's favor.

I appreciate the time you took to talk with me today.

After your discussion of service-attitude in selling, I was glad that I had chosen selling for my career. You "sold" me on the Farnsworth company!

Thank you very much.

In each of the thank-you examples cited, the candidate reveals that he or she *remembered* something from the interview. Isn't that a much more original way to please the interviewer than to say you "enjoyed" the interview? Observe, too, that the thank-you letters are relatively short; presenting too much of anything else de-emphasizes the gratitude.

Regardless of whether we are writing *about* employment or *for* employment, we have an obligation to do our best. Our letter of application represents us as no other letter does. Employers justifiably assume that it represents our best effort.

SUMMARY

Application letters and résumés assist employers in selecting applicants for interviews. Before preparing the letter and résumé, the applicant should make two lists: what the employer wants and what the applicant has to offer. The jobseeker's goal is to convince the employer that the two lists match.

Like sales letters and other persuasive letters, application letters and résumés need to include enough details to be convincing. The bulk of detail may be in the letter, or it may be in the résumé. If the letter presents specifics of job and educational experiences, the résumé may be a relatively brief listing of facts. If the résumé presents the specifics, the letter may be a relatively short introduction. Either way is acceptable.

Solicited application letters are a little easier to write because the employer has invited them.

Recommendation letters may be written deductively or inductively. If the applicant is being endorsed strongly, deductive presentation is preferable. Recommendation letters should be fair, they should include pertinent information, and they should include legal safeguards.

If the purpose of a letter is to find out whether a job is open, a short letter is sufficient. Deductive presentation is preferable.

If a few weeks have passed without response to an application, a follow-up letter is appropriate.

Job-acceptance letters should be short and deductive. Job-refusal letters should be inductive.

After an interview, a short thank-you letter is appropriate.

EXERCISES

Questions about Résumés

1. Why should a jobseeker prepare a résumé before writing the letter that accompanies it?

2. On a résumé that uses "Education" and "Experience" as headings, what determines which one should be presented first?

3. In the experience section, what are the advantages and disadvantages of listing experiences in chronological order?

4. What is the advantage of dividing the "Objective" into two parts: immediate and eventual?

5. Should a list of references be included? Explain.

6. In the "Education" section, which is better—just list pertinent courses, or identify some principles that were *learned* from those courses? Why?

7. What messages are communicated by poor typing and poor arrangement on the page?

8. Which is the more serious error—giving too many details, or giving too few details? Why?

9. To an employer, which is more important: *when* an attribute was developed, or *whether* an applicant possesses the attribute?

10. An applicant has developed a point of view that would be very beneficial in the performance of the job sought. To an employer, is it more important to know whether the point of view was developed in school or at work, or to know that the applicant possesses that viewpoint?

11. Should a long résumé accompany a long application letter? Explain.

12. Which places more emphasis on the match-up between qualifications and job requirements—use of "Education" and "Experience" as headings, or use of attributes as headings?

13. From which can an employer get a more vivid answer to the question "What does this applicant have to offer"? (a) A résumé that employs "Education" and "Experience" as headings? or (b) A résumé that employs such headings as "Ability to Communicate," "Dependability," "Aptitude for Learning Quickly," etc.?

14. For an applicant whose formal education is rather scant, which type of résumé is recommended—one with attributes as headings, or one with "Education" and "Experience" as headings?

15. On a résumé, should an applicant try to account for all time spent since entering the work force? Explain.

Questions about Employment Letters

1. Libby Garrett observed that the principles she was applying on her present job were directly related to principles that would lead to success on the job she was seeking. If her résumé is the listing type, should those principles be incorporated into the application letter? Explain.

2. Should a long application letter follow the basic outline recommended for sales and persuasive letters? Explain.

3. Should the word "I" be avoided completely? Explain.

4. As a *first* sentence in an application letter, is the following sentence effective: "In May of this year, I will graduate from City College"? Explain.

5. As a *last* sentence, is the following sentence effective? "May I have an interview at your earliest convenience?" Why?

6. Should the following sentence be included in an application letter? "I definitely feel qualified for the position." Why?

7. List some advantages of sending unsolicited letters.

8. Should a letter employ the narrative approach? Explain.

9. Although discussing salary in an application letter is normally inadvisable, under what condition should salary be discussed?

10. Do recommendation letters usually have a bias in favor of the applicant? Explain.

11. List some expressions that would be useful in incorporating legal safeguards into a recommendation letter.

12. What is the recommendation writer's obligation to the prospective employer?

13. How can word-processing equipment be useful in getting information about prospective employees?

14. How do job-inquiry letters assist in the job-getting effort?

15. What can be accomplished by writing application-letter follow-ups?

Questions about the Job-Hunting Process

1. List some qualities that employers would like their employees to have.

2. Which is the more common cause for dismissal—failure to do a job well, or failure to get along with others?

3. In a written application for a job as an operator of heavy equipment, why should an applicant try for perfection in grammar, spelling, punctuation, and typing?

4. For students who are enlisting the services of a university placement bureau in finding a job, what are the advantages and disadvantages of waiving the right to see statements made by those invited to write letters of recommendation?

5. What incentive does a private employment agency have to help an applicant get a high-paying job?

6. Before applying for a job, how can a jobseeker benefit from preparing a two-column worksheet—one column being *what the job requires;* the other, *what the applicant can offer?*

7. Assume an applicant had a nervous breakdown, was unemployed for 18 months, but is now completely recovered. Should these facts be discussed in the written materials that precede an interview? Explain.

8. Why should an applicant keep a record of the firms to which applications have been sent, those from which responses have been received, date and nature of response, etc.?

9. For what reasons must an applicant refrain from falsification?

10. List some of the library sources of job information.

11. Before addressing a letter to a personnel director, why is it worth the effort to find out (and use) the personnel director's name?

12. Compared with seeking employment information by telephone, what is the advantage of going directly to the firm and asking?

13. Before applying for a job, why should an applicant study the firm's annual report and pamphlets distributed by its employment office?

14. George has learned that his brother's employer is in the market for new employees. Before applying, why should George try to find out whether the firm has a written policy on nepotism?

15. Why is it essential that a jobseeker keep a positive attitude?

Letter-Analysis Problems

Consider the ten numbered letters in this section. As directed by your instructor (1) write a sentence-by-sentence critique, (2) make a list of ways in which a letter applies and violates principles discussed in this chapter, (3) rewrite a letter in such a way as to overcome its weaknesses, *or* (4) be prepared to discuss the letters in class. (Sentences in each letter are numbered for reference.)

Letter 1.

(1) Please consider me as an applicant for the buyer's position you advertised in last nights issue of the Gazette.

(2) The primary advantage I would have as a buyer is my educational background. (3) Among the courses I have taken are Buyer Behavior, Retailing, Marketing, Public Relations in Business, and Advertising. (4) I am sure you realize the many ways in which these courses can prepare one for a career in marketing.

(5) In addition to my classes, my educational background includes work in the University bookstore, service on the school yearbook, and president of my fraternity.

(6) I will be receiving my degree on May 5, 1982. (7) If you can use an energetic young man with my educational background, I will appreciate you studying the data sheet which you will find enclosed. (8) May I have an interview at your earliest convenience. (9) So I can put my educational background to work for you.

Letter 2.

(1) Your company again has won esteem in the public eye in its handling of the recent political convention. (2) I have watched your company in working with other conventions and public contacts.

(3) This last June 16, 1980, I graduated from City University's Business School. (4) I have a Bachelor of Science degree and majored in public relations. (5) At the present time, I am attending graduate school to further my knowledge in this field.

(6) While attending college I worked for three summers with Landsworth Public Relations Company, where I have received good experience.

(7) I would like to arrange an interview at your earliest convenience. (8) Your company has long been of interest to me, and I would like to be part of your company staff.

Letter 3.

(1) In June of this year, I shall graduate from City University. (2) I have majored in Small Business Management and minored in Mathematics. (3) I have had cources in retailing, advertising, display of merchandise, and personell relations.

(4) I have worked as a delivery man, salesman, and manager for one of the leading West Coast furnature chains. (5) The details of these jobs are on my attached datta sheet.

(6) In lieu of my experience and schooling, I feel that I would be an asset to your firm and I would appreciate an opportunity for a personal interview. (7) I can meet with you any time at your convenience. (8) You may contact me any evening at 555-9040.

Letter 4.

(1) Please consider me for the insurance position you advertized in yesterday's paper.

(2) As you can see from the attached, I have worked for a real estate firm for the last fifteen years. (3) As you know, real estate experience is very similar to insurance experience.

(4) An insurance man needs (above all else) dependability. (5) He needs to be accurate, courteous, and understanding. (6) He needs to be able to communicate, both orally and written. (7) I have written many letters in conection with my work in real estate. (8) Actually, I do most of the correspondence for the other persons in this office. (9) As a student in college, you will observe that I have been exposed to Marshall McLuhan's theories in my various courses. (10) I have observed the influence of his thinking in all the writing I do.

(11) While in school (where I compiled a 3.621 average as a business major) I took some very valuable courses in insurance. (12) Work in real estate has kept me in constant contact with insurance matters.

(13) References (and details of my qualifications) are presented in organized form on the enclosed data sheet which is attached for your convenience.

(14) I shall look forward to the opportunity of meeting you personaly and discussing my qualifications.

Letter 5.

(1) It is my desire to be employed as an instructor with your institution commencing this forthcoming semester.

(2) Enclosed you will find a Data Sheet to further elaborate upon my qualifications.

(3) I am desirous of instructing in such particular courses as: Business management; (organization, industrial, methods and techniques); business correspondence and reports; business and professional speech; business machines; typing; and business psychology (industrial, personnel, human relations).

(4) A complete résumé, concerning my degrees and recommendations is available from the University Placement Office, City University, Northwood, CA 93114.

(5) Arrangements for an interview, at your convenience, will be made upon request.

(6) Your prompt attention and consideration given this request will be greatly appreciated.

Letter 6.

(1) I am interested in being considered as the new purchasing agent advertised for in the November issue of Maintenance Management.

(2) I have been employed by Jackson's, Inc., for the past six years as a wharehouse manager and purchasing agent. (3) It is a small company (fourteen employees) engaged in the sale of janitorial supplies. (4) Through my work, I have learned the importance of keeping a well-rounded inventory, introducing new products, and maintaining competitive prices.

(5) Chuck's Floor Finishing is a company that I formed to serve some of the needs that I saw through my work with Jackson's, Inc. (6) It was part time work, but it was helpful in financing of my college career.

(7) I will be graduated from City University on May 20. (8) Although my first year shows some poor work, throughout my last three years I have maintained a grade point average of 3.6.

(9) Among the references on the enclosed data sheet are the president of Jackson's, Inc., an architect, and a school principal for whom I have done floor maintenance through Chuck's Floor Finishing. (10) As they have all exhibited a willingness to divulge information about me, please write to them.

(11) I shall appreciate you writing me to name a date when we may discuss the job that you advertised for and my qualifications as a purchasing agent.

Letter 7.

(1) As a person who had done much direct work with people, The Emporium's emphasis on maximizing customer services motivates me to seek management level positions enabling a continuation of this tradition for a growing company to best serve their customers. (2) Education and employment on many different levels and areas at The Emporium has prepared me to tackle problems that your managers are responsible for solving.

(3) During day-to-day operations at The Emporium the relationship between managers and fellow employees is easily seen as the cohesive or destructive force in obtaining desired goals. (4) This relationship can be used as a cohesive force if the manager understands the employees point-of-view. (5) Therefore, an employee who has grown with the company both in related education and as an experienced worker is best suited to manage others.

(6) I offer both of these two special requirements to be an effective manager at The Emporium. (7) A management-oriented education gives me the necessary background to carry on as a manager; my previous work experience has taught me the importance of getting along with people for success.

(8) Careful planning and staffing are some theoretical determinates of a successful organization, but these determine success only to the extent the manager believes in the employees. (9) As an employee, I was surprised at the amount of work I could do when my supervisor said that I could get such a large amount done. (10) And, when a manager asked me for advice, I felt important. (11) As a manager, I would take advantage of such experiences and believe in my employees. (12) They really can do what a manager asks, if they know he believes they can, and he seeks their advice. (13) After all, the employee is the expert in their particular area and the manager should treat the employee accordingly.

(14) Let's work together to serve the customer. (15) I'm ready to do my part to reach this goal in the successful future of The Emporium. (16) Please contact the references on the attached data sheet; I hope that this additional background will convince you of the degree of dedication I have. (17) Thank you for your time and consideration.

Letter 8.

(1) Since I have a four-year Real-Estate degree and two years of applicable work experience in sales, I can help you with your business. (2) I can serve West Realty in a productive and enthusiastic manner.

(3) Along with the necessary courses, taken to fulfill my real-estate curriculum I held several jobs. (4) A position in sales taught me that close attention and polite consideration of potential customers is

always important. (5) As an assistant manager, my experience was strengthened in the management operations of a business. (6) I supervised employees, made bank deposits, and gave on-the-job training to new employees. (7) My real-estate and business courses, along with my work experience taught me the elements of accounting, finance, management, and the laws of the real-estate business.

(8) For affirmation of my real-estate-related background, please study the attached résumé.

(9) Can you arrange to talk with me at some convenient time, to discuss employment with West Realty as a real-estate agent.

Letter 9.   Assume the following letter was written by a person who had written an application, had been interviewed (the firm had paid his travel expenses), and had received a turndown letter:

(1) I certainly appreciate the time you took to write to me on March 14. (2) Thank you for keeping my personal data sheet on file.

(3) Compared with other resumes you may have on file, mine undoubtedly shows some educational and experience data that few others can show. (4) From the demand analysis study and the market research project, I came to appreciate the importance of sales forecasting; in-depth research in the areas of demographics and customer expectations; and decisions concerning price, promotion, and distribution.

(5) From my work experience with The Emporium, I've learned to integrate duties with peers and superiors to accomplish my assignments. (6) Primarily, my duties were to sell directly to the consumer, keep inventory records, train employees, set displays, stock, and handle money. (7) Daily, I saw opportunities to develop my ability to get along with colleagues, be courteous to customers, increase sales, and determine promotional themes.

(8) Of all retailing firms to which I could apply, I prefer to work for The Emporium as an assistant buyer. (9) The combination of my abilities, familiarity with the "Valley of the Sun" area, and my desire to do a professional job has prompted me to write this letter.

(10) May I return (at my expense) to The Emporium to talk with you again? (11) The week of March 29 would be ideal, but I can arrange any time you suggest. (12) Thank you.

Letter 10.

(1) Part-time writing for a collection agency and a year's university instruction in business writing--how well do these experiences prepare me for entrance into your Correspondence Services Section?

(2) When you need a new sales series to promote engineering success, an individual adjustment refusal, or a new collection series,

you could have me prepare them; I have worked with all three. (3) My school writing courses included the writing and criticizing of all types of letters.

(4) We analyzed letters from every angle. (5) My sales letters seemed to be most effective when I chose a central theme and stuck with it, placing the product in the prospect's hands and describing the benefits he or she would get from using it. (6) Both students and teachers were very critical of my refusal letters until I started giving the reasons behind refusals, then following with a logical refusal and an attempt to preserve goodwill.

(7) As a part-time worker in the Smith Collection Department while earning my B.S. degree, I helped Mr. Albert Smith prepare an entire collection series. (8) We know how much hard work goes into such a writing project; we know the pleasure that goes with it, too.

(9) Mr. Smith tells me this year's loss from bad debts is almost 30 percent less than last year's, and he thinks the new letters are primarily responsible.

(10) After you have studied the attached résumé, I would appreciate your writing me to name a time when we can talk over the correspondence work you have to do and the correspondence work I have done.

Letter-Writing Problems

1.　Prepare an application letter and a résumé for the job you hope to get after graduation. Even though graduation seems far into the future and your specific job objective may be somewhat vague, writing the letter and résumé now will be well worth the effort: the thinking required may help to identify goals more clearly, instructor's comments can help you to write more clearly, and having a completed application on which modifications could be made will enable you to respond quickly when an application is to be sent.

2.　If you hope to get a part-time or summer job before graduation, prepare an application letter and résumé. Before sending the two, incorporate your instructors' suggestions.

3.　Write an inquiry letter. You want to find out about job openings in the type of work you want to do, and you want the firm's application form.

4.　Assume you have been interviewed for a job. Write a thank-you letter to the interviewer. Your letter of gratitude could allude to a specific point or two that was stressed by the interviewer, include some reminder of your major qualification, and convey any additional point you want to add. For example, your grades were reported the day after the interview and you got A's in your major subjects.

5.　Assume you have applied for a job and did not get it. The job was more closely related to your minor field of study than to your major field of study. After taking two more courses related to that job, you plan to apply again. Write to the firm that did not hire you.

6.   Assume you are applying for the job you want most of all. Select a person whom you would list as a reference. Write the recommendation letter you think the reference should send. Of course, you are not going to write the letter and ask the reference to sign it! But doing this exercise will help you to see yourself as you think others see you, and it will allow you to write about an applicant whom you know very well.

7.   Assume you were graduated three years ago. A former professor of yours is being considered for promotion to the rank of full professor, and you have been randomly selected to express yourself on that issue. The promotion committee is interested primarily in your evaluation of the professor's effectiveness as a classroom teacher. From classes you have already completed, select a certain teacher and assume your letter is about him or her; use a pseudonym. Address: Dr. Sue Jones, Chairperson, Faculty Promotions Committee, College of Business Administration, City University, Wellstown, VA 23578.

8.   Assume two months have passed since you sent an uninvited letter of application. It brought no response. Since then, the job market may have changed and you have accumulated some additional experience and education that are related. Write a follow-up letter.

9.   Assume you have just received a letter saying you were selected for the job you want. You have a week to accept. If you accept, some enclosed personnel forms are to be completed and returned. Write the acceptance letter.

10.   Assume you have received a letter saying that you were selected, but you have decided to accept a different job. It is more compatible with your background and professional objectives. Write a refusal letter.

TALKING ABOUT EMPLOYMENT— LISTENING AND THE INTERVIEW

Listening as an Interview Skill
Detrimental Listening Habits
Effective Listening Suggestions
Types and Styles of Interviews
The Job Interviewer's Role
Preparation
Meeting Face to Face — The
Interchange
Evaluating the Interview
Taking Action
Some Interviewer Guidelines
**The Interviewee's Role in the Job
Hunt**
Preparing to Take the Interview
Meeting Face to Face — The
Interchange
Following up the Interview
Practicing for Interviews
Summary

If the preceding paperwork is unimpressive, is an interview likely to take place?

Interview comes from Latin and Middle French words meaning to "see between" or "see each other." The interview between two people may be the epitome of applied interpersonal communication. For the jobseeker, an interview with a prospective employer is the logical outcome of having prepared an effective, successful résumé and letter of application. In this chapter, we examine the importance of listening, the role of the person conducting an interview—the interviewer—and the role of the person being interviewed—the interviewee.

LISTENING AS AN INTERVIEW SKILL

People who fail to listen are actually communicating something about themselves. What is it?

Although listening should consume half of all the interviewing time, it probably doesn't in most interviews simply because one person or the other fails to listen. For example, a meeting between a boss and employee might go something like this: "Boss, I really have a problem." "That so, George? Well, take a seat and let me hear about it," the boss says in a friendly tone. As George takes a seat, the boss goes on, "George, you think you have a problem, eh? How would you like to have the one I'm faced with now? Just listen to this!" Then the boss recites his own woes for several minutes while George listens. As he finishes, the boss says, "Well, George, I have another appointment now, and we didn't get your problem solved, so come on in here tomorrow and we'll take another crack at it. You know I always want to help—my door's always open." George leaves completely frustrated, his problem still on his mind and untalked about.

This little scenario may seem unusual, but it represents a common communication breakdown. The boss simply failed to listen to George's opening statement. He heard it, but he wasn't really listening. If he had been, he would have responded to George's need for advice rather than take advantage of the opportunity to air his own frustrations.

What keeps people from listening effectively?

Failure to listen may result from a variety of personal habits. We speak at rates of 100 to 200 words a minute, read at two or three times our speaking rate, and think several times faster than we can read. As a result, a listener can move through a discussion much faster than can a speaker. In fact, the mind has lots of spare time to spend in other-than-listening activities. Because all of us are ego centered, we frequently lose control of our minds during the listening process and end up thinking about our own concerns rather than about the message.

Detrimental Listening Habits

Do most people listen effectively?

Really good listeners are rare. They have the ability to block out distractions and focus their eyes, ears, and minds on the message. Poor listeners, or average ones for that matter, have developed one or more bad listening habits.

Several of the habits detrimental to effective listening have been listed by Ralph Nichols and Leonard Stevens:[1]

1. *Faking attention:* Trying to look like a listener to give the speaker assurance.

2. *I-get-the-facts listening:* Trying to listen for each and every fact and, as a result, missing the main point.

3. *Avoiding difficult listening:* Turning off the radio or the television—or our minds—if the subject seems too difficult.

4. *Dismissing a subject as uninteresting:* Rationalizing our poor listening as being caused by an uninteresting subject.

5. *Criticizing delivery or physical appearance:* Deciding in advance that the speaker has little of importance to say because his or her delivery style or appearance does not coincide with our standards.

6. *Yielding easily to distractions:* Seeking a distraction to release us from listening.

Although these bad habits apply to listening in a wide range of circumstances, they are of particular importance to both the interviewer and interviewee. If one or the other fails to listen, the interview will doubtless fail to achieve its purpose.

The first of these bad habits, faking attention, is one all people are guilty of at one time or another. We have all had the experience of listening—or supposedly listening—only to discover later that we had absolutely no idea what was said. We looked at the speaker, smiled, frowned, nodded, leaned forward and gave the speaker all sorts of feedback. Yet, we were faking attention. Faking attention happens in the classroom, at work, and at home. Our minds tend to become preoccupied with our own concerns, and we may daydream or spend much of our listening time formulating what we are going to say when it is our turn to speak.

On the other hand, we often overlisten—a characteristic of the I-get-the-facts bad listening habit. It is often practiced in the classroom when students are so intent on not missing a thing that might later appear in the examination that they attempt to remember or record every detail, every statistic, every story. They listen so intently that they are still trying to concentrate on details when the professor makes the major point—the generalization that was critical to the presentation. Later in reviewing for the examination, the overlistener must arrive at the major point or generalization by inductive analysis of all the details. And this can be difficult.

We might also avoid listening when the spoken message is about a complex, difficult subject. Our minds are forced to accept more than we are willing to work for, so we turn off our listening equipment as easily as we might unplug a hearing aid or turn off a light switch. Some people blame modern technology for this apparent listening laziness. Television, for example, provides many options: If the subject is difficult or not entertaining, we simply change channels. Obviously, listening is

What are some of the bad habits that keep people from listening effectively?

Do interviewer and interviewee have an equal obligation to listen?

Is planning what you are going to say more important than listening to what is being said?

The mind is capable of receiving messages much faster than they come. Could the spare capacity be devoted to distinguishing between major and minor points?

1. Ralph G. Nichols and Leonard A. Stevens, *Are You Listening?* (New York: McGraw-Hill, 1957).

related to interest. We can listen to things of interest and switch listening channels from uninteresting subjects to interesting ones.

The bad habit of writing off subjects as uninteresting usually results from our preliminary perception of the subject. Some people will not go to the opera simply because they have never developed a taste for opera. They probably have never given themselves a chance to do so. Or an adult may say "I hate asparagus!" only to respond when asked when was the last time he or she tried asparagus, "When I was in the sixth grade." We do the same thing when we write off speakers as uninteresting. Even little things turn us off: unusual dress, awkward gestures, poor grooming, mannerisms or tics unacceptable to us. People who do not come up to our standards are often placed in the uninteresting category. We effectively stereotype others based on our prior experience. Conversing and listening can be pictured graphically:

How do prior experiences influence listening?

What are some of the most common barriers to effective listening?

Barriers
Distractions
Negative feelings about subject
Speaker ⟷ Thinking only about self ⟷ **Listener**
Low interest level
Negative feelings about speaker

Effective Listening Suggestions

What mental processes are involved in effective listening?

Through his research in effective communication, Ralph Nichols has defined four mental processes going on in the mind when the listener is doing a good job of receiving and understanding the spoken word:[2]

1. The listener thinks ahead of the talker, trying to guess where the discourse is leading.

2. The listener weighs the verbal evidence used by the talker to support points as they are made.

3. Periodically, the listener reviews the portion of the talk completed thus far.

Should listening between the lines be avoided?

4. Throughout the talk, the listener reads between the lines for meaning that is not necessarily put into spoken words.

From the communication process described in Chapter 1, we know that the availability of feedback and the opportunity to observe nonverbal aids such as gestures and other bodily motions are the critical factors in determining communication effectiveness. For the listener, this knowledge translates into the following suggestions:

1. *Watch the speaker.* Gestures, facial expressions, and eye movements can add much to the words used and the meaning intended. If the speaker can't look

2. Ibid., p. 82.

the listener in the eye, the sincerity of the remarks made may be questioned. Of course, the opposite is probably true: firm eye contact may be interpreted as added sincerity or firmness.

Can eye contact be overdone? Is staring objectionable?

2. *Provide listener feedback.* The listener can acknowledge understanding, agreement, disagreement, and a variety of other feedback responses through facial expressions, sounds, and gestures. In this way, the speaker can either provide whatever restatement or added information may be necessary or continue on with the discussion.

3. *Take the time to listen.* Because people in a communication transaction are simultaneously serving as both senders and receivers, the receiver may become occupied with thoughts about what to say when it is his or her turn to speak and fail to listen.

In conversation, when do you get time to think?

Listening is not only a valuable business skill, it is also a desirable social trait. Because people have a basic need to be heard, to be appreciated, to be wanted (Maslow would describe this as a social-ego need), they really want someone to listen to them. If they have problems, chances are people will solve the problem themselves when given a chance to talk it out. Thus, by taking the time to listen, we can provide others with a valuable service. In fact, others will like us because we are considered good listeners. Aren't most of your close friends also good listeners? Probably they are close friends because together you provide each other with a forum.

How does listening satisfy a social-ego need?

One of the major distractions during interviews is the desk that separates the two participants. First, the desk itself may place the participants in an unequal-status relationship; the person sitting behind the desk is more secure—it's *her* desk. Second, the desk often holds mail, books, even mementos such as pictures, that are distracting. Good interviewers will attempt to eliminate the desk as a barrier either by having it clear of distracting materials or by moving to side chairs for the interview.

How is a desk a barrier to effective listening?

In summary, listening is at least half of the oral communication process. In fact, studies have shown that we spend about as much time listening as we do reading, writing, and speaking *combined.* Good listening applies to more than a person's role in the interviewing process. It's a major tool for learning in school, for finding out what goes on in business, and for creating close friendships. As the interviewing process is discussed, you'll be able to see just how listening may be used by both participants to achieve the goal of the interview.

TYPES AND STYLES OF INTERVIEWS

As many interview styles exist as there are people engaged in the process. People's interview styles tend to parallel their leadership styles in other managerial activities. Some are democratic; some are autocratic; some range between the extremes. Some tend to mix their behavior to adjust to varying situations. With some knowl-

Would an autocratic leader do most of the talking in an employment interview?

edge and a little experience, a person being interviewed can adapt to the interviewer's style and use it to his or her advantage.

Some terms used to describe styles and types of interviews are

In an exit interview, should the interviewer do more listening than talking?

1. *Personnel interviews.* Personnel interviews include those used in the employment process (hiring) and in the exit process (retirement, resignation, firing). Of course, the employment interview is designed to obtain information through discussion and observation about how well the applicant will perform on the job, fit in effectively as a member of a task team, and participate as a part of the total organization. The exit interview is a means of obtaining feedback that will assist the organization in developing an improved environment for employees. Information about why people leave is a valuable resource for constructive changes.

What is the goal of an evaluation interview?

2. *Evaluation interviews.* Evaluation interviews take the form of regular performance-appraisal discussions between superiors and subordinates. The goal of the evaluation interview is to provide an opportunity for each member of the organization to grow professionally through an analysis of the member's strengths and weaknesses.

Would a persuasive interview proceed in accordance with the basic sales-letter plan?

3. *Persuasive interviews.* Persuasive interviews are designed to sell someone a product or an idea. When a sales representative talks with a prospective buyer, persuasion takes the form of convincing the prospect that the product meets a need. In this kind of interview, the distinction between interviewer and interviewee may be blurred. For example, the prospective buyer may convince the seller that the product doesn't meet a need, just as the opposite may occur and result in a purchase. The employment interview may also be considered a persuasive interview because the job applicant must convince the prospective employer that he or she meets the company's need.

4. *Structured interviews.* Structured interviews tend to follow formal procedures; the interviewer follows a predetermined agenda, such as a checklist of items or questions.

5. *Unstructured interviews.* Unstructured interviews tend to be less formal than structured ones. The discussion will probably be free flowing and may shift rapidly from one subject to another, depending on the interests of the participants.

For what reason might an interviewer resort to a stress interview?

6. *Stress interviews.* Stress interviews are designed to place the interviewee in a stress situation in order to observe the interviewee's reaction. Each of the preceding interview types may become a stress interview, depending on the purpose of the interviewer.

Obviously, the personnel, evaluation, and persuasive interviews will also be either structured or unstructured as well as stressful or relaxed. The person being interviewed should assess the nature of the interview quickly and adjust her or his behavior accordingly. In reviewing the role of the interviewer, the following discussion explains how you, as an interviewee, can make the most of your interview opportunity.

THE JOB INTERVIEWER'S ROLE

The success of any interview depends on the communication skills of the participants and how strongly each wants to practice them. As a guide, these following four steps apply to almost all interviewing and will vary with the types of interviews:

1. Preparation

2. Interchange

3. Evaluation

4. Action

Preparation

Preparation may be the most ignored of the four steps, yet it may be the most important. It involves these elements:

1. *Purpose.* What is the purpose of the interview? What are the expected outcomes? What style is most appropriate, and what atmosphere is best — relaxed or stressful?

2. *Physical arrangements.* Is the physical setup consistent with the purpose? Is privacy adequate? What distractions should be eliminated?

3. *Self-understanding.* Does the interviewer have an awareness of his or her own strengths and weaknesses, prejudices, biases, perceptions, and other possible barriers to effective communication?

4. *Understanding the other.* What is known or should be known about the interviewee? What are her or his values, aspirations, motives and background?

Is there a parallel between getting ready to write and getting ready to interview?

Through effective preparation, the interviewer can set the stage for whatever kind of interviewing situation he or she might desire. If the interview is to be structured, have items to be discussed been arranged in proper sequence? Will the nature of the questions elicit information-revealing responses? Will the sequence lead to a relaxed interview or to a stressful one? When you, as a job applicant, plan for your interview, keep in mind that most personnel interviewers have probably gone through these preparatory steps. This reminder will help you determine the interview style, so you can adapt your behavior appropriately.

Meeting Face to Face— The Interchange

What are the important elements in face-to-face interchange?

During the interview, both the interviewer and the interviewee should pay particular attention to these factors:

1. *Rapport:* How well have you reached a common ground to establish a climate consistent with the purpose of the meeting? Does an air of mutual respect exist?

2. *Flexibility:* Can the interviewer redirect the flow of discussion when it strays from the purpose and disrupts the original plan?

3. *Two-way flow:* Are the participants engaged in two-way communication, or is one or the other turning it into a one-way situation?

As either the interviewer or the interviewee, you can become far more effective than the usual participant if you develop some simple techniques for providing feedback and for clarifying issues. Listening in the classroom, for example, is relatively easy to do because you assume a listening role as your primary activity. In an interview, however, you will be both a listener and a speaker; and some of your listening time will be spent preparing what you will say when it is your turn to speak. Interviewing as a process is much like ordinary one-to-one conversation, differing primarily in the higher degree of tension that normally goes with interviewing. Thus, you should work to make your shift from listener to speaker as smooth a transition as possible. If you haven't listened thoroughly enough to understand completely, your response to the other person will probably be inadequate. Effective, active listening involves mental concentration and good physical posture. It is not a passive activity as many people believe.

How does posture affect interviewing?

Questioning is one technique used by good conversationalists and interview participants to gain more information before making a complete response. It can also encourage a shy person to participate more fully. An example of a question to get more information:

Bob: I had no idea I would be invited to run for office.

Jane: What did you say to them after being invited?

A question to clarify word meaning:

Mariette: Jerry has been pusillanimous about this.

Bill: How can you tell? (pusillanimous = cowardly)

A question to seek feeling:

George: Then I was promoted to a job I didn't like.

Mac: Were you disappointed enough to refuse?

Questions are effective feedback forms and tend to keep the interview moving when it might otherwise fall flat. *Direct* questions can be answered easily and briefly.

They ask for yes or no answers or for factual information. *How old are you? When will you graduate? Have you traveled overseas?* Because they call for factual information, direct questions don't help much in encouraging the dialogue of the interview. *Indirect* questions, however, do contribute to dialogue because they call for answers that call for thought on the part of the receiver. *Why do you feel accounting is the career for you? What experience have you had in working as part of a team or group?*

Questions or statements are often a form of paraphrasing—restating the content or the intent of the sender's message to check one's own understanding.

What is a paraphrase?

Tamara: I'm looking forward to the Christmas vacation.

Alice: You'll get caught up on your school work.

Tamara: No, I'm caught up on that. I'll have time to spend with my parents.

You can see that the techniques of questioning and paraphrasing are things we practice most of the time in conversation. The thoughtful use of these techniques, however, can contribute much to interviewing situations and to the two-way flow.

Evaluating the Interview

Decision-making time arrives at the close of the interview. Is the interviewer prepared to analyze the alternatives? Should the decision be made or postponed? Should the interviewee be asked back for further interviews? Should the interviewee be told a letter will be mailed to him or her at a later time?

Taking Action

The interviewer should know what action to take simply because arriving at some kind of decision or outcome was considered in the preparation step. Does each of the two participants know exactly what is to be done? Has a mutual understanding been developed?

Should an interview close with an agreement?

Some Interviewer Guidelines

The interviewee should be told the interviewer's guidelines, since they can help both parties in the meeting.

How could note-taking be offensive?

If the interviewer plans to take notes during the interview, for example, she or he must forewarn the interviewee. Otherwise, the interviewee might freeze when the interviewer takes notes. On the other hand, if notes are not made, the job applicant in a personnel interview might feel that he or she is not receiving fair consideration. The interviewer should introduce the note-taking idea with a statement such as: "I like to take a few notes during the interview to jog my memory later and to make sure we cover everything we should. We can also use them near the end of the interview to make sure your comments and my understanding are in agreement. Do you mind?'' Following agreement, note taking will not be a barrier of consequence, particularly if the notes are not considered secret and if they are for the interviewer's use only. Even leaving the notes in a visible place will help assure the interviewee. Of course, the interviewer can always add personal impressions to the notes after the interviewee leaves.

Should interviews be strictly question and answer?

The interviewer can help establish the style of the interview by proper use of voice tone and volume. A friendly tone may put the applicant at ease. A harsh, aggressive tone may frighten the applicant and result in a stress situation. In the same way, the interviewer can set the stage for a relaxed or stressful interview simply by organizing questions. Asking the most difficult question first, for example, may throw the applicant into a frenzied state. Body posture is also an important element. By paying attention through eye contact and by appearing interested through the use of acknowledging head motions and a general body posture indicating concern, the interviewer has a better opportunity to pursue the goals of the interview.

Should a difficult question be asked at the beginning?

These guidelines have much to do with the effectiveness of the interview, but the kinds of questions asked can determine its success or failure. Questions that can be answered with a simple ''yes'' or ''no'' don't contribute much and may leave interviewees in a position of having to stray from the subject to put themselves in a better light. Questions that ask how, what, or why provide openings for genuine discussion.

Should questions that can be answered with "yes" or "no" be used sparingly?

In general, interviewers must describe all working conditions to any job candidate, but the candidate must decide whether she or he is willing and able to meet those conditions. Of particular interest to interviewers and to women applicants are some of the guidelines for interviewing and hiring compiled by the Women's Association of the Harvard University Graduate School of Business Administration as adapted from Equal Opportunity Commission guidelines and various court rulings. These guidelines can be adapted, of course, to possible discriminatory actions related to race or religion.

What are some of the legal considerations for employment interviewing?

1. To turn down an applicant because customers would not want to deal with a particular sex, because company coworkers might object, because the position requires travel with members of the opposite sex, or because of unusual working hours or lack of restroom facilities is illegal.

2. To offer a woman a lower salary than is offered to a male applicant of equivalent background is illegal.

3. During an interview, such questions, statements or actions as the following are considered discriminatory:

What types of questions are considered discriminatory?

a. Questions about marriage plans, child-bearing plans, and marital status asked of a woman applicant and not of men applicants.

b. Any statement showing hiring preference for either married or unmarried women.

c. Discussing a stereotyped female job with a female applicant, especially if the applicant is applying for another job.

d. Job benefits or conditions that pertain only to heads of households or principal wage earners.

e. Company literature that refers to all employees as *he* as well as comments about the *girls* in the office.

Therefore, employment interviewers must be well prepared and must use appropriate language in their meetings with women candidates. These discriminatory actions apply equally to racial minorities.

For you as an interviewee, these guidelines indicate that the professional personnel interviewer must be thoroughly prepared for the interview. No matter how casual of how formal the interview may seem to be, you can rest assured that considerable effort went into planning it. Obviously, interviews can never be identical. Participants change as a result of each interview experience, and each experience gives them greater self-confidence. Competent interviewing is one of the most satisfying and rewarding management skills.

Is preparing for an interview with a woman different from preparing for an interview with a man?

THE INTERVIEWEE'S ROLE IN THE JOB HUNT

Just as the interviewer proceeds through a step-by-step process, so should the interviewee. As the interviewee, you'll want to engage in some pre-interview activities, prepare to perform well during the interview, and take appropriate action after the interview.

College students generally engage in on-campus interviews with a variety of business organizations. Following the on-campus interviews, successful candidates are often invited for further interviews on the company premises. The purpose of the second interview is to give executives and administrators, other than the personnel interviewer, an opportunity to appraise the candidate. Whether on campus or on company premises, interview methods and practices apply to the situation. When the interview is with company executives, the candidate will probably encounter a wide variety of interview styles. Preliminary planning can pay rich dividends.

Preparing to Take the Interview

Pre-interview planning involves learning something about the company or organization, doing some studying about yourself, and making sure your appearance and mannerisms will not detract from the impression you hope to make.

How should applicants get ready for interviews?

Study the Company

Nothing can hurt the candidate more than knowing little about the organization. No knowledge probably indicates no sincerity, and the interviewer doesn't want to waste precious interview time providing the candidate with information that should have been gathered long before. As discussed in Chapter 11, several sources are available for information about companies.

Where can applicants find information about companies?

Those with publicly traded stock are required to have annual reports. Many business school libraries have a file of annual reports and several financial service reports. Other information can be obtained from brokerage houses, from periodicals and from financial newspapers. Employees of the company or other students who have been interviewed may be of particular help to the interviewee. Some major schools have prepared videotape interviews with representatives of a variety of company recruiters and make the tapes available to students. Attempt to prepare a guide similar to that shown in Figure 12–1 for each company with which you interview.

Study Yourself

Does self-analysis help in preparing for an interview, as it does in preparing for writing an application letter?

What types of information might an interviewer expect an interviewee to know about a company?

When you know something about the company, you'll also know something about the kinds of jobs or training programs they have to offer. The next thing is to assess your own abilities. Determine your interest and ability to work in an office versus working outside the office. Do you like to work intimately with people or do you prefer to work primarily alone? Are you an extrovert? Do you like detailed work? Can you develop a career plan that you can achieve with the company? The answers to these questions about yourself can provide you with an arsenal of material to use during the interview. If you can't see a relationship between yourself and the job or company, you won't be able to demonstrate the interest or enthusiasm necessary to sell yourself. A good method is to list the company and job characteristics in one

---

Company Information

The name. Know that *IBM* stands for *International Business Machines,* for example.
Status in the industry. Know the company's share of the market, its Fortune 500
  standing if any, its sales, its assets, and its number of employees.
Latest stock market quote.
Recent news items and developments.
Scope of the company. Is it local, national, or international?
Corporate officers. Know the names of the Chairman, President, and the Chief
  Executive Officer.
Products and services.

Job Information

The job title. Know what the typical entry-level positions are called.
The job qualifications. Understand what specific knowledge and skills are desirable.
The probable salary range.
The career path of the job.

Figure 12-1 Interviewee's guide for studying the company.

column and attempt to place your qualifications in a corresponding column such as the following illustration:

Company and Job Requirements   **My Qualifications and Needs**

Detailed or broad
Inside-outside
People orientation
On a career path
High or low pay
Educational requirements
Travel requirements
Job security
Prestige level

Of course, you'll probably never find the job and the organization that will satisfy all your needs and meet all your requirements. Additionally, you'll personally place greater weight on some factors than on others. In any case, the analysis you give such factors before you embark on each interview may save problems later.

Normally, can an applicant expect job requirements and personal qualifications to match completely?

Plan Your Appearance

An employment interviewer once made the observation that if the job applicant did not meet her *extremities* test, the interview might as well not take place. She went on to explain that the extremities were the candidate's fingernails, hair, and shoes. The fingernails had to be clean and neat, the shoes shined, or at least clean, and the hair clean and well-groomed. Long hair on men met the standard, incidentally, if clean and well groomed. She simply felt that if the candidate did not take care of those items, the candidate could not really be serious about, or fit into, her organization. Another interviewer turned down an otherwise outstanding applicant because the applicant could not look him in the eye when he answered a question. Interviewers are subject to their personal perceptions and biases just as are all other people.

In a series of words, first and last positions are emphatic. Does this parallel the *extremities* test of appearance?

The job applicant, of course, cannot be prepared for everything, but must be adequately groomed and attired so as not to call negative attention to something that may or may not be job related. In terms of appearance, then, one should

Failure to look someone in the eye — what kinesic communication is transmitted?

1. Be as clean and well groomed as possible.

2. Wear appropriate footwear.

3. Select appropriate clothes for the interview.

If you must, borrow clothes from a friend. Avoid gaudy colors. Research the company dress code — real or implied — ahead of time. And remember that if you *look* and *dress like* the people who already work at the company, the interviewer will be able to visualize your working there. In many cases, your college placement officer may be able to provide helpful hints.

Writing style should not call attention to itself. Is the same statement true of clothing?

Plan Your Time

What kinesic communication is transmitted by being late for an interview?

One of the worst things you can do is be late for an interview. Another is to miss the interview entirely. Therefore, plan your time so you will arrive early. This planning allows you to unwind and mentally review the things you plan to accomplish. At the same time, don't sit in a waiting room just making yourself nervous. Move around a little to keep loose. But by all means, be on time. Should something happen to prevent your doing so, do telephone your apology.

Meeting Face to Face — The Interchange

Before an offer is made, should interviewees normally expect to have more than one interview?

Now that you have gone through the planning stages, you are ready for the interview. Your job is to sell yourself so successfully that you are invited to proceed to whatever the next step in the hiring process might be. If the first step was an on-campus interview, the next step will be an interview with company executives. You should not expect to receive a firm job offer in the first interview, but one may be made occasionally.

Opening Formalities

When you meet the interviewer, use the interviewer's name if you are sure you know how to pronounce it correctly. Usually, the interviewer will initiate the handshake, although you may do so. In either case, apply a firm handshake. You don't want to leave the impression that you are weak or timid. At the same time, you don't want to overdo the firm grip and leave an impression of your being overbearing. Once the introduction is over, wait for the interviewer to invite you to be seated. These common courtesies—using the correct name, applying a firm handshake, and waiting to be seated—can contribute to a favorable first impression. Use your body language to add to that impression. Sit erect with a slight forward lean to express interest. A slouchy posture can do nothing for your image—nor can smoking or gum chewing.

At the beginning of the interview, is a bit of small talk a waste of time?

The interviewer will begin the conversation and effectively set the stage for the interview. You might expect some nonbusiness talk or a direct opening into the business of the interview.

Interviewing Guidelines

Should an interviewer's questions be expected to parallel information already given on the résumé?

Much of the information about you will appear on your résumé or company application form, already available to the interviewer. Thus, the interviewer will most likely seek to go beyond such things as your education, work experience, and extracurricular activities and attempt to assess your attitudes toward work and the probability of fitting you successfully into the organization.

The best way to prepare for the interview discussion is to study the company and yourself, of course. Additionally, though, you can prepare to answer such questions as these:

1. What do you know about our company?

2. Why do you want to work for us?

3. Why should we hire you?

4. Can we offer you a career path?

5. What are your greatest strengths?

6. What are your greatest weaknesses?

7. What do you think are the real qualifications for this job?

8. What is important to you in a job?

9. How do you spend your spare time?

10. How does what you have accomplished outside the classroom add to your education?

What could be an interviewer's purpose in asking you about your weaknesses?

Your answers to these and other variations of the same questions can help you proceed to the next step. First of all, your education is your foremost attribute if you are a student. You should point out its relationship to the job for which you are being considered. Even more important, the fact that you have succeeded in school indicates that you have the ability to learn. Because most companies expect you to learn something on the job, your ability to learn and, thus, to become productive quickly may be your greatest asset. So your most important response to the interviewer's questions may be about your ability to learn. Even no work experience may be an asset. You have acquired no bad habits through work experience that you will have to unlearn!

Which would be better, saying you can learn quickly, or relating an incident that seems to confirm the statement?

Second, your skill in getting along with others may be an important attribute. What did you do in college that helped you get along with others? Were you a member, an officer, or a president of an organization? What did you accomplish? How did others perceive you? Were you a leader? The extracurricular activities listed on your résumé give an indication of these traits, but how you talk about them in your interview helps. "I started as corresponding secretary and was subsequently elected to higher office for four semesters, eventually becoming president" may be a statement that proves your leadership qualities. If at the same time your organization went on to greater heights, all the more power to you.

Third, a degree of humility is important in all interviews. If you are being interviewed by a representative of General Motors, don't suggest that you can turn the company around. A candidate for the presidency of a university was not considered further when he said he could turn the university around when the university was already successful. Incidentally, he had been president of another university for only six months and claimed he had turned that university around. Obviously, the candidate for president hadn't become familiar with the problems of

Why are employers interested in humility?

the university. The candidate had failed to take even the first step toward a successful interview: study the company.

"Why do you want to work for us?" is really not a difficult question to handle if you give it a little planning. In addition to your study of the company from the literature, you can usually locate someone who works for the company to tell you about it. You can often visit a local office of the firm, as well. Then you can make a favorable impression simply by referring to the people you have talked with about the working conditions, company achievements, and career paths. You'll also show that you are strongly interested in the company and not just taking an interview for practice. The interviewer not only attempts to develop an impression of you, he or she also evaluates you in comparison with others being interviewed for the position. Your responses can indicate your sincere interest in getting a job with this company rather than just any company.

Your response to inquiries about why you should be hired will be a composite of some of the things already discussed. You have the proper education, you have proved you have the ability to learn, and you are enthusiastic about working for the company. If you really understand the job requirements, you should have little difficulty relating your skills and knowledge to the job. If the immediate job will lead to supervisory or management responsibilities later, make certain that you stress your skill in getting along with others and working successfully as part of a team.

A question about whether the company can offer you a career path is probably best answered with a question such as: "I believe someone like me has a future with your company, but I would like to discuss the normal progression within the company. Can you tell me about it?" Most candidates for positions with public accounting firms are familiar with the steps from staff accountant to partner; but the steps are not so clearly defined in marketing, finance, and management paths. An open discussion can provide you with new information.

When asked about your greatest weaknesses and strengths, your study of yourself will help. An answer that you have no weaknesses is lacking humility. You may indicate that you occasionally become overcommitted to extracurricular activities, particularly if your résumé shows a high level of extracurricular participation. But use this response only if you also have a strong academic record. Don't confess that your overcommitment resulted in a failure to pursue your education properly. Thoughtless answers can sometimes screen you out of further consideration. Your greatest strength probably is easy to identify: (1) the ability to learn, (2) the ability to work with others and to assume leadership roles, (3) the ability to organize your time in such a way that you can achieve academically while still participating in non-class activities or work, (4) and skill in problem solving. Because the question asks for your *greatest* strength, you should focus on a single point rather than brag about all your strengths.

Questions about how you spend your spare time and about how your extracurricular activities have added to your education are designed to make you elaborate on résumé items. Give some thought to these items so you can appear to have broad, balanced interests rather than a single, time-consuming avocation.

Finally, what is important to you in a job? Although we are all interested in a paycheck, any job satisfies that need—some will pay more, some less, but the paycheck is a part of the job and should not be your primary concern. Intrinsic

---

In answering the question "Why do you want to work for us?" would flattery be advisable?

Should inter- viewees ask questions as well as answer them?

Might a weakness confessed by the applicant be a strength in the eyes of the employer? (Being overcommit- ted, driving yourself too hard, being overly concerned about detail.)

Could an appli- cant profitably tell what is being done to overcome a weakness?

rewards such as personal job satisfaction, the feeling of accomplishment, and making a contribution to society are things you should think about discussing in the interview. You should like what you are doing. You should look forward to a challenge. A job that will satisfy these needs is important to almost everyone.

One of the major reasons for college graduates' changing jobs is lack of challenge and the resulting dislike for the job. Research has shown that most of us change jobs two or three times before finding our career occupation. So, as you engage in the interview, look for things that will satisfy your immediate needs and lead to future challenges. Job changes usually involve hardships of some sort, and careful consideration of how the job and the company will meet your needs can prevent later problems.

To a job seeker, which is ultimately more important? The pay, or the intrinsic rewards?

Handling Salary Discussion

For most entry-level positions the beginning salary is fixed. However, if you have work experience, excellent scholarship records, or added maturity, you may be able to obtain a larger salary. The interviewer should initiate the salary topic. What you should know is the general range for candidates with your qualifications so that your response to a question about how much you would expect is reasonable. If your qualifications are about average for the job, you can indicate that you would expect to be paid the going rate or within the normal range. If you have added qualifications, you might say "With my two years of work experience, I would expect to start at the upper end of the normal salary range."

Should the interviewee introduce a discussion of salary?

If you have other job offers, you are in a position to compare salaries, jobs, and companies. In this case, you may suggest to the interviewer that you would expect a competitive salary and that you have been offered X dollars by another firm. If salary hasn't been mentioned, and you really want to know about it, simply ask courteously how much the salary would be for someone with your qualifications. In any case, though, if you really believe the job offers the nonmonetary things you seek, don't attempt to make salary a major issue.

Closing the Interview

The interviewer will provide the cues indicating that the interview is completed by rising from the chair or making a comment about the next step to be taken. At that point, don't prolong the interview needlessly. Simply rise, accept the handshake, thank the interviewer for the opportunity to meet, and close by saying you look forward to hearing from the company. The neatness with which you close the interview may be almost as important as the first impression you·made.

If gratitude has been expressed in the interview, should a thank-you letter be sent?

Following Up the Interview

After the interview, don't take too long to send a thank-you letter to the interviewer. The letter should be similar to the thank-you letter described in Chapter 11. If you were asked to submit some statement or further information, the prompt follow-up action becomes all the more important.

Practicing for Interviews

Are prac-
tice interviews
really worth the effort?

Essential to presenting yourself favorably is your display of sincerity. Although most of us tend to be nervous during our first interview, we gain confidence with experience. Therefore, practice and rehearse your own interviewing style. Work with someone else in mock interviews, alternating roles as interviewer and interviewee. Then follow each practice interview with a constructive critique of each other's performance. A few such mock interviews will give you some experience and will make the first real interview more effective.

SUMMARY

The job interview may be the most important face-to-face interaction you will have. You will be selling yourself in competition with others. How you listen and how you talk are characteristics the interview will be able to measure. Your actions, your mannerisms, and your appearance will combine to give the total picture of how you come across. Added to the obvious things you have acquired from your education, experience and activities, your interview performance can give a skilled interviewer an excellent picture of you.

Practice leads to perfection, so the time you devote to preparing for the interview may determine the payoff by making you stand a little higher than your competition.

EXERCISES

1. Indicate whether each of the following items is a direct or an indirect question:
    a. When did you move to Michigan?
    b. How would you react if you were asked to travel for long periods while working for us?
    c. What is your grade-point average in business courses?
    d. Why do you want to work for us?
    e. What was your favorite course in college?
    f. Can you give me an example of your interpersonal skill?

2. Prepare questions to respond to each of the following statements:
    a. I prefer to work with things rather than with people.
    b. A job in a bank would be perfect for me.
    c. If I had only a bachelor's degree, I'd try to stay in school for a couple of years.

    d. I'm scared when I meet someone at the executive level.

    e. I hate coffee.

3. Prepare paraphrases (reflecting sentences rather than questions) as responses for the items in exercise 2.

4. Make a list of things you'd like to learn about a company from an interviewer. Do not list things you can learn from other sources.

5. Make a list of things about you that you would like to have the interviewer learn. Do not list things that are apparent from your personal data sheet.

6. Form groups of four for practice job interviews. Each person should have available a copy of his or her résumé. Alternately play the roles of interviewer and interviewee with the two additional people serving as critical observers. Change places until all four have had an opportunity to serve as interviewer and interviewee. You may assume the jobs being applied for are the ones you have selected and designed applications for; or you may use one or more of the following positions:

    a. A part-time job visiting high schools to sell seniors on the idea of attending your school.

    b. A full-time, summer job as a management intern in a local bank.

COMMUNICATING THROUGH MEMORANDUMS AND REPORTS

OBJECTIVES

1. To develop an analytical approach to problem solving.

2. To understand the role of reports and memorandums in business.

3. To strengthen skills in outlining and organizing.

4. To provide practice in the preparation of both long and short reports

5. To develop skill in objective, nonpersonal writing.

THE REPORT PROCESS AND RESEARCH METHODS

Characteristics of Reports
  What is a Report?
  A Problem Is the Basis for a Report
Recognize and Define the Problem
  Using Hypotheses
  Limiting the Problem
  Defining Terms Clearly
Select a Method of Solution
  Doing Library Research
  Doing Normative Survey Research
  Doing Observational Research
  Doing Experimental Research
Collect and Organize the Data
Arrive at an Answer
  Collecting Data
  Interpreting Data
Summary

Institutions of all types—business, governmental, service, and charitable—are faced with daily problem-solving and decision-making tasks. Whether at the policy-making executive level or at the operational management level, decision makers and problem solvers require a steady supply of information on which to rely. This information may be supplied orally or in written form. The term used to describe the body of information is *a report.* The process of developing the information and preparing it for presentation is *reporting.*

CHARACTERISTICS OF REPORTS

Hello, Pete. This is Walters in customer services. The boss wants to know how things are going with the 400-case Sleepwell order. Are we going to make the 4 P.M. shipping deadline?

Oh, hi, Walt. We *are* going to make the deadline, with time to spare. We have about 250 cases on the loading dock, another hundred on the box line, and fifty going through the labeling process. They'll all be ready for the loader at 2:00.

This brief exchange illustrates a simple reporting task. A question has been posed; and the answer given (along with supporting information) satisfies the reporting requirement. Although Pete may never have studied report preparation, he did an excellent job; so Walters, in turn, can report to his boss. Pete's oral report is a very simple illustration of five main characteristics of reports:

1. Reports are generally requested by a higher authority. In most cases, people would not generate reports unless requested to do so.

2. Reports typically travel upward in the organization structure. The upward direction of reports is a result of their being requested by higher authority.

Does logic lead to orderliness?

3. Reports are orderly. Orderly, in this sense, means that reports are logically organized. In Pete's case, he gave Walt an answer to his question first and then supported the answer with evidence to justify it. Our study of the organization of letters showed us the difference between deductive and inductive organization. Pete's report was deductively organized. If Pete had given the supporting evidence first and followed that with the answer that he would meet the deadline, the organization of his reply would have been inductive and would still have been logical.

4. Reports stress objectivity. Because reports contribute to decision making and problem solving, they should be as objective as possible; when nonobjective (subjective) material is to be included, the reporter should make that known.

5. Reports are generally prepared for a limited audience. This characteristic is particularly true for reports traveling within an organization. This characteristic means that reports, like letters, can be prepared with the receiver's needs in mind.

What Is a Report?

On the basis of these five characteristics, a workable definition of a report is that it is an orderly, objective message used to convey information from one organizational area to another to assist in decision making and problem solving.

Reports have been classified in numerous ways by management and by report-preparation authorities. These classifications use the form of the report, the direction, the functional use, and the content as the bases for classifying. A brief review of several classifications is helpful in understanding the scope of reporting in organizations and in establishing a departure for report study.

Formal or Informal Reports

The formal-informal classification is particularly helpful, because it applies to all reports. Formal reports are carefully structured; they stress objectivity and organization, contain much detail, and are written in a style that tends to eliminate such elements as personal pronouns. Informal reports are usually short messages with natural, casual use of language. The internal memorandum generally can be described as an informal report. All reports lie on a continuum as shown here:

Formal ⟵————————⟶ *Informal*

Scientific Research

Routine Business Research

Informational Messages

Later chapters will explain more fully the distinction among the degrees of formality of various reports.

Short or Long Reports

"Short-or-long" can be a confusing classification for reports. A one-page memorandum is obviously short, and a term paper of twenty pages is obviously very long. What about in-between lengths? One important distinction generally holds true: as a report becomes longer, it takes on more characteristics of formal reports. Thus, the formal–informal and short–long classifications are closely related.

Informational or Analytical Reports

Informational reports carry objective information from one area of business to another. Analytical reports present attempts to solve problems. The annual report of a company is an informational report, and a report of scientific research is an analytical report.

Vertical or Lateral Reports

The vertical-lateral classification refers to the directions reports travel. Although most reports travel upward in organizations, many travel downward. Both represent vertical reports and are often referred to as upward-directed and downward-directed reports. The main function of vertical reports is to contribute to management *control.* (See Figure 13–1.) Lateral reports, on the other hand, assist in *coordination* in the organization. A report traveling between units of the same organizational level, as between the production department and the finance department, is laterally directed.

Can coordination also mean cooperation?

Internal or External Reports

Internal reports travel within the organization; external reports, such as annual reports of companies, are prepared for distribution outside the organization.

Periodic Reports

When reports are classified as periodic, they are reports issued on regularly scheduled dates. Periodic reports are generally upward directed and serve management control purposes. Daily, weekly, monthly, quarterly, semiannual, and annual time periods are typical of those covered by periodic reports. Preprinted forms and computer-generated data contribute to uniformity of periodic reports.

Why do periodic reports generally travel upward?

Functional Reports

The functional classification includes accounting reports, marketing reports, financial reports, personnel reports, and a variety of other reports that take their functional designation from the ultimate use of the report. For example, a justification of the need for additional personnel or for new equipment is described as a justification report in this classification.

As you review these report classifications, you will very likely decide that almost all reports could be included in most of these categories. If this thought does cross your mind, you are correct. A report may be formal or informal, short or long, informational or analytical, vertically or laterally directed, internal or external, periodic or nonperiodic, functionally labeled, or any combination of these classifications. Although authorities have not agreed on a universal report classification, these report categories are in common use and provide a nomenclature for the study and use of reports.

A Problem Is the Basis for a Report

The upward flow of reports provides management with information to use in problem solving and decision making. If problems did not exist, reports would be

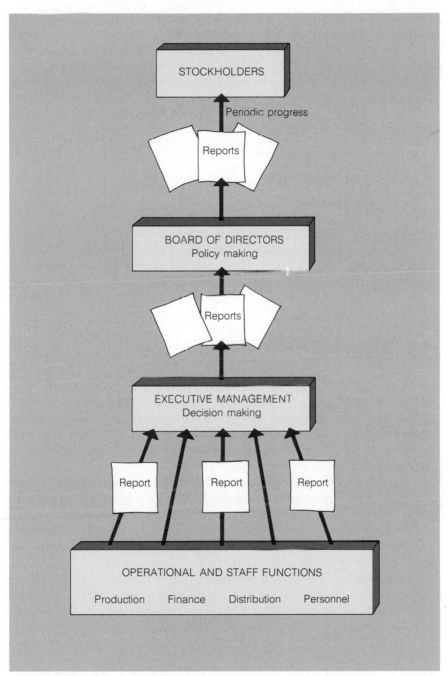

Figure 13-1   The general upward flow of reports.

Does
unique imply
a one-time event?

unnecessary. Some problems are recurring and, hence, call for a steady flow of information; other problems may be unique and call for information on a one-time basis. If we can accept the idea that a problem is the basis for a report, the preparation, organization, and writing of the report all become much easier.

Whatever the problem—business or otherwise—human reason has developed the following steps for finding a solution:

1. Recognize and define the problem.

2. Select a method of solution.

3. Collect and organize data.

4. Arrive at an answer.

Only after all four steps have been completed is the report written for presentation. Reports represent an attempt to communicate how a problem was solved and what the solution was. Let's take a closer look at the four steps in problem solving and in successful report preparation.

RECOGNIZE AND DEFINE THE PROBLEM

Before any logical analysis can take place, we must pinpoint the problem to be solved. We should take a good look at the instructions accompanying the report request. Specifically, what is wanted? We must attempt to divide the major request into subrequests: *"what, why, when, where,* and *who?"* This kind of analysis enables us to break a large problem into several small ones. The solutions to the parts can lead to the solution of the major problem.

Is this statement similar to
which came first,
the chicken or the egg?

The important questions are *what?* and *why?* Only we can tell which question should come first. Unless we know specifically what is wanted, it is pretty difficult to explain why it is wanted. On the other hand, unless we can say why the information is wanted, it is difficult to define what is wanted. Insight enables us to answer both the what and the why. Once these two elements are isolated, we must write them down. The problem is on its way to solution.

At this point, we establish a hypothesis. That is, we attempt to state a tentative solution to the problem. Then research is directed toward testing the hypothesis. The research and tests prove or disprove the tentative answer. But the early definition and analysis of the problem gives the study direction.

Using Hypotheses

A *hypothesis* is a statement to be proved or disproved as a result of research. For example, a study of skilled manufacturing employees might be made to determine whether production would increase if the employees were given a bonus or incentive pay for production in excess of a standard. The researcher could formulate a hypothesis in the following way: "The productivity of skilled manufacturing employees will increase if the employees are given added pay for production in excess of the standard." This is a *positive* statement whose validity the researcher would attempt to test through research. However, many research people object to the use of a positive hypothesis because it may indicate a built-in prejudice on the part of the researcher toward a result favoring the hypothesis. To them, a *null* hypothesis is more desirable. The null hypothesis takes the form of a statement indicating no prejudice toward an answer. For example, the null hypothesis on the productivity of manufacturing employees could be stated in this way; "No significant difference will exist between productivity of workers on an incentive pay plan and productivity of workers on a regular wage plan."

Does a null hypothesis remove prejudice toward possible solutions?

Limiting the Problem

One of the major shortcomings of research planning is the failure to establish or to recognize desirable limitations. Assume, for instance, that we want to study clerical salaries. Imagine the scope of such a task. Millions of people are employed in clerical jobs. And perhaps a thousand or so different types of jobs fall into the clerical classification. To reduce such a problem to reasonable proportions, we should use the *what, why, when, where,* and *who* questions to limit the problem. Here's what we might come up with if we were in the position of the personnel manager in a metropolitan banking institution:

What: A study of clerical salaries.
Why: To determine whether salaries in our firm are competitive and consistent.
When: Current.
Where: Our metropolitan area.
Who: Clerical employees in banking institutions.

Now we can phrase our problem this way: "The purpose of this study is to survey clerical salaries in local banking institutions to determine whether our salaries are competitive and consistent." Notice that this process of reducing the problem to a workable size has also established some pretty firm limits to our research. We've limited the problem to current salaries, to the local area, and to a particular type of business. Notice, too, how important the *why* was in helping establish the limitations. Once we can clearly state the purpose of our research, many of the other elements important in formulating the problem fall into place.

Defining Terms Clearly

One of the great demons in developing understanding, of course, is the vague term. In the study of clerical salaries, it is clear that a comparison of our bank's salaries

Why define terms
when everyone has
access to a dictionary?

with those paid by other firms would be valid only if the information gathered from other firms is related to identical jobs in our organization. A job description defining the duties performed by a clerk-typist, for example, would help ensure that all firms would be talking about the same job tasks. It is very possible, and quite probable, that persons with different job titles perform the same tasks. Again, we'd have to be quite clear about the term *salary*. Is it hourly, weekly, monthly, yearly? A conversion table would probably be needed to provide consistency in converting amounts to the pay period we want to use. In all research leading to reports, the researcher should be certain to make a careful analysis of the terms used to ensure against misunderstanding.

SELECT A METHOD OF SOLUTION

After the problem has been defined, the researcher must plan an attack to arrive at a solution. He or she selects from the following recognized research methods one or more that will permit collection of the necessary information:

1. library research
2. normative survey research
3. observational research
4. experimental research

Doing Library Research

Library research is an essential part of all studies. It is a way to discover what other research in the area of our problem has uncovered. It is also a way to avoid investigating problems that have already been definitely answered. For example, an electronics engineer needs to develop a new airborne navigation system. From her knowledge and experience in the field, she knows that a body of knowledge exists about airborne electronic navigation. But she also knows that the boundaries of this body of knowledge are constantly expanding. Other scientists have worked in the same area and have, no doubt, contributed new information to the field. Therefore, she seeks to identify these new contributions and add them to the established body of knowledge before she conducts her own experiments. Figure 13–2 attempts to illustrate this constant development of knowledge.

Why is library
research not a need-
less duplication of effort?

Within the confines (white area) of a field of knowledge, certain truths have been established. These truths are treated as principles and reported in textbooks and other publications. However, because knowledge is not static and is constantly expanding, the researcher knows that new information is available. The job, then, is to become familiar with the library, canvass the literature of the field, and attempt to redefine the boundaries of knowledge (shaded area). This redefinition is the function of library research. Researchers then explore the unknown (dark area). Through

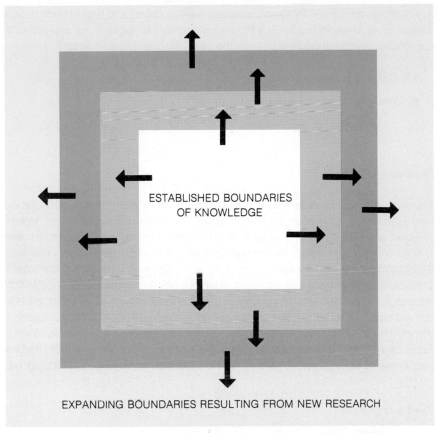

ESTABLISHED BOUNDARIES
OF KNOWLEDGE

EXPANDING BOUNDARIES RESULTING FROM NEW RESEARCH

Might this figure
be better as a series
of concentric circles?

Figure 13-2   The constant broadening of the boundaries of knowledge.

redefinition of boundaries, library research accomplishes the following functions:

1. It establishes a point of departure for further research.
2. It avoids needless duplication of costly research efforts.
3. It reveals areas of needed research.

One other point should be made: library research makes a real contribution to our body of knowledge.

Applied to business problems, library research involves the investigation of books, periodicals, and any records stored by the business because they might be needed for future information. Because it involves material already created, library research contributes *secondary* research data. Data created as a result of research from observation, surveys, and experiments are known as *primary* data.

When beginning to collect data for a study, we must beware of one of the major deterrents to good reporting—the problem of collecting too much information.

Although we want to be thorough, we don't want to collect and record such a large volume of information that we will hardly know where to begin in our analysis or in our writing. Try these devices to keep the volume of data at a minimum:

1. Use suggestive or cue notes.

2. Develop a card system.

3. Learn instead of accumulate.

The Suggestive Note or Cue Note

Would abbreviations qualify as symbols?

The suggestive or cue note is an abbreviated longhand or shorthand symbol that will help us recall the information we want to remember. It may consist of letters, words, phrases, sentences, symbols, or other abbreviations. For example, the chemist uses H_2O as a symbol for water; the shipper uses *bbl* for barrels; the teacher uses *A* for excellent; and the medical doctor uses $\bar{c}$ for with. And everyone uses *$* for dollars. These are commonplace symbols, but all writers develop some system of symbols meaningful to themselves. The point is that we should reduce bulky information to conveniently usable data. It is a way to protect ourselves from too much material. If something can be recorded easily on a small file card, why use a sheet of typewriter paper? Remember, the suggestive note is the smallest record we can make that will later serve as a recall cue. An example of a recall cue is the grocery shopping list.

The Card System

The card system is particularly useful in library work. Regular 3-by-5 or 5-by-8 cards can be used effectively. When library information is needed, we go first to the card catalog and to one or more of the reader's indexes to compile a bibliography. We should become familiar with sources such as those shown in Figure 13–3. After we have used the library's card catalog and located the references we need, we should attempt to make as complete a bibliographical entry as possible for each potential reference item. This practice may save a lot of time later when we might otherwise have to return to the library to look for missing items. Notice in Figure 13–4 how the essential items are included:

1. Author's name followed by a period.

2. Title of the book followed by a period.

3. Location and name of the publisher with a colon following the location and a comma following the publisher.

4. Year of publication followed by a period.

5. Total pages in the reference followed by a period. Total pages may also be abbreviated as *pp.* preceding the number of pages.

On Locating Information

Business Periodicals Index
Education Index
New York Times Index
Readers' Guide to Periodical Literature
Social Science and Humanities Index
Wall Street Journal Index

General Factual Information

Bureau of the Census publications, particularly the *Statistical Abstract of the United States*
Dictionary (any major publication)
Encyclopedia Americana
Encyclopedia Britannica
Fortune Directory
Rand McNally World Atlas
The World Almanac and Fact Book

Biography

Who's Who in America (and a variety of sub-who's who's by geographic areas, industries, and professions)

Report Style and Format

Form and Style in Thesis Writing, by William Giles Campbell, Houghton Mifflin Company
A Manual of Style, University of Chicago Press
A Manual of Style for the Preparation of Papers and Reports, by Irwin M. Keithley, South-Western Publishing Company
A Manual for Writers of Term Papers, Theses, and Dissertations, by Kate L. Turabian, University of Chicago Press
Style Manual for Written Communications, by Arno Knapper and Loda Newcomb, Grid, Inc.

Figure 13-3   Useful reference and source books.

It is generally easier to make notes from references in paraphrase style; that is, in our own words. We should be extremely careful, however, not to change the meaning intended by the author. We should record the page number or numbers on which our paraphrased or quoted material was found. Recording the library call number will help us find the reference rapidly and make check-out cards for the librarian.

Should a paraphrase be cited in footnote form? Why?

Definitions   LC 75-18006
Flexner, Stuart B. (ed.). Family Word Finder. Pleasantville,
N.Y.: The Reader's Digest Association, 1975. pp. 896.

p. 161--communicate (verb). make known, inform of, announce,
apprise of, tell, notify, advise, pass on, convey, disclose,
divulge, reveal, relate, bring word, proclaim, broadcast,
publish, publicize; state, declare, say, mention; show, exhibit,
signify. . . . Antonyms: keep secret, hush up, suppress,
repress, withhold, hold back, cover up.

Figure 13-4 Cue card showing classification, bibliographical reference, and noted material.

As we work with each reference, it is useful to develop a subject classification (shown at the top of Figure 13–4). Subject classifications are very helpful when compiling the report; they allow us to organize our cards rapidly. We could put all the definitions cards together, for instance.

What does *plagiarism* mean?

When using library materials in written work, we should give credit where credit is due. To commit plagiarism by not footnoting the source of the material is foolish. Many college students have received failing grades, even been accused of cheating, simply because they don't document their work. In a later chapter, suggestions will be made for proper citation of materials used in reports, term papers, and other written work.

The Goal of Library Research

The primary purpose of library research is *to learn,* not to accumulate. The following technique is especially effective: (1) read an article rapidly, (2) put it aside, (3) list main and supporting points *from memory,* and (4) review the article to see whether all significant points have been included. Rapid reading forces concentration. Taking notes from memory reinforces learning and reduces the temptation to rely heavily on the words of others. If you really learn the subject matter of one source, you will (as research progresses) see the relationship between it and other sources. You will see yourself growing toward mastery of the subject.

Doing Normative Survey Research

Normative survey research is a method used to determine the status of something at the time of the research. It utilizes survey instruments: questionnaires, opinionnaires, checklists, or interviews. The opinion polls reported in our daily newspapers use normative research methods to obtain information. These forms of research are not used to determine facts already obtainable through library research. They may be used, however, to test the validity of the information reported in the literature. The United States census is conducted periodically to establish an actual population count. In effect, the census tests the validity and reliability of projection techniques used to estimate population during the ten-year periods between official censuses.

The term *normative* is used to qualify surveys because surveys establish current norms or standards. The survey discovers "what is"—the present status of something. For example, suppose we want to determine the attitude of employees in a plant toward labor unions, compulsory insurance, or any of a variety of items affecting employee welfare. About the only way these can be determined is through the use of surveys. The questionnaire or personal interview would help reveal the necessary information. But would management be using good judgment if it decided to use the results of such a survey a year or two after the survey? Would the information still be current? Would all the employees still be there? It is easy to see that survey information is valid only at the time of the survey. Later studies are necessary to bring the data up to date.

Whether the survey is made by personal interviewing or by distributing devices such as checklists or questionnaires, some principles of procedure and preplanning are common to both methods. These principles assure the researcher that the data gathered will be both valid and reliable. Data are *valid* (said to possess *validity*) when they measure what they are supposed to measure. Data are *reliable* (said to possess *reliability*) when they give assurance that they are reasonably close to the truth; that is, when they measure accurately.

Validity generally results from careful planning of questionnaire or interview questions (*items*). Cautious wording, preliminary testing of items to detect misunderstanding, and some statistical techniques are helpful in determining if the responses to the items are valid.

Reliability results from asking a large enough sample of people so that the researcher is reasonably assured the results would be the same even if more people were asked to respond. For example, if you were to ask ten people to react to a questionnaire item, the results might vary considerably. If you were to add ninety more people to the sample, the results might tend to reach a point of stability, where more responses would not change the results. Reliability would then be assured.

Thus, *reliability* is a sign that whatever you have attempted to measure would give the same results even if more people were surveyed. *Validity* is a quite different element. It refers to the idea that what you attempted to measure is actually what you intended to measure. Validity results from careful planning of questionnaire items. The good researcher tests survey items to detect misunderstanding on the part of respondents. Reliability is an outcome of sampling.

Use of Sampling

In all surveys, the research assumes that the people asked to respond are either representative of a larger group or constitute the entire group that is to be surveyed

Can the term *par* be considered a synonym for *normative*?

Is the United States census both valid and reliable?

and about whom generalizations are to be drawn. The researcher normally can't survey everyone in the population; but through sampling techniques, he or she can be confident that only a small part of the total population can fairly represent the total population. *Sampling,* then, is a survey technique that saves the time and trouble of questioning 100 percent of the population.

The sampling process is based on the principle that a sufficiently large number drawn at random from a population will be representative of the total population; that is, the sampling group will possess the same characteristics in the same proportions as the total population. For example, public opinion polls actually survey only a few people, but they are considered valid if the sample of people surveyed has the same percentage of butchers, housewives, Democrats, Republicans, cab-drivers, schoolteachers, retired persons, mothers, and so on, as the entire population does.

Sampling is thus a vital part of effective surveys. If, for example, we survey the members of our class on the value of this course, we will have surveyed the entire population of the class. Our results will be reliable because we do not plan to make generalizations about a larger population. But could we survey our class and then make generalizations about the feelings of the entire student body toward the course? We would certainly first have to answer questions such as these: Do all members of the student body have to take this course? Would students who did not have to take it think it was valuable? Would science majors consider it as valuable as business majors might? Is there more than one section of this course? Does the same teacher always teach it? Are the students in our class representative of the student body in general?

When sampling methods may be necessary because of the size of the population involved, several options are available. These include (1) random sampling, (2) stratified random sampling, and (3) systematic random sampling. The researcher's primary task is to select the best sampling technique for the study.

Is the nature or makeup of a sample a limitation on a study?

1. *Random sampling* is perhaps the most desirable technique. It gives all members of the population an equal chance to be included in the sample. For example, if we want to survey all the members of a college student body, it might be too time consuming to survey everyone in a large school. We could, instead, use random sampling by putting the name of each student on a piece of paper, putting all the names in a container, and drawing out a predetermined number of names. Because the entire student body was included, each name would have an equal opportunity to be drawn.

Does random-ness mean chance?

2. *Stratified random sampling* is the method public opinion poll organizations use. In surveying the student body with this method, for example, we would continue to draw names until we had the same percentage of seniors, juniors, sophomores, and freshmen as in the total student population. If we decided to include in our sample 1,000 students in a student body of 10,000, composed of 30 percent freshmen, 27 percent sophomores, 23 percent juniors, and 20 percent seniors, we would need to include 300 freshmen, 270 sophomores, 230 juniors, and 200 seniors.

Does stratifying the sample reduce chance? If so, why are public opin-ion polls often incorrect?

3. *Systematic random sampling* is a form of random sampling in which, to use our college survey as an example again, every tenth name might be drawn from the files of the register. To ensure randomness, we would place in a hat the numbers 1 through 10, and then draw one. If 3 is drawn, for example, we would use the third name in the files, then the thirteenth, then the twenty-third, and so on until we reached the number we wanted to sample. Again, the technique ensures that each member of the student body has an equal chance to be selected.

These techniques are used in surveys that attempt to determine shopper preferences, buying habits, attitudes, and similar marketing-oriented studies. Again, of course, the researcher must be cautious about drawing conclusions from a sample and applying them to a population that might not be represented by the sample. For example, early-morning shoppers may differ from afternoon or evening shoppers, young ones may differ from old ones, men may differ from women. The good researcher defines the population as distinctly as possible and uses a sampling technique to ensure that the sample is representative.

Achieving sophistication in surveys requires considerable study of the field. Findings are only as reliable and valid as are the methods of selecting and surveying the sample.

Even when the sampling technique results in a representative sample, the construction of the survey instrument—usually a questionnaire or interview guide—is critical to the process.

Use of Questionnaires

Effective handling of data gathered through surveys depends very much on the format of the questionnaire. Prior to formulating the items for the questionnaire, the researcher should attempt to visualize the ways data are to be assembled and included in the final report. Then, questionnaire items that concern the same subject should be grouped together, making responses easy. This same grouping also makes tabulation of replies much easier. For example, if name, age, sex, family size, and income are important to the study because it will include an analysis of the respondents to the questionnaire, these items should be grouped together.

Provide enough space for respondents to record their answers to questionnaire items. An open-ended quesiton, such as "What effect would an additional tax on oil and natural gas have on the economy?" may require a lengthy answer. To provide only one line for the answer would be unfair to the respondents, and it might result in responses that would be impossible to interpret. On the other hand, some items may require only check marks in columns:

Techtonics Inc. should have a company newspaper to keep employees informed.

Agree _____   Disagree _____   No Opinion _____

Should the respondent's ease in answering and the researcher's ease in tabulating responses receive equal consideration in questionnaire construction?

Here are a few general rules to keep in mind for effective questionnaires:

1. Ask for factual information as much as possible. Of course, opinions may be needed in certain studies; however, opinions may change from day to day. As a general rule, too, the smaller the sample, the less reliable are conclusions based on opinion.

2. Ask for information that can be recalled readily. To ask for information going back over time may not result in sound data.

3. Test the wording of items with others before preparing a final survey instrument. For example, how would someone be expected to respond to the following item?

Have you stopped beating your spouse?

Yes ———   No ———   Don't Know ———

Obviously, items can be phrased in ways that put people in very awkward positions. We should avoid wording items in such a way that personal, sensitive characteristics are involved in the answers. This approach is of especial importance when questionnaires require the respondent to give his or her name, for even questions about age, income, or church-going habits may not be answered accurately.

Should age, income, sex, and occupation be a part of all questionnaires?

4. In determining the sequence of items, try to arrange the questionnaire so the easiest-to-answer items come at the beginning. People are inclined to delay responding when the material requested is difficult. On the other hand, easy items at the beginning will probably get the respondent involved to the point where he or she will want to complete the entire questionnaire, even though more difficulty is encountered in later terms. Easy items, of course, are those with which respondents are most familiar. If you place the most difficult item first, the questionnaire may end up in the wastebasket.

5. Try to design a format that will make the job of tabulating information easier. Ask for only one piece of information for each item. Notice how the format of the questionnaire in Figure 13–5 makes responses easy. Because the questionnaire is not to be signed, the questions asking for age, income, and occupation will probably be answered honestly. Additionally, tabulating responses should be facilitated because the layout makes computer input easy if the study has a large sample. Even manual tabulation is simple since only the final item on stereo brands has more than one response.

6. Prepare a letter to accompany the questionnaire. People must be convinced they are doing something worthwhile when they tackle a survey instrument. The instructions for filling out the questionnaire may be included in the letter or may be incorporated as part of the questionnaire.

What would be your reaction if you were asked to complete a questionnaire and to return it with your own stamp?

7. If the questionnaire is mailed, enclose a stamped return envelope. This courtesy is expected and helps increase the percentage of returns.

MARKETING SURVEY OF STEREO
PURCHASING PREFERENCES

Please check the appropriate space in each of the items.

Your Age Group (1)   Your Occupation (2)
a. under 20   _____   a. Student   _____
b. 20-29   _____   b. White Collar   _____
c. 30-39   _____   c. Blue Collar   _____
d. 40-49   _____   d. Professional   _____
e. 50-59   _____   e. Retired   _____
f. Over 59   _____   f. Unemployed   _____
                                            g. Other _____

Your Sex (3) a. Female _____ b. Male _____

Marital Status (4) a. Married _____ b. Single _____

Household Income Group (5)
a. Below $10,000   _____
b. $10,000-19,999   _____
c. $20,000-29,999   _____
d. $30,000-39,999   _____
e. $40,000-49,999   _____
f. $50,000+   _____

Do you presently own a stereo? (6) a. Yes _____ b. No _____

If not, do you plan to purchase one? (7) a. Yes _____ b. No _____

If you have a system, do you plan to add to it within the next
year? (8) a. Yes _____ b. No _____ c. Uncertain _____

If you own a stereo system, please check the appropriate spaces
in the following items:

Your Estimate
of the Value
of Your
Present System (9)
a. Under $200   _____
b. $201-400   _____
c. $401-600   _____
d. $601-800   _____
e. $801-1000   _____
f. $1001-1200   _____
g. Over $1200   _____

Figure 13-5   Questionnaire keyed for computer input.

Please check from the following list up to five brands with which you associate quality: (10)

a. Advent _____	e. Harmon-Kardon _____	i. Pioneer _____
b. Bose _____	f. JBL _____	j. Sony _____
c. Dual _____	g. Kenwood _____	k. Teac _____
d. Garrard _____	h. Marantz _____	l. _____

Figure 13-5 continued.

Use of Rating Scales

Rating scales are similar to questionnaires because they pose problems or questions that can be responded to simply. Suppose you want to determine the most pressing problems faced by employees in a production line. You could ask them to list the problems, but the responses might be so ambiguous that tabulating them would be impossible. A rating scale such as the following illustration would be an improvement:

For each of the following problems, please circle the degree to which the problem affects you:

Acceptance by others

1	2	3	4	5	6

Little	Moderate	Great
effect	effect	effect

Interest in the job

1	2	3	4	5	6

Little	Moderate	Great
effect	effect	effect

Similar information could be obtained by listing the potential problems and by asking respondents to rank the problems in order of their importance.

Please rank the following problems in order of their importance to you. Place a 1 in the space following the most important problem, a 2 in the space following the second most important problem; proceed in this manner until all have been ranked. Two blank lines have been left for you to write in a problem area that may have been omitted.

Acceptance by others   _____
Interest in the job   _____
Economic security   _____
Concern for health   _____
_____   _____
_____   _____

Even though most of us are familiar with ranking scales because we have encountered them both at work and at school, when we do use them in research, we should first test them on a small sample to see if they are clearly understood and produce the kind of information we seek.

If we are interested in determining which of the problems is most critical to the production employee, a *forced answer* question can be used:

Of all the problems listed, which is the single most critical problem for you personally? _____

_____

This question could also have been posed in multiple-choice form, much like the multiple-choice items used in school tests.

Which of the following problems is the single most critical problem for you personally? Please check.
    a. Acceptance by others   _____
    b. Interest in the job   _____
    c. Economic security   _____
    d. Concern for health   _____
    e. Other   _____

Researchers must select from the several choices available the one best suited to the situation. Criteria for selecting one alternative over the others might include (1) Which format leaves the least chance for misinterpretation? (2) Which format provides information in the way it can best be used? (3) Can it be tabulated easily? (4) Can it be cross referenced to other items in the survey instrument?

Doing Observational Research

Observational, or statistical, research describes research involving statistical analysis of one or more sets of data. Suppose we wanted to know if scores on college aptitude tests really had any relationship to grades made in a college history course. We would gather the grades of students in the history class, obtain the college aptitude scores of those same students, and perform statistical correlations of the two sets of data to seek information about the relationship.

Frequently, businesses use both observational and survey methods to solve problems. Market analysts may use survey methods to determine buying habits of certain income groups. Then statistical analyses are used to determine the most desirable markets.

The name *observational research* is used because this type of analysis involves observing certain phenomena to assist in establishing new principles.

Several studies have used the observational method to determine the differences between business letters rated good or rated bad. One study used a random sample of 500 letters obtained from the files of various companies. Copies of the 500 letters were sent to five experts in written communication who served as a rating jury. Each jury member was asked to sort the letters into five sets. The first set was to include the 100 best letters in the jurist's opinion; the second set, the second-best 100; the third set, the middle 100; and so on. The reports of the five jury members were then combined to determine the 100 letters with the highest ratings and the 100 with the lowest ratings. Three hundred letters fell in the middle and were discarded. Thus only the best and worst 100 remained. Then, the two groups of letters were analyzed in terms of planning, writing style, tone, sentence length, spelling, punctuation, and length. Statistical tests of significant differences between the two groups were used to determine the characteristic differences between good and bad letters.

In this study, the observational method was used because certain phenomena were observed, counted, and analyzed statistically to help establish principles.

> Would a traffic count of automobiles using a specific route be an observational study?

Doing Experimental Research

Experimental research is familiar to most of us as the test-tube research conducted in a laboratory by a scientist wearing a white smock. Scientists are conducting experimental research when they put exactly the same materials into two test tubes and then add one new ingredient to only one of the two original tubes. After the new ingredient is added to one tube, the changes that take place in that tube are measured. Any change is due, of course, to the addition of the new ingredient.

Basically, then, *experimental research* involves two samples that have exactly the same ingredients before a variable is added to one of the samples. The differences observed are due to the variable.

How is experimental research used in business? As a simple example, assume an office has a great number of clerk-typists doing the same routine job. Management decides to make a study of the effects of incentive pay (extra pay for production in excess of a minimum standard). It separates the clerk-typists into two groups about equal in experience, skill, and previous productivity rates. Then one group is placed on an incentive-pay basis. During the time length of the study, the difference in the two groups is noted. Because the incentive pay is assumed to be the only variable, any difference is attributed to its influence. Of course, we can criticize such a study; but the point is that the business used the experimental research method just as the laboratory scientist used it.

> How can experimental research be used to determine the effects of drugs on the performance of race horses?

COLLECT AND ORGANIZE THE DATA

Having decided on a method, researchers must outline a step-by-step approach to the solution of the problem. The human mind is an inquiring mind. But it is also susceptible to digressions. Although these may be short-lived, they distract from the job at hand; and, if given free rein, they can lead to obliteration of the real object of the study.

Therefore, *keep on the right track*. Plan the study and follow the plan. Question every step for its contribution to the objective. Keep a record of actions. In a formal research study, the researcher is expected to make a complete report. Another qualified person should be able to make the same study, use the same steps, and arrive at the same conclusion.

Tabulation techniques should be used to reduce quantitative data such as numerous answers to questionnaire items. Suppose we have made a survey and have collected several hundred replies to a twenty- or thirty-item questionnaire in addition to many cards or notes from library sources. What do we do next? As shown in Figure 13-6, the report process is one of reducing the original information to a convenient size that can be handled in a written message.

Visualize the report process as taking place in a huge funnel. At the top of the funnel, pour in all the original information. Then, within the funnel, through a process' of compression,

How does condensation of material assist in reaching conclusions?

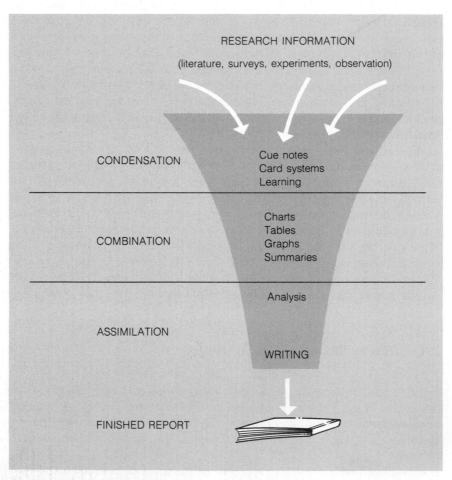

RESEARCH INFORMATION

(literature, surveys, experiments, observation)

CONDENSATION

Cue notes
Card systems
Learning

COMBINATION

Charts
Tables
Graphs
Summaries

Analysis

ASSIMILATION

WRITING

FINISHED REPORT

Figure 13-6   The Report Process.

1. Evaluate the information for its usefulness.

2. Reduce the useful information through the use of suggestive notes, card systems, or learning.

3. Combine like information into understandable form through the use of tables, charts, graphs, and summaries.

4. Report in written form what remains.

ARRIVE AT AN ANSWER

Even if valid and reliable data have been collected, a report can be worthless if the interpretation is faulty. Although success at interpretation may be very closely related to mental ability, even the most intelligent person cannot be expected to draw sound conclusions from faulty information. Sound conclusions can be drawn only when information has been properly (1) collected and (2) interpreted.

Is a good writing style of muoh value if conclusions are weak?

Collecting Data

If acceptable data-gathering techniques have been employed, data will measure what they are intended to measure (have validity) and will measure it well (have reliability). Some common errors at the data-gathering stage that seriously hamper later interpretation are

What are some of the common errors in the gathering of data?

1. Using samples that are too small.

2. Using samples that are not representative.

3. Using poorly constructed data-gathering instruments.

4. Using information that came from biased sources.

5. Failing to gather enough information to cover all important aspects of a problem.

6. Gathering too much information and then attempting to use all of it even though some may be irrelevant.

Interpreting Data

If we avoid data-collecting errors, we are more likely to reach sound conclusions. But sound conclusions are unlikely if interpretation is faulty. Some common mental

What are some common errors in the interpretation of data?

errors seriously handicap the interpretation of data:

1. Trying, consciously or unconsciously, to make results conform to a prediction or desire. Seeing predictions come true may be pleasing, but objectivity is much more important. Facts should determine our conclusions.

2. Hoping for spectacular results. People often need ego satisfaction. But an attempt to astonish our superiors by preparing a report with revolutionary conclusions can only have a very negative effect on accuracy.

3. Attempting to compare when commonality is absent. Concluding that a certain product would sell well in Arizona because it sold well in Massachusetts would be risky. Because of differences in geography, climate, and economic factors, relationships might not be at all comparable.

4. Assuming a cause-effect relationship when one does not exist. A company president may have been in office one year and sales may have doubled. But the sales might have doubled *in spite* of the president rather than *because* of her.

5. Failing to consider important factors. A college professor returned from a tour of the educational institutions in Mexico. Speaking to a group of high school teachers, he cautioned against modifying the school curriculum to include four years of science and math, four years of foreign language, four years of social studies, and four years of English. That curriculum, he said, is Mexico's curriculum; and in Mexico last night two-thirds of the babies went to bed hungry. He apparently neglected to consider the influence of such factors as geography, climate, natural resources, tradition, and politics.

6. Basing a conclusion on lack of evidence. "We have had no complaints about our present policy" does not mean that the policy is appropriate. And, conversely, lack of evidence that a proposed project will succeed does not necessarily mean that it will fail. The old adage that "No news is good news" is not applicable in research.

7. Assuming constancy of human behavior. A survey indicating 60 percent of the public favors one political party over the other in March does not mean the same thing will be true in November. Because some people paid their bills late last year does not mean a company should refuse to sell to them the next year. The reasons for slow payment may have been removed.

SUMMARY

In arriving at an answer (a conclusion), report writers must have the results of their research before them. They should be able to see the problem as a whole. If they defined the problem, selected an appropriate method of research, and gathered and analyzed the data, they can arrive at a sound conclusion. Throughout the entire process, however, researchers must protect themselves not only against their own human failings but also against their material. That is the nature of objectivity. As you approach the report-writing task, your success will rest primarily on your ability to reason objectively.

EXERCISES

1. For each of the following research topics, write a positive hypothesis and then restate it as a null hypothesis. Thus, you have two items to write for each topic. Solutions to topic (a) are given.

    a. A study to determine the relationship existing between the FOG Index readability rating of business textbooks and student interest in courses using the textbooks.

    Hypothesis: Students show more interest in courses using textbooks with low FOG Indexes than in courses using textbooks with high FOG Indexes.

    Null Hypothesis: Readability levels of course textbooks has no relationship to student interest in those courses. *Or:* No relationship exists between readability of textbooks and student interest in courses using those textbooks.

    b. A survey to determine whether the occupations of people twenty years after college were the occupations they prepared for in college.

    c. A study to find whether office workers produce more, less, or the same after background music is provided in the office.

    d. A study to determine whether access to a home computer improves a student's college grades.

2. List the limitations you might have for any of the studies in exercise 1. What uncontrollable factors might influence your findings? How universally would your findings apply? What factors might change if the study were to be repeated?

3. Using a library, prepare annotated bibliography cards covering four recent items related to one of the following subjects:

    a. Accounting

    b. Personnel management

    c. Computer technology

    d. Word processing

    e. Marketing

4. Explain why a single report might fit several of the report classifications described at the beginning of this chapter.

5. If you were a professor and a student came to you with the statement "I am going to make a study to prove that all students should have a course in economics," how would you respond in terms of the objective nature of the research process?

For the research studies in exercises 6 to 10, prepare a one-page description of your attack on the problem. Use the following headings for the problem assigned:

Statement of the Problem
Research Method and Sources of Information
Nature of Data to Be Gathered and Analyzed
Hypothesis or Hypotheses to Be Proved or Disproved (if feasible)

Think ahead to the nature of the questionnaire or other type of research instrument or technique you might use.

6. As research director of Glow-Stern, a stock brokerage firm, you have the task of determining investment practices for your clients. Your goal is to learn how different age groups manage their investment or savings dollars. Because this subject could be quite sensitive to many clients, your survey is to be anonymous. You've also decided that your age groups should be adults under the age of thirty, people between thirty and fifty, and those over fifty.

7. As marketing director of Club Carib, proprietor of a chain of resort hotels in the Caribbean, you want to determine what former customers liked and disliked about their vacations at your resorts.

8. MacDonald's fast-food company plans to open a new outlet in one of three possible locations: (1) on an interstate highway, (2) in a downtown shopping district, (3) in a neighborhood shopping mall. All locations are within a three-mile radius of the center of a city. You are to submit a recommendation.

9. As marketing promotion director for the Ajax Cosmetics Company, you are planning to advertise your new line of high-priced cosmetics in either *Vogue* or *Cosmopolitan* magazines. Only one can be selected because of budget. You plan to run ads of a full page in color for the next 12 months.

10. As promotion-advertising director of City First Thrift and Loan, you have the job of determining whether the firm should give gift certificates or actual gifts (of items such as calculators, pens, or hand kitchen mixers) as incentives to encourage people to open accounts. In either case, the incentives cannot exceed a value of $5 for each $1,000 deposited in the new account.

11. For any of the problems in exercises 1 through 5 that might require a survey, prepare an appropriate questionnaire.

MANAGING DATA AND USING GRAPHICS

Managing Quantitative Data
Measures of Central Tendency
The Range
Using Tables and Graphics
Using Tables
Using Graphics
Introducing Tables and Graphs in the Text
Using Common Language to Describe Data
Summary

355

Once we have defined the problem and selected a method of solution, our next step is to gather and analyze the findings of the research. The analysis of findings is greatly enhanced when we follow a few easy steps to protect ourselves against being overwhelmed by the material gathered. The steps cover two broad areas: managing quantitative data and selecting the best means of presenting it in the final written report.

MANAGING QUANTITATIVE DATA

Does analysis precede tabulation?

In most studies, particularly in surveys, much of the data gathered lends itself to statistical analysis. A number of people responded "yes," a number said "no," and some replied "no opinion." Of course, we must count these responses in some way. Whether they are counted manually or by a computer, the counting process is called tabulation. Analysis can only follow this process.

Assume, for example, that you have been given the task of determining family income by the age of the head of the household. Your sample of 356 respondents was a stratified random sample representing the various age groups in the population studied. One item in the questionnaire asked for the respondent to indicate his or her age; another item asked for family income. It would be easy to tabulate all the ages and then to tabulate all the incomes. However, your analysis would be much more effective if you could relate age to income. You could feed all your questionnaire information into a computer and use a simple program to obtain your information. On the other hand, you could do a manual tabulation using a form similar to that shown in Figure 14-1 to accomplish the same goal. Notice that the tabulation covered the responses to two questionnaire items: age and income.

In the upper left-hand corner, or cell, of the tabulation sheet in Figure 14-1, three persons who were nineteen or under also had incomes below $5,000. The person doing the tabulating simply looked at both items, age and income, and placed a mark in the appropriate cell. Now, as you look at Figure 14-1, you can make several broad generalizations even without applying any statistical techniques. You can see, for example, that

1. Incomes range from under $5,000 to over $35,000.

2. Ages range from under nineteen years to over seventy years.

3. The largest group of people earned between $20,000 and $24,999.

4. The largest age group was between forty and forty-nine years.

5. Only a very few had incomes under $5,000, and only a very few were under nineteen or over sixty-nine.

But your analysis can go beyond these readily apparent observations if you use a simple statistical treatment of the data. First, sort out the kinds of information you will want to report. Let's take the right-hand total column, for example, to analyze

Income	19 and under	20–29	30–39	40–49	50–59	60–69	70 and over	Totals
Under $5,000	|||	||						||	8
$5,000–9,999	⊞		⊞ |||	||||	||		||	⊞ ||	29
$10,000–14,999	||	⊞ ⊞ |||	⊞ ||	||||	||||	⊞ ||	⊞	42
$15,000–19,999			⊞ ⊞ ⊞	⊞ ||||	⊞ ⊞ ||	⊞ |||	⊞		||	53
$20,000–24,999		⊞ ⊞	⊞ ⊞ ⊞ ||	⊞ ⊞ ||	⊞ ⊞ ⊞ |||	⊞ ⊞			83
$25,000–29,999		⊞ ||	⊞ ⊞ ⊞	⊞ ⊞ ⊞ ||	⊞ ⊞ ⊞	⊞			65
$30,000–34,999		⊞		⊞ ⊞ ||	⊞ ⊞ ⊞		⊞ ||||	|||		45
$35,000 and over		||	⊞		⊞ ⊞ ||	⊞ ||||	||		31
Totals	12	63	71	90	67	36	17	356

AGE GROUPS

Figure 14-1 Tabulation sheet with count.

just what the distribution of incomes might reveal. (*Distribution* is a term used to describe how the total sample was divided among the various income categories.) By using both the number of responses for each category and the percentage each group is of the total, we can develop a table as follows:

Income Distribution of 356 Respondents

Income	Number	Percent
$35,000 and over	31	9
30,000–34,999	45	13
25,000–29,999	65	18
20,000–24,999	83	23
15,000–19,999	53	15
10,000–14,999	42	12
5,000–9,999	29	8
Under $5,000	8	2
Total	356	100

As you look at this table, you can quickly make some observations using the percentage column. A percentage is a common language symbol. People have difficulty understanding what is meant by 83/356, which is the number of people with incomes between $20,000 and $24,999. When the 83/356 is converted to a percentage and shown as 23, most people can readily see that almost one out of four responses was in that income class. Thus, your analysis of data proceeds by reducing 356 questionnaire responses to two items to a one-page tabulation, as shown in Figure 14-1. Then you further reduced some of the information on the tabulations sheet to a simple table showing easy-to-understand percentages. In effect, you have protected yourself against your masses of data by constantly reducing them to usable size.

Further inspection of the table reveals that only 10 percent of the people had incomes below $10,000; well over half—in fact, 63 percent, or almost two out of three—had incomes over $20,000. Notice that even percentages can be rounded to simple ratios like one-out-of-four and two-out-of-three. How much simpler those ratios are to grasp than such statements as 83-out-of-356! In most social-science research, the report writer can round off items to the nearest percentage and convert percentages to approximate ratios. Additional analysis can be made using statistical measures of central tendency.

Measures of Central Tendency

Measures of central tendency are simple statistical treatments of distribution that attempt to find a single figure to describe the entire distribution. The three most commonly used measures are the *mean,* the *median,* and the *mode.* Selecting which measure to use is up to the report writer.

The Mean

The *mean* is the figure we get when the total of all the values in a distribution is divided by the number of values in the distribution. If, for example, eight people score 60, 65, 70, 75, 80, 85, 90, and 95 on a test, the total of these values would be 620. Dividing 620 by 8 gives an arithmetic mean of 77.5. Most people would call 77.5 the *average* score, but *mean* is a more appropriate term.

When figures are grouped as they are in the previous income distribution table, the *midpoint* of each class serves as the figure to describe the entire group of responses in that class. For example, 42 people had incomes in the $10,000–14,999 class. We must assume that the 42 were distributed evenly throughout the class. If we assume this even distribution, then the midpoint of the class—halfway between $10,000 and $14,999.99—is $12,500. To obtain a single figure to describe that class, we multiply 42 (the number of people) by $12,500 (the number of dollars each was assumed to have as income—the midpoint) to arrive at a total income for that class of $525,000. We then repeat the process for each income class, total all the class incomes, and divide by 356 to get a mean income for the entire distribution.

To the sophisticated statistician, however, the mean for the distribution is a questionable figure because we do not know much about the 31 respondents who had incomes over $35,000. Because no upper limit is shown, some could have incomes far beyond $35,000 or $37,500 or $40,000. What if someone had an income of several million dollars? If so, that income could make the mean far too high to describe the distribution very accurately. For example, if 9 people in a group each earns $10,000, and a tenth person earns $110,000, the total is $200,000 and the mean ($200,000 divided by 10) is $20,000. That's not a very good measure of central tendency to use in this case.

How does a mean differ from a median?

The Median

The *median* is the middle value in a distribution. For example, test scores of 60, 65, 70, 75, 80, 85, and 100 would have a middle value of 75, the middle score of the seven. The median in the example of 9 people each earning $10,000 and one earning $110,000 is $10,000, a far better descriptive value for the 10 people than $20,000. Medians are found by counting values from the highest or the lowest to the middle value. In grouped data, such as the income distribution of the 356 respondents, the median would be a value between the 178th and 179th incomes. Half of the 356 incomes would be below the median and half above the median. To find this value, begin with the 8 people who have incomes under $5,000 and count upward to the 178th income. A total of 132 people are in all the classes below the $20,000–$24,999 class. You then count an additional 46 people of the 83 in the $20,000–$24,999 class. In effect, you take 46/83 of the $5,000 range of the class, or $2,770, and add it to the bottom of the class, $20,000, for a median of $22,770. Then you can say that the total distribution has a median income of $22,770.

When a distribution contains some extreme values, which is better, the mean or the median?

Because the median is only concerned with the middle value, the possible extreme incomes over $35,000 are ignored. Thus, the median is useful when very extreme values exist or may exist. The mean, on the other hand, is an accurate measure of arithmetic averages when *all* values are known. Additionally, the mean is used to calculate other statistical measures.

When a sample is extremely large, which would a statistician probably use, the mean or the median?

The Mode

The *mode* is the value found most frequently in a distribution. For example, test scores of 65, 70, 75, 75, 75, 80, 80, 90, and 95 would have a mode of 75 because it is the most frequent value in the distribution. In grouped data, the mode is not a single value or figure but is the range of the entire class having the highest frequency. In Figure 14-1, the *modal* class for income is $20,000–24,999 because 83 people were in that class. The modal class for age is forty to forty-nine years because the 90 people in that age group represent the single largest class.

In general, the mean is the most stable of these three measures of central tendency. That is, from distribution to distribution developed from the same population, the mean will fluctuate less widely than will the median or mode. It is also useful in calculating standard deviations and is extremely reliable when the sample is large. Even a person 110 years old (or with an income of $1 million) would not have much effect on the mean when several hundred persons are included in the sample.

On the other hand, the median is less sensitive to extreme cases. In either case, good judgment must be used in what descriptive measure to use or whether to use one at all.

The Range

Because extreme values may influence measures of central tendency, the *range* — the difference between the lowest and highest values — is frequently used to describe the limits of the distribution. The range of our income groups was from under $5,000 to over $35,000. Test scores of 20, 30, 75, 75, 75, 80, 85, 90, and 95 would have a range of 20 to 95, or 76 points (95 minus 20 plus 1, to count both the 20 and the 95).

The range is important in determining the number of classes for a tabulation sheet. In Figure 14-1, the tabulation was done with seven classes for age groups and eight for income groups. Without a knowledge of the range, the researcher's classes could be too small or too large to lend themselves to effective statistical treatment and later presentation.

To eliminate further the distortion created by extreme figures, the *interquartile range* may be used. The interquartile range is the spread of the middle 50 percent of the values. For example, in a distribution such as 7, 19, 21, 23, 24, 25, 29, and 41, the interquartile range is 21 to 25. Because eight items are included, two are in each quarter of the distribution. The second and third quartiles (the middle half) include the figures 21, 23, 24, and 25. Even though the total range is from 7 to 41, the interquartile range shows that most figures are grouped tightly. Thus the influence of the extreme values, 7 and 41, is decreased.

Therefore for each distribution we must use our judgment to determine how best to manage the data. Too few classes will put too many values in each class. Too many classes will result in a distribution with only one or two cases in each class, so that tabulation may be of no more value than a simple listing of individual values. In general, in most studies using quantitative data similar to the ones used in this chapter, five to ten classes would be adequate and permit reasonable data management.

USING TABLES AND GRAPHICS

Managing data effectively protects a report writer from being overwhelmed by the data collected. To protect readers from also being overwhelmed, report writers must select appropriate means of presenting the data. "One picture is worth a thousand words" is an old but meaningful saying. Material that can be reported in a table, picture, graph, or chart will make your written analysis of it clearer to the reader. Imagine trying to put in composition style all the information available in a modern financial statement. Several hundred pages might be necessary to explain all the material that could otherwise be contained in three or four pages of balance sheets and profit and loss statements. And even then, the reader would no doubt be thoroughly confused! When graphics are used, they go hand in hand with the written discussion to achieve clarity. As you proceed through the remainder of this chapter, ask yourself if the discussion would be effective if the accompanying graphic figures were not included.

Using Tables

A *table* is a presentation of data in column form. Very simply, 2 plus 3 plus 5 plus 6 plus 11 equals 27 is better represented:

$$
\begin{array}{r}
2 \\
3 \\
5 \\
6 \\
\underline{11} \\
27
\end{array}
$$

Typically, the preparation of tables is concerned with labeling techniques to make the content clear. Here are some helpful practices in table preparation:

1. Number tables and all other graphics consecutively throughout the report. This practice enables you to refer to "Figure 1" rather than to "the following table" or the "figure on the following page." Incidentally, the term "figure" should be used to identify all tables, graphs, pictures, and charts. In this chapter, for example, notice that all illustrations are identified as figures.

2. Give each table a title that is complete enough to clarify what is included without forcing the reader to review the table. Table titles may be quite long and even extend beyond one line. A two-line title should be arranged on the page so that neither line extends into the margins. The second line should be shorter than the first and centered under it. Titles may contain sources of data, numbers included in the table, and the subject of the table; for example, "Opinions of 350 School Administrators Toward Appointive Boards of Education." The title of a table can be written in all capital letters for emphasis.

3. Label columns of data clearly enough to identify the items. Usually, column headings are short and easily arranged. If, however, they happen to be lengthy, use some ingenuity in planning the arrangement.

4. Labels for the rows (horizontal items) in a table are easy to arrange with two exceptions. First, if the label requires more than one line, indent the second line two or three spaces. Labels that are merely subdivisions of more comprehensive labels should be indented, and summary labels such as *total* should also be indented. The sample table, shown in Figure 14-2, illustrates effective layout,

COMBINED FIRST-YEAR COSTS FOR THREE POSSIBLE SITES **(b)**

(d) Cost	**(e)** Fullerton	**(c)** Location San Pedro	Glendale
Lease **(f)**	$ 90,000	$ 75,000	$ 72,000
Property Taxes	14,000ᵃ	22,000	22,000
Trucking	64,000	60,000	64,000
Site Preparation	30,000	50,000	30,000
(g) Totals	$198,000	$207,000	$188,000

ᵃ Real property in Fullerton is to be reappraised in March, and an increase of about 40 percent is expected. **(h)**

Key:

(a) Figure number. Number figures consecutively throughout the report. Effective placement is achieved by centering the table number over the title of the table.

(b) Title. Titles should be long enough to identify clearly the contents of the table. Placing the title in all capital letters lends emphasis.

(c) Caption head. When several columns, such as the names of the three cities, are to be used, a caption head clarifies their meaning.

(d) Line identification. The line identification, in this case *Cost,* clarifies the meaning of the line titles and the content of the lines.

(e) Subcaptions. Subcaptions identify the breakdown in each column falling under the caption head (c).

(f) Line captions. Line captions identify the horizontal line content.

(g) Summary line caption. Even though it may seem obvious that columns have been totaled, this caption ensures reader understanding.

(h) Footnote or source placement. Frequently, something must be said about one or more elements in a table. The explanation should be placed immediately after the table in footnote fashion. If the source of information in the table is to be identified, place it in the same format as the footnote. When both footnotes and sources are used following the same table, the footnote should generally precede the source. Notice that the item to be footnoted, the $14,000 in the Fullerton column, is indicated by ᵃ (the superior letter a). An asterisk could also be used.

Figure 14-2 Appropriate table layout with parts labeled.

good title placement, and appropriate captions for the vertical columns and horizontal rows of items.

A major problem for amateur typists is arranging a great amount of data on one page. Keep in mind that two-page tables are often necessary, that scissors and paste are fair to use in making large tables, and that when the material won't fit on the page vertically, it might very well fit horizontally. In other words, a little creativity helps. Notice in Figure 14-3 that the table is "turned" on the paper, its width running from the bottom of the page to the top. And note that because the table was copied in its entirety from another source, the source is included; and it is shown a double space after the last line in the table.

In reports, the most commonly used graphic forms are bar charts, line charts, pie charts, maps, pictograms, and actual pictures. These graphic presentations are also often used as aids during oral reports. But, whether the report is written or oral, several guidelines can be used to determine whether a graphic presentation should be used at all and to make the graphic effective. We can ask ourselves

1.   Does the graphic presentation contribute to the overall understanding of the subject? Would a graphic assist the reader?

2.   Can the material be covered adequately in words rather in visual ways? Graphics, both in written and oral reports, should be saved for things that are difficult to communicate in words alone.

3.   Will the written or spoken text add meaning to the graphic display?

4.   Is the graphic easily understood? Extreme use of color, complicated symbols, confusing art techniques, and unusual combinations of type faces only detract from the impact of the material presented.

5.   Is the graphic honest? The hand is often quicker than the eye; and, as we will discover later in this chapter, data can be distorted rather easily.

6.   If the visual presentation is part of an oral report, can it be seen by the entire audience? Flip charts, poster boards, and overhead-projector transparencies are the visual means most often used to accompany oral reports.

Bar Charts

The simple bar chart is perhaps the most effective graphic device for comparing quantities. The length of the bars, whether they are horizontal or vertical, indicates quantity, as shown in Figure 14-4. The quantitative axis should always begin at zero. The gradation spaces should be equal. Also, of course, the width of the bars should be equal, or the wider bar will imply that it represents a larger number than the narrower bar.

Could total federal budget amounts, year by year, be represented in bar charts?

In bar charts, shadings, cross-hatchings, or variations in color can be used to distinguish among the bars.

Figure I

COMPARISON OF PEBBLE AND JORDAN PROCESSES

Item	Process--Pebble Mill	Process--Jordan
Power consumption per ton of rubber	127.2KW	9.06 KW
Recovery of rubber	65 percent	95 to 100 percent
Dirt in rubber (insolubles)	10 to 11 percent	1 percent or less
Rubber tensile strength	3,720 psi	5,200 psi
Aging-resistance to oxygen	Poor	Excellent
Elongation	Good	Excellent
Shrub condition for milling	Seasonal, must be preconditioned for one to eight months	Use any time, no preconditioning
By-products	None	Paper pulp, resin for industrial uses
Resin content before deresination	20 to 24 percent	12 to 15 percent
Deresination	Costly batch process	Continuous process
General operation	Intermittent batch with much "down" time	Little "down" time, continuous operation, faster

Source: Hugh H. Anderson, Pacific Rubber Growers, to Dr. John Hatchett, U.S. Department of Agriculture, Pacific Rubber Growers' Correspondence File.

Figure 14-3 Effective table layout.

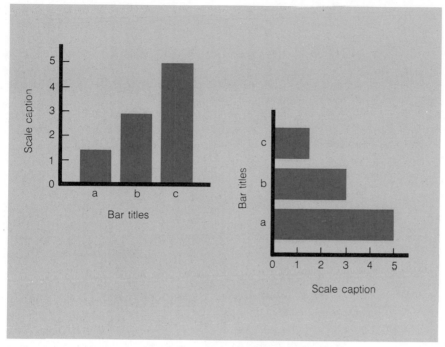

Figure 14-4   Simple bar-chart layout for vertical and horizontal bars.

If some quantities are so large that the chart would become unwieldy, the bars may be broken to indicate that some parts have been left out, as in Figure 14-5.

Component Bar Charts.   The component bar chart, also called a segmented or subdivided bar chart, is shown in Figure 14-6. When we want to show how different factors (components) contribute to a total figure, the component bar chart may be desirable. This graphic is particularly useful when components for two different time periods are being compared. Different colors or cross-hatchings may be used to distinguish the different components, with a key included at the bottom of the chart.

Positive and Negative Bar Charts.   Sometimes negative quantities are involved in our data. Then we must break the rule about beginning the quantitative scale at zero on the vertical axis, and place the zero at some midpoint on the scale. As shown in Figure 14-7, both positive and negative amounts can be illustrated and relationships shown clearly.

Line Charts

Line charts, such as the one shown in Figure 14-8, depict changes in quantitative data over time and illustrate trends. When constructing line charts, keep these principles in mind:

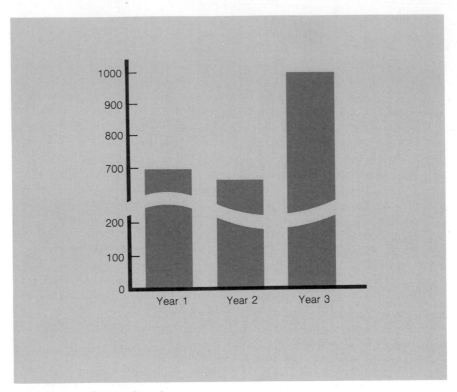

Figure 14-5   Broken-bar chart.

1.   Use the vertical axis for amount and the horizontal axis for time.

What would
be the result
of failing to use
zero as the base
for the vertical axis?

2.   Begin the vertical axis at zero. When the height of the chart may become unwieldy, break it in the same way the vertical scale was broken in Figure 14-5.

3.   Keep all vertical gradations equal, and keep all horizontal gradations equal. The vertical or amount gradations, however, need not be the same as the horizontal or time gradations. In any case, use your judgment in determining the size of gradations so the line or lines drawn will have reasonable slopes. (By using unrealistic gradations, you would develop startling slopes that could mislead readers.)

Cumulative line charts are similar to component bar charts, because they show how different factors contribute to a total, as shown in Figure 14-9. This chart might represent the components that make up the assets of a savings institution. The cumulative total of net worth, borrowings, and savings is illustrated by the top line on the chart. Cumulative line charts enable us to represent the amount of each component and the total amount of those components at any time.

Line charts differ from bar charts in that bar charts show only the total amount

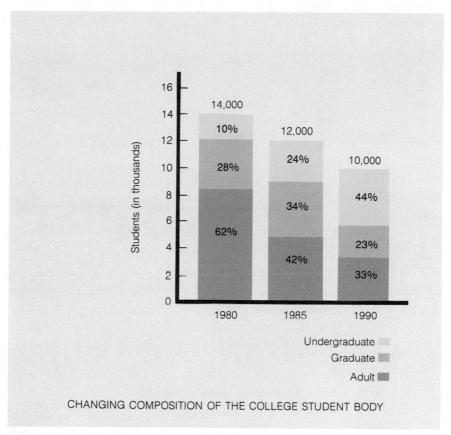

Figure 14-6   Component bar chart with key.

for a time period, whereas line charts show variations within each time period. In oral presentations, a cumulative line chart can be used effectively by having a separate transparency made for each component. During the presentation, each transparency could be laid over the previous one for a cumulative effect. In the example shown in Figure 14-9, for instance, a first transparency may show only the net worth; then a second could be added to show borrowings and a third could be added to show savings and complete the chart.

Pie Charts

Like a component bar chart and a cumulative line chart, pie charts are used to show how the parts of a whole are distributed. As the name indicates, the whole is represented as a pie, with the parts becoming slices of the pie, as shown in Figure 14-10. The pie on the left shows that the three slices representing durable goods,

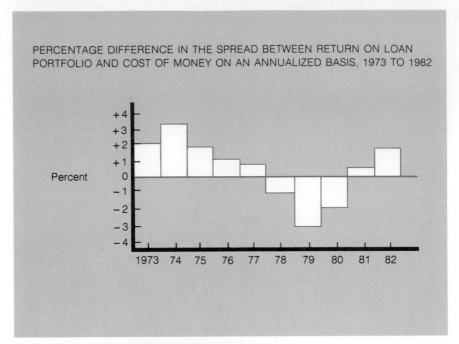

Figure 14-7   Positive-negative bar chart.

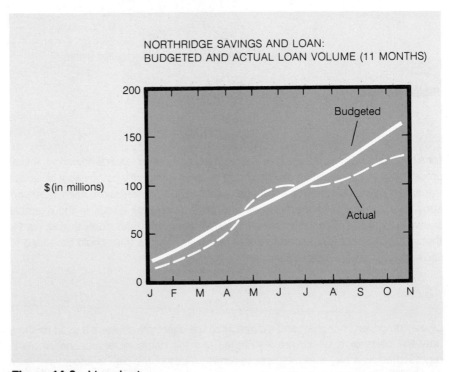

Figure 14-8   Line chart.

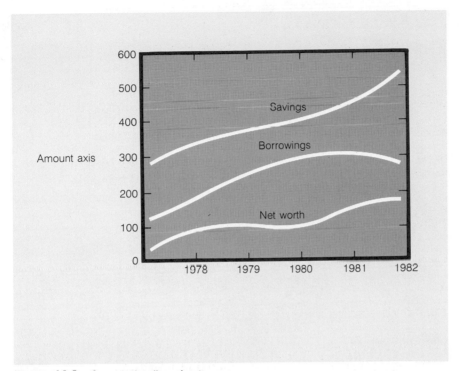

Figure 14-9 Cumulative line chart.

nondurable goods, and services account for over 80 percent of the distribution of the personal income dollar. Then, the pie on the right shows how that 80 percent is distributed when it is considered 100 percent of the personal consumption expenditures. Notice that the pie on the right is the same size as the pie on the left even though it represents only 80 percent. Pies are effective in showing percentages (parts of a whole), but they are not effective in representing quantitative totals or comparisons for two or more time periods when numerical totals are different.

When constructing pie charts, we should begin slicing the pie at the 12 o'clock position and work toward the right (that is, clockwise). Generally, the largest piece should be sliced first, with other large pieces following. For emphasis or contrast, however, the pieces do not have to be in descending order of size. The chart should be large enough to contain descriptive material. Of course, unless at least three pieces of pie are to be shown, the pie chart is not necessary. A simple statement in a report can be effective in demonstrating the relationship of two items. Frequently, however, this guideline is violated for dramatic effect, as shown in Figure 14-11.

Which type of graph is particularly useful in showing percentages?

Pictograms

A pictogram uses pictures to illustrate numerical relationships. Pictograms are frequently used in newsmagazines. Unfortunately, pictograms can be more dra-

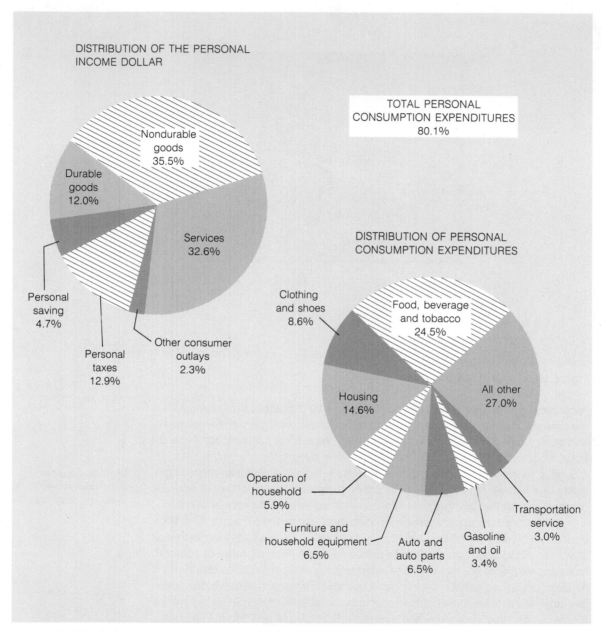

DISTRIBUTION OF THE PERSONAL
INCOME DOLLAR

Nondurable
goods
35.5%

Durable
goods
12.0%

Services
32.6%

Personal
saving
4.7%

Personal
taxes
12.9%

Other consumer
outlays
2.3%

TOTAL PERSONAL
CONSUMPTION EXPENDITURES
80.1%

DISTRIBUTION OF PERSONAL
CONSUMPTION EXPENDITURES

Clothing
and shoes
8.6%

Food, beverage
and tobacco
24.5%

All other
27.0%

Housing
14.6%

Operation of
household
5.9%

Furniture and
household equipment
6.5%

Auto and
auto parts
6.5%

Gasoline
and oil
3.4%

Transportation
service
3.0%

Figure 14-10   Complex pie charts (*Source:* U.S. Department of Commerce).

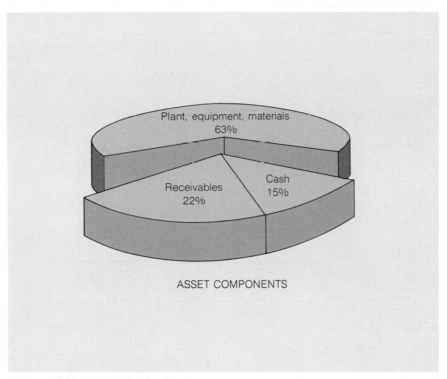

Figure 14-11 Dramatic pie chart.

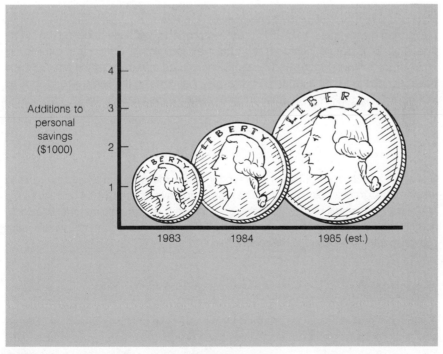

Figure 14-12 Pictogram with misleading symbols.

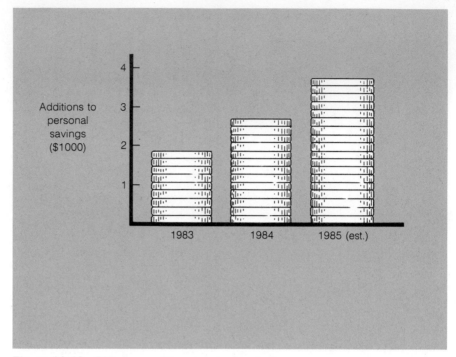

Figure 14-13   Pictogram with same-size symbols.

matic than meaningful if they aren't planned properly, because doubling the height and width of a picture increases the total area four times. Notice that the relative sizes of the coins in Figure 14-12 are misleading and make the actual amounts and relationships hard to understand. On the other hand, using the same size figures, as in Figure 14-13 makes both amounts and relationships instantly clear.

Maps

Maps are effective as graphics particularly when the reader may not be able to visualize geographic relationships. The maps shown in Figures 14-14 and 14-15 are taken from an annual report; they effectively present geographic material for stockholders who are scattered throughout the country and perhaps are not familiar with the geography discussed in the report.

Flow Charts

A variety of problems can be resolved through the use of charts to support written analysis. For example, most companies have procedures manuals to instruct em-

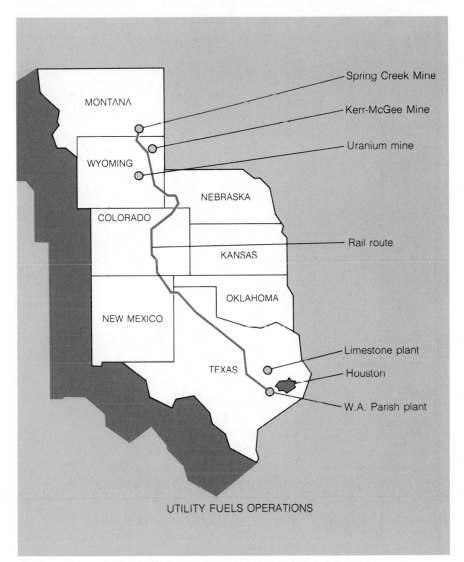

Figure 14-14 Map presentation (courtesy of Houston Industries, Inc.).

ployees on how to accomplish certain work tasks. As shown in Figure 14-16, the routing of copies of a form can be made clearer through the use of a flow chart. If the same information were presented only in a series of written steps, we would have to rely not only on the employee's reading ability but also on the employee's willingness to read and study. When the chart accompanies written instructions, chances of errors are lessened.

Organization charts are widely used to provide a picture of the authority

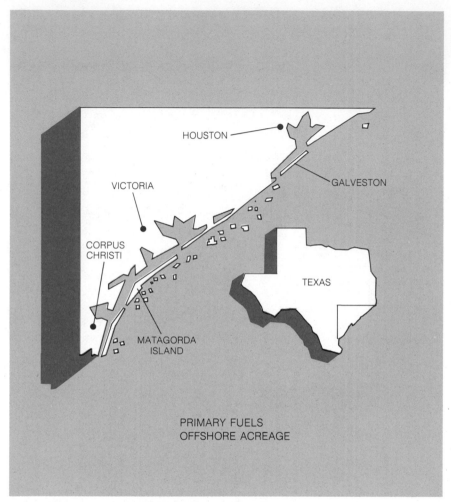

Figure 14-15   Map presentation (courtesy of Houston Industries, Inc.).

structure and relationships within an organization; they provide employees with an idea of what their organization looks like in terms of the flow of authority and responsibility.

INTRODUCING TABLES AND GRAPHS IN THE TEXT

Under no conditions should a table or graph be included in the report without being referred to in the textual material. Ideally, each table or graph should be introduced in the text *before* the reader comes to it. That ideal simply means that the illustration

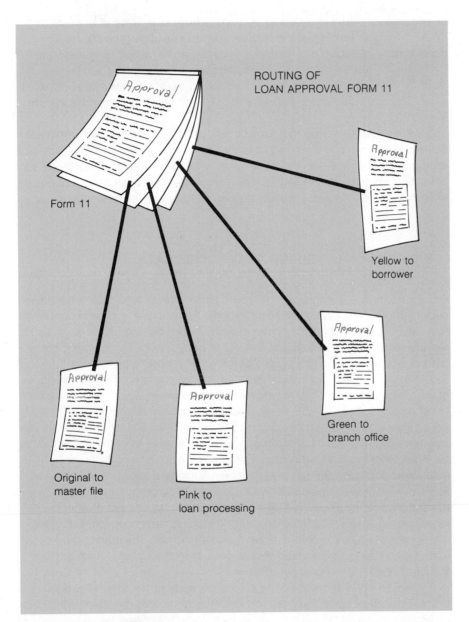

Figure 14-16 Flow chart.

comes *after* the text mentions it. If the illustration can be integrated in the text of the report, it should come immediately after its introduction. If the illustration occupies an entire page, it should appear on the page following the page on which it was introduced.

Notice how the language used in the following sentences introduces illustrative material.

Acceptable: About two thirds of the consumers preferred to shop in suburban areas rather than in the city. (See Figure 1.)

Improved: As shown in Figure 1, about two thirds of the consumers preferred to shop in suburban areas rather than in the city.

Best: About two thirds of the consumers preferred to shop in suburban areas rather than in the city, as shown in Figure 1.

The first is acceptable because it does the job, but it builds parentheses into the text material and doesn't tie the introduction into the sentence. The second sentence is an improvement, but it puts the introduction at the beginning of the sentence, thus detracting from the real message. The third is best because it talks about the illustration and also includes the introduction but only after stressing the message.

USING COMMON LANGUAGE TO DESCRIBE DATA

Every industry has a language of its own, *jargon.* When reports or letters travel outside the industry, jargon should be avoided. For example, someone outside the real estate appraisal field may have difficulty understanding jargon such as *the residual techniques, economic life,* and *unit-in-place factors.* For internal communications, however, jargon may be one of the writer's most helpful aids.

The common language recommended for reports is not jargon-slanted language. It is language that communicates to all people because it reduces complicated data to understandable terms. Take, for example, a report to stockholders saying that sales for this year have been $13,765,425.62, and for the previous year they were $11,655,772.80. Very few people can visualize amounts of these sizes, but most people understand percentages and ratios. Using a common language to report this information, we can say that for every six units sold last year, seven were sold this year. Or we can say that sales increased 18 percent over last year. We can assist the reader by providing a table or graph; but in our analysis of what the data mean, we should use a common language. We should remember, too, that changes in the value of money make the dollar a shaky indicator. The automobile industry uses the number of automobiles sold as the common language. Railroads talk of freight-car loadings and cost per ton-mile.

When only two items are being compared, such as the sales of two years, a simple percentage comparison is sufficient. Simply say that one item exceeds the other. For more than two items, graphic presentation becomes feasible.

Is a percentage a ratio?

Suppose that a survey of employee opinion results in 51 percent of the employees favoring a proposed project, 19 percent opposing the project, and 30 percent giving an undecided response. Instead of percentages, an even clearer picture might be given by reducing the 100 percent base to fractions of ten, as in this statement: "Of every ten employees, five favored the proposal, two opposed it, and three were undecided." Just as reports result from a gradual condensing of original data and methods, report writing at its communicative best is the result of condensing large, difficult concepts into concise, common-language statements.

SUMMARY

How difficult would it be to drive across the country for the first time without the aid of a road map? We'd probably have to ask directions frequently. And in a large city, finding a specific street address without assistance would be almost impossible. Tables and graphics add clarity to reports just as a map aids a traveler. Protecting oneself against a deluge of data through good data management and use of tables and graphs has a great deal to do with effective report preparation.

Fortunately, we live in an age in which much of what we have discussed can be aided by computers. If you plan to make a study involving the collection and analysis of considerable quantitative data, talk to an expert in your computer facility. Questionnaires and other data-gathering devices can be designed so that a respondent's answers can be fed to computers through optical scanning equipment directly from the answer sheet. A variety of easy-to-use programs are available for doing much of the data management mathematics described earlier. Properly designed, the work of data management can be reduced hundreds, even thousands, of times. Many computers also have graphic ability; they can produce the tables and other graphic figures so important to reports.

For many reports, you'll find it an easy task to prepare the tables and graphics on your own. The important thing in terms of your study of this chapter is that you must know what you want and how to construct it. Then you can either do the work on your own or tell the computer what to do.

The skilled report writer knows not only what graphics to use but also when to use them. When people read about number relationships and ratios, they understand only when they have visualized in their minds what is involved. Your use of tables and graphics to complement your written words makes the visualization easy.

Although this discussion has emphasized the use of graphics in written reports, you'll also make use of them as supports for oral presentations. Very often the writer of a report will be called on to make oral presentations about the written report; and many times, of course, graphic materials are used in oral presentations that will not have a research basis. Speeches designed to inform, to entertain, and to persuade are often built around the use of visual materials. Chapter 19 on oral presentations includes material on the types of visual techniques and their construction; the principles presented in this chapter apply equally to the use of visuals in oral presentations.

EXERCISES

Review Questions

1. What broad generalizations may be developed about a distribution simply by observing it and analyzing it without using statistical methods?

2. If a distribution consisted of amounts such as 8, 65, 68, 72, 73, 79, 81, and 88, which measure of central tendency would be most appropriate? Why?

3. What is meant by *common language* in relation to report preparation?

4. In most charts and graphs, the vertical axis is used for amounts and the horizontal axis for items or time. Must the size of the vertical gradations be equal to the size of the horizontal gradations? Should each of the vertical gradations be equal to the other vertical gradations in the same chart? What impressions might the reader be given if gradations were of varying sizes?

5. What is meant by a *broken* chart? Why should it ever be used?

6. Give two or three guidelines for the preparation of pie charts.

7. What is the difference between a component bar chart and a cumulative line chart? Give an example of how each might be used.

8. How can a pictogram mislead the reader?

9. Can some data be presented more efficiently and effectively in words rather than in graphics? Give an example.

10. People read from left to right and from top to bottom. What does this statement have to do with the preparation of graphics?

Problems in Using Graphics

1. Select what you think is the most effective graphic means of presenting each of the following sets of data. Then prepare the graphic and write a sentence that would introduce the graphic effectively in a report.
   a. The registration of voters in a community is 45 percent Democratic, 38 percent Republican, 12 percent uncommitted, and 5 percent minor political parties.
   b. Average interest rates on home mortgage loans for a ten-year period are

1976	8.4 percent	1981	14.2 percent
1977	9.1 percent	1982	15.0 percent
1978	9.7 percent	1983	13.0 percent
1979	11.0 percent	1984	12.0 percent
1980	12.2 percent	1985	12.0 percent

   c. Grades received by students in a beginning accounting course showed 12 A's, 22 B's, 40 C's, 14 D's, 8 F's, and 4 IN's (incompletes) for the 100 students enrolled.

2. From the following English scores of twenty-five first-year students, compute the mean, median, and mode:

36	48	66	74	82
38	49	68	74	87
38	53	70	78	90
42	57	74	80	92
42	62	74	82	96

3. To discover the differences in computing central tendencies from an array of individual items, as in exercise 2, and from grouped data, tally the scores in exercise 2 in seven classes beginning with 30–39, 40–49, 50–59, and on to 90–99. When you have tallied the scores, compute the mean and the median and indicate the modal class. How do you account for the differences between the answers for this exercise and those in exercise 2?

4. Prepare a simple table for the data used in exercise 3 and indicate the appropriate percentages for each class.

5. From the following array of estimated annual visits to a shopping center from a sample of 75 people, prepare whatever you think is necessary to *manage* the data:

14	7	41	52	24	23	46	28	14	21
9	27	52	38	27	27	22	21	13	19
12	14	36	21	31	41	18	24	21	23
17	31	41	9	33	47	23	34	28	
35	11	6	3	20	48	24	37	20	
8	18	5	11	24	33	35	22	11	
8	3	27	17	17	18	21	27	16	
10	29	19	23	18	22	24	20	24	

6. Prepare a component bar chart and a pie chart, each of which would represent the table data developed in exercise 4. Can a graphic be prepared to present the data in exercise 5?

7. Obtain a copy of a corporate annual report. Prepare a one-page written memorandum to your instructor telling to what degree you think the graphics in the report agree or disagree with the principles contained in this chapter.

8. Prepare introductory sentences for the tables or graphics developed in exercises 4 and 5.

9. Write summary sentences using common language to describe your interpretation of the materials developed in exercises 4 and 5.

10. Improve the following statements taken from reports:
   a. As can be seen in Table 5, the correlation between verbal scores on admissions tests and achievement in English was .57.
   b. Land values in the southern part of the state have increased about 32 percent while those in the northern portion have increased 19 percent. (See Figure 6.)
   c. Take a look at Figure 3, where a steady decline in the price of farm products during the past quarter is shown.
   d. The data reveal (Figure 4) that only one of seven voters is satisfied with the performance of the City Council.

11. Prepare a graphic or tabular presentation for the following paragraph:

   CONSUMER CREDIT
   Total consumer credit at end of March was $184.3 billion, of which $32.8 billion was noninstallment. The $151.5 billion of installment credit was composed of $51.6

billion for personal loans, $50.5 billion for automobiles, and $49.4 billion for other consumer goods.

12. Prepare whatever graphic or tabular presentations you think would be desirable for the following discussion:

URBAN FAMILY BUDGETS

Costs of three hypothetical family budgets for an urban family of four rose about 16 percent from the autumn of 1979 to the autumn of 1980, according to the Bureau of Labor Statistics. An urban family consisting of a 38-year-old husband employed full time, his nonworking wife, a boy of 13, and a girl of 8 could expect the average cost of an intermediate budget to amount to about $19,866. Average cost of the lower budget amounted to $13,250, with the higher budget $24,780.

Family-consumption items comprised 76 percent of the intermediate family budget with the remaining 24 percent composed of gifts and contributions, occupational expenses, life insurance, and social security and personal income taxes. Total family consumption at the lower and higher budget levels comprised 82 percent and 70 percent of the family budget, respectively. During the year, consumption costs rose by approximately 11.4 percent for all three budgets. Food costs accounted for 38 percent of total family consumption at the lower level, 33 percent at the intermediate, and 28 percent at the higher level. Food costs represented the largest single component for the lower and intermediate budget levels, but the largest component of consumption at the higher level was housing expenditures.

13. Prepare graphic or tabular presentations for the following information:

JOB GROWTH RATE (figures are fictitious)

The rate of government jobs opened and filled in the last decade was almost two times that in private industry, according to the Tax Foundation. Between 1970 and 1980 the number of federal, state, and local government workers increased 50 percent from 10.6 million to 15.9 million compared to a 27 percent job growth rate in private industry. Total nonfarm payroll employment in the U.S. rose from 62.0 million to 80.0 million in the ten-year period. Of this increase, 12.7 million jobs were added by the private sector and 5.3 million by the government.

14. Prepare graphic presentations for the following:

ANNUAL INCOME/EXPENSES OF COLLEGE STUDENTS (figures are fictitious)

Median expected educational expenses for full-time college students in October 1982 varied from about $1,100 for those in public junior colleges to $5,800 for students in private universities. Breakdown of the median amount of educational expenses — including tuition and fees, books and supplies, and transportation — for all full-time and part-time students was about $1,900 for attending four-year colleges, $1,600 for universities, $1,010 for vocational schools, and $840 for two-year colleges. For students attending private institutions, median expenses were considerably higher than for those attending public schools: $4,700 compared with $2,100 for universities; $4,600 compared with $2,210 for four-year colleges; and $1,400 with $820 for two-year colleges.

Students' earnings and aid from parents were the most common sources of income for all undergraduates, with about 44 percent earning an average of $4,100 during the school year, but 42 percent were given an average of $2,800 by their parents. Other major sources of income for students were personal savings, 34 percent; spouse's earnings, 15 percent; and veteran's benefits, 11 percent.

15

PREPARING MEMORANDUMS

Qualities of Memorandums
    Orderliness
    Logical Organization
    Natural, Informal Writing Style
    Graphic Support When Necessary
Informational Memorandums
Procedures and Instructions
Persuasive Memorandums
Helpful Guides for Memo Writers
Summary

Although previous chapters on report preparation have stressed the research methods used and techniques for managing and presenting data, we should take a break here in order to examine a rather informal report—the memorandum—before studying the preparation of formal research reports. The memorandum, also called the memo, is the medium of written communication most used by managers.[1] Also, as a message form used almost exclusively internally (within an organization), the memorandum serves the purposes of communicating policies, providing information, and attempting to persuade. To achieve these purposes, the well-conceived memorandum uses both letter-writing and report-writing techniques.

QUALITIES OF MEMORANDUMS

An important thing to remember about organizations is that, theoretically, everyone is a member of a team striving to achieve the goals of the organization. Thus, all team members should be looked on as peers. Status in the organization is easy to recognize—the chief executive is at the top of the organization chart, and the beginning office worker is probably near the bottom. Communication is improved, however, when messages flowing upward or downward are prepared with the welfare of the organization in mind and not so much with the status of the communicators as a guide.

Do you question this idea?

A century ago, American industry was characterized by small businesses. Internal communication was simple because of the proximity of management and employees. As business grew in size and complexity, reliance on spoken communication became impossible; and the memorandum developed. Memorandums are characterized by the following qualities:

1. Orderliness.

2. Logical organization.

3. Natural, informal writing style.

4. Graphic support when necessary.

Orderliness

The quality of orderliness in memorandums is a product of the traditional headings used in their preparation. Some time in the distant past, someone came up with the following introductory items for memorandums:

Date:

To:

1. Marie E. Flately, "A Comparative Analysis of the Written Communication of Managers at Various Organizational Levels in the Private Business Sector," *The Journal of Business Communication* 19, no. 3 (Summer 1982): 41.

From:

Subject:

When these items are filled in, orderliness permits easy filing reference, the reader's immediate recognition of the writer (not possible with regular letters, where the name of the writer is at the end), and establishment of the subject before the reader comes to the content. The quality of orderliness is something like standardization of automobile parts and of one-size-fits-all hosiery. When everyone in the organization uses the standard memorandum format, uniformity is achieved; the memorandum becomes a part of the business routine.

Might the receiver answer "Dear Desk"?

An interesting sidelight about memorandums is the tendency of some people in the organization to have their own note or memo forms printed with "From the desk of . . . ." Taken literally, this heading implies the memo was written by the desk!

Logical Organization

From your study of letter planning, you'll recall that inductive (indirect) and deductive (direct) plans applied to all letters. Both plans are logical and apply to memorandums as well as to letters and formal reports. Thus, the memo writer has a choice and can plan messages in terms of the expected reader reaction. Because internal communication is a tool to help achieve organizational goals, the inductive plan is probably used only infrequently. We need to be direct in a memo. Besides, inductive presentation is best suited to writing about disappointing information and for persuasion; the indirectness would be relatively ineffective when the subject line of the memorandum has already revealed the topic.

Are subject lines necessary?

An important part of the logic of memorandums comes from the use of the subject line in the heading. If you think through the reasons for your memorandum and what you intend to achieve by it, you should be able to write a good subject line. If you can't phrase the subject properly, chances are you don't really know what you are writing about. Nonetheless, you should not rely on the subject line for thought in the message to follow. For example, opening statements in a memorandum should not include such wording as "This subject . . .", "The above mentioned subject . . ." or "This is a very interesting. . . ." The message that you prepare to follow the subject line should stand by itself and should not rely on what preceded it. In other words, even if the subject line were omitted, the message should still be clear, logical, complete, and understandable. The subject line assists in communication, but it is not part of the message.

Natural, Informal Writing Style

The natural, informal writing style of memorandums distinguishes them from formal research reports. Although all writing styles should be natural, they are not all informal. The writing style you used in letters is the same writing style you should use in memos. When we examine the writing style of formal reports, you'll note the distinctions. Because memorandums are internal and addressed to peers, you should write in such a way that you don't focus attention on your writing at the expense of having the reader lose your message.

Informal writing talks to readers and involves them in the message through the use of personal pronouns, contractions, and jargon. As we have seen, *jargon* refers to the specialized vocabulary and idioms of people in the same profession or business. For example, terms such as "byte," "cursor," "modem," and "CPU" are common language to those in the computer and word-processing businesses but not understandable to most outsiders. In many cases, you'd have to use several sentences to say the same thing as said in one word of jargon.

Is slang a part of jargon?

Graphic Support When Necessary

Although you probably didn't use any graphics in your letter-writing problems, you should know that graphics are appropriate whenever they may strengthen your efforts to communicate. Tables, graphs, charts, and even pictures may be either integrated in the content of a memorandum or attached as supporting material. Additionally, the practice of numbering items in a list may improve communication. For example, "the four qualities of memorandums are orderliness, logical organization, informal writing style, and graphic support when necessary" was used earlier in this chapter but was much clearer, we assume, when the four items were numbered this way:

1. Orderliness.

2. Logical organization.

3. Natural, informal writing style.

4. Graphic support when necessary.

Although this technique, called tabulating items, is not a graphic, such as those described in Chapter 14, it is closely related and very effective in memorandum and formal report preparation.

When memorandums contain only one table or graphic, the illustration need not carry a number label such as "Figure 1" (as was recommended in Chapter 14 on graphics). Reference to the graphic is made simply by saying ". . . as shown in the following figure:" in the text material preceding the figure.

Should graphics be mentioned prior to the reader's coming to them?

INFORMATIONAL MEMORANDUMS

Informational memos are the most frequently used of all internal written messages, and they are the easiest to compose. When the subject of the memo is about personnel problems and involves personal emotions, the message must be planned in terms of reader reaction, of course. In such cases, the memorandum is actually a pleasant, unpleasant, or persuasive letter in a different format. When the memo is used simply to convey information about business operations and personalities are not involved, the direct plan of pleasant-news messages is appropriate. The concept that many memorandums are simply letters dressed in memo format should be a helpful guide.

Notice the format and the tabulation of items used in the memorandum shown in Figure 15-1. The heading is only one of many "to-from-subject" formats possible. The memorandum has three purposes: first, it serves as the transmittal for a report to a committee of faculty and trustees; second, it conveys information about the use of the report; and third, it ends with a statement about the next step to be taken by announcing a possible meeting of the committee.

The short message included in Figure 15-2 is all that is needed to convey a policy message to employees. As a general principle, directives or policy messages carry information determined by management and do not call for feedback from employees. Thus, they do not usually include a complete discussion of reasons for the policy.

Incidentally, the normal practice for signing memos is to initial them following the name of the writer; but it is also appropriate to sign them at the end of the memo, as was done in Figure 15-1.

As mentioned in Chapter 13, periodic or progress reports are part of the normal routine in most businesses of providing information to upper management. The periodic report shown in Figure 15-3 uses headings within the body as an organizational technique. Headings are a necessary part of longer, formal reports and a desirable way of helping make long memorandums understandable. They actually assist the writer as much as they do the reader by dividing content into easy-to-write sections. Informational memos may be as short as one sentence and as long as several pages. The longer your memo, the greater the need for division of material. In fact, even a one-page, single-spaced memo without headings may be difficult to read. Headings provide attractive breaks for the reader.

PROCEDURES AND INSTRUCTIONS

Because much of business is accomplished through the use of routines, systems and procedures manuals are designed as guides for recurring problems. The memo shown in Figure 15-4 reports the development of a new procedure and requests approval for implementing it. The step-by-step procedure is simple but detailed and was probably prepared after much discussion and even a "walk-through" testing by members of the committee.

As you read through the "procedure" portion of the memorandum, note that all six steps begin with active verbs. This technique involves the reader in the steps by defining the action to be taken by the understood subject (you) of each item. When *people* are the critical factor in carrying out a procedure, active voice can be the key

June 7, 198-

MEMORANDUM TO: Members, Long-Range Planning Committee

William F. Butland
Alice J. Sentoro
William J. Daw
Ruth L. Steiner
Katherine C. Bryan
Harvey Simpson

FROM: Richard H. Van Kirk, Chairman

SUBJECT: University Goals

Enclosed is a consolidated listing of the goals for the college, as suggested by committee members. I have attempted to avoid duplication. In the process, I may have inadvertently left something out or missed the meaning of a particular suggestion.

Please review the attached list with an eye toward

1. other goals we should include
2. suggested revisions to specific goals
3. areas of disagreement
4. possible priorities

I would like to have the committee meet in early July to work out more explicit and concise overall college goals. If we can do this, it might be possible to present a draft statement of goals to the Board of Trustees at its August meeting.

Richard Van Kirk

RHVK:rhd

Enclosure

Figure 15-1   Informational memorandum using deductive organization.

October 20, 198-

To All Employees of Carson Bank

From Robert Dickerson, President *RD*

THANKSGIVING HOLIDAY RECESS

The headquarters office will be closed Thanksgiving Day, November 23, and Friday, November 24. All branch offices will be closed Thanksgiving Day and open as usual on Friday, November 24.

Figure 15-2 Policy memorandum.

March 31, 198-

To: R. H. McAfee, Vice President

From: Sylvia Glass, Marketing Director

Subject: Monthly Marketing Activity Report for March

Following is the activity report of the marketing division for the month of March.

Advertising

Three meetings were held with representatives of the Bart and Dome agency to complete plans for the fall campaign for Fluffy Buns. The campaign will concentrate on the use of discount coupons published in the Thursday "food sections" of sixty daily newspapers in the Pacific states. Coupons will be released on the second and fourth Thursdays of both September and October.

The estimated costs of the program are

Publication costs	$180,000
Redeemed coupons	
(2.2 million @ .20)	440,000
Bart and Dome	25,000
Total	$645,000

A point-of-sale advertising display, shown on the attached sheet, has been developed for retail grocery outlets. Our sales reps are pushing these in their regular and new calls. The display is flexible to permit stores to feature a different product from our line on a weekly basis. We do, however, give them a suggested time schedule for changing the display.

Figure 15-3   Informational memorandum with headings.

Sales Staff

We have dropped one sales rep from the extreme northern section of California and divided that territory between the southern Oregon and Sacramento sales reps. We have also added a rep to our Los Angeles area staff.

During the month, our 52 reps made 8,320 calls and solicited $6,330,000 in new orders in addition to servicing their continuing accounts.

Figure 15-3   continued.

M E M O R A N D U M

DATE: July 1, 198-   FILE NO.: 2410

TO: Harold Johnston   CC: J. Dent
                                            D. Sturm

FROM: Isabel Higginbotham

SUBJECT: Procedure for Handling Payroll Advances

The ad hoc committee assigned the task of developing a procedure for handling payroll advances proposes the following:

Policies

    1.   All employees may request payroll advances of up to 80 percent of their normal net pay for a payroll period in case of an emergency.

    2.   Payroll advances are limited to one every two months.

Procedure (Instructions to Employee)

    1.   Obtain Form PR-7, Request for Payroll Advance, from your supervisor.

    2.   Complete Form PR-7 by filling in all blanks in the Employee Section of the form.

    3.   Have your immediate supervisor approve your request by signing on the Supervisor Approval line.

Figure 15-4 Informational memo covering a procedure.

Harold Johnston
Procedure for Handling Payroll Advances
July 1, 198-
Page 2

4.   Take the approved Form PR-7 to the receptionist in the Payroll and Benefits Office, Room 1620.

5.   Pick up your check at the time designated by the receptionist.

6.   Sign the receipt form in the presence of the receptionist.

With your approval, we will incorporate this material in the Personnel Manual.

Figure 15-4 continued.

to developing easily understood instructions. When *things* are the critical factor, passive voice is appropriate. For example, let's rewrite items 1 and 2 of the procedure in passive voice:

1. Form PR-7, Request for Payroll Advance, should be obtained from your supervisor.

2. The Employee Section of Form PR-7 should be completed by filling in all the blanks.

The technique of using passive voice places the things acted on as the subject of each sentence. Writers have a choice about voice usage; a good way to make the choice is to have others read the two versions of the procedure and express an opinion about which is better.

Is the use of active voice always better?

As you review these first four memorandums, note the different to-from-subject heading layouts. We have purposely used four different ones to emphasize the point that no single format is universal. In most companies, internal memorandum forms are preprinted to achieve uniformity and to save typing time.

PERSUASIVE MEMORANDUMS

Persuasion in objective memorandums is developed more by careful, logical presentation of information than by the use of emotion-laden words as in advertising and some sales letters. For example, the memorandum in Figure 15-5 attempts to justify the need for an additional employee; so in that sense, it is persuasive. Deductive organization is used by placing the recommendation first and following it with supporting evidence. Notice that the writer was requested to make the study apparently to assist the reader in solving a problem. When the message has an element of persuasion but is written to a busy person who has decision-making responsibilities, deductive organization can save reader time. This organization is particularly appropriate when you are confident your request will be granted.

Do you believe deductive organization may conserve reading time?

As an example of a somewhat persuasive message being adapted to the reader's needs, the writer of the message in Figure 15-6, after analyzing the problem, used an inductive organization to convey his message. Apparently the writer felt the reader might object to the total cost of the project if the details were not presented first. In fact, the reader might never read the details if the conclusion came first!

HELPFUL GUIDES FOR MEMO WRITERS

As you approach the task of preparing memorandums, you may find some of these suggestions helpful:

MEMORANDUM

TO: Paul R. Williams, Vice President

FROM: Robert Shaw, Internal Auditing

DATE: October 17, 198-

SUBJECT: Coping with the Billing Increase

Recommendation

Because of the backlog created by increased business, I suggest the addition of one key-punch machine and one operator in the Accounts Receivable Department. This recommendation is made following my study of the department, as you requested.

Discussion

The following observations underlie the recommendation:

1. During the past three months, the four operators have produced at normal rates. Yet about five hours of overtime a week for each operator have been necessary to achieve current volume.

2. Total billings have increased at a compounded rate of 5 percent a month; and with an increase in sales expected during the warm summer months, a larger backlog is expected.

3. Overtime costs have reached about $200 a week. Operators indicated they prefer not to work overtime on a régular basis.

4. The salary for an operator is $240 a week, and machine rental is $75 a month. Any summer increase in billing volume can be handled by the additional operator, and a saving in total labor cost can be expected within a short time.

Figure 15-5   Persuasive memorandum using deductive organization.

April 4, 198-

TO: Wilma Evans, School of Architecture
FROM: Robert T. Smith, Physical Plant Operations
SUBJECT: Air-conditioning Installation Costs for East Hall

As you requested in your memo of March 15, we have studied
the costs of installing air conditioning for the seven offices and
two studio classrooms in East Hall. As you suggested, we also
sought information on the additional cost of air conditioning
access halls and stairways.

Office and Classroom Installation

Estimates were obtained from three contractors on the costs of
covering the offices and classrooms. All three were in the
$20,000 to $25,000 range. The work would take about three
weeks.

Because the central unit would be installed on the roof, some
noise problems might occur during a four- or five-day period.
However, class interruption should be minimal. Sheet metal
work to install outlets in the classes could be done on weekends,
and the overtime labor costs of about $1,500 have been included
in the estimates.

Arrangements were not made to do the office space installation
on weekends. Each faculty member could expect to have workers
in the office for about one day.

Additional Installation

Because a larger installation, including a more powerful central
unit, would be necessary to handle the halls and stairways, an
additional $6,000 would be required for the equipment. Labor
costs would be an additional $5,000, bringing the total cost of
the addition to $11,000.

If this additional work were delayed until a later time, a new
central unit would be required along with changes in conduit
routing. This later installation would cost about $20,000.

Summary

The total job for the building would be about $35,000 if done at
one time. A two-stage installation would cost about $55,000. I
can get official bids at your request.

Figure 15-6   Memorandum using inductive organization.

1.   Plan your message before you begin to write.

    a.   What do you want to accomplish through the message?
    b.   Who is the reader(s)? What will be the reader reaction? Does the reader have any special needs familiar to you?
    c.   Select either the inductive or deductive plan.

2.   Prepare a comprehensive subject line. Use as many words as you find necessary—even two-line subjects are appropriate.

3.   Keep in mind that the message should stand by itself and should not rely on the subject line for thought. Therefore, if you believe your first sentence is almost a repetition of the subject line, you are on the right track.

4.   If you are presenting considerable quantitative information, see if you can first prepare it in table or graphic form. Make a rough draft of the table or graphic and decide what you can or must say about it.

5.   If your message is lengthy, try to divide it into logical sections. Then, use headings to help the reader. When headings are used, you may find that you can write one section in rough draft form on a separate sheet of paper before proceeding to the next section. When all sections have been written, you can arrange them in any sequence you like before final typing.

6.   If you have several items that lend themselves to tabulation (i.e., numbering, as in a procedure) do so. Tabulating adds to communication.

7.   As you write, remember you are writing to communicate for the good of the organization and not to impress the reader.

SUMMARY

As the primary written communication tool in organizations, the memorandum deserves our careful attention. Its primary purposes are to inform and to assist in decision making. Although they are described as "informal," memorandums emphasize objectivity to achieve their purposes.

EXERCISES

Review Questions

1.   In what ways are memorandums like letters?

2.   In what ways do memorandums differ from letters?

3.   What is meant by logical organization as a quality of memorandums?

4. Do you believe using a reader's first name in the body of a memorandum would be appropriate? Why or why not?

5. Is the plan for a persuasive sales letter also a good plan for a persuasive memorandum? Why or why not?

6. What is meant by "don't rely on the subject line for thought" in memorandum writing?

7. Is the memorandum format a form of standardization?

8. In what directions do memorandums flow in the organization? Describe.

Cases in Communication and Memorandum Writing

Following are two case problems that call for memorandum-writing activity. Read the case and then read the situations requiring memorandum solutions. Prepare whatever solutions might be assigned.

The Prime First Savings Case

Prime First Savings and Loan, Inc., has 123 branches in your state and another 68 branches in other states. Its assets are $8.5 billion. Karen Grillo, the manager of the Condonville branch, has been with the company for five years, is 30 years of age, and plans to make the savings and loan industry her career. Condonville is a community of about 40,000 people and is served by three other savings and loan associations and three banks. Condonville is a rather conservative, rural community; its residents prefer to have their money in insured savings accounts rather than to invest in risk ventures.

Prime First is organized into regions, and the Condonville branch is one of eight supervised by a regional vice president, John Eddie. The manager of the Condonville branch holds the title of assistant vice president. In addition to the manager, the Condonville branch has seven other employees: (a) four tellers, who staff the customer service windows, update accounts for interest earned, and handle deposit and withdrawal transactions; (b) an assistant manager, who supervises the tellers in addition to serving as a new-accounts representative; (c) a loan officer, who handles both home and consumer loans; and (d) a new-accounts clerk, who is primarily responsible for handling the paperwork associated with new accounts. This person reports to the assistant manager.

Part of the manager's responsibilities include public relations and the solicitation of local businesses for pension fund deposits and for corporate checking and savings accounts. Manager Karen Grillo belongs to the Condonville Gourmet Club, Soroptomists, Better Business Bureau, and the Chamber of Commerce. She is vice president of the Chamber of Commerce and should be president next year. Prime First looks on her as a candidate for a leading position in the organization soon. Grillo's next step would probably be to take a regional vice presidency, and her MBA degree in finance should be an asset. But she does have problems.

She seems to be the favorite target for criticism by John Eddie, the regional VP, who is 65 years of age. Several times when he has visited her office unannounced (he calls these visits "informal"), she has been out on company business or community service. Although the policy of the company is for branch managers to spend much of their time in these activities, Mr. Eddie calls himself "from the old school" and thinks managers should spend their time "tending the store."

The assistant manager, Herman Harvey, is about the same age as Karen Grillo. According to the tellers and the loan officer, he tends to be overly domineering and abusive when the manager is out of the office and he is in charge. He has been with the firm for a year and a half; his previous experience was in sales; and he too has an MBA, but in marketing.

The tellers and their ages are Mabel Henson, 57; Martin Blatt, 19; Rosemary Jones, 18; and Steve King, 20. All have been with the firm for less than two years. All except Henson attend the local county community college in the evening for at least two courses.

The loan officer is James Burns, 46, an employee of the company for 20 years. He knows the loan business well and is the second highest paid employee in the branch. Although he theoretically reports to the manager, his real responsibility for his function is to the senior vice president in charge of lending in the corporate office. Burns has the authority to approve and order checks for consumer loans up to $7,500. He prepares the papers for home loans, but he does not have approval authority. The completed applications are sent to the corporate office with his recommendations for approval or disapproval, then the corporate loan committee makes the final decision. Because the guidelines are fairly rigid, his recommendations are usually accepted.

The new-accounts clerk, Margaret Swenson, 23, has a bachelor's degree in business and will probably be with this branch for only a few months as part of her management training program. She is attractive, likable, and very effective in dealing with new customers. She is a frequent luncheon companion of the manager, who likes to work closely with management trainees even though they usually report to the assistant manager, as in this case.

Prime First is fully computerized. All branch financial transactions are recorded on terminals linked to the home office. Although employee problems can usually be resolved within branches, managers are responsible for documenting personnel actions that violate company policies. Copies of the documentation are reviewed with the employee before they are sent to the home office of the company.

Prepare memorandums for the following situations:

1. As manager, you have observed that the four tellers are constantly busy. In fact, long lines of customers seem to occur during the first hour you are open each day (9:30 A.M. to 10:30 A.M.) and during the noon hour. Your office closes each day at 4:00 P.M. to enable workers to complete their work for the day without the problem of serving customers. The office closes at 5:00 P.M. Tellers hours are 9:00 A.M. to 5:00 P.M., with a morning rest break of 15 minutes, a half-hour lunch period, and a 15-minute afternoon break. Employees Harvey, Burns, and Swenson are exempt from these times as salaried officers. They are usually in the office by 8:30 A.M. and tend to work beyond the 5:00 P.M. closing time, as you do. Because of frequent customer complaints about the lines, you propose to add a part-time teller trainee to work from 9:00 A.M. to 1:30 P.M. each day. You can easily recruit such a person through the community college placement office. You have phoned John Eddie and he has asked you to prepare a memorandum supporting your request. He will have to obtain permission from the home office to add new employees.

2.   After you, the manager, have prepared and sent the memo to Eddie, he writes you — although he could have phoned — that he'd rather not send the request to the home office. He'd like to try opening the office to the public at 9:00 A.M. to ease the morning rush and to have two tellers take their lunch periods before noon and two take lunch between 1:00 P.M. and 2:00 P.M. Your concern is that tellers need at least 20 minutes to prepare their work stations before opening the doors to the public. They would have to be paid overtime (time and a half) for the 20 minutes; that amount, times two tellers, would be enough money to hire the part-time teller. Additionally, employees already take their lunch breaks when the customer traffic subsides; they are quite flexible and usually bring their own food to eat in the employees' back room where a refrigerator and coffee maker are available. Additionally, you don't like the idea of imposing specific hours on the tellers. The pre-noon lunch would follow the morning rest break closely; and the tellers who had to eat after 1:00 P.M. would have almost four consecutive hours on their feet handling a constant flow of customers. You discussed the proposal with the tellers and the assistant manager, and they are the ones who expressed many of these concerns. Write a memo to John Eddie.

3.   You are the manager. John Eddie phones you about three days after receiving your memo; his good news is that you have permission to hire a 20-hour-a-week teller trainee. Authority to hire is being sent directly to you from the home office personnel department. Write a letter to the placement office at Condonville Community College describing your needs.

4.   After interviewing several candidates for the part-time position, you have selected Gordon H. Fernandez. Prepare a brief memo to the home office personnel department to accompany all the necessary personnel and payroll papers that you, as manager, have prepared for Fernandez.

5.   After Fernandez is on the job, you notice that Mabel Henson doesn't seem to be at a teller's window regularly. When she is there, she seems to be bored and unfriendly. A discussion with Herman Harvey reveals that she has been late to work four times in the past two weeks and has taken half-hour rather than the 15-minute rest breaks every day during that time. Harvey says he thinks she has some personal problems and will soon be herself again. As manager, you feel you should document these violations of work rules just in case Mabel doesn't correct her problems and must be dismissed. She does have seniority over two of the tellers, so any move to fire her would have to be thoroughly justified. Write a memo for her personnel file. You'll show the memo to Mabel before sending it to the home office.

6. Herman Harvey comes to you, the manager, with the request that you send John Eddie a letter recommending Harvey for the position of assistant manager of the branch in North Bend; this position will become available in two weeks. You believe Harvey has the potential to become a branch manager, particularly in terms of recruiting new business because of his sales and marketing background. But you are very conscious of his need to develop skill in handling people. You'll write the memo, because you think the experience of working under Bob Trout, a 20-year veteran manager with good "people" skills, will be valuable.

7. You receive news that James Burns is being promoted to assistant loan department head and vice president in the home office. His replacement in the branch of which you are manager has been appointed. You like Jim Burns very much and appreciate the friendly attitude he has shown the young employees, as well as the support and advice he has given you. You plan to say more in person, but you think it would be nice to write him a special memo.

8. You are now Herman Harvey, the newly appointed assistant manager of the North Bend branch. Today is your last day at Condonville. Write a parting memo to the branch manager, Karen Grillo.

9. Margaret Swenson, as a management trainee, has frequently filled in at tellers' windows during rush periods. In addition to the other things you know about her (see the introductory material), she is enthusiastic. As manager, you must submit monthly progress reports on her. Now is the time to send one to R. R. Jenks, Personnel VP.

10. As manager you are required to prepare a written report in memorandum form on the status of your branch at the end of the month. The report is to cover volume of transactions, changes in total deposits, and personnel. Your deposits increased $244,800 from $7,200,000 to $7,444,800, a percentage increase of 3.4. Deposit and withdrawal transactions amounted to 8,441, an average of 384 a day for the 22 days the bank was open. The personnel report should be a summary and not a detailed listing of people. Simply report the number of continuing employees, the transfers, and new hires. The report should be addressed to John Eddie, who prepares a combined report for the region.

The Kappa Psi Foundation Case

Paul Stiglitz is president of the Kappa Psi Foundation, a charitable organization founded by Kappa Psi Fraternity members to promote better understanding of the private enterprise system. Contributions to the Foundation are tax deductible to donors, most of whom are members of Kappa Psi Fraternity. The Foundation is governed by a seven-member board of directors. Officers are elected by the board from its own members, but the directors are elected by delegates to the national convention of the Fraternity. In addition to Stiglitz, the other officers are Vice

President of Finance, Charles "Chuck" Hansen; Vice President of Grants, William "Bill" Wilson; Vice President of Administration, Mary Ann Harris. The four officers constitute the executive committee; the three other directors do not hold office but are kept informed of the actions of the executive committee and attend annual meetings of the board.

The current financial statements of the foundation are as follows:

Balance Sheet

Assets	
Cash	$ 4,000
Investments	188,000
Accrued interest	3,000
Total Assets	$195,000
Liabilities and Fund Balance	
Payable to Fraternity	$ 200
Fund balance	194,800
Total	$195,000

Statement of Revenue, Expense & Changes in Fund Balance This Year

Revenue	
Interest	$ 12,300
Dividends	4,600
Contributions	11,400
Total	$ 28,300
Expenses	
Awards	$ 9,000
Professional services	1,400
Board meeting	3,400
Administrative	1,800
Taxes	600
	$ 16,200
Excess of Revenue over Expense	12,100
Fund balance beginning of year	182,700
Fund balance end of year	$194,800

The home office of Kappa Psi Fraternity handles most office and recordkeeping work, and the Foundation pays $1,800 yearly to the Fraternity for this service. As a private foundation, the Kappa Psi Foundation must pay income tax on retained interest and dividends. In other words, it must distribute at least that amount or be subject to tax. The $600 in taxes was paid for a previous year. No tax liability is expected for the current year.

The Foundation's investments shown on the balance sheet consist of certificates of deposit (CDs), corporate bonds, and common stocks. The common stock holdings are as follows:

Shares	Company	Original Cost
100	American T & T	$ 6,360
300	Firestone Tire & Rubber	6,187
100	General Motors	6,937
200	Gulf Oil	5,600
200	Panhandle Eastern	6,400
200	Rockwell International	7,200
200	Texaco	5,800
100	United Technology	4,000
300	F. W. Woolworth	6,900
		$55,384

The Foundation, although only a few years old, has developed a program of awards and fellowships that has made it prominent in educational circles. Currently, awards of $500 each and an engraved, framed certificate are given annually for outstanding articles in major journals in the fields of accounting, marketing, policy, and finance. The awards are presented at regional or national conferences of practitioners in those fields. Additionally, fellowship awards of $1,000 each are made to doctoral students in business who are planning on teaching careers. One award is made annually to a student in each of seven prominent universities.

During the coming year, the Foundation plans to provide $500 awards to six high school teachers to enable them to attend training seminars sponsored by the Council on Economic Education. As funds become available, all programs will be expanded.

As president, Paul Stiglitz is involved in carrying out policies established by the board of directors, in personally presenting as many of the awards as possible, and in planning meetings of the board of directors. He also keeps the other officers informed about his activities and plans. Chuck Hansen keeps an eye on the investments and anticipates the amount of money to be available for the various awards programs. Bill Wilson is responsible for doing the research needed to begin new awards, and Mary Ann Harris coordinates activities related to award presentations and public relations. She is also responsible for the preparation of press releases when awards are made. Because the seven members of the board live in widely scattered parts of the country, most of the communication Stiglitz initiates is by mailed memorandums. When he holds a board meeting, he tries to have it in a central location to keep travel expenses to a minimum.

Prepare appropriate memorandums for the following situations:

1.   You are Charles "Chuck" Hansen. Prepare a memo to inform the board of directors of the current status of your stock holdings. You will show the original cost and the latest stock market quote. All stocks are listed in the New York Stock Exchange daily trades.

2.   You are Mary Ann Harris. Prepare a memo to the people involved to process the award for the outstanding article in the *Journal of Marketing*. The editorial board of the *Journal* has selected Dr. Sigrid Johnson of Northern University for the award. Her article was "Coupons Versus Price Cutting as Consumer Incentives," which appeared in the July issue of the *Journal*. The certificate will be prepared by the home office of the Fraternity.

3. As Chuck Hansen, prepare a memo to Mary Ann to accompany the $500 check you have prepared for presentation to Dr. Sigrid Johnson.

4. As President Paul Stiglitz, you have arranged for a board meeting for the third weekend of next month at the Airport Hilton Hotel in Chicago. Your meetings usually begin with an informal dinner at the hotel on Friday evening about 7:00 P.M. Then, you meet all day (9:00 A.M. to 6:00 P.M.) on Saturday, following which members are free to depart for home. The Foundation will, however, pay for Saturday night lodging if members must stay until Sunday for return flights. Prepare a memo announcing the board meeting and include a tentative agenda of items to be considered. You'll also want to make sure members can attend. The Executive Director of Kappa Psi Fraternity, Frank Brie, is always invited to attend Foundation meetings. (See a sample agenda in Figure 19-4, p. 553.)

5. As President Stiglitz, respond to the stock memo you received from Chuck Hansen (exercise 1). You may make any comments you like about the portfolio of stock holdings and about Chuck's work.

6. As President Stiglitz, write Mary Ann Harris to find out what is happening about the award for an accounting article. This is just about the time of year when the editors of the *Journal of Accounting* report their selection to us. You don't want any delays or other difficulties; you've had problems before in handling the accounting award.

7. As Mary Ann Harris, respond by memo to the one you have received from the president about the accounting award. You are a little upset about receiving the memo because you have communicated with the accounting award selection people. They have promised to send you the name of the winner within ten days.

8. As Bill Wilson, send the board a memorandum reporting on your progress in establishing a $1,000 doctoral fellowship award at Potter University. You have met with the dean of business at Potter, and he is eager to begin the award program this year. Potter U has a good reputation, its doctoral program is small (about five people receive doctorates each year) but of high quality. The dean is sending a Potter catalog or bulletin to each foundation director. In two weeks, you will poll the board for its decision about beginning the award program at Potter.

9. As Bill Wilson, prepare the memo you will use to poll the board (as mentioned in exercise 8).

10. As Chuck Hansen, analyze the Statement of Revenue and Expense. Interest and dividends totaled $16,900. Total investments were about $185,000 when averaged for the year. Thus, you are earning about 9 percent on your investments. If you have the background, prepare a memo to the executive committee suggesting ways to maximize your investment income and seeking other suggestions. You should check the dividends paid by your common stock holdings. They may be the reason for the modest return on total investments. Use the latest New York Stock Exchange listings to determine the dividends paid per share.

Memorandum Problems

For each of the following situations, prepare a memorandum solution.

1.   You were hired six months ago as a department head for XYZ, Inc. The home office, in which you work, is quite small in area and in number of employees — about fifty. Because the office area is generally open, all employees are aware of any unusual events. The company president, Mr. James Dix, has a short temper. In fact, he loses his temper so often and raises his voice to such a pitch that absenteeism in the office is very high. He has taken notice of the absenteeism and has requested each department head to prepare a memo suggesting solutions to the problem. As one of the four department heads, and the youngest, prepare the memo you would send to Mr. Dix.

2.   Assume now that you have been with XYZ, Inc., since Mr. Dix organized it twenty years ago. You have been close friends through the years, and Mr. Dix respects your forthrightness. Write the memorandum you would send Mr. Dix (see problem 1).

3.   Prepare a memorandum to be placed on all bulletin boards in the American Aircraft plant. A bus service between the airport plant and the production plant, which are located five miles apart, will be put in service on June 16 to transport the many employees whose jobs make it necessary to travel back and forth between the plants. Two buses will operate and will load and unload employees at the main gates of each plant. One will leave the airport plant at 8:30 A.M., and the other will leave the production plant at the same time. They will leave each plant every twenty minutes thereafter. No buses will leave between noon and 1:00 P.M. The afternoon schedule will begin at 1:20 P.M. and the last bus will leave each station at 4:20 P.M.

4.   As chief payroll accountant for the Kon Tiki Manufacturing Company, you believe it necessary to establish a procedure for handling errors in employee paychecks. At present, whenever an employee believes an error has been made in a paycheck, he or she takes the check to the payroll office for correction. Too many employees stand around and wait for the error to be checked and for action to be taken. As a result, much employee time is wasted, and the work of the accounting office is disrupted. The new procedure will be for the employee to complete a Payroll Claim Form that can be obtained from any department head. The department head will check the form for completeness and accuracy, sign it on the appropriate line, and send it to the payroll office within five days after payday. The received claims will be processed with those for the following payroll period. Small payroll adjustments will be included in the paychecks for the next period. Separate checks will be prepared only if the adjustment involves $15.00 or more. Sort through the information presented here, and prepare a report presenting the new procedure. The memorandum will be distributed to all department heads for the information of all employees.

5. Select any article from *Fortune* magazine. Prepare a synopsis of it in about 250 words, the equivalent of a full-page, single-spaced memorandum. Address the memorandum to your instructor.

Condensing articles is a regular assignment for many assistants to top executives, because the condensations assist executives in their efforts to keep up with their business reading.

6. Select ten stocks listed on the New York Stock Exchange and reported in your daily paper or in the *Wall Street Journal.* Assume that you will purchase 100 shares of each of the ten stocks at the prices listed at the market close on a particular day. You are going to keep a record of changes in the stocks for a one-week period— five trading days. Submit a memorandum to your instructor on the purchase date reporting your ten stocks according to the following format:

Name of Stock	Price per Share	Total Cost (x 100)

At the end of the five-day period, submit another memorandum to your instructor detailing how your investment fared during the week. This memorandum should include a statement about how your investment compared with the performance of the Dow Jones Industrial Average of thirty stocks. You will need the Dow Jones figures for both your purchase data and the end of the five-day period. The percentage change in the value of your portfolio should be compared with the percentage change in the Dow Jones average.

7. As a marketing trainee for the Safeside Supermarket Company, you work directly with the vice president of marketing, Ms. Clara Brandon. One of the tasks of trainees is to keep Ms. Brandon informed about what the competition is doing in different areas of the city. This is done by shopping a grocery list at other stores. The grocery list normally contains canned foods, paper goods, and fruit or vegetables. You are to shop—simply obtain prices—for the following items at three different grocery outlets and to prepare a memorandum report for Ms. Brandon showing the prices for each item at each store and the total cost of the list:

Pork and beans	Dog food
Peanut butter	Gatorade or other canned drink
Napkins	Fresh apples (pound)
Oven cleaner	Catsup
Applesauce	Fresh lettuce or cabbage
Canned peas	

You must make certain that your comparison includes only comparable sizes, weights, and quantities. You should use the same brands in all three stores.

What are Formal Reports?
The Growth of a Report
    The Letter of Transmittal
    The Title Page
    The Contents Page
    The Summary or Synopsis
    The Body of the Report
    Addenda
Complete Report Outline
Organizing Reports
    Being Systematic
    Using the Right System
A Sample Problem
Using Outline Symbols
Organizing Data
Summary

The memorandums we studied in Chapter 15 were examples of reports written at the informal end of the informal–formal continuum of reports. As we move toward the formal end of the continuum, we should first consider what things are involved in the distinction between formal and informal reports.

WHAT ARE FORMAL REPORTS?

The degree to which a report stresses formality versus informality depends on these variables:

1. The use to be made of the report.
2. The nature of the research prior to the report preparation.
3. The complexity of the subject matter.
4. The status, needs, and temperament of the reader or readers of the report.

All reports—formal and informal—are also either informational or analytical reports, and they may involve research as outlined in Chapter 13. Informational reports are not expected to solve problems, but they are expected to provide information to assist in problem solving or decision making. Analytical reports, on the other hand, are expected to contain conclusions of a problem-solving nature.

When a report contains complex subject matter that is based on the four steps in problem solving (as outlined in Chapter 13) and is to be used by higher management, it will require thorough detail to support the findings, conclusions, or recommendations. Therefore, the report writer will no doubt put it together as a formal report. At this point, we should understand that reports are written *after* the research and analysis have been completed. Thus, the written report is simply a statement or description of things that have already occurred. A report writer cannot begin with the first sentence and continue to write, synthesize, and analyze as he or she continues to write. When the time for writing comes, the problem is not one of analyzing data but rather one of organizing and explaining the procedures and analyses that preceded the writing task.

What are the four steps in problem solving?

THE GROWTH OF A REPORT

Because we do write to affect others, we usually fall into a habit of making our work even more impressive as the number of pages increases. College students usually add a cover page, which includes name and class, to a routine assignment, or perhaps a plastic report cover to a three- or four-page document. So do report writers. Much of this dressing-up activity is actually necessary to achieve the goals of the writer and to place the report in its proper place in the informal-formal continuum.

For example, refer to the step-by-step growth of a report, shown in Figure 16-1. In the first step, (a), a simple memorandum, which may call attention to a meeting or problem, may require only one page or less. As the material required to cover the problem expands, additional pages may be required (b and c). At some predictable point, based on the number of pages, the writer will decide that the report is large enough to warrant a little dressing and add a title page (d). Another page or two may be added; at that point, the writer will probably attach a letter to the readers (e) to indicate that the report is complete and is being transmitted to them. If the report is organized with headings to assist the reader, a formal outline of the headings may be inserted as a table of contents (f).

As the size of the body of a report increases, so does the number of assisting items. When the report reaches sizable proportions, the writer will attempt to assist the readers — and possibly save them time — by adding a summary page which puts the entire report in capsule form (g). If the report includes such items as a bibliography, sample questionnaire, raw data, or illustrations not appropriate for the body of the report, an appendix will be added at the end of the report (h).

Although some of this material may be considered window dressing, a good report writer uses only those elements that help achieve clear understanding of the report. Certainly, a one-page memorandum does not require any of these added items. On the other hand, a report containing a hundred pages would quite likely be incomplete without all of them.

On the formal-informal report continuum, the memorandum is at the informal end. As the length of the report increases, more formal methods of presentation are introduced. At the most formal end of the continuum, the report can include tables, graphs, and other aids to communication; and the writing style may tend to be very formal by eliminating the use of personal pronouns and appearing to be scientific. Because it is important to picture the formal report parts to get a picture of all the ingredients in the report, let's look at some of them.

The Letter of Transmittal

A letter is usually attached to the report when it is sent to readers. Although the letter of transmittal is sometimes placed after the title page, the letter is actually the greeting accompanying the report. It serves the same purpose as an oral introduction would if we were to carry the report to the reader.

Do "summary" and "synopsis" have the same meaning?

Frequently, a brief summary or synopsis of the study is incorporated in the letter of transmittal. In this case, the report may very well omit the separate synopsis or summary. In general, the length of the report and the space needed to prepare the summary should determine whether the summary is included in the letter.

In addition to its use as a greeting or transmittal, the letter of transmittal enables

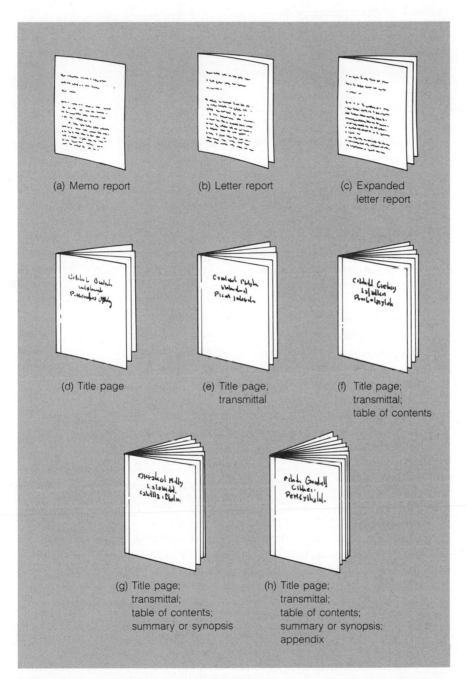

(a) Memo report

(b) Letter report

(c) Expanded letter report

(d) Title page

(e) Title page, transmittal

(f) Title page; transmittal; table of contents

(g) Title page; transmittal; table of contents; summary or synopsis

(h) Title page; transmittal; table of contents; summary or synopsis; appendix

Figure 16-1 As the size of a report increases, so does the number of assisting items.

the writer to talk to the reader in letter-writing style. Here is an effective plan for the letter of transmittal:

1.   Open directly with a statement establishing the subject:

Dear Mr. Jones:

    Here is the report you requested on May 15 about a desirable location for. . . .

2.   Follow the opener with an overall review of the report. If the report is to include a separate summary, make the review brief.

3.   Acknowledge those who have assisted with the study.

4.   Thank the authority (the person who requested the report) for the opportunity to help. An effective closing is a look forward to helping again, if the writer is sincere about doing so.

Since the letter of transmittal is a business letter, we should use personal pronouns, first person, active voice; and we should use the opportunity to express our personality and sincerity, as shown in Figure 16-2. When the report is prepared by someone within the organization, the letter of transmittal may be written in memorandum form similar to that shown in Figure 16-3.

The Title Page

Format for a title page is important, of course. Because the title page may be the first thing the reader sees, it should be as attractive as possible. As a minimum, the title page should include

1.   The title of the report. The title should be as thoroughly descriptive of the study as possible. Short titles are often extremely vague. A title such as "Marketing Survey: Donuts" leaves the reader confused when the title could have been "Donut Flavor Preferences of Teenagers in Midville."

2.   Full identification of the authority for the report. The authority for the report is usually the reader of the report; that is, the person who requested the study. On some title pages, the authority line is preceded by a "prepared for" heading.

Prepared for
Mr. William R. Johnston
Chairman
Western Savings and Loan Association
Fresno, California

R. R. LERNER, INC.
1234 Madison Street
San Francisco, California 94118

January 24, 198-

Mr. William R. Johnston
Chairman of the Board
Western Savings and Loan Association
784 Yosemite Boulevard
Fresno, CA 93112

Mr. Johnston:

Here is the report of the study you requested on the feasibility of opening a branch office in the city of Porterville.

In making the study, we surveyed the social and economic factors of the community within 15 miles of Porterville. Savings patterns of community families were analyzed as was the mortgage volume for each of the past ten years. A study of your potential competition for the savings dollar indicates that Porterville could accommodate an additional savings and loan branch office.

The image of Western Federal is excellent in the community; and with much of your radio and television advertising already going into the area, promotion would not be a problem.

We at Lerner were pleased to make this study, Mr. Johnston; and we hope it assists you in making a decision. Should you wish to discuss the report in any way, please let me know.

Sincerely,

Donald R. Jessup

Donald R. Jessup
Research Associate

Figure 16-2   The letter of transmittal.

MEMORANDUM

AJAX COSMETIC COMPANY

April 15, 1983

TO: Mr. Sidney Smith, Director of Sales Promotion

FROM: Barbara Lambert-Knipe, Advertising Manager

SUBJECT: Selection of a Women's Magazine for Advertising

Here is the report you requested regarding in which of three women's magazines--Vogue, Harper's Bazaar, or McCall's--it would be best for us to purchase advertising space.

Briefly, it was necessary to determine what the readership of each magazine was like to decide which would be best suited for our high-quality cosmetic line. Based on the nature of the products advertised, the appeals used, cost and circulation, the answer to your question is "Vogue." The report presents justification for this answer.

Doing this research was both interesting and informative. Thank you for assigning me the study.

BLK/vet

Figure 16-3 Transmittal in memorandum form.

3. Full identification of the person who prepared the report, as in the following example:

Prepared by
Donald R. Jessup, Research Associate
R. R. Lerner, Inc.
1234 Madison Street
San Francisco, California

4. The date on which the report was presented to the authority.

Why do we include all this information on the title page when most of it is included in the letter of transmittal? Because the transmittal letter may be separated from the report and lost or filed separately. Since the formal report may be retained for some time, the title page provides essential and immediate information. Note the placement of the key items in the title page shown in Figure 16-4.

The Contents Page

When a report is long, a contents page helps the reader locate information. Additionally, it indicates the organization of the report since, with only slight changes, the report outline is the basis for the contents page. The contents should include each heading in the report to at least the third level of headings if the organization extends that far. The wording of headings should be identical with the wording in the body of the report.

Can a contents outline reveal something about a writer's skill in organizing?

The writer has several options available in the design of the contents page. Outline symbols may be used before each item in the contents. However, if the contents page items are arranged so that each major heading has its subdivisions indented on succeeding lines, the outline symbols are not necessary. Variations, too, are possible. The contents page illustrated in Figure 16-5 uses Roman numerals to indicate the major divisions of the report. Subheadings under those major divisions are indented (if there were subsections within the subheadings, they would be indented farther). Thus the content outline is clear without the use of excess outline symbols.

The sample contents page also demonstrates how communication can occur without the use of words or symbols. For example, the far right-hand column is obviously a column of page numbers. It was unnecessary to use the word *page* as a caption for that column. A simple glance at the page makes it obvious that it is a table, so we can title it simply as *Contents* rather than as *Table of Contents*. Of course, it isn't incorrect to label the page *Table of Contents*. The choice is simply one of writer preference.

The contents page shown in Figure 16-6 eliminates the Roman numerals and page column heading. Dots connecting headings and page numbers are desirable because of the two-line headings. Additionally, this page includes a list of figures contained in the report. When the content outline and the list of figures will fit on one

THE FEASIBILITY OF OPENING A BRANCH SAVINGS
AND LOAN
OFFICE IN PORTERVILLE

Prepared for

Mr. William E. Johnston
Chairman
Western Savings and Loan Association
Fresno, California

Prepared by

Donald R. Jessup, Research Associate
R. R. Lerner, Inc.
1234 Madison Street
San Francisco, California 94118

January 24, 198-

Figure 16-4 The title page.

CONTENTS

I. Introduction 1

    Purpose of the Study 1

    Method and Sources of Data 1

    Scope of the Report 2

II. The Stereo User 3

    Youth Dominates the Market 4

    Likely Prospects: White-collar
    Males 5

III. Purchasing Preferences 6

    Quality and Power Leading
    Criteria 7

    Speakers and Amplifiers Desired
    Components 8

    Brand Names Preferred Items 10

    Moderate Range Desired Price 13

IV. Conclusions and Recommendations 15

V. Appendix 17

Figure 16-5 The contents page.

CONTENTS

Introduction. 1

    Why This Study Was Undertaken 1

    How Data Were Collected 1

Evaluating the Three Locations 3

    Cost Is Comparable in Sites B and C 4

    Location and Access Favor Site C. 4

    Lack of Competition Favors Site C 6

    Movie-Goer Population Points to Site C 7

    Weekly Family Entertainment Expenditures
      Favor Community C. 8

    Population and Growth Trends Make No
      Distinction 9

Site C Is the First Choice 10

Bibliography. 12

Appendices 13

LIST OF FIGURES

1. Distances from the Center of Orange 2

2. Total Expected Expenditures for Sites A,
   B, and C 4

3. Percentage of Movie-Goers in Each
   Community 7

4. Population and Growth Trends in the Three
   Communities 9

Figure 16-6 One variation in the contents page format.

page, the page serves as a total reference or guide to the report. When either content outline or list of figures is lengthy, they should be placed on separate pages.

The Summary, or Synopsis

In a long report, some means is necessary to let the reader know what the report is all about. Even though the contents page reveals the organization of the report, and the letter of transmittal may indicate something about the findings and conclusions, it helps to include a separate, brief condensation in the preliminary part of the report to give the reader some information about the contents. This brief condensation is called variously a *summary,* a *synopsis,* a *précis,* an *epitome,* or a *brief.* The most commonly used terms are *summary* and *synopsis.*

This condensation is an excellent indicator of a writer's ability to synthesize the work. It requires the ability to see the problem as a whole; to put this whole view into understandable, precise language; and to organize key points logically. Although the summary may seem redundant in that it repeats information in the body of the report, do not underestimate the value of repetition in reporting. Many reports are technical and complex. Would it be more economical to read a long report twice or a summary and long report only once? The famous answer given by a preacher when he was asked how he got his points across so well is appropriate. He replied, "First I tell them what I am going to say, then I say what I have to say, then I tell them what I have said."

Might some readers read only the summary and omit the body?

The summary reviews the four steps in problem solving as covered in the body of the report. Two types of organization, familiar by now, may be used in the summary. The deductive or direct sequence of organization places the conclusion(s) first and then presents the substantiating data. The inductive plan of organization follows the problem-solving steps. Compare the following plans:

Indirect	**Direct**
1. Purpose	1. Conclusion
2. Method	2. Purpose
3. Findings	3. Method
4. Conclusion	4. Findings

Obviously, the direct sequence lets the reader know the ultimate result right away. A long report is usually organized according to the indirect plan, but it achieves an overall direct organization by using a summary at the beginning. A summary using direct organization adds impact to the conclusions. Notice how the sample summary, shown in Figure 16-7, uses the problem-solving steps as the basis for its indirect organization. To convert the summary to direct organization, simply rephrase the last paragraph and place it at the beginning.

SYNOPSIS

On March 1, Mr. Charles Martin, vice president of marketing, authorized a study to determine (a) the characteristics of those planning to purchase additional stereo components, (b) the types of components desired, and (c) the general range of dollars to be expended for additional components.

A questionnaire study was conducted to achieve the goals of the study. Over 7,000 persons were consulted at ten stores selling stereo components in the Kansas City area. In all, 2,350 owned stereo systems and participated in the study by completing the questionnaire. Over 75 percent planned to add components to their current systems. No effort was made to question those who did not own stereo systems because they fell outside the scope of this study.

Some highlights of the findings are

  --Over half of the owners were in the 25-to-35 year age
    group, were white-collar or skilled laborers, and had
    incomes between $20,000 and $26,000 a year.
  --Three out of four owners were men.
  --Tape components, including 8-track players, were the most
    desired additions to systems.
  --Components contributing to increased power and to noise
    reduction were also strongly desired additions.
  --Although the average investment in their present systems
    was about $300, owners still planned to spend an average
    of $200 to improve their systems. Added quality was the
    primary motivation for planning added expenditures.

Based on these and other findings presented in the report, advertising should be focused on a young, relatively affluent male age group. Emphasis should be placed on tape components and on those components contributing to improved power and tone. At the same time, the packages of components should not exceed $300. Desirably, three packages should be planned with prices of about $125, $190, and $275, respectively.

Figure 16-7 The summary, or synopsis.

The Body of the Report

The heart of the report is, of course, the body. Within the body, the writer presents the entire scope of the research. In addition, all the expository techniques possible are used to convey to the reader a picture of the research model, the analysis and solution of the problem, and the conclusions and/or recommendations on which management can base some future action. Writing methods for constructing the body of the report are discussed in Chapters 17 and 18.

Addenda

In addition to the preliminary parts, a report may include a variety of items after the body. Some of these parts are well known.

1. The *bibliography* is the listing of all published and unpublished documents used in preparing the study and the report. When oral interviews with authorities are part of the research, documentation of them is included in the bibliography.

2. The *appendix* is a section containing a variety of items that are concerned with the study but that would probably hinder the reader's ability to grasp the message if presented in the body of the report. Appropriate items for the appendix are cover letters for questionnaires and the survey instruments themselves. Such materials as maps, summaries of raw data, and explanations of complex mathematical formulas are also frequently included as appendix materials.

3. The *index* is an alphabetic guide to the subject matter included in the report. Although it is not a part of most business reports, an index may be necessary in proposal reports, prospectuses, and annual reports. The easiest way to prepare an index is to record each key term and its page number on 3-by-5 cards while reading the report from beginning to end. Even if the same term is found more than once, make a card for it. When a card has been made for each key term, simply alphabetize the cards. Where the same term has been found more than once, transfer the page numbers to the single card containing the first page on which the item was located. Then the index will include the term followed by a list of all the page numbers on which the term is used.

COMPLETE REPORT OUTLINE

The following outline includes the detailed parts of a complete report:

I. Preliminary parts
    A. Letter of transmittal
    B. Title page

      C. Contents page
      D. Synopsis or summary (when not included in the letter of transmittal)
II. Body of the report
      A. Purpose
      B. Method
      C. Findings (in as many sections as necessary)
      D. Conclusions (and recommendations if requested)
III. Addenda
      A. Bibliography
      B. Appendix material
      C. Index

To find all these parts included in a business report would be extremely rare. They are included here simply to illustrate all the possible parts. The preliminary parts and addenda are mechanical items that only support the body of the report. The body contains the report of the research and covers the four steps in the research process. The organization of the body of the report leads to the construction of the contents page.

ORGANIZING REPORTS

Now that the preliminary and addenda parts of the report have been described, the problem for students of report writing is to discover just how the Roman numeral II, Body of the Report, came to be in the form described in the contents page. The body of the report is the actual account of how the subject was approached, what was found, and what the results should be.

We have seen that the preliminary portions of the report provide the busy executive with an overview of the body—in effect, they tell what the report is all about and may save reading time if the reader is willing to accept the statements and analyses (if any) in them. If the reader does not accept the conclusions presented in the transmittal letter or the synopsis, the reader will proceed to the body, perhaps ultimately to the addenda, before accepting the report.

Just as letters employ either inductive or deductive outlines, so do reports. Normally, executives who read reports prefer the deductive report (introduction reveals the overall conclusion and paragraphs basically present major ideas followed with details). However, the inductive approach is justified if the writer wants to employ an interest-holding, curiosity factor. Between the lines, it says something like this to the reader: "Keep on reading and you'll see the answer. Only then can you know whether you have correctly guessed where the facts are leading." Also, the inductive approach is preferred if the reader is known to have a bias contrary to the conclusions. In this case, the facts-first approach (as in refusal and sales letters) is recommended.

Because reports contain more information than letters, outlining is more complicated. The typical report contains many pages of facts and figures. A haphazard presentation would be frustrating to both reader and writer. A poor outline (or no outline at all) results in messages in which the reader has difficulty seeing relationships among points. A writer who has no outline (or an outline that has not been made carefully) is going to have an unpleasant experience in composition: insecurity about the order of points to be discussed, worry over the possibility of returning to topics previously touched upon, and fear of failure to discuss certain topics sufficiently.

Is faulty organization a symptom of faulty thinking?

Typically, a person who has a report to write is doing some organizing and interpreting while gathering information. By the time all the information has been interpreted and a conclusion reached, the writer already has some idea of major categories into which the report can be divided. That division must be systematic.

Being Systematic

Examine the following list of major headings (outline) to see whether a serious weakness can be detected in each list:

List A
- I. Book Alpha
- II. Book Beta
- III. Results of a Survey
- IV. Book Gamma

List B
- I. Interviews
- II. Questionnaires
- III. Readability
- IV. Publisher's Pamphlets

List C
- I. Readability
- II. Cost
- III. Questionnaires
- IV. Subject Coverage
- V. Reader Aids

List D
- I. Problem
- II. Method
- III. Results of Survey
- IV. Findings
- V. Conclusions
- VI. Recommendations

Assume each of the preceding outlines was designed for a report that was to answer the question "Which real estate text would be appropriate for the upcoming seminars?" In each of the four lists of possible major headings, which item does not belong?

In each list, item III does not belong. In list A, all the units except III are possible books. Because item III is not also a book, it does not belong in a list of books. In list B, item III ("Readability") is not a source of information, as are the other three units, and does not belong. In list C, "Questionnaire" does not belong in a list of book features. In list D, "Results of Survey" is out of place in a series of steps that constitute the scientific method.

Observe the relationships within the following columns:

Readability	1/4
Cost	3/4
Questionnaire	2/3
Subject Coverage	5/4
Reader Aids	1/4

The column of fractions does not have a common denominator. Before the column can be added, the fractions must be changed so that they have a common denominator. The word "Questionnaire" is to the column of words what the "2/3" is to the column of figures; the word doesn't belong. Just as a column of fractions needs a common denominator before the fractions are added, so do major headings in an outline need a common denominator before the report is written.

When considering major headings for an outline, a writer can profitably ask "If I think of my major headings as numerators, what is my common denominator?" Actually making the diagonal and writing in the common denominator helps:

Readability/feature
Cost/feature
Questionnaire/source
Subject coverage/feature
Reader aids/features

What writing problems will arise if a report's major headings do not have a common relationship to one another?

Because "Questionnaire" is clearly out of place, it should be removed from the outline. If it is not, two very serious writing problems will result: (1) some topics will contain overlapping information, or (2) some topics will not be covered completely. Suppose, for example, the questionnaire results reported some information about readability. If the write-up on readability does not include the questionnaire's information on readability, the topic "Readability" is not completely discussed. If the questionnaire's readability data are included under the "Readability" heading *and* under the "Questionnaire" heading, the topic is discussed in two places. Circular writing (returning to a topic previously put aside) is one of the most serious criticisms of writing. Writers who repeat themselves unnecessarily get credit for being disorganized, illogical, careless, or even unaware of what they have written previously.

Find some additional ways to state this important outlining principle.

If a plot of land is to be divided or if a cake is to be cut into small pieces, the division is expected to be systematic. After division of the major unit, the small units would be expected to have commonality in shape and size. The same principles apply to division of ideas. *The ideas into which a report is divided must have a common relationship to one another.*

Sometimes a concept is more vivid if expressed in more than one way. The preceding principle could be stated as "If the major headings are thought of as numerators, they must have a common denominator," "The ideas must employ a single basis for division," "Each unit in the series must be something that the other units are also," or "The *ideas* must be parallel."

When that principle is employed, each item III in the preceding examples must be removed; it does not belong. In a report outline, the principle of the common denominator applies to the parts that appear between the introduction and the conclusion.

Do the findings of the study fall between the introduction and the conclusion?

The common-denominator principle applies at all levels of an outline. Just as major units must have commonality, so must the subunits that appear under each major unit. For example, assume that "Reader Aids" in List C from page 421 were to be subdivided:

Reader Aids
  Graphs
  Charts
  Tables

Reader Aids
  Emphasize points
  Add clarity
  Provide variety

The basis for division (common denominator) of the list on the left is *type* of reader aids. Among the three subheadings that appear in the group on the right, the common denominator is *advantage* of reader aids. A violation of the common-denominator principle at the subdivision level results in the same writing problems that are encountered when the violation is at the major division level: some topics will overlap, or some topics will not be discussed completely.

Using the Right System

Writers sometimes succeed in employing a common denominator, but they choose the *wrong* one. Studying the same outlines that appeared on page 421, try to answer the question "If I were going to write the report on which real estate text to use, *which* of the following outlines (A, B, C, or D) would I choose?"

List A
Introduction
Book Alpha/title of text
Book Beta/title of text
Book Gamma/title of text
Conclusion

List B
Introduction
Interviews/source of information
Questionnaires/source of
  information
Publishers' pamphlets/source
  of information
Conclusion

List C
Introduction
Problem/step in scientific method
Method/step in scientific method
Findings/step in scientific method
Conclusions/step in scientific
  mothod
Recommendations/step in
  scientific method
Conclusion

List D
Introduction
Readability/book feature
Cost/book feature
Subject Coverage/book feature
Reader Aids/book feature
Oonclusion

The preceding outlines were prepared for an *analytical* report designed to present a solution to a problem.

For an Analytical Report

In preparing the outline for an analytical report, the writer can benefit greatly from asking two questions:

1. If I had this proposed report finished and handed it to the person who asked for it, what would that person's first question be? Almost surely, it would be "Good, what is your solution to the problem?"

What is a reader of
a report looking for?

2. And what would the second question be? It would be "Why?" or "For what reasons did you select that solution?"

Everyone who requests a problem-solving report wants to know the solution and the supporting reasons. Most of the report will be devoted to the latter. If the reasons seem valid and are well presented, the report will be well received; so a writer needs to choose an outline that will emphasize the reasons that support the conclusion. Major divisions in the outline become major topic titles (headings) in the typewritten report. Like newspaper headlines, ideas that are placed in report headings receive emphasis.

Assume that in the preceding illustration book Beta is best. The person who receives the report wants to know *why*. Would the major headings from list A ("Book Alpha," "Book Beta," etc.), list B ("Interviews," "Questionnaires," etc.), list C ("Problem," "Method," etc.) give the reader a clue? They would not. Now re-examine the headings in list D. Each heading ("Readability," "Cost," "Coverage," "Aids") represents a factor that had to be taken into account before the decision could be made. Each factor is one of the criteria by which all the books had to be judged.

The person who reads a report that employs list D as major headings could hardly do so without seeing vividly how each major heading is associated with reasons for the decision. By looking through the report and glancing at headings, the recipient becomes aware of the *reasons* for the decision.

Because reasons for the decision are so important, *the best common denominator for major headings in an analytical report is reasons for the decision.*

Compared with the three other choices, list D has these advantages:

1. It emphasizes reasons for the decision.

2. It makes comparison easy.

3. It employs headings that have an obvious relationship to the problem being solved.

4. It ensures headings that appear to have originality.

Under the heading "Readability," all three books can be discussed and a conclusion drawn on that criterion. Likewise, the other headings facilitate easy comparison of all three. The reader who sees the headings "Readability," "Cost," "Coverage," etc., has no difficulty recognizing them as characteristics of books — the problem being reported upon. The writer employing these headings on the book-selection report will have a totally new and different set of headings for the next report written.

Having seen the advantages of using an outline that employs criteria as the basis for division, look at the disadvantages of the other three possibilities.

Are criteria the things on which selections are based?

If list A were employed as major divisions, comparison would be difficult. Under the heading "Book Alpha," the other books should not be discussed. By the time a reader sees costs and readability figures for book Gamma, the figures for book Alpha may have been forgotten. Pages previously read will have to be re-examined. Also, each feature (readability, cost, etc.) would have to be discussed in three different places. If subheadings were used, the same subheadings that were used under "Book Alpha" would be repeated under "Book Beta" and "Book Gamma." The monotony and the scattered information make the reading less pleasant and less effective.

If list B were employed as major divisions, each source would become a major heading. Although readers do need confidence that information came from appropriate sources, they are more interested in the *outcome* of the research and the *reasons* for the conclusion. List B gives more emphasis to the sources than the sources deserve. Also, list B invites overlap. For example, some of the same ideas that came from questionnaires could also come from interviews. Reporting the same ideas under both headings constitutes circular writing. In attempting to avoid overlap, a writer can make the error of failing to cover completely a topic that a heading suggests will be covered.

If list C were employed as major divisions, each step in the problem-solving process would become a heading. As such, each step would get more emphasis than it deserves. Readers do need confidence that a problem was solved systematically, but that confidence can be established without de-emphasizing the reasons for the decision. Too much emphasis on method of research may detract from the criteria for the decision.

Another weakness in list C is that the headings used for this report can be used for *any* analytical report. Because the headings are so general, their direct relationship to the specific problem is not obvious. A report writer can seldom expect to devote the same amount of space to each major division; but, when steps in the scientific method are employed as the common denominator, the space devoted to findings is likely to be much more than the space devoted to all other divisions combined. Because the "Findings" division includes so much detail, it is likely to need numerous subdivisions. The major headings of list A or list D could appear as subheadings under "Findings." Just as an idea that appears in a heading gets more emphasis than an idea that appears in a sentence, an idea that appears in a subheading gets *less* emphasis than an idea that appears in a major heading. If readability, cost, coverage, etc., appeared as subheadings under "Findings," they would not get the emphasis they deserve.

Is "Findings" a weak heading?

Note that in the preceding outlines the last division is "Conclusions" or "Recommendations." These headings are appropriate for a problem-solving report; but, if the report were informational, the final section would be more appropriately called "Summary."

For an Informational Report

What is the
difference between
analytical and
informational reports?

Because an informational report is not expected to solve a problem and present a solution, the common denominator can hardly be *reasons for the conclusion.* Yet informational reports need a common denominator just as analytical reports do. What should the common denominator be? The possibilities are numerous.

Assume the assignment is to gather and report information about federal land grants to railroads. Before making an outline, the writer could profitably ask "What area is of primary interest?" If the primary interest is the government's purposes for giving away land, each major heading will be a purpose. If the primary interest is which geographic region benefited most from land grants, each of the major headings will be a geographic region.

Again, failure to employ a common denominator will result in overlapping topics or failure to cover some topics completely. Establishing commonality among major headings is the most critical problem in outlining. Other outlining techniques are easy to employ.

For Both Informational and Analytical Reports

Regardless of whether a report is informational or analytical, the number of major divisions should be carefully controlled. If the initial attempt at outlining resulted in eighteen major divisions, each division could not seem particularly significant. Division into parts is essential and helpful, but division into too many parts can be harmful. Usually, a limited number of good reasons is much more impressive than a large number of insignificant reasons. Just as reasons need to be emphasized, they need to be remembered. If they are to be remembered, they should not be too numerous. When the number of major divisions reaches seven, the list is on the verge of being too long. On the other hand, a long report that is divided into only two major divisions may require many subdivisions; and some points that appear in subheadings may actually need more emphasis than subheadings afford.

Is overoutlining possible?

If the initial attempt at outlining yields too many major divisions, some of them will have considerable commonality and can be grouped under one general term. Because the major points should be emphasized and easy to remember, *the number of divisions must be carefully controlled.*

The sequence of those divisions should not be left to chance. If the divisions are time periods, *time* can be used in determining which division is presented first. Other possibilities: *place* (moving from one place to the next contiguous place), *amounts* (with the highest figure first and progressing to the lowest, or vice versa), *importance* (from most to least or least to most), or *psychology* (with impressive points at beginning and ending positions). Whatever the basis for sequence is, *the sequence of divisions must be justifiable, not haphazard.*

Not only must the divisions be related to one another, the wording of each division should confirm that relationship. Division titles (which become headings when a report is typed) can be presented as statements, questions, phrases, or single words; but they must be consistently presented. If three headings are in question form and one is in statement form, the one in statement form appears out of place. Its presence is distracting; the writer's logic may even be questioned.

Especially in an analytical report, talking headings can be used. Instead of the topical heading "Readability," a writer can use "Book Beta Is Easiest to Read." Such headings go beyond identifying the nature of the subject matter to be discussed and reveal the nature of the conclusion presented in the paragraphs that follow. Effective use of the common denominator assures that each major division belongs with the others. The use of parallel construction (stating each heading in a similar way grammatically) helps to confirm the relationship. The principle of parallel construction applies to subdivisions as well as to major divisions. Subdivisions A and B under a major division must be worded the same way. Likewise, 1 and 2 under A must be worded the same way. At each level of division, *the units must be worded in a similar way.*

What makes a "talking" head desirable?

Outlining (organizing) is essentially a process of division. Naturally, after any unit has been divided, at least two parts will remain. Subdivision A must be followed with subdivision B. Subdivision 1 must be followed with subdivision 2. Some units are simply not divisible; but *if a unit is divided, it must be divided into two or more units.*

Is a single subheading under a major heading appropriate?

The mental exercise of making a satisfactory outline is excellent preparation for the writing that is to follow. And the same outlining principles that are applied in preparing letters and reports are applicable in other presentations.

A SAMPLE PROBLEM

Because a report is written to present information or to present the analysis of a problem, the first part of the report should tell the reader about the research problem or purpose of the study. Then it will be necessary to tell the reader about the method used in solving the problem. Next, we can tell what our findings are and what conclusions are finally drawn. Thus, the body of a report covers the four steps in problem solving presented in Chapter 13:

1. Recognize and define the problem.
2. Select a method of solution.
3. Collect and organize data.
4. Arrive at an answer to the problem.

Generally, the findings and the conclusions are of most importance to the researcher and to the reader. Therefore, they should receive the greatest attention in the written presentation. The definition of the problem and the description of the research method used are of secondary interest in most cases, but they provide necessary background for the other material. As a result, these topics become subheadings rather than major headings. An outline of a report including these four elements, then, could look like this:

I.   Introduction
   A.   Definition of the Problem
   B.   Description of the Research Method
II. Findings
III. Conclusions

This outline includes all four items, but it combines the problem and the method in one section. These become relatively less important in the outline than the findings and conclusions. But reports would be pretty dull reading if they came from outlines as lifeless as this. Let's take a hypothetical problem; assume we've thought it through, conducted the research, and are ready to put it all down in a written report. In this way, we can take a closer look at some outlining refinements that will be of value to us in writing. Keep in mind at this point that the final outline for a report, a book, or other sizable pieces of writing will probably become the familiar table of contents page.

Here's the problem: as a management trainee of the Arvon Company, you have been assigned to work on special problems delegated by the executive vice-president. This assignment involves the company's eight-year-old, eight-passenger airplane, which is used to take executives around the country on company business. The plane should be traded in on a new one; and you are to make a recommendation from three that would possibly fill the bill: the Bobcat, the Birch, and the Clark. You obtain prices and trade-in offers for the old plane from dealers of the three others. You study such factors as range, speed, operating costs, and safety factors. You ask six executives to take test rides in each plane and to complete a checklist covering their reactions to each. In addition, you ask the two company pilots to write reports on their reactions to the flying habits of each plane. After much consideration, and considerable arithmetic, you know we are going to recommend the Bobcat.

Your outline for the written report to the vice-president might look like this:

I.   Background for the Study
   A.   Problem
   B.   Method
II. Performance Factors of Three Fine Planes
   A.   The Bobcat
   B.   The Birch
   C.   The Clark
III. Conclusion and Recommendation

But some things are missing. Where is the heading for trade-in value? For the opinions of the executives who took the test rides? For the reactions of the company pilots? For the criteria you used to reach your decision? Maybe you should analyze the problem again and see how you can make a more effective outline.

As shown in the analysis schematic in Figure 16-8, two options are available for analysis. You could discuss all features of the Bobcat, follow with a discussion of all features of the Birch, and finally present all features of the Clark. On the other hand, you could present and compare the cost of the three planes in one section of the report body, follow with an analysis of the trade-in factors of the three, and proceed in this way until each of the criteria being used to analyze the problem was covered.

If the three planes were each to be the heading of a major part of the findings, consider for a moment the reader's difficulty trying to recall the range of the Bobcat

Have you seen this idea earlier?

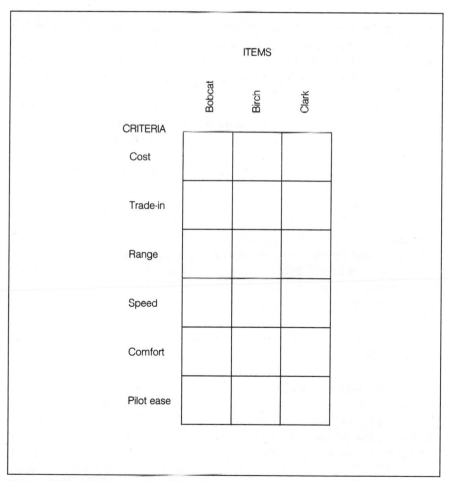

Figure 16-8   Analysis schematic: use of criteria, rather than items, as comparison elements.

when reading the later section on the Clark. Comparison and analysis would be much simpler if the range of all three were covered in a single section. Note in this revision of the outline how criteria, rather than the planes (items), have been used for subdivisions of the body.

    I. Introduction
        A. The Problem
        B. The Method
   II. Cost and Trade-in Favor the Bobcat
 III. Range and Speed Are Comparable in the Bobcat and Clark
 IV. Executives Prefer Bobcat's Comfort
  V. Pilots Like the Bobcat and Birch
 VI. The Bobcat Is the Plane for Arvon

Items II through V are actually subdivisions of the findings section of the report, and item VI is the conclusion section of the outline. But staid terms, such as findings and conclusions, have not been used. In their places are headings far more descriptive of the content. They'll help the reader through the report, too, because when used as headings, descriptive language tells the reader more about what is to come.

Many report writers prefer to omit the introduction material in the outline. Because everything really has an introduction anyway and because the reader expects the first part of the report to be an introduction, you can prepare effective content outlines by deleting items I, IA, and IB from the preceding outline. In this case, you would still include the problem and the method in the opening portion of your report, but you'd not identify them with headings. Then the content outline would look like this:

    I. Cost and Trade-in Favor the Bobcat
   II. Range and Speed Are Comparable in the Bobcat and Clark
 III. Executives Prefer Bobcat's Comfort
 IV. Pilots Like the Bobcat and Birch
  V. The Bobcat Is the Plane for Arvon

This outline becomes a contents page simply by adding page numbers and omitting the Roman numerals:

Cost and Trade-in Favor the Bobcat	2
Range and Speed Are Comparable in the Bobcat and Clark	4
Executives Prefer Bobcat's Comfort	5
Pilots Like the Bobcat and Birch	6
The Bobcat Is the Airplane for Arvon	8

Had this outline included the introduction, the problem, and the method as headings, they would have been listed as beginning on page 1:

Introduction	1
The Problem	1
The Method	1
Cost and Trade-in Favor the Bobcat	2

Therefore, you have a choice about your outlining style. In either case, the content will be the same; and whatever items you have on the contents page will become headings within the report.

USING OUTLINE SYMBOLS

Styles of outline symbols other than Roman numerals are increasing in popularity. Any symbol system may be used to classify, sort, and organize information so long as the system is expandable and understandable. *Expandable* means that a whole element can be divided into its components, that those components can be further subdivided into their parts, and that the parts can be subdivided into their parts— and the system will not run out of symbols to identify these divisions. *Understandable* means that people who might refer to the system later will be able to understand the levels of organization.

For example, the Dewey decimal system, developed more than 100 years ago, has been able to accommodate the tremendous number of publications produced since the system was developed. A library call number such as 524.816f can be used to identify a single book from among over five million. However, since reports seldom go beyond two or three divisions and subdivisions, elaborate symbol schemes are usually unnecessary.

In the following illustrations of commonly used symbol systems, note the similarity of symbols and the logical relationship among the three schemes:

Roman numeral	Decimal	Alphanumeric
I.	1.0	A.
A.	1.1	1.
1.	1.11	a.
2.	1.12	b.
B.	1.2	2.
II.	2.0	B.

The Roman numeral item IA2, the decimal item 1.12, and the alphanumeric item A1b designate the same item in all three outlines. Roman numeral outlines are used widely in schools and industry, decimal outlines are found frequently in engineering and other technically oriented firms, and variations of the alphanumeric outline are used by many governmental organizations. All three systems enable us to organize our material in a logical way, are expandable so that we can create additional subdivisions without disrupting the basic outline, and clearly indicate to readers the various levels of importance. No matter which system we choose, the outline is a key tool for a writer.

ORGANIZING DATA

After we have decided on our major headings, we still have the problem of arranging our information in an orderly, understandable fashion. This is when — if we haven't been careful with our conceptualizing — we will have to make decisions and narrow down the possible ways of viewing our data. For example, suppose we were doing a report on new automobile models. How would we classify the automobiles?

1. By size; for example, subcompact, compact, standard-sized, luxury.

2. By manufacturer; for example, American Motors, Chrysler, Fiat, Ford, General Motors, Toyota, and so on.

3. By model; for example, two-door, four-door, station wagon, and so on.

4. By country; for example, American, French, German, Italian, Japanese, and so on.

5. By price; for example: under $8,000; $8,000–12,000; $12,000–16,000; and so on.

We could even begin to combine these classifications, and arrive at designations such as "foreign-made, two-door subcompacts costing under $8,000."

Obviously, the combinations are endless. And, just as obviously, whatever mental gymnastics we go through at the beginning of our study to decide on our categories will save us considerable effort at the end. That is, if we make our decisions about classifications as early as when we are designing the questionnaire, our final task will be easy.

The process of classifying is one of taking the entirety of the problem, dividing it logically, and then subdividing to the point where each single unit making up the whole of the problem has its own special niche or class. A further consideration is involved for the report writer, however. The classification system should reflect the relative importance of the item in the final report. That is, if one classification occupies far more space in the report than another, the reader will automatically assume that it is more important than the item that has less space. Since this assumption may well not be true, we should make sure our classes are balanced in importance.

In some reports, classification will be provided for in the directions given the report writer by management. Routine departmental reports on such things as personnel, sales, and activities may be made on prepared forms with printed headings for classifications, as shown in Figure 16-9.

Because skill in classification is a function of how well an individual can perceive

CALIFORNIA FEDERAL
INCOME PROPERTY

APPRAISAL REPORT

Applicant _____ Date _____

Property Address _____

City _____ County _____ State _____ Map Ref. _____

LOCATION_____ Blks N/S of _____ and _____ Blks E/W of _____

Surrounding Structures _____

Built-Up: Residential ☐ Commercial ☐ Industrial ☐ Conformity _____

Trend _____ Built-up _____%

Competition Existing and Potential _____

Transportation _____ Freeways _____ Shopping _____ Schools _____

Cultural _____ Locational Obsolescence _____

LOT Size _____ X _____ X _____ X _____ = _____ Sq. Ft.   Corner ☐   Inside ☐

Curb & Gutter_____ Pub. Walks _____ Street _____ Alley _____Paved ☐

Sewer _____ Contour _____ Drainage _____ Zoning _____

Gas _____ Electricity _____ Comment _____

BLDG. Type _____ Sched. Gross $ _____ Taxes $ _____ Ins $ _____

Bach _____ Sgls _____ 1 BR _____ 2 BR _____ 3 BR _____ Furn ☐ Unf. ☐

Age _____ Yrs.   Stories _____ Ext. Walls _____ Elevtr. _____ Constr. _____

Features _____

Parking Ratio _____ : _____ Type _____

Year Blt. _____ Rem. Econ. Life _____ Yrs. Appeal _____ F/S ☐ Msnry. ☐ Roof _____

Plaster ☐ D.W. ☐   Kit. Flr. _____ Bath Flr. _____ Heat _____

Panel ☐ Paper ☐ Paint ☐ Cabinets _____ Pullman _____ Air Cond. _____

LR Flr. _____ Snack Bar _____ Tub Encl. _____ Hot Water _____

Features _____ R & O _____ Stall Shr. _____ Laundry _____

DR Flr. _____ H & F _____ Elec. Htr. _____ Trash Chute _____

BR Flr. _____ Drainbd. _____ Sauna _____ Special _____

Closets _____ Disposal _____ _____

Dr. Room _____ Dishwash. _____ _____

Balcs. _____ Driveway _____ Walks _____ Patios _____

Pool _____ Walls _____ Fences _____ Landscaping _____

Other _____

Land $ _____	Sq.Ft.	A/V $ _____	Sq.Ft.	Net Income $ _____	
Land $ _____	Unit	A/V $ _____	Unit	1 TD Yrly. $ _____	
Unit Area _____	Sq.Ft.	Loan $ _____	Sq.Ft.	2 TD Yrly. $ _____	
Rental $ _____	Sq.Ft.	Loan $ _____	Unit	Net Spend. $ _____	
Rental $ _____	Aver.	Gross Mult. _____		N.S. Ratio _____	%
Rooms _____ BRs _____		Ins. Req. $ _____		Pmt + Exp = _____	% EGI
Baths _____		_____		Breakeven _____	%
_____		_____		Annual Constant _____	%

Requirements _____

VALUE APPROACHES	VALUE CONCLUSION $ _____
INCOME: $ _____	Certified by:
COMPARISON: $ _____	
COST: $ _____	
	APPRAISER DATE

CF 726 E   **APPRAISAL (1)**

Figure 16-9 Form appraisal report (courtesy: California Federal Savings and Loan Association).

Is skill in class-
ifying related to
mental vizualization?

a whole and its parts, no cut-and-dried rules can be prescribed. However, our job will
be easier if we pay attention to the following procedures:

1. Attempt to perceive the whole of the data gathered.

2. Divide the whole into its major components in agreement with the primary
purposes of the research.

3. Divide each major component into its constituent parts.

4. Continue dividing as long as it contributes to the purposes of the study.

Remember, however, that something has to divide into at least *two* parts, or it
can't be divided. So in outlines, for example, the symbol *A* must have at least
divisions symbolized as *1* and *2* or it can't be divided. That is, we must decide if *A* is
an entity by itself or if it has parts.

A final caution about the process of classifying: We should not become so
involved with the process that we lose sight of our original purpose. The proper
number of divisions to use is one of judgment. Five different people might come up
with five different classifications for the automobile industry example included in this
discussion. Each of the five might be very well correct, too, in terms of the judgment
of each and the ultimate use each perceived for the report. The important thing is
that we understand why we chose to classify as we did.

SUMMARY

The degree of formality in a report depends on (1) the length and complexity of the
report, (2) the needs or expectations of potential readers, and (3) the ultimate
disposition of the report. As you evaluate these factors, you arrive at conclusions
about the final report format.

Because reports are logical presentations of problem-solving efforts, organizing them involves the ability to perceive the process of identifying and solving a
problem as well as skill in outlining and classifying. Beginning and ending items in
formal reports—the letter of transmittal, title page, contents page, summary or
synopsis, bibliography, and appendix—reflect the care and detail put into preparing
the report. Remember that they are prepared after the research has been completed
and, except for the contents page (which is based on the outline), after the body of
the report has been written. Their purpose is to support the body of the report. In
succeeding chapters, you'll study how the report body is developed.

EXERCISES

Review Questions

1. Would a report be understandable if it had no preliminary parts or addenda? If
so, why are such parts included?

2. Why might a complete, formal report seem repetitious?

3. What is the general purpose of a summary at the beginning of a report?

4. When might a letter of transmittal also include a summary?

5. If the summary of a report is included in the letter of transmittal, should it be repeated as a separate item?

6. What is meant by the statement "Something divides into at least two parts or it is not divisible" in relation to report outlining?

7. Are outline symbols necessary in the contents page?

8. Explain what is meant by using criteria (rather than items) for divisions of the findings portion of a report.

9. In a report outline, major units must have a common denominator. If this principle is not followed, what difficulties will be encountered in composing the report?

10. What is meant by the process of classifying?

11. In an analytical report, which serves better as a common denominator— sources of information, or criteria?

12. In a ten-page report, would twelve major headings be too many? Explain.

13. What might be the reaction of a reader if one major division of a report takes up as much space as several other major divisions combined?

14. Will several skilled report writers classify the same information in the same way? Explain.

15. In your opinion, should definitions of unusual terms used in the report be included in the appendix? Why or why not?

16. What is the peculiar characteristic of talking headings?

Problems

1. Assume you have made a study of three brands of 19-inch television sets for a hotel corporation that wants to select one brand to install in each of 300 rooms in a new hotel. The brands were General Electric, Zenith, and RCA. You found that Zenith had the lowest cost, RCA had the longest warranty, RCA used the least power, and GE had the best color tuning. Prepare a table of contents for a report you might present. Use "talking" headings.

2. Assume you are to prepare an informational report on your school that will be mailed to prospective students. List some headings for your report.

3. Using the content of Chapter 2 as a guide, prepare a list of criteria you might use in selecting word processing equipment.

4.   Assume you have been assigned a report that is to answer the question: "Shall we institute a formal merit-rating system for employees of a bank?" Which of the following outlines would you prefer? Why?

A. Introduction
        History of Merit Rating
        Need for a New Sys-
            tem
        Results of a Survey
        Conclusion

B. Introduction
        Morale
        Efficiency
        Public Relations
        Conclusion

PREPARING SHORT REPORTS

Characteristics of Short Reports
A Sample Short Report
Letter Reports
A Sample Letter Report
Proposals
Summary

Somewhere in the gap between a memorandum and a long, formal report lies a communication means we can describe as a *short report*. A short report, as distinguished from most memorandums, is a research-based or research-oriented messsage. In this respect, the short report, then, is a report of research that does not require all the separate preliminary and addenda items associated with formal reports, as described in Chapter 16.

CHARACTERISTICS OF SHORT REPORTS

The planning and organizing steps discussed in Chapter 16 apply to both short and long formal reports; and as you study the short report, you'll detect much similarity. Recall that formal reports have several possible parts organized in three distinct sections:

> *Preliminary parts:* Transmittal letter, title page, contents page, synopsis or summary.
>
> *Body of the Report:* Purpose, method, findings, and conclusion.
>
> *Addenda:* Bibliography, appendix, index.

A short report may include some of these parts as separate, distinct items, of course. But any report that includes most of them would be described as formal.

Additionally, the short report may be written in either personal or impersonal style through the use of either personal or impersonal pronouns. It may be written in first person with the writer as the subject of sentences; in second person with the reader as the subject; or in third person with the thing written about as subject. As you no doubt have noticed, we have written much of this text with *you,* the reader, as the subject of sentences. Some has been written with *we,* the writers and readers as subjects, and much has been written with the things talked about as subjects. Variations in person add interest to writing. On the other hand, consistency of person aids clarity. Needless changes of person are not desirable; in fact, the reader will probably be distracted by them, wondering to whom the writer is referring.

If the reader can accept the short report as a research-based message, then she or he must accept the idea that the short report should include the steps in problem solving. When executives receive reports of research, they want to see concise, logical material with enough supporting evidence to help in decision making. To present this material effectively, the writer of a short report will rely on graphic materials when desirable, on headings within the report, and on logical organization.

In terms of format, a short report may take the form of a letter, a memorandum, or an abbreviated formal report. Form is determined by the writer and should involve an evaluation of reader needs, purpose of the report, and complexity of the subject.

A SAMPLE SHORT REPORT

The short report (included in this book as Figure 17-1 on the following pages) encompasses the four main steps in problem solving. Apparently the student group responsible for the report decided that it should be in memorandum form and should not include all the preliminary and addenda parts included in formal reports. Actually, however, they did have the option of preparing it as a long, formal report. Had the seven pages been typed double spaced, rather than single spaced, the report would have been about fourteen pages in length. Then, if the preliminary and addenda items had been included, the total report might have been about twenty pages. A bibliography and a copy of the questionnaire used were included in the addendum to the original report but have been omitted from this example.

At any rate, let's examine the report to see how it incorporates good organization and report preparation methods and techniques.

Page 1

a. The first page is actually a letter of transmittal and a synopsis in memorandum form. The first sentence transmits the report and states the purpose of the research study. The second and third paragraphs describe the research methods used in the study, and the tabulated highlights of the findings reveal much about the conclusions.

b. Because the date-to-from-subject heading of page 1 Includes the necessary elements, it also serves as a modified title page.

Page 2

a. The heading at the top of page 2 is appropriate for multiple-page memorandums; but it is optional in a report such as this and is included here for illustrative purposes. When used, the heading should include the name of the reader, the date, and the page. The subject is optional.

b. The centered title of the body of the report can also be considered the first of three major headings—the others are "Conclusions" on page 6 and "Recommendations" on page 7.

c. Second-level headings, as divisions of the first major heading, are found on pages 3 and 5.

d. If all the headings in the report were combined to form a content outline, the contents page would look like this if included as a separate page in a formal report:

Textbook-Course Relationship   2
   Managerial Accounting Text Is Difficult   3

January 15, 198-

TO: Dean Melvin Smith

FROM: Student Advisory Board

SUBJECT: Study on Textbook-Course Relationships

We are pleased to submit the following study you requested on the relationships among textbook readability, course and text difficulty as perceived by students, and student interest in courses.

The study involved an opinion survey of students in the school and an assessment of textbook readability as measured by Robert Gunning's Fog Index formula.

We think the sampling method used gave us a population sample adequate to represent the entire student body, and the results of the survey should be considered reliable. At the same time, we have some reservations about the adequacy of measuring readability only in terms of sentence length and word difficulty. Readability can also be affected by other language elements, but no formula exists to include a variety of other factors.

Some highlights of the findings of the study are

1.   Heavily quantitative or technical and theoretical courses are considered more difficult than the behavioral courses, which are primarily verbal.

2.   Courses in which students show a high degree of interest are considered easier than courses in which interest is low. This observation is also true of student interest in textbooks used.

3.   Although a positive relationship does exist between measured reading difficulty and student perception of course and textbook difficulty, further study is desirable to (a) investigate the relationship between teaching performance ratings and the factors considered in this study and (b) determine the influence of the student's career plans on his or her perceptions about courses.

Figure 17-1   Short report with body and memorandum (reproduced over the next several book pages).

TEXTBOOK-COURSE RELATIONSHIP

The purpose of this study was to determine the relationships between course difficulty and interest as perceived by students, and the reading difficulty of textbooks as measured by Robert Gunning's Fog Index and as perceived by students.

The major hypothesis is that core-course difficulty as perceived by students is directly affected by the reading-level difficulty of textbooks.

A questionnaire survey was administered to business students at the University. The questionnaire, appended to this report, was designed, tested, and revised for final use by students in the business communication course.

A random sampling resulted in 22 percent of the total business student body being included. Demographic information was solicited from respondents to establish the reliability of the sample. Of the 235 respondents, 62 percent were male and 38 percent female, as shown in Figure 1. Also, as shown in Figure 1, 53 percent of the respondents were juniors and 44 percent were seniors. In both cases, the sample closely resembled the male-female ratio of 2:1 and the junior-senior ratio of 10:9 of the actual student body. Thus, the sample can be considered representative.

The questionnaire was designed to determine student opinion about textbook difficulty, course difficulty, and course interest through the use of an intensity rating scale. Students could select from five choices on the rating scale with 1 being very easy, or very low interest in the case of course interest, to 5 being very difficult, or very high interest in the case of course interest. These responses were made on computer-readable answer sheets and processed through the school's computer facility.

Additionally, because students might rate more than one course or text as having the same difficulty, a forced-answer

Figure 17-1   continued.

Dean Smith
Textbook - Course Relationships, January 15, 198-
Page 3

Figure 1.   Respondents by school class and sex.

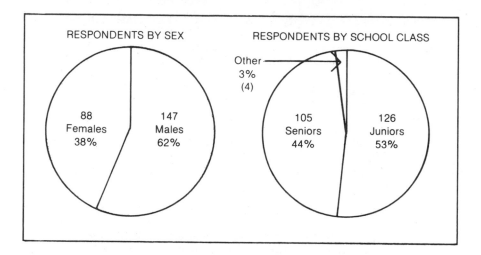

item asked students to name the single most difficult course
and the single most difficult text. This item served as a
check against the opinions given on the rating scales.

Robert Gunning's Fog index (2:2-15) was used to measure
reading difficulty. The index is a useful tool, but it should be
noted that it measures reading difficulty levels based only on
percentage of difficult words and on sentence length. It does not
measure the quality of writing. All readability formulas
concentrate on these two elements; but because of the wide
popularity of the Fog formula, it was selected as appropriate for
this study.

Managerial Accounting Text Is Difficult

Students view the Managerial Accounting text as the most
difficult and the Business Communication text as the easiest, as
shown in Figure 2. The weighted average is simply the

Figure 17-1   continued.

Dean Smith
Textbook - Course Relationships, January 15, 198-
Page 4

arithmetic total of responses weighted 1, 2, 3, 4, and 5 on the intensity scale divided by the total number of students who were taking or had taken the course using the appropriate textbook.

Figure 2.   Weighted opinions of text difficulty.

Course Number	Course Title	Weighted Average
301	Managerial Accounting	3.80
350	Macroeconomics	3.79
351	Microeconomics	3.78
310	Operations Management I	3.54
403	Business Law	3.44
311	Operations Management II	3.29
306	Business Finance	3.17
280	Financial Accounting	3.07
304	Organizational Behavior	2.75
307	Marketing Management	2.64
302	Business Communication	2.36

The Managerial Accounting text and the two economics texts do have about the same degree of difficulty as expressed by students. At the "easy" end of the scale are texts for Organizational Behavior, Marketing Management and Business Communication. Of interest is the observation that quantitative and highly theoretical course texts are considered difficult and the more "verbal" course texts are considered relatively easy.

To simplify the study, a decision was made to measure the Fog Index difficulty of the two texts considered most difficult; the Operations Management II text, which fell in the middle of the distribution; and the two texts considered easiest. As shown in Figure 3 (see page 5), some relationship does appear between student opinion and the Fog Index of the books. The Fog Index is based on a sampling of 15 pages from each book drawn from a table of random numbers.

Figure 17-1   continued.

Dean Smith
Textbook - Course Relationships, January 15, 198-
Page 5

Figure 3.   Fog Index levels of texts.

Course Number*	Course Title	Fog
301	Managerial Accounting	13.7
350	Macroeconomics	16.6
311	Operations Mgmt.	12.6
307	Marketing Mgmt.	13.4
302	Business Communication	12.6

* Courses are listed in order of difficulty as perceived by
  students, as shown in Figure 2.

Despite the slight relationship that seems to exist, it appears
that student opinion of text difficulty may be influenced by
something other than the readability difficulty as measured by
the Fog Index.

When asked to name the single most difficult text, students
responded with rankings similar to the weighted rankings. In
terms of percentage of students selecting a text as the single
most difficult, texts for Macroeconomics, Managerial
Accounting, and Microeconomics ranked first, second, and
third, respectively. Texts for the behavior, marketing, and
communication courses ranked ninth, tenth, and eleventh
among the eleven courses.

Interest Is Related to Course Difficulty

To obtain a clearer picture of the relationships that might exist
among student-perceived course difficulty, student-perceived
text difficulty, student course interest, and the Fog Index, a
composite table was developed. As shown in the previous
sections, Macroeconomics and Managerial Accounting courses
and texts were perceived as most difficult by students.
Additionally, the texts for the courses were ranked as most
difficult by the Fog Index. However, when asked to rank courses
in order of interest, students selected those with the most

Figure 17-1   continued.

444

Dean Smith
Textbook - Course Relationships, January 15, 198-
Page 6

difficult books and course requirements as the least interesting,
as shown in Figure 4.

Figure 4. Composite Rankings of Course and Texts*

Course Number and Title	Fog Index Rank	Perceived Text Rank	Perceived Course Rank	Course Interest Rank
350--Macro-economics	1	2	2	5
301--Managerial Accounting	2	1	1	4
307--Marketing Mgmt.	3	4	5	1
311--Operations Mgmt.	4	3	3	3
302--Business Communication	5	5	4	2

* These rankings are restricted to the five courses for which the
Fog Index was applied to the text. Overall, the Business Law
course ranked first in interest, fifth in perceived text difficulty,
sixth in Fog difficulty, and fourth in course difficulty.

On the other hand, the courses indicated as "high interest"
tended to rank low on text and course difficulty scales.

CONCLUSIONS

An inverse relationship appears to exist between course and
text difficulties, as perceived by students, and course interest.

Figure 17-1 continued.

A positive relationship appears to exist between easy-to-read texts and measured Fog indices. These measures also tend to show an effect on student interest in courses. High course interest might be related to "easy" teaching-learning materials; but an equally strong hypothesis might be that when students have a strong interest in a course, they perceive the course as easier and the textbook as less difficult. Other than the high Fog of 16.6 for the macroeconomics text, not much difference really exists among the other four texts in terms of Fog measurements.

As mentioned earlier, the Fog does not measure writing quality. A well written text with a high Fog Index might be easier to read than a poorly written text with a low Fog. And both might be easy to read if student interest is high in the subject.

The major hypothesis that core course difficulty as perceived by students is directly affected by the reading difficulty of textbooks cannot be accepted or rejected on the basis of the findings of this study. A positive relationship does appear, but other factors such as interest are involved. The study does, however, suggest recommendations for further investigation.

RECOMMENDATIONS

Using this study or a similar one as a basis, the following areas seem desirable for further research:

1. How do student evaluations of their teachers affect student perceptions of course and text difficulty?

2. How do such elements as students' career plans and teaching performance affect course interest and course or textbook difficulty as perceived by students?

Figure 17-1 continued.

Interest Is Related to Course Difficulty   5

Conclusions   6

Recommendations   7

e. The purpose and the method of research are covered in far greater detail on page 2 than in the introductory summary on page 1.

f. The sentence in the middle of the page, "Of the 235 respondents. . . ," introduces Figure 1 in proper style, as you'll recall from the introduction of Figures in Chapter 14.

Page 3

a. Figure 1 at the top of page 3 is too large to be placed immediately following its introduction on page 2. Thus, the writer continued to write to the bottom of page 2 and to place the figure on page 3. This placement is consistent with the guiding rule that figures should be placed as near as possible *following* their introduction in the narrative, or written, part of the report.

b. The notation of (2:2–15) is a footnote form that refers to item 2, pages 2–15, in the bibliography. Optional forms of footnotes as well as bibliography forms are covered in detail in Chapter 18.

c. The heading "Managerial Accounting Text Is Difficult" is a talking heading. It reveals something about the analysis, and this technique is advocated by most report-writing authorities. Notice also that the sentence following the heading is repetitive of the heading. Thus, the report could stand by itself without the use of headings.

Page 4

a. Figure 2 is arranged properly with a descriptive title and captions for each of the three columns. Notice that the courses are arranged in a sequence of most difficult to least difficult textbook.

b. The discussion of information in Figure 2 talks about broad generalizations. The paragraph immediately following the table is inductively organized to lead the reader to the conclusion that "quantitative and highly theoretical course texts are considered difficult and the more 'verbal' course texts are considered relatively easy."

c. In the last paragraph, the opening phrase "To simplify the study" provides transition from the discussion of Figure 2 to the introduction of Figure 3.

Page 5

a. To be consistent with the content of Figure 2, the writer has listed the courses in Figure 3 in the same order they were listed previously. Using this technique, the writer is able to show some relationship between student opinion of course difficulty and the Fog Index levels of texts used in those courses. At the same time, the Fog Index figures are not consistent in terms of course difficulty.

b. The paragraph at the bottom of the page begins a discussion of student interest in the various courses. Notice how the opening phrase in the paragraph "To obtain a clearer picture of the relationships" leads the reader easily into the discussion by providing effective transition to the new topic.

Page 6

a. The sentence introducing Figure 4 precedes the figure and includes a conclusion about the analysis of the figure data.

b. As in Figure 3, Figure 4 contains a footnote for clarification. An asterisk (*) is placed following the title and preceding the footnote. Notice that the footnotes for both Figures 3 and 4 are followed by quadruple spacing to separate the end of the figure from the report discussion that follows (the text). An alternative to this extra spacing would have been to enclose the figures, and their footnotes, in a ruled "box" to separate them from the text.

c. The last sentence before the heading "Conclusions" effectively summarizes the analysis of the data in Figure 4.

d. "Conclusions" is centered and in all capital letters, thus making it a major heading parallel to the first major heading on page 2.

Page 7

a. The discussion under "Conclusions" effectively brings together several things found in the research. These same ideas were reported in the opening of the report on page 1.

b. The last sentence before the heading "Recommendations" provides the transition between the conclusions and recommendations sections.

c. Recommendations are not always appropriate for reports. In this case, however, the writers felt two recommendations for further study warranted inclusion.

Perhaps a unique feature of research reports is the apparent repetition that occurs in their final development:

1. The transmittal message usually includes a brief summary of the research including the statement of the purpose, something about the method of research, and highlights of the findings or the conclusions.

2. The body of the report contains detailed descriptions of the research, greatly expanded over the items in the transmittal. Actually, the transmittal can be prepared only after the body is complete.

3. Finally, the concluding part of the body brings together in generalized terms the details of the findings.

The reader is exposed three times to the results of the research and is therefore able to read the summary, scan the body, and concentrate on the conclusions in whatever order he or she finds convenient. Because it is an accepted form of learning, repetition is appropriate.

LETTER REPORTS

When a report is to go outside the organization, the memorandum form would be inappropriate; therefore, such reports are designed either as complete formal reports or as letter reports. The letter report is ordinarily used when the report is short—about one to five pages in length. It is written on letterhead paper, makes use of headings as organizational devices, and may include graphic or tabular figures. Essentially, the letter report is a short report dressed as a letter.

What determines whether a short report should be a letter or a memo?

A general plan for a letter report includes the following parts:

1. Use an inside address, a salutation, and a subject line following the salutation:

Ms. Martha Weston
Word Processing Supervisor
ABC Company
Post Office Box 7190
Ventura, CA 93888

Dear Ms. Weston

Performance of the CPT Equipment

Is the subject line also the report title?

2. Use the opening paragraph as a transmittal and introduction to the report:

I'm pleased to tell you about our experience with the CPT Word Processor as you requested recently. We are pleased with its performance and versatility. . . .

3. Build the body of the report around key factors, using whatever headings would assist in your organization and in the reader's understanding. This portion of the report should be as objective as you can make it.

4. Close the letter report with a forward-looking, friendly statement.

A SAMPLE LETTER REPORT

Assume you have been requested by another firm to comment on the performance and reliability of, and your general satisfaction with, your CPT word processor which you have used in your department for about 18 months. The CPT company suggested to the potential buyer that you used the equipment and might be a good reference.

As you review the request, some thoughts quickly come to mind. Although the word processor can interface with computers, you use yours solely for word processing and not for computer functions — in the jargon, this is called a *dedicated* word processor. Much of the success you have had with the CPT you credit to the thorough indoctrination given your staff *before* the equipment was used operationally. You began operating with two word-processing machines and have since increased to four. The additional word processors were added as replacements for electric typewriters. However, you still have a couple of typewriters available for light typing jobs. In addition, your library of software programs has grown as you learned more about the equipment and its application to a variety of office needs.

The letter report you have prepared is shown in Figure 17-2. It is a short report because it is essentially based on research of an informal nature. You were given the problem of reporting on your experience with equipment, so you recalled the necessary information, drew the conclusion that you were satisfied with equipment, and then prepared the report.

PROPOSALS

Proposals are written documents designed to obtain business and are a critical part of many businesses. The federal government, for example, *requires* proposals as a part of its procurement process for the acquisition of services and supplies. College and university teachers and administrators prepare a constant flow of proposals to obtain research funding and other types of monetary grants.

Some proposals, particularly those for major projects such as the manufacture of military equipment for the government, may be hundreds of pages in length and call for extreme formality. In these cases, a proposal team may work together over long time periods in the development of the proposal. The greatest number of proposals, however, consist of short, informal presentations. But in either case, the proposal follows the same general plan related to the problem-solving process. The easiest way to understand the nature of a proposal is to picture yourself as having something to offer that is helpful to someone else. In effect, you must write a sales message in a logical, objective way without applying the persuasive and emotional techniques used in persuasive letter writing.

Your first step is to analyze the problem to determine how you can help solve it by providing your service or product. Next you attempt to put together a plan about how your product or service will solve the problem. If such things as materials or

June 15, 198-

Ms. Martha Weston
Word Processing Supervisor
ABC Company
Post Office Box 7190
Ventura, CA 93888

Dear Ms. Weston

Performance of the CPT Equipment

I'm pleased to tell you about our experience with the CPT Word
Processor as you requested recently. We are pleased with its
performance and versatility. I assume you have looked at
several machines and have narrowed down your choices. Here
are my observations.

An approach to adopting word processors

Eighteen months ago we adopted CPT equipment on a limited
scale with the idea in mind that we could phase out our reliance
on electric typewriters a little at a time as we became familiar
with the potential of word processing. We began with two work
stations and now have four. The stations are actually in pairs
so each pair can share a common printer. The Rotary VIII
printer with a speed of 45 characters a second can easily handle
two input stations.

We use the equipment as dedicated word processors, although
we do have the ability to link up with our computer installation.

The step-at-a-time development of our word-processing center
has, we think, saved us money and training time, and has
lessened the confusion that exists about buying software
packages.

Performance

In terms of performance, the CPT equipment is excellent. We
have not experienced mechanical problems, and our service
contract and warranty have covered all maintenance costs.

We have software packages that check spelling and signal when
a typo occurs. Our routine letters are prepared from disc-stored
masters. Using both printers, we recently prepared 1200
individually typed form letter mailings in under four hours. We
have no complaints about our preparation of executive reports.

Figure 17-2 Letter report (continued on next page).

Versatility

When we installed our equipment as dedicated word processors, we did not anticipate its application to different areas of our business. We now process all customer billing on an after-hours basis through a specially designed program. All customer and supplier address lists are maintained in our department, and we can update them regularly as changes occur.

General Satisfaction

As you can tell, we are satisfied with our CPT installation. In eighteen months we've learned a lot, and we learn more every day. The equipment can do far more than we have asked it to do, I'm sure.

Although this is a brief and generalized commentary on our use of CPT, I hope it will be of help to you in making your selection. Please call on me again if you'd like; and if you'd like to visit our office, please let me know.

Sincerely

Martin Sloan
Director, Word Processing

Figure 17-2 continued.

Dear _____

As a follow up to our discussion of the need for training in the area of oral and interpersonal communication for your supervisory and middle-management personnel, I am pleased to present the following proposal.

The Problem

Management has perceived a need for improved communication performance on the part of supervisory and middle-management personnel to strengthen relationships between them and their subordinates.

A Proposed Course of Instruction

Based on our experience, the following broad concept should be effective in producing better understanding and improved performance:

Teaching-learning Method. The acquisition of interpersonal skills results from an activity-oriented training program in which students have an opportunity to apply theory through role playing, case discussion, and critical feedback.

In this approach, the instructor is a learning facilitator rather than a lecturer. Frequent use of our video playback accompanied by instructor and group feedback reinforces learning.

Content. The following topics constitute the content core of the program:

1. Perception and self-concept
2. A positive communication climate
3. Sending skills
4. Receiving skills
5. Nonverbal skills
6. Reducing communication barriers
7. Resolving conflict
8. Interviewing
9. Small-group communication
10. Power and persuasion

Learning Materials. Because students seem to feel more comfortable when they have a textbook to guide them, we use the Verderber book, Interact. Additionally, case-problem handouts are provided for role playing and discussion.

Figure 17-3 Short proposal (continued on next page).

Length of Course. The course consists of twelve 2-hour sessions over a six-week period.

Number of Participants. Because of the activity orientation of the program, a maximum of 12 students (participants) is desirable.

Cost

All teaching-learning materials will be provided by us and include textbooks, handouts, video camera and playback equipment. Based on a 12-session, 12-participant program, the total cost is $1,800. When two courses are offered on the same days, the total cost is $3,300.

Should you like to discuss implementation of the program, I will be pleased to meet with you at your convenience.

Sincerely

R. M. McNitt
R. M. McNitt

Enclosures: Biographical sketches of instructional staff.

Figure 17-3 continued.

equipment are critical to your proposal, you must present them. If people or services are critical, the reader will want to know exactly who the people are, their qualifications, and how a service will be provided. Finally, of course, the potential buyer of goods or services will want to know the cost. Thus, the cost typically is presented only after the other items are presented. When the proposal is extremely long, a final summary is appropriate.

The format of a proposal will be a short memorandum report when the proposal travels within the organization, a letter report when it is short and travels outside the organization, and a formal report when it is long, whether it travels outside the organization or remains within it.

A variety of headings may assist in proposal preparation, and you have these general ones to select from:

Problem

Purpose

Scope

Method or Procedures

Materials and/or equipment

Personnel

Follow up or evaluation

Cost or budget

Summary

Some proposals will include all and some short ones (such as the letter proposal from a consulting firm, as shown in Figure 17-3) may include only a few.

SUMMARY

Short reports written in memorandum format are distinguishable from routine memorandums by their research-based nature. In this respect, short reports should contain the elements of the research process, should be objective, and should reflect the organizational qualities of what we have called formal reports. As a form of short reports, the letter report takes its label from its letter format used for short reports going outside the organization.

Because these reports are based on research, they lend themselves to the report-writing techniques of the use of headings, graphic and tabular support, and objective writing. At the same time, when the reports are used within the organization, they can reflect the teamwork aspects of groups through the use of informal, personal language—a style that we should minimize in the formal report (which we examine next in Chapter 18).

EXERCISES

Review Questions

1. What differences exist in the format of short reports in memorandum form and letter reports? What is the reason for these differences?

2. What is the difference between memorandums and short reports written in memorandum form?

3. Who has the responsibility of deciding whether a report should be prepared as a short report or as a long, formal report? What criteria help in this decision making?

4. How does the heading on a memorandum do the work of a title page in a formal report?

5. Is the sample short report in this chapter organized in inductive or deductive fashion?

6. Why is "Managerial Accounting Text Is Difficult" a talking heading?

7. If reports should stand by themselves without the use of headings, what implication does this rule have for the first sentence following the heading?

8. What is your understanding of *transition* as a composition technique as practiced in the sample short report in this chapter?

9. Why do reports seem repetitious?

10. What factors might cause a report going outside the business to be written as a letter report rather than a formal report?

Cases

A. The Food Service Case

Preptech University is located in a community of 60,000 and has an enrollment of 8,500 students. As a private school with relatively high tuition, Preptech enrolls many students from upper-level income groups. At the same time, about 60 percent of the students receive some form of financial aid in the form of government loans, work-study funds, and university grants. Of the 8,500 students, about 6,000 live in campus dormitories, fraternities and sororities, and nearby off-campus apartments. The remainder are commuters living within about 25 miles of the campus.

The University Food Service operates a cafeteria, a deli shop, and a restaurant with a combined capability of serving about 3,000 people at each of the three daily meals. Meals at fraternities and sororities accommodate about 1,200 students. For those living in dormitories, the university has three board-and-room plans and a room-only plan. The room-only plan is $180 a month, and monthly board-and-room plans are as follows:

A. Room with 3 cafeteria meals daily Monday–Friday: $360

B. Room with a cafeteria meal ticket worth $100 monthly: $280

C. Room with one meal daily—lunch or dinner, Monday–Friday: $260

During the past four school terms (semesters), the number of people selecting the plans has been as follows:

	Room Only	Plan A	Plan B	Plan C
This Term:	685	285	700	1280
Last Term:	520	405	770	1140
A Year Ago:	450	560	840	960
1½ Years Ago:	385	836	950	880

The University Food Service manager, Carla Perkins, is concerned about the decline in use of campus food facilities and has been pressured from higher university administrators to do something about the problem. Overall, the total university enrollment has remained stable in the neighborhood of 8,500 during the four terms.

Although off-campus eating facilities have been around for a number of years, two years ago a MacDonald's, a Taco Bell, a Joe's Pizza Parlor, and a full-service restaurant (the University Club) opened within a short walk of the campus.

Ms. Perkins asks your business communication instructor if a group from your class can assist her by making a study of student opinion about the university food services compared with the off-campus eating facilities. The university will pay $1,200 for the study. Because your class is organized in four-person teams, your instructor decides that the teams should compete for the job by submitting proposals. Assume that your team has submitted a proposal and received the job.

Your study plan is to determine the cost of meals for board-and-room plans A, B, and C and the cost of average meals in the four new eating facilities. Additionally, you then plan to conduct a survey of student opinion using a rating scale for the eating facilities. You will sample about 20 percent of the student body during meal hours in the various eating facilities. The rating scale will make use of a 5-point scale similar to the 6-point scale illustrated in Chapter 13. Your team has decided to obtain student opinion about these items:

Cost of meals

Convenience

Variety

Food Quality

Atmosphere

After you have completed your research, you come up with some useful facts and attitudes.

1.   The average cost of meals in the off-campus establishments:

	Breakfast	Lunch	Dinner
MacDonald's	$1.65	$2.20	$2.30
Taco Bell	None	2.10	2.45
Joe's Pizza	None	2.50	3.45
University Club	$2.80	3.75	6.00

2.   Your rating scale was tested for clarity in class and was refined to look something like the following for the item of cost:

For each of the eating facilities, circle the appropriate number to indicate how you feel about the cost of food for each facility:

	Low Cost		Average Cost		High Cost
Campus	5	4	3	2	1
MacDonald's	5	4	3	2	1
Taco Bell	5	4	3	2	1
Joe's Pizza	5	4	3	2	1
University Club	5	4	3	2	1

For the measures of convenience, variety, food quality and atmosphere, you designed a similar scale—so that, there too, the most favorable rating would be a 5.

After you had administered the rating scale to 2,050 students, you felt you had a fair sample; so you put the ratings of each rating scale in the computer which totaled the results and divided the total by 2,050 to obtain a weighted index for each quality, with 5.0 being the most favorable rating.

Here are the results:

	Campus	MacDonald's	Taco	Joe's	Univ. Club
Cost	2.1	4.2	3.8	3.0	1.7
Convenience	4.3	3.8	3.8	2.9	2.5
Variety	3.3	2.5	2.7	1.7	4.2
Food Quality	2.7	2.4	2.4	2.8	4.5
Atmosphere	1.8	1.3	1.4	3.8	4.8

3.   The following facts about the campus eating facilities undoubtedly affected the attitudes of the students you polled: (a) The delicatessen section of the campus eating facilities is open on weekends. (b) None of the campus facilities is open after 7:00 P.M. on any day. (c) All the campus facilities are painted a cream color with little trim. (d) They are also brightly lighted, and the furniture is primarily metal tables and chairs.

Your final short report will have a copy of your rating scale as an appendix. You should complete any of the following items as assigned by your instructor:

1.   Your proposal that got you the job.

2.   The rating scale.

3.   The short report.

In addition to the information provided in item 3, you may make any assumptions you find necessary to complete the tasks.

B. The Foremost Savings & Loan Case

As assistant vice president of the Foremost Savings and Loan Association, you are part of a team that is concerned with disposing of real estate that may come into possession of the association through foreclosure, purchase, or trades. One property owned is at 4312 Main Street, a vacant corner lot. Your appraisers have determined that the corner property has a best-use value (a term used to describe the most effective economic use of the land) to the association as the location for a restaurant. Your job is to survey the people in the community to determine their dining-out habits to decide whether an effort should be made to interest a fast-food chain, an enclosed sit-down restaurant chain, or a firm specializing in combination indoor-outdoor restaurants in the location. You have conducted a survey of families living in the area, of workers in nearby stores and other firms, and of passersby. The survey included a total of 400 people, and you feel confident that the sample is representative of potential users of a dining or eating facility in the area. Prepare a memorandum report addressed to your boss, G. J. Jenks, vice president of real estate. Here are the results of your survey:

1. What kind of prepared-food service should be located at 4312 Main Street? Enclosed sit-down restaurant 70; Restaurant with indoor and outdoor seating 165; Fast-food service with indoor and outdoor seating 165.

2. On the average, how often do you eat out each week?
52   1 or 0 times   112   2 or 3 times
212   4 to 7 times   24   8 or more times

3. What meal would you most often have outside the home?
96 Breakfast   168 Lunch   136 Dinner

4. When you eat out, how much per person would you usually spend?
Breakfast: Under \$1 34; \$1-2.50 242; Over \$2.50 124.
Lunch: Under \$2 48; \$2-3 198; \$3-4 147; Over \$4 7.
Dinner: Under \$4 75; \$4-6 185; Over \$6 140.

C. The Noble Oil Case

As an outside consultant in communications for the Noble Oil Corporation, you have just completed administering a reading-improvement program for sixty middle-management officials of the firm. The officials taking the experimental program used the Craig Controlled Reader, which flashes written material on a small screen at varying speeds. The officials spent fifteen hours each at the reading machines. The following distribution of reading rates is from a reading test given at the beginning of the program:

Rate in Words per Minute	Number of People Reading at the Rate Shown
Over 600	3
500–599	8
400–499	14
300–399	32
200–299	2
Under 200	1
	60

A comprehensive test on the material included in this beginning test revealed an average comprehension score of 65 percent for the group.

At the conclusion of the fifteen lessions, the participants were given similar final reading examinations and a comprehension test. The average comprehension score was 87 percent. Here is the distribution of reading rates on the final examination:

Rate in Words per Minute	Number of People Reading at the Rate Shown
900–1000	4
800–899	7
700–799	10
600–699	12
500–599	18
400–499	6
300–399	3
	60

Prepare a report giving your analysis of the success of the experimental program. Include evidence. Generally, a reading rate of 450 is considered good. The company had indicated that the program would be offered to each of the 700 supervisory and administrative personnel if the experimental program proved successful. Address the report to Ms. Jean Tobler, executive vice president.

D. The Grading System Case

As assistant dean in the College of Business Administration at Mideastern University, your tasks are many and varied. One of them is to analyze the grading practices of faculty by departments and to send a report to the department heads. You have just finished tallying the grades given last term by the faculty of the Department of Marketing.

Instructor Orange is a nationally known marketing authority and head of the department. Instructors Blue and White are senior faculty who have traditionally been quite popular with students. Instructors Red and Green are new faculty and in their first year of teaching at Mideastern after receiving their doctoral degrees. Instructor Black is a powerhouse personality who is in great demand for speech making and consulting. He, too, is popular with students and spends more than the appropriate amount of class time telling about his own exploits in the business world.

Course and Section	Instructor	Number of Final Grades by Letter				
		A	B	C	D	F
Principles of marketing (1)	Blue	7	3	10	2	0
(2)	Blue	11	0	7	0	0
(3)	Red	1	3	16	5	1
(4)	Green	3	6	10	6	3
(5)	Green	2	7	9	5	1
Advertising	White	3	6	7	0	0
Retailing	Red	2	6	6	4	0
Sales management	Black	5	5	6	0	0
Advanced advertising	White	4	8	5	0	0
Market research	Black	6	9	3	0	0
Market logistics	Orange	1	4	11	3	1

The Principles of Marketing course with its five sections is required as a prerequisite course for the other offerings in the department. The generally recommended distribution of grades in the university is A = 10 percent, B = 30 percent, C = 50 percent, and D and F together another 10 percent. This distribution is not official and no one knows where it came from, but for years It has been followed rather religiously by some faculty. Your own school policy in business is that instructors should be able to grade as they see fit. Theoretically, grades are assumed to be a little lower in basic courses required of all students, such as Principles of Marketing, and a little higher in the advanced courses.

You always send, as part of the report to each department head, a summary of the grade distribution for the entire school. For this same term, your total distribution for the entire school was

A = 225 grades
B = 346 grades
C = 781 grades
D = 125 grades
F = 23 grades

Prepare a report to send to Dr. Orange, the head of the department.

E. The Textbook Readability Case

Assume that you are the associate dean for academic affairs in your school. One of your concerns is for good textbook selection by faculty. Students complain frequently about books being unusually difficult, particularly for the subject matter involved. Using the Fog Index, you undertake a study to determine the readability levels of textbooks in selected business and economics courses. Choose six texts normally used in these areas and determine their average Fog Index. In the process of conducting your study, you should refer to some library references to establish that your selection of the Fog Index is appropriate. Here are some suggestions in addition to the discussion of the Fog Index in this text:

Flesch, Rudolf. *The Art of Readable Writing.* New York: Harper and Brothers, 1949.

Flesch, Rudolf. *How to Test Readability.* New York: Harper and Brothers, 1951.

Gunning, Robert. *The Technique of Clear Writing.* New York: McGraw-Hill Book Company, 1968.

The work of Rudolf Flesch was instrumental in the development of readability indexes, and he has been considered a leading authority in this area.

Although Flesch recommends about forty separate samples as necessary to determine the readability level of a book, you may plan on using only ten samples for this study. Your sampling method should be a random one in which, for example, you take a sample from every fiftieth page in a 500-page book, every sixtieth page in a 600-page book, and so on. Review the process of selecting such samples (systematic sampling) in Chapter 13.

When you have determined the Fog Index for each of the ten samples in a book, simply average the ten to determine the Fog level of the entire book. Use whatever tabular or graphic displays you think necessary in the report you will prepare to present to your immediate superior, Dean James K. Thederos.

PREPARING FORMAL REPORTS

Composition
Procedures for Writing
Techniques of Conviction
Techniques of Style
Special Parts
The Introduction
The Body
The Summary or Conclusion
Physical Presentation
Documentation
Typing
Report Critique
A Formal Report Checklist
Summary

Composition is easy if you have taken the preliminary steps carefully. Before you begin composition, you need confidence that (1) you understood the problem clearly, (2) your information came from the most appropriate sources, (3) you have properly interpreted your information, and (4) you have prepared an ideal outline.

At this stage, your attitude should be something like "I know I have the right answer to the problem. The report is actually done; all I have to do is begin expressing it in words. Then I can present it in written form." Apprehension about whether preliminary steps meet high standards will probably keep the composition from reaching high standards. Superlative writing techniques cannot overcome the effects of poor research. Above all else, an analytical report must contain a good answer that is properly supported. A well-written report that contains a bad answer may actually be more harmful than a poorly written report that contains a bad answer.

Could good writing be a liability?

Confident that a report contains a good answer, you can approach the final steps (composition and presentation) with enthusiasm.

COMPOSITION

By the composition stage, the thinking has been done. Ideas to be included have already been identified. Because the decisions have been made already, your mind is free to concentrate on the problem of expressing ideas. Success is now dependent on writing procedures and techniques.

Procedures for Writing

Understandably, a procedure that works well for one person may not work so well for another; but consider the following suggestions:

How does outlining simplify composition?

1. *Begin writing only after you have solved the problem satisfactorily and have prepared a good outline.* Any worries about the validity of points made or about the order in which to make them will interfere with expression. On the other hand, confidence about the validity and sequence of points generates a positive attitude that will simplify expression.

2. *Select a good writing environment.* Naturally, a suitable environment for one person may be completely unsuitable for another; but each writer can, through experience, identify conditions that work best for him or for her. Such factors as room decor, noise level, presence or absence of music, time of day, possibility of interruptions, etc., do influence creativity. Each writer should find a good place and time for composition and try to avoid unnecessary environmental changes.

3. *Get started early.* The date for submission is set by the person who assigns a report. The date for completion should be set by the writer. If the self-imposed completion date is a few days before the submission date, you can relax. If some unforeseen problem causes a delay, you can still submit the report on schedule. If you need additional time for writing or rewriting, the time is available. Not only does a late start ensure a late finish, it may result in a substandard report. By getting started early, you can possibly avoid sacrificing quality for time.

Does the pressure of starting late create quality problems?

4. *Begin at an easy section.* In writing, as in other activities, the beginning is often difficult. If you perceive all points of the outline to be of about equal difficulty, you may as well begin with the introduction and proceed through to the conclusion. But if any section appears to be especially easy, writing it first will have advantages: (1) Looking back over the first few minutes' effort, you will see genuine evidence of progress. (2) Early success generates a positive attitude that assists in bringing more success. (3) The momentum you achieve in an easy section often carries over into the composition of a difficult section. (4) Chances for success on the most difficult section are improved if you do it last: because all other sections are now considered in the bag, concentration may be easier on the last section; because your enthusiasm for the task may be increased; and because toward the end of a composition, inhibitions may be easier to overcome. For example, in the early sections you may feel inhibited by the numerous ways in which ideas can be expressed. You can waste time considering and reconsidering alternatives. In the later sections, you will have overcome these inhibitions.

Why begin writing with an easy section?

5. *Set aside relatively long blocks of uninterrupted writing time.* For most writers, numerous half-hour periods for composing a long report would be unsatisfactory. After an interruption, you can consume too much time getting back your train of thought. For each individual, experience will soon demonstrate the most satisfactory block of writing time (perhaps two, three, four, or even five hours).

6. *Write rapidly with the intention of rewriting where necessary.* Mary and Sheila have different approaches. Before Mary makes a decision, she likes to consider various possibilities. Because she has high standards, she is willing to spend considerable time thinking about an idea before choosing one of the many possible ways of expressing it. She likes efficiency. "Why not be right the first time," she says, "and avoid any necessity of writing anything a second time?" Overall, Mary sees composition as an unpleasant, time-consuming task. Even after pondering the various ways of expressing each idea, she worries that she may have chosen a bad way after all. After taking time to consider various ways, she frequently chooses the first way and condemns herself for having wasted so much time. To Mary, the unpleasant part of composition is not typing or writing a sentence; rather, it is those moments or minutes between her sentences. They are frustrating.

Sheila wastes little time between sentences. Like Mary, Sheila likes efficiency, too; but, instead of trying to achieve perfection in one step, Sheila is willing to take two steps: write rapidly and rewrite portions later. Writing rapidly gives her a positive feeling of progress. Moving almost constantly, she keeps her mind on the subject; whereas Mary's long pauses between sentences are an invitation to think about other problems. By the time Sheila has written one sentence, another closely related sentence occurs to her. By moving right on to record the next sentence quickly, she achieves coherence easily.

What advantages do rapid writers have?

Sheila says "If I find myself stopping and wasting time, I just pretend that my report is the answer to an essay question on a final examination. I know I have no time to squander; it's either get going or fail."

Sheila finishes her draft in far less time than Mary. When Sheila has written her last paragraph, she has a sense of accomplishment. All her ideas are now on paper; the hard part is over. Everything that remains to be done will result in improvement, and she can work with enthusiasm on remaining steps.

7. *Skip difficult passages and return to them later.* In her rapid writing, Sheila may encounter a paragraph in which she has some doubts about the idea to be included or about the way to express it. She ponders for a short time, but the problem is not resolved. Instead of taking time to consider and reconsider (perhaps fruitlessly), she skips a few lines on the page and continues to compose the remaining paragraphs in the section. After completing the entire report, she returns to the skipped portions. Usually, she is very gratified to discover that the problem is now resolved. What seemed difficult earlier now seems easy, and she fills in the blank space. Because the main burden of the entire report has been lifted, and perhaps because a lapse of time has enabled her to see the problem in a new perspective, filling in all blank spaces is not a time-consuming task. She has saved all the wheel-spinning time that would have been spent if she had sat and waited for inspiration to solve the problem before moving on.

8. *Put the report aside for a day or two.* Having done the research, interpreted, outlined, and written the report, you can become so involved that you overlook obvious weaknesses. Forgetting about the report for a day or two can be very beneficial. Then, you can review the report almost as objectively as another person. If you find weaknesses, you can remove them.

Does a late start prohibit this step?

9. *Review for possible improvement.* A review should determine if the main ideas are sufficiently supported and effectively expressed. The two problems *could* be solved by *one* review; but separate reviews for each question permit greater concentration and thus better answers.

The first review may reveal that occasionally a little more detail is needed before the point becomes convincing. Perhaps another reference to research or some more facts and figures can be inserted. Some paragraphs may have been overwritten; they include too much detail. Marking through a few lines that have been carefully written may be objectionable; but if doing so results in improvement, the lines should be deleted.

The second review will reveal any errors in style, grammar, spelling, or punctuation. Whereas the first draft was primarily designed to get ideas on paper, the purpose now is to improve upon the way the ideas are expressed. Because total concentration is directed toward this effort (whether a thought should have been included and how well it has been supported are no longer questioned), some improvements can be made.

Why review twice?

This second review can also be a rewarding experience. When reading a certain passage, you may recall the experience of composing it. At first you may have had some apprehension about the best way to express an idea. Instead of wasting time considering various ways, you selected the first possibility and moved on quickly. Now, the sentence expresses the idea with sufficient clarity; its style and grammar are perfectly acceptable. As Sheila (preceding illustration) can say about many sentences as she reviews her own work: "This sentence is fine. Glad I didn't waste a half hour trying to improve it."

10. *Rewrite where necessary.* Of the two procedures presented earlier, Mary preferred to write to perfection in one step. Sheila preferred to write rapidly with complete willingness to rewrite where necessary. Mary's approach is less desirable because it is more likely to waste time and because it forces you to engage in too many mental activities at once. When you are simultaneously concerned with which thoughts to include, how you should support them, stylistic matters, grammar, spelling, and punctuation, you have only a limited chance of reaching high levels of performance on any of these standards.

The net result is that Mary may actually need do more rewriting than Sheila. Slow, careful writing does not necessarily imply better writing any more than slow, careful reading implies better comprehension. Typical speed-reading programs do not achieve speed at the expense of comprehension. Rather, the faster the reading the greater the comprehension. Similarly, reports that are written rapidly may actually need less rewriting than reports that are written slowly. Because rapid composition reduces the time between ideas, their relationships may be all the more vivid in your mind; and you can, in turn, make them more vivid to the reader.

These procedures do not ensure report-writing success, but completely ignoring them can mean failure. Typically, those who see themselves as poor writers, and those who say they do not like to write, suffer from failure to proceed in the right way. They make such mistakes as trying to write before they have completely solved a problem, getting started too late, writing a difficult section first, using time periods that are too short, and trying to write to perfection in one step. These problems are not encoding problems; they are procedural problems. Encoding problems can be at least partially avoided if certain conviction techniques are employed.

What are some of the typical habits of poor writers?

Techniques of Conviction

Of all qualities that a report should possess, none is more important than *conviction*. If a report is convincing, the reader will accept it as valid and reliable. From the first step to the last, all efforts are directed toward production of a report that contains good ideas that are presented convincingly. If the report is analytical, the person who assigned it wants to know *what the answer is* and *how the writer knows* what the answer is. By providing details, a writer achieves conviction.

How do we achieve conviction?

At the writing stage, conviction is easier to achieve if care has been exercised in gathering and interpreting information at earlier stages (see Chapter 13). Some further suggestions that will help you achieve conviction:

1. *Avoid emotional terms.* Instead of writing "Sales increased *tremendously,*" "The increase was *fantastic,*" or "The *amazing* increase was attributed to . . . ," simply state the percentage of increase. By so doing, you are neither passing judgment nor trying to make the reader pass judgment. You should be content with stating what the facts *are;* labeling them as good or bad is unnecessary and unwise. Emotional terms introduce the possibility of bias in the research as well as bias in the reporting.

2. *Identify assumptions.* An *assumption* is a fact or condition that is taken for granted. For example, one group is exposed to a training program at ten o'clock; another, at two o'clock. If an investigator *assumes* that fatigue caused by the day's prior activities is not a factor for the two o'clock group, the assumption should be called to the reader's attention. Satisfied with the explanation behind the assumption, the reader is more likely to be convinced that differences are unrelated to fatigue.

3. *Label opinions.* Generally, facts are strongly preferred over opinions. Sometimes, however, opinions add conviction. The opinions of specialists may be available when facts gleaned from research are not available. When presenting opinions, elevate their respectability by revealing the background of the person presenting the opinion. For example, "In the opinion of our attorney, *who has prosecuted almost 300 such cases*. . . ." An opinion from a person with that experience has a ring of authenticity.

Why identify assumptions and opinions?

In an effort to be factual, some writers make the mistake of trying to omit opinions entirely. An opinion (appropriately labeled as such) can be very beneficial. Depending on a report writer's record of credibility, a reader may actually appreciate a writer's statement of opinion. After all, the writer has done considerable research and thinking on the subject and may be well qualified to state an opinion. Sometimes, data are such that no solid conclusion can be drawn, or a variety of explanations could exist. A writer can sometimes stimulate beneficial thinking or open new areas of research by making such statements as "These facts introduce three possibilities," or "One possible explanation is . . . ; another is. . . ."

4. *Use documentation.* By using footnotes and bibliographies, you reveal their relationship to the subject matter of the report. You also imply "If you want to check on the facts being presented, here are the sources and page numbers."

Composition **469**

Techniques of Style

For a more thorough treatment of stylistic techniques, return to Chapters 4 and 5. Some more common problems peculiar to report writing are summarized here:

1. *Use concrete nouns.* Although abstract nouns are certainly useful at times, they should not be used frequently as sentence subjects. Notice the difference between these two sentences:

> Authorization for the study was received from President Jones.
> President Jones authorized the study.

The second sentence is more vivid because its subject is easier to visualize.

2. *Use active voice.* Although the passive voice is certainly useful at times, it should not be used unnecessarily. Because active voice is more vivid, a writer (or speaker) should try to stay principally in active voice and switch to the passive only when doing so serves a purpose. For example, "President Jones authorized the study" is probably best; but "The study was officially authorized" would be appropriate if the specific person who did the authorizing is not to be revealed. Likewise, "The project was authorized by President Jones" is appropriate if the writer wishes to place a little more emphasis on *project* than on *Jones.* (The subject normally is more emphatic than the object.)

When might passive voice be appropriate?

3. *Avoid personal pronouns.* "Avoid all pronouns" would be questionable advice. Suppose, for example, that a report is based on questionnaires returned by maintenance personnel. Notice effective use of the pronoun: "Thirteen mechanics expressed concern about safety. *They* reported. . . ." Such use of the pronoun is legitimate; it saves repetition of a word and serves as a coherence technique.

However, pronouns that refer to the reader or to the writer should be used very sparingly or not at all. When *I* is used, it serves as a sentence subject and thus risks placing more emphasis on the author than on the ideas being presented. When *you* is used, it may not be interpreted as intended. The person who authorized the report could wonder whether *you* is used to mean that person only or whether it includes *all* those who read the report. *You* is sometimes used to mean people in general or even the author. For example, "You can hardly extract meaning from the data collected" could mean "*Scarcely anyone* can extract meaning," "The *person who assigned the report* can hardly extract meaning," or "The *author of the report* has difficulty extracting meaning." "The data are difficult to interpret" would be an improvement.

Why is use of second person risky?

4. *Use tense consistently.* Consistency in tense does not mean choose a certain tense and do not deviate from it. Notice the legitimate use of three tenses:

> The policy *was established* last year, it *is* now *suffering* severe criticism, and it *will* be discussed thoroughly at the next board meeting.

**Why write about
the method of
research in past tense?**

The changes in tense are realistic and essential. However, *unnecessary* changes in tense are distracting and confusing. For example,

> Secretaries *said* the rules are too strict; stenographers *say* they are too lenient.

Seeing the change in tense, a reader may wonder whether it is accidental or whether secretaries have in fact *stopped* saying the rules are too strict and now agree with the stenographers.

One way to solve the problem of tense consistency is to decide whether the report is primarily about an *act* or about *results.* You have gone through the act of writing, and interviewees or questionnaire respondents have gone through the act of supplying information. These are past events. Therefore, the writing can be consistently in the past tense:

> Only one author disagre*ed.* . . .
>
> Almost 80 percent of the interviewees *said.* . . .

Having reported the information gathered, you can legitimately switch to the present tense in reporting the interpretation of data:

> "These figures clearly *show* that. . . ."

If you choose to write about *results,* the present tense will serve. The results of research are now before you, and are now being shared:

> Only one author disagree*s.* . . .
>
> Almost 80 percent of the interviewees *say.* . . .

Because the title page contains a date, readers of a present-tense report can see that information presented is applicable to the time of the writing; during the interval between the writing and the reading, results could change.

5. *Use transition sentences.* If you prepared your outline well, the major portions of your report have a common relationship to one another. If you write carefully, that relationship will be apparent. If you include transition sentences, the reader will expect a heading, and it will seem logical as the next point for consideration. Between major headings, transition sentences summarize the preceding section and lead a reader to expect the upcoming section.

**What purpose
do transition
sentences serve?**

> The costs are more than predicted, but the benefits are numerous.

This sentence helps the reader to put the preceding section (costs) into perspective and leads the reader to expect a discussion of the next section (benefits).

The following sentence does serve as a link between topics, but such a transition should be avoided:

> Now that costs have been discussed, the next topic is benefits.

This sentence states the obvious.

6. *Use a variety of coherence techniques.* Just as transition sentences bind portions of a report together, certain coherence techniques bind sentences together: repeating a word, using a pronoun, using a conjunction. If such devices are employed, each sentence seems to be joined smoothly to the next. The words and phrases here are particularly useful:

Is "The next topic is price." an effective transition into a discussion of price?

Time Connectors
finally
further
furthermore
initially
meanwhile
next
then
thereafter
while
at the same time

Contrast Connectors
although
despite
however
in contrast
nevertheless
on the other hand
on the contrary
yet

Similarity Connectors
for instance
for example
likewise
In the same way
just as
similarly

Cause-and-effect Connectors
but
conversely
as a result
because
consequently
hence
since
therefore
thus

These words and phrases keep you from making abrupt changes in thought. The lists could be extended.

7. *Use tabulation and enumeration.* Because the preceding lists are tabulated (arranged in columns), they are emphatic and reference to them is easy. Notice the difference when the same words are presented in sentence form: "as a result, at the same time, because, consequently, etc." In a similar manner, points can be made to appear more emphatic and reference to them can be simplified by assigning a number to each point. Notice the difference:

What advantages accrue from tabulation?

> Problems fall into three categories: men, materials, and money.
>
> Problems fall into three categories: (1) men, (2) materials, and (3) money.

Enumeration *and* tabulation makes the three categories all the more emphatic:

> Problems fall into three categories:
> 1. men
> 2. materials
> 3. money.

8.   *Use parallel construction.* A list or series of items should be presented in the same way grammatically. Otherwise, the inconsistency will be distracting and certain items will not appear to belong with the others. Failure to use parallel construction is especially obvious when items are enumerated or tabulated. Notice the effect of failure to use parallel construction:

> Problems fall into three categories: (1) men, (2) source and quality of materials, and (3) money.

The reader may wonder why some details about materials problems are given and none are given about the men and money problems. Of course, tabulation and enumeration are not recommended for presentation of ideas that are to be de-emphasized.

9.   *Define terms carefully.* Instead of merely telling what a word *is about, is related to,* or *has to do with,* a definition should tell what a word *means.* For example, the following definitions of the word *dictionary* would be unsatisfactory:

> You can look up words in it.
>
> It has to do with the words in the language.
>
> A dictionary is useful in determining correctness in word usage.

Making a true statement *about* something is different from telling what that something *is.*

Although a reader can be led to know the meaning of a new term through indirect means, formal definitions are easy to present (and to understand) if presented in three parts: term, family, and point of difference. Observe these parts:

> A dictionary (term) is a book (family) that contains an alphabetized list of all words in a language (point of difference).

Bacon (term) is meat (family) taken from the side of swine, smoked, and cured with certain spices (point of difference).

A platitude (term) is a statement (family) that is common knowledge (point of difference).

Define definition.

To make certain a word is understood completely, you may need to add further details or examples.

10. *Check for variety.* At the time of composition, primary attention should be directed toward presenting the right ideas and support. Later review may reveal that certain portions have a monotonous sameness in sentence length or construction. Changes are easy and well worth the effort.

The preceding stylistic techniques become habitual through experience. Without much awareness of them, you can simply use them while concentrating primarily on presenting and supporting ideas at the first-draft stage. Necessary improvements can be made later.

SPECIAL PARTS

Generally, stylistic techniques that apply in one section of a report can be applied in another section. Likewise, stylistic techniques that can be used in an informational report can be used in an analytical report. The difference between an informational report and an analytical report is not *style* but *content.* Informational reports contain an introduction, a body, and a summary. Analytical reports contain an introduction, a body, and a conclusion.

What is
the difference
between analytical
and informational reports?

The Introduction

In answering the question "What points should I include in the introduction?" you have but to ask "If I were the reader, what questions would I want answered before reading the body of the report?" Before beginning composition, answer the question "*Who* will the reader or readers be?" Will the report be read by one person (the one who assigned it), by a few, or by many? What are their backgrounds? The answers to such questions will help you determine the amount of detail you should present.

If your report is informational, your introduction needs to let the reader know (1) *what* the topic is, (2) *why* it is being reported upon, (3) *where* the information came from, (4) *how* the topic is divided into parts, (5) and the order in which the parts will be presented. It may also identify related topics that will *not* be included in the report.

What information
should be included
in any introduction?

If your report is analytical, your introduction needs to let the reader know (1) the problem the report purports to solve, (2) the circumstances that brought the problem about, (3) the research technique and sources of information, (4) the answer to the problem, (5) the major points that will be presented, and (6) the order in which the points will be presented.

These last six items do not necessarily have to be presented in any certain order, but putting points 5 and 6 at the end of the introduction serves as a good transition into the first division of the report. Normally, readers of analytical reports like to discover the answer right away; hence, the answer is usually included in the introduction. However, if the answer is expected to come as a disappointment to the reader, omitting it from the introduction has advantages. By withholding the answer until supporting reasons have been presented, you can improve your chances of getting the reader to study the report carefully and accept its conclusions.

In the introduction, not every reader will need to review the circumstances that brought the problem about. The person assigning the report may not need the review at all. On the other hand, other readers will benefit greatly from a review. A review should not be greatly detailed, and it should be worded in such a way as to recognize that the review is not necessary for all readers. Sentences like "For those who have not been working closely with the problem, ..." or "To review recent events that have led to this investigation, ..." should enable you to present helpful background information without being offensive to those who have no need for it.

Why is the
heading
Introduction
sometimes used?

Although reports need an introductory section, they really do not need a title that says *Introduction.* The first paragraph is *expected* to be introductory. Headings are helpful in finding information, but most readers can find an introductory paragraph without the heading *Introduction.* However, the heading is sometimes used as a matter of custom.

The Body

Likewise, reports do not need the heading *Body.* Without seeing the heading *Body,* readers will know that the body is the portion between the introduction and the summary or conclusion.

What subjects
are desirable for
major headings in the
body of analytical reports?

In analytical reports, the composition of each major division is simplified if each major heading represents one of the criteria used in reaching a conclusion. Before writing the paragraphs that appear under each major division, keep in mind that the purpose of this division is to present and support a conclusion (the support may come *before* the conclusion). Nothing more is needed, other than a transition sentence into the next major division.

In informational reports, conclusions are not included. By keeping your outline in view, you can tell when enough information has been presented to cover each major division.

The Summary or Conclusion

Because the headings *Introduction* and *Body* are not needed, their omission is recommended. However, the heading *Summary* or *Conclusion* is recommended so that readers who want to review (or turn immediately to) the final section, can find exactly where it begins.

In an informational report, the summary should include a condensation of the major points presented earlier. This emphasizes the main points and adds unity.

In an analytical report, the conclusion also adds unity. This section presents the overall conclusion and the supporting reasons for it (though not necessarily in this order). The conclusions drawn previously under each major heading represent supporting reasons. The reasons can be presented in paragraph form; or, for the sake of emphasis, they can be tabulated and enumerated.

What is meant by "adds unity"?

Sometimes the last major heading of an analytical report is *Conclusions and Recommendations.* Or, *Conclusions* is one heading and *Recommendations* is a separate heading. The heading *Recommendations* is unnecessary when implementation is taken for granted.

By the time you write the last paragraph, you should feel confident that the report meets high standards. If effective, a report will meet these high standards:

1. *Content:* the report must convey the necessary ideas convincingly.

2. *Organization:* the report must have a good outline.

3. *Style:* the report must employ language effectively and convey ideas clearly.

4. *Mechanics:* the report must effectively present the ideas on paper.

PHYSICAL PRESENTATION

After you have written and revised a report, your remaining tasks are mechanical—physically presenting ideas on typewritten or printed pages. Correct any spelling and punctuation errors before you begin typing. Check carefully afterward, too. These errors can take attention away from your ideas. They can cause a reader to get the wrong message, they can raise questions about your pride of workmanship, and they can reduce a reader's confidence in your findings and conclusions.

During the composition process, you will have employed documentation as a means of presenting and supporting ideas. And you will have made decisions about whether certain ideas should be best presented in nonverbal forms (charts, graphs, etc.). During the typing process, documentation and nonverbal devices present special problems.

Documentation

In footnotes and bibliographies, the key word is consistency. Most readers are familiar with a variety of styles for presenting footnotes and bibliographies; but although they may have a preference, they probably won't resent any form that is used consistently. Therefore, you should look on the following suggestions as guides rather than as an "only way." Whether you follow a particular part of a documented reference with a period or a comma really doesn't matter. What does matter is that succeeding items of the same type follow the same format.

Writing and research carry with them the obligation to give credit where credit is due. Documenting your sources not only helps your reader understand more about your reporting, but it also protects you in three ways:

1. It protects against plagiarism, which is taking things from others without giving credit. Keep in mind that literature is real property. When we use it without permission or giving credit, we are guilty of theft. In general practice, two to three lines (50 words) of another person's work may be quoted and referenced by footnote without the necessity of requesting permission to use the material.

2. It protects your professional reputation by giving credit where credit is due. Someone is reputed to have said "Not documenting a source is plagiarism, but documenting it is scholarship." Additionally, so much is available in literature today that we can prove almost anything if we look long enough. In that case, giving credit where credit is due may take on the nature of passing the buck — or at least of sharing responsibility. Unfortunately, many students make the mistake of believing that anything in print is true. They blithely quote anything, footnote it, and then stand behind it as fact. It's a good idea to attempt to verify the authority of authors by referring to publications such as *Who's Who,* or to quote from publications of learned societies and from factual sources such as the *Statistical Abstracts of the United States,* which are considered authoritative.

In what way does documentation serve the writer?

3. It supports statements. If recognized authorities have said the same thing, your work takes on credibility; and you put yourself in good company.

Using Footnotes

At least three methods of citing documented sources in footnote form are available to the report writer. First, in formal papers and books, the source is normally given at the bottom of the page on which the cited material is used, as in the following example:

"Comparisons between countries are always tendentious to some extent and thus suspect."[1]

---

[1] Edwin J. Feulner, Jr., Congress and the New Economic Order (Washington: The Heritage Foundation, 1976), p. 53.

A second method relies on a separate listing of footnotes at the end of the paper, much as you would list a bibliography. As in the previous example, the raised footnote number—called a superscript—is placed in the same position, and the number indicates that the footnote is number one in a list of footnotes following the text material. Rather than use the raised superscript, some authorities recommend using a citation such as (1) on the line of writing. This method makes typing easier but may create a problem if the paper contains several listings or tabulations that contain numbers in parentheses because it becomes awkward to refer to those numbers in the text.

The third method is to designate footnote items by their listings in the bibliography, where all sources are listed in alphabetic order. A notation such as (4:24) in the text tells the reader that the cited material is from page 24, reference number 4 in the bibliography. This method essentially eliminates the need for either bottom-of-the-page footnotes or separate footnote lists in the addendum portion of the report.

Which of the four footnote styles appeals to you?

A possible fourth method (rarely used in business reports) is to place what could have been a bottom-of-the-page reference directly after the superscript, as in

"Comparisons between countries are always tendentious to some extent and thus suspect."[1]

---

[1]Edwin J. Feulner, Jr., Congress and the New Economic Order (Washington: The Heritage Foundation, 1976), p. 53.

However, if countries with a similar economic. . . .

This method is primarily used in papers prepared for publication—to assist the editors and typesetters in arranging copy for printing.

The choice of style is up to you as the writer, although you can never be incorrect to use the bottom-of-the-page method. In that method, the footnote must be planned for in advance so you won't run off the bottom of the page. An underscored line about 1½ inches long separates the footnote from the text material. The footnote begins with the same identifying superscript as used in the text material and is followed by the author's name, in normal order. When footnotes are used for explanatory purposes rather than for reference to a source, the explanation follows the superscript. The order of information in footnotes is illustrated in the following examples:

1. For a book reference:

William C. Himstreet and Wayne Murlin Baty, *Business Communications,* 7th ed. (Boston: Kent Publishing Company, 1984), p. 201.

For a book with only one author, simply list that author. When three authors are involved, list all three; but for a book with more than three authors, list the first author's name followed by the Latin abbreviation "et al." which means "and others" as in

> Harold R. Jones et al., *The Age of Man* (New York: Archibald Press, 1980), p. 24.

2.   For an edited book:

> Brent D. Rubin, ed., *Communication Yearbook I* (New Brunswick, NJ: Transaction Books, 1977), pp. 48–50.

3.   For a magazine or journal article:

> Betty R. Ricks, "The Neglected Managerial Communication Skills," *The A. B. C. A. Bulletin,* December 1981, pp. 22–25.

4.   For unpublished speeches, interviews, and letters:

> Wayne L. Miller, Personal letter to Mary Ellen May, July 31, 1983.
>
> Ronald R. Reagan, Radio address to the Nation, May 14, 1982.

5.   For unpublished papers

> Homer Lawrence, "Behavior Patterns in Rigid Organizations," (Doctoral dissertation, Arizona State University, Tempe, June 1976), p. 145.

6.   For a government publication:

> United States Department of Agriculture, *Dry-Farming Possibilities for Guayule in California* (Washington, D.C.: United States Government Printing Office, 1968), p. 75.

In each of the foregoing examples, the letter *p* is placed before the page number when only one page is cited. When the information is included in a series of pages, the citation uses *pp.* before the page numbers, to indicate the multiple-page reference. Because most readers know the final part of a footnote citation refers to page or pages, some authorities omit the *p* or *pp.* For example, the book reference for Harold R. Jones et al. would appear like this:

What is the difference between *p* and *pp* in footnotes?

> Harold R. Jones et al., *The Age of Man* (New York: Archibald Press, 1980), 24.

This method is used in the sample report shown in this chapter.

Although these represent some of the frequent types of citations, several others are possible. For example, a footnote to support a statistical table might describe the mathematics involved, as in

> * The weighted opinion was arrived at by assigning responses from high to low as 5, 4, 3, 2, and 1; totaling all responses; and dividing by the number of respondents.

In this case, the asterisk (*) was used rather than a number to identify the footnote both in the text and in the footnote citation. This method is often used when only one or two footnotes are included in the paper and, in the case of two, they do not fall on the same page.

The primary concern for the report writer is to maintain consistency. Footnotes are designed to permit the reader to locate the original source if desired. Here are some suggestions for handling footnotes:

1. If in doubt about whether to include certain information, follow the rule that it is better to include more than enough rather than too little.

2. Place explanatory information in footnotes when the information is not easily incorporated as part of the text.

3. Be consistent. Simply because our examples may include a comma or period to separate parts of the footnote citation does not necessarily mean that is the only way to prepare the entry. Any good style manual will have its own method. Four widely used manuals are cited here (each in the style it recommends). You should attempt to locate the latest edition, so dates have been omitted in these bibliographical entries.

> Campbell, William Giles, and Stephen Vaughan Ballou. *Form and Style: Theses, Reports, Term Papers.* 4th ed. Boston: Houghton Mifflin, 19___.
>
> Knapper, Arno F., and Loda I. Newcomb, *Style Manual for Written Communications,* Grid, Inc., Columbus, Ohio, 19___.
>
> The Modern Language Association of America. *MLA Style Sheet.* New York: Modern Language Association of America, 19___.
>
> Turabian, Kate L. *A Manual for Writers of Term Papers, Theses, and Dissertations.* 4th ed. Chicago: University of Chicago Press, 19___.

4. Become familiar with many of the Latin abbreviations used in documentation work. Here are a few of the most common ones:

Abbreviation	Latin Word(s)	Meaning
et al.	et alibi	and elsewhere
et al.	et alii	and others

Abbreviation	Latin Word(s)	Meaning
ibid.	ibidem	in the same place; from the same work
id.	idem	the same
loc. cit.	loco citado	in the place cited; in the message last referred to
op. cit.	opere citato	in the work cited

Latin abbreviations are now used infrequently.

Using Bibliographies

Using bibliographies differs in two respects from using footnotes. First, bibliography entries refer to the entire work cited and not simply to the specific page or pages from which material came. Thus, a footnote might cite a specific page from a book, but the bibliography entry would include the entire book without page references. A magazine article in a bibliography would include the beginning and ending pages of the article. Second, bibliography entries are written with the author's last name first; footnotes with the given name first.

Is listing the total pages in a book entry required or optional? (See Figure 18-1.)

Just as footnotes provide references to specific quotes, paraphrases, and information sources, bibliography entries give evidence of the nature of sources from which the author has obtained information. All footnote sources are included in the bibliography as well, but informational, explanatory footnotes that do not refer to literature or other verbal sources would not appear. In addition, a researcher often uses sources that provide broad information but do not result in footnote citations. Your judgment should tell whether to list them in the bibliography; but when in doubt, include them.

The bibliography, shown in Figure 18-1, contains both book and article references in separate sections. When the bibliography contains only five or six references, division is not necessary; simply combine books, articles, and other citations in a single alphabetic listing. On the other hand, extremely long bibliographies may contain several headings such as books, articles, publications of learned societies, unpublished documents and papers, government publications, newspaper articles, interviews, and personal letters.

When more than one bibliography entry is by the same author, the second entry substitutes an underscored line for the author's name or names, as in this example:

Jones, Joseph J., <u>The New Communication,</u> . . . .
_____, "Hearing is No Good Without Listening," . . . .

Several variations are acceptable in the internal mechanics of bibliography entries. For example, some authorities place the location of the publisher before the name of the publisher and others reverse them. When the city is well known, the state need not be indicated. The use of parentheses to separate some items such as

BIBLIOGRAPHY

<u>Books</u>

Aronson, Elliott, <u>The Social Animal</u>, San Francisco: W. H.
Freeman and Company, 1972.

Clark, Virginia, <u>Language</u>, New York: St. Martin's Press, Inc.,
1972.

Gay, Kathlyn, <u>Body Talk</u>, New York: Charles Scribner's Sons,
1974.

Harris, Thomas A., <u>I'm OK--You're OK</u>, New York: Avon Books
(published by arrangement with Harper & Row, Publishers),
1973.

Lewis, Phillip V., <u>Organizational Communication: The Essence of
Effective Management</u>, 2nd ed., Columbus, Ohio: Grid
Publishing, Inc., 1980.

Williams, Frederick, <u>The Communications Revolution</u>, Beverly
Hills, Calif., Sage Publications, 1982.

<u>Articles</u>

"Body Language: Student and Teacher Behavior," <u>Saturday
Review of Education</u>, Vol. 1, No. 5 (May 1973), pp. 78-84.

Cater, Douglass, "The Communications Revolution--What
Social-Political Consequences?" <u>Current</u>, Vol. 3, No. 155
(October 1973), pp. 36-40.

Davis, Keith, "The Care and Cultivation of the Corporate
Grapevine," <u>Dun's Review</u>, Vol. 102, No. 7 (July 1973), pp.
44-47.

James, Muriel, and Dorothy Jongeward, "Born to Win," <u>Family
Circle Magazine</u>, June 1975, pp. 18-28.

Swift, Marvin H., "Clear Writing Means Clear Thinking
Clear . . .," <u>Harvard Business Review</u>, Vol. 51, No. 1 (January
1973), pp. 59-62.

Figure 18-1 Bibliography format.

location and name of the publisher is optional, as is the use of periods or commas to separate parts of the entry. Notice, too, that the location of the publisher is not included in journal or magazine articles.

Despite the possible variations, the guiding rule for bibliography entries is the same as for footnote entries: Give enough information in consistent form so the reader can understand what has been used and where to find it.

Typing

Now that word-processing equipment is becoming common, reports can be typed quickly and efficiently from relatively rough drafts. Word processors can make the right margin straight, divide words between syllables at the ends of lines, and check spelling.

Generally, a typewritten page should have one-inch margins except on the side where pages are bound. A report that is to have pages bound on the left should be typed with a one-and-a-half-inch left margin. A report that is to be bound at the top should be typed with a one-and-a-half-inch top margin.

Why have a wider left-hand margin?

Although the bottom margin should be about an inch, it can vary somewhat. Since paragraphs are natural division places, a typist should let a bottom margin be slightly less than an inch if doing so allows the typist to reach the end of a paragraph. A narrow bottom margin is less distracting than the last line of a paragraph by itself at the top of a next page. Likewise, a wide bottom margin is less distracting than the first line of a paragraph by itself at the bottom of the page.

Reports may be single spaced or double spaced. When you use single-spaced typing, skip a line between paragraphs, and do not indent the first line. When you use double spacing, indent the first line of the paragraph five spaces and skip no additional lines between paragraphs.

The location of a heading depends on whether the heading is major or minor. Assume that the units in the following outline are headings in a written report:

```
Major Heading One
   Minor Heading One
   Minor Heading Two
      Subheading One
      Subheading Two
Major Heading Two
```

Observe the location of each heading in the typewritten report shown in Figure 18-2. The x's represent lines of writing. The diagonals (/) represent lines on which nothing is to be typed in a double-spaced report. Assume that the first major heading is preceded by the last line of the introductory paragraph.

Notice that major headings are placed in the visible center of the page. When the report is to be bound on the left, major headings should be typed about a half

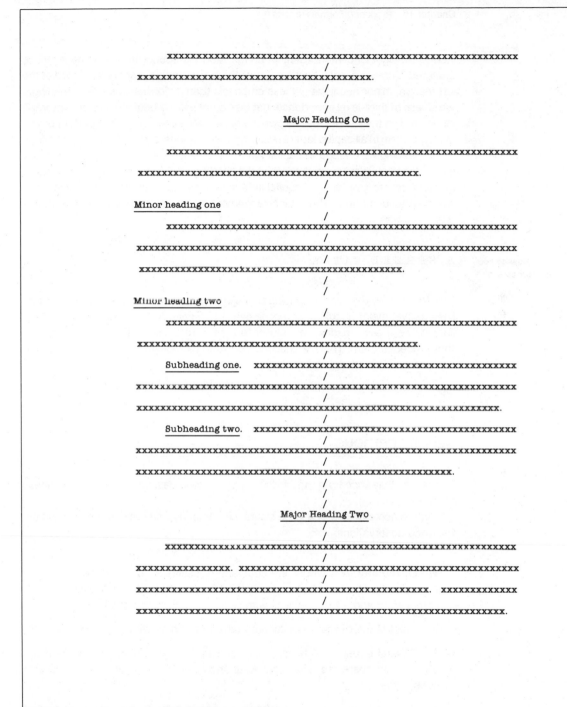

Figure 18-2 Placement of headings on a page.

inch to the right of center. Then, when the report is bound, they will appear to be centered. Centering major headings gives them appropriate emphasis. Placed at the left margin, minor headings get less emphasis than major headings. Subheadings, which are of third-level importance, get less emphasis by beginning on a paragraph indent and on the line of type. To give major headings even greater importance, you can type them in all capital letters rather than in the underscored, lowercase style. If major headings are typed in capital letters, the report's title should be typed in a manner that looks more emphatic than the headings: either typed in all capital letters *and underscored,* or typed in capital letters with a space after each letter and three spaces after each word. The latter arrangement is called a "spread" title. It looks like this:

How do you construct a "spread title"?

A S P R E A D T I T L E

Notice also the vertical spacing of major and minor headings. With three blank lines above, major headings do not appear to be crowded in. With only two blank lines below, major headings are closer to the line that follows them than to the line that precedes them. This distance indicates the relationship of the heading to the content that follows.

REPORT CRITIQUE

The report that appears on the following pages was designed to solve a business problem.

In the home offices of a large insurance company, the president has made the following observations:

1. Of the fifty men whom the company classifies as being in some type of managerial capacity, most appear to be overworked. Yet policy holders are complaining about the slowness with which the company adjusts claims.

2. Most of the executives habitually take work home with them at night.

3. Several department heads have regularly passed up vacations. Reasons given: can't spare the time, no substitutes available, lack of faith in available substitutes.

4. Sudden illness of one or two key personnel in a department seems to disrupt the whole department.

5. Turnover among young men and women who aspire to higher executive positions is high.

The president thinks the problems center around delegation of authority. He knows overworked people are unhappy and not so efficient as they might be. He believes most of his executives would not be overworked if they delegated more of their work. He believes many young employees have left the firm because they have not had a chance to grow, a chance to broaden their scope of authority.

The president asks Robert Smith, of the research department, to prepare a report answering the following questions: (1) Should the company train executives in delegation of authority? and (2) What type of program is generally recommended?

Smith learns that the president will circulate the report among several key personnel, that it is due in two weeks, and that the president expects him to do more than just present information. Smith is to analyze the information and make recommendations. Of course, the decision rests with the president; but Smith knows the president will give his recommendations thorough consideration.

As you review the report, note that some of the pages have numbered items in the left-hand margin. These numbers correspond to the numbers on the facing page that list descriptions, instructions, or suggestions to assist you in preparing your own reports. Only selected pages of the total report are presented because they present most of the critical items in report preparation and presentation covered in this and previous chapters on report writing.

Following the sample report is a checklist summarizing important things to remember when preparing a formal report.

Transmittal Memorandum or Letter

1.   If the report is prepared for someone in the organization, use the memorandum form (see Figure 18-3); if for someone in another organization, use letterhead paper and prepare the transmittal in letter form. For example, if Robert Smith works for a consulting firm and conducted the study as an outsider, the letter of transmittal might well take the following form and tone:

Dear Mr. Jackson

I am pleased to submit the following report of the study you asked our firm to conduct in an effort to answer your questions about delegation of authority.

After surveying 50 of your management people and evaluating possible ways to meet their needs for training, we have concluded that some training in delegation is essential and that this could best be provided in seminar form conducted by an outside consultant.

We appreciate the opportunity to serve you. Your staff was most helpful and courteous to us.

Cordially

2.   If the report includes a synopsis or a detailed introduction, as this one does, keep the letter of transmittal short. The body of the transmittal memorandum follows an appropriate sequence:

   a.   Let the first sentence present the report and remind the reader that he or she requested it.
   b.   Attempt to establish the subject of the report in the first paragraph.
   c.   Briefly present the conclusions and, if called for, the recommendations.
   d.   Close cordially. The closing paragraph of the transmittal letter also expresses appreciation for the cooperation given by the company. In the transmittal memorandum, it appears that Smith conducted the study by himself; the tone tends to reflect the nature of internal memos.

1

MEMORANDUM

WESTERN INSURANCE COMPANY

January 4, 198-

To: William H. Jackson, President
From: Robert Smith, Assistant, Research Department
Subject: Program of Instruction in Delegation of Authority

2   My answer to your question, "Should we have some form of executive training in delegation of authority?" is "Yes." The answer to your second question, "What type of program is generally recommended?" is "a seminar conducted by an outside consultant." The report presents justifications for these answers. Doing the research was both interesting and informative. Thank you for assigning me the study.

R. Smith

Figure 18-3   Transmittal memorandum.

The Title Page

1.   Divide the title page into four parts and arrange them in order of descending importance (see Figure 18-4):

a.   The title in all capital letters. With all letters capitalized, this title looks more significant than major-division titles. Although not a requirement, this title reflects findings; it is as specific as space and consistency permit.
b.   The name and title of the person who authorized the report.
c.   The name and title of the person who did the report.
d.   The city in which the report was prepared and the date. (As years go by, the date on a filed report may become increasingly important.)

2.   Use systematic vertical and horizontal placement.

a.   If the report is to be bound on the left, let all lines appear one-half inch to the right of center. They will then appear centered when bound.
b.   For horizontal placement of each line, move the typewriter carriage to a point one-half inch to the right of the center of the page. Backspace once for each two letters in the line.
c.   For vertical placement, count the number of vertical lines consumed from the top line to the bottom line, subtract from 66 (total lines possible on an 11-inch page), and divide by 2. The resulting figure indicates how far the title line should be from the top of the page. (The first four categories include blank lines between text in the totals.) For example:

Title lines	5
Authorization lines	5
Writer's lines	5
Place-date lines	3
Space between parts (8 $\times$ 3)	24
	42

Subtracting 42 from 66 leaves 24; dividing that by 2 equals 12, meaning that the title line should be 12 lines from the top of the page.

3.   Use a courtesy title before the name of the person for whom the report is written; do not place a courtesy title before the name of the writer.

1-2   FOR WESTERN INSURANCE COMPANY,

A CONSULTANT DIRECTED PROGRAM

OF INSTRUCTION IN "DELEGATION OF AUTHORITY"

3   Presented to

Mr. William H. Jackson, President

Western Insurance Company

by

Robert Smith, Assistant

Research Department

Los Angeles, California

June, 198-

Figure 18-4   The title page.

Table of Contents

1. Prepare the contents page (Figure 18-5) from the outline after writing the report.

2. If the report is analytical, strive for an outline that uses criteria as a basis for classification. These headings and subheadings not only reveal what the answer is, but they also show how the answer evolved.

3. Arrange the outline to indicate the importance of the headings. For example, minor divisions appear less significant because they are indented five spaces. Before each heading, its outlining symbol *could* be typed (*I, II, III,* before major headings); but indented lines sufficiently distinguish minor from major headings. Observe from the remaining pages that within the context of the report each heading has a position commensurate with its significance in the outline.

4. Use capital and lowercase letters for major headings; capitalize only the first word of a subheading. This technique helps demonstrate that subheadings are less important than major headings.

5. Type titles and subtitles exactly as they appear within the body of the report.

6. Between each title and its page number, type leaders by striking the space bar and period alternately. For a neat, uniform appearance, type all the periods on the even numbers of the typewriter scale; or, type them all on the odd numbers. For example, after typing the title of the first major division, on the first line, hit the space bar and then look at the small scale beneath where the keys strike. Remember whether the number is odd or even. If it is even, begin all the rest of the leader lines by hitting a period on even numbers of the scale.

7. If the report contains numerous graphs, tables, or figures, list them separately at the bottom of the page or on a separate page under a heading such as List of Figures.

8. If the contents page is short, use double spacing.

Contents

A Formal Program of Instruction Is Recommended 2

Morale Is Best Achieved Through Outside-the-Firm
Consultant. 5
    Consultants present broader point of view 5
    Consultants are specialists in instruction 5
    Consultants provide Western executives with
      an opportunity to exchange views 6
    Consultants' advice may be more readily accepted
      than fellow executives' advice 6

Specific, Company-Oriented Instruction Is Best
Achieved Through Company Director 7
    Company director would know Western's specific
      problem 7
    Company director would know Western's
      executives and their backgrounds. 8

Daily Work Schedule Is Least Affected by Night
Classes at State University. 8
    No company time is lost 9
    Some can gain credit toward advanced degrees . . . 9

Cost of Instruction Is Least Through Outside
Consultants 10
    Direct instructional costs are low. 10
    Indirect instructional costs are low 11
      Cost of room 12
      Lost time 12
      Interruption of work 12

Summary of Reasons for Recommending a Seminar
Conducted by Outside Consultants 13

Figure 18-5 Table of contents.

Synopsis

Skill in preparing synopses or summaries is very much a function of the writer's ability to synthesize the material and to select specific highlights of the study on which the report was based. (See Figure 18-6.) Notice how this synopsis includes only four items from the survey of executives and four statements to support recommendations. Yet, as the contents page shows, the entire report covers at least thirteen pages. The report itself includes discussion or analysis of the subject; the synopsis should not also do so. It reports the results of the discussion and analysis.

1.   The opening sentences create a deductively organized synopsis by giving the conclusions of the study.

2.   The first paragraph also contains the "authority" for the report—the name of the person authorizing it.

3.   The second paragraph explains the problems leading to the need for the study, thereby taking the first step in problem solving.

4.   The opening sentence in the third paragraph briefly describes the method of research—the second step in the problem-solving process.

5.   Highlights of the findings, the third step in problem solving, are presented following the description of the method.

6.   The fourth paragraph introduces the second part of the research, the determination of the most desirable way to solve the problem. Notice how the use of enumerated sentences assists the reader. Each of the numbered items could have been listed one under the other by indenting them and beginning each item on a new line. Of particular interest to you should be the use of parallel construction in each list. The three methods all begin with a participle: (1) paying. . . , (2) holding. . . , and (3) holding. . . . Each of the four reasons for selecting the outside-consultant method is a complete sentence.

7.   The closing paragraph repeats the conclusion in recommendation form as a logical last step in the problem-solving report process.

1   Western Insurance Company can benefit from a formal program of instruction in delegation of authority. For Western, the most efficient method of conducting the program is through an outside consultant. These conclusions emerged as the result

2 of research authorized by President William H. Jackson.

     The research arose in attempting to solve such problems as workload for executives, speed in adjusting claims, disruptions caused by illnesses and vacations, and turnover

3 among younger executives.

     The recommendation of a formal program of instruction is

4 based on 50 executives' responses to a questionnaire and on interviews with 15 of them. (1) Almost 90 percent spend more time executing details than planning. (2) About 75 percent are frequently interrupted to give advice or make decisions for subordinates. (3) About 75 percent say they have no subor-

5 dinates whom they would trust to make decisions. (4) Over 50 percent take work home at night. These percentages are much higher than what management specialists say is desirable.

     Three different methods were considered: (1) paying tuition for night courses in management at State University, (2) holding a seminar directed by a company executive on company

6 time, or (3) holding a seminar directed by an outside consultant on company time and premises. The last was chosen for four reasons: (1) Consultants present a broad, theoretical point of view, yet can apply the theory to specific company problems. (2) Consultants are specialists in instruction. (3) Consultants' advice may be more readily accepted than fellow executives' advice. (4) The consultant-directed program is least expensive.

     For these reasons, a consultant-directed, formal program of instruction in delegation of authority is recommended for

7 Western Insurance Company.

Figure 18-6 Synopsis.

Page 1 of Report Body

1.   The first page of a report (Figure 18-7) has about twice as much space at the top as do other pages, so leave about two inches of blank space. Either omit the page number or center it at the bottom of the page.

2.   Type the title in capital letters, exactly as it appears on the title page. If the title requires more than one line, break it so that it is attractive.

3.   Leave two blank lines between the title and the first typewritten line. An *Introduction* heading is not needed; readers expect the first page or two to be introductory material.

4.   Let the first paragraph identify the purpose of the report, which can be done without using the word "purpose."

5.   Lead coherently from one part of the introduction to the next. "These questions" (in the second paragraph) are tied to the questions in the first paragraph.

6.   Review the background of the problem if doing so will prepare the reader to understand the report, but don't present pertinent facts about the firm as if no one knows them. Some people who read the report may know about the branch offices; others may not. The sentence beginning "For the information of those . . . " informs everyone about branch offices but does not talk down to those who already know about them.

7.   Always report the method of research employed. The reader with faith in the method and sources of information has greater faith in the findings.

8.   Use *Purpose, Background, Method,* or *Scope* as subheadings only if the introduction occupies more than a page or two. A one-page introduction only with subheadings looks as though division has been carried too far.

9.   Do not end with a single line of a paragraph appearing by itself; let the page end either one line shorter or longer.

1   FOR WESTERN INSURANCE COMPANY,
             A CONSULTANT-DIRECTED PROGRAM
2   OF INSTRUCTION IN "DELEGATION OF AUTHORITY"
3
4   This study was designed to answer two questions: (1)
Should Western Insurance Company have a formal program of
instruction in delegation of authority? (2) If so, what is the
preferred method of conducting such a program?

5   Company officials have posed these questions because of
the following observations: (1) Many executives appear
overworked and rushed. (2) An executive's absence for illness
or vacation disrupts work. (3) Many younger workers have
left the firm complaining of lack of work, authority, and
responsibility. (4) Average claim-adjustment time is 40 days
after submission.

6   For the information of those who do not work directly
with branch offices, Western maintains 14 branch offices in 7
states. Branch managers refer all claims to executives in the
home office for adjustment.

7   Information for this report came from questionnaires
filled out by 50 home office executives, from interviews with 15
executives and 3 professional consultants, and from a survey
of management texts and journals. That survey provided
background for the study and ideas for the questionnaire. The
interviews added depth to the information gathered from the
survey.

8–9   1

Figure 18-7   Page 1 of report body.

Note: See preceding number 8. Some people prefer to use some of these headings in the introduction, so Figure 18-8 shows how an alternative first page would appear under these circumstances. In this case, "Introduction" is used as the first-page heading rather than the title of the report which is also included on the title page. The use of the minor headings decreases the content that can be placed on the page. When this method is used, the contents page would, of course, be revised to contain the added headings.

Introduction

Because of several observations, Western Insurance Company is concerned about the need for increased delegation of authority by its executive staff.

Purpose

This study was designed to answer two questions: (1) Should Western Insurance Company have a formal program of instruction in delegation of authority? (2) If so, what is the preferred method of conducting such a program?

Background

Company officials have posed these questions because of the following observations: (1) Many executives appear overworked and rushed (2) An executive's absence for illness or vacation disrupts work. (3) Many younger workers have left the firm complaining of lack of work, authority, and responsibility. (4) Average claim-adjustment time is 40 days after submission.

For the information of those who do not work directly with branch offices, Western maintains 14 branch offices in 7 states. Branch managers refer all claims to executives in the home office for adjustment.

1

Figure 18-8 Alternative first page of report body.

Page 2 of Report Body

1.   Number the second page in the upper right-hand corner (Figure 18-9).

2.   Let the last part of the introduction reveal the answer (if the report is deductively written) and the major points to be discussed. By the time readers have reached the last part of the introduction, they know the problem, its background, the method of solving it, and the solution. They are now ready to receive the supporting details. To provide coherence, before presenting the supporting details, remind readers of the points to be presented and the sequence they will follow. End the introduction with a short preview of things to come to provide coherence. After reading that a discussion of a problem contains four major topics, the reader expects the report to discuss the first one immediately.

3.   Leave three blank lines above a major topic heading, two blank lines below.

4.   Use a consistent plan for paragraphing. "Western executives have had. . . ." is obviously a topic sentence that is to be developed in the remaining sentences.

5.   If a page contains a reference, leave enough room at the bottom of the page for the footnote without having a narrow bottom margin.

6.   If a quotation is more than two lines long, single space it and make the lines five spaces shorter on each side. Quotation marks are not necessary in this arrangement. When quotations are two or fewer lines, include them in the double-spaced regular text within the paragraph and use quotation marks.

7.   If you omit any words in a quotation, use ellipses: three periods, with spaces between and before and after, when the omission is within a sentence; use four periods when the omission is at the end of a sentence.

8.   When typing a footnote, double-space below the last line and place a solid line about one-and-a-half inches long. Double-space beneath the line to the footnote, which is to be typed single spaced. Use a consistent form for footnotes throughout the report.

2   From these sources came information related to these questions: (1) Do we need instruction in delegation? (2) Which type of instruction would (a) best promote morale and relate to company problems, (b) least interfere with daily work schedules, and (c) cost least? The following sections discuss each of these questions in detail.

3   <u>A Formal Program of Instruction Is Recommended</u>

4   Western executives have had very little formal instruction in delegation. None has had a college course in delegation. They appear to be somewhat familiar with principles; they admit

5 weakness in application. They agree with a Stanford professor:[1]

6   We all know that merely to understand and accept a principle is not enough; implementation is the major obstacle. It is particularly difficult in this instance of

7   delegation because for a great many people . . . almost a change of personality or at least of deep habit may be involved.

        If an understanding of the principles were all that Western Insurance executives needed, the firm could supply them with books and magazine articles written on delegation. However, seminars can best contribute to understanding the function of implementation.

---

8   [1] John S. Ewing, "Patterns of Delegation," <u>Harvard Business Review</u>, XXXIX, No. 4 (July-August 1961), 33.

Figure 18-9 Page 2 of report body.

Page 10 of Report Body

1.   Include a transition sentence between major topics. In the sentence before the heading, this report writer is about to take the reader from a consideration of the daily work schedule to the problem of cost. The sentence bridges the gap between them. It lets the reader know what to expect. It serves about the same purpose as a highway marker that says "Right Lane for Highway 99."

   A good transition ordinarily includes two ideas — that which was just considered and that which is about to be considered. Smooth transitions are fairly good proof of logical organization. If it's easy to write a sentence that leads from work schedule into costs, the sequence of topics in the outline is evidently logical.

2.   Be sure to have a lead-in sentence or paragraph between a major heading and the first minor heading. If the topic is sufficiently broad to warrant division, the topics warrant an introduction.

3.   Place the major topic's division titles at the left margin, underscore them, but begin only the first word with a capital letter. The left-margin position and lowercase letters help de-emphasize the minor heading. Every minor heading typed in this position should have been indented five spaces on the contents page.

4.   If several numbers appear in a paragraph, strive for consistency in typing them. (When two numbers appear together, however, as in ten 2-hour sessions," spell out the first number.)

1   Our daily work schedule, then, would be least affected by having executives take management courses at State University night school; but for this advantage, Western would have to pay a higher price.

Cost of Instruction Is Least Through Outside Consultants

2   Of the three approaches to delegation training, outside consultants are the least expensive when only direct instructional costs are considered. Indirect costs are difficult to establish.

3   Direct instructional costs are low

4   The optimum number of participants in any one seminar appears to be 10, according to the executives and consultants interviewed. More than 10 executives away from their offices at one time could handicap our daily operations; seminars with more than 10 participants could restrict opportunities for exchanging views. If 50 are to receive instruction, they should be divided into 5 separate groups.

4   Each of the consultants thought ten 2-hour sessions would be adequate for each group. Each charges a fee of $70 an hour ($1,400 for 20 hours of instruction). Of the half dozen Western executives whose backgrounds and interests are such that they could conduct the seminars, each is earning over $50,000 a year--about $25 an hour. Since none of these men has conducted a previous seminar in delegation, company officials have arrived at a conclusion that for each class hour spent in

Figure 18-10   Page 10 of report body.

Page 11 of Report Body

1.   Introduce figures in sentences that say something analytical about the content of the figure. The introductory sentence should always precede the figure, and the figure should follow as closely as possible (see Figure 18-11).

2.   Because this report contains only tables as graphic presentations, table numbers are used for all tables in the report rather than "Figure" designations. In introductions of figures, refer to the figures by number — rather than in language such as "a table is presented below." (After the final typing, a figure designated as "below" may actually be on the following page.)

3.   Give the figure a title that is specific enough to assist readers who merely thumb through the report. For instance, the title of Table 7 could have been lengthened to include the number of persons to be instructed, as in "Cost of Instruction for 50 People in Delegation of Authority."

4.   Have some logical reason for the sequence of tabular data. The alternative instructional methods shown in Table 7 are arranged in order of least expensive to most expensive, but the sequence would also have been logical in order of most expensive to least expensive.

5.   When the table is integrated in the text, rather than being placed on a page by itself, follow the table with whatever further interpretation is necessary.

6.   Use figures to show conviction anywhere in the report; amount or dollar figures are not confined to tables and other graphics.

7.   Unless a report is exceptionally long, do not strive for transition sentences between subdivisions. Of course, natural coherence is expected, but summarizing sentences between *all* minor divisions may make the report too wordy.

Note: Although the data in Table 7 could have been presented as a bar chart, the table form is superior because of the detail included. For example, the information about 50 persons at $120 each, 5 classes at $1,400 each, and 5 classes at $1,500 each would probably be too unwieldy to incorporate in a graph unless used as explanatory footnotes.

seminar a company executive would have to spend at least two hours of company time in preparation. Some would probably devote other hours at home. Thus, the cost of 20 hours of seminars would be $1,500. Expenses for supplies and films would be about the same for company instructors as for consultants, as shown in Table 7, which summarizes the direct

1-2   costs of instruction.

Table 7

3   Cost of Instruction in Delegation of Authority

Method	Instruction	Supplies	Total
Night classes at State University (50 persons at $120 each)	$6,000	--	$6,000
Outside consultant (5 classes at $1,400 each)	7,000	$500	7,500
Company instructor (5 classes at $1,500 each)	7,500	500	8,000

5
6   Since not all Western executives could attend night classes, tuition expense would actually be less than $6,000. Obviously, the night-class approach would be the least expensive; but many executives would not be exposed to instruction in delegation. Additionally, the instruction might not be specifically designed for our needs.

Indirect instructional costs are low

7   Technically, costs for on-the-premises instruction should include allowances for use of a conference room, time lost by executives, and interruption of work. However, these factors are discounted because of the difficulty in measuring them.

Figure 18-11 Page 11 of report body.

Page 12 of Report Body

Since this report discounts the costs of the room, lost time, and work interruption, inclusion of these words as headings is questionable. Headings probably provide more emphasis than these factors deserve, but they are included here to illustrate format when minor divisions are still further divided (Figure 18-12).

When a subdivision is broken into still smaller divisions, indicate de-emphasis by (1) typing the smaller division titles at the paragraph indention point, and (2) beginning the paragraph on the same line.

Note: This page of the report also shows the application of some principles of punctuation:

1.   *The colon.* The lead-in sentence under "Cost of room" employs a colon because the words preceding the numbered points form a complete sentence. The lead-in sentence under "Lost time" does not employ a colon because the words preceding the numbered points do not form a complete sentence.

2.   *The semicolon.* Under the "Lost time" heading, a semicolon follows "delegating" because each of the independent clauses contains commas. Thus, a semicolon (a stronger mark of punctuation than a comma) is necessary for separating the clauses. Under "Interruption of work," a semicolon follows "return" because no conjunction is employed in the compound sentence. A semicolon follows "difficult" because the compound sentence employs a conjunctive adverb "furthermore". In both of these cases, using a comma would create a run-on sentence.

3.   *The comma.* In the last paragraph, notice the comma between "accurately" and "but." It separates two independent clauses, neither of which contains a comma. On the sample page, what *other* uses of the comma can you identify?

4.   *The hyphen.* In the last line, "consultant-directed" is used as a single-word modifier of the noun "instruction." Compound adjectives are to be hyphenated.

<u>Cost of room</u>.   Cost of the seminar room was discounted
1   for two reasons: (1) Western maintains a conference room
already, and its present schedule is light enough to accommodate delegation seminars without serious scheduling
problems. (2) Light or power expenses would be about the same
regardless of who is teaching the course.

<u>Lost time</u>.   Cost of lost time was discounted because (1) as
salaried workers, executives may find means of making up for
2   lost time, hopefully, by delegating; and (2) through spending
two hours in a single seminar, executives may learn ways to
increase their efficiency, thus enabling Western to recoup many
times the value of the time lost.

2   <u>Interruption of work</u>.   Understandably, executives'
absences could cause subordinates to lose time in waiting for
their return; their absences could cause delays that result in a
loss of goodwill. But measuring these factors was too difficult;
furthermore, the seminars would be designed to give instruction in surmounting such problems.

Both direct and indirect costs should be regained in
terms of dollars saved. The amount of savings realized from
3   instruction in delegation cannot be estimated accurately, but
some figures presented in another insurance company's annual
4   report may be helpful.[9] After a formal program of consultant-
directed instruction in delegation, the company reported savings

---

[9] Westfield Insurance Company, <u>Annual Report for 1979</u>,
March 1980, 4.

Figure 18-12   Page 12 of report body.

Page 13 of Report Body

1. Try for a smooth transition from the last major topic into the summarizing section (Figure 18-13). Because several reasons are to be listed as justification for the recommendations, note the use of the word "equally" to indicate that even though the reasons are numbered in the summary the numbers have nothing to do with the degree of importance of each item.

2. Because the report is designed to solve a problem, the final heading could be simply *Conclusion* or *Summary.* Because preceding headings are talking headings that convey the conclusion reached under each major heading, this final heading is presented in a consistent manner. Also note the placement of the two-line heading.

3. Have nothing in the summary that the report did not discuss. By definition, a summary *summarizes* what has gone on before. Introducing a new idea in the summary can cause these problems: (1) It may make the reader wonder why the point was not developed earlier; (2) the summary, which is expected to be fairly short, does not provide space for developing a new idea; (3) it may suggest that the study was not adequately completed; (4) it suggests that the writer did not adequately plan the report before beginning to write.

4. Let the summary reveal the decision, but devote most space to summarizing the reasons behind the decisions.

5. For emphasis and clarity, enumerate points. Also notice that the reasons are rather broad generalizations from the findings portion of the report and are not repetitive about specific details or findings. As an example, reason number 4 simply says that consultant-directed programs are less expensive and does not include actual dollar amounts.

far beyond the cost of the program, more time for executives to think and plan, and generally improved morale. No one can tell whether Western would have a similar experience, but similarities in goals and size give much cause for optimism. Although dollar savings is one justification for recommending the use of consultants, other factors discussed are equally important.

Summary of Reasons for Recommending a Seminar Conducted by Outside Consultants

The following percentages, which authorities say are exceedingly high, suggest a need for training in delegation:

1. Almost 90 percent of Western executives spend more time executing details than planning.
2. About 75 percent are frequently interrupted to give advice or make decisions for subordinates.
3. About 75 percent say they have no subordinates whom they trust to make decisions for them.
4. Over 50 percent take work home with them.

A professional consultant is recommended as the preferred means of conducting a training program in delegation because

1. Consultants can present theoretical principles while pointing out specific applications.
2. Consultants are specialists in seminar instruction.
3. Consultants' advice may be more readily accepted than the advice of fellow executives.
4. Consultant-directed programs are less expensive than either night courses or firm-directed programs.

Figure 18-13 Page 13 of report body.

A FORMAL REPORT CHECKLIST

The following checklist provides a concise, handy guide for you as you prepare a report. It covers in condensed, outline form many of the principles and practices suggested in the last few chapters.

I. The Transmittal Memorandum or Letter
(Use the following points for a letter-style transmittal in reports going outside the organization. For internal reports, use a memorandum transmittal.)
   A. Let the letter of transmittal carry a warm greeting to the reader.
   B. Open quickly with a "Here is the report you requested" tone.
   C. Establish the subject in the first sentence.
   D. Follow the opening with a brief summary of the study. Expand the discussion if a separate summary is not included in the report.
   E. Acknowledge the assistance of those who helped with the study.
   F. Close the letter with a thank you and a forward look.

II The Title Page
   A. Include on the title page
      1. The title of the report.
      2. Full identification of the authority for the report (the person for whom the report was prepared).
      3. Full identification of the preparer of the report.
      4. The date of the completion of the report.
   B. Use an attractive layout. If the items are to be centered, leave an extra half-inch on the left for binding. In other words, make sure the point from which the items are centered is a little to the right of the actual center of the paper.

III. The Contents Page
   A. Use *Contents* or *Table of Contents* as the title.
   B. Use a tabular arrangement to indicate the heading degrees used in the report.
   C. If many graphs or tables are used, list them in a separate *List of Figures*. Otherwise, the graphs or tables should *not* be listed because they are not separate sections of the outline but only supporting data within a section of the report.
   D. Center the entire contents outline horizontally and vertically on the page.

IV. The Synopsis
   A. Use a one-word title, such as *Synopsis, Summary, Epitome, Brief,* or *Précis.*
   B. Prepare the synopsis as a condensation of the major sections of the report.
   C. Concentrate on writing effective, generalized statements that avoid detail available in the report itself. Simply tell the reader what was done, how it was done, and how it all ended.

V. The Body of the Report
  A. In writing style, observe the following rules:
    1. Avoid the personal *I* and *we* pronouns. Minimize the use of *the writer,* *the investigator,* and *the author.*
    2. Use active construction to give emphasis to the *doer* of the action; use passive voice to give emphasis to the *results* of the action.
    3. Use proper tense. Write naturally about things in the order in which they happened, are happening, or will happen. Try to write the report as though the reader were reading it at the same time it was written.
    4. Avoid ambiguous pronoun references. If a sentence begins with *This is,* make sure the preceding sentence employs the specific word for which *This* stands. If the specific word is not used, insert it immediately after *This.*
    5. Avoid expletive beginnings. Sentences that begin with *There is, There are,* and *It is* present the verb before presenting the subject. Compared with sentences that employ the normal subject-verb-complement sequence, expletive sentences are longer.
    6. Enumerate lists of three items or more if the tabulation will make reading easier. For example, a list of three words such as *Ivan, George,* and *Diana* need not be tabulated; but a list of three long phrases, clauses, or sentences would probably warrant tabulation.
    7. Attempt to incorporate transition sentences to ensure coherence.
  B. In physical layout, observe the following rules:
    1. Use headings to assist the reader by making them descriptive of the contents of the section. Talking headings are preferred.
    2. Maintain consistency in the mechanical placement of headings of the same degree.
    3. Use parallel construction in headings of the same degree in the same section of the report.
    4. Try to incorporate the statement of the problem or purpose and method of research as minor parts of the introduction unless the research method is the unique element in the study.
    5. Use the picture-frame layout for all pages. Recommended margins are *top* = 1 inch; *right* = 1 inch; *bottom* = 1½ inches; *left* = 1½ inches (the extra half-inch is for binding).
    6. Number all pages, with the first page of the body of the report being page 1. For pages, such as page 1, that have a major title at the top, omit the number or place it in the center of a line a double space below the last line on the page. For all other pages, place the number in the center of the top line, or in the upper right corner a double space above the first line on the page, or centered a double space below the last line on the page.
  C. In using graphics or tabular data, observe the following rules:
    1. Number consecutively the figures used in the report.
    2. Give each graph or table a descriptive title.
    3. Refer to the graph or table within the text discussion that precedes its appearance.

      4. Place the graph or table as close to the textual reference as possible and limit the text reference to analysis. It should not merely repeat what can be seen in the graph or table.

      5. Use effective layout, appropriate captions and legends, and realistic vertical and horizontal scales that help the table or graph stand clearly by itself.

  D. In reporting the analysis,

      1. Question each statement for its contribution to the solution of the problem. Is each statement either descriptive or evaluative?

      2. Reduce large, unwieldy numbers to understandable ones through a common language such as units of production, percentages, or ratios.

      3. Use objective reporting style rather than persuasive language; avoid emotional terms. Identify assumptions and opinions. Avoid unwarranted judgments and inferences.

      4. Document the report wherever necessary.

      5. Tabulate or enumerate items when it will simplify the reading or add emphasis.

  E. In drawing conclusions,

      1. State the conclusions carefully and clearly, and make sure they grow out of the findings.

      2. If it seems necessary, repeat the major supporting findings for each conclusion.

      3. If recommendations are called for, make them grow naturally from the conclusions.

VI. Documentation

  A. When using footnotes,

      1. When in doubt, footnote the material or the source.

      2. Plan the placement of the bottom-of-the-page footnote in advance so it doesn't run off the page or below the bottom margin.

  B. When preparing the bibliography,

      1. When in doubt about whether a reference should be included, make the entry.

      2. If in doubt about what to include for an entry, include more information than you believe might be necessary.

      3. Prepare the bibliography in alphabetic sequence by author from index cards.

      4. If the bibliography is lengthy, include separate sections for books, articles, governmental publications, and unpublished references.

VII. Appendix Material

  A. Include cover letters for survey instruments, the survey instruments, maps, explanations of formulas used, and other items that should be included but are not important enough to be in the body of the report.

  B. Label each item beginning with *Appendix A, Appendix B,* and so on.

  C. Identify each item by giving it a title.

SUMMARY

When you are ready to put your words on paper, proceed in the following manner:

1. Begin writing only after you have solved the problem satisfactorily and have prepared a good outline.

2. Select a good writing environment.

3. Get started early.

4. Begin at an easy section.

5. Set aside relatively long blocks of uninterrupted writing time.

6. Write rapidly with the intention of rewriting where necessary.

7. Skip difficult passages and return to them later.

8. Put the report aside for a day or two.

9. Review for possible improvement.

10. Rewrite where necessary.

To give a reader confidence that your answer is the right answer, use the following techniques:

1. Avoid emotional terms.

2. Identify assumptions.

3. Label opinions.

4. Use documentation.

For effective writing style, use the following techniques:

1. Use concrete nouns.

2. Use active voice.

3. Avoid personal pronouns.

4. Use tense consistently.

5. Use transition sentences.

6. Use a variety of coherence techniques.

7. Use tabulation and enumeration.

8. Use parallel construction.

9. Define terms carefully.

10. Check for variety.

If your report is informational, let your introduction reveal what the topic is, why it is being reported on, where the information came from, how the topic is divided into parts, and the order in which the parts will be presented.

If your report is analytical, let your introduction reveal the problem the report purports to solve, the circumstances that brought the problem about, the research technique and sources of information, the answer to the problem, the major points that will be presented, and the order in which the points will be presented.

The body of a report includes everything between the introduction and the final sentences or paragraphs. In an analytical report, these final elements are called *Conclusion;* in an informational report, they are called *Summary.* The conclusion presents the overall answer to a problem and the supporting reasons. The summary presents a condensation of the points presented earlier.

For physical presentation and documentation, refer to the preceding pages or to standard style manuals.

EXERCISES

Review Questions

1.   What are the advantages of composing an easy portion first and a difficult portion last?

2.   Which is normally better, composing a report in two 4-hour sittings, or composing a report in eight 1-hour sittings? Why?

3.   Which is better and why? (a) Writing rapidly and rewriting where necessary, or (b) writing slowly with the intention of achieving perfection in the first draft?

4.   Which is better and why? (a) In one review of a draft, look for ways to improve both content and style; or (b) In one review of a draft, look for ways to improve content; and, in another review, look for ways to improve style.

5.   How does a writer achieve conviction?

6.   Comment on the point of view expressed: "Research reports should not contain any statements of opinion."

7.   Why should the pronouns *I* and *you* be avoided in reports?

8.   Should all verbs be the same tense? Explain.

9.   Write a definition of the word *bicycle.*

10.   List the ideas that normally appear in an introduction.

11.   Is the heading *Introduction* essential?

12.   What is the advantage gained by presenting items in list form and placing a number before each of them?

13. What are the advantages and disadvantages of placing footnotes at the bottoms of pages instead of at the end of the report?

14. Should ideas presented in graphic form be presented also in paragraph form? Explain.

15. For all pages, should the bottom margin be the same width? Explain.

16. If a report is to be bound on the left, should major headings be typed in the center of the page? Explain.

17. How much space is left above and below major headings?

18. Which is better as an introductory sentence for a table or graph?
- (a) Figure 4 shows the distribution of days absent for sickness by department.
- (b) More days were lost because of sickness by employees in the Operations Department than in any other department, as shown in Figure 4.

19. Must a formal report always have a synopsis? Must it always have an appendix? Explain.

20. Explain the concept of a talking heading in a report.

21. Why do some reports have letters of transmittal and others have memorandums as transmittals? How do they differ?

22. Explain how writer preference may lead to differences in the format of the first page of the body of a report.

Complete Formal Report Problems

Report the following problems in formal style. Even though survey results are included in some problems, prepare a questionnaire in appropriate form. The sequence in the problem questionnaires is purposely random.

1. As director of research for Karl Turkan and Associates, a prominent public relations consulting firm, you have been asked to determine how college-age people perceive men and women from different professions on some selected characteristics. Your instructions are to determine how people in the following professions are perceived:

Accountants	Medical Doctors
Dentists	Attorneys
College Professors	Members of the Clergy
Engineers (Electrical)	Commercial Aviators
Business Executives	Elected Officials

Four characteristics have been isolated by Mr. Turkan for investigation. He wants to know how people in these professions are perceived in terms of (a) honesty, (b) personality, (c) intelligence, and (d) physical appearance.

You should develop and test an appropriate survey instrument to help you gather information. Prepare a report. You should consult secondary (library) sources to assist you in your analysis of the findings. Your instructor might assign this problem as either a short or a long formal report. The results will be used by the firm to design public relations programs for some professional people who need image improvement.

2. As office administrator at the Wilmoth Company, you must make a recommendation for the selection of a single photocopying machine, or a variety of machines, for use throughout the organization's seven offices—one home office and six branch offices.

Each branch has 30 employees, and the home office has 210 employees. Copying load for work orders, incoming and outgoing invoices, checks, and typewritten materials is about 600 pages a day in all six branch offices. In the home office, the number of copies a day is about 4,000. In the branches, copies may be made on any kind of paper. About 10 percent of the copies made in the home office must be on bond paper.

All employees in the home office are located on two floors of a large office building. Letters and reports are prepared in a word-processing center, which uses bond paper for some of its work. The word-processing center is within easy walking distance of any department.

Investigate the products of three different copying-machine manufacturers and prepare a report making a recommendation to the operations vice president, Eric Bondesson. You know Mr. Bondesson likes formal reports with adequate supporting evidence for whatever recommendations are made.

3. See problem 2. Conduct a similar study and prepare the report for any of the following problems:

a. Selection of a word processor.
b. Selection of a personal computer.
c. Selection of a heavy-duty, electronic typewriter.

In any of these problems, make the selection from a choice of three major brands. You are the office administrator, and your report will be prepared for Eric Bondesson, the operations vice president for your firm, the Wilmoth Company.

4. As summer-tour coordinator for the Beverly Hills Travel Bureau, you have to plan vacation travel tours and to promote them. The tours are usually made by charter flight to reduce travel costs. The Beverly Hills Travel Bureau is one of the largest firms of its kind in the nation. Before you can promote a tour, you submit a report to Mr. Sidney Rosenfeld, president, for consideration by the executive committee. Once approval is given, you then work out the fine details of specific dates, travel itinerary, meal and hotel arrangements, and final costs. Prior to submitting the report, you survey a selected list of former tour customers about their desires. The survey helps establish interest in tours and the broad guidelines for specific travel. For the coming year, a tour of the Far East has been proposed. As a result, you surveyed by mail 600 former tour customers, and 300 replied. Following are the cover letter, the questionnaire material, and the tabulated results of the 300 respondents:

Dear Traveler:

Because you have traveled with us before, we would greatly appreciate your taking the time to complete the following questionnaire. Your ideas will help us plan a charter trip to the Far East. As a seasoned traveler, your ideas are valued even though you may not be planning such a trip. Please simply respond as if you could plan your own trip.

For a tour of the Far East, when would you like to leave?
Late spring: <u>40</u>   Midsummer: <u>196</u>
Late summer: <u>64</u>

What length trip would you prefer?
11 days/nights <u>111</u>   21 days/20 nights <u>189</u>

Would you prefer a stopover at
Hawaii: <u>184</u>   Guam: <u>28</u>   Anchorage: <u>76</u>

Which cities would you prefer to visit? (Check all that apply.)
Seoul: <u>162</u>   Bangkok: <u>291</u>   Osaka: <u>136</u>
Taipei: <u>281</u>   Singapore: <u>138</u>   Manila: <u>214</u>
Tokyo: <u>264</u>   Hong Kong: <u>275</u>

If it could be arranged, would you be interested in a one- or two-day side trip to Peking on mainland China?

Yes: <u>272</u>   No: <u>28</u>

Would you prefer to stay at
First-class hotels: <u>191</u>
Local tourist hotels: <u>109</u>

Please indicate the number of meals you would prefer the tour have together each day:
3 meals: <u>27</u>   2 meals: <u>212</u>   1 meal: <u>48</u>
Meals open: <u>13</u>

Would you like your evenings
Planned: <u>74</u>   Open: <u>226</u>

Would you prefer
Only American tour leaders: <u>84</u>
Native, English-speaking guides: <u>52</u>
A combination of American and native guides: <u>164</u>

Check the price range most acceptable to you personally for the tour you have visualized in your responses.

	10-11 days	20-21 days
Under $2,000	114	30
$2,001-$2,500	184	112
$2,501-$3,000	2	148
$3,001-$3,500	0	8

5. Using the design of the study in problem 4 as a guide, prepare your own questionnaire for a tour of any one of the following areas: Europe, the Mediterranean, South America, Scandinavia, Australia–New Zealand, Africa. Use the members of your student body as your population for the survey. Then prepare an appropriate report for Mr. Rosenfeld. A visit to a travel agency or two might give you background information available in current tour brochures.

6. As an independent planning consultant to the general manager of Capitol Theater Industries, Inc., you have accepted the assignment of making a study of available land sites for an outdoor drive-in theater. About thirty acres are necessary for construction of the theater and entry and exit roads. Studies have shown that most drive-in theater patrons come from within seven miles of the theater. The company plans to purchase the land, pave the parking area, install the necessary equipment, and erect a snack bar with lounges. Its total expenditure should not exceed $1,000,000. Experience has shown that the cost of improvements on the land run about $500,000.

Three sites have been selected for study. Each is about eight miles from the center of Orange, the shopping and business center for the region. You have made an on-the-site study of the three sites. With the help of real estate people, a building contractor with experience in outdoor theater construction, and representatives of the chambers of commerce in three communities, you have gathered the following data:

Site A. Site A is located seven miles from the center of Orange, adjacent to the Southern Expressway, a major commuter highway. The surrounding seven-mile area has a population of about 40,000, with an expected population of about 60,000 within the next five years. Thirty-two acres are available; all must be purchased at a total cost of $280,000. Young families predominate. The average age of the head of the household is thirty-five. Each family contains about four people. Average income is $24,400 a year. Most families are buying their own homes. Two drive-in theaters are already located in the area.

Site B. Site B is located eight miles from the center of Orange and is about one mile off Highway 32, a major through highway from Orange to the north. It is in a suburban community of 50,000. The anticipated population in five years is 65,000. Thirty acres will cost $7,000 each. A suitable highway sign attracting attention to the theater will cost $25,000. The average family size is 4.5 persons. The head of the household is about forty-two years of age on the average. Average income per family is $35,000. Most families are well on the way to owning their own homes. Three other drive-in theaters are now operating in the general seven-mile area.

Site C. Site C is located ten miles from the center of Orange. It is adjacent to a suburban shopping area near the industrial area of Orange. The population of the area is about 50,000, and only modest growth is foreseen in the next five years.

Thirty acres of land will cost $240,000. The average income is $27,500 for each family. The average age of the head of the household is thirty-five, and about four people constitute a family. The residential market is dominated by rental apartments. One other drive-in theater is now serving the population.

A representative sampling technique was used in conducting a questionnaire survey in each community. From the questionnaire, you gathered the following data:

(1) What is your favorite form of evening family entertainment?

	TV:	Movies:	Other:
Community A.	447	153	100
Community B.	326	124	200
Community C.	505	180	15

(2) How much do you normally spend each week on family entertainment outside the home?

Community A. Mean expenditure: $6.00
            Median: $7.00
Community B. Mean expenditure: $8.00
            Median: $12.00
Community C. Mean expenditure: $10.00
            Median: $12.00

(3) How long have you lived in your present home?

Community A. Mean: 4 years
Community B. Mean: 9 years
Community C. Mean: 1½ years

Prepare your report attempting to evaluate the three sites. Recommend the sites in first, second, and third order. Transmit the report to Gina Munson, general manager of Capitol.

7. Assume you are involved in selecting advertising outlets and preparing advertisements for the Ajax Cosmetic Company. Your supervisor is Mr. Brian McDermott, director of sales promotion. He has asked you to select a national magazine from three magazines of your choice as a probable place to purchase advertising space for an initial new-product sales campaign. The product is a new line of women's competitively priced cosmetics. Ajax has long been a leader in low-priced facial cosmetics, but this new product represents an attempt to break into the high-style field. Your new product line consists of skin, eye, and lip cosmetics.

Although you have been told to select from three magazines of your choice, you know that for proper exposure you should select from magazines such as *Vogue, Harper's Bazaar, McCall's, Mademoiselle, Cosmopolitan,* and other fashion-oriented magazines including some of the newer publications such as *Playgirl* and *Working Woman.* From the three magazines you select for study, your final choice will be based on the nature of appeals used in advertisements in each magazine, the kinds of products advertised, and the cost of advertising. You can find information about cost of ads and circulation of all national magazines in the most recent issue of *Consumer Magazine and Farm Publication Rates and Data.*

Your plan is to use three recent issues of each of your three magazines to analyze the nature of advertisements. Ajax plans to use only full-page, color or black-and-white ads. You plan to begin your study of each magazine with the inside cover and to analyze the first 30 or 40 ads of each of the three issues until you have at least 100 ads in your total sample. Thus, you'll analyze at least 300 ads by the time you have covered three issues of each of the three magazines.

A couple of assumptions must be made here. First, you are an expert in determining the basic appeal of an advertisement and; second, a sample of 100 ads is adequate to determine the nature of products advertised and appeals used in each magazine.

Here are some of the product categories you may find convenient in tabulating your count of ads:

Automobiles	Travel
Cosmetics and beauty aids	Personal services (nonproduct)
Office equipment and supplies	Household appliances
Convenience items	Furniture
Clothing	Food

You may add others, of course. Some of the suggested product groups may not apply in certain magazines. If you find only a small number of ads in a product area, you may want to combine two or more areas such as household appliances and furniture. Should some ads not fit in any category, you could have a *Miscellaneous* or *All Other* grouping.

Advertising appeals typically fall into one or more categories.

Security	Quality
Love	Sex
Safety	Elegance
Beauty	Economy
Health	Comfort
Pride	Goodwill

Again, these are suggested appeal groupings only. You may find it convenient to combine closely related ones, such as safety and security or pride and quality.

After selecting your magazine, make a trial analysis to test the nature of the categories you'll want to use. Keep in mind that the purpose of your study is to determine the products most advertised and the appeals most used for those products. For instance, your findings should indicate that the four or five most advertised product groupings were. . . . At the same time, you'll report that the four or five most used advertising appeals were. . . . To keep a record of which appeals were used for each product, you'll find it helpful to make a chart similar to the following one for your initial tabulation of each magazine. All three issues of each magazine may be included in one chart.

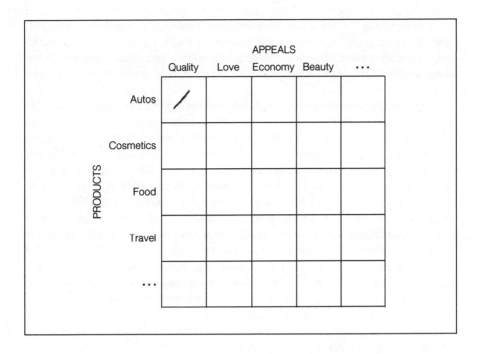

Your charts will be much larger, no doubt. Using the charts will simplify your analysis and lead to better information for your written report. For example, an automobile advertisement using an appeal to quality would be recorded by making a slash mark (/) in the counting cell, as shown. After you have tabulated all the advertisements on the chart, you can total across each row to get the number of automobile ads, the number of cosmetic ads, the number of food ads, etc. By totaling down the columns, you can determine the total number of each appeal used. And by inspecting the cosmetic ads across the chart, you can determine the frequency with which each appeal was used in cosmetic advertisements.

A neat revision of your three tabulating charts would be appropriate appendix items. You'll also use the totals in the charts for construction of tables and other figures to be used in the body of your report. For example, a figure showing the percentage of total ads devoted to cosmetic products from each of your three magazines would be an excellent table in the body of your report. As you study your tabulation charts, you'll find almost an endless combination of items that lend themselves to table and graphic presentation.

You hope to be able to recommend a magazine and a major appeal or appeals to be used in the advertising campaign. The magazine and its readership should be compatible with your product. Prepare a formal report.

8. A major manufacturer of typewriters and related equipment, M.B.I., has made a presentation to your boss, Ms. A. J. Wainwright, executive vice president of the American Automobile Association Club in your area. The presentation encouraged the club to establish a Communication Center (or Word Processing Center) which would bring all but five of the current twenty-three secretaries together in one area. Each of the eighteen departments that previously had personal secretaries would simply pick up a telephone, push the dictation button, and dictate material to the center where a supervisor would distribute dictated tapes to typists for transcription.

The manufacturer has claimed that twelve of the eighteen secretaries moved to the center could handle the entire work load, thus creating a savings of six secretarial salaries if the six were released or assigned to other clerical duties in the organization. The cost of installing the system is about $75,000. The total yearly salaries of six secretaries is about $95,000. The manufacturer points out that replacement of the equipment would be necessary only about once every five years. Thus, the savings would be significant; quality control over secretarial production would be improved because individual secretaries would then be working in a common area under one supervisor; morale too, it is claimed, would be high once the secretaries adapted to the idea of working in the center.

The morale problem is one that bothers Ms. Wainwright. Rumors about the proposed center have started, and the grapevine message is that the secretaries are up in arms and several plan to quit if the center becomes a reality. Additionally, several of the departments and executives who have private secretaries are very upset about having their routines changed. Ms. Wainwright has asked you to take a survey of the secretaries involved and their supervisors to determine just what their attitudes are.

You have developed a questionnaire which you fill out yourself following an interview with each of the twenty-three secretaries. To open each interview, you describe briefly what the center will be like in terms of physical facilities. If it comes to reality, the center will include soundproofing, air conditioning, music, plush carpet, and all-new secretarial desks and chairs. Here's the questionnaire with total responses of the twenty-three secretaries as you subjectively recorded them after each interview.

1. Do you believe you'll be one of those moved to the Center?
   Yes: _19_   No: _4_

2. Do you think the work load will be greater in the Center than it is for you now?
   Yes: _22_   No: _1_

3. Have you talked with other secretaries about the Center?
   Yes: _23_   No: _0_

4. Do the ones you talked with like the idea of the Center?
   Yes: _0_   No: _23_

5. Have you thought about leaving if the Center becomes a reality?
   Yes: _9_   No: _14_

6. Would you definitely leave if transferred to the Center?
   Yes: _5_   No: _18_

7. Miscellaneous sample comments:

    "We'll certainly lose a lot of our present harmony with our bosses."

    "Will we get a raise if we're assigned to the Center?"

    "Who'll be fired if we reduce the number of secretaries?"

    "Aren't we doing a good job now?"

    "Who'll answer the phone in here when the executives are out of the office? That seems terrible--letting the phone ring and all that, you know."

    "With all the money you'll spend, why can't we just put better stuff in our present offices?"

    "I'll bet those secretaries who work for Wainwright and her crowd don't get transferred. They aren't all that good either."

    "Have you asked the executives about this? I'll bet some of them can't dictate to a machine."

    "Sure sounds great to me. I'd like to work in a nice place."

    "Wearing those earphones all day is a sure way to drive someone crazy."

    "I suppose we'd really be regimented--like punching time clocks and lacking freedom to move about as we have now."

    Your interviews with executives were a little more direct, and you tabulated their responses as follows:

1. Do you like the idea of the Center?
    Yes: <u>5</u>   No: <u>10</u>   Undecided: <u>8</u>

2. Are you satisfied with the current arrangement?
    Yes: <u>11</u>   No: <u>12</u>

3. If the answer to item 2 was "no," what is not satisfactory?
    (Several listed more than one unsatisfactory item.)

    a. Quality of work: <u>4</u>
    b. Secretary is often busy with others when needed: <u>4</u>
    c. Answering the phone keeps the secretary busy when there are typing jobs to do: <u>7</u>
    d. Secretarial hours of 9 to 5 are such that I have to write my letters in longhand at night and in the early morning and leave them for typing on days when I am out in the field (out of the office): <u>7</u>

4. How would your office be affected if the secretary were moved to the Center?

   a. Need a clerk-typist for the office: <u>18</u>
   b. Need a receptionist for the office: <u>12</u>
   c. Need a system to make sure we'd always have an open line to the Center: <u>18</u>
   d. Need a system to permit dictation outside of normal office hours: <u>7</u>

Prepare a report for Ms. Wainwright outlining your findings and making recommandations for her consideration.

9. You have been hired by a major building firm, Watt Construction Company, to make a survey of what college students would prefer in nearby apartment complexes. The following data were developed as a result of your study, which included 200 students selected at random. The figures in parentheses following each item are the numbers of female responses. Male responses are covered in the figures preceding the parentheses. Thus, you have the data covering the responses of males and females separately; and, by combining them, you have the total response. Prepare the report for R. A. Watt, President.

I. Personal Data (check one alternative in each part of this section)

   A. Sex:
   Male: <u>112</u>   Female: <u>(88)</u>

   B. Marital status:
   Married: <u>27 (2)</u>   Single: <u>85 (86)</u>

   C. Age:
   18 & less: <u>4 (6)</u>   26-30: <u>8 (12)</u>
   19-21: <u>63 (47)</u>   31-40: <u>6 (6)</u>
   22-25: <u>27 (17)</u>   41 & more: <u>(10)</u>

   D. Current residence:
   Dormitory: <u>23 (24)</u>   Off-campus
   On-campus   apartment: <u>13 (11)</u>
     apartment: <u>16 (7)</u>   With
   Fraternity or   parents: <u>22 (20)</u>
     sorority: <u>38 (26)</u>   Other
                                      (specify): <u>0 (0)</u>

   E. School standing:
   Graduate: <u>16 (8)</u>   Undergraduate: <u>96 (80)</u>

II. Recreational Facilities

   A. Outdoor facilities (check all that you would like to have provided)

Pool: 85 (80)   Badminton-volleyball
Jacuzzi: 51 (70)   courts: 40 (37)
Tennis courts: 78 (53)   Barbecue area: 25 (67)

B. Indoor facilities

1. Recreation room (check one)
    Should be provided: 84 (50)
    Should not be provided: 28 (38)

    If you think that a recreation room should be provided,
    check all recreation room facilities that you would want:

    Billiards tables: 37 (10)
    Ping-pong tables: 25 (15)
    Television sets: 10 (27)
    Lounging area: 55 (36)
    Fireplace: 31 (48)
    Cocktail area: 70 (50)
    Party area: 78 (50)
    Kitchen: 52 (21)

2. Gymnasium (check one)
    Should be provided: 60 (30)
    Should not be provided: 52 (58)

    If you think that a gymnasium should be provided, check all
    gymnasium facilities that you would want:

    Weights: 45 (15)
    Conditioning machines: 33 (27)
    Mats: 20 (30)
    Ropes or rings: 50 (2)
    Slant boards: 42 (30)

3. Sauna (check one)
    Should be provided: 75 (31)
    Should not be provided: 37 (57)

C. Organized recreation (check one)
    Should be provided: 32 (20)
    Should not be provided: 80 (68)

III. Parking Facilities

A. Number of parking spaces per apartment that should be provided:

1. Spaces per one-bedroom apartment (check one)
    One: 57 (31)   Two: 54 (55)
    Three: 1 (2)

2. Spaces per two-bedroom apartment (check one)
    One: _18 (16)_   Two: _88 (71)_
    Three: _6 (1)_

B. Type of parking lot that should be provided (check one)
    Conventional: _75 (38)_   Underground: _37 (50)_

    If you chose underground, check one:
    Secured: _28 (40)_   Unsecured: _9 (10)_

IV. Security Facilities (check all that you would like to have provided)

None: _0 (2)_   Watch dog: _16 (27)_
Locks on all doors   Security guard: _79 (75)_
   to complex: _93 (80)_

10. As part of a team selected from your class, make a one-hour survey of the nature of shoppers in your school bookstore. Each member of your team will also survey shoppers during a one-hour period, and you'll pool your data to provide a comprehensive sample. The purpose of your study is to determine (a) what kind of people shop in the bookstore during certain hours, (b) what items seem to sell to certain categories of shoppers, (c) what services or products not now offered would be desirable additions. In other words, your team will make a survey to determine how to provide better services. Organize your team in any way you like. Keep in mind sampling techniques. Don't survey only between 8 and 9 A.M. each day of the week. And don't limit your study to Friday afternoons. Outline the kinds of information you'll need and can get. Your team will make an oral presentation to the class in addition to a written presentation to the instructor.

11. Following is a brief list of studies concerned with communication. Each may be completed individually or in teams and should be presented in formal report form.
   a. Collect sixty copies of letters written by business firms. You will have to ask for them personally to explain why you want them. You can also offer each donor of letters a copy of your report when it is finished. Naturally, the letters will be held confidential; and if desirable, you'll be happy to take copies with no identifying information on them. For example, the inside address and the name of the writer may be deleted. When you have the copies, analyze them according to whatever criteria you can establish from earlier chapters in this book. For example, you might use planning, grammar and usage, spelling, consideration of the reader, Fog Index, and adequacy of detail as criteria. Keep track of the kinds of exceptions you find that would violate writing principles. Another approach would be to have a knowledgeable jury—a team of students in your class—select the fifteen best and the fifteen worst letters. Forget about the thirty letters that fall in the middle. Then attempt to determine what things distinguish between the good and bad letters. Prepare a report for your instructor.
   b. Collect several samples of news items and analyses from *Time, Newsweek,* and a local newspaper that discuss the same topic. Analyze each in terms of

readability, pictorial presentation, and quality of writing. You might again use the jury approach. Attempt to use some quantitative basis—for example, a rating scale as described in Chapter 13—to determine which publication is best in terms of your study.

c. We are bombarded constantly with sales slogans and the use of personalities to promote products and services advertised on television. Bob Hope represents Texaco with "We deserve your trust." Mrs. Olson represents Folgers. Develop a list of slogans and personalities with a matching list of products. Then attempt to determine from people in your age group which seem to be best known by having people attempt to match the products with the advertising theme or personality. Analyze why some are better recognized than others. You may find help in advertising or marketing textbooks and periodical literature. You can also ask respondents to indicate the amount of time they watch television each week, which television shows, games, and news reports they watch most, and whether they are really conscious of television advertising.

12. Here are some topics for research reports. Previous report assignments in this section have provided data for report preparation. For the following topics, you will be required to develop an entire report from your own research findings. This list is only suggestive, of course. In the process of reviewing it, you may discover ideas of your own simply by adapting the general theme as you see fit.

College Bookstore Traffic and Desirable Reorganization

Student Political Attitudes

Items for a Student Handbook

Student Evaluation of Teachers

Campus Parking and Traffic

How Students Spend Their Out-of-Class Time

Readability of Popular Books vs. Textbooks

Career Ambitions of Students

How to Select a Photocopy Machine

Personal Profile of a Typical Student

Part-time Employment Opportunities

Communicating on Campus

Student Opinion of Campus Eating Facilities

Teachers' Views of Their Profession

Characteristics of Student Leaders

Risk and Investments

Savings Opportunities in Commercial Banks, Savings and Loans, and Thrift Institutions

The Most Desirable Small Car

Campus Housing

What Students Want in Housing

Library Services and Problems

Survey of First-Year Accountants

The Legalization of Marijuana

Consumer Tax Burdens

Merit Rating as a Form of Employee Evaluation

Organization of a Textbook Exchange

ORAL COMMUNICATIONS AND COMMUNICATION MANAGEMENT

OBJECTIVES

1. To understand the need for preparation in a variety of oral communication activities.

2. To provide a framework for building oral communication skills.

3. To develop an appreciation for the scope and cost of communication in business, government, and industry.

4. To develop an understanding of the manager's role in controlling communication practices.

SPEECHES, ORAL REPORTS, AND GROUP COMMUNICATION

Controlling Voice Qualities
  Phonation
  Articulation
  Pronunciation
Knowing the Audience
Making A Speech
  Speech Organization
  Speech Content
  Delivery Style
  Some Final Comments on Speaking
Making an Oral Report
  Planning the Presentation

  Using Visual Aids
  Keeping Within the Limits
Communicating in Groups
  Purposes of Group Interaction
  Factors in Group Communication
Leading Conferences
Leading Committee Meetings
  Preparing the Discussion
  Role of the Presiding Officer
  Role of Members
Running Banquets
Summary

When people begin to speak, they reveal much about their personalities and their backgrounds—educational and social. But the trauma that most people feel when asked to speak before an audience often leads to a fumbling performance that reflects negatively on their personalities and backgrounds. George Jessel, famed emcee and comic, said "The human brain is a wonderful organ. It starts to work as soon as you are born and doesn't stop until you get up to deliver a public speech." And Eddie Rickenbacker, World War I flying ace (and later president of Eastern Airlines), returned from that war to an appropriate ticker-tape parade and public acclaim. At a banquet in his honor, he stood up to a tumultuous ovation, opened his mouth to speak, and was absolutely terrified. He stumbled through a few words in poor grammar and sat down. The next day, he hired a speech coach, a speech writer, and a grammar tutor. Later he became a popular speaker on the lecture circuit and became a wealthy person.

Someone has said that death is most people's second greatest fear; the first is having to speak before an audience. But if we do our homework by studying voice control, learning the development of a speech, and practicing effective speaking techniques, we can become members of the elite who actually relish the opportunity to speak before an audience.

CONTROLLING VOICE QUALITIES

Knowledge about and skill in three important qualities of speech—phonation, articulation, and pronunciation—are necessary to the development of effective speaking habits.

Phonation

Define phonation.

Phonation involves both the production and variation of the speaker's vocal tone. We project our voices and convey feelings—even thoughts—by varying our vocal tones. Such elements as pitch (how high or low the tones are), intensity (how loud the tones are), and duration (how long the tones are held), are factors in phonation. These factors permit us to recognize other people's voices over the telephone. Anyone who studies oral communications should also remember that changes in vocal quality occur with emotional moods.

Do high-pitched voices make listening pleasant?

In general, good voices have medium or low pitch, are easily heard but not too loud, carry smooth sounds, and are flexible in conveying emotional moods. Weak or poor voices, on the other hand, have a very high or monotonous pitch, are too soft or too loud for comfortable listening, are jerky and distracting, or may lack flexibility.

Practicing the following exercises can be helpful to anyone trying to achieve good voice qualities.

Breathe Properly and Relax

A nervous person usually loses control of his or her normal breathing. Although no one can avoid nervousness completely, we can eliminate some of our nervousness in speaking situations by preparing in advance. Study your audience, your subject, and yourself. Self-confidence is your most valuable asset. Even a casual focus on the self-confidence of national television news announcers will reveal its role. Their training in phonation is also evident.

Might too much self-confidence be just as harmful as too little?

Listen to Yourself

A tape recording of your voice reveals much about pitch, intensity, and duration. Most people, on hearing themselves, react with "Oh, I didn't know I sounded like that." To be a good speaker, though, you must do more than simply listen — you must attempt to alter some factors. Nasal twangs, for example, usually result from a failure to speak from the diaphragm, which involves taking in and letting air out through the larynx where the vocal cords operate. Letting air out through the nose leads to the nasal sound and prohibits resonance — the rich vibrations that make a voice pleasant. Several well-known voices in the entertainment field exemplify what a person can do by varying vocal qualities.

Develop Flexibility

The good speaking voice is musical, with words and sounds similar to notes in a musical scale. Read each of the following sentences aloud and emphasize the italicized word in each. As you practice saying the sentences, notice the change in meaning as the emphasis is changed.

What makes written messages harder to interpret than oral messages?

I am happy you are here. (Maybe I'm the only happy one.)
I *am* happy you are here. (I really *am*.)
I am *happy* you are here. (Happy best expresses my feeling.)
I am happy *you* are here. (Yes, *you* especially.)
I am happy you *are* here. (You may not be happy, but I am.)
I am happy you are *here*. (Here and not somewhere else.)

Articulation

An articulate speaker produces smooth, fluent, and pleasant speech. Articulation is the way in which a speaker produces and joins sounds. Faulty articulation is usually caused either by (1) organic disorders of the teeth, mouth, tongue, lips and other speaking equipment; (2) lack of education; or (3) personal carelessness. *Snoo* for *What's new* is an example of carelessness. *Dis, wid,* and *dem* for *this, with,* and *them*

What causes faulty articulation?

may result from a lack of knowledge and education. Various forms of lisping may result from organic disorders. These examples should not be confused with *dialect,* which people informally call "an accent." A dialect is a variation in pronunciation, usually of vowels, from one part of the country to another. Actually, everyone speaks a dialect; and speech experts can often identify, even pinpoint, the section of the country from which a speaker comes. In the United States, people often describe dialects as New England, New York, Southern, Texan, Ozark, Midwestern, Mountain, and Western. Within each of these, minor dialects may arise regionally or from immigrant influence. The simple fact is that when people interact, they influence each other even down to speech sounds. Yet, many prominent speakers have developed a rather universal dialect that seems to be effective no matter who the audience is.

To improve your articulation, most authorities suggest that you become aware of common errors. Make your tongue, lips, and teeth do the jobs they should to produce proper sounds. Next, understand the speech sounds. Vowels, for example, are always sounded with the mouth open and the tongue clear of the palate. Consonants are responsible primarily for the distinctness of speech and are formed by an interference with or stoppage of outgoing breath.

Pronunciation

The dictionary provides the best source to review pronunciation. People may articulate perfectly but still mispronounce words. The best rule to follow, perhaps, is to pronounce words in the most natural way. The dictionary often gives two pronunciations for a word. The first one is the desired pronunciation and the second an acceptable variation. To adopt, for example, a pronunciation commonly used in England such as *shedule* for *schedule* or *a-gane* for *again* could be considered affected speech. In other cases, the dictionary allows some leeway. The first choice for pronouncing *data* is to pronounce the first *a* long, as in *date;* but common usage is fast making pronunciation of the short *a* sound, as in *cat,* acceptable. Good speakers use proper pronunciation and refer to the dictionary frequently in both pronunciation and vocabulary development.

KNOWING THE AUDIENCE

Obviously, a speaker should know the audience, the subject, and the purpose before making any kind of oral presentation. A research scientist should not attempt to give a highly technical talk to a group of laymen who are interested only in the general findings, conclusions, and implications of research. At the same time, a scientist should probably not give a nontechnical report to a group of his or her peers. Many speakers have fallen flat simply by misjudging the interests and needs of the audience. Whether the group be a conference hall full of delegates or a small committee, you must size up your audience. Then decide whether the presentation should be factual, persuasive, inductive, deductive, logical, psychological, humorous, serious, and so on. A brief review of the sending and receiving skills can assist you in audience analysis and in planning your speech.

MAKING A SPEECH

One of the most satisfying experiences you can have is giving a speech successfully before a large audience. At the same time, the thought of making such a presentation is often frightening. You may recall the times in elementary school when you attempted to give a memorized presentation and words would just not come out. Or you may recall excellent speakers you have heard and you think, "I could never do that."

Only in rare cases, though, does good public speaking come as a gift. It is mostly a matter of preparation and practice. Edward R. Murrow, the late, famous newscaster, said he always developed some nervousness before speaking and called the moisture in his palms the "sweat of perfection." Speakers never get rid of nervousness; they simply learn to control it. Those who can speak competently are well recognized, are usually highly respected, and may earn substantially from their speaking activities. The higher a person rises in the ranks of business, education, government or community affairs, the more that person will be called on to make speeches. As a means of promoting institutional images and individual prestige, a speech is one of the most effective tools.

How can nervousness have positive effects?

Public speaking for most professionals is really an act—half content and half showmanship. Almost anyone can improve platform speaking skill by studying speaking principles, practicing, and learning some of the tricks of the trade. Three elements determine the effectiveness of the formal speech: organization, content, and delivery.

Speech Organization

Just as written presentations must be planned to develop a topic effectively and to appeal to reader interests, so must oral presentations. Like reports, speeches are organized in parts: an introduction, a content body, and a conclusion. All speeches fall into one of two categories based on the purpose of the speech:

Expository Speeches	Persuasive Speeches
Narration	Appeals to reason
Description	Appeals to emotion
Explanation	

How is outlining for a speech similar to outlining for a letter?

Expository speeches are usually organized deductively because their purpose is to describe a situation, to narrate a story, or to explain the reasons for an action already taken. Persuasive speeches, on the other hand, are likely to be organized inductively because the audience must be persuaded before being asked to take action. Both types of speeches may involve elements of the other, of course; but the purpose of the speech places it in one class or the other.

In a thirty-minute talk, could seven major points be sufficiently emphasized?

In a typical after-dinner talk of thirty to forty-five minutes, you can plan on two things. First, time permits only a few major points to be developed to back up the thrust of the speech. Second, your audience can absorb only a few major points regardless of the length of the speech. Thus, a presentation might be outlined as follows:

I. Introduction
   A. Purpose
   B. Justification of or importance of the topic
II. Major point 1 with support
   A. Anecdotes
   B. Statistics
   C. Quotes of authorities
III. Major point 2 with support
   A. Anecdotes
   B. Statistics
   C. Quotes of authorities
IV. Major point 3 with support
   A. Anecdotes
   B. Statistics
   C. Quotes of authorities
V. Summary and conclusion

Note how anecdotes, statistics, and quotations are used to support each major point. Making every statement in a talk into a major point—something to be remembered—is impossible, unless the talk lasts only two or three minutes. Consider a speaker who must get contributions to a highway safety campaign in the school system. The major purpose of the talk is to persuade people to give to the program. To develop this point, however, the speaker will probably build the talk around two or three major points such as

Highway safety must be improved.
Young people are the most susceptible to effective safety education.
Highway safety is everyone's business.

To develop these points, the speaker might use statistics on accidents, injuries, and fatalities; stories about local citizens involved unnecessarily in highway accidents; information about the cost of highway accidents to families, businesses, and the community; and evidence about the increasing rates of automobile insurance for all drivers. With these points developed, the speaker might spend only two or three minutes of the total time encouraging people to contribute.

Although stories, statistics, quotations, and the like may seem to be incidental trivia, they are critical to effective speech making. They retain listener interest, provide proof and evidence supporting major points, and often provide the humor and enlightenment that turn an otherwise dreary topic into a stimulating message. They are one of the professional speaker's most important inventory items. How does a speaker accumulate these items? Most obtain them from personal reading. When they come across something that seems worth remembering, they write it down.

Of course, the broader the reading, the greater the supply of material. Additionally, libraries contain references with titles like *Stories for All Occasions* and *A Speaker's Handbook of Illustrations*. Many speakers find miscellaneous items in publications such as *The Reader's Digest* valuable. The best source is everyday reading and research within your field of specialization. Small-talk items provide you with something to say in support of the content of the speech.

In a serious speech on an important topic, should small talk be completely omitted?

Speech Content

The field of specialization just mentioned is something worth talking about. Too many new speakers commit the blunder of accepting speaking engagements on topics they know little about and fail to recognize that expertise in a field cannot be feigned. As a general rule, you should only choose subjects about which you are knowledgeable and enthusiastic. Couple a lack of knowledge with a lack of enthusiasm, and the speech will be a total failure.

Many college commencement speeches fail in effectiveness because the speakers resort to the time-worn practice of telling graduates and their parents what the real world is like rather than sticking to their fields of expertise. These speakers have failed to analyze their audiences. College students have spent fifteen or more years of study preparing themselves to cope with the real world, and twenty or thirty minutes of more of the same isn't going to change the course of their lives one little bit.

These guides may be useful in selecting speech content:

1. Choose topics of personal interest.

2. Select topics about which you are enthusiastic.

3. Try to speak on a subject on which the audience credits you as an expert. Good speakers know more about the subject than does the audience.

Then, of course, the critical test is to deliver the talk with enthusiasm and confidence.

Delivery Style

Assuming your speech has been prepared and practiced adequately, you should take a few precautions to ensure that your delivery will be effective. Arrive at the speaking location early enough to get accustomed to the environment. What kind of amplifying equipment is to be used? Is it working? Can people in the back of the room see and hear comfortably? If you plan to use visual materials, can they be seen? The attention you pay to these physical considerations will have much to do with the effectiveness of your presentation.

How can a speaker get the type of introduction desired?

Good speakers also make certain that they will get an appropriate introduction. Some speakers have an introduction they have written personally for use on all occasions. They hope the person introducing them will read it verbatim. They almost never give the introducer a complete lifetime vita from which the introducer may select appropriate items. This technique puts the introducer on the spot and frequently leads to a poor or inadequate introduction.

Follwing the introduction comes the delivery of the speech. Speakers follow four different speech styles:

Why should an impromptu speech be relatively short?

1. *The impromptu speech.* The impromptu speech is frightening to most people, because the speaker is called on to say a few words without forewarning. In some cases, speakers can anticipate the request and are able to formulate some ideas. These ideas can often be designed around a cause-effect, historical, advantage-disadvantage or problem-solution basis. In any case, impromptu delivery style should be simple, conversational, and direct. If you feel inadequately informed or unprepared, simply thank the person for calling on you and explain why the opportunity is being declined.

How do impromptu and extemporaneous speeches differ?

2. *The extemporaneous speech.* Extemporaneous speaking is not impromptu speaking. Although the impromptu speech is totally unrehearsed, the extemporaneous speech is prepared, outlined, rehearsed, but not written in detail. This is the kind of speech most often delivered by professionals. Simple cues written on 3-by-5 index cards may provide enough material for the speaker to talk meaningfully for long periods. Extemporaneous style enables the speaker to adapt material to the audience as the audience reacts during the talk. Most teachers employ this type of preparation. Through experience they have compiled a reservoir of material so that they can adapt to varying class and individual reactions. One class may understand a concept readily so that little "small talk" is necessary, but another class may indicate that it won't understand without considerably more background and developmental material.

What are the limitations of a memorized speech?

3. *The memorized speech.* Of all the speech styles, the memorized speech has the greatest limitations. First, the speaker is almost totally unable to adjust to audience feedback. Second, as everyone who attended elementary school knows, when the speaker forgets a point or blocks out, the entire speech may be lost. At best, a long embarrassing pause may occur. Generally, people giving memorized speeches sound monotonous, use unnatural body gestures, and lack the sincerity necessary to convince the audience. For short roles in church or in club initiation rites, however, the memorized presentation is often impressive.

4. *The written-and-read speech.* A written-and-read speech is appropriate for many technical-conference speaking engagements and for occasions when the material is extremely complex. Everyone is familiar with the written-and-read

speeches made by high governmental and business officials. Two reasons underlie choosing this form of address. First, if the speaker holds high office or position, the written speech provides the speaker protection against being misquoted. Second, when time constraints are exact, as with television programming, the written speech can be designed to fit the schedule.

However, written-and-read speeches have some drawbacks. They may frighten or alienate audiences. Nothing makes an audience fidget more than a stack of manuscript pages on the podium and the feeling that the speech will last for hours. Many speakers use large longhand writing or triple-space typing to make the manuscript easy to read. For some large gatherings, speakers use one-way glass on both sides of the podium. The manuscript is then projected on both screens, a page at a time, unseen from the audience's side of the glass. This method permits the speaker to make eye contact with the audience and gives the impression of an extemporaneous speech. When writing a speech, keep in mind the following suggestions:

What are the drawbacks of a written-and-read speech?

a. Write large enough and with wide spacing to avoid becoming lost in the manuscript.

b. Avoid unusual words. It's easy to stumble over or mispronounce words you would not normally use.

c. Keep sentences relatively short, but be sure to use conjunctions and other transitional devices for coherence.

d. Write in the first person, active voice, and use contractions. These techniques lend a natural tone to the speech and help ease delivery.

How do contractions and the use of first-person pronouns assist in making a speech effective?

When your speech can be assisted by graphic aids, use them to your advantage. Be forewarned that the audience will pay more attention to the graphic than to your comments, but we'll look more closely at the use of graphics in the part of this chapter on oral reports. For now, keep the following suggestions in mind as you prepare your public speech; although most of these suggestions apply to extemporaneous speaking, most are helpful in all four styles:

1. As the time approaches for the speech, try to work up a little nervous tension if you are not already nervous. Good speakers admit to being nervous prior to speaking and claim a touch of anxiety helps them make a better opening.

Can nervousness be an asset instead of a liability?

2. Once standing, try to gain eye contact with the audience. It's much easier to address only a few people than to attempt to meet everyone in the audience eye-to-eye. Select about six people from the entire audience and talk to them. A good technique is to select a person in the middle of the front row, one at each side of the front, one in the center, and one in each corner of the back. As you look at each of them, as shown in Figure 19-1, eye contact appears to be made with the entire audience. You will get better feedback, and your delivery will seem more natural.

3. Use gestures naturally, and don't overdo them. Some people have trouble talking without using their hands, and others appear motionless — a sign of fear. Gestures will come naturally as you gain confidence in yourself.

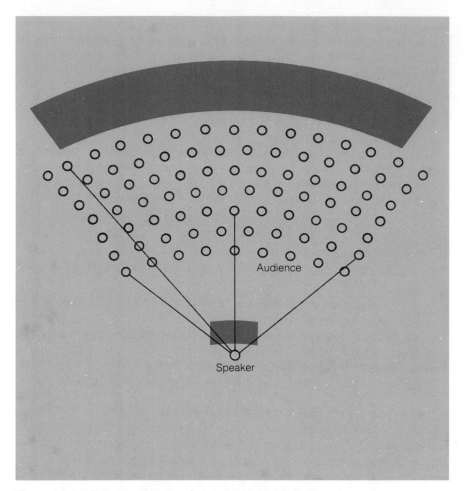

Figure 19-1   Selecting listeners for eye contact.

4. Insist on having a podium. A podium not only holds your notes, it can be grasped to prevent a trembling hand from showing. The podium serves as your security blanket.

5. Avoid annoying speech habits. Some people follow every statement with a word or phrase such as "Okay," "Ya know," "See," or "Right." Other habits such as clearing your throat or uttering a soft cough continually shift the audience's focus from the subject of the speech to the speaker.

Can a joke be counted on to loosen up an audience?

6. Use jokes or humorous stories appropriately. These should be closely related to the subject matter, or they are totally out of place. Inexperienced speakers often misunderstand the use of an opening joke. It has only one purpose: to capture audience attention and focus it on the subject. It seldom loosens up the audience or lets them know the speaker is superior. When poorly integrated into a talk, a joke can shift the focus from the subject. It might even alienate the entire audience. Of course, off-color stories are taboo, unless the subject of the talk is off-color stories.

7.   Work hard on the preparation of the opening and closing sections of the speech. A good opening sets the stage for speaker-audience rapport, and a good ending will solidify the theme of the speech.

8.   Adjust both content and length by audience reaction. Shortening the talk by ending it is better than continuing on despite negative audience feedback. Restlessness is shown by an increase in audience motion, coughing, moving of chairs, and sounds of talking in the group.

9.   Dress carefully. Appropriate clothing and good grooming won't alienate anyone. Appearance has a significant effect on the audience.

10.   Appear confident and seem to enjoy making the speech.

Some of these points need clarification. First, as you work up a little mental tension or nervousness, also try these ways to reduce your physical tensions:

1.   Breathe rhythmically, slowly, and deeply.

2.   Move your body whenever possible; don't stay motionless.

3.   Don't grit your teeth; rather try to relax your jaw, shoulders, and throat.

4.   Loosen your arms and neck by moving them about so the audience is not aware.

Second, as you gain confidence, don't worry about eye contact with only a selected few in the audience. You'll know when you can speak to the entire group. Third, although jokes are the stock-in-trade of the professional, you should know the professional has practiced them over and over again. What you should do when you think you have a good joke is try it on friends. If their laughter is merely perfunctory —a matter of courtesy—forget it because you're better off without it. Good story tellers have a superb sense of timing; so if you don't, jokes aren't your strength. Lastly, remember you are the professional if you've selected your topic properly in terms of your own background. You know more about it than anyone in the audience does.

Additionally, graphics are a genuine strength in oral reporting, as will be discussed in the following section; but they should be used sparingly in public speaking where *you* are the "star" and the graphic is only a very minor supplement.

Some Final Comments on Speaking

The importance of careful planning for any speaking engagement cannot be over-emphasized. If reading a speech makes you feel more confident, it's better to read than to give a poor extemporaneous speech. Through practice, you can learn to vary

Is it possible
to convey credibility
while putting on an act?

tone, speed, and manner in such a way as to make the audience think you are speaking without a manuscript. Don't consider effective public speaking merely an act, however. Sincerity is a prime requisite. Insincerity leads to ineffectiveness. Strong presentations combine planning, content, sincerity, and technique.

Effective speakers let the audience know that they don't take themselves too seriously. Some degree of informality in manner is important on every occasion. Ad libs and other asides can contribute to this impression. The one thing most prominent speakers have in common is the ability to speak *to people* rather than *down to them.* Stand-up speaking is face-to-face communication. You and your audience are engaged in a constant flow of feedback activities, and your ability to adapt determines how effectively the message goes over. As mentioned, nervousness is part of the game and shouldn't be used as an excuse for avoiding speaking opportunities.

MAKING AN ORAL REPORT

Oral reporting differs from public speaking in that it isn't "public." Although public speaking is designed to inform, to persuade, and to entertain, oral reporting is similar to written reporting: an objective presentation in either an informational or analytical form. Oral reporting to groups within the organization is a far more common practice than new employees imagine.

On one occasion, you might give a presentation to your peers in committee work, to subordinates as part of a training or information program, or to superiors at a board of directors meeting or at a stockholders' meeting. In any case, your reputation is on the line. If you get the respect of those to whom you are reporting, you achieve status, and managing others becomes relatively easy; and if you get the respect of the board of directors, promotion to higher rank is a strong possibility.

Planning the Presentation

Oral reports differ from stand-up, public speeches in at least these aspects:

1. Much more is usually known about the audience for an oral report, and the speaker is probably known personally by most members of the audience.

2. Because the audience is smaller in number, the setting for the oral report will be more intimate than the setting for a formal speech.

3. Questions are more likely to be asked *during* the oral report.

4. The time allotted tends to be shorter. Thus, you must plan the presentation in a way that develops points fully, yet concisely, before interruptions occur or time expires.

Usually, oral reports fall within the normal speech categories of expository or persuasive. Within these two, the reports should be limited to the descriptive, explanatory, and appeals-to-reason categories and should not include narration and appeals to emotion. Because reports are logical and involve problem solving, oral reports should be organized in the same way as written reports. They should use much the same language and should take advantage of graphic aids. In general, oral reports should follow the inductive plan. A broad outline should include the following points:

1. Purpose of the report
2. Discussion, including
   a. Method of research and other background material
   b. Presentation of the findings
3. Summary including the conclusion and implications

Among the reports that can be planned around this outline are reviews of economic conditions; development of new methods, practices, or policies; periodic progress reports; affirmative action and other personnel studies; financial reports; and reports of research.

As you plan your report, keep in mind the principles that apply to report writing and particularly be aware that your oral report will not contain a table of contents and headings to guide the listener as they guide the reader of a report. Therefore, you have the task of leading the audience through your report. As you plan, you should develop topic sentences to introduce each major section and subsection of the report. Statements such as "Next, I'll present some of the major findings of our study" are helpful. You can also make a larger-than-normal pause as you move from one topic to the next, or you can make a change in your bodily position or a distinct gesture, such as a visible motion as you move from one page of your notes to another. Additionally, remember the transition phrases and other techniques of coherence that apply to report writing.

More will be said about the use of graphics; but for transitional purposes, you might have a list of topics you'll cover printed on a chalkboard or flip chart and simply point to each topic as you begin to talk about it. As a general observation, your oral report audience will have a built-in interest in your presentation, which is an advantage over the public speech where the speaker must build the interest of the audience as the talk develops. Let's look at some differences between public speeches and oral reports as they apply to the introduction, the body, and the summary or conclusion.

Would a list of topics serve the same purpose as headings in a written report?

The Introduction

In both oral reports and speeches, the speaker should thank the one who made the introduction. "Thank you, Mr. Chairman" after the introduction for an oral report and "Thank you for your kind introduction, Mrs. Garcia" for a speech are adequate. Then you follow with your own introduction to your presentation. The public speaker uses the opening as an effort to capture the attention of the audience. Startling statements, jokes related to the topic, famous quotations, and anecdotal stories are familiar speech openings.

For the oral report, you might use one of those speech openings if you believe it appropriate; but because your purpose is to report—not to entertain—you should seek to stay with your subject. An opening statement such as ''When we were granted the approval to open a new branch office in Watson, we assigned a team to select the best possible inner-city location'' introduces the subject immediately and sets the stage for the rest of the report. If you want to organize your report in deductive sequence, you might begin with ''I want to inform you about why and how we selected the corner of Main and First in Watson as the location for our newest branch office.''

Is the opening of an oral report important?

The Body

You'll recall from the discussion of speech organization that major points are supported by anecdotes, statistics, and quotes. As you prepare your oral report, however, you'll have to support your major points with factual information. Persuasive, emotional talk is out—unless, of course, you want to give the board of directors the idea that you'd make a good used-car salesman. The design of your paragraphs will become readily apparent to your listeners if you begin with a topic sentence and follow with the supporting material. For example, ''Three possible sites for the branch were available—Main and First, the Roseburg Mall, and the City National Bank building at Main and Twelfth. As this chart shows, pedestrian foot traffic is . . .'' uses the topic sentence and follows with an introduction to the factual data to be presented.

Why use para- graphing tech- niques in an oral report?

The Summary

In a public speech, the ending is often an urgent plea for the members of the audience to take some action or to look on the subject from a new point of view. In the oral report, the terminal or summary section is like that of the written report. First, state your conclusion and support it with the highlights from your supporting evidence; ie.; ''In summary, we selected the Main and First location because it had. . . .'' As we discuss the use of visual aids in oral reports, try to picture not only how effective they can be in conveying your message but also how much easier they can make your own job of planning your report.

Using Visual Aids

Visual aids are developed from the variety of graphics discussed in Chapter 14 and are important to oral reports because they reinforce the spoken word. Through the use of visuals, a speaker hits the listener (receiver) with doubled impact—through the eyes and the ears. An ancient Chinese proverb says, ''Tell me, I'll forget. Show me, I may remember. But involve me and I'll understand." Thus, the use of visuals approaches desirable audience involvement. Additionally, graphics provide the audience with a means of resolving possible communication problems with the speaker by providing answers in advance of the questions.

How does a visual aid contribute to double impact?

Skilled speakers generally develop a set of graphic aids before they determine exactly what to say about each one. Graphs, tables, and pictures are the most-used items, and here are some guides for using them:

1. Make the graphic large enough to be seen by everyone in the audience. Either large paperboard displays or overhead transparencies are effective. In some organizations, great care is taken in the preparation of 35-millimeter projection slides which can be used with a carousel projector and controlled by the speaker with a hand-held slide changer. This is an expensive method, but it may be desirable depending on your analysis of the audience or the number of times the materials might be used.

2. Keep the graphics simple. Too much detail may lead the audience to concentrate on unimportant items and often makes letters and figures too small to be effective.

Is a simple graphic effective?

3. Use a small file card to record what must be said about each graphic. Then, as you proceed from one graphic to another, simply move to the next file card. Sometimes you may write notes lightly in pencil directly on paperboard materials and refer to them without the audience's seeing them.

4. During the presentation, step to one side of the graphic so the audience may see it. Use a pointer if necessary; but in any case, direct your remarks to the audience and not to the graphic—maintain eye contact.

Let's examine some of the visual devices available to speakers. The most common are posterboard graphs and outlines, overhead transparencies and projectors, flip charts, blackboards (chalkboards), and 35-millimeter slides.

Posterboard Displays

Posterboard can be purchased in a variety of sizes, colors, and weights from most bookstores, art supply stores, and stationers. Size and weight determine the price, but you should know that the lighter weight boards have a tendency to bend and fall forward when placed on easels or chalk trays. It is embarrassing to have one begin to sway and then fall loudly to the floor during your presentation.

You can use poster paints to develop your visual, and you can also purchase paste-on letters if you are not a good letterer. Perhaps most important in terms of your presentation is to make sure your visual is large enough to be read by the entire audience.

Notice visuals A and B in Figure 19-2. They could be effective on posterboard; and, incidentally, they are the type of graphic that can be on display for quite a long time, providing an outline for the items to be covered in all or part of a presentation.

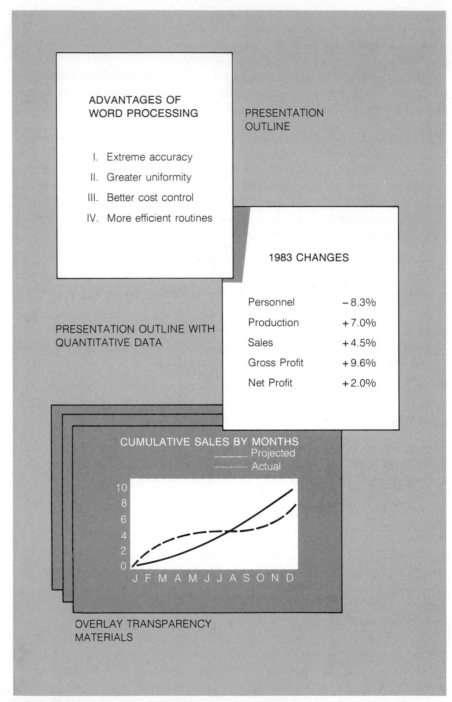

Figure 19-2   Visuals to accompany oral presentations.

For an audience of about a hundred, graphics should be on posterboard at least 16″ × 22″ and in large lettering. During the presentation, the speaker simply points to each item as it comes up during the talk.

Make certain that you do point accurately even if you have to touch the board with your finger or wooden pointer. Experience has shown that people will go to great pains to make a good visual and then fail to make effective use of it. Inexperienced speakers often fall into the habit of simply nodding their heads toward the visual, and that is not enough to keep the audience with you.

Overhead Transparencies

You have certainly been exposed to overhead transparencies during your education, but you may not have learned to prepare them. You can make a transparency of almost anything from free-hand drawings to book pages simply by running your materials through a transparency-making machine, although some machines will not produce transparencies from anything but a photocopy.

During your presentation, you can point to specific parts of the transparency by pointing specifically to the part either on the projection screen or on the overhead projector plate that holds the transparency. Additionally, you can quickly remove a transparency and replace it with another because the projector is usually within arm's reach. An advantage of the use of transparencies is their adaptability to overlay presentations. For example, visual C in Figure 19-2 consists of two transparencies. First the speaker displays a transparency with only the headings and projected sales line; second, the speaker places the second transparency which contains only the actual sales line over the first. This is an effective technique when you want to talk about projected sales before getting the audience involved in actual sales and the reasons for the discrepancies. Other times that overlays are helpful are when you want to show the step-by-step development of a procedure or a process, such as a flow chart or the manufacture of a product. Incidentally, you can write on transparencies with a greased pencil or with some pens designed for the purpose. In this sense, then, you can do some of the same things that overlays accomplish.

Chalkboards

We are all familiar with chalkboards in the classroom and the varying degrees of teachers' ability to use them. For oral presentations outside the classroom, you can use portable chalkboards. Some of the major problems presented by chalkboards are the slickness and lack of cleanliness of some, poor penmanship of the user, and the failure of the user to erase items once they have been covered.

Can you recall any sloppy use of chalkboards?

If you plan to use this method to present visual assists to your presentation, practice beforehand and make certain the equipment is satisfactory. If your chalk board display is sizable or complex, you'll find it helpful to place it on the board before your presentation. Most portable boards have two sides, thus permitting you to keep your material from view until you need it.

Flip Charts

Flip charts consist of a pad of paper with sheets about 2' × 3', fastened at the top, and mounted on an easel with a tray for crayons or colored pens. The speaker can prepare a series of visuals before the presentation and simply "flip" from one visual to the next as the talk progresses. Additionally, flip charts are often used to record ideas during a discussion. Although they serve many of the same purposes as a chalkboard, flip charts permit the speaker to use color to advantage and to prepare material in advance, a factor not always available when chalkboards are used.

35-Millimeter Slides

Presentations built around the use of 35-millimeter slides usually involve several visuals in a planned sequence and are displayed by means of a carousel or other slide projector. A major disadvantage is that the room should ordinarily be darkened.

For sophisticated presentations, however, slides add a great deal of impact. The slides are often prepared by graphic artists before being reduced to projector size, and this process can be very expensive compared with other visual methods. For presentations involving ordinary photography pictures, of course, the slide method is most appropriate.

Keeping Within the Time Limits

If your presentation is part of a busy program, be prepared to complete the presentation within the allotted time. In many organizations, speakers have one or more rehearsals before making reports to groups such as a board of directors. These rehearsals or dry runs are made before other executives, critiqued, timed, revised, and rehearsed again. In some organizations, video-taped sessions are held so participants can see how they come across.

Questions often disrupt carefully laid plans. At the same time, questions provide feedback, clarify points, and ensure effective understanding. More often than not, people ask questions that will be answered in a later part of the presentation. In these cases, you should say something like "I believe the next slide will clarify that point. If not, we will come back to it." If the question can be answered quickly, the speaker should do so while indicating that it will also be covered later in the presentation. If necessary, the speaker might also indicate that questions will be answered following a certain portion of the presentation. In any case, rehearsal should include a session on questions that might be raised. Then, the talk may be altered to anticipate the questions.

Do you become flustered by interruptions?

The importance of oral reports cannot be overstressed. College students, for example, often wonder about why they should engage in oral report practice; yet, many find themselves called on early in their careers to make such presentations. Their futures may hinge on the effectiveness of their performance.

COMMUNICATING IN GROUPS

Most of your oral communication in business will be spent in one-to-one relationships, to which we gave significant attention in Chapter 1. Another form of oral communication you will undertake at least occasionally is the making of speeches and oral reports. But your second most frequent oral communication activity will occur when you are a participant in groups—primarily committees formed within your work environment. The human relations orientation of business and government is a democratic one and has made the committee meeting a permanent part of those institutions. Yet, when a participant is asked for feedback about committee meetings, more often than not he or she will confide that the meeting was boring, the leader talked too much, one or two people dominated, time was wasted, the group didn't stick to the subject, and no conclusions were drawn. Nevertheless, group meetings can be productive when members understand something about the nature of groups and how they should operate.

Purposes of Group Interaction

Groups form or are formed for synergistic effects; ie., through pooling their efforts, groups can achieve more collectively than could the group members working individually. Groups also may serve either or both of two major purposes: First, they have a work or *task purpose*—to get the job done. Second, they have a *maintenance purpose* that grows out of the social nature of groups—to maintain group morale and to feel better about themselves individually. Although this second purpose may not have been designated as a responsibility of the group, all groups spend some time working to achieve it. According to Huseman, most experimental literature about small groups indicates that "small group communication and decision making is usually motivational for the individual, conducive to attitude change, improves thinking, and results in group decisions that are superior to individual decisions."[1] Thus, groups have both task and maintenance goals, and the emphasis they put on either is a result of several factors in group communication.

Do you belong to groups that spend time on maintenance?

Factors in Group Communication

As you review the following factors in group communication, try to visualize their relationship to some of the groups you have belonged to through school, church, athletics, and social activities.

Group Goals

Both task and maintenance goals are common to groups of all kinds, but the relative emphasis a group places on each results from several other factors. One important

1. Richard C. Huseman et al., *Readings in Interpersonal and Organizational Communication*, 2nd ed. (Boston: Holbrook Press), 1973, p. 413.

factor is the ability of the leader to work toward task goals while, at the same time, contributing to the development of group maintenance goals.

Longevity

Some groups are formed to perform for only a short time, such as to select a location for a dinner meeting. Others may be assigned such tasks as monitoring a firm's compliance with equal opportunity standards, serving for extended periods. Short-term groups generally spend almost all their time on task goals and little on maintenance goals. The reverse is obviously true of long-time groups inasmuch as relationships are long lasting.

Are groups studying for exams primarily task oriented?

Size

The smaller the group, the more the opportunity to communicate with one another; conversely, large groups inhibit communication. When broad input is desired, large groups may be good; and when expert opinion is the goal, smaller groups may be desirable. An interesting observation about groups is that when large groups meet they generally divide into smaller groups for maintenance purposes, even though the large group is task oriented. Although much research has been conducted in the area of group size, no single number of members has been identified as optimum. Considerable support exists for groups of five to seven members as being desirable in decision-making and problem-solving circumstances. When groups grow larger, opportunities for individuals to participate is limited. Odd numbers of participants are preferred because deciding votes are possible and tie votes are infrequent.

Perception and Self-Concept

Do all group members have the same perception of the group?

People who become part of groups have perceptions of how the group should operate and what it should achieve. The member also has a self-concept that dictates fairly well how the member will behave. A funny or humorous person tries to preserve the image; a person with an aggressive-type reputation attempts to maintain that reputation. Whenever expectations and perceptions are not met, the entire group may suffer. Very often, when expectations and satisfaction of self-concept fall short, individuals may seek and find a sort of ''emergent'' behavior to compromise the conflict.

Status

Because groups are composed of a variety of people, some are more qualified than others to speak on certain subjects—even though everyone should have input. Consider a group in which the chief executive or president of the organization is a member: group members tend to direct their remarks to that person; and when that person speaks, group members almost to a person agree. People are inclined to communicate equally with peers, but they tend to speak upward to superiors and downward to subordinates. Nonetheless, groups require balance in status and expertise, not homogeneity.

Group Norms

A norm is a standard or average for behavior, and all groups possess norms. How members behave is largely a result of norms the group has established. In your classroom, for example, a norm probably is that students keep quiet while the teacher is talking. Another norm is that if the teacher is generally five minutes late to class, the students may start coming late to class too. In your everyday life you'll notice that families have a normative seating order at family dinners and that changes make members uncomfortable. People conform to norms for several reasons: (1) Conformity makes them comfortable, and nonconformity makes them uncomfortable. (2) Conformity leads to their acceptance by the group and to status. (3) By conforming, they benefit from the feedback of others.

Can you list some norms for student behavior?

Communication Networks

Communication networks describe the structural makeup of a group. These networks are usually described in terms of schematic models such as those shown in Figure 19-3. Five people are in each group configuration for illustrative purposes. In the *star* network, one person is the "star performer" and can communicate with each of the others; but they can only communicate with the leader. The *circle* describes a group in which each participant can speak to two others, and the *chain* provides two relationships for each of the three intermediate positions, but only one contact for the extreme positions. In the *all-channel* network, everyone can communicate with all members of the group. The *subgroup* model represents the situation when "cliques" form within the group. Obviously, in such a situation, group performance is impaired.

What group network applies in your class?

Which of these is best under which conditions? Much research about group structure and performance has involved experiments in which groups of various structures have been given identical problem-solving tasks. Performance is measured in terms of time and participant morale. Results have generally shown that the *star* network, with one centralized participant, is most effective in terms of speed and controllability. For short-term tasks — collecting and compiling information from a variety of sources — the star is effective. In terms of morale, however, only the "star" or leader is likely to get great satisfaction out of the group's accomplishment.[2] The star network does not meet the personal needs and perceptions of the other members.

2. Harold J. Leavitt, *Managerial Psychology*, 3rd Ed. (Chicago: The University of Chicago Press), 1972, p. 192.

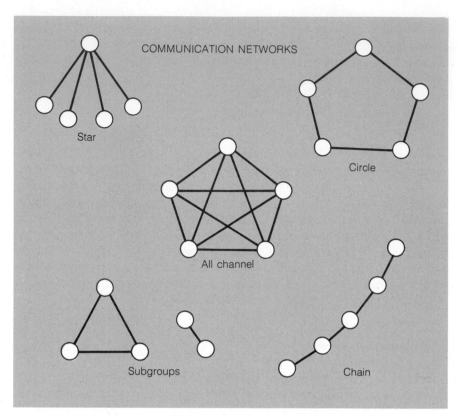

Figure 19-3 Group communication networks.

In terms of group morale, networks providing multiple relationships and variety in feedback are superior. The greater the number of relationships, the greater is participant satisfaction. The *chain* provides two relationships for the intermediate participants but only one for those at the ends of the chain. The *circle* provides two for all group members, but the *all-channel* has four for each participant.

What do these networks imply for group work? First, the strong leadership in a star network is effective for short-term tasks when little attention needs to be given to the group-maintenance goal. The all-channel network provides for the greatest amount of individual member input into the discussion or work of the group; but at the same time, leadership might be lacking and considerable time could be devoted to determining such things as who will be the leader, how the group will operate, and even what is to be the purpose of the group. The nature of multiple-relationship groups is that participants may learn about the needs and perceptions of others while satisfying their own. The multiple-relationship network would probably be more effective in handling complex, long-term tasks. Incidentally, one of the major advantages of group processes in general is that people who have an opportunity to participate in problem solving and decision making also engage more enthusiastically in implementing the results of the group decision.

When is the star network effective?

Beyond these somewhat obvious conclusions, research evidence about structure on group performance is limited. The influences of styles of leadership and complexity of group tasks, for example, are aspects yet to be resolved. As we review some group leadership tasks, keep in mind some of the factors that affect group performance.

LEADING CONFERENCES

Parliamentary law has come down through the years little changed from its original use in the English Parliament; hence, it has been a successful means of controlling large meetings. Presiding over meetings governed by parliamentary rules can frighten the untried. Of course, a good group leader should know parliamentary procedures, and, in large group meetings, should appoint a parliamentarian to advise the chair and give rulings when necessary. Chairing a meeting involves a variety of problems that can distract the presiding officer from parliamentary details. The following basic suggestions should assist in the presiding officer's preparation for the task:

1. Become familiar with basic parliamentary procedures, including the order of business, the procedure for offering and acting on motions and amendments, and techniques for limiting discussion or debate.

Is Roberts' Rules of Order a good guide?

2. Plan the agenda carefully, so one item leads naturally to another.

3. Use the parliamentarian judiciously; do not lean on her or him for every decision. Doing so simply lowers prestige in the minds of the other participants.

LEADING COMMITTEE MEETINGS

Large and small committee meetings are frequent in business, government, and civic affairs. Many fall flat simply because the presiding officer lets control of the meeting slip away. Essentially, the purposes of group discussion are to solve a problem common to the group or to reach agreement or improved understanding of a subject. The prime characteristic of effective discussion is a permissive attitude toward contributions of group members. Unless people feel free to make contributions, little will be accomplished in the way of discussion; and the meeting may become merely a dialogue or even a monologue.

What is a prime characteristic of a discussion leader?

Preparing the Discussion

Aimless wandering and repetitious, irrelevant contributions to group discussion can be avoided by careful planning. Either the leader or a committee should prepare a plan for distribution prior to the meeting or for first consideration at the meeting. The plan or agenda should begin with a statement of the purpose of the meeting or a clear definition of the problem to be solved. This process of stating objectives at the beginning of a meeting helps define the parameters for the discussion. One of the problems of getting a discussion off in the right direction is securing agreement on the definition of terms used in describing the purpose of the meeting. Semantics enters into almost any discussion, and an early attempt to avoid misunderstandings should be made by the leader.

Next, an analysis of the topic should be made to get members to focus on the nature of the problem with its ramifications. These ramifications may be included as agenda items for early consideration. Then, if disagreement on the goals exists, many later problems and perhaps much discussion can be avoided. This preliminary discussion actually helps define the final agenda, which should be agreed on before discussion of solutions begins.

Role of the Presiding Officer

In all types of committee or conference meetings, you have several responsibilities as the presiding officer:

1. Arranging the time and place.

2. Preparing and distributing an agenda. (See the sample agenda in Figure 19-4.)

3. Calling the meeting to order on time.

4. Making clear the purpose of the meeting and of each agenda item.

5. Keeping the discussion on course.

6. Eliciting contributions from each participant.

7. Controlling overenthusiastic members.

8. Creating an atmosphere of ease.

9. Summarizing discussion from time to time.

10. Working to end the meeting on schedule.

Ideally, you should have studied the problem or subject of the meeting thoroughly. This preliminary preparation enables you to describe concisely the nature of the problem and the purpose of the meeting before calling attention to the agenda. If you have ultimate authority for decision making after the group discussion, use discretion in presenting views during the preliminary statement. Subordinates might feel inhibited about speaking freely or doing much reflective thinking if they think you have an unchangeable point of view. After the preliminary discussion, talk will undoubtedly begin on the agenda items. If voluntary contributions are not forthcoming, call on various members for their comments.

Should the chairperson express strong views?

AGENDA

Management Committee

Tuesday, March 15, 10:30 am

Presiding--Mr. Maurice L. Hall, Chairman

1. Call to order.
2. Approval of minutes of meeting held February 18 (previously distributed).
3. President's Report.
4. Committee Reports
   a. Executive Committee (Mrs. Franks)
   b. Social Responsibility Committee (Mr. Washington)
   c. Budget and Fiscal Planning Committee (Ms. Lee)
   d. Development Committee (Mr. Archibald)
   e. Long-range Planning Committee (Mrs. Fluent)
   f. Personnel Committee (Mr. Robbins)
5. Decisions on Recommendations to the Board (Mr. Hall).
6. Old Business.
7. New Business.
8. Adjournment.

Attachments:

1. Long-range plans A and B.
2. Recommendation Items for Board Consideration.

Figure 19-4 Sample meeting agenda.

Keeping a freewheeling discussion on course takes skillful handling. Although group members have agreed on the agenda items and sequence, some will stray, bring in irrelevant ideas, jump to later items in the agenda, or state relevant ideas in such a way that they appear to be out of order. Some techniques of value to leaders are

1.   Recall the agenda item or the purpose of the meeting when irrelevant talk appears.

2.   Take the opportunity to summarize the discussion from time to time.

3.   Restate, if possible, the snarled and unclear ideas of a group member.

4.   Ask for a contribution from one member when it appears that another is beginning to do all the talking.

Of course, a well-controlled voice used with understanding and tact is vital. Sarcasm and other offensive behavior should be used sparingly or not at all.

Although the talkative member presents problems, sometimes the shy, quiet ones present even greater problems, for they may not contribute when they do have a valuable thought. Often a simple interjection indicating that views from noncontributors are wanted is enough to bring them into the discussion.

When violent disagreement on a topic is apparent, make sure that each side has an opportunity to present its story without interruption. Other group members should be cautioned to listen carefully for gaps in logic, lack of information, and other shortcomings. Very often the disagreement is resolved when the two arguments are combined to fill in the missing or weak areas each contained. Then it is your responsibility to summarize, as carefully as possible, the areas of general agreement and those still in disagreement. This control of the discussion leads to a resolution of the problem by eliminating the areas of disagreement one by one. Frequently areas of disagreement can be resolved by bringing additional authoritative information into the discussion. Do not hesitate to assign a member to leave the meeting to consult reference materials or resource people.

Should a good leader sense consensus?

Once it appears that members are reaching agreement, you should attempt a summary and move on to the next agenda item. Just as a sales representative might try several times to close a sale, a leader should attempt to consolidate agreement as the discussion proceeds. Often it might be necessary to isolate an area of disagreement for later consideration when it is apparent that discussion of a later item might lead to a solution.

After agenda items have been covered, a summary is in order. This summary should include an analysis of action yet to be taken. For instance, the discussion and conclusion of a board of directors on the feasibility of acquiring another firm would necessitate further discussion about how to put the recommendation into effect.

Role of Members

Members, like the presiding officers, should discover all they can about the subject prior to the meeting. Each member should be prepared, even with notes, to make contributions as direct and pertinent as possible. Just as important are the attitudes members bring with them. Members should resolve to be patient and understanding about other points of view. They should present their ideas objectively without sounding argumentative or emotional. Above all, each member should attempt to be a good listener. As mentioned earlier, irrelevant ideas and repetition are avoided when effective listening is involved. Some leaders have found it effective to establish a ground rule at the very beginning of meetings: no one can speak unless he or she can first summarize what the previous speaker said.

RUNNING BANQUETS

Committee meetings and banquets have much in common. Both should start and end on time. Both should be kept on course, and an atmosphere of ease should prevail at both.

Although many banquet meetings have both a presiding officer and a toastmaster, it is nevertheless true that the skill of the man or woman acting as toastmaster is usually critical to the success of the meeting. When the jobs of presiding officer and toastmaster are combined, the responsibility becomes much greater. The presiding officer, of course, is responsible for seating arrangements, the agenda, the time and place, and all matters not directly related to the actual flow of the program. The toastmaster is the person who keeps the show on the road. All too often, the toastmaster may be someone who has the job because of some high office held in the organization. Then the planning of the banquet may be given to subordinates, and the toastmaster may not be well informed about the program, seating, or even the time schedule. If the toastmaster is unfamiliar with the schedule, the banquet will probably not be a success. Therefore, it's a good idea for the presiding officer to go over the schedule with the toastmaster prior to the banquet.

Must the presiding officer be the toastmaster?

The good toastmaster has an engaging personality. He or she must also run the meeting with an iron hand. Introductions of guests to the audience should be brief but impressive. Frequently these head-table introductions may be made prior to the start of the program if time is a problem. If given the role of toastmaster, make careful notes. When the time comes to introduce the speaker, remember that all speakers need good introductions. An impressive introduction establishes the authority of the speaker and helps capture the early attention of the audience. Never introduce the speaker as ''a person who needs no introduction.''

Because the success of banquets depends on the toastmaster, these points are appropriate:

1. Let humor seem spontaneous. Vulgar or borderline jokes are inappropriate and often indicate that the toastmaster is trying to upstage the speaker. Keep in mind that the speaker is considered the star of the show. Your responsibility is to make certain that the speaker is actually the star.

Should the toastmaster be "the star"?

2. Keep the meeting moving, but don't try to be the life of the party—you may drag out the meeting and counteract all the good things that might have been said.

3. Introduce the invited head table guests and the speaker with enthusiasm and dispatch. Do not, however, tell the audience what a great or funny speech they are about to hear. The speaker may not live up to the introduction.

4. Don't comment on the speech. When the speaker has finished the presentation, simply thank him or her warmly and move to the next part of the agenda. The response of the audience will provide enough comment on the speech. As toastmaster, however, you may initiate the applause for the speaker.

5. Keep an eye on the heat, lighting, and ventilation in the banquet room. If the audience is uncomfortable, the program will not be successful.

SUMMARY

When you make a speech, give an oral report, or run a meeting, you are on center stage as a star performer. Performing in these capacities gives you great visibility and can contribute to your success both in your career and in your community activities.

How well you perform will be directly related to the preparation time and effort you devote to practice. As you experience success in your speaking activities, you'll also become more proficient and self-confident. By using some of the methods and techniques discussed in this chapter, you will have a head start on others. Good speakers seldom acquire their speaking ability naturally. They work at it!

EXERCISES

Review Questions

1. What is the difference between articulation and pronunciation?

2. What is the difference between an impromptu speech and an extemporaneous speech?

3. In your opinion, would a memorized speech be easier to deliver than a written-and-read speech? Why?

4. What is the function of a joke when used in a speech?

5. What *differences* distinguish public speaking from oral reporting?

6. In committee meetings, what is the role of the presiding officer? What suggestions would you have for the preparation of committee members?

Oral Presentation Problems

1. Observe a television newscaster. Prepare a one-page memorandum on your opinion of his or her speaking skill. What elements of voice quality are easily observable in terms of phonation, articulation, and pronunciation? What speech style does the newscaster use? Close your eyes for a few minutes to evaluate how effective the reporting is without whatever gestures or other nonverbal cues are available.

2. List your own speaking strengths and weaknesses. If nervousness before groups is a problem, how can you go about controlling it?

3. Obtain a copy of an annual report for a corporation. (Many business school libraries have some reports.) Prepare a five- to seven-minute talk on the company, its goals, and its financial status. Prepare whatever visual aids you think would assist.

4. Prepare an outline for a speech encouraging high school students to select your school and major for their college work.

5. Use a tape recorder to record a lecture or speech in which the speaker used visual aids and play the speech in class. What effect did the lack of visual materials have on the play back?

6. Prepare a five-minute oral report or speech on a topic of your choice. Organize the presentation in such a way that you can develop a visual outline on a poster-board similar to that in Figure 19-2.

COMMUNICATION IN ORGANIZATIONS

Three Levels of Communication

**Characteristics of Formal
   Organizations**

  Goal Orientation

  Specialization of Individuals
   and Units

  Interdependence of Individuals
   and Units

  Formalized Hierarchy

**Organizational Structure
   and Communication**

External and Internal Systems

**Communication Flow in
   Organizations**

Downward Communication

Upward Communication

Horizontal or Lateral
   Communication

A Supportive Climate

  Recognize the Nature
   of the Organization

  Use the Internal System
   Appropriately

  Assume an Exemplary Role
   in Communication

Summary

Although the purpose of this book is to assist in the development of your personal communication skills, we must consider the normal environment in which much of our communication takes place: the organization.

THREE LEVELS OF COMMUNICATION

The discussion of communication theory and foundations in Chapter 1 focused on the one-to-one idea of interpersonal communication. When two people engage in a communicative transaction, they have two goals: (1) They want to accomplish whatever task confronts them. (2) They each want to feel better as a result of the exchange. These two goals are commonly referred to as *task* goals and *maintenance* goals, and they exist side by side in most of our daily activities.

A second level of communication is that of communicating in groups. A group includes more than two people: a committee, a club, or all the students enrolled in a class. Groups are formed usually because the combined efforts of a number of people result in greater output than the individual efforts of the same number of people. In other words, groups can do more for the individuals than the individuals can do for themselves.

What is the motivation for forming groups?

The third level of communication arises when groups discover that they are unable to accomplish their goals without some kind of organization. Thus, organizations, as we know them, are really combinations of groups ordered in such a way that large tasks may be accomplished. Businesses, colleges, and governments are examples of organizations.

How is an organization different from a group?

Despite the differences in size and complexity, each of these levels of communication continues to have task and maintenance goals. But the idea of maintenance goals can be expanded, or divided, into two distinct goals: (1) a self-maintenance goal that describes the individual's need to maintain his or her personal worth or psychological well being, and (2) a group-maintenance goal that describes the group's need to maintain its *esprit de corps* — the non-task relationships they have established by interacting with one another as a team.

What is the difference between a task goal and a maintenance goal?

The study of organizational communication is a subject on which entire books have been written, but a brief review of communication in the organization should help us understand the role of management in the organizational communication process.

CHARACTERISTICS OF FORMAL ORGANIZATIONS

What elements distinguish a formal organization from a group? Both are made up of individuals, and both have goals. Some groups may exceed the size of some organizations in terms of individuals. Essentially, large organizations are distinguishable not by a single factor but by a combination of the following four factors:

Goal Orientation

Organizations can accomplish some things individuals and groups cannot do by or for themselves. The task goals, for example, of individuals and groups may evolve into such complex and sizable endeavors that more complex entities are necessary to accomplish them. Take the example of the small-business person whose business expands beyond the personal ability to cope with it.

Try to visualize the one-druggist pharmacy that concentrates on filling prescriptions. Ultimately, the pharmacist's son or daughter graduates from college with visions of taking over the family business and developing it into something big. Soon, greeting cards, confections, toiletries, and a variety of other items fill the shelves. Business is good. More space is needed. As a result, a larger building is leased in a more desirable location. Additionally, more employees are needed to handle the expanded business. In fact, it isn't too long before the store is handling clothing, housewares, toys, stationery, food, beverages, garden supplies and the great variety of things available in many modern drugstores. The prescription department is now far at the rear of the store—so those customers using it must pass all the impulse items on the way to pick up their prescriptions—and it occupies only a small portion of the total space. Thus, the goal orientation of the store has changed to the point where individuals or groups could not achieve those goals by themselves.

Specialization of Individuals and Units

Does complexity lead to specialization?

The new drugstore calls for more employees and for some skills not available to the family operation. Purchasing merchandise for resale, maintaining inventories, maintaining accounting and other office records, developing displays and exercising control over a variety of activities have all required some specialization. Business has become so good that management—the family—is thinking of expanding the business into a branch or chain operation. They add to all those other jobs a specialist in market research and locate a consultant for site selection.

To exercise the necessary control over the wide range of activities, management has also organized its personnel into functional units called departments: purchasing and marketing, finance and accounting, warehousing and inventory control, prescriptions, and planning. Within these departments, specialization of labor further occurs. Purchasing and marketing have specialists in cosmetics, paper products, outdoor products, clothing, and so on. Obviously, as the complexity of the undertaking increases, greater specialization is required. It is this specialization that leads to the next characteristic of the large organization.

Interdependence of Individuals and Units

Because of the specialization in the large, formal organization, each of the departments is dependent on each of the others to some extent. Sales efforts on the part of the marketing staff are very much dependent on a steady and uninterrupted flow of merchandise provided by the warehousing and inventory-control department. Regular reports from these units to finance and accounting provide the basis for an efficient record-keeping system that can, in turn, provide information to assist management in planning and decision making.

Within each of these departments, too, specialization of people leads to interdependence of individuals. Therefore, the dependence of units on one another in the large organization is also a characteristic of the internal structure of the smaller units. The large organization is now composed of smaller units, and these units are composed of individuals. All, however, are organized so that the goals of the organization can be achieved. The organization grew or matured in step with changes in goals. Keep in mind, however, that in the everyday work of the organization the task goals of the total organization exist side by side with the group-maintenance goals of the departmental units and the self-maintenance goals of the individuals involved. The interdependence characteristic of units and individuals applies equally to both task goals and maintenance goals.

Does inter-
dependence mean
"mutual dependence"?

Formalized Hierarchy

To achieve its goals, the organization needs to direct and coordinate the interdependence of units and individuals toward a desired end. Formal organization structure results from efforts to achieve coordination. As shown in Figure 20-1, the original pharmacy has grown into a sizable super-drugstore operation with a formalized hierarchy.

The formalized hierarchy ensures that communication occurs effectively as an element in coordination. Coordination results from effective communication and well-organized programs or systems.

The large, formal organization is characterized by

1. Goal orientation

2. Specialization of individuals and units

3. Interdependence of individuals and units

4. Formalized hierarchy

These characteristics are acquired as the organization develops, and they are probably acquired in the order listed. As goals expand beyond the capacity of the current organization, additional specialization is necessary to achieve these goals. As specialization increases, interdependence also increases. And as interdependence of individuals and units increases, the greater the need for formalized structure or hierarchy to ensure communication and hence coordination.

ORGANIZATIONAL STRUCTURE AND COMMUNICATION

Almost any knowledgeable person can sketch an organization chart similar to the one for The Super Drugstore. But not everyone can describe what the chart represents. Traditionally, organization charts have been used to describe the au-

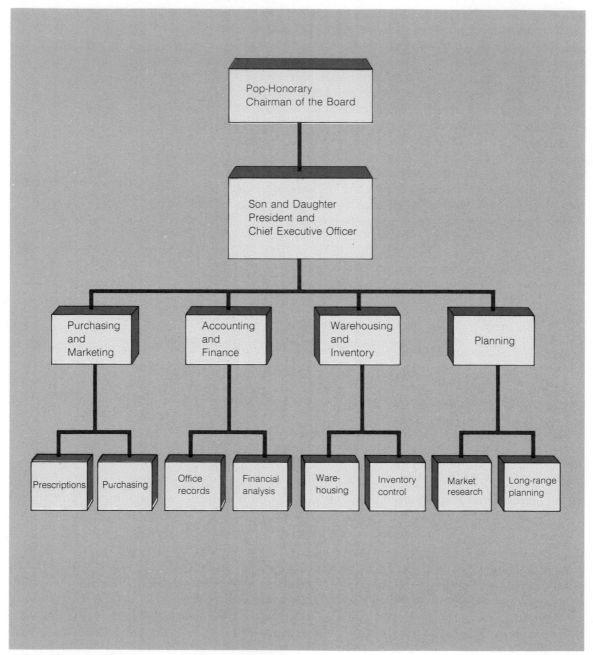

Figure 20-1 Organization chart: the super drugstore.

thority structure of the organization. People included in positions high in the chart appear to have greater authority than those located at lower levels. If used to describe communication in the organization, however, the chart may be entirely inadequate. May people talk only to those immediately above or below them, employees whose positions on the chart are connected to theirs by an uninterrupted line? Is each department on the chart autonomous and shielded from relationships with other departments? If units and individuals depend on one another, the chart does not define the communication structure.

Nor does the chart necessarily define the role structure—the relative importance of each department or individual participating in the organization. The honorary chairman of the board occupies the highest spot on the chart, but the actual role may have little to do with the success or failure of the organization. Someone in the lowest level on the chart, for example in financial analysis, may play a role of considerably greater importance than the status position on the chart would indicate.

Organization charts help define the scope of the organization and assist people in getting a total view. Because people generally occupy roles and perform functions in all those spaces in the organization chart, the pictured structure could seldom be considered a final answer. At the same time, the organizational structure is much easier to talk about when the same graphic presentation is used by all.

The organization structure does affect the behavior of individuals and units within it. Most organizations are pyramid shaped. The higher a person is on the pyramid, the greater the apparent authority and rewards. Most people probably strive for a higher position on the pyramid; and this striving may determine relationships with peers, subordinates, and superiors. Competition has become a characteristic of the American way of life. People and organizations compete for a greater share of scarce resources, for a limited number of positions at the top of organizations, and for esteem in their professions. Such competition is a healthy sign of the human desire to succeed; and in terms of economic behavior, competition is fundamental to the private-enterprise system. At the same time, when excessive competition replaces the cooperation necessary for success, communication may be diminished, if not eliminated.

Is competition for promotion a likely barrier to effective communication?

Just as we want to look good in the eyes of our peers, superiors, and subordinates, units within organizations want to look good to one another. Behavior may then take the form of "I win, you lose" and replace cooperative behavior, which could be characterized by "I win, you win." As a result, excessive competition may have a negative influence on the performance of the organization—everybody loses.

At the same time, the organization may change behavior when effective communication takes place. Most conflict among people and groups results from a lack of understanding. When one unit is uninformed about the importance or function of another, needless conflicts may occur as the groups attempt to better themselves at the expense of others. Interestingly enough, groups engaged in competition tend to solidify and become more cohesive with great internal group morale. As a consequence, the competitive spirit of the group may intensify and lead to further deterioration of communication with other groups. It is easy to visualize what such activity may do to cooperative efforts in the total organization. Therefore, although

Do family conflicts arise from lack of understanding?

competition is appropriate and desirable in many situations, management must take steps through open communication to reduce competition and to increase cooperation. When the competitors have an understanding of others' importance and functions, cooperation is more likely. This statement is as true of cooperation among individuals as it is of cooperation among groups within organizations.

Organization structures are designed by management as a means to control members' and units' behavior. Some of the previous comments have pointed to problems introduced by rigid organization structures, but other problems occur when individual- or group-maintenance goals mix with the task goals of the organization.

EXTERNAL AND INTERNAL SYSTEMS

Is automobile driving behavior subject to external systems?

Two systems of organizational communication simultaneously influence human behavior. The *external* system is typified by the formal organization chart, which is created by management to control individual and group behavior and to achieve organization goals. Essentially, the external system is dictated by the technical, political, and economic environment of the organization. Within this external system, people are required to behave in certain ways simply to get the work done. Because it is dictated by environmental forces existing outside the needs of the individuals in the organization, the system is called external.

The *internal* system develops as people interact within the formal, external system and certain behavior patterns emerge, patterns which accommodate social and psychological needs. To distinguish between the two systems, return to The Super Drugstore and its organization chart. The owner/pharmacist works full time in the prescription department, which is subordinate to and apparently has a reporting relationship to the purchasing and marketing department. Quite likely, however, the people in the purchasing and marketing department don't give the owner a bad time. Their behavior in the external system is minimal and just enough to get the work done. In the internal system, however, their behavior is adapted, depending on their personal perceptions of the owner.

As another example, if the work hours for office staff are 8:00 A.M. to 5:00 P.M., that is part of the external system. But if one office employee begins at 4:50 P.M. to clear the desk, put on outdoor clothing, and get ready to run for the door promptly at 5 P.M., this behavior may spread to all others in the office and become a part of the internal system. The external system, then, requires certain behaviors to get the work done, nothing more. The internal system develops from emergent behaviors and assists in achieving maintenance goals. These two systems operate concurrently in all organizations but to varying degrees, and management must recognize and work with both.

When participants rely almost entirely on the formalized external system as a guide to behavior, the system might be identified as a *bureaucracy*. Procedures manuals, job descriptions, organization charts, and other written materials dictate the required behavior. Communication channels are followed strictly, and red tape is abundant. Procedures are generally followed exactly; terms such as *rules* and *policy* serve as sufficient reasons for actions. But even the most formal of organizations cannot function long without an internal system emerging. As people operate within the external system, they must interact on a person-to-person basis and create an environment conducive to satisfying their personal emotions, prejudices, likes and dislikes.

Take the college classroom, for example. The student behavior required to satisfy the external system is to attend class, take notes, read the text, and pass the examinations. On the first day of class, this behavior probably is typical of almost all students, particularly if they did not know one another prior to attending the class. As the course progresses, however, the internal system emerges and overlaps the external system. Students become acquainted, sit next to people they particularly like, engage in horseplay, and may even plan ways to beat the external system. Cutting class and borrowing notes is an example. Soon, these behaviors become norms for class behavior. Students who do not engage in the internal system may be looked on with disdain by the others. Obviously, the informality of the internal system is good for people because it helps satisfy maintenance goals. At the same time, it affects communication.

The grapevine is perhaps the best known informal communication system. It is actually a component of the internal system. As people talk casually during coffee breaks and lunch periods, the focus usually shifts from topic to topic. And one of the topics most certainly would be work — job, company, boss, fellow employees. Even though the external system calls for very definite communication channels, the grapevine tends to develop and to operate within the organization.

As a communication channel, the grapevine is reputed to be speedy but inaccurate. If the building is on fire, the grapevine may be the most effective way, in the absence of alarms, to let occupants know of the problem. It certainly beats sending a written memorandum.

As an inaccurate channel, the grapevine may be mislabeled. Even formal communication may become inaccurate as it passes from level to level in the organizational hierarchy. Perhaps the inaccuracy of the grapevine has more to do with the message input than with the output. For example, grapevines are noted as carriers of rumor, primarily because they carry informal messages. If the input is rumor, and nothing more, the output obviously will be inaccurate. But the output may be an accurate description of the original rumor.

For the college student, the grapevine carries much valuable information. Even though the names of the good teachers may not be published, students learn those names through the grapevine. How best to prepare for certain examinations, teacher attitudes on attendance and homework, and even future faculty personnel changes are messages traveling over the grapevine. In the business office, news about promotions, personnel changes, company policy changes, and annual salary adjustments are often communicated via the grapevine long before being disseminated by formal channels.

A misconception about the grapevine is that the message passes from person to person until it finally reaches a person who can't pass it on — the end of the line. Actually, the grapevine works through a variety of channels. Typically, one person

Does an internal system exist in your school?

To most people, would the word *grapevine* be thought of as negative?

What are some benefits of a grapevine?

tells two or three others who each tell two or three others, who each tell two or three others, and so on. Thus, the message may spread to a huge number of people in a very short time. Additionally, the grapevine has no single, consistent source. Messages may originate any place and follow various routes. More will be said about sources and routes later in this chapter.

Management must recognize that an informal, internal system will emerge from even the most carefully designed formal, external system. To ignore this fact is to attempt to manage blindfolded. Yet, some managers do try to work exclusively with the external system. For them, the achievement of organizational goals must be extremely difficult. As long as people interact, the organization will have both systems.

Instead of trying to squelch grapevines, should management accept them and even use them to advantage?

COMMUNICATION FLOW IN ORGANIZATIONS

Within the external system, communication may flow downward, upward, or horizontally; and because these terms are used frequently in communication literature, they deserve some clarification.

Downward Communication

Downward communication is that from superior to subordinate — from boss to employee, and from policy makers to operating personnel. One study has identified or distinguished five elements in downward communication:[1]

1. *Job instruction.* Teaching new or current employees how to do a particular task.

2. *Rationale.* The justification for the organization and its goals; how a particular task or function fits into the total organization.

3. *Information.* Orientation to the company — its rules, practices, procedures, and history.

4. *Feedback about job performance.* Supervisor's evaluation or appraisal of employee performance.

5. *Ideology.* The effort to convey to and instill in employees a degree of enthusiasm, loyalty, or support for the organization.

Why do messages seem to get larger as they move downward?

Downward communication flow is, of course, related to the hierarchical structure of the organization. Messages seem to get larger as they move down through successive levels of the organization. A simple instruction given at the top of the

1. Daniel Katz and Robert Kahn, *The Social Psychology of Organizations* (New York: John Wiley and Sons, 1966), pp. 239–243.

hierarchy, for example, may become a formal plan for operation at lower levels. Much of this growth of messages is also related to the relative knowledge of the total organization and its goals possessed by those at each level. An objective established by people at the policy level—the board of directors or executive officers—to "capture a larger share of the consumer market for our product" would doubtless result in detailed plans at the sales-promotion level.

As they move downward or upward through successive levels, messages tend to change in meaning as well as in size simply as a result of being transferred from one station to another. This transfer process could be called *serial* communication and is often demonstrated by having a message given to one person in a room relayed from person to person through several transfer stations. The last to receive the message then reports it orally. Typically, the message bears little similarity to the original. This variation is particularly true of oral messages. Written messages, on the other hand, probably expand when rewritten and transmitted downward, through the addition of greater detail as one means of preventing distortion. Sometimes, of course, these attempts to prevent distortion only lead to misinterpretation and thus magnifiy distortion.

Upward Communication

Feedback about downward communication is one of the items that is communicated upward. In fact, when broadly interpreted, feedback may be a characteristic of all upward communication. Employees talk to superiors about themselves, their fellow employees, their job satisfactions, their perceptions of their work and how it should be done, and their perceptions of the organization and its goals. These topics are related to the broad flow of downward information carried both orally and in written form by group meetings, procedures manuals, personnel handbooks, company newspapers and magazines, and other messages from higher levels. The feedback management receives from upward communication is often extremely critical to decision making as well as to labor–management relations, and it should be encouraged. All too often, however, employees may not provide upward communication freely and accurately. Later in this chapter, a climate that is conducive to upward communication will be discussed.

Why is feedback from subordinates vital to management?

Horizontal or Lateral Communication

Horizontal or lateral communication is often used to describe exchanges between organizational units on the same hierarchical level. This description is one of the major shortcomings of organization charts. Charts really don't leave much room for horizontal communication when they picture authority relationships by placing one box higher than another and define role functions by placing titles in those boxes. But horizontal communication is the primary means of achieving coordination. In The Super Drugstore, for instance, the chart implies that people in finance and accounting can't communicate directly with people in purchasing and marketing without going through the president. Obviously, that would be a pretty difficult way to operate a complex organization.

In fact, horizontal communication would probably exist as part of the internal system even though it was not defined by the formal chart. Workers at the same level tend to talk with one another about their work, their superiors, and their working condtions. No doubt, they also talk with one another about various personal, nonwork problems. As a result, horizontal communication can contribute to self-maintenance goals as well as to task goals.

Why is horizontal communication a necessity?

In this respect, management must recognize that informal horizontal communication takes place in any system or organization where people are available to one another. The informal communication and behavior that is not task oriented develops alongside formal task communication and behavior, contributing to morale, to improvements in ways to accomplish tasks, and to clarification of upward and downward communication. Formalized horizontal communication serves a coordinating function in the organization. Units coordinate their activities to accomplish task goals just as adjacent workers in a production line coordinate their activities.

A SUPPORTIVE CLIMATE

Just as elements such as empathy and trust influence the effectiveness of interpersonal communications, certain elements combine to create an environment in which organizational communication can develop positively. The combination of these elements contributes to the *climate* in which communication occurs. Additionally, since communication in a one-to-one setting is an integral part of organizational communication, the factors leading to effective interpersonal communication must be present.

From a managerial view, much can be done to strengthen the environment for organizational communication. The following three broad steps are examples:

1. Recognize the nature of the organization.

2. Use the internal system appropriately.

3. Assume an exemplary role in communication.

Recognize the Nature of the Organization

All organizations are not alike, and no single set of guiding principles can apply to all. Some organizations are static and predictable. For example, governmental organizations tend to be bureaucratic—static and predictable. The day-by-day work is routine; systems and procedures are fixed and are perhaps revised only infrequently. Many banking and savings institutions as well as public utilities tend to fall in this same category. On the other hand, some organizations are dynamic and unpredictable. High-technology industries such as those involved in aerospace or computer development are typically dynamic, unpredictable organizations. Within both extremes of organization—static to dynamic—some units will vary from the definition. Record-keeping units in either tend to be static, but research and development units tend to be dynamic. Burns and Stalker[2] have labeled the static organization *mechanistic* and the dynamic organization *organic*. Perhaps the following outline will clarify the differences between the two organizational extremes:

Static (Mechanistic)	Dynamic (Organic)
Relies on the external system	Relies on the internal system
Commands and directs	Involves participation
Uses formal communication	Uses informal communication
Places a small communication load on the organization	Involves a heavy communication load
Tends toward a well-defined difference between task and maintenance goals	Tends toward greater integration of task and maintenance goals

Obviously, the static or mechanistic organization reduces the need for interpersonal relationships and communication and the dynamic or organic organization relies heavily on such relationships. The static organization relies on the external system heavily; that is, rules and procedures are fixed, little interpersonal communication of an informal nature is necessary, and individual and group maintenance activities are quite separate from task activities. Nothing is wrong with this type of organization. It developed because of the nature of the tasks involved and simply happens to be the most effective type of organization for accomplishing those tasks.

The dynamic organization also developed as the most effective way to accomplish its tasks. Rapid changes in technology and in market demands for improved products necessitate a reliance on the internal system. Problem solving requires personal exchange and input from various units of the organization. Formalized rules and procedures may be outdated shortly after having been developed. The communication load in the organization is extremely heavy because individuals and units must be constantly informed quickly and accurately about changes.

Although this could not be a universal distinction, the typical coffee break in the two organizations might be somewhat characteristic. In the static organization, the coffee break discussion may be primarily individual- and group-maintenance oriented. Discussion would be about people and nonwork activities. The mechanistic nature of the organization requires little informal communication related to work. On the other hand, the coffee-break discussion in the dynamic organization would probably involve task-maintenance items. In a sense, individuals in the dynamic organization achieve individual- and group-maintenance goals through activities that seem primarily task-goal oriented.

2. Tom Burns and G. M. Stalker, *The Management of Innovation* (London: Tavistock Publications, Ltd., 1961).

Use the Internal System Appropriately

Two aspects characterize the internal communication system: the grapevine and the self- or group-maintenance activity. The combination of these two elements may lead to effective communication and can often be used by management to achieve task purposes.

Do you think key communicators enjoy their participation in grapevine communication?

Within the grapevine network, certain individuals may be identified as sources or intermediaries in the communication process. They are called *key* communicators because of their roles in the process. Input of information to key communicators can assist in communication. And at the same time, the accuracy of messages may be determined by checking with these same individuals. In instances of emergency, individual or group insecurity, and task pressures, the informal communication network may be used to help achieve task goals. The manager who takes the time to chat casually outside the office may end up better informed and may clarify messages more readily than he or she could in any other way.

Circumvent the communication or organizational hierarchy when necessary. Permitting horizontal communication, although not a part of the external system, may assist you in pressure and emergency situations related to either task or maintenance purposes.

Assume an Exemplary Role in Communication

To establish an effective communication environment for the organization calls for management to lead by example. The manager who is skilled in interpersonal relations provides a model for subordinates. Many of the practices and techniques spread to others in the organization as a result of the manager's interaction with them.

In addition to many of the practices covered in chapters on interpersonal and group communication, the exemplary role can be strengthened by

1. Avoiding unilateral changes in the external and internal systems.

2. Involving all levels in problem solving.

3. Indicating a receptivity to information exchange.

Avoiding unilateral changes in the organizational systems is critical. Obviously, a change in the external system that threatens internal behavior norms may have an impact on task achievement. Because people have a tendency to fight back or to become defensive when threatened, the communication-oriented manager will attempt to involve those affected in the decision to make changes. Skill in group communication leadership assists greatly in encouraging and directing participation in the decision-making process. In turn, the apparent receptivity of management to information exchange encourages employees to contribute to the process.

SUMMARY

Communication in the large, formal organization is actually an extension of person-to-person and group communication, because the organization is made up of interdependent and often overlapping groups. The organization exists because it can accomplish more than individuals and groups can by themselves. As an entity, the organization develops when task complexity and size require increased specialization and, thus, greater interdependence of units. A formalized hierarchy is usually designed to assist in the coordination of organizational activities.

The formalized organization along with the rules, procedures, and practices designed to accomplish the purposes of the organization constitute the external system. However, alongside and operating simultaneously in most organizations is an internal system that results from the needs of individuals and groups to achieve their own purposes, self- and group-maintenance. As these two systems interact, a system emerges that is a combination of both.

Communication flows upward, downward, and horizontally through the emergent system and often defies the ability of management to describe it graphically. To cope with communication problems in the organization, management should attempt to create a supportive climate by recognizing the nature of the organization as it actually exists, by using the internal system appropriately, and by assuming an exemplary role in the communication process.

Management should recognize that effective organization is built on a knowledge of human behavior and on both knowledge of and skill in interpersonal communication.

EXERCISES

Review Questions

1. What is the difference between task and maintenance goals?

2. How does an organization differ from a group?

3. Why do organizational charts often fail to describe the communication process in the organization?

4. What is the cause of most conflict among groups in organizations?

5. What is the difference between external and internal systems?

6. Why is the term *grapevine* suitable for describing some informal communication systems or networks?

7. Why do downward messages tend to increase in size as they move through the organization?

8. What is the primary function of lateral communication?

9. What major communication differences exist between static and dynamic organizations? Why?

10. How do McGregor's X and Y styles of management (described in Chapter 1) relate to a manager's communication behavior in the organization?

Problems in Organizational Communication

1. What factors may exist in the organization that could impede the achievement of the individual's self-maintenance goal?

2. Be prepared to discuss the following topics:
   a. The inflexibility of the formal organization.
   b. The effect of job specialization on organizational communication.
   c. The "I win, you lose" philosophy and the achievement of task, self-maintenance, and group-maintenance purposes.
   d. The effect of horizontal communication on the internal system.

3. Assume you are the chief executive officer of an electronics wholesaling firm. Your firm sells radios, stereos, television sets, tape recorders, calculators, cameras, and watches to retail outlets. The firm has annual sales of about $150,000,000, and about 350 employees. You purchase products in about equal dollar amounts from manufacturers in the United States and the Orient—primarily Japan, South Korea, and Hong Kong. Yours is a publicly held company and must have a board of directors responsible to your 10,000 stockholders. Sales representatives deal directly with retailers in your part of the country. You do business in your own state as well as in the five states nearest you. Your only union contract is limited to the fifty employees in your warehouse.

   Prepare a chart showing your formal organization. Describe how the distinctive characteristics of organizations are involved in your organization chart. Describe how you would involve employees in each of the following areas:
   a. Your nonunion pension fund, to which the firm contributes an amount equal to 5 percent of each employee's earnings. The employee contributes 5 percent through payroll deduction.
   b. The adoption of new products.
   c. The annual company awards dinner, which is held to recognize and reward employee performance and longevity with the firm.
   d. The company accident prevention and safety program.
   e. Board of directors' policies on pay increases and paid holidays.

4. Select one of the following organizations for study:

   A branch bank having at least fifteen employees
   A manufacturing company
   An educational institution such as a college, university, or public school system

A school of business administration that is departmentalized

A retail department store

A large hotel

A departmentalized C.P.A. firm

An automobile dealership having a full-service department

Any other familiar large organization

Prepare the following items:

a. An organization chart depicting the formal structure.

b. An organization chart showing by dotted lines variations in communication flow from the formal organization.

c. A list of key communicators in the informal communication system.

d. A description of the use of committees or other groups for short- or long-range policy planning or decision making.

e. Examples of horizontal or lateral communication.

f. Examples of the types of information communicated downward as distinguished from the types of information communicated upward.

g. Other communication elements in the organization.

You will probably have to conduct interviews. You may also obtain an organizational chart to accompany your own work. Whether you work alone or in groups, retain your material for class oral reports and for the possibility of preparing a formal written research report. You should record in step-by-step detail the method you used in conducting your study.

COMMUNICATION MANAGEMENT

**Communication Problems in the
        Organization**
  A Need for Openness
  A Need for Education or Training
  A Need for Communication
        Management
Tips for the Individual Manager
Suggestions for the Organization
Managing Written Communications
  Decreasing the Volume of Written
        Communications
  Planning Educational and Training
        Programs
  Developing Substitutes for
        Individually Written Messages
  Using Technology
Summary

In *Changing Organizations,* Warren Bennis[1] attempted almost twenty years ago to make a prediction about what organizational life might be like in the 1990–2020 era. He predicted an environment characterized by accelerated technological change, greater diversity, increased relationships between industry and government, large organizations rather than small, greater interdependence and less competition, and dynamism rather than stability.

Within this environment, the typical worker would be college educated, have more mobility, and perhaps less loyalty to the organization than at present. At the same time, with more education, workers would be more deeply committed intellectually to their jobs. Although the group or organizational orientation would be weaker, people would seek an increase in interpersonal communication. Bennis foresaw that the job of tomorrow's manager would be an imposing one.

Preparing to become a manager presents us with several problems. Should the preparation consist solely of acquiring tools to be used in the future? Predicting the future is shaky at best: the future might not correspond to the predictions, and the tools might never be used. Should the preparation consist solely of acquiring the tools used today? In that case, might not the educated people—instruments of change—be unable to effect change? Either course alone would be inadequate. But some things about the future are fairly certain.

Organizations will change—only the form they will take is unknown. Communication processes will not change fundamentally. People will still send messages to be received and decoded by others. These messages will consist primarily of spoken and written words and the nonverbal aids that accompany them. Speaking, writing, listening, and reading will continue to be the elements of human communication. In a sense, then, the person best prepared to cope with today's world may also be the person best prepared to adapt to the changes of tomorrow. Those people inadequately prepared for today will probably have to spend so much time keeping pace that they will have little time to spend on coping with change, let alone have anything to do with creating it. Therefore, this chapter is devoted to things that can be done to improve your communication skills in industry and to some things that may pose future problems.

COMMUNICATION PROBLEMS IN THE ORGANIZATION

Reflecting on the state of the art of organizational communication, Gary Richetto[2] cited a parable related by Peter Drucker:

> An old story tells of three stonecutters who were asked what they were doing. The first replied, "I'm making a living." The second kept on hammering while he said, "I am doing the best job of stonecutting in the entire country." The third one looked up with a visionary gleam in his eyes and said, "I am building a cathedral."

1. Warren G. Bennis, *Changing Organizations* (New York: McGraw-Hill Book Company, 1966), pp. 10–13.
2. Gary Richetto, "Organizational Communication: An Overview," in *Communication Yearbook I* (Austin, Tex.: International Communication Association, 1977), p. 343.

Richetto indicates that some important stonecutting in theory and research has been done, but that the building of a cathedral is only just beginning. This observation seems accurate. Scholars and researchers have long studied the organization and what makes it function. But few universal findings or principles have emerged, perhaps because organizations have already begun the accelerated change that inevitably accompanies rapid changes in technology, governmental relationships, and increased understanding of human elements. In other words, organizations simply don't stand still long enough to provide static subjects for analysis.

How can organizational communication be improved?

What is really needed to improve communication—ranging from interpersonal to total organizational communication—is a strong commitment by management and employees to work toward good communication. The climate for effective communication in the organization, as suggested by W. Charles Redding,[3] results from a combination of factors such as supportiveness; participative decision making; trust, confidence and credibility; openness and candor with respect particularly to upward and downward communication; and emphasis on high performance goals. These factors look very much like some of the factors leading to good communication discussed in Chapter 20. The things that contribute to interpersonal effectiveness are similar to the factors that contribute to organizational communication effectiveness.

When interpersonal communication factors are conducive to effectiveness, organizational factors will also fall into place and communication in the organization will be more effective. The two are woven inextricably together. Yet, at times, either management or employees are blind to these factors and indicate they are not in tune with each other.

A Need for Openness

Employees have a tendency to tell superiors what the superior wants to hear. John Powell[4] makes the point that we are afraid to tell people who we are because we are afraid others will not like us. Therefore, we pretend to be someone we think others might like. As a result, we play roles, play games, and wear masks. Ultimately, the situation becomes so confusing that we may not be able to distinguish our false roles from our real selves.

Do management and subordinates tend to agree on which morale factors are important?

Bormann, Howell, Nichols, and Shapiro[5] report a study in which a group of managers ranked those morale factors most important to their subordinates from a list of ten items. The subordinates were asked to do the same in terms of importance to themselves. The managers ranked "full appreciation of work done," "feeling in on things," and "sympathetic help on personal problems" as the *last* three in importance to their subordinates. The subordinates, on the other hand, ranked these same items as the *first* three in importance to themselves.

3. W. Charles Redding, *Communication Within the Organization: An Interpretive Review of Theory and Research* (New York: Industrial Communications Council, 1972).

4. John Powell, *Why Am I Afraid to Tell You Who I Am?* (Niles, Ill.: Argus, 1969), p. 13.

5. Ernest G. Bormann et al., *Interpersonal Communication in the Organization* (Englewood Cliffs, N.J.: Prentice-Hall, Inc., 1969), p. 190.

Thus, the establishment of openness and trust becomes almost paramount in the development of a good communication climate. Perhaps a lay-the-cards-on-the-table approach is best. Simply sit together and talk about communication in understandable terms.

A Need for Education or Training

People are not going to understand communication terms without some education or training in their meaning and application. Training itself is a motivational influence simply because, when given the opportunity to participate in training programs, people feel accepted and recognized. Employees want to be accepted and recognized by superiors; to be informed about company policies, practices, and progress; and to be given the opportunity to be heard. Employees also often have considerable anxiety about who should report to whom and who should do or does what in the organization. To satisfy these wants, management itself is frequently in need of appropriate training or education. It doesn't do any good for management to provide training programs for employees if it doesn't know, or appreciate, what goes on in the training program. One of the most frequent comments from employees who have taken part in such programs is, "This would really be a good program for my boss!"

What are the benefits of training programs in communication?

A Need for Communication Management

An important element in the total commitment of management to improving internal communication is fixing responsibility on a broad scale. Some firms have people with titles such as *communication manager, director of communication,* or *vice president —communication* with responsibility for various components of the communication function. Employee relations, personnel, company publications, communication training programs, advertising and public relations may all fall within the authority and responsibility of the office. Although every manager, ideally, should be a model communicator, the emphasis placed on communication when a corporate officer is broadly involved is probably healthy for the entire organization. That officer should never use the excuse that she or he is too busy to be involved in such a nonproductive thing as communication.

TIPS FOR THE INDIVIDUAL MANAGER

At the departmental or small-group level, individual managers can practice some tactics helpful not only to their own communication problems but also to the problems of the total organization. Here are some suggestions:

1. Share information with employees in the morning if possible. Employees are more receptive to information when they are fresh.

2.   Emphasize to subordinates how each topic affects them personally. People are mostly concerned with "what's in it for me?"

3.   Share information promptly. This technique helps dispel rumors that may circulate on the grapevine, and it helps convince subordinates that you really want to communicate.

4.   Provide instant feedback. When you don't know the answer to a question, say so. If some information is not available, follow up on the information.

5.   Attempt to be objective about controversial topics. Give other viewpoints in addition to those of the organization. Employees want an opportunity to draw some conclusions of their own.

6.   Use supporting staff to make presentations. Often the manager is not an expert on certain topics. It's better to have help than to leave a poor impression.

**Is small
talk a waste of
a manager's time?**

7.   Talk to employees about things other than work occasionally. Keep in mind that employees have self-maintenance goals as well as task goals.

8.   Be available when a subordinate wants to talk.

SUGGESTIONS FOR THE ORGANIZATION

No matter how skilled the manager is in using communication tools personally, certain organizational elements inhibit effective operational communication. The following suggestions may contribute to improved internal communication:

**Can a man-
ager adhere to the
chain of command
and still encourage
horizontal communication?**

1.   *Adhere to the chain of command.* The organizational structure establishes desirable routes for communication. Despite all that has been said to this point, when employees follow the prescribed route in communicating both upward and downward, effective communication is probable. Continued violations indicate that something is probably wrong with the organizational structure in the first place.

2.   *Label jobs effectively.* Everyone likes a nice job title. Stenographers like to be called secretaries, and secretaries like to be called administrative assistants. In many savings institutions, titles are given to individuals to help create better public relations rather than to indicate authority and responsibility. For example, in a bank or savings and loan office, the customer frequently has the opportunity to talk with an assistant vice president. But that assistant vice president may lack the authority to make the decisions the customer seeks. In fact, the assistant vice president may have to seek the permission of the bank secretary (another corporate title) to make a commitment to the customer. To a new employee at the beginning teller level, the titles may be confusing and result in a violation of the chain-of-command principle.

3.   *Designate authority and responsibility clearly.* "I thought Joe was going to do it." "No," says Joe, "I thought it was left up to George." Such comments arise frequently in work situations and can often be avoided by holding regularly scheduled group meetings, by planned orientation of new employees, and by clearly written job descriptions.

4. *Maintain sensible work loads.* Overloading some employees with work while underloading others contributes to poor communication. Just as overloading a communication channel creates static or noise, work overloads and underloads build barriers to organizational as well as to interpersonal communication.

5. *Maintain effective spans of control.* The principle of a span of control involves keeping the number of people reporting to a single person within reasonable limits. Some work assignments allow a supervisor to supervise twenty or thirty employees easily, particularly if all are doing the same task. Other assignments allow the supervisor to handle only three or four subordinates effectively. This suggestion, then, is similar to the sensible work loads mentioned previously. One applies to everyone in the organization and the other to supervisory personnel.

6. *Consider all communication requirements of the position during employment interviews.* Technical skills such as accounting, statistical ability, typewriting, and dictation-transcribing are generally assessable during employment interviews and testing. The willingness and ability of a person to function in a position calling for considerable communication activity are seldom pursued during interviews. Yet, if the interviewer is familiar with the communication requirements of the job, the interview can reveal much about the qualifications of the applicant.

Would job seekers improve chances of employment if they stressed communication skills on their application forms?

7. *Use house organs effectively.* A house organ is the term given to company newspapers or magazines. These publications keep employees informed about company achievements and plans; employee promotions; and personal news such as marriages, births, deaths, retirements, bowling league standings, and a variety of nonwork-related items. The recognition given employees through the personal-column approach may improve the morale of the individuals involved. Employees are generally more strongly motivated when they know the company itself is achieving and they are part of the team. Company achievements can be promoted through business magazines, trade journals, and association publications. Additionally, local newspapers are generally receptive to company news releases. The organization has an opportunity to help build a desirable image through these outlets. And when employees take pride in the accomplishments of their organization and in their colleagues, the environment for better organizational communication is improved. Thus, the house organ should seek to report a balance between individual and organizational accomplishments.

What is the purpose of a house organ?

MANAGING WRITTEN COMMUNICATIONS

The United States Postal Service maintains the largest postal system in the world, handling almost half of the world's volume of postal traffic. In 1960, the Postal Service handled slightly over 60 billion pieces of mail. By 1970, the total had increased to about 85 billion, and the total in 1980 was about 100 billion.[6] Because about three out of five pieces were first-class mail, that is about 500 pieces for every person in the country. Many of the first-class pieces are printed matter, personal letters, or household payment of bills. However, the cost of each letter dictated, transcribed, and mailed by business is significant. For a firm operating on a profit margin of 5 percent of sales, one letter that needn't have been written may consume the profit margin on a hundred dollars in sales. Add to this expense the cost of preparing all the internal messages—those that are never mailed—and the cost of writing can be critical to many organizations. What might the time to read all those messages cost?

Cost, of course, cannot be the only criterion for measuring writing. Quality is even more important. Thus, the steps available to improving and controlling written communication must be cost and quality directed. Management can select from several alternatives, which are probably best implemented in combination:

1. Decrease the volume of written communications both in total number of items and in length of items.

2. Plan educational and training programs to improve the efficiency and effectiveness of those preparing messages.

3. Develop substitutes for individually written messages.

4. Install a word-processing center and use other modern technology.

Decreasing the Volume of Written Communications

The major expense item in written communication is labor: the cost of the time involved in planning what to say, in dictating it, in recording it, and in typing it. Although the cost of paper can be significant in some organizations, paper is a minor item in the total cost. Decreasing the volume and the number of words written results primarily in saving labor costs.

Some old habits must be changed to decrease written communication. In many growing businesses, of course, decreasing the total volume of communications would be impossible. But it is within the ability of any organization to decrease the *average* number of letters and reports per employee. The need to get something in writing has permeated business and government for many years. People believe they protect themselves by putting things in writing. Essentially, this belief results from a lack of trust in others. Many things are written formally when they could better be handled by a telephone call or a brief longhand memorandum.

For example, a response to a memorandum announcing a committee meeting can be handled simply by jotting an answer on the original memo and returning it. A phone call would also do the job. The problem becomes compounded when the formal writer dictates the simple message to a secretary for typing. No doubt, this type of writer also insists on a carbon copy which must be filed!

6. Statistical Abstracts of the United States, U.S. Printing Office, 1980.

When matters can be handled by telephone calls, and the need for formal records doesn't exist, the telephone should be used, even for long-distance calls. A three-minute, transcontinental call may cost far less and accomplish more than a dictated and transcribed letter. The telephone call also permits instant feedback — a critical element in message effectiveness — and probably avoids the need for two more letters, one to provide the feedback and the other to respond to it.

What are the advantages of telephoning instead of writing?

Within the firm, programs to determine how many copies of reports and memorandums should be prepared can greatly reduce the proliferation of copies. In almost every firm, people receive copies of communications they don't know a thing about and really don't care about. The letter or report that shouldn't be written and the copy that shouldn't be directed to others are costly and time consuming. Just the cost of filing such items is immense. The four square feet of floor space taken up by a filing cabinet may cost between $25 and $60 a year for rent in many major cities. The filer's time might be better spent on some other more productive activity. All too often, the top management of a firm is so involved with policy matters that it doesn't have the time for or interest in paperwork and cost-reduction programs. Internal audit staffs should be as concerned with these items as they are with accounting and other work-procedure controls. Simply placing controls over the use of modern copying machines can go a long way toward reducing paper waste. Some firms have completely given up the practice of using carbon paper for copies — a practice which is far cheaper than using copying machines.

Decreasing the length of written items is a function of good training in organizing ideas, composition, and human relations.

Planning Educational and Training Programs

The business employee operates in the best communication laboratory in the world, the business office. In the office, you will have opportunities every day to apply what you learned in the classroom. The training approach to communication control can be effectively practiced by business, much as it is in the college classroom; but in the business office, daily practice also takes place in an actual business setting with real problems.

Some other differences exist between the college classroom and the business office. Business workers acquire maturity through experience, and their familiarity with business practices enables them to cope more quickly with the circumstances surrounding writing problems. In general, too, business workers use language far more effectively than they give themselves credit for. As a result, formal grammar instruction may not be needed. On the other hand, the study of proper usage and mechanics is generally helpful.

Study after study has recommended that the courses in business communication that are generally rated by expert panels should include these principles:

1. Letters should be planned for their potential effect on the reader. Interestingly enough, the functional letter-planning process used in this text was recom-

mended by Sherwin Cody in 1906 and has been followed or only slightly modified by textbook authors since that time.[7]

2. Letters should be long enough to ensure clearness, completeness, and effectiveness of message. This is not to say that letters should be long in the literal sense. They should be long enough to accomplish the purposes of the writer and nothing more. All too often, the writer will dictate back the message of the sender and then follow with his or her own message. This practice can only lead to longer messages than usual, and it is evidence that the writer has no understanding of the basics of communication. Almost all people know what they have already written, and they do not want to read their entire message before they read something original.

3. Old-fashioned jargon and stereotyped expressions should be eliminated. Modern letters do not begin with "enclosed herewith please find" and "pursuant to your request" any more than they would begin with "yours of the 10th inst. received." Phrases that should have gone out with button shoes and the celluloid collar still remain in many places.

4. Letters should have a positive, friendly tone. Phrases that say "You can't," "we regret to inform," and "you neglected" are symptomatic of poor human-relations understanding.

5. Proper use of punctuation and other grammatical points that contribute to readability, clarity, and effectiveness should be emphasized. For example, the run-on sentence or sentence splice, as used in this sentence, "Mr.Smith was upset, therefore, he left the meeting," misuses the punctuation before *therefore* and leaves the reader confused about which clause the *therefore* belongs with. Although a semicolon on the appropriate side of *therefore* would clear up the problem, many writers are unaware of the error in punctuation.

Interesting studies have been made about what distinguishes good letters from bad. These studies usually have a jury of experts examine a sampling of letters and place them in several piles which they would rate from *good* to *bad*. Then a postmortem is conducted on the extremes — the 20 percent rated good as opposed to the 20 percent rated bad. The middle 60 percent are ignored; thus, only those that are separated by the middle 60 percent are included, ensuring that some validity is established between good and bad. The previously mentioned five qualities usually distinguish between good and bad. Although misspelling may not be a distinguishing factor, it would surely affect a reader negatively.

A study of business letters written by business and office executives who were members of a professional management association found that almost 60 percent of the letters studied were written at a reading-difficulty level of 11th grade and below.[8] This low reading-difficulty level was deemed desirable; but even at that, only

Can lengthy letters result from lack of planning?

Summarize some important principles of letter writing.

7. Gayle A. Sobolik, "A History of Business Letter-Writing Theory as Revealed in an Interpretive Analysis of American Collegiate Business Communication Textbooks" (Doctoral dissertation, University of North Dakota, 1970).

8. Caroline M. B. Otwell, "Analysis of Business Letters Written by Selected Administrative Management Society Members" (Doctoral dissertation, Georgia State University, 1970).

6 percent of the letters were rated as acceptable because of other errors in grammar, punctuation, and tone.

With the characteristics of the business worker and the environment of the business office in mind, a competent training officer or consultant can plan an education program to provide effective in-service training in business writing. The three essentials for a training program are a motivated student, a competent teacher, and adequate teaching materials. All are readily available to most firms. Business people are generally motivated to improve communication skills, and survey after survey has found "ability to communicate" an employee deficiency. Executives often wish they had developed greater competence in communication while in college. The business office provides the laboratory for practice in communicating, and the everyday work of the office can provide the materials of instruction.

The teacher may be a regular employee who is qualified to direct and instruct. Or, in consultation with management, training directors can employ excellent instructors or consultants from outside the firm. The advantage of using an outsider is that employees tend to look on outside professionals as more competent than their peers in the firm, although this difference in competence may not actually exist.

Several approaches are available to help determine instructional content for training programs in written communication:

What is the disadvantage of using company personnel as directors of in-service training programs in communication?

1. Select from standard college textbooks those elements deemed desirable for an industry-wide or in-house course of study.

2. Purchase programmed texts from among several on the market to enable individuals to progress at their own pace.

3. Conduct a study of strengths and weaknesses in actual business communications prepared by employees.

4. Consult with the continuing-education division of a college about the possibilities or availability of courses for employees, particularly if the firm is too small to offer its own course economically.

The program need not be so lengthy as the typical college course. "If some is good, more is better" does not necessarily apply to employee training. A program as long as a typical college term can drag in the minds of employees. Much of the college time, for example, is concerned with discussion of the background material for particular types of messages. In business, credit people already understand credit; sales people understand sales; collection people understand collections; and adjustment people understand adjustments. They do not need to study the background. They are concerned with planning for reader reaction, with proper use of grammar and mechanics, and with current practices in letters and reports.

What are the disadvantages of having a training program that extends beyond a few weeks?

Training programs are typically limited to from four to ten hourly sessions. The programs may concentrate on only one phase of the college course—report writing, for example. In effect, the training program limits itself to one of several modules of the college course. Some in-service courses may be limited to executives only, to secretaries only, or to middle-management personnel only. Each group may have different needs, and mixing the groups may inhibit questioning or result in instruction not suited to the needs of one group or the other.

What are the disadvantages of having executives and their subordinates attend the same communication seminar?

No matter what form it takes, the training program requires follow-up procedures if it is to be effective. Before-and-after evaluations of student work should be attempted. Because of employee turnover, programs should be established on a continuing basis. Follow-up can take the form of periodic refresher sessions or review of written work by the instructor after employees have completed the program. One program incorporated follow-up by sending a random sampling of copies of written work to the instructor each month for several months after the classwork was completed. The instructor commented directly on the copies in a way similar to the comments made on college papers. Because of the random selection of copies, writers were never certain which of their papers would be submitted for review. Thus, employees were probably careful in preparing every message. This follow-up process was accompanied with occasional personal consultations between the instructor and each writer.

Industry-wide programs such as those used by the Institute of Financial Education of the savings and loan industry and the American Institute of Banking are beneficial. Because they require regular classroom instruction, they usually take employees away from their places of employment for instruction and enable them to engage in an exchange of ideas with employees from similar firms with similar interests. These programs involve broad principles rather than specific how-to methods and would be classed as educational rather than as training programs. They provide a sound base on which to build skills adapted to the particular policies and practices of each employee's firm.

Developing Substitutes for Individually Written Messages

Control over the quality and cost of written communications may also be achieved through carefully developed form or guide letters, through standardization of practices, and through a procedure called the editorial approach.

Form and Guide Letters

A form letter is a complete letter on which only the name of the addressee and perhaps a few items such as dates and amounts of money need filled in. It is intended to be used only when the situation calling for a letter is routine and repetitious. Replies to requests for information, collection problems, and credit requests are examples. Form letters may be printed or reproduced in quantity or prepared on automatic typewriters so they appear to be individually written. Individually typed form letters do not fool many people. Most people know when the situation calls for a form-letter response and are not gullible enough to believe that it is a personal message, even when their name appears in the body.

Guide letters, on the other hand, are composed from several optional sentences or paragraphs that can be combined to produce a single letter. These letters are individually typed.

Both form and guide letters reduce dictation and transcription time. The writer

What are the advantages and disadvantages of form letters?

How do form letters and guide letters differ?

simply jots down a notation about which form or guide letter to use in handling a situation, avoiding considerable expense. In the case of a printed form letter, both dictation and typing time are saved. Conservatively, about three fourths of the executive and secretarial time could be saved. When guide letters are used, the time usually spent dictating and taking dictation is saved; only the research time of the dictator and the transcribing time of the secretary remain the same as for dictated letters.

Additionally, copies of form or guide letters need not always be made because the notation on the incoming letter or in the file can indicate that a message has been sent. If this practice were applied to only 1 billion of the 100 billion first-class letters prepared each year, almost 200,000 file drawers would not be needed to file the carbon copies! A billion letters ready for mailing and stacked one on the other would reach 390 miles into the stratosphere; laid end to end they would circle the earth five times.

Standardization

In addition to the time savings created by substitute letters, quality control is also developed. Simply by applying some of the principles of industrial management to the written communication problem, management helps assure control. People prefer to find things orderly. They like to find things in the same place each time they look for them, and they appreciate anything that will assist their memories and lead to better job performance. One of the major principles underlying the use of substitutes, then, is *standardization.* Anything that is repetitious can be organized as a routine and made uniform so it is done the same way each time. Interoffice memorandum forms with printed headings for *To, From,* and *Subject* are examples of standardization.

Form and guide letters lend uniformity to business operations. Neither business people nor consumers object to form letters when properly used. They do object to poorly prepared form letters or to letters that do not fit the situation.

Colored paper for various copies of forms or messages is another approach to standardization. Copies can be quickly routed to the proper work station when they are prepared on the colored paper designated for that station. Colors are frequently used to control distribution, to designate the urgency of the communication, and to facilitate filing. A worker receiving a message on colored paper intended for someone else can quickly reroute the message.

The office or communication manual may indicate management concern for effective communication and include sample form or guide letters. An index should be prepared covering the variety of situations calling for written communications and should be keyed in such a way that the worker can refer easily to the appropriate letter covering each situation. The preparation of form- or guide-letter manuals is not an easy task. The following steps should be taken in sequence to develop a manual:

1. *Collect samples.* Request an extra copy of each letter written. The request should be specific and should ask for a count of the number of times each

currently used letter is prepared. Collect the samples for a long enough period to ensure a thorough sample. For example, a firm with a heavy correspondence volume might require only a week or two to assemble the necessary information. Others with less volume should collect samples for a month.

2.   *Sort the sample.* Prepare a list of key subjects of letters included in the sample and establish a file folder for each subject.

3.   *Inventory the letters.* Take each key file and prepare a list of repetitive letters by topics. This step involves making an outline through second-degree headings of all items in the file. As each item in the file is reviewed, label it with a topic heading and keep a tally of the number of items under each heading.

4.   *Prepare an index.* When all items have been sorted and inventoried, prepare an index of all subdivisions created from the total sample. This step should reveal form or guide letter possibilities. When several individually prepared letters were written to cover a single repetitive subject, a form letter will probably be useful.

5.   *Prepare form or guide letters.* For each repetitive situation, prepare a single substitute. This step is important and calls for a consultation with the writers of the individual letters to make certain the substitute will be effective.

6.   *Test the substitute letters.* Try the substitutes for a long enough time to reveal problems. The period may be roughly equivalent to the time used to collect the original sample.

7.   *Prepare a manual of form and guide letters.* The manual may be prepared in notebook style with reference tabs or in a rotary card file large enough to include a letter on each card. Substitutes should be numbered systematically to assure uniformity in their use.

Because the development of a manual is a major task, and one that requires constant follow-up, the responsibility for development and maintenance should be given to one individual, perhaps with a supporting committee or staff. The system should be regularly reviewed and revised when necessary. Any form letters used should emanate from the manual. Control is lost when people decide to invent their own form letters without going through the person responsible for the manual.

The Editorial System

In some firms, the editorial approach is used to ensure control over written communication. Letters going outside the firm are edited by someone who is qualified to evaluate a written item. Usually the editor is free to make suggestions and to return the communication for rewriting. This practice may seem time consuming, but it leads to uniformity and consistency. Firms using this practice have found the amount of editing and the volume of rewriting decrease as employees become accustomed to the practice.

Over long periods, employees develop their own form letters because they learn how to prepare messages that will receive the editor's approval. This approach has an element of training as well as elements of the form or guide letters. The approach is used by many high-technology firms, where all material leaving a department of the business must be signed by the person in charge of the department. As a result, the employees become ghost-writers who must prepare material that will meet the satisfaction of the signer. The advantage to the large company is that the editorial system leads to the fixing of authority and responsibility.

Using Technology

The communication-technological explosion of the past few years has had a dramatic effect on office productivity. The original concept of word processing involved automatic typewriting with error-free copy. Now word processing involves computerized copy preparation and storage—along with automatic centering, right-hand margin alignment, decimal alignment, spelling checks, and a variety of type styles. Additionally, optical scanners, storage units, and transmission devices make possible the integration of the word-processing function into a total information system.

With the use of such equipment, guide and form letter systems can be automated, filing and retrieval methods of the past will become antiquated, and the status of many clerical workers will be raised.

Any sizable business can find areas where electronic mail can increase efficiency and reduce costs in the long run. Facsimile equipment for long-distance communication and computer terminals for intraoffice messages form the core of the electronic mail system.

As with any drastic change from traditional methods, people present the major obstacle to innovation. But with the increasing use of personal computers at school and in the home, the mysteries that seem to go along with the computer age should soon become only a part of history alongside the development of high-speed printing, the telephone, and air travel. These developments took place over relatively long periods, but the era of office electronics has occurred so quickly that we are still groping to understand it and its implications. The adoption of wide-scale electronic technology within an organization should be made cautiously and only after considerable study.

SUMMARY

Managing communications is primarily a job of educating or training people. Whether it be interpersonal, group, organizational, or written communication, effectiveness rests with individuals. Attempts to achieve controls through routines and standardization are helpful, of course. But management really creates the environment for more effective communication by setting good communication examples and by providing the means for employees to develop personally.

EXERCISES

1. Who has the larger span of control, a bank president with four executive vice presidents reporting, or a foreman of a crew with twenty ditch diggers? Explain your answer.

2. Who should be responsible for internal corporate communications? Explain.

3. If you were in charge of a group of people concerned primarily with credit-collection problems for an oil firm, what things would you include in an educational program? In a training program?

4. Comment on the state of affairs in organizational knowledge. What external conditions support your answer?

5. What conditions contribute to an ideal organizational communication climate?

6. Management wants some control over communication effectiveness. List some things management might do.

7. What is the difference between education and training?

8. Your collection department has communication problems. It doesn't seem to be able to collect past-due accounts. Each person is assigned a certain alphabetic section of customers and is totally responsible for collection. What would you do?

9. You are president of a company with four senior vice presidents and seven vice presidents reporting to you. Most of the thirty-two assistant vice presidents work outside the office about 90 percent of the time, consulting customers and sales representatives. Each of these officers has a private secretary. Most of the secretaries have little to do. What would be your course of action, and why?

10. As dean of admissions at your college, you learn that each applicant receives a personal letter from each of your assistant deans telling about his or her admissions status. You turn down about 50 percent of your applicants. Suddenly, you learn that your assistant deans, who should be visiting schools and recruiting prospects, are spending most of their time dictating letters about admission status and not spending much time recruiting. You have eight assistant deans. How would you get them back in the field? Explain.

APPENDIX

Pretest
I. Grammar
Words Frequently Misused
Nouns
Pronouns
Verbs
Adjectives and Adverbs
Sentence Structure
II. Mechanics
Abbreviating
Capitalizing
Writing Numbers
Dividing Words
Punctuating
Spelling
Typing
Word Processing
Letter Placement
Posttest
Grading Symbols

If messages do not meet high standards of grammar and mechanics, they have negative consequences. The receiver may (1) misunderstand the message, (2) lose time by stopping to review the message, (3) think more about the error than the message, or (4) think negatively about the sender's background or respect for the receiver.

The following pages review some of the common problems that confront business writers. The subject matter is basic. Regardless of job level (from the lowest entry level to the highest managerial level), a knowledge of basics is beneficial. Mastery of the following pages is exceedingly beneficial for those engaged in (or associated with) word processing. For both administrative personnel and correspondence personnel, knowledge of basic English usage is considered a necessity.

The following review of basics seeks to answer frequently encountered questions about grammar, spelling, punctuation, and typing. For more thorough reviews, consult standard reference books on grammar or transcription.

PRETEST

Take the following pretest to determine your present level of mastery. Proceed in this manner:

1. Place a cover sheet beneath the first line of sentence 1.

2. With a pencil, make the necessary corrections in sentence 1 (look for mistakes in grammar, spelling, punctuation, and manner of expressing numbers).

3. Move the cover sheet downward and check your answers against the corrected sentence (making an unnecessary change is a mistake; failing to make a necessary change is also a mistake).

4. Record the number of mistakes in the space provided at the left.

5. Continue this procedure for the remaining sentences.

1. Of 63 people who recieved questionaires only eleven responded before the designated date; December 16th.

    Of 63 people who received questionnaires, only 11 responded before the designated date: December 16. (Instead of the colon that follows "date," a comma or a dash would be correct, also.)

    _____

2. While conclusions were based on highly subjective data; the students were not asked to repeat they're survey.

    Although conclusions were based on highly subjective data, the students were not asked to repeat their survey. *Or,*
    Conclusions were based on highly subjective data, but the students were not asked to repeat their survey.

    _____

3. The 14-page document was prepaired by Helen and me, it was the most difficult report we had ever writen.

     _____ The 14-page document was prepared by Helen and me; it was the most difficult report we had ever written.

4. Only one of our employee's know the combination but he is on a three week vacation.

     _____ Only one of our employees knows the combination, but he is on a three-week vacation.

5. If I had began the task earlier I would have completed it today, but the new target date for completion has been set for Febuary 2nd.

     _____ If I had begun the task earlier, I would have completed it today; but the new target date for completion has been set for February 2.

6. Shipments which were recieved last week have been tagged, shipments which were received this week will not be tagged untill tomarrow.

     _____ Shipments that were received last week have been tagged; shipments that were received this week will not be tagged until tomorrow. *Or,* Shipments received last week have been tagged, but shipments received this week will not be tagged until tomorrow.

7. Neither the office manager or his assistance has been invited to the party, this has had a negative effect on the morale of office personnell.

     _____ Neither the office manager nor his assistants have been invited to the party; this oversight has had a negative effect on the morale of office personnel. (Some other noun could be used instead of "oversight.")

8. Did you read "What Russia Wants" in the last issue of *U. S. News and World Report?*

     _____ Did you read "What Russia Wants" in the latest issue of *U. S. News and World Report?*

9. The responsibility is ours, the authority is yours'.

     _____ The responsibility is ours; the authority is yours. *Or,*
The responsibility is ours, but the authority is yours.

10. Before we discuss this issue further lets invite our guests to sit their briefcases in the adjoining room.

     _____ Before we discuss this issue further, let's invite our guests to set their briefcases in the adjoining room.

11. Our principle reason for making this request is because the firm has revised its' position on reemployment.

     _____ Our principal reason for making this request is that the firm has revised its position on re-employment. *Or,*

We are making this request primarily because the firm has revised its
_____   position on re-employment.

12. The company has reversed their decision to meter 2nd, third, and 4th class
mail.

The company has reversed its decision to meter second-, third-, and
fourth-class mail. *Or,*
The company has reversed its decision to meter 2nd-, 3rd-, and 4th-
_____   class mail.

13. Our methods were different than your's but, as you can see from the
inclosed sheet, our result's are simular too your's.

Our methods were different from yours; but, as you can see from the
enclosed sheet, our results are similar to yours. *Or,*
Our methods were different from yours; but as you can see from the
_____   enclosed sheet, our results are similar.

The preceding test provides approximately 70 opportunities for error. The more
errors you made, the more profitably you can study the following pages.

Since the following review is intended for *study* or for *reference,* the terminology found in English textbooks is employed. For those who have forgotten, many of
the basic grammatical terms are defined. Principles are followed with illustrations.
For best results, (1) read the principles, (2) examine the illustrations that follow, and
(3) *then read the principles again.* Returning to the principle after seeing the
illustrations increases the clarity of the principle and reinforces learning.

In the following pages, principles fall conveniently into two categories: grammar
and mechanics.

I. GRAMMAR

For a *complete* review of grammar, other sources would be needed; but knowledge
of the words frequently misused, the parts of speech, and sentence structure
prevents a high percentage of errors that appear in business writing.

Words Frequently Misused

1. *Above* and *below.* In referring to material that comes before or after, avoid
use of *above* and *below.*

Not: *the above statement*
But: *the preceding statement*

Not: *the graph below*
But: *the following graph*

Above and *below* are especially distracting when they appear in unfortunate positions on a typewritten page. Too often, *below* appears in the last paragraph of a page and the reference is *not* in fact below (it's at the top of the next page); or *above* appears in the first paragraph of a page and the reference is *not* in fact above (it's at the bottom of the preceding page).

2. *Accompanied by, accompanied with. Accompanied by* is used when *people* are involved. *Accompanied with* is used when *objects* are involved.

> She was *accompanied by* her secretary.
> The letter was *accompanied with* a check.

3. *All together, altogether. All together* means ''in one group''; *altogether* means ''completely'' or ''wholly.''

> The answer is *altogether* correct.
> The employees were *all together.*

4. *Already, all ready. Already* means ''at a previous time''; *all ready* means ''inclusively ready.''

> The employee had *already* left for home.
> The machines are *all ready* for use.

5. *Amount, number.* Use *amount* when speaking of money or of things that cannot be counted; use *number* when speaking of things that can be counted.

> The *amount* of grumbling has been troublesome to the supervisors.
> The *number* of workers has been increased.

6. *Anxious, eager.* Use *anxious* only if great concern, doubt, worry, or anxiety is involved.

> The manager is *eager* to participate.
> He is *anxious* about the lack of security.

7. *Anyone, any one.* Use *anyone* if the *any* is to be accented; use *any one* if the *one* is to be accented. *Any one* will usually be followed by *of.*

> Does *anyone* have a pencil?
> *Any one* of our machines will be satisfactory.

8. *As . . . as, so . . . as.* Use *as* good *as* when comparing positive qualities; use *so* good *as* when comparing negative qualities.

The old machine is *as* good *as* the new one.
The old machine is not *so* good *as* the new one.

9. *As to, about,* and *on.* Use *about, on*, or some other single-word preposition instead of *as to.*

Do you have any remarks *about* (not *as to*) the contract?
May we have your comments *on* (not *as to*) the proposal?

10. *Balance, remainder.* Use *balance* to refer to the difference between the debit and credit sides of a ledger account or when referring to an amount of money owed. Use *remainder* to refer to that which is left over.

The unpaid *balance* is $60.
Our staff can complete the *remainder* of the work in an hour.

11. *Can, may. Can* indicates capability or power. *May* indicates permission.

We *can* do this work easily.
You *may* talk with the superintendent now.

12. *Complement, compliment. Complement* means ''to complete'' or ''that which completes or suits another.'' *Compliment* means ''words of praise.''

The clerk was *complimented* for his success.
This shipment is a *complement* to our latest series of orders.

13. *Continual, continuous.* If an action is *continual,* it will have planned-for breaks in continuity; if an action is *continuous,* it will be constant, without breaks.

The clock has run *continuously* for four years. (It has not stopped.)
The mechanism for raising and lowering the garage door has given *continual* service for four years. (It provided service over a four-year period, but it did not raise and lower the door constantly.)

14. *Correspond to, correspond with.* If one thing *corresponds to* another, it matches or has a similarity. To *correspond with* is to write, to exchange letters.

His recommendations *correspond to* mine.
Mr. Woods has *corresponded with* us about a job.

15. *Contact. Contact* means ''to touch'' or ''to meet.'' It is used only colloquially to mean ''to communicate with.''

Please *write to us* (not *contact us*) when we can help.
Call us (not *contact us*) for an estimate.
Talk with us (not *contact us*) before making your decision.

16. *Criteria, criterion.* A *criterion* is a standard for judging, a yardstick by which something is measured. The plural form is *criteria.*

> The most important *criterion* was cost.
> Three *criteria* were developed.

17. *Data, datum. Datum* is a singular noun meaning "fact," "proposition," "condition," or "quantity" from which other facts, etc., may be deduced. *Data* is the plural form.

> This *datum* suggests. . . .
> These *data* suggest. . . .

Use of *data* as a singular form is gaining some degree of acceptance. Some people use the word in the same way in which they would use *group.* Although composed of more than one, *group* is singular:

> The group *has* decided.

Until (and if) *data* becomes generally accepted as a singular, the word should be used carefully. Because *data is* may sound incorrect and distracting to some and *data are* equally incorrect and distracting to others, an alternative expression may be preferred. Instead of "This data is," or "These data are," such expressions as "This *set* of data is," "These facts are," "This information is," or "These figures are" can be used to avoid the risk of alienating certain readers or listeners.

18. *Deal. Deal* is not a good substitute for *transaction* or *exchange.*

> We reaped a profit from the *transaction* (not *deal*).

19. *Differ from, differ with.* Use *differ from* in discussing characteristics; use *differ with* to convey the idea of disagreement.

> This machine *differs from* that machine.
> The manager *differs with* the president.

20. *Eminent, imminent. Eminent* means "well known." *Imminent* means "about to happen."

> An *eminent* scientist will address the group.
> A merger seems *imminent.*

20. *Enthused. Enthusiastic* is preferred. *Enthused* is colloquial.

> The gentleman is *enthusiastic* (not *enthused*) about his work.

22. *Except, accept. Except* means "to leave out," "to exclude"; *accept* means "to take what is offered," "to accede," "to assent."

All columns have been added *except* one.
I *accept* your offer.

23. *Farther, further.* Use *farther* when referring to distance. Use *further* when referring to extent or degree.

Let's go one mile *farther.*
Let's pursue the thought *further.*

24. *Following, preceding.* These words are not nouns; they are adjectives and should be followed by nouns. Avoid "the following is" or "the preceding is." Instead, write

The *following* list is up to date.
The *preceding* idea is ascribed to the president.

25. *Forward, send.* Use *send* to convey the idea of *initiating* movement of an item toward its receiver; use *forward* to convey the idea of *redirecting* an item that has already been sent on its way to the receiver.

After the contract is signed, I shall *send* it to you.
The package came to my address, but I *forwarded* it to you.

26. *If, whether.* Use "if" to mean "on the condition that." Use "whether" with implied or stated alternatives.

If I make high grades, I will be admitted.
I don't know *whether* he plans to go. (The implied alternative is "or stay.")
She asked *whether* I would prefer Monday or Wednesday for the appointment.

27. *Impact.* Use *impact* as a noun, not as a verb.

The cost increase had a serious *impact* on our decision. Avoid such expressions as "cost will *impact* our decision," or "the decision will seriously *impact* performance."

28. *In, into.* Use *in* to denote location. Use *into* to denote action.

The keys are *in* the vault.
He fell *into* the water.

29. *Kindly.* Avoid using *kindly* for "please."

Please (not *kindly*) fill out the attached form.

30. *Latest, last.* Use *latest* to refer to something that is still in effect; use *last* to refer to something that came after all the others.

> The *latest* model has a twelve-inch carriage. (The series has not necessarily ended; other models could follow.)
> The *last* model had a ten-inch carriage. (The series has ended; no other models will follow.)

31. *Lie, lay.* In the present tense, *lie* means "to rest" and *lay* means "to put."

Lie	**Present:**	He *lies* on the sofa.
	Past:	He *lay* down for an hour.
	Perfect Participle:	He *has lain* there for an hour.
Lay	**Present:**	She *lays* the book on the table.
	Past:	She *laid* the book there yesterday.
	Perfect participle:	She *has laid* it there many times.

32. *Lose, loose. Lose* means "to fail to keep"; *loose* means "not tight."

> Don't *lose* the moneybag.
> The cap on the fountain pen is *loose.*

33. *Majority.* Avoid use of *majority* in referring to a singular.

Not:	The *majority* of the contract is acceptable.
But:	The *major portion* of the contract is acceptable.
Or:	The *majority* of the provisions are acceptable.

34. *Media, medium.* A *medium* is a means for transmitting a message. Letter, telephone, radio, newspaper, and telegraph are examples. The plural form is *media.*

> The best *medium* for advertising this product *is* the radio.
> The news *media* are very objective in *their* coverage.

35. *Myself, me. Myself* is used to intensify *I* or *me.* It should not be used in place of these words.

> I *myself* would like to have a vacation.
> The manager and *I* (not *myself*) have investigated this plan.
> Give the report to Ms. Smith and *me* (not *myself*).

Use of such pronouns as *myself, herself,* and *themselves* is appropriate when the pronoun has been used already in the sentence.

> I taught *myself* to type.
> She sees *herself* as a perfectionist.
> They were criticizing *themselves.*

36. *Nor, or.* Use *nor* with *neither;* use *or* with *either.* (*Or* is also used in sentences that don't contain *either.*)

> Use *neither* pen *nor* pencil.
> Use *either* pen *or* pencil.
> You may pay now, *or* you may wait until January.

37. *Only.* Place *only* as close as possible to the word it is intended to modify.

> *Only* Carol takes dictation. (No one else takes dictation.)
> Carol *only* takes dictation. (She does nothing more than take it; she does not transcribe.)
> Carol takes dictation *only.* (Dictation is the only thing she takes.)

38. *Party.* Except in legal documents, do not use *party* as a synonym for person. Technically, a *party* is a group of people.

> Another *person* (not *party*) is interested in buying this house.

39. *Practical, practicable. Practical* means "useful" or "not theoretical." *Practicable* means "capable of being put into practice." Do not use *practicable* in describing a person.

> The manager is a *practical* person.
> This is a *practical* tool.
> The plan appears to be *practicable.*

40. *Quiet, quite. Quiet* means "silent"; *quite* means "entirely" or "completely."

> This room is *quiet.*
> The instructions are *quite* clear.

41. *Raise, rise. Raise* means "to lift up" or "to move something upward." *Rise* means "to go up" or "to come up."

Raise	**Present:**	We do not want to *raise* prices.
	Past:	We *raised* our prices last year.
	Perfect participle:	Our prices have been *raised* this year.
Rise	**Present:**	I do not expect prices to *rise*.
	Past:	Prices *rose* slightly last year.
	Perfect participle:	Prices have *risen* this year.

42. *Reason is because.* Since *because* means "for the reason next presented," *reason is because* constitutes a form of redundancy.

Not: The *reason is because* losses from bad debts tripled.
But: The reason is *that* losses from bad debts tripled.
Or: Profits decreased *because* losses from bad debts tripled.

43. *Same.* Do not use *same* as a pronoun in business letters and reports.

   Thanks for lending me the book; I have read *it* (not *same*) thoroughly.

44. *Set, sit. Set* is "to place"; *sit* is "to rest one's body on the buttocks."

Set	**Present:**	*Set* your briefcase on the counter.
	Past:	She *set* the briefcase there yesterday.
	Perfect participle:	She *has set* the briefcase there previously.
Sit	**Present:**	Please *sit* on the bench.
	Past:	He *sat* there yesterday.
	Perfect participle:	He *has sat* there for ten minutes.

45. *Sometime, some time.* Use *sometime* to refer to a point of time on the clock or calendar. Use *some time* to refer to a number of time units.

   Come to the office *sometime* this afternoon.
   Try to pay the account *sometime* next month.
   We have not seen him for *some time.*
   Some time has elapsed since we saw him.

46. *Stationary, stationery. Stationary* means "without movement" or "remaining in one place." *Stationery* is "writing paper."

   The machine is to remain *stationary.*
   Order another box of *stationery.*

47. *Sure, surely. Sure* is an adjective; *surely* is an adverb.

   I am *sure.*
   We *surely* (not *sure*) appreciate that attitude.

48. *Suspicion. Suspicion* is a noun; it should not be used in place of the verb *suspect.*

   Her actions aroused *suspicion.*
   We *suspect* (not *suspicion*) her.

49. *That, which.* Use *that* when a relative clause is essential in conveying the basic meaning of the sentence. Use *which* when a relative clause is not essential in conveying the basic meaning of the sentence.

The books *that* were on the shelf have been sent to the bindery.

The apparent purpose of the sentence is to identify certain books as having been sent to the bindery; therefore, "that were on the shelf" is essential. Because the clause restricts the discussion to certain units, it is called a *restrictive* clause.

Multigrade oil, *which* is only slightly more expensive than one-grade oil, will serve your purpose better.

The apparent purpose of the sentence is to convey the superiority of multigrade oil; therefore, "which is only slightly more expensive than one-grade oil" is not essential. Because the clause does not restrict the discussion to certain units, it is called a *nonrestrictive* clause. Notice that nonrestrictive (*which*) clauses employ punctuation; restrictive (*that*) clauses do not. Notice the difference in meaning:

Return the papers *that* are marked "passing." (Return "passing" papers only; keep the others.)
Return the papers, *which* are marked "passing." (Return all papers; incidentally, they are marked "passing.")

50. *Unique, complete, perfect.* These adjectives have neither comparative nor superlative forms. *Unique* means "the only one of its kind"; therefore, something that is unique is not comparable. Anything is either unique or not, complete or not, perfect or not.

Her score is *perfect.* (Not *more perfect* or *most perfect.*)
The plan is *unique.* (Not *very unique* or *more unique.*)
His report is *complete.* (Not *fairly complete.*)

51. *Very, real. Very* is an adverb; *real* is an adjective. Do not use *real* to modify verbs, adjectives, or adverbs.

The report was *very* (not *real*) effective.

52. *Wait for, wait on. Wait for* means "to await." *Wait on* means "to serve."

We are *waiting for* the report.
The waitress will *wait on* us next.

53. *Was, were.* Use *was* with the singular and *were* with the plural. However, use *were* with the singular when the mood is subjunctive (when the sentence speaks of doubt, probability, sorrow, wishfulness, or conditions that do not actually exist).

She *was* present.
They *were* present.

I *wish* the story *were* true. (Not "I wish the story *was* true.")
If I *were* old enough, I *would* apply. (Not "If I *was* old enough. . . .")

54. *Without, unless. Without* is a preposition; do not use it for the conjunction *unless.*

Your credit privileges will be revoked *unless* (not *without*) you pay within ten days.

55. *You.* Do not use *you* to mean "I" or "people in general." "You can scarcely interpret these data" is incorrect if it is intended to mean "I can scarcely interpret these data" or "People can scarcely interpret these data." Such misuses of *you* can make a reader think his or her abilities have been underestimated.

Nouns

Nouns (words that indicate people, places, or things) may be either specific or general, concrete or abstract, proper or not proper.

1. Specific Versus General. For most business writing, use *specific* nouns because they let a reader see exactly what is meant. "She types 70 words a minute" gives a clearer picture than "She types fast"; "She telephoned the boss" is clearer than "She contacted the boss."

When you do not want (or need) to convey a vivid mental picture, you can use general words. "I appreciated your letting me know about the accident" is less vivid (and better) than ". . . about your sprained ankle, your broken ribs, and the smashed-up car."

2. Concrete Versus Abstract. *Concrete* nouns are word labels for that which is solid—something that can be seen, touched, and so on. *Abstract* nouns are word labels for that which is not solid—something that cannot be seen, touched, and so on. *Tree* is a concrete noun. *Thought, confrontation,* and *willingness* are abstract nouns.

As sentence subjects, concrete nouns are normally preferred because they help to present ideas vividly. "Joe explained the procedure" is more vivid than "Explanations were given by Joe." Since "explanations" are harder to visualize than "Joe," the idea in the second sentence is more difficult to see. However, if a writer does not want an idea to stand out vividly, an abstract noun can be used as the subject of a sentence: "His weakness was well known" is less vivid than "He was known to be weak."

3. Proper Versus Not Proper. A proper noun begins with a capital letter; other nouns do not. Capitalize special names of geographic locations: the *Near East,* the *South,* the *Great Plains.*

Do not capitalize words that simply indicate direction: *southern* Arizona, *west* of Kansas City, an *easterly* direction.

Pronouns

Pronouns (words used in place of nouns) enable us to make our writing smoother than it would be if no pronouns were used. For example, compare these versions of the same sentence:

Without pronouns: Mr. Smith had some difficulty with Mr. Smith's car, so Mr. Smith took Mr. Smith's car to the corner garage for repairs.

With pronouns: Mr. Smith had some difficulty with his car, so he took it to the corner garage for repairs.

Grammatically, selecting pronouns of the appropriate gender is simple. Socially, the problem is more complicated. See pages 57–58. Pronouns do present three grammatical problems: (1) how to get agreement in *number,* (2) how to use the appropriate *case,* and (3) how to use *relative* and *interrogative* pronouns.

1. Agreement in Number. (*Number* indicates whether a pronoun involves one or more than one. An *antecedent* is the specific noun for which a pronoun stands.)

a. When a pronoun represents two or more singular antecedents connected by *and,* the pronoun must be plural:

The secretary *and* the treasurer will take *their* vacations. (The article *the* before the word *treasurer* indicates that the sentence is about two people.) The secretary *and* treasurer will take *his* vacation. (Lack of the article *the* before the word *treasurer* indicates that the sentence is about one person.)

b. Parenthetical remarks (remarks that can be omitted without destroying the basic meaning of the sentence) that appear between the pronoun and its antecedent have no effect upon the form of the pronoun:

The manager, *not the secretaries,* is responsible for *his* correspondence. (Since *his* refers to manager and not to *secretaries, his* is used instead of *their.*)

c. *Each, everyone, no,* and their variations are singular and take singular pronouns:

Each student and *each* teacher will carry *his or her* own equipment. *Everyone* is responsible for *her or his* work.

d.   When two or more singular antecedents are connected by *or* or *nor,* the pronoun must be singular:

> *Neither* David *nor* Bill can complete *his* work.
> Ask *either* the file clerk *or* the secretary about *his* in-service training.

e.   When a noun represents a *unit* that is made up of more than *one,* use a singular pronoun:

> The *company* stands behind *its* merchandise.
> The *group* wants to retain *its* goals.

f.   Collective nouns take pronouns that agree in number with the intended meaning of the collective noun:

> The accounting *staff* has been asked for *its* contributions. (Here the staff is thought of as a *unit;* thus, the singular *its* is appropriate.)
> The accounting *staff* have been asked for *their* contributions. (Here the *staff* is thought of as more than one individual; the plural pronoun *their* is appropriate.)

2.   Pronouns and Case. *Case* tells whether a pronoun is used as the subject of a sentence or as an object in it.

a.   Use nominative-case personal pronouns (*I, he, she, they, we, you, it*) as subjects of a sentence or clause:

> The manager and *he* are working on the report.
> *You* and *I* must work together.

b.   Use objective-case personal pronouns (*me, him, her, them, us, you, it*) after transitive verbs (active verbs requiring an object):

> Mrs. Kellegher telephoned *him.*
> Mrs. Kellegher telephoned Mr. Horn and *me.*
> I wish she had assigned the problem to *you* and *me.*

c.   Use objective-case pronouns after prepositions:

> The information is valuable only to *you* and *me.* (*You* is still *you* regardless of whether it is used in the nominative or objective case.)
> This is a secret between *you* and *me.*
> The increase in salary is for the manager and *her.*

d.   When forms of the linking verb *be* require a pronoun to complete the meaning, the pronoun should be in the nominative case.

It is *I*.
It was *he* who should receive credit for the sale.

e.   Use the possessive form of a pronoun before a gerund (a verb used as a noun):

Incorrect: We were delighted at *him* taking the job.
Correct: We were delighted at *his* taking the job. ("Taking the job" is used here as a noun. "His" in this sentence serves the same purpose it would serve in "We are delighted at *his* success.")

Incorrect: I shall appreciate *you* helping me.
Correct: I shall appreciate *your* helping me.

Since problems with possessive pronouns involve apostrophes, possessive pronouns are discussed in the punctuation section.

3.   Interrogative and Relative Pronouns. An *interrogative* pronoun is used to form a question.

Who is there?
Which one is correct?

A *relative* pronoun joins a subordinate clause to its antecedent:

The woman *whom* we choose must have experience. ("Whom we choose" is the subordinate clause; it is less significant than "The woman must have experience." "Whom" is the relative pronoun that joins "woman" and "we choose"; it is *whom* because it is the object of the choosing.)

a.   Place relative pronouns as near their antecedents as possible:

Incorrect: The *members* were given receipts *who* have paid.
Correct: The *members who* have paid were given receipts.

Incorrect: The agreement will enable you to pay *whichever* is lower, *6 percent or $50.*
Correct: The agreement will enable you to pay *6 percent or $50, whichever* is lower.

b.   Use *who* as the subject of the sentence; use *whom* as an object:

Who does the work?
Those *who* work will be paid (Although "who" is not itself the subject,

"who" refers to the subject.)

We are working for *whom*?

To *whom* shall we send the report? ("We" is the subject; "whom" is the object of "for" in the preceding question and of "to" in this question.)

c.   To determine which pronoun to use, restate the subordinate clause introduced by *who* or *whom:*

> She is the type of secretary *whom* we can promote. [Restating "whom we can promote" gives the proper form of the pronoun: "We can promote *her* (*whom*)."]
>
> She is the type of secretary *who* can be promoted. [Restating "who can be promoted" gives the proper form of the pronoun: "*She* (*who*) can be promoted."]

Notice that in the first example the pronoun is the object; in the second example, the pronoun is the subject.

d.   To determine the correct form of an interrogative pronoun such as *who, whom, which,* or *what,* change the question to a statement:

> *Whom* did you call? (You did call *whom.*)
>
> *Whom* did you select for the position? (You did select *whom* for the position.)

e.   Use *who* or *whom* to refer to persons; *which* to refer to things or animals; and *that* to refer to things, animals, or persons.

f.   Instead of risking a vague pronoun reference, restate a noun:

> **Vague:**   The patrolman captured the suspect even though *he* was unarmed.
>
> **Clear:**   The patrolman captured the suspect even though *the patrolman* was unarmed.
>
> **Or:**   Even though the patrolman was unarmed, *he* captured the suspect.

g.   Do not use a pronoun to refer to a phrase, clause, sentence, or paragraph. (*A pronoun should stand for a noun, and that noun should appear in the writing.*)

> **Incorrect:**   He expects to take all available accounting courses and obtain a position in a public accounting firm. *This* appeals to him.
>
> **Correct:**   He expects to take all available accounting courses and obtain a position in a public accounting firm. *This plan* appeals to him.

Verbs

Verbs present problems in mood, number, person, tense, and voice.

1. Mood. *Mood* reveals the writer's attitude toward the idea expressed, indicating whether the idea is to be thought of as a fact; a command; or a supposition, desire, or possibility.

The *indicative* mood makes a statement of fact or asks a question:

> The merchandise *arrived* today.
> When *is* the delivery date?

The *imperative* mood states a request or a command:

> *Send* us your check today.
> *Wait* until the end of the month.

The *subjunctive* mood talks of conditions that do not necessarily exist. It suggests doubt, supposition, probability, wishfulness, or sorrow.

    a. In the subjunctive mood, use *were* for the present tense of *to be:*

> **Incorrect:** I wish the story *was* true.
> **Correct:** I wish the story *were* true.

> **Incorrect:** If I *was* he, I would try again.
> **Correct:** If I *were* he, I would try again.

    b. Consider the subjunctive mood for communicating negative ideas in positive language:

> I wish I *were.* (In response to someone who asks if you are going to the company picnic, the sentence sounds better than "No, I am not.")
> We *would* make a refund if the merchandise had been used in accordance with instructions. (The sentence conveys "Since the merchandise has *not* been used in accordance with instructions, we are *not* making a refund" but avoids negative words.)

2. Number. *Number* is used to describe how many people, things, items, and so on are being discussed.

    a. Do not switch unnecessarily from singular to plural:

> **Incorrect:** *We* shall appreciate your returning the contract to me. *I* am glad you are joining Burdon's.
> **Correct:** *I* shall appreciate your returning the contract to me. *I* am glad you are joining Burdon's. (Both *I* and *we* are frequently over-

used, but changing from one to the other just for variety may cause confusion about whether one is speaking for oneself only or for oneself and others.)

b. If the subject is singular, use a verb form that fits the singular; if the subject is plural, use a verb that fits the plural:

Incorrect: Good material *and* fast delivery *is* essential.
Correct: Good material *and* fast delivery *are* essential.

Incorrect: The gentleman *and* his son *is* in charge of the business.
Correct: He *and* his son *are* in charge of the business.

c. Remember that parenthetical words coming between the subject and the verb have no effect on the verb used:

Incorrect: *You,* not the carrier, *is* responsible for the damage.
Correct: *You,* not the·carrier, *are* responsible for the damage.

Incorrect: *The manager,* as well as her three secretaries, *were inclined* to agree with the statement.
Correct: *The manager,* as well as her three secretaries, *was inclined* to agree with the statement.

d. When *or* or *nor* comes between two subjects, determine the verb form by inspecting the number of the noun closer to the verb:

Incorrect: Only one or *two* questions *is* necessary.
Correct: Only one or *two* questions *are* necessary.

Incorrect: Several paint brushes or *one* paint roller *are* necessary.
Correct: Several paint brushes or *one* paint roller *is* necessary.

e. Determine the verb by the subject, not by modifiers that come between the verb and subject:

Incorrect: The *attitude* of these people *are* receptive.
Correct: The *attitude* of these people *is* receptive. (*Attitude* is the subject; *of these people* is simply a phrase coming between the subject and the verb.)

Incorrect: *One* of the clerks *were* dismissed.
Correct: *One* of the clerks *was* dismissed. ("One" is the subject; "of the clerks" is simply a phrase coming between the subject and the verb.)

f. Use singular verbs with plural nouns that have a singular meaning.

The *news is* good.
Economics is a required course.
Mathematics is to be reviewed.

g.   Use a singular verb with plural subjects that are thought of as singular units:

Twenty *dollars is* too much.
Ten *minutes is* sufficient time.

h.   Even if titles of articles, firm names, and slogans are plural, use a singular verb:

"Understanding Computers" *is* an interesting article.
Stein, Jones, and Baker *is* the oldest firm in the city.
"Free lunches for all" *is* our campaign slogan. (In each sentence, the subject is singular: one article, one firm, and one slogan.)

3.   Person. *Person* is used to describe the quality of the verb that indicates whether the subject is (1) speaking, (2) being spoken to, or (3) being spoken about:

First person (the writer or speaker):   *I am, we are*
Second person (receiver of message):   *You are*
Third person (person being discussed):   *He is, she is, they are*

a.   Choose verbs that agree in *person* with their subjects:

Incorrect: *She don't* attend class regularly.
Correct: *She doesn't* attend class regularly.
Correct: *They don't* attend class regularly.

b.   For vivid, emphatic writing, choose second person instead of third person:

Less vivid: Next, *the operator* takes the film in *his* right hand, swings the gate open with *his* left, and. . . .
More vivid: Next, *you* take the film in *your* right hand, swing the gate open with *your* left, and. . . .

c.   Try to avoid second person in formal reports.

Poor: *You* would have difficulty interpreting such data.
Improved: Such data would be difficult to interpret.

To the reader, "you" could have three different meanings: the one who asked for the report, all readers of the report, or the writer of the report.

d.   Try to avoid third person in referring to yourself. In business letters, *I* is preferable to *the writer* or *the undersigned.* However, *I* should be used sparingly because its overuse usually places too much emphasis on the one who writes. In business reports, *I* is almost always avoided; it has the effect of emphasizing the writer and thus taking emphasis away from the subject matter.

4.   Tense. *Tense* indicates time. Tenses are both simple and compound.

a.   Simple tenses:

Present: I *see* you. (Tells what is now happening.)
Past: I *saw* you. (Tells what has already happened.)
Future: I *shall* see you. (Tells what is yet to happen.)

b.   Compound tenses:

Present Perfect: I *have seen* you. (Tells of past action that extends to the present.)
Past Perfect: I *had seen* you. (Tells of past action that was finished before another past action.)
Future Perfect: I *shall have seen* you. (Tells of action that will be finished before a future time.)

c.   When something *was* and *still is* true, write about it in present tense:

Incorrect: The speaker reminded us that Rhode Island *was* smaller than Wisconsin.
Correct: The speaker reminded us that Rhode Island *is* smaller than Wisconsin.

d.   Avoid unnecessary shifts in tense:

Incorrect: The deliveryman *brings* my package but *left* without asking me to sign for it.
Correct: The deliveryman *brought* my package but *left* without asking me to sign for it.

(Verbs that appear in the same sentence are not required to be in the same tense. For example, "The contract that *was prepared* yesterday *will* be signed tomorrow.")

5.   Voice. *Voice* is the word used to indicate whether a subject *acts* or whether it *is acted upon.* If the subject of a sentence acts, the verb used to describe that action is called an *active verb:*

The typist *made* an error.
The woman *asked* for an adjustment.

If the subject of the sentence is acted upon, the verb used to describe that action is called a *passive verb*. See the examples on page 63.

An error *was made* by the typist.
An adjustment *was asked* for by the woman.

For most business writing, active voice is preferred. But sometimes passive voice is more appropriate. Use passive voice:

a. to emphasize the receiver of action more than the doer:

Say: Dinner *is* now *being* served.
Not: The waiters *are* now *serving* dinner.

b. to avoid a tone of accusation:

Say: Three errors *have been made* on this page.
Not: You *made* three errors on this page.

c. to avoid revealing names:

The procedure *has been criticized* severely. (The sentence is appropriate if the writer does not want to reveal who has been criticizing.)

Adjectives and Adverbs

Adjectives modify nouns or pronouns. *Adverbs* modify verbs, adjectives, or other adverbs. Although most adverbs end in *ly*, some commonly used adverbs do not end in *ly: there, then, after, now, hence,* and *very*. Most words that end in *ly* are adverbs; but common exceptions are *neighborly, timely, friendly, gentlemanly*. Some words are both adjective and adverb: *fast, late,* and *well*.

1. **Adjectives**

a. Use an adjective to modify a noun or pronoun:

She wrote a *long* letter.
I prefer the *little* one.

b. Use an adjective after a linking verb when the modifier refers to the subject instead of to the verb. (A linking verb connects a subject to the rest of the sentence. ''He *is* old.'' ''She *seems* sincere.'')

The salesperson seemed *enthusiastic*. (The adjective "enthusiastic" refers to "salesperson" and not to "seemed.")
The president looked *suspicious*. (The adjective *suspicious* refers to *president* and not to *looked*.)

c. Use comparatives and superlatives carefully:

Incorrect: She is the *fastest* of the two workers.
Correct: She is the *faster* of the two workers.
Correct: She is the *fastest* of the three workers.

Incorrect: He is the *best* of the two operators.
Correct: He is the *better* of the two operators.
Correct: He is the *best* of the three operators.

2. Adverbs

a. Use an adverb to modify a verb:

The salesperson looked *enthusiastically* at the prospect. (The adverb "enthusiastically" refers to "looked" and not to "salesperson.")
The president looked *suspiciously* at the cash register. (The adverb "suspiciously" refers to "looked" and not to the "president.")

b. Use an adverb to modify an adjective:

The committee was *really* active. (The adverb "really" describes the adjective "active.")

c. Use an adverb to modify another adverb:

Worker A progressed *relatively faster* than did worker B. (The adverb "relatively" modifies the adverb "faster.")

Sentence Structure

1. Be sure to state the subject of each sentence (unless the sentence is a command):

Incorrect: *Received* the foreman's request today.
Correct: *I received* the foreman's request today.

In such imperative sentences as "Return the forms to me," the subject (*you*) is understood and therefore appropriately omitted.

2. Rely mainly on sentences that follow the normal subject-verb-complement sequence:

> We (*subject*) withdrew (*verb*) for three reasons (*complement*).

People are accustomed to sentences that employ this sequence. Sentences that expose the verb *before* revealing the subject have three disadvantages: they slow down the reading, they present less vivid pictures, and they employ more words than would be required if the normal sequence were followed:

Original:	There are *two reasons* for our withdrawal.
Better:	*Two reasons* for our withdrawal are. . . .
	We withdrew for two reasons.

Original:	*It* is important that we withdraw.
Better:	*Our withdrawal* is important.
	We must withdraw.

There and *It* are called *expletives* — filler words that have no real meaning in the sentence.

3. Do not put unrelated ideas in the same sentence:

> The *coffee break* is at ten o'clock, and the company plans to purchase additional *parking space* for its employees. (These ideas appear to have little relationship. Therefore, they should certainly not be introduced in the same sentence; they should be discussed in different paragraphs or even in different messages.)

4. Put pronouns, adverbs, phrases, and clauses near the words they modify:

Incorrect:	I saw his *performance* at the Christmas party, *which* I certainly enjoyed watching.
Correct:	I saw his *performance, which* I certainly enjoyed watching, at the Christmas party.
Correct:	I certainly enjoyed watching his performance at the Christmas party.

Incorrect:	He *only* works in the toy department for $3.25 an hour.
Correct:	He works in the toy department for *only* $3.25 an hour.

Incorrect:	The *secretary* stood beside the mimeograph machine *in a white dress.*
Correct:	The *secretary in a white dress* stood beside the mimeograph machine.

Incorrect:	He put a new type of *oil* on his hair, *which* he had just purchased at the drugstore.
Correct:	He put a new type of *oil, which* he had just purchased at the drugstore, on his hair.

5. Do not separate subject and predicate unnecessarily:

Incorrect: *He,* hoping to receive a bonus, *worked* rapidly.
Correct: Hoping to receive a bonus, *he worked* rapidly.

6. Attach an introductory phrase to the subject of an independent clause. Otherwise, the phrase dangles. Remedy the dangling phrase in one of two ways: change the subject of the independent clause, or make the phrase into a subordinate clause by assigning it a subject:

Incorrect: *When* a little boy, *my mother* took me through a milk-processing plant. (Implies that the mother was once a little boy.)
Correct: *When* a little boy, *I* was taken through a milk-processing plant by my mother.
Correct: *When I was a little boy,* my mother took me through a milk-processing plant.

Incorrect: *Working* at full speed every morning, *fatigue* overtakes me in the afternoon. (Implies that "fatigue" was working at full speed.)
Correct: *Working* at full speed every morning, *I* become tired in the afternoon.
Correct: *Since I work* at full speed every morning, *fatigue* overtakes me in the afternoon.

Incorrect: *After working* four days on the financial statements, *they* were finally completed. (Implies that "financial statements" were "working four days.")
Correct: *After working* four days on the financial statements, *the accountants* finally completed the task.
Correct: *After the accountants* had worked four days, the financial statements *were* finally *completed.*

Incorrect: *To function* properly, *you* must oil the machine every hour. (Implies that if "you" are "to function properly," the machine must be oiled hourly.)
Correct: *To function* properly, *the machine* must be oiled every hour.
Correct: *If the machine* is to function properly, *you* must oil it every hour.

7. Express related ideas in similar grammatical form (use parallel construction):

Incorrect: The machine operator made three resolutions: *(1) to be punctual, (2) following* instructions carefully, and *third, the reduction* of waste.
Correct: The machine operator made three resolutions: *(1) to be punctual, (2) to follow* instructions carefully, and *(3) to reduce* waste.

Incorrect:	The personnel manager is concerned with *the selection* of the right worker, *providing* appropriate indoctrination, and *the worker's* progress.
Correct:	The personnel manager is concerned with *selecting* the right worker, *providing* appropriate indoctrination, and *checking* the worker's progress.

8. Do not end a sentence with a needless preposition:

Incorrect:	Where is the plant to be located *at*?
Correct:	Where is the plant to be located?

Incorrect:	The worker did not tell us where he was going *to*.
Correct:	The worker did not tell us where he was going.

9. End a sentence with a preposition if for some reason the preposition needs emphasis:

I am not concerned with what he is paying *for*. I am concerned with what he is paying *with*.

The prospect has everything—a goal to work *toward*, a house to live *in*, and an income to live *on*.

10. Avoid clumsy split infinitives. (Two words are required to express an infinitive: *to* plus a *verb*. The two words belong together. An infinitive is split when another word is placed between the two.)

Incorrect:	The superintendent used *to occasionally visit* the offices.
Correct:	The superintendent used *to visit* the offices *occasionally*.

Incorrect:	I want *to briefly summarize* the report.
Correct:	I want *to summarize* the report *briefly*.

II. MECHANICS

Writers do not encounter *mechanical* problems until they put their thoughts on paper. Which ideas to include, the order in which to present them, the amount of support needed, and the words to be used are problems of definition and organization. Mechanical problems, on the other hand, are the problems encountered when ideas are placed on paper: abbreviating, capitalizing, writing numbers, dividing words, punctuating, spacing, spelling, and arranging on the page.

Abbreviating

Style manuals are not in complete agreement on rules of abbreviation, but the following conventions are generally accepted:

1. **Abbreviate**

    a. titles that come before proper names: *Dr., Mr., Mrs., Ms.*

    b. titles that come after proper names: *D.D.S., Esq., Jr., M.D., Ph.D., Sr.*

    c. commonly known governmental agencies: *FDIC, FCC, FHA, TVA*

    d. commonly used business expressions: *f.o.b., C.O.D., A.M.,* or *P.M.* (Note: Use *A.M.* and *P.M.* only when a specific time is mentioned):

Incorrect	Come to the office this *A.M.*
Correct:	Come to the office at 10:15 *A.M.*
Correct:	Come to the office this *morning.*

    e. the names of businesses when their own letterheads contain abbreviations: Smith *&* Company; Jones and Smith, *Inc.;* The John C. Andrews *Co.*

    f. the word *number* when it is used with a figure to designate something:

    Go to room *No.* 7.
    May we have a carton of *No.* 10 envelopes.
    Refer to Policy *No.* 384862.

    g. the names of states when they appear as parts of envelope addresses or inside addresses. The post office prefers the following abbreviations for states:

Alabama	AL	Kansas	KS	Ohio	OH
Alaska	AK	Kentucky	KY	Oklahoma	OK
Arizona	AZ	Louisiana	LA	Oregon	OR
Arkansas	AR	Maine	ME	Pennsylvania	PA
California	CA	Maryland	MD	Puerto Rico	PR
Canal Zone	CZ	Massachusetts	MA	Rhode Island	RI
Colorado	CO	Michigan	MI	South Carolina	SC
Connecticut	CT	Minnesota	MN	South Dakota	SD
Delaware	DE	Mississippi	MS	Tennessee	TN
District of		Missouri	MO	Texas	TX
Columbia	DC	Montana	MT	Trust Territories	TT
Florida	FL	Nebraska	NE	Utah	UT
Georgia	GA	Nevada	NV	Vermont	VT
Guam	GU	New Hampshire	NH	Virgin Islands	VI
Hawaii	HI	New Jersey	NJ	Virginia	VA
Idaho	ID	New Mexico	NM	Washington	WA
Illinois	IL	New York	NY	West Virginia	WV
Indiana	IN	North Carolina	NC	Wisconsin	WI
Iowa	IA	North Dakota	ND	Wyoming	WY

2. Do Not Abbreviate

a. the names of cities, states (except in envelope and inside addresses), months, and days of the week.

b. the words *avenue, boulevard, drive,* and *street* (except in envelope and inside addresses where abbreviations will make line lengths more uniform):

Send to our Main *Street* office.
Go south on Mill *Avenue.*

Mr. Cy Wood
230 Loma Vista *Blvd.*
Tempe, *AZ* 85282

c. points on the compass (except on envelopes, in inside addresses, and in legal documents):

Tom has been in the *West* for seven years.
Go *east* one block and turn *south.*

Mr. Henry Lopez
1150 *W.* Adams Street
Atlanta, GA 30305

. . . the *northeast quarter* of the *southwest quarter* of Section 21, containing 40 acres more or less.

d. the word *Christmas.*

e. names of school subjects:

Use	Instead of
physical education	phys. ed.
corporation finance	corp. fin.
vocational agriculture	vo. ag.
economics	econ.

f. a person's name (unless you know that he or she abbreviates it):

Use	Instead of
Charles	Chas.
Barbara	Barb.

Capitalizing

Style manuals are in general agreement on the rules of capitalization.

1. Capitalize

a. names of people, animals, places, geographic areas, days of the week, months of the year, holidays, deities, publications, and other special names.

b. the first word of a direct quotation:

The sales representative said, "*We* leave tomorrow."

c. the first word of a title (book, magazine, article, theme) and all other words of a title or heading except conjunctions (*and, for, but*), articles (*a, an, the*), and short prepositions (*in, on, of, to*):

"*The* Story of My Life" (article)   "Cost of the Land" (Heading in
The Prince and the Pauper (book)   a report)

d. the first word following a colon when a formal statement or question follows:

Here is an important rule for report writers: *Plan* your work and work your plan.
Each sales representative should ask himself or herself this question: *Do* I really look like a representative of my firm?

e. pronouns that refer to the deity:

The clergyman asked *His* guidance.

f. father, mother, brother, sister when used as names:

Make the suggestion to my *father.*
Make the suggestion to *Father.*

g. only the first and last words in salutations and only the first word in complimentary closes:

My dear Madam: *Respectfully* yours,

h. the names of documents and historical events:

The Missouri Constitution   *Battle of Bunker Hill*

i. titles that come before or after a name:

Editor Smith   *Mr.* John Smith, *Editor*

President *King*   *Dr.* John King, *President*

Used with a person's name, such words as "editor" and "president" are capitalized when they are used as *titles;* they are not capitalized when they are used as *explanations:*

Helen Platt, *President,* Broadmor PTA (Her title in the organization.)
Helen Platt, *president* of a local speakers' club, offered to serve as MC. (Explanation of her credentials.)
Eugene Jenkins, *Editor, Sun City Daily* (His title.)
Eugene Jenkins, a newspaper *editor,* will serve as judge in the essay contest. (An explanation.)

j. a one-word sentence.

Yes!   *Certainly.*

k. the word *number* when used with a figure to designate something:

Policy *No.* 8746826

2. Do Not Capitalize

a. the first word of an indirect quotation:

He said that *it* was time to part.

b. such words as father, mother, uncle, or cousin when they are preceded by a possessive pronoun:

He has taken the position formerly held by his *father.*
Please mail the check to my *mother.*

c. the names of school courses that are not proper nouns:

The student is taking French, *mathematics, science,* and English.

d. the names of seasons (except when they are personified):

We make most of our profits during the *winter.*

Note: When a season is used to designate a school term or semester, the season is ordinarily capitalized.

Summer session   *Spring* semester

e. the first word in the last part of an interrupted quotation:

"We shall proceed," he said, "*with* the utmost caution."

   f. the first word of a parenthetical sentence:

The president said (*you* will probably agree) that production could be increased by 10 percent.

Writing Numbers

Since business people use quantitative data often, numbers appear frequently in business writing. *Accuracy* is exceedingly important. The most frequent problem in expressing numbers is whether to write them as figures or to spell them as words.

1. Use Figures

   a. in most business writing, use figures not spelled-out words, because (1) figures are important and get deserved emphasis; (2) figures are easy for readers to locate if they need to reread for critical points; and (3) figures provide economic use of time and space — *12* can be typed faster and in less space than *twelve.*

     Regardless of whether a number has one digit or many, use figures to express dates, sums of money, mixed numbers and decimals, distance, dimension, cubic capacity, percentage, weights, temperatures, and page numbers. (With the preceding exceptions, numbers one to ten are normally spelled out if no larger number appears in the same sentence: "Only *three* people were present." "We need *five* machines." "Send *5* officers and *37* men.")

   b. with ordinals (*th, st, rd, nd*) only when the number precedes the month.

The meeting is to be held on *May 10.*
The meeting is to be held on the *10th of May.*

   c. without the ciphers when presenting an even-dollar figure that is not accompanied with a figure that includes both dollars and cents.

He paid *$30* for the cabinet.
He paid $31.75 for the table and *$30.00* for the cabinet.

2. Spell Out

   a. numbers if they are used as the first word of a sentence:

Thirty-two people attended.

   b. numbers that represent time when *o'clock* is used:

Please be there at *ten o'clock.*
Meet me at *10:15 P.M.*

c.   names of streets up to and including twelve:

Fifth Street, *Seventh* Avenue

d.   the first number when two numbers are placed together in the same sentence:

We need *four 17-cent* stamps.
We need *seventeen 4-cent* stamps.

Note: If one number in a sentence follows another, style manuals agree that *one* of the numbers should be spelled ("4 17-cent" or "17 4-cent" may cause a reader to ponder). Manuals do not agree on *which* number is to be spelled. Be consistent. Note also that a hyphen joins the second number with the word that follows it, thus forming a compound adjective that describes the noun "stamps."

e.   numbers in legal documents, following them with figures enclosed in parentheses:

For the sum of *four hundred dollars ($400),* . . .
For the sum of *four hundred (400)* dollars, . . .
. . . including *forty (40)* acres, more or less.

Dividing Words

In typewritten material, right margins are not expected to be exactly even. If one line is a few spaces shorter or a few spaces longer than the lines above and below it, no harm is done; but if a line is exceedingly long or short, it detracts from the overall appearance. A divided word at the end of the line would be less distracting.

Try to avoid dividing words at the end of a line. Too many lines that end with divided words will be just as distracting as lines that extend too far into the right margin. If words *must* be divided, the following rules apply:

1.   Divide words between syllables only. (Words with only one syllable cannot be divided: *through, hearth, worked.*)

2.   Do not divide a word if it has fewer than seven letters. (Lines on a typewritten page can vary as much as six or seven letters in length; therefore, division of such short words as *letter* or *report* is pointless.)

3.   Do not separate the following syllables from the remainder of a word:

a.   A syllable that does not include a vowel: would/*n't.*

b.   A first syllable that contains only one letter: *a*/greement.

c.   A last syllable that contains only one or two letters: pneumoni/*a,* apolog/*y.*

4. Divide a word after a single-letter syllable, unless the word contains successive single-letter syllables: semi-nary, congratu-late, extenu-ate, semi-aquatic.

5. Try to avoid dividing hyphenated words at any place other than the hyphen: self-employed, semi-independent.

6. Avoid dividing proper names.

7. Do not divide a word at the end of a page.

Punctuating

In business writing, punctuation is basically the same as in other writing. Clarity is a primary consideration. Convention is another.

1. Use an Apostrophe

a. to form the possessive singular: *Smith's, company's, Utah's.* (Add an apostrophe and an *s*.)

b. to form the possessive plural of words ending in *s*: *boys', students', dealers', Smiths'*. (Add *s* and an apostrophe.)

c. to show possession of a proper noun: *Mr. Wilson's* boss, *Mr. Brandt's* statement. (Add an apostrophe and an *s*.)

d. to form the possessive singular when the last letter in a proper noun is an *s*. Determine placement of the apostrophe by the number of syllables in the noun:

When the singular form of a one-syllable noun ends in *s*, form the possessive by adding *'s*: *Jones's, Ross's.*

When the singular form contains more than one syllable and ends in *s* or in an *s* sound, form the possessive by adding an apostrophe only: for *goodness'* sake, *Moses'* words.

e. in expressions that indicate ownership. (The apostrophe shows omission of a preposition): Last *year's* reports (reports of last year).

f. when the noun presents time or distance in a possessive manner: an *hour's* visit, three *weeks'* vacation, a *mile's* journey.

g. when a noun precedes a gerund:

Miss *Bowen's* receiving the promotion caused. . . .
Mr. *Green's* taking the gavel indicated. . . .

h.   to show whether ownership is joint or separate:

To indicate joint ownership, add an *'s* to the last name only: *Olsen* and *Howard's* accounting firms.
To indicate separate ownership, add an *'s* to each name: *Olsen's* and *Howard's* accounting firms.

i.   to form the plural of figures, letters, unusual words, or characters: *7's,* the *why's* and *wherefore's, %'s, a's, b's,* and *c's.*

2.   Do Not Use an Apostrophe

a.   in the titles of some organizations. Use the name as the organization uses its name.

National Business *Teachers* Association
National Sales *Executives* Association

b.   to form the possessive of a pronoun (most pronouns become possessive through a change in spelling; therefore, an apostrophe is not employed)

yours (not *your's*)
ours (not *our's*)

3.   Use Brackets

a.   to enclose words that are inserted between words or sentences of quoted material:

"How long will the delay be? No longer than this: [At this point, the speaker tapped the podium three times]. That means no delay at all."

b.   as required in certain mathematical formulas.

c.   to enclose parenthetical material that contains parentheses:

The motion passed. [The vote (17 for and 4 against) was not taken until midnight.]

4.   Use a Colon

a.   to suggest that a list will follow a statement that appears in complete-sentence form:

For three reasons, we have decided to move to a new location: (1) We need an expanded market. (2) We need an inexpensive source of raw materials. (3) We need a ready source of labor.

Three factors influenced our decision: an expanded market, an inexpensive source of raw materials, and a ready source of labor.

We need to (1) expand our market, (2) locate an inexpensive source of materials, and (3) find a ready source of labor. (A colon does not follow *to* because the words preceding the list do not constitute what could be a complete sentence.)

b.   When the verb that would complete a sentence is sufficiently understood and thus omitted:

The proposal was rejected. The reasons: (1) no money, (2) no technicians, and (3) no work space.

(Such verbs as "are presented," "are given," and "are stated" could be employed after "reasons"; but they are not essential. Since the thought is complete without them, a colon is used.)

c.   to stress an appositive (a noun that renames the preceding noun) at the end of a sentence:

His heart was set on one thing: promotion.
Our progress is due to the efforts of one man: Mr. Keating.

d.   after the salutation of a letter (when mixed or closed punctuation is used):

Dear Dr. Gorga: Dear Miss Campbell:

e.   after a word or phrase followed by additional material in ads or signs:

No Parking: Reserved for executives
For Rent: Two-bedroom apartment

f.   between hours and minutes to express time in figures:

5:45 *P.M.*   11:05 *A.M.*

5. Use a Comma

a.   between coordinate clauses joined by *and, but,* and *for:*

He wanted to pay his bills on time, *but* he did not have the money.

b.   after participial phrases or dependent clauses:

Believing that her earnings would continue to increase, she sought to borrow more money.

Sentences that begin with prepositions or such words as *if*, *as*, and *when* almost always need a comma.

> Under the circumstances, we think you are justified.
> To get the full benefit of our insurance plan, just fill out and return the enclosed card.
> Whatever you do, please explain it to your supervisor.
> As you may know, Mr. Smith has been ill for three weeks.
> If you can meet us at the plane, please plan to be there by six o'clock.
> When I left the building, doors were being closed.

c. to separate words in a series:

> You have a choice of gray, green, purple, and white. (Without the comma after ''purple,'' no one can tell for sure whether there are four choices, the last of which is ''white,'' or whether there are three choices, the last of which is ''purple and white.'')
> You have a choice of purple and white, gray, and green. (Choice is restricted to three, the first of which is ''purple and white.'')

d. between coordinate adjectives (two separate adjectives that modify the same noun):

> New employees are given a long, difficult examination. (''Long'' and ''diffi-cult'' both modify ''examination.'')

> We want factual, up-to-the-hour news. (''Factual'' and ''up-to-the-hour'' separately modify ''news'' and are separated by a comma.)

> The supervisor is an excellent public speaker. (Do not place a comma between two adjectives when the second adjective may be considered as part of the noun that follows. Technically, ''excellent'' and ''public'' are both adjectives. In this sentence, however, ''excellent'' modifies the noun ''public speaker.''

e. to separate a nonrestrictive clause (a clause that is not essential to the basic meaning of the sentence) from the rest of the sentence:

> Mr. MacMurray, who is head of the collection department, is leaving for a vacation. (The parenthetical remark is not essential to the meaning of the sentence.)
> The man who is head of the collection department is leaving for a vacation. (Commas should not be used because ''who is head of the collection department'' is essential to the meaning of the sentence.)

f. to separate parenthetical expressions from the rest of the sentence:

p.   between the typewritten name and the title on the same line beneath a signature line.

Roy Murr, President   Cathryn W. Edwards
                                        President of Academic Affairs

q.   between the city and the state in an address:

Belmont, CA 94002

r.   after a conjunctive adverb:

The check was for the right amount; however, it was not signed.

6.   Use a Dash

In typewritten material, the dash is constructed by striking the hyphen key twice with no space before or after. The dash is thus twice as long as the hyphen and has a slight break in the middle. (In typeset material, as follows, it is longer than a hyphen but has no break.)

a.   to place emphasis on appositives:

His answer—the correct answer—was based on years of experience.
Compare the price—$125—with the cost of a single repair job.
She was concerned with one thing—promotion.

b.   when appositives contain commas:

Their scores—Mary, 21; Sally, 20; and Jo, 19—were the highest in a group of 300.

c.   when a parenthetical remark consists of an abrupt change in thought:

The committee decided—you may think it's a joke, but it isn't—that the resolution should be adopted.

7.   Use an Ellipsis

to indicate that some words have been omitted from a quotation:

Mr. Thomas reported, "We believe . . . that our objectives will be accomplished."
Mr. Thomas said, "The time has come when we must provide our employees with in-service training. . . ." (Ellipses at the end of a quotation employ four periods, one of which indicates the end of the sentence.)

Miss Watson, speaking in behalf of the entire department, accepted the proposal.

g. before and after year dates when the month and day precede:

On July 2, 1977, Mr. Kababik made the final payment.

h. before and after the name of a state when the name of a city precedes:

I saw him in Kansas City, Missouri, on the 12th of October.

i. after a direct address:

John, I believe you have earned a vacation.

j. after the words *No* and *Yes* when they introduce a statement:

Yes, you can count on me.   No, I shall have to decline.

k. to set off appositives:

The group heard a speech from Mr. Matthew Welch, a recruit.
Mr. Herbert Jackson, former president of the Jackson Institute, spoke to the group.

A comma before an appositive is used for neutral emphasis; a dash would emphasize the appositive more.

l. between contrasted elements:

We need more money, not less.
The job requires experience, not formal education.

m. to show the omission of words that are understood:

Miss Reno scored 96 percent on the pre-employment examination; Mr. Mehrmann, 84 percent.

n. before a question that solicits a confirmatory answer:

It's a reasonable price, isn't it?
Our bills have been paid, haven't they?

o. between a name and a title on the same line of an inside address:

Mr. Eugene Partridge, President   Mrs. Janet W. Shallhammert
                                         Director of the Budget

8.   Use a Hyphen

a.   in such compound words as *self-analysis* and *father-in-law*.

b.   between the words in a compound adjective. (A *compound adjective* is a group of words joined together and used as a single word to describe a noun that follows.)

an *attention-getting* device

a *page-by-page* description

an *up-to-date* record

a technical, *hard-to-follow* lecture

Observe that each of the hyphenated expressions precedes a noun. Hyphens would not be required in "a lecture that was hard to follow," a "record that is up to date," and so on. Do not use a hyphen in such expressions as "*commonly accepted* principle," "*widely quoted* authority," "*rapidly advancing* leader": since the first word in each expression ends in *ly*, no compound adjective is involved. *Commonly,* for example, is an adverb modifying *accepted.*

c.   to prevent misinterpretation:

a *toy-machine* man (a man concerned with toy machines)
a *toy machine* man (a toy man of the machine type)
guaranteed used tires (used tires that are guaranteed)
guaranteed-used tires (tires that are guaranteed to have been used)
twelve *foot-soldiers* (twelve soldiers who travel by walking)
twelve-foot soldiers (soldiers twelve feet tall)
eight inch blades (eight blades, each of which is an inch long)
eight-inch blades (blades eight inches long)
recover a chair (to obtain possession of a chair once more)
re-cover a chair (to cover a chair again)

d.   after a prefix that ends with the same vowel with which a root word begins:

semi-independent   *de-emphasize*   *re-educate*

Readers frequently encounter double vowels that are to be pronounced as one (*been, feed, good, root, see*). A hyphen between a prefix ending in a vowel and a root word beginning with the same vowel assists readers in seeing the two vowels separately and pronouncing them separately. Perhaps because certain words (such as *co-operate* and *re-enter*) are used frequently, most publishers are now omitting the hyphen. For questionable words, consult a recently published dictionary.

e.   to express fractions that precede a noun:

a two-thirds interest   a three-fourths majority

Figures—⅔ and ¾—are acceptable. Spelled-out fractions not followed by nouns are not hyphenated: *two thirds* of the members.

f.   in spelling out compound numbers:

thirty-one   *ninety-seven*

g.   to avoid repetition of a word.

first-, second-, and *third-class* mail
short-, medium-, and *long-range* missiles

''Short-range, medium-range, and long-range missiles'' would have the same meaning; but repetition of ''range'' is not necessary. The hyphens after ''short'' and ''medium'' show that these words are connected to another word that will appear at the end of the series.

h.   to divide words at the end of a line. (See the discussion of dividing words.)

9.   Use Parentheses

a.   for explanatory material that could be left out:

Three of our employees (Mr. Bachman, Mr. Russo, and Mr. Wilds) took their vacations in August. (Dashes may be used instead of parentheses to precede and follow parenthetical material. Dashes have the effect of emphasizing; parentheses, de-emphasizing.)
All our employees (you'll not believe this, I'm sure) have perfect attendance records. (Sentences within sentences neither begin with a capital letter nor end with a period.)

b.   for accuracy in writing figures:

For the sum of three thousand five hundred dollars ($3,500). . . .

c.   To enclose figures when parts of a sentence are enumerated:

The clerk has authority to (1) issue passes, (2) collect membership fees, and (3) sign checks.

d.   *after* a period when an entire sentence is parenthetical; *before* a period when only the last part of a sentence is parenthetical:

The board met for three hours. (The usual time is one hour.)
Success can be attributed to one man (Earl Knott).

e.   both before and after that which is parenthetical:

Incorrect: authority to 1) issue passes, 2) collect fees
Correct: authority to (1) issue passes, (2) collect fees

10.   Use a Period

a.   after imperative and declarative sentences:

Complete this report.   We shall attend.

b.   after a courteous request:

WIll you please complete the report today.
May I have your answer this week.

Technically, the sentences are questions; but they do not suggest a verbal answer. They do suggest an *action* answer.

c.   after an abbreviation:

Dr.
M.D.
Mrs.
Ms.
Miss (not abbreviated when used as a title; it's a complete word)

d.   to end a sentence in which the last word is abbreviated:

Incorrect: Send to John Cook, Jr..
Correct: Send to John Cook, Jr.

Two periods look too much like an ellipsis.

11.   Use Quotation Marks

a.   to enclose direct quotations:

The supervisor said, "We shall make progress."
"We shall make progress," the supervisor said, "even though we have to work overtime." (Note that the period and comma are typed within the quotation marks. All other punctuation is typed outside —unless it is part of the quotation.)

b. before the first word and after the last word of a multiple-sentence quotation:

> The president said, "Have a seat, gentlemen. I'm dictating a letter. I should be through in about five minutes. Please wait."

c. to enclose titles of songs, magazine and newspaper articles, and themes:

> "Home on the Range"   "Progress in Cancer Research"

(Underscore or italicize the titles of books, magazines, and newspapers.)

d. to define terms:

> As used in this report, *syntax* means "the branch of grammar that has to do with sentence structure."

e. to enclose slang expressions:

> Gentlemen, we can describe the attacks against our policies with one word—"hogwash."

f. to enclose nicknames:

> And now for some comments by Ray "Skinny" Johnson.

g. to imply that a different word may be more appropriate:

> our "football" team (hints that the team appears to be playing something other than football)
> our football "team" (hints that "collection of individual players" would be more descriptive than "team")
> out for "lunch" (hints that the reason for being out is something other than lunch)

h. to enclose quoted material that contains other quoted material:

> The budget director said, "Believe me when I say 'A penny saved is a penny earned' is the best advice I ever had."

Note: A quotation that appears within another quotation is enclosed in *single* quotation marks.

i. before and after a word that is used in an unusual way. The last word in each of the following sentences is used in the usual sense:

The presentation was effective.
May I please have your recommendation.

In the first sentence, the last word conveys the idea of a presentation that accomplishes its purpose; in the second, the last word conveys the idea of a proposed alternative or course of action. No quotation marks are needed. However, the following sentences employ the same words in unusual ways; therefore, quotation marks are used:

The word "effective" was used in describing his presentation.
In this sentence, "effective" is used as an adjective.
He had difficulty learning to spell "recommendation."

In the preceding sentences, the words included in quotation marks could (instead) be presented in italics (if the typewriter is equipped with keys for italics).

j. in their proper position within a sentence. Place periods and commas *inside* quotation marks:

"Take your time," she said, "and the work will be easier."

Place semicolons *outside* quotation marks:

She said, "Take your time"; but within five minutes she was urging people to work as fast as possible.

Place question marks *inside* quotation marks when the question is within the quotation:

The contractor asked, "When shall we begin?"

Place question marks *outside* quotation marks when the question is not within the quotation:

Did the contractor say, "We shall begin today"?

12. Use a Semicolon

a. when a conjunction is omitted:

Our workers have been extraordinarily efficient this year, and they are expecting a bonus.
Our workers have been extraordinarily efficient this year; they are expecting a bonus.

b. in a compound sentence that contains a comma:

We prefer delivery on Saturday morning at four o'clock, but Friday night at ten o'clock will be satisfactory.

As you may know, we prefer delivery on Saturday morning at four o'clock; but Friday night at ten o'clock will be satisfactory.

We prefer delivery on Saturday morning at four o'clock; but, if the arrangement is more convenient for you, Friday night at ten o'clock will be satisfactory.

c. before conjunctive adverbs:

The shipment arrived too late for our weekend sale; therefore, we are returning the shipment to you.

Other frequently used conjunctive adverbs are "however," "otherwise," "consequently," and "nevertheless."

d. in series that contain commas:

Some of our workers have worked overtime this week: Smith, 6 hours; Hardin, 3; Cantrell, 10; and McGowan, 11.

e. before illustrative words, as in the following sentences:

We have plans for improvement; for example, we intend to. . . .

The engine has been "knocking"; that is, the gas in the cylinders explodes before the pistons complete their upward strokes.

13. Use Symbols

a. for convenience in filling out such forms as invoices and statements, but not in sentences of letters and reports. The dollar sign ($), in contrast with such symbols as %, ¢, @, and #, should be used in letters and reports.

b. in sentences of letters and reports:

31 *percent* (not "31%")
80 *cents* a foot (not "80¢ a foot")
21 *cases at* $4 a case (not "21 cases @ $4 a case")
to policy *No.* 468571 (not "to policy # 468571")

14. Use an Underscore or Italics

a. to emphasize a word that is not sufficiently emphasized by other means.

b. to indicate the titles of books, magazines, and newspapers:

Gone with the Wind
The Reader's Digest
The Evening Star

Spelling

The following words appear often in business letters and reports. To avoid frequent references to the dictionary and to avoid embarrassing errors when a dictionary is not available, study and try to memorize the list.

acceptable	accessible	accommodations
accompanying	accumulate	accurate
acknowledging	acknowledgment	across
advisable	allowance	announcement
announcing	apparently	appealing
argument	arrangement	attorneys
automatically	available	bargain
beginning	believing	beneficial
benefited	bookkeeper	bulletin
calendar	cancellation	changeable
changing	chargeable	collectible
column	commodities	competent
competitive	congratulations	consent
controlled	controlling	convincing
deductible	deferred	deficiency
definite	describe	description
desirable	developing	development
difference	disbursement	discrepancy
distribute	distribution	efficiency
eligible	embarrassing	enclosed
enforceable	enforcing	equipped
exceed	excellent	exchangeable
exhausted	existence	existent
extension	facilities	factories
feasible	February	finally
forcible	furniture	getting
grateful	guaranteed	handling
helpful	incidentally	independent
indispensable	inquiring	installation
interfered	introducing	issuing
journeys	labeled	legible
leisure	license	making
management	mistake	modern
movable	moving	noticeable
notifying	occasion	occupies

occurred	occurrence	offered
offering	officially	omitting
organizing	original	overestimate
pamphlet	parallel	perform
permanent	permissible	personnel
persuade	pleasant	policies
possibilities	precede	preceding
predictable	preferred	preparing
prevalent	privilege	procedure
putting	quantity	questionnaire
receive	recipient	referred
reinforcement	repetition	reputable
requirement	research	retrieve
separate	signature	similar
suffered	supersede	surprise
transferring	traveling	truly

Typing

For the following reasons, a typewritten message must look attractive and conform to accepted standards:

1. First impressions are emphatic. People are influenced by the appearance of a page *before* they become aware of its content. If the very *first* impression is poor, this reaction may remain in the reader's mind, even though he or she may be unaware of its cause.

2. People are inclined to judge ability to do one thing by performance of another. With some justification, the reasoning goes something like "He takes no pride in the appearance of his letters; therefore, he takes no pride in other aspects of his business," "Since she has no respect for appearance, she has little or no respect for me," or "Since he does not know or care about the details of letter placement, he does not know or care about the details of his business."

3. A poor appearance is distracting; it takes a reader's mind away from the message itself. Such thoughts as "This looks messy" or "She doesn't care about appearance" can actually interfere with the reader's comprehension of what is being read.

Word Processing

Thanks to technological advances and innovative office management, typing is now being done at greatly increased speeds and at much higher standards of accuracy and appearance.

The standard procedure for transferring words to the typewritten page has changed drastically in recent years. Typically, a letter, memo, or report went through the following steps: (1) written in longhand or dictated to a secretary; (2) typed in rough form—on a manual or electric typewriter—by a secretary or typist who was subject to interruption; (3) edited and proofread; (4) corrected by use of an erasure or other correcting devices; and (5) typed again—in final form. The system has many disadvantages:

1. Longhand is time consuming for the writer and sometimes difficult for typists to read.

2. Dictation to a stenographer requires the time and efforts of *two* people.

3. Transcription of cold shorthand notes (notes taken so long ago that memory is of little assistance) is often slow and error prone.

4. Transcription of notes taken by another stenographer is sometimes impossible.

5. Interruption of typists can cause errors and waste time required for reorientation.

6. Correction of errors is time consuming, and improperly made corrections can be damaging to appearance.

7. Final-form typing (a relatively slow process when typewriters are manual or electric) may also suffer from interruptions, as well as new errors that did not appear on the first draft.

These weaknesses are being remedied through a relatively new approach—word processing. Technically, anything that happens to words between their selection by a writer and their interpretation by a reader could be thought of as word processing. When business people use the term *word processing*, however, they usually mean a system that employs (1) dictation to a voice-recording machine; (2) typing on an automated typewriter; (3) reproduction of copies (if needed) on convenience copiers, which make high-quality copies almost immediately; (4) distribution of messages through electronic mail (teletypewriter); and (5) electronic storage of messages.

When advanced electronic equipment became available for word processing, office procedures had to be changed accordingly. Standardization and specialization are paramount in word processing. Although the traditional title *secretary* still exists, word processing has brought with it such job specialties as *correspondence specialist* or *word-processing operator* (titles for employees whose responsibilities are primarily typing) and *administrative assistant, administrative secretary, lead secretary,* or *administrative specialist* (titles for employees whose responsibilities are much broader than typing).

With all the technological and procedural changes brought about by word processing, the heart of the system is (1) the automated typewriter and (2) a skilled, specialized operator.

In a firm that uses a word-processing system, letters go through the following steps: (1) dictated into a recording machine (magnetic tape, such as cassettes, is typical); (2) typed by a correspondence specialist on an automated typewriter (as a specialist, the typist is not interrupted by other tasks); (3) edited and proofread; (4) corrected on the screen (a correction is made by backspacing and typing over the word incorrectly typed, very much as a correction can be made on a cassette tape by returning the tape to the incorrect word and saying the correct word); and (5) setting the typewriter to make a final typewritten copy, which it will type automatically at speeds from 150 to 600 words per minute.

Compared with the conventional system of putting words on paper, word-processing systems have the following advantages:

1. Dictation to a machine requires the time and effort of only *one* person.

2. Typing is done by a specialist who will not make mistakes caused by interruption and who knows how to use the automated typewriter to full advantage.

3. Corrections made on the screen result in perfect copy when the page is typed in final form; distracting erasures and other evidences of correction efforts do not appear.

4. The operator types only the rough draft, which appears on the screen, and makes corrections; the final copy is typed by the automated typewriter.

5. Production expenses are greatly reduced. With an automated typewriter, words can be processed five or six times faster than is possible by conventional means.

6. Automated typewriters can store form paragraphs, reproducing them perfectly at speeds up to 600 words per minute. For frequently recurring messages, form paragraphs greatly reduce dictation time. In some letters, for example, a manager may dictate only the first and last sentence. The typewriter is instructed to place certain form paragraphs between them.

Businesses are moving rapidly to word-processing equipment and procedures. Managers and managers-to-be can very profitably read recent books and articles on word processing—or take a word-processing course at a college or university.

Letter Placement

The following suggestions on letter placement will assist in achieving conformity to accepted practices, but conformity should not be sought for its own sake. Rather, it should be sought because it helps in making a good first impression, it implies pride and efficiency in business, and it reduces the chances of reader distraction.

Before beginning to type, a typist needs to know which *style* of letter placement to use. Ordinarily, a business selects one style and uses it for all letters. Although other styles are sometimes used, the most frequently used are the *full-block* and the *modified-block* styles. The *simplified* style is not widely used, but is illustrated here because its features deserve attention.

The Full-Block Style

This style, shown in Figure A-1, is simple in appearance. Since every line begins at the left margin, a typist has a minimum of machine adjustments to make before beginning to type and while typing. But the style has a visual disadvantage; it looks heavy on the left side. (Use of "Dear" in a salutation is a matter of personal preference.)

The Modified-Block Style

In the modified-block style in Figure A-2 (page 639) the date is begun at the horizontal center of the page. The complimentary close, the typewritten name, and the title begin at the center of the page, too.

The Simplified Style

The simplified style shown in Figure A-3 (page 640) includes neither salutation nor complimentary close. In place of a salutation, a subject line is used. All lines begin at the left margin.

The advantages of the simplified style are (1) it is easy for the typist because all lines begin at the left margin, (2) it is economical because salutations and complimentary closes — which convey little or no message — are eliminated, (3) it avoids the risk of selecting a salutation that the reader would consider inappropriate, and (4) it makes the subject easy to identify.

The disadvantages are (1) it looks a little heavy on the left, (2) it gives emphasis to a negative idea if it should appear in the subject line, and (3) it omits two parts that (although not necessary) have come to be expected.

Typed Return Address

Writers who do not have letterhead paper need to include a return address. It is placed at least one and a half inches from the top edge of the paper; lines should begin at the center of the page or be arranged so that the longest line ends at the right margin. The date is placed immediately beneath the city, state, and zip code line.

The amount of space between the date and the inside address is determined by the length of the letter. The complimentary close and signature lines are begun at (or five spaces to the left of) the center of the page. See Figure A-4.

Date Line

Spell out the month. Type the date at least a double space beneath the lowest part of the letterhead. (See Figures A-1, A-2, and A-3.) Begin at the left margin if the

COPPER MATERIALS, INC.
Post Office Box 3274
Scottsdale, Arizona 85384

June 15, 198-

Mr. Carl F. Johnson
Johnson Hardware Store
Post Office Box 347
Denver, CO 80223

Dear Mr. Johnson:

The nationally advertised copper ice buckets you ordered should reach your store within the week.

Because of your prompt payment habits with your other suppliers, you may pay according to our usual terms: 2/10, n/30. Pay by June 25 if you wish to take advantage of the cash discount on this order; otherwise, by July 15.

The normal markup on these eye-catching ice buckets is 43 percent. For similar copper items that should sell rapidly during the summer months, see the enclosed brochure.

Cordially,

Keeman Todd

Keeman Todd
Sales Manager

lp

Enclosure

Figure A-1 Full-block style.

COPPER MATERIALS, INC.
Post Office Box 3274
Scottsdale, Arizona 85384

June 15, 198-

Mr. Carl F. Johnson
Johnson Hardware Store
Post Office Box 347
Denver, CO 80223

Mr. Johnson:

The nationally advertised copper ice buckets you ordered
should reach your store within the week.

Because of your prompt payment habits with your other
suppliers, you may pay according to our usual terms: 2/10,
n/30. Pay by June 25 if you wish to take advantage of the cash
discount on this order; otherwise, by July 15.

The normal markup on these eye-catching ice buckets is 43
percent. For similar copper items that should sell rapidly
during the summer months, see the enclosed brochure.

Cordially,

Keeman Todd

Keeman Todd
Sales Manager

lp

Enclosure

Figure A-2   Modified-block style.

COPPER MATERIALS, INC.
Post Office Box 3274
Scottsdale, Arizona 85384

June 15, 198-

Mr. Carl F. Johnson
Johnson Hardware Store
Post Office Box 347
Denver, CO 80223

YOUR ORDER FOR ICE BUCKETS

The nationally advertised copper ice buckets you ordered
should reach your store within the week.

Because of your prompt payment habits with your other
suppliers, you may pay according to our usual terms: 2/10,
n/30. Pay by June 25 if you wish to take advantage of the cash
discount on this order; otherwise, by July 15.

The normal markup on these eye-catching ice buckets is 43
percent. For similar copper items that should sell rapidly
during the summer months, see the enclosed brochure.

Keeman Todd

Keeman Todd, Sales Manager

lp

Enclosure

Figure A-3 Simplified style.

235 West Thomas Road
Kenton, KY 41053
June 14, 198-

Wright County Department of Parks
302 County Court Building
Hartville, KY 41052

SUBJECT: The lanterns used in your landscaping

Will you please tell me who made the small Japanese-type
lanterns that you have recently placed near the entrance of
Cartwright Park.

The small ones (about 1-1/2 feet high with a wide top and small
base) would fit very well into my landscaping pattern.

I shall appreciate your sending me the name and address of
their manufacturer.

Cordially,

Benson Lee

Benson Lee

Figure A-4   Business letter with typed return address.

full-block or simplified style is used. Begin at the center if the modified-block style is the style used.

Punctuation

Choose either open or mixed punctuation. *Open* includes no punctuation after the date, lines of the inside address, salutation, complimentary close, typewritten name when it appears on a line by itself, title, or reference initial. *Mixed* also includes no punctuation after these lines, with two exceptions—a colon is placed after the salutation, and a comma is placed after the complimentary close. If the salutation is followed by a colon, a comma is placed after the complimentary close. If the salutation is *not* followed by a colon, the complimentary close is *not* followed by a comma.

Salutations

Make the salutation agree with the inside address. Use of *Dear* in salutations is beginning to diminish. Although it may convey politeness, its absence hardly conveys *im*politeness. Present-day usage has almost eliminated *Gentlemen* as an appropriate salutation when the letter is addressed to a company. A better practice is to skip the salutation altogether and to use a subject line:

Personnel Director
Wilson Chemical Company
Hartville, NY 11052

Dear Director

Ms. Jane Day
The Waxo Company
Walls, KS 76644

Dear Ms. Day

Jackson Manufacturing Company
1334 West Devonshire Road
Bolivar, MO 65613

SUBJECT: Your order of January 13, PO #1447

Attention Lines

Place the attention line between the address and the salutation. The best practice is to omit an attention line when a salutation is involved, addressing the letter to the

enclosure, the word

n the first place. If you use
r with or without a subject

he typist's initials
one person and
n the foregoing
nal may appear

g. Important ideas that appear in the
letter, a reader can easily spot impor-
s. Therefore, a writer should rely mainly
ood *average* for business letters. But, of
e short, even one short sentence. Short
nable a reader to read rapidly.

ldom need to
for emphasis
ertical space
enclosure. If
re and the

of film.

ript

ere included in signature sections to assist In
hat its employee wrote. After some court cases
regardless of whether the company name ap-
any name began to decline. If we are using the
capital letters a double space below the
e their company name in the signature
plain paper, the company name is
letter than in a one-page letter:

of film.

son's name is the last

Charles Jones

erence initials and one space
st businesses need to know who
ase) begin at the left margin, a double

space below the dictator's name and title. If a letter contains an
Enclosure is typed below the reference initials:

```
sld                    KTB:sld              BLB/sld

Enclosure              Enclosure            Enclosur
```

Normally, letters are dictated by those who sign them; only t
appear (*sld* in the column on the left). If a letter has been dictated b
signed by another, the initials of the dictator (*KTB* and *BLB*
illustrations) precede the initials of the typist. Either a colon or a diag
between the dictator's initials and the typist's initials.

Postscripts

Because we should plan carefully before we write, we should very se
include a postscript as an afterthought. Rather, a postscript is used
(whatever appears last on a page gets special attention). Leave one v
between the reference initials and the postscript if the letter includes no
an enclosure is included, leave one blank line space between *Enclos*
postscript:

```
Enclosure

P.S.  If you order before December 1, you will receive a free roll
```

Because a sentence added at the bottom of a letter will be thought of as a
regardless of whether the letters *P.S.* appear, those letters may be om

```
sld

Enclosure

If you order before December 1, you will receive a free rol
```

Copies

When a copy of a letter is sent to an interested person, that pe
word typed on the page. It is preceded by *cc:* or *Copy:*

```
sld                              sld

Enclosure                        Copy:   Mr.

cc:   Mr. Charles Jones
```

Second Page of a Letter

Space the heading for the second page of a letter six lines from the top; and in the heading include the addressee, the page number, and the date. The second page needs a heading that will identify it with the first page. Any of these three forms may be used:

Miss Judy Miller   -2-   March 8, 19--

Miss Judy Miller, March 8, 19--, page 2

Miss Judy Miller
March 8, 19--
Page 2

     Letters seldom extend beyond two pages; but when they do, a similar heading (with appropriate page number) should appear at the top of subsequent pages.

Envelope Addresses

Because use of Optical Character Readers is increasing, the post office prefers that all envelope addresses be single spaced. Include the zip code number. If the first line is begun at the center (horizontally and vertically) of an envelope, an address will normally be well placed.

Mr. Edward Smith, President
The Jackson Manufacturing Company
1334 West Devonshire Road
Bolivar, MO 65613

     The commercial-size envelope No. 6¾ (6½ by 3⅝ inches) is used primarily for letters that are typed on pages smaller than the standard 8½-by-11 size. The official size, No. 10 (9½ by 4⅛ inches) is normally used for standard-size sheets and especially for letters that include an enclosure.

Letterhead Paper

The trend in letterhead design is toward simplicity. The name of the business, and the address and zip code are essential. Paper can be bought in various weights. However, less than sixteen-pound weight seems too flimsy.

Placement Guide for Letter Typing

If a letter is too high or low on the page, or if the margins are too wide or narrow, the impression is unfavorable. Balance on the page can be achieved through (1) varying the distance between the date and the inside address and (2) varying the width of the margins.

Experienced typists can estimate these points. Others can benefit from a guide sheet. A letter placement guide like the one on the left of Figure A-5 can be inserted into the typewriter immediately behind the sheet upon which the typing is done. The dark lines will show through; thus, the typist can easily see the points at which to begin typing the date, the inside address, and the complimentary close.

To construct such a guide sheet, draw on an 8 ½-by-11 sheet with a soft-lead pencil to make the lines that appear in the figure. (Dimensions, which are not to be put on the guide sheet, are indicated on the figure.)

The *x* at the center of the top line and the broken line in the lower center assist in getting the date and signature sections in proper position.

To use the guide sheet, place it behind the sheet on which typing is to be done, and decide whether the letter is long, medium, or short.

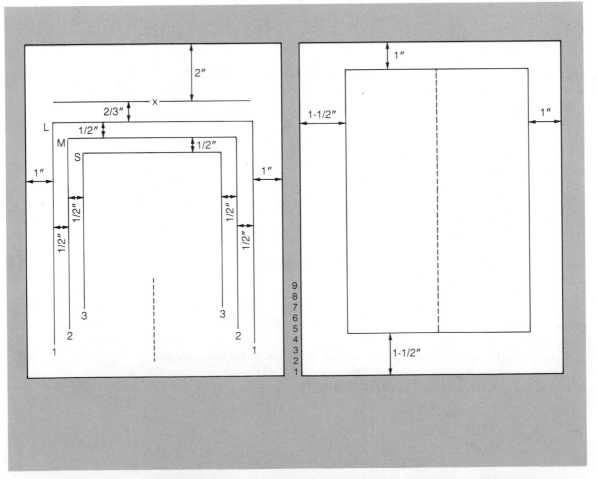

Figure A-5 Letter placement guide (left); report placement guide (right).

If a letter is *long* (200 to 300 words in the body), set the left and right margins at vertical lines *1.* Type the date at the top line (at the left margin for a block-style letter, at the center for a modified-block letter). Begin typing the inside address at point *L.* Continue typing until the letter is completed. Let the right vertical line serve as a *guide* for ending the lines. Lines may end a few spaces before or after the line; just try to avoid extremes. If a letter is *medium* in length (100 to 200 words), set the margins at vertical lines *2.* Type the date, and begin typing the first line of the inside address at point *M.* If a letter is *short* (50 to 100 words), set left and right margins at vertical lines *3,* type the date, and begin the inside address at point *S.*

Placement for Term-Paper Typing

In reports or term papers, a typist's problem in achieving proper placement on the page is simplified by using a guide sheet. The guide sheet shown at the right in Figure A-5 can be inserted into the typewriter immediately behind the page on which the typing is done. Since the heavy lines will show through the page on which the typing is done, the typist can easily determine where to set margins, type the page number, begin the first line, end a line of typing, type a heading that is to be centered, begin the typing of footnotes, and type the last line of a page. Such a guide sheet is easy to prepare:

1. Use standard-size, 8 ½-by-11 paper.

2. With a soft-lead pencil and a straight edge, make the same lines that appear in the figure. The left margin is one-and-a-half inches wide because at least half an inch will be obscured when the pages are bound on the left. If the pages should be bound at the top, then right and left margins should be equal—one inch. The bottom margin is one-half inch wider than the top margin for better appearance—pages look better balanced if the bottom margin is slightly wider than the top margin. Place the broken line three inches from the two vertical lines. This line is used as a guide for placing headings that are centered horizontally.

3. Place a small *x* halfway between the upper-right corner and the top edge of the paper. Except for the first page of a report, page numbers are typed at this point.

4. Insert the page into a typewriter and type numbers *1* through *9,* beginning with *1* at the lower left and placing the next higher number on the line above it. These numbers are helpful in determining whether to type additional lines before removing the page. When using this guide sheet, a typist would not type below line 1. If the page contains footnotes, the numbers would be helpful in determining the appropriate line on which to stop the typing of sentences and begin the footnotes.

Paragraphs in a term paper are normally double spaced, but footnotes are single spaced. If two or more footnotes appear at the bottom of the same page, a space is left between them. To type a two-line footnote at the bottom of a page, stop on or at the end of line 6. Then move to line 4 and with the underscore key make a solid line one-and-a-half inches long to separate the lines of the paragraphs from the footnote. Then move to line 2 for typing the first line of the footnote; line 1 for the last. If two footnotes are to appear at the bottom of a page and if each requires two lines, no part of the paragraph should be typed lower than line 9.

To achieve acceptable form and consistency in typing footnotes, use the style manual recommended by your company, college, or professor. For acceptable footnote layout, see page 476. Note placement of the footnote numbers. To raise a number slightly above its normal position on a line, grasp one of the cylinder knobs on the typewriter carriage. Looking at the lines that have already been typed on the page, turn the knob until the lines have moved downward about half a line and strike the number key. Then, return the knob to its previous position.

Spacing Properly with a Typewriter

To achieve right margins that are straight, printers can vary the amount of space between words, punctuation marks, and sentences. Since this arrangement is not possible with standard typewriters, the following guidelines will help the appearance of our letters:

1. Space twice after a period, question mark, or colon at the end of a sentence.

```
Step two was completed.   Then. . . .
When will he arrive?   Regardless of the time. . . .
We have three questions:   (1) Where is. . . .
```

2. Space once after a comma and a semicolon:

```
When the end of the month comes, we shall be prepared.
The operator left at three o'clock; he was ill.
```

3. Space once after a period following an initial:

```
Mr. Warren H. Ragsdale          Mr. W. H. Ragsdale
```

4. Space once after a period following such abbreviations as No., Co., and Corp.:

```
Send a case of No. 6 nails to the Johnson Co. of Chicago.
```

5. For proper vertical spacing in business letters, leave

    a. one blank line between (1) the inside address and the salutation, (2) the salutation and the first paragraph, (3) each paragraph, and (4) the last line of the last paragraph and the complimentary close.

    b. at least three blank lines between the complimentary close and the typewritten signature.

6. Leave a 1-inch margin at the top and right-hand side of a page in a typewritten report. If the page is to be bound at the left, leave 1½ inches at the left; otherwise, leave 1 inch on each side.

7. When typing a report that is single spaced, indicate paragraphs by skipping a line. When typing a report that is double spaced, indicate paragraphs by indenting the first line. Five-space indentions are most common; ten-space indentions are acceptable.

POSTTEST

Exercise 1

Select the correct word. (See pages 592 to 601 for review if necessary.) Your instructor will tell you whether (a) the sentences are to be recopied and the correct word employed, (b) the correct word is to be written beside the number of each sentence, or (c) the correct word is to be underscored in the book.

1. The answers are shown in (*the table below, the following table*).

2. The president was accompanied (*with, by*) an attorney.

3. Your conclusions are (*all together, altogether*) correct.

4. They have (*all ready, already*) asked our permission.

5. The (*number, amount*) of applications is increasing.

6. The sales representatives were (*anxious, eager*) for a vacation.

7. Has (*anyone, any one*) heard today's weather report?

8. My watch is not (*so, as*) accurate as yours.

9. Do you have any comments (*about, as to*) my proposal?

10. The (*balance, remainder*) of the work can be completed within three hours.

11. For this week, you (*may, can*) have 20-minute coffee breaks.

12. I thought his (*compliments, complements*) were very sincere.

13. Miss Woods danced (*continually, continuously*) for three hours — a new record in her club for constant motion.

14. The report from the accounting department does not correspond (*with, to*) the report from the finance department.

15. If the report needs to be re-edited, please (*contact, call*) me.

16. The committee could not agree on a (*criteria, criterion*) of success.

17. Will you please try to interpret this (*data, set of data*) for me.

18. The proposed (*deal, transaction*) is being discussed with our attorneys.

19. Tom agreed with the statements about procedure, but he differed (*from, with*) the statements about policy.

20. After fifteen years, some changes in our rules are (*eminent, imminent*).

21. The personnel department seemed to be (*enthusiastic, enthused*) about the technique.

22. John's report was (*accepted, excepted*), but mine was rejected.

23. The report is designed to provide (*further, farther*) insight into the proposal.

24. Please alphabetize the (*following, following words*):

25. When you have finished analyzing the findings, please (*send, forward*) a copy of your report to me.

26. I don't know (*if, whether*) he will choose the army or the navy.

27. The variable did not (*impact, influence*) costs.

28. The folders are already (*in, into*) the file.

29. (*Please, Kindly*) prepare these documents for signature.

30. The article appeared in the (*last, latest*) issue of *Fortune.*

31. The administrative assistant (*lay, laid*) the minutes on the presiding officer's desk.

32. Don't (*lose, loose*) your balance.

33. The (*majority, major portion*) of the book is interesting.

34. The news media (*have, has*) taken little interest in the subject.

35. The request was signed by Mr. Elsden and (*me, myself*).

36. Neither the text (*or, nor*) the manual was printed on schedule.

37. (Assume the following sentence is intended to reveal that Tom's work is limited to one location.) Tom (*only works here, works here only*).

38. Only one (*party, person*) has applied for the job.

39. George impresses me as a very (*practicable, practical*) person.

40. The leader's suggestions were (*quite, quiet*) clear.

41. If we get the contract, we will (*raise, rise*) our bid.

42. The reason is (*because, that*) our budget was reduced.

43. When I became aware of the error, I reported (*it, same*) to the judge.

44. Just (*set, sit*) your briefcase in the closet.

45. We have already spent (*some time, sometime*) discussing the technique.

46. The printer suggested that we use off-white (*stationery, stationary*).

47. The representative (*sure, surely*) wanted to please his constituency.

48. The detective (*suspected, suspicioned*) collusion.

49. The report (*which, that*) was on my desk this morning has been edited; the others will be edited tomorrow.

50. I liked your presentation; it was (*unique, very unique*).

51. I like this book; it is (*very, real*) interesting.

52. If you plan to go to the game, please wait (*for, on*) me.

53. If I (*was, were*) Bill, I would reapply.

54. (*Unless, Without*) payment is received before June 1, the account will be turned over to a collection agency.

55. After reading that paragraph several times, (*you, a reader*) would still not understand it.

Exercise 2

Nouns. (Review page 601.) For each pair of sentences, (1) select the better sentence, and (2) give your reason for thinking it is better than the other sentence.

1. a. I received a call from Mr. Stinson last week.
  b. I heard from Mr. Stinson last week.

2. a. Carlos types 75 words per minute.
  b. Carlos is a fast typist.

3. a. We appreciate your writing to us about your divorce and your declaration of bankruptcy.
  b. We appreciate your writing to us about your current problems.

4. a. Clarification of the issues was achieved by Mr. Veroni.
  b. Mr. Veroni clarified the issues.

5. a. The errors were made by George.
  b. George made the errors.

6. a. Go straight East for 11 miles.
  b. Go straight east for 11 miles.

Exercise 3

Pronouns. (Review pages 602 to 605.) Select the correct word.

1. The typists, not the administrative assistant, (*is, are*) responsible.

2. In the boys' group, everyone is being asked to state (*their, his*) point of view about the contest rules.

3. Among the women employees, each receptionist and each typist has been asked to bring (*her, their*) calculator.

4. Neither Maria nor Sophie could remember (*her, their*) seat number.

5. The board has made (*their, its*) decision.

6. The superintendent and (*me, I*) have been invited.

7. Packages were delivered to Tom and (*me, I*).

8. The proposal interested Mary and (*I, me*).

9. Divide the money between you and (*him, he*).

10. That message is for you and (*she, her*).

11. We are pleased about (*his, him*) completing the job so soon.

12. Tom appreciated (*us, our*) talking with his supervisor.

13. I appreciated (*you, your*) returning the questionnaire.

14. (*Whom, Who*) is calling?

15. He (*who, whom*) works most should be paid most.

16. For (*whom, who*) were the remarks intended?

17. To (*whom, who*) was the letter addressed?

18. Jim is a person (*who, whom*) we can trust.

19. Tom is a person (*who, whom*) can be trusted.

20. (*Who, Whom*) did you invite?

21. (*Whom, Who*) was invited?

22. Make a list of the horses (*who, that*) need to be shod.

23. The tires had 16 pounds of pressure; (*this, this underflation*) caused unnecessary damage.

24. Materials were delivered three days late. (*It, This tardiness*) has delayed our completion date.

25. The columns were added incorrectly. (*This, This error*) explains the lack of agreement.

Exercise 4

Verbs. (Review pages 606 to 610.) Select the correct word.

1. If I (*was, were*) a year older, I would vote.

2. If the price (*was, were*) reasonable, I would buy.

3. The mother and her daughter (*were, was*) invited to the banquet.

4. The typists, not the office manager, (*is, are*) responsible.

5. The office manager, not the typists, (*is, are*) responsible.

6. Neither the supervisor nor her secretaries (*was, were*) expected to attend.

7. Neither Julia nor Misha (*is, are*) interested.

8. Neither the secretaries nor their supervisor (*was, were*) expected to attend.

9. So far as inflation is concerned, the news (*is, are*) encouraging.

10. Only one of these machines (*is, are*) being repaired.

11. Only one person in fifty (*is, are*) that accurate.

12. "The Profit Takers" (*is, are*) a very interesting article.

13. The latest firm to sign the agreement (*is, are*) Weston & Jones, Inc.

14. "Save the Pieces" (*were, was*) adopted as their slogan.

15. (*I, The undersigned*) will conduct the investigation.

16. She (*don't, doesn't*) want a promotion now.

17. Alice observed that Rhode Island (*was, is*) smaller than Connecticut.

18. Two of the applicants (*were, was*) admitted.

19. Karen stopped the machine and (*starts, started*) talking.

20. Karen types rapidly and (*makes, made*) few mistakes.

Exercise 5

Voice. (Review pages 609 to 610.) Change the following sentences from passive to active voice:

1. That device was purchased by our office manager.

2. The report was written and edited by Mr. Cho.

3. The driver was stopped by the officer.

4. This car has been washed thoroughly.

5. The papers were discarded.

Exercise 6

Voice. (Review pages 609 to 610.) Change the following sentences from active to passive voice:

1. The cook will soon serve dinner.

2. Sally made a mistake.

3. Tom gave me the wrong answer.

4. You sent me the wrong set of figures.

5. I will report the incident to authorities.

Exercise 7

Adjectives and adverbs. (Review pages 610 to 611.) Select the correct word.

1. Cal seemed (*enthusiastic, enthusiastically*) about the offer.

2. The officer looked (*suspiciously, suspicious*) at the driver.

3. The driver looked (*suspicious, suspiciously*).

4. The test is (*real, unusually*) difficult.

5. The speakers were (*real, really*) interesting.

6. The timing was (*very, real*) good.

7. Of the three tellers, Juanita does the (*best, better*) work.

8. Ellen is the (*oldest, older*) of the two sisters.

9. Of the ten bricklayers, Hector is the (*faster, fastest*).

10. Mr. Bonser spoke very (*slow, slowly*).

Exercise 8

Sentence structure. (Review pages 611 to 614.) Write (1) the weakness of each sentence and (2) an improved version.

1. There are some parts that malfunction.

2. Received the instructions this morning.

3. It was decided to adjourn the committee.

4. When a little girl, my uncle taught me to play tennis.

5. The story was reported in the *Examiner,* which was written by Edward Jones.

6. Kathy only works on weekends; Sheryl works every day except Sunday.

7. By skipping the rest periods, the job can be completed in two days.

8. Take the steps in this sequence: (1) find average sentence length, (2) find the

number of difficult words per 100, and (3) then you will need to add the two figures obtained in the first steps.

9. Jim excelled in running, throwing, and with the bat.

10. To do this job well, a two-week training period is necessary.

11. Where is the information at?

12. Joan tried to quickly revise her answer.

Exercise 9

Abbreviating and capitalizing. (Review pages 615 to 619.) In recopying each of the following sentences, make whatever changes are necessary in abbreviating and capitalizing.

1. My Mother is planning to take an english course next semester.

2. Before beginning to write, answer the following question: "am I satisfied with my outline?"

3. Have you read "the Status Ruiners," which appeared in last Week's issue of *City Tribune?*

4. I encouraged Mistress Woods to apply for an F. H. A. loan.

5. From the speaker's remarks, I concluded that We should proceed with caution.

6. At 8:15 A.m., you are to receive a call from William Jones, jr.

7. Be sure to call our L. A. office before Jan. 1.

8. The president's only comment was "we'll consider the plan."

9. Wm. spent his Xmas. vacation in N. Y.

10. Chas. plans to enroll in two courses next semester: Corp. Fin. 321 and Prin. Of Ins.

Exercise 10

Writing numbers. (Review pages 619 to 620.) Assume the following sentences appear in a letter or a report. If a number is presented in appropriate form, copy the sentence as is. If a number is presented in inappropriate form, change the number to correct form as you recopy the sentence.

1. Our loss from bad debts has decreased by twenty-one percent.

2. The appointment is at 2:45 p.m. on May 7th.

3. The price has been raised from $15 to $17.73.

4. At the store on East 4th Street, the price has been reduced by fifteen dollars.

5. We replaced twenty-one four-cylinder engines last year.

6. The program begins at 7 o'clock on Tuesday evening.

7. Twenty-two new members were admitted.

8. For a quick review, turn to page eight.

9. Only 6 people were absent.

10. Mix 1 quart of oil with twelve gallons of gasoline.

Exercise 11

Use of apostrophe. (Review pages 621 to 622.) Which is correct?

1. **a.** Three month's pay.
   b. Three months' pay.

2. **a.** We got a response from one supply store: Tom and Jerry's.
   b. We got a response from one supply store: Tom's and Jerry's.

3. **a.** First person was overused (17 "I's" were detected).
   b. First person was overused (17 "Is" were detected).

4. **a.** We appreciated Marisa's responding so quickly.
   b. We appreciated Marisa responding so quickly.

5. **a.** That organization's retirement plan.
   b. That organizations' retirement plan.

6. **a.** Last month's decline.
   b. Last months' decline.

7. **a.** Mr. Morris's comment.
   b. Mr. Morris' comment.

8. **a.** Mr. Jones' comment.
   b. Mr. Jones's comment.

9. **a.** Mr. Smith's address.
   b. Mr. Smiths' address.

10. **a.** This boy's father.
    b. This boys' father.

Exercise 12

Use of colon. (Review page 623.) In each pair of sentences, which sentence employs the colon correctly?

13. Prices on these calculators have decreased not increased.

14. Yes we do plan to be in Tulsa, Oklahoma on May 1.

15. We bought the house on January 2 1983 and lived in it for six months.

Exercise 14

Use of dash, ellipsis, hyphen, parentheses, period, and quotation marks. (Review pages 626 to 631.) What is the difference in meaning?

1. a. Have you read *The Road to Riches*?
   b. Have you read "The Road to Riches"?

2. a. The reward went to Scooter Jones.
   b. The reward went to "Scooter" Jones.

3. a. The president said the project is complete.
   b. The president said, "The project is complete."

4. a. Our team has had a losing streak.
   b. Our "team" has had a losing streak.

5. a. The task was completed in one week by one clerk — Sue Brown.
   b. The task was completed in one week by one clerk (Sue Brown).

6. a. Mrs. Hughes
   b. Ms. Hughes

7. a. . . . because of Tom's two-base hits.
   b. . . . because of Tom's two base hits.

8. a. Divide the group into four-man teams.
   b. Divide the group into four man teams.

9. a. Put the materials in the new equipment shed.
   b. Put the materials in the new-equipment shed.

10. a. According to the boss, "These orders . . . came from headquarters."
    b. According to the boss, "These orders came from headquarters."

Exercise 15

Use of semicolon. (Review pages 631 to 632.) In each sentence, place a semicolon where it is needed.

1. The last questionnaire was returned on November 20 however tabulation was not begun until December 1.

2. The following dispatchers worked more than 40 hours last week: Ellis, 43 Jones, 47 Williamson, 49 and Thomas, 50.

1. **a.** We bought the machine for one reason: to save mone
   b. We bought the machine for one reason; to save mone

2. **a.** The session starts at: 3:15 p.m. on March 1.
   b. The session starts at 3:15 p.m. on March 1.

3. **a.** Wanted: four cords of wood.
   b. Wanted; four cords of wood.

4. **a.** I like this model because it: (1) is less expensive, (2) re
      and (3) produces better copies.
   b. I like this model because it (1) is less expensive, (2) re
      and (3) produces better copies.

5. **a.** I like this model for three reasons: (1) it is less expensiv
      up-keep, and (3) it produces better copies.
   b. I like this model for three reasons (1) it is less expensiv
      up-keep, and (3) it produces better copies.

6. **a.** Dear Mr. Lorenzo:
   b. Dear Mr. Lorenzo;

Exercise 13

Use of comma. (Review pages 623 to 626.) If a sentence nee
after the appropriate word. (Some sentences may need mo
others, none.)

1. Miss Edwards, Secretary of Mortar Board gave a brief

2. This unit which is powered by the sun, is almost comple

3. All questionnaires that were sent last month have been

4. The report was plagued by long complicated paragraph

5. The package contains three kinds of dried fruit: peache

6. When the letter was received the president was out of

7. As you can see from the enclosed folder utility bills have

8. If you can spare time for the tour you should take it.

9. Because only 5 percent of the questionnaires were
   project was abandoned.

10. The project was scheduled for completion on Janua
    completed until January 20.

11. The building has been inspected, hasn't it?

12. Mary completed the task in 12 minutes; John 15.

3. The team has improved in many ways, for example, the team's free-throw percentage is now 89.

4. Only one proposal was considered, it was accepted.

5. If copper tubing had been delivered on schedule, the project would have been completed today, but the most likely completion date is February 4.

Exercise 16

Grammar and mechanics. (Review pages 592 to 634.) Examine each of the following sentences for errors in word usage, spelling, punctuation, and manner of expressing numbers. If a sentence contains no error, copy it as it is. If a sentence does contain one or more errors, make the needed corrections as you copy the sentence. Do not divide a sentence into two sentences.

1. I appreciated you sending the report on December 14th, this allowed me time to study the majority of it before Xmas.

2. This set of data was gathered by Trisha and I; but, consensus of opinion is that it will have little effect on our pay-as-we-go policy.

3. Please cancel the request for 16- and 24-page booklets, they are to long for this advertising media.

4. Miss. Jarvis's Mother wants me to buy a ticket for her, she thinks our team has a real good chance of winning.

5. In the last issue of The Reader's Digest the longest artical is What does Russia Want?

6. Their objectives were different than our's, but irregardless of the objectives, we had similiar results.

7. If I was prepaired for the test I would be more enthused about taking it but compared to my classmates, I have studied very little.

8. Two-thirds of the applicant's were eligible to take the preemployment test, therefore the test was given in a 69-seat room.

9. Of 51 members only thirteen were present; this was definately insufficient for transacting business.

10. While I like to study independantly my friends seldom allow me such a priviledge.

11. Three criteria were established by the five member committee; scholarliness of research, effectiveness of instruction and service.

12. With only two days notice Bill was unable to produce a outline which would be accepted by the instructor.

Exercise 17

Write brief answers to each question.

1. How many times should a typist hit the space bar after typing

    a. a period at the end of the sentence?
    b. a question mark at the end of a sentence?
    c. a period following an abbreviation that is somewhere other than at the end of a sentence?
    d. a colon that precedes a list?
    e. a semicolon?
    f. a comma?

2. How many vertical spaces should be left between

    a. an inside address and a salutation?
    b. a salutation and the first line of a letter?
    c. each paragraph?
    d. the last line of a letter and the complimentary close?
    e. the complimentary close and the typewritten signature?

3. In business reports, how much space should be left for margins?

4. In single-spaced reports, are paragraph indentions necessary?

5. In double-spaced reports, how many spaces constitute the standard indention?

6. Describe the typewriter that is commonly used in word-processing units.

7. On an automated typewriter, how are corrections made?

8. What is the primary advantage of dictating to a machine instead of to a stenographer?

9. Is use of form paragraphs to be discouraged? Explain.

10. List some of the job titles held by workers in a word-processing unit.

Exercise 18

Write answers to the following questions:

1. Why is a letter's appearance so important?

2. Which two letter styles are most frequently employed, and what are the principal characteristics of each?

3. What are the principal characteristics of the simplified letter?

4. If writers do not have letterhead paper, where should they type the return address and the date?

5. What does *mixed punctuation* mean?

6. If the first line of an inside address is "Personnel Director," what should the salutation be?

7. If the first line of an inside address is "Mr. Buford Adams," what is the preferred salutation?

8. Between which two lines is a subject line placed?

9. Why should *Mr.* be used before a man's name in an inside address but not before a man's name in the typewritten signature line?

10. What is a satisfactory *average* length for paragraphs in a business letter?

11. For what reason would you choose to place an idea in a postscript instead of in a paragraph?

12. What three items are included in the heading for the second page of a letter?

13. Is the word *Enclosure* typed above the reference initials, or is it typed below the reference initials?

14. Does the post office prefer envelope addresses to be single spaced?

15. If a letter is to include an enclosure, which envelope is preferred — No. 10, or No. 6¾?

16. Are term papers normally double spaced, or single spaced?

17. Why should a typist normally leave 1½ inches for a left margin of a term paper but 1 inch for the top and right margins?

18. Should the bottom margin of a page that contains no footnote be the same as one that contains a footnote?

19. If two footnotes appear on the same page, should a typist leave a space between them?

20. Where should a page number be typed?

In Exercises 19 through 25, the first sentence of each pair contains one or more errors. In the second sentence, the errors have been corrected. Parenthetical numbers identify pages where explanations can be found. For maximum benefit, use a cover sheet. After trying to identify errors in the first sentence, slide the cover sheet downward and study the corrected sentence. To review reasons for changes, refer to the parenthetical numbers. Within each set of parentheses, the first number is a page number in the text; the second number or letter identifies a certain place on that page.

Caution: Remember that the sentences have been deliberately designed to reinforce knowledge of word usage, grammar, spelling, punctuation, and manner of expressing numbers. Just make the changes necessary for correctness in these categories. Do not attempt to revise a sentence and present its idea in an entirely different way.

Each exercise is designed to reinforce between twenty and forty principles. For *mastery* of these principles, do exercises 19 through 25 repeatedly throughout the semester. Students who want to form *habits* of correctness will find these exercises (which invite frequent re-exposure to principles) exceedingly beneficial.

Exercise 19

1. I have made a three-week study of this recommendation, however I cannot make a decision before March 5. (627, 8-b) (632, 12-c) (626, r) (619, 1-b)

> I have made a three-week study of this recommendation; however, I cannot make a decision before March 5.

2. If we could help you prepare that report; we would be glad to do so but not one of us have had experience in your field of specialization. (623, 5-b) (632, 12-b) (607, e)

> If we could help you prepare that report, we would be glad to do so; but not one of us has had experience in your field of specialization.

3. After we got the business re-establish in the community; our sales began to rapidly increase. (623, 5-b) (627, d) (614, 10)

> After we got the business reestablished in the community, our sales began to increase rapidly.

4. If I was Edward I would write a formal report to the superintendant. (623, 5-b) (606, 1-a)

> If I were Edward, I would write a formal report to the superintendent.

5. The students, not the teacher, are directly responsable. (624, f) (607, c)

> The students, not the teacher, are directly responsible.

6. Only one of these reports is to be bound, all others are to be stapled. (607, e) (631, a)

> Only one of these reports is to be bound; all others are to be stapled.

7. I appreciate you're helping, however, I will not be able to pay you now. (604, e) (632, c) (626, r)

> I appreciate your helping; however, I will not be able to pay you now.

8. There are many reasons for us beginning the project before the 5th of March. (612, 2) (604, e) (619, 1-b)

> For many reasons, we should begin the project before the 5th of March.
> He gave many reasons for our beginning the project before the 5th of March.
> He gave many reasons for beginning the project before March 5.

9. Time sheets must be sent on Friday mornings', this works a hardship on the time keepers office. (621, a) (631, a) (605, g)

> Time sheets must be sent on Friday mornings; this requirement works a hardship on the time keeper's office. (Also correct: ". . . on the time-keeper's office.")

10. Please review the reports that have a stamp on the front; and I will review the reports which have a stamp on the back. (599, 49) (631, a) (623, a) (624, e) (631, a)

> Please review the reports that have a stamp on the front, and I will review the reports that have a stamp on the back.
> Please review the reports that have a stamp on the front; I will review those that have a stamp on the back.

Exercise 20

1. I accept your invitation too attend all the meetings. (595, 22)

> I accept your invitation to attend all the meetings.

2. Will you please make sure the report is accompanied by a diagram? (593, 2) (629, 10-b)

> Will you please make sure the report is accompanied with a diagram.

3. We could not escape from his discovering us. (604, e)

> We could not escape his discovering us.

4. He sure gave a good report. (611, 2-b)

> He surely gave a good report.

5. Please let us know whether or not their books are different from ours'. (80) (70, 7) (622, 2-b)

> Please let us know whether their books are different from ours.

6. The money is to be divided equally between John, Eleanor, and William. (69, 3) (624, c)

The money is to be divided equally among John, Eleanor, and William.

7. He acted as if he was pleased. (606, 1-a)

He acted as if he were pleased.
He acted as though he were pleased.

8. The superintendent approved the report, so we had it duplicated. (632, c) (626, r) (631, a)

The superintendent approved the report; therefore, we had it duplicated.
Because the superintendent approved the report, we had it duplicated.
The superintendent approved the report; we had it duplicated.

9. The first report was independent from the 2nd report. (619, 1-a) (613, 7)

The first report was independent of the second report.
The first report was independent of the second.

10. I read in the "State Press" where enrollment is raising. (630, c) (632, 14-b) (598, 41)

I read in the *State Press* that enrollment is rising.
In the *State Press,* I read the article about increasing enrollment.
(Could be stated in other ways; just avoid the "I read . . . where" expression.)

Exercise 21

1. We recommend that you exercise this privilege before 10:00 o'clock tomorrow morning. (619, 2-b)

We recommend that you exercise this privilege before ten o'clock tomorrow morning. (Also correct: ". . . before 10:00 A.M. tomorrow.")

2. More than 60 per cent of the superintendent's use machines for their correspondence. (619, 1-a) (602, a) (621, 1-a)

More than 60 percent of the superintendents use machines for their correspondence.

3. If the price is still 21 cents each; please ship us four thirteen ounce weights. (619, 1-a) (632, 13) (623, 5-b) (619, 1-a) (620, d) (627, b)

If the price is still 21 cents each, please ship us four 13-ounce weights.

4. May we have an up to date report on your efforts to reestablish definate lines of communication. (627, b) (627, d) (629, 10-b)

May we have an up-to-date report on your efforts to re-establish definite lines of communication.

5. The personnell in our department benefitted grately from the experience. (633) (634)

The personnel in our department benefited greatly from the experience.

6. The local station plans to carry a play by play account of the game on the 13th of June. (627, 8-b) (619, 1-b)

The local station plans to carry a play-by-play account of the game on the 13th of June.

7. As the clerk reported we received a check for $250, but the check was returned because of insufficient funds. (623, 5-b) (632, 12-b) (619, 1-c)

As the clerk reported, we received a check for $250; but the check was returned because of insufficient funds.

8. Send the report to Mister Gould and me, we will try to interpret it. (615, 1-a) (603, 2-c) (631, 12-a) (623, 5-a)

Send the report to Mr. Gould and me; we will try to interpret it.
Send the report to Mr. Gould and me, and we will try to interpret it.

9. Did you say this data was complete and up to date. (595, 17)

Did you say these data were complete and up to date?
Did you say this set of data was complete and up to date? (According to the newest dictionaries, the word *data* can be used as a singular word. Thus, *This data was* is considered correct if the writer is thinking of the word *data* as being similar to *group,* which is treated as a singular.)

10. The players spent to much time in the huddle, they recieved a 5-yard penalty. (631, 12-a) (627, 8-b) (619, 1-a)

The players spent too much time in the huddle; they received a 5-yard penalty.
Because the players spent too much time in the huddle, they received a 5-yard penalty.

Exercise 22

1. This correspondence has resulted in some heated, time consuming discussions, however the results have been real beneficial. (624, d) (626, r) (632, c) (611, 2-b)

> This correspondence has resulted in some heated, time-consuming discussions; however, the results have been very beneficial. (Also correct: ". . . have been really beneficial.")

2. From the presidents speech I inferred that this years' rejections are fewer than last year's rejections. (621, 1-a) (621, 1-f) (70, 10) (70, 13)

> From the president's speech, I inferred that this year's rejections are fewer than last year's rejections.

3. Neither the father nor his son have offerred to pay for damages; however, it will be payed by a friend-of-the-family. (603, 1-d) (607, d) (632, c) (626, r) (627, 8-b) (59)

> Neither the father nor his son has offered to pay for damages; however, they will be paid by a friend of the family. (Also correct: ". . . for the damage; however, it will be paid by a friend of the family.")

4. In John's three page report each of the following words was used less than ten times; advisable, 7, equipped, 8 gratefull, 9, seperate, 9, and convenience, 9. (621, 1-a) (627, 8-b) (623, 5-b) (602, 1-c) (70, 13) (625, m) (632, d) (622, d)

> In John's three-page report, each of the following words was used fewer than ten times: advisable, 7; equipped, 8; grateful, 9; separate, 9; and convenience, 9.

5. I suspicion he will ask "what are your primary reasons? (617, b) (599, 48) (617, 1-b) (631, j)

> I suspect he will ask "What are your primary reasons?"
> I have a suspicion he will ask "What are your primary reasons?"
> (A comma after "ask" would be correct also.)

6. Were his exact words "The goods are in process?" (617, b) (629, 11-a) (631, d)

> Were his exact words "The goods are in process"? (Also correct. . . .
> words, "The goods. . . .)

7. Between you and me, are principle problem is energy; but if we can believe the personnel director, are principle problem is health. (603, c) (623, 5-b) (70, 14) (632, 12-b)

> Between you and me, our principal problem is energy; but if we can believe the personnel director, our principal problem is health. (Also correct: ". . . energy; but, if we can believe. . . .")

8. The women's game schedule has been changed; but the girls' game schedule remains unchanged. (623, 5-a) (631, 12-a) (621, 1-b)

> The women's game schedule has been changed, but the girls' schedule remains unchanged.

9. If I was the professor I would read all term papers, except those which were handed in after June 27th. (606, 1-a) (623, 5-b) (595, 22) (619, 1-b) (624, e) (599, 49)

> If I were the professor, I would read all term papers except those that were handed in after June 27. (Also correct: ". . . except those handed in after the 27th of June.")

10. Will you please place five 18 cent stamps on each package. (620, d) (629, 10-b)

> Will you please place five 18-cent stamps on each package.

11. While I am convinced the decision is definate I am also convinced of its' negative effect on our pre-employment procedures. (71, 15) (623, 5-b) (622, 2-b) (627, 8-d)

> Although I am convinced the decision is definite, I am also convinced of its negative effect on our pre-employment procedures.
> I am convinced the decision is definite, but I am. . . .
> I am convinced the decision is definite; I am also convinced. . . .
> I am convinced the decision is definite, and I am also convinced. . . .

12. Put all 16 and twenty pound weights in the display cabinets; put all others in the storage room. (628, g) (619, 1-a) (631, 12-a) (623, 5-a)

> Put all 16- and 20-pound weights in the display cabinets; put all others in the storage room. (Also correct: ". . . display cabinets, and put all others. . . .")

13. My objectives are different than your's, but my techniques are similar to yours'. (70, 7) (622, 2-b) (623, 5-a) (623, 12-a)

My objectives are different from yours, but my techniques are similar to yours.

My objectives are different from yours; my techniques are similar.

14. In last weeks edition of "Time"; I read where use of ain't is becoming acceptable. (621, 1-e) (623, 5-b) (632, 14-b) (630, i)

In last week's edition of *Time,* I read an article that said use of "ain't" is becoming acceptable.

Last week's edition of *Time* reported that "ain't" is becoming an acceptable word in our language. (Other solutions are acceptable; just avoid use of "I read where.")

15. Only one of my colleagues object to me resigning; but consensus of opinion is that I should proceed as planed. (607, e) (604, e) (623, 5-a) (69, 5)

Only one of my colleagues objects to my resigning, but consensus is that I should proceed as planned.

Only one of my colleagues objects to my resigning, but opinion is that I should proceed as planned.

Exercise 23

1. He did spend some time in field work, that is, he was not always at a desk. (599, 45) (632, e)

He did spend some time in field work; that is, he was not always at a desk.

2. The dictator, not the secretaries, are responsible. (607, c) (624, f)

The dictator, not the secretaries, is responsible.

3. He was instructed to go East, not West. (601, 3) (625, l)

He was instructed to go east, not west.

4. The company assures us of their determination too meet financial commitments. (603, e)

The company assures us of its determination to meet financial commitments.

5. Of the two drivers; Jeannette is the one in whom we have most confidence. (623, 5-b) (605, c) (611, 1-c)

Of the two drivers, Jeannette is the one in whom we have more confidence.

6. Our activities are divided into three categories; planning, organization, and how to activate. (622, 4-a) (623, c) (613, 7) (624, c)

> Our activities are divided into three categories: planning, organizing, and activating.

7. The phys. ed. department has no need for no. 10 envelopes. (616, e) (615, f) (618, k)

> The physical education department has no need for No. 10 envelopes. (Just as *boy* or *girl* is used to categorize a youngster, so is *physical education* used to categorize a department; no capital letter is employed. Of course, when the *name* of the child is used, it is begun with a capital letter (*John*). When intent is to identify the *name* of the department, capital letters are employed. (*Physical Education*).

8. Two-thirds of the members were absent, consequently no decisions were made. (619, 2-a) (628, e) (632, c) (626, r)

> Two thirds of the members were absent; consequently, no decisions were made.

9. Our activities are divided into: 1) planning, 2) organizing, and 3) activating. (622, 4-a) (629, e) (624, c)

> Our activities are divided into (1) planning, (2) organizing, and (3) activating. Our activities are divided into planning, organizing, and activating.

10. Thank you for assisting Sue and I, we can now proceed with haste. (603, 2-b) (631, 12-a)

> Thank you for assisting Sue and me; we can now proceed with haste.

Exercise 24

1. Only one of the applicants were excepted, therefore; another add is being placed in Sundays "Republic." (607, e) (632, c) (626, r) (621, e) (632, 14-b)

> Only one of the applicants was accepted; therefore, another ad is being placed in Sunday's *Republic*.

2. Were Mistress Jones' roports actually marked "Return For Editing?" (615, 1-a) (621, 1-d) (617, c) (631, j)

> Were Mrs. Jones's reports actually marked "Return for Editing"? (A comma after "marked" is also acceptable.)

3. Management is not enthused about the rapidly forming union; however, no resistants is being planed. (595, 20) (611, 2-b) (627, 8-b) (632, c) (626, r)

> Management is not enthusiastic about the rapidly forming union; however, no resistance is being planned.

4. Will you please send 7 thirteen pound weights before Xmas? (619, 1-a) (620, d) (616, 2-d) (629, 10-b)

> Will you please send seven 13-pound weights before Christmas.

5. The Houston Corporation is anxious to reestablish it's market in the area East of the Mississippi river. (593, 6) (627, 8-d) (70, 12) (601, 3)

> The Houston Corporation is eager to re-establish its market in the area east of the Mississippi River.

6. Concensus of opinion was that a three day convention would be appropriate; but a formal vote was not taken. (69, 5) (627, 8-b) (623, 5-a)

> Consensus was that a three-day convention would be appropriate, but a formal vote was not taken. ("Opinion" could be substituted for "Consensus.")

7. Of the 79 questionaires that was returned only fourteen was useable. (623, 5-b) (619, 1-a) (607, b) (634) (613, 7)

> Of the 79 questionnaires that were returned, only 14 were usable.

8. Send copies of your results too I and Bill, we can evaluate it before February 21st. (603, 2-c) (631, 12-a) (602, 1-a) (619, 1-b)

> Send copies of your results to Bill and me; we can evaluate them before February 21. (Also correct: ". . . before the 21st of February.")

9. Of the articles I read before the test the most beneficial was 'Check for Errors in Research Design', which was printed in last weeks issue of "Time." (623, 5-b) (630, c) (629, 11-a) (599, 49) (624, e) (621, f) (632, 14-b)

> Of the articles I read before the test, the most beneficial was "Check for Errors in Research Design," which was printed in last week's issue of *Time*.

10. Each of the following are too be added to you're list; privilage, recomend, recieve, offered, greatfull, interfered, and extention. (607, e) (622, 4-a) (596, 24) (633, 634)

Each of the following words is to be added to your list: privilege, recommend, receive, offered, grateful, interfered, and extension. *Or:* the following words are to be added to .. . .

Exercise 25

1. Data that was supplied on February 21 has been evaluated, the remainder will be evaluated before the 28th of February. (595, 17) (595, 49) (631, 12-a) (619, 1-b)

Data that were supplied on February 21 have been evaluated; the remainder will be evaluated before February 28.
The set of data that was supplied on February 21 has been evaluated, and the remainder will be evaluated before February 28.

2. Such a conclusion is highly questionable, the reason is because an important variable was not controlled. (631, 12-a) (598, 42) (627, 8-b)

Such a conclusion is highly questionable; the reason is that an important variable was not controlled.
Such a conclusion is highly questionable because an important variable was not controlled.

3. The ten year decline was relatively steady, as depicted in the graph below. (627, 8-b) (592, 1) (624, e) (622, 4-a)

The ten-year decline was relatively steady, as depicted in the following graph:

4. Their conclusions were different than our's because different criteria was employed. (70, 7) (622, 2-b) (595, 1-b) (607, b)

Their conclusions were different from ours because different criteria were employed.
Their conclusions were different from ours because a different criterion was employed.

5. When you have completed modification of this plan please forward them directly to me. (623, 5-b) (596, 25) (491, e)

When you have completed modification of this plan, please send it directly to me. *Or:* When you have completed modifications of these plans, please send them directly to me.

6. While the majority of this 12 point agreement is acceptable; an additional point is being recomended. (71, 15) (597, 33) (627, 8-b) (619, 1-a) (595, 22) (623, 5-b) (623, 5-a)

Although the major portion of this 12-point agreement is acceptable, an additional point is being recommended.

The majority of these 12 points are acceptable, but an additional point is being recommended.

7. The media has been extremely critical, this has caused serious reconsideration of the proposal. (597, 34) (631, 12-a) (605, g)

The media have been extremely critical; this reaction has caused serious reconsideration of the proposal. ("Reaction" is one of several nouns that could be used after "this.")

8. Cabinets, which were purchased last year, are to remain in this building; all others are to be moved to the new building. (599, 49) (631, 12-a) (624, e) (623, 5-a)

Cabinets that were purchased last year are to remain in this building; all others are to be moved to the new building.

Cabinets purchased last year are to remain in this building, but all others are to be moved to the new building.

9. The above figures supports the primary hypothesis; however, an additional factor needs to be considered. (592, 1) (626, r) (632, 12-c)

The preceding figures support the primary hypothesis; however, an additional factor needs to be considered.

10. Each of the articles were reviewed by the secretary and I. (607, b) (607, e) (603, 2-b)

Each of the articles was reviewed by the secretary and me.
Each article was reviewed by the secretary and me.

GRADING SYMBOLS

In placing comments on students' papers, teachers can save time by using symbols instead of words. By learning the symbols or referring to them when they appear on returned papers, you will discover ways in which your work can be improved.

ACE	Avoid copying examples	AEB	Avoid expletive beginnings
ACP	Avoid copying problems	AOS	Avoid obvious statements
ADE	Avoid doubtful expressions	ARW	Avoid repeating words
ADP	Avoid dangling participles	ASI	Avoid split infinitives

AWE	Avoid worn expressions	UAW	Use another word
BMS	Be more sincere	UCL	Use capital letters
GRF	Give reasons first	UCS	Use correct spelling
HCA	Hyphenate compound adjectives	UDS	Use deductive sequence
		UFN	Use firm name
ISS	Improve sentence structure	UFP	Use first person
ITI	Interpret this idea (give concrete evidence to illustrate the point)	UFW	Use fewer words
		UIS	Use inductive sequence
LC	Lowercase (don't capitalize)	UPC	Use parallel construction
LTI	Leave to implication	UPL	Use positive language
MIL	Make introduction logical (action taken or spoken of in an introductory phrase is attributed to the noun that follows)	UPV	Use passive voice
		USS	Use shorter sentences
		USW	Use specific words
PRA	Put reader in action	UTS	Use transition sentence
SSQ	Single space quotes	#	Insert space
STP	Subordinate this point	ℓ	Delete
UAC	Use antecedents correctly	∿	Reverse order of letters or words
UAE	Use action ending (an action ending tells what and how, makes action seem easy, and encourages quick action)	⊂	Close up (leave no space)
		↑→↓←	Move copy this direction (up, down, across)
UAS	Use appropriate salutation	/	Divide word here
UAV	Use active voice		

INDEX

Abbreviating, 615–16
Abbreviations of states, 615
Abstract nouns, 56, 601
Acceptance letters, job, 295
Acknowledgment, letters of, 151
Action
  in application letters, 282
  in sales letters, 204–6
Active verbs
  defined, 62–64, 610
  in sales letters, 197
Active voice, 91–92
Addenda, 419
Adjectives
  compound, 64–65, 96, 98
  coordinate, 65–66
  defined, 64–66, 610–11
  punctuation of coordinate, 97
Adjustment letters, 141–44
Adjustment refusals, 166–71
Adverbial conjunctions, 67–68
Adverbial conjunction, punctuation of,
  97, 626
Adverbs, 66–67, 611
Agenda, sample of, 553
Agreement
  in person, 62

of pronouns and numbers, 602–3
  in pronoun usage, 59
  of subject-verb, 61
Alphabet
  derivation, 25
  phonetic, 126
Alphanumeric outline, 431
American values and stereotypes, 39
Analytical report organization, 424
Antecedents of pronouns, 59, 604
Apologies, 171
Apostrophe, 621
Appeals in collections, 218, 221
Appendix, 419
Application follow-ups, 295
Application letters
  common errors in, 276
  preparation of, 271–91
  solicited, 285–91
  unsolicited, 276–85
Appositives, 94–95, 97, 623, 625, 626
Armstrong, Neil, 25
Articulation, vocal, 531
ASCII, 34
Attention
  in application letters, 277
  in sales letters, 192–93

Attention line, 642
Attributes résumé, 267–71, 290–91

Banquets, 555–56
Bar charts, 363
Barnlund, Dean C., 6
Basic computer language, 34
Behavioral concepts, 12
Bennis, Warren G., 575
Bibliography
    format, 481, 483
    need for, 480–82
Bidirectional, 34
Binary, 34
Bit, 34
Blind ads, 285
Bormann, Ernest G., 576
Brackets, 622
Brevity, 95–96
Byte, 34

Capitalizing, 617–18
Card system, 338
Career service, 257
Caret, in proofreading, 129
Case, pronoun, 603–4
Cause-and-effect connectors, 471
Central selling feature, 194
Central selling point
    emphasis in sales, 199
    stressing in sales, 197–98
Central tendency, measures of, 358
Certainties, 77
Chalkboards, 545
Character, as basis for credit, 147
Character printer, 35
Charts and Graphs
    bar charts, 363
    broken bar chart, 366
    component bar chart, 365
    cumulative line charts, 366
    flow chart, 372
    line charts, 365
    maps, 372
    pictogram, 369
    pie charts, 367
    positive-negative charts, 365
Chip, 35
Ciphers, with whole numbers, 619
Circuit board, 35

Claims
    favorable response to, 141–44
    persuasive, 211–12
    routine, 140–44
Classifying, process of, 432
Clause
    defined, 86
    dependent and independent, 86
    emphasis and de-emphasis, 92–93
Clichés, 80–84, 148
Climate, organizational, 576
Closure, in collections, 218
Cobol, 35
Cody, Sherwin, 582
Coherence
    in application letters, 283
    in sales letters, 196
    techniques, 98–99, 104–5
Collections
    appeal letter, 218
    form letters in, 223
    inquiry letter, 217
    language of, 225
    related letters, 223–25
    reminder messages, 216
    series in, 215–16
    ultimatum letter, 222
Colon
    with appositives, 94–95, 97
    to precede series, 97
    usage rules, 622–23
Comma
    after adverbial conjunction, 97
    with appositives, 94–95, 97
    in compound sentence, 97
    after coordinate adjectives, 97
    after dependent clause, 97
    in series, 97
    usage rules, 623–26
Commendation letters, 242–44
Common denominator in reports, 422
Common language, 376
Communication
    brief history of, 25
    defined, 6
    process of, 10
Company policy
    in credit refusals, 175
    in refusals, 180
    in request refusals, 180
Comparatives, 611

Comparisons incomplete, 200
Complement, in sentences, 85
Complex sentences, 86
Component bar charts, 365
Composition methods in reports,
     464–67
Compositions, 103–7
Compound adjectives
   to achieve brevity, 64–65, 96
   with hyphen, 98
   punctuation of, 627
Compound object, 60
Compound sentences
   defined, 86
   punctuation of, 97, 632
Compound-complex sentences
   defined, 86
   punctuation of, 98
Computer glossary, 34–36
Computers, personal, 27
Concrete language, in sales, 199
Concrete nouns, 56, 601
Condolence, letters of, 240
Congratulations letters, 234
Conjunctions
   adverbial, 97
   punctuation of, 67–68
   usage rules, 67–68, 631
Conjunctive adverbs
   punctuation of, 626, 632
   usage of, 67–68
Connecting words, 99
Connectives in reports, 471
Consistency in tense, 62
Construction, parallel, 613
Contents page, 413, 490–91
Contrast connectors, 471
Conviction techniques in reports, 467
Coordinate adjectives
   punctuation of, 97
   usage rules, 65–66, 624
Coordinate clauses, 623
Coordinate conjunctions, 67
Counterproposals
   in refund adjustments, 169
   in response to credit request, 172
Credit letters
   favorable responses to, 146
   responses to routine requests,
      145–46
   routine requests, 146

Credit refusal letters
   principles summarized, 174–75
   stating reasons for , 172
Credit terms, 148
Cue card, 340
Cue note, 338
Cultural environment, 38
Culture
   body communication, 44
   economic development, 38
   legal aspects of, 38
   religion in, 38
   semantic problems, 42
   translation problems, 42
   values and attitudes, 38
   written communication problems, 40
CPU, 35
CRT, 35
Cursor, 35

Dangling phrases, 87–89, 613
Dash
   with appositives, 94, 97
   usage rules, 626
Data collection errors, 351
Data interpretation errors, 351
Decimal outline, 431
Decoding, defined, 9, 54
Deductive letters
   in favorable responses, 156
   in job acceptances, 295
   outlines for, 116, 118, 140
   in recommendations, 236, 292
Deductive paragraphs, 101–2, 104
De-emphasis
   in credit refusals, 174
   through general language, 93
   in inductive letters, 117, 119
   in long, complex sentences, 181
   through punctuation, 97
   in refused adjustments, 169
   with the subjunctive mood, 91
Definitions
   punctuation of, 630
   in reports, 472
Deity, capitalization, 617
Demeaning expressions, 77–78
Dependent clause
   for de-emphasis, 92–93
   defined, 86

Dependent clause *(continued)*
  punctuation of, 623–24
  usage, 613
Details in applications, 273
Dictating messages, 121–31
Dictation
  methods of, 121
  post-dictation practices, 128
  pre-dictation practices, 122
  procedures, 123–27
  process of, 122
  requisites for, 121–22
Disc, 35
Disk, 35
Disk drive, 35
Division of words, 621
Documentation, 476–82
Documentation, as conviction, 468
Doubt, expresions of, 84–85
Doubtful expressions
  in refusals, 171
  in request refusals, 180
Drucker, Peter, 575
Dysphemism, 78

Editorial system, 586
Education, on résumé, 262, 264, 265,
  269
Educational training programs, 581–84
Educational television, 33
Ego states in TA, 15
Electronic mail, 31
Ellipsis, 626
Empathy, intercultural, 39
Emphasis
  in applications, 283
  of appositives, 94
  in compositions, 105
  in deductive letters, 116, 118
  in paragraphs, 102–3
  by position in outline, 114
  by position in paragraphs, 102
  by position in sentence, 93
  through punctuation
    in resumes, 261
  in sentences, 92–95
  through specific language, 93
Employees needs, 255–59
Employees qualities, 254–55
Employment agencies, 257

Employment letters, 253–97
Enclosures
  dictating about, 131
  notations of, 643
  in sales letters, 203
Encoding, defined, 9, 54
Enumeration
  before dictating, 123
  for emphasis, 102
  in letters about negatives, 245
  of points in applications, 274
  in recommendation letters, 236
  in reports, 471
Envelope adresses, 645
Euphemisms, 78
Evaluation interview (see interview)
Evaluation letters, 242–46
Evaluations
  negative, 244–46
  positive, 242–44
Evidence
  in application letters, 281
  in sales letters, 198–204
Exaggerations, 243, 245
Executive work station, 27
Experience, in résumés, 262–63, 265,
  269, 290
Experimental research, 349
Explanations
  in credit refusal, 172
  in refusal letters, 165
  in refused adjustments, 169
Expletives, 89–90, 612

Facsimile transmission, 31
Fair play in collection appeals, 218–19
Fake inside address, 193
Familiarity as basis for sequence, 103
Favor requests
  persuasive, 212–15
  refusal of, 179–81
Fax, 31
Fear, in collection letters, 218
Feedback, defined, 9
Feminine pronouns, 57–59
Figures
  introducing in reports, 375–76
  labeling in memorandums, 385
  manner of expressing, 619

numbering sequence in reports, 362
placement in reports, 447
File, 35
First person, 59, 83
Flately, Marie E., 31
Flip charts, 546
Flow charts, 372
Fog Index, 99–100
Follow-ups, 295
Footnotes, 476–80
Form letters
  in acknowledgments, 151
  in collections, 223
  about credit, 147
  development and preparation,
    584–86
  about people, 292
  for refused orders, 176
  in word processors, 179
Format of data sheet, 263–70
Fortran, 35
Fragments of sentences, 86
Full-block letter style, 637–38

Gender, in pronouns, 58
General language for de-emphasis,
  93–94
General nouns, 601
General words, in commendations, 242
Gerund, 57, 604, 621
Good-news letters, outline for, 140
Gould, John W., 45
Grammar (see specific parts of speech)
  importance of, 105–6
  review of, 592–614
Graphics, guides for, 363
Graphs (see charts and graphs)
Group communication
  composition of groups, 548
  factors in, 547–51
  goals of, 547
  maintenance purpose in, 547
  members status in, 548
  networks in, 549
  norms of behavior in, 549
  perceptions of, 548
  size of group in, 548
  task purpose of, 547
Group interaction purposes, 547
Group norms, 549

Guarantees, in sales letters, 204
Guide letters, developing, 584–86

Hall, Edward T., 44
Handwritten letters, 234, 239, 241
Handicapped job applicants, 291
Haneda, Saburo, 42
Headings
  for emphasis, 105
  in letter reports, 449
  preceded by transition, 105
  in reports, 424–31, 481–84
Hierarchy of communication levels, 19
Hierarchy of needs, 13
Hildebrandt, Herbert W., 45
House organs, 579
Human communication theory, 10
Human relations
  through predicting reactions, 115
  and tone, 90–91
Hyphens
  in compound adjectives, 65
  usage rules, 627–28
Hypothesis, 334

Impatience, 166
Imperative mood, 606
Imperative sentences, 611
Implication, in letter being answered,
  177–78
Importance, as basis for sequence, 103
Independent clauses
  defined, 86
  for emphasis, 92–93
  punctuation between, 97
  usage rules, 613
Index, in reports, 419
Indicative mood, 606
Individualized credit letters, 145–46
Inductive letters
  adjustment refusals, 166–71
  credit refusals, 171
  job refusals, 295
  order refusals, 175
  outline for, 165
  persuasive, 189–226
  persuasive claims, 211–12
  planning of, 165–81
  in recommendations, 236
  special favors, 212–15

Inductive outline
    advantages of, 181
    in persuasive letters, 191–92
Inductive paragraphs, 101–2, 104
Infinitives
    defined, 62
    split, 614
Information, defined, 8
Information theory, 7
Informational memorandums, 385
Information report, 426
Input, 9
Inquiry, in collections, 217
Inside address, 193, 642
Instruction, 35
Instructions in communication process,
    12
Integrated circuit, 35
Integrity
    in application letters, 291
    in employees, 255
Intent in unworded messages, 53
Intercultural training programs, 45
Interface, 35
Interpretation in sales leters, 201
Interrogative pronouns, 604
Interviews
    conduct of, 314, 320–23
    defined, 308
    employment, 312, 579
    evaluation, 312, 315
    personnel, 312
    persuasive, 312
    practice for, 324
    preparation for, 313, 317–20
    stress, 312
    structured, 312
    types and styles, 311–13
    unstructured, 312
Interviewee's role, 317
Interviewer guidelines, 315
Interviewer's role, 313
Introducing graphics, 374
Introduction, letters of, 238
Introductory phrases, 613
Invitations, 238–40
Italics, 632

Job
    acceptance letters, 295
    inquiry letters, 294

objectives on resume, 262
    refusal letters, 295
    requirements matched with
        qualifications, 258
    résumé, 260–71
Johari window, 17
Judgment, expressions of, 84–85
Judgmental terms, in evaluation letters,
    246

Katakana, 31
Keyboard, 35
Keyboarding, 27
Kilobyte, 35
Kinesic communication, 52
Kraar, Louis, 45

Language and culture, 20
Leading committee meetings, 551–55
Leading conferences, 551
Leavitt, Harold J, 549
Length of paragraphs in sales, 195
Length, résumé, 261
Letter outlines
    bad news, 117
    deductive, 116, 118
    good news, 116
    inductive, 117, 119
    neutral, 118
    persuasive, 119
Letter placement, 636
Letter-placement guide, 646
Letter reports, 449–52
Letter styles, 637–41
Letterhead paper, 645
Letters
    of application, 271–91
    application follow-up, 295
    collection, 215–25
    commendation, 242–44
    condolence, 240
    congratulatory, 234–35
    deductively written, 140–57
    employment, 253–97
    evaluation, 242–46
    handwritten, 234, 239, 241
    of introduction, 237–38
    of invitation, 238–40
    job acceptance, 295
    job inquiry, 294

job refusal, 295
about negative qualities, 244–46
persuasive, 189–226
recommendation, 235–38, 291–94
reservation, 238
sales, 189–211
special, 234–46
sympathy, 240
thank-you, 241, 296
transmittal in reports, 408
Libel, 292
Libraries as job sources, 256
Library research, 336
Line charts, 365
Line printer, 35
Linguistics, 21
Linkage, 35
Linking verbs, 603–4
Listening
barriers to effective, 310
detrimental habits, 308–10
effective, 310–11
Luft, Joseph, 18

McGregor, Douglas, 14
Machine dictation, 121
Magazines, as job information source,
256–57
Maintenance purpose, 547
Managers, communication tips for,
577–78
Maps, 372
Masculine pronouns, 57–59
Maslow, Abraham, 13
Mean, 358
Meaning-centered approach, 6
Mechanics, 614–34
Median, 359
Memorandums
informational, 385
persuasive, 393
policy, 386
procedural, 386
qualities of, 383
subject line of, 384
writing guides, 393
Memory, 35
Message
defined, 9
nonverbal, 52
without words, 52

Message-centered approach, 6
Metacommunication, 52
Misused words, 69–71
Mode, 359
Modem, 35
Modified-block letters, 637, 639
Modifiers, misplaced, 612
Mood, 90, 606
Morphology, defined, 21
Morse, Samuel F. B., 7
Motivating action, 204–6
Motives in metacommunication, 53
Murrow, Edward R., 533

Negative evaluations, 244–46
Negative ideas
with euphemisms, 78
and general language, 94
in inductive letter outlines, 117, 119
with third person, 59
Negative language in refusals, 170, 175
Negative tone, 90
Nepotism, 258
Neutral beginnings, in refusals, 168
Neutral ideas, outline for, 140
Neutral messages, outline for, 118
Newspapers, as job information
source, 256–57
Nicknames, punctuation of, 630
"No" letters
characteristics of, 181
response to adjustment request,
166–71
response to favor request, 179–81
response to order, 175–79
response to request for credit,
171–75
Nominative case, 60
Nominative-case pronouns, 60
Nominative pronouns, 603–4
Nonrestrictive clauses, 624
Nonverbal communication, 52
Nonverbal devices, for emphasis, 105
Normative survey, 340
Nouns
abstract versus concrete, 56
usage rules, 601–2
Number
agreement in, 61
with verb agreement, 606–7

Numbers
  spelled out, 619
  used in a series, 94

Objective case, 60
Objective-case pronouns, 60
Objective pronouns, 603
Objectivity in sales letters, 199
Observational research, 348
O'clock, in expressing time, 619
Off-line, 35
On-line, 35
Oral reports
  body of, 541
  introduction, 541
  outline, 541
  summary in, 541
  visual aids in, 541–46
Order letters
  favorable responses to, 151–53
  outline for, 150
  planning and purpose, 149–52
Order refusals, 175–79
Ordinals in expressing numbers, 619
Organization, defined, 114
Organizational communication guides,
    578–79
Organizing
  data in reports, 432
  letters, 115–20
  reports, 434
Originality, in attention getting, 195
Otwell, Caroline M. B., 582
Outline
  application letter, 274
  deductive letter 116, 118, 140
  before dictating, 122
  inductive letter, 117, 119
  in promoting human relations,
    115
  necessity of, 114
  for "no" letters, 165
  order letter, 150
  in persuasive letters, 192
  persuasive letters, 215
  response to credit request, 146
  routine claim letter, 141
  routine request letter, 153
  routine request for credit information,
    144–45

symbols, 431
Output, 9, 35
Overhead transparencies, 545
Ownership, joint and separate, 622

Paragraphs
  deductive-inductive, 104
  emphasis within, 101–3
  length of, 101
  length in sales letters, 195
  sequence of, 103
  summarized, 107
  type of, 101–2
Parallel construction
  in compositions, 78–79
  in reports, 472
  usage rules, 613
Parallelism, 78–79
Parentheses
  with appositives, 97
  for de-emphasis, 95
  usage rules, 628–29
Parenthetical remark, punctuation of,
    97, 626
Parenthetical sentence, 619
Parenthetical words, between subject
    and verb, 607
Participial phrases, 87–89, 613
Passive verb, 62–64, 610
Passive voice, 91–92
Perception and self concept, 548
Period, usage rules for, 629
Peripherals, 35
Person
  agreement in, 62, 608
  in application letters, 275
  first-person pronouns, 59
  in pleasant and unpleasant ideas, 63
  in sales letters, 194
Personal computers, 27
Personnel interview, 312
Persuasive interview, 312
Persuasive letters
  attention getters, 192–93
  collection, 215–25
  outline for, 119
  preparing to write, 190–92
  principles of style in, 190–91
  reasons for resistance, 189
Persuasive memorandums, 393

Persuasive requests, 211–15
Phatak, Arvind, 40
Phonation, 530
Phonetic alphabet, 126
Phonology, defined, 21
Phrases
    in composition, 77–85
    dangling, 87–89
    defined, 86
    parenthetical, 97
    summarized, 106
Physical presentation of reports, 475
Pictogram, 369
Pie charts, 367
Placement bureaus, 257
Plagiarism, 476
Pleasant ideas
    with active voice, 91
    letter outline for, 140
    outline for, 116
Position, emphasis by, 105
Positive evaluations, 242–44
Positive ideas
    in deductive letter outline, 116
    with second person, 59, 63
    and specific language, 94
Positive language
    in credit refusals, 173
    in refused orders, 177
Positive-negative bar charts, 365
Positive tone, 90
Possessive pronouns, 604
Possessives, punctuation of, 621
Posterboard displays, 543
Postscripts, 644
Posttest, grammar and mechanics, 649
Powell, John, 576
Predictions, 575
Prefixes, for brevity, 95–96
Prepositions
    at end of sentence, 614
    placement of, 68–69
    before pronouns, 60, 603
    repetition of, 69
Pretest, grammar and mechanics,
    590–91
Price, in sales letters, 202
Pride appeal, 218, 220
Problem-solving steps, 334
Procedures, 386

Product, introduction of in sales,
    196–98
Program, computer, 36
Pronouns
    agreement in number, 59
    defined, 57
    first, second, third person, 59
    as objects, 60
    in positive and negative ideas, 59
    as subjects, 60
    usage rules, 602–5
    after verbs, 61
Pronunciation, 532
Proofreader's marks, 129–30
Proofreading, before signing, 128–31
Proper nouns, 601
Proper noun capitalization, 618
Proposal sample, 453–54
Proposals, 450–55
Punctuation (see specific marks)
    of conjunctions, 67–68
    in dictating, 127
    importance of, 105
    usage rules, 621–32

Question mark, 631
Questionnaires
    preparation of, 344
    use of, 343
Quotation marks, 629–31

RAM, 36
Random sampling, 342
Range, 360
Rating scales, 347
Readability, 99–101
Reader interest, in sales letters, 195
Reader reaction
    displeased, 116
    interested, 118
    not interested, 119
    pleased, 116
Recommendation letters, 235–38,
    291–94
Recommendations, solicited and
    unsolicited, 236
Redding, Charles W., 576
Redundancies, 79–80
Reference initials, 643
References, on résumés, 262, 266, 271

Refusal letters
    adjustment, 166–71
    characteristics of, 181
    credit, 171–75
    favor request, 179–81
    impatience in, 166
    job, 295
    of orders, 175–79
    outline for, 117, 165
Refused adjustments, common errors
        in, 169–71
Registered mail, in collections, 226
Regularity, in collections, 215
Reliability, defined, 341
Relative pronouns, 604
Reminder, in collections, 216
Repetition
    for emphasis, 105
    versus redundancy, 80
Reports
    active voice in, 469
    addenda to, 419
    appendix in, 419
    assumptions in, 468
    bibliography in, 480–82
    body, 419, 474
    characteristics, 330
    check list for, 508–10
    classifications, 331–32
    coherence in, 471
    common denominator in, 422
    conclusion in, 475
    concrete nouns in, 469
    contents page, 413
    continuum, 331
    conviction techniques, 467
    data collection errors, 351
    defining the problem, 334
    definitions in, 472
    documentation in, 468, 476–82
    emotional terms in, 468
    enumeration in, 472
    flow of, 333
    footnotes in, 476–80
    growth of, 407
    headings in, 424–31, 481–84
    index in, 419
    interpretation errors, 351
    introduction, 473–74
    letter of transmittal, 408

limiting the problem of, 335
    opinions in, 468
    oral (see oral reports)
    organizing, 420–34
    organizing data, 432
    parallel construction in, 472
    personal pronouns in, 469
    physical presentation, 475
    process, 350
    proposals, 450–55
    recommendations in, 475
    reference and sources books, 339
    research methods in, 336
    sample first page, 495, 497
    sample of letter, 451–52
    sample of short, 439–48
    sample title page, 489
    short, 437–62
    summary, 417, 475, 492–93
    synopsis, 417, 492–93
    table of contents, 490–91
    tabulation in, 471
    techniques of style, 469–73
    tense in, 469
    title page, 410, 488–89
    transition in, 470
    transmittal, 486, 487
    variety in, 473
Request letters
    refusal of, 179–81
    routine, 153–54
Requests
    for credit information, 145
    persuasive, 211–15
    for recommendation, 235
Resale
    in credit letters, 149
    in credit refusals, 172
    defined, 142
    in refused adjustments, 169
    in refused-order letters, 177
Reservation letters, 238
Restrictive clauses, 624
Résumé
    attributes, 290–91
    attributes résumé, 267–68
    job, 260–271
    types of, 261
Return address, 637
Richetto, Gary, 575

Ricks, David A., 42
Roles, defined, 11
ROM, 36
Roman numeral outline, 431
Routine letters
  claims, 140–44
  credit, 144–46
  orders, 149–51
  outline for, 140
  requests, 153–54
  responses to requests, 154–56
Routine requests, outline for, 153
R. S. V. P.'s, 239
Ruesch, Jurgen, 11
Rules in communication theory, 11
Run-on sentences, 87

Sales letters *See also* Persuasive letters
  illustrated, 206–10
  solicited and unsolicited, 211
Sales-promotional material
  in credit refusals, 174
  defined, 142
  illustrated, 144
  in refused adjustments, 169
  in refused orders, 179
Salutations, 642
Salutations punctuated, 623
Sampling
  defined, 342
  random, 342
  stratified, 342
  systematic, 343
Sarcasm and euphemisms, 78
Second page of letter, 645
Second person
  with active voice, 63
  defined, 59
  with pleasant ideas, 63
Semantics, defined, 21
Semicolon
  before adverbial conjunction, 97
  in compound-complex sentence, 98
  when conjunction is omitted, 98
  usage rules, 631–32
Sentence structure, 611–14
Sentences
  categories of, 86
  length of, 101
  parenthetical, 619

run-on, 87
structure, 85–89
subjunctive, 91
summarized, 106–7
transition, 104
Sequence of ideas
  in bad-news letters, 117
  for good-news letters, 116, 140
  in neutral letters, 118
  in persuasive claims, 212–15
  in persuasive letters, 119
  in refusal letters, 165, 171
  for routine letters, 140
Sequence of paragraphs, 103
Series
  collection letter, 215–16
  parallelism in, 78–79
  punctuation of, 97, 624
  tabulation of, 94
Sexist language, 60
Shannon, Claude, 8
Short reports, 437–62
Similarity connectors, 471
Simple sentences, 86, 92
Simplicity in word usage, 54–55
Simplified letter style, 640
Slang, punctuation of, 630
Slides, 546
Sobolik, Gayle A., 582
Social situation, 11
Software, 36
Solicited application letter, 277, 285–91
Solicited sales letters, 211
Space
  as basis for sequence, 103
  the language of, 44
Spacing, with a typewriter, 648
Special letters, 234–46
Specific words in commendations, 242
Speech, parts of, 57–69
Speeches
  annoying habits in, 538
  content of, 535
  delivery styles, 535–37
  expository, 533
  extemporaneous, 536
  gestures in, 537
  impromptu, 536
  jokes in, 539
  knowing the audience for, 533

Speeches *(continued)*
memorized, 536
organization, 533
outline for, 534
persuasive, 534
stories in, 534
suggestions for delivery, 537–39
types, 533
written-and-read, 536
Spelling
commonly misspelled words, 633
importance of, 105
Split infinitives, 62, 614
Spread title, 484
State abbreviations, 615
Status
defined, 11
symbols, 11
Stereotypes, American, 39
Stratified random sampling, 342
Stress interview, 312
Stringency, in collections, 216
Stroking in TA, 16
Strong appeal, in collections, 221
Structure in sentences, 85–89
Structured interview, 312
Style, in writing, 51–71, 77–107
Subject, agreement with, 61
Subject line, 154
Subjects in sentences, 85
Subjunctive mood, 90, 606
Subordinate conjunctions, 67
Subordinate clauses, with pronouns,
605
Suffixes, for brevity, 95–96
Suggestive note, 338
Sullivan, Jeremiah, 42
Summary, in reports, 417
Superlatives, 66, 200, 611
Surprise, expressions of, 84–85
Symbols, typing of, 632
Sympathy letters, 240
Synopsis, 417, 492–93
Syntax, defined, 21

TA, 14
Table of contents, 490–91
Tables, planning of, 361–63
Tabulation
defined, 94
for emphasis, 102

in order letters, 150
in reports, 385, 471
in series, 94
Tact, and subjunctive mood, 91
Talking heading, 430
Task purpose, group, 547
Technology in the organization, 587
Technophobia, 27
Teleconferencing, 33
Telegram, in collections, 225
Telephone, in collections, 225
Tense
changes in, 62
and passive verbs, 64
usage guide, 609
Term papers, typing of, 647
Terminal, 36
Testimonials, in sales letters, 203
Thank-you letters, 241, 296
Theory X, 14
Theory Y, 14
Third person
defined, 59
with unpleasant ideas, 63–64
Time
as basis for sequence, 103
connectors, 471
language of, 43
Timeliness, in collections, 215
Title page in reports, 410, 488–89
Titles
articles and firms, 608
capitalized, 618
Toastmaster, 555
Tone, 90–91, 123
Training programs, 581–84
Transactional analysis, 14
Transition sentence, 104
Transmission-centered approach, 6
Transmittal, in reports, 486–87
Typing
letters and reports, 634
need for accuracy, 105

Ultimatum, in collections, 222
Underscore, 632
Understanding, in collections, 216
United States Postal Service, 579
Unity
in application letters, 283
in compositions, 103

Unpleasant ideas, with passive voice, 91
Unpleasant messages, outline for, 117
Unsolicited application letters, 276–85
Unsolicited sales letters, 211
Unstructured interview, 312
Urgency, in collections, 221

Validity, defined, 341
Value, as basis for sequence, 104
Values, American, 39
Variety in reports, 473
Variety in sentences and paragraphs,
    101
Verbs
   active versus passive, 62–64
   agreement in number, 61
   linking, 603–4
   in sentences, 85
   usage rules, 606–10
Verderber, Kathleen, 39
Verification agencies, 291
Vocabulary, value of, 54
Voice, 63, 91–92, 609–10

Weiner, Norbert, 21
Who-whom, 604–5
Williams, Frederick, 25
Word division, 620–21
Word processing
   advantages, 30
   centers, 28
   in collections, 223
   and dictation, 121
   equipment, 28, 30
   for form letters, 147
   network, 29
   problems, 30
   review, 634–36
Words
   categories of, 56
   frequently misused, 69–71, 592–601
   misspelled, 633
   simplicity, 54
Worn expressions, 80–84
Writing suggestions in reports, 464–67

Zong, Baolin, 45